Human Sexuality

Cross Cultural Readings

Fifth Edition

Brian M. du Toit

University of Florida

The McGraw-Hill Companies, Inc.
Primis Custom Publishing

*New York   St. Louis   San Francisco   Auckland   Bogotá
Caracas   Lisbon   London   Madrid   Mexico   Milan   Montreal
New Delhi   Paris   San Juan   Singapore   Sydney   Tokyo   Toronto*

McGraw·Hill

A Division of The McGraw·Hill Companies

Human Sexuality
Cross Cultural Readings

McGraw-Hill's Primis Custom Publishing consists of products that are produced from camera-ready copy. Peer review, class testing, and accuracy are primarily the responsibility of the author(s).

2 3 4 5 6 7 8 9 0 HAM HAM 9 0 9 8

ISBN 07-229658-5

Editor: Mae Kraich
Cover Designer: William C. Whitman Jr.
Printer/Binder: HAMCO/NETPUB Corporation

Foreword

In spite of excellent textbooks dealing with most facets of the human biosexual make-up and experience, none adequately places this in a cross-cultural context. Earlier texts were devoid of cross-cultural references or any recognition that most of the world lives and behaves differently. These texts could better be titled "American Sexuality." Increasingly we find brief references in boxed format and designated "cross-cultural perspective", "other times, other places", or something similar, or even a separate concluding chapter especially for this purpose. None of these is satisfactory since it smacks of an afterthought to recognize the rest of the world and especially more traditional societies where we can trace many of our own organizational and behavioral roots.

This reader is not meant to stand alone but to be used in concert with a more technical textbook. Subject titles introduce each section and readings can be required in the context of the treatment of that particular subject. This collection of readings is neither final nor perfect. It will be adapted and expanded in an attempt at highlighting the diversity and broadening our understanding of *human sexuality*.

Each photograph in this volume is by Brian M. du Toit

Table of Contents

Introduction

Sexuality is fundamental to the continuation of every species. Among most animals, sexual behavior is governed by seasonal changes and hormonal secretion, and its expression restricted by their anatomical construction. Among the higher primates, and especially hominids, sexual attractiveness and expression is less controlled by hormones and thus becomes more complex. Bipedal locomotion, grasping hands, and an innovative brain have produced a diversity of behavioral patterns and actions concerning sexual expression. Human sexuality is at once a part of culture and influenced by other aspects of culture. Human sexuality underlies not only the perpetuation of the biological group as well as a range of related richly diverse behaviors and institutions, but also much of the emotional and aesthetic expression which is uniquely human.

This collection of readings explores and illustrates, in the limited context of a small book, some of the ways people experience and express their sexual feelings. It also relates some of the organizational and institutional results of sexuality. The outline follows essentially a life cycle approach, but the use of section headings allows students to read these in any order required by a course outline or desired by their own interests. The attempt has been to present some historical, some exploratory, and some cross-cultural information.

x

Section I

PAIR-BONDING

In his book *Love and Love Sickness*, John Money explains that pair-bonding can occur between any two people and last for an undetermined duration. When two people pair-bond and an intimate relationship develops, it always involves others—particularly relatives. Worldwide, intimate relationships involve members of opposite genders. In some form or other we find that through arranged marriages, infant betrothal, preferred marriages, or free choice there always are stages in the relationship. These are referred to as courtship and marriage, and involve a growing intimacy and interactions of a sexual nature. But, as already suggested, others are always involved. These may be siblings, parents or other relatives. Anthropologists have encountered in many communities relationships which are patterned and in which specific behaviors are expected. These relationships may be very free and unrestrained, permitting persons ready access to each other, thus also involving sexual overtones, innuendos or even acts. We normally refer to these as *joking relationships* and they exist between persons who stand in specific kinship or affinal relationships to each other. There are, however, other persons who also stand in specific relationships to each other who are expected never to look at each other, never to be in each other's company, never to use each other's name, or some combination of these actions. These we call *avoidance relationships*. One of the most widespread avoidance relationships pertains to a man and his wife's mother. But the reasons, or explanations, for such formal avoidance have not met with the same explanations.

The two readings included in this section approach the avoidance of the mother-in-law from completely different points of view. In the first, the father of psychoanalysis ventured away from the couch and into anthropology. Sigmund Freud explained that in the book *Totem and Taboo* (1912) he was attempting "to apply view-points and results of psychoanalysis to unexplained problems of racial psychology". The result of Freud's argument and his explanation of the Oedipus complex is that the fear of incest and temptation produced the avoidance by a man of his wife's mother. This first section then is from a chapter he titled "The savage's dread of incest"; we read only the second part of that chapter.

Approaching the subject from a diametrically opposed point of view, the social anthropologist Radcliffe-Brown explains that social behaviors must be seen in the context of other social behaviors. Thus the avoidance between persons must be investigated in the social context and in terms of personal relationships which produce attachment or separation. The diagram below will allow us to look at the persons being discussed as they appear in actual relation to each other.

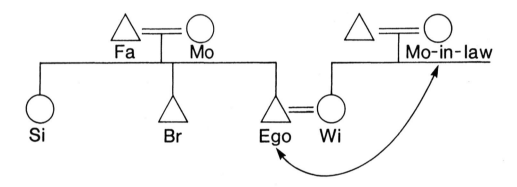

Avoidance Relationship

TOTEM AND TABOO: THE SAVAGE'S DREAD OF INCEST

Sigmund Freud

The most widespread and strictest avoidance, which is perhaps the most interesting one for civilized races is that which restricts the social relations between a man and his mother-in-law. It is quite general in Australia, but it is also in force among the Melanesian, Polynesian and Negro races of Africa as far as the traces of totemism and group relationship reach, and probably further still. Among some of these races similar prohibitions exist against the harmless social intercourse of a wife with her father-in-law, but these are by far not so constant or so serious. In a few cases both parents-in-law become objects of avoidance.

As we are less interested in the ethnographic dissemination than in the substance and the purpose of the mother-in-law avoidance, I will here also limit myself to a few examples.

On the Banks Islands these prohibitions are very severe and painfully exact. A man will avoid the proximity of his mother-in-law as she avoids his. If they meet by chance on a path, the woman steps aside and turns her back until he is passed, or he does the same.

In Vanna Lava (Port Patterson) a man will not even walk behind his mother-in-law along the beach until the rising tide has washed away the trace of her footsteps. But they may talk to each other at a certain distance. It is quite out of the question that he should ever pronounce the name of his mother-in-law, or she his.[17]

On the Solomon Islands, beginning with his marriage, a man must neither see nor speak with his mother-in-law. If he meets her he acts as if he did not know her and runs away as fast as he can in order to hide himself.[18]

Among the Zulu Kaffirs custom demands that a man should be ashamed of his mother-in-law and that he should do everything to avoid her company. He does not enter a hut in which she is, and when they meet he or she goes aside, she perhaps hiding behind a bush while he holds his shield before his face. If they cannot avoid each other and the woman has nothing with which to cover herself, she at least binds a bunch of grass around her head in order to satisfy the ceremonial requirements. Communication between them must either be made through a third person or else they may shout at each other at a considerable distance if they have some barrier between them as, for instance, the enclosure of a kraal. Neither may utter the other's name.[19]

Among the Basogas, a Negro tribe living in the region of the Nile sources, a man may talk to his mother-in-law only if she is in another room of the house and is not visible to him. Moreover, this race abominates incest to such an extent as not to let it go unpunished even among domestic animals.[20]

Reprinted by permission of the editors from *Totem and Taboo,* New York: Random House, 1946, pp. 17-25.

Whereas all observers have interpreted the purpose and meaning of the avoidances between near relatives as protective measures against incest, different interpretations have been given for those prohibitions which concern the relationship with the mother-in-law. It was quite incomprehensible why all these races should manifest such great fear of temptation on the part of the man for an elderly woman, old enough to be his mother.[21]

The same objection was also raised against the conception of Fison, who called attention to the fact that certain marriage class systems show a gap in that they make marriage between a man and his mother-in-law theoretically not impossible and that a special guarantee was therefore necessary to guard against this possibility.

Sir J. Lubbock, in his book *The Origin of Civilization*, traces back the behaviour of the mother-in-law toward the son-in-law to the former "marriage by capture." "As long as the capture of women actually took place, the indignation of the parents was probably serious enough. When nothing but symbols of this form of marriage survived, the indignation of the parents was also symbolized and this custom continued after its origin had been forgotten." Crawley has found it easy to show how little this tentative explanation agrees with the details of actual observation.

E. B. Tylor thinks that the treatment of the son-in-law on the part of the mother-in-law is nothing more than a form of "cutting" on the part of the woman's family. The man counts as a stranger, and this continues until the first child is born. But even if no account is taken of cases in which this last condition does not remove the prohibition, this explanation is subject to the objection that it does not throw any light on the custom dealing with the relation between mother-in-law and son-in-law, thus overlooking the sexual factor, and that it does not take into account the almost sacred loathing which finds expression in the laws of avoidance.[22]

A Zulu woman who was asked about the basis for this prohibition showed great delicacy of feeling in her answer: "It is not right that he should see the breasts which nursed his wife."[23]

It is known that also among civilized races the relation of son-in-law and mother-in-law belongs to one of the most difficult sides of family organization. Although laws of avoidance no longer exist in the society of the white races of Europe and America, much quarrelling and displeasure would often be avoided if they did exist and did not have to be re-established by individuals. Many a European will see an act of high wisdom in the laws of avoidance which savage races have established to preclude any understanding between two persons who have become so closely related. There is hardly any doubt that there is something in the psychological situation of mother-in-law and son-in-law which furthers hostilities between them and renders living together difficult. The fact that the witticisms of civilized races show such a preference for this very mother-in-law theme seems to me to point to the fact that the emotional relations between mother-in-law and son-in-law are controlled by components which stand in sharp contrast to each other. I mean that the relation is really "ambivalent," that is, it is composed of conflicting feelings of tenderness and hostility.

A certain part of these feelings is evident. The mother-in-law is unwilling to give up the possession of her daughter; she distrusts the stranger to whom her daughter has been delivered, and shows a tendency to maintain the dominating position, to which she became accustomed at home. On the part of the man, there is the determination not to subject himself any longer to any foreign will, his jealousy of all persons who preceded him in the possession of his wife's tenderness, and, last but not least, his aversion to being disturbed in his illusion of sexual over-valuation. As a rule such a disturbance emanates for the most part from his mother-in-law who reminds him of her daughter through so many common traits but who lacks all the charm of youth, such as beauty and that psychic spontaneity which makes his wife precious to him.

The knowledge of hidden psychic feelings which psychoanalytic investigation of individuals has given us, makes it possible to add other motives to the above. Where the psycho-sexual needs of the woman are to be satisfied in marriage and family life, there is always the danger of dissatisfaction through the premature termination of the conjugal relation, and the monotony in the wife's emotional life. The ageing mother protects herself against this by living through the lives of her children, by identifying herself with them and making their emotional experiences her own. Parents are said to remain young with their children, and this is, in fact, one of the most valuable psychic benefits which parents derive from their children. Childlessness thus eliminates one of the best means to endure the necessary resignation imposed upon the individual through marriage. This emotional identification with the daughter may easily go so far with the mother that she also falls in love with the man her daughter loves, which leads, in extreme cases, to severe forms of neurotic ailments on account of the violent psychic resistance against this emotional predisposition. At all events the tendency to such infatuation is very frequent with the mother-in-law, and either this infatuation itself or the tendency opposed to it joins the conflict of contending forces in the psyche of the mother-in-law. Very often it is just this harsh and sadistic component of the love emotion which is turned against the son-in-law in order better to suppress the forbidden tender feelings.

The relation of the husband to his mother-in-law is complicated through similar feelings which, however, spring from other sources. The path of object selection has normally led him to his love object through the image of his mother and perhaps his sister; in consequence of the incest barriers his preference for these two beloved persons of his childhood has been deflected and he is then able to find their image in strange objects. He now sees the mother-in-law taking the place of his own mother and of his sister's mother, and there develops a tendency to return to the primitive selection, against which everything in him resists. His incest dread demands that he should not be reminded of the genealogy of his love selection; the actuality of his mother-in-law, whom he had not known all his life like his mother so that her picture can be preserved unchanged in his unconscious, facilitates this rejection. An added mixture of irritability and animosity in his feelings lead us to suspect that the mother-in-law actually represents an incest temptation for the son-in-law, just as it not infrequently happens that a man falls in love with his subsequent mother-in-law before his inclination is transferred to her daughter.

I see no objection to the assumption that it is just this incestuous factor of the relationship which motivates the avoidance between son- and mother-in-law among savages. Among the explanations for the "avoidances" which these primitive races observe so strictly we would therefore give preference to the opinion originally expressed by Fison, who sees nothing in these regulations but a protection against possible incest. This would also hold good for all the other avoidances between those related by blood and by marriage. There is only one difference, namely in the first case the incest is direct, so that the purpose of the prevention might be conscious; in the other case, which includes the mother-in-law relation, the incest would be a phantasy temptation brought about by unconscious intermediary links.

We have had little opportunity in this exposition to show that the facts of folk-psychology can be seen in a new light through the application of the psychoanalytic point of view, for the incest dread of savages has long been known as such, and is in need of no further interpretation. What we can add to the further appreciation of incest dread is the statement that it is a subtle infantile trait and is in striking agreement with the psychic life of the neurotic. Psychoanalysis has taught us that the first object selection of the boy is of an incestuous nature and that it is directed to the forbidden objects, the mother and the sister; psychoanalysis has taught us also the methods through which the maturing individual frees himself from these incestuous attractions. The neurotic, however, regularly presents to us a piece of psychic infantilism; he has either not been able to free himself from the childlike conditions of psycho-sexuality or else he has returned to them (inhibited development and regression). Hence the incestuous fixations of the libido still play or again are playing the main rôle in his unconscious psychic life. We have gone so far as to declare that the relation to the parents instigated by incestuous longings is the central complex of the neurosis. This discovery of the significance of incest for the neurosis naturally meets with the most general incredulity on the part of the grownup, normal man; a similar rejection will also meet the researches of Otto Rank, which show in even larger scope to what extent the incest theme stands in the centre of poetical interest and how it forms the material of poetry in countless variations and distortions. We are forced to believe that such a rejection is above all the product of man's deep aversion to his former incest wishes which have since succumbed to repression. It is therefore of importance to us to be able to show that man's incest wishes, which later are destined to become unconscious, are still felt to be dangerous by savage races, who consider them worthy of the most severe defensive measures.

Notes

17 Frazer, *Totemism and Exogamy,* II, p. 76.

18 Frazer, *l.c.,* II, p. 113, according to C. Ribbe: *Two Years Among the Cannibals of the Solomon Islands,* 1905.

19 Frazer, *l.c.,* II, p. 385

20 Frazer, *l.c.,* II, p. 461

21 *v.* Crawley: *The Mystic Rose* (London, 1902), p. 405

22 Crawley, *l.c.,* p. 407

23 Crawley, *l.c.,* p. 401, according to Leslie: *Among the Zulus and Amatongas,* 1875.

ON JOKING RELATIONSHIPS[1]

A. R. Radcliffe-Brown

The publication of Mr. F. J. Pedler's note[2] on what are called 'joking relationships', following on two other papers on the same subject by Professor Henri Labouret[3] and Mademoiselle Denise Paulme,[4] suggests that some general theoretical discussion of the nature of these relationships may be of interest to readers of *Africa*.[5]

What is meant by the term 'joking relationship' is a relation between two persons in which one is by custom permitted, and in some instances required, to tease or make fun of the other, who in turn is required to take no offence. It is important to distinguish two main varieties. In one the relation is symmetrical; each of the two persons teases or makes fun of the other. In the other variety the relation is asymmetrical; A jokes at the expense of B and B accepts the teasing good humouredly but without retaliating; or A teases B as much as he pleases and B in return teases A only a little. There are many varieties in the form of this relationship in different societies. In some instances the joking or teasing is only verbal, in others it includes horse-play; in some the joking includes elements of obscenity, in others not.

Standardised social relationships of this kind are extremely widespread, not only in Africa but also in Asia, Oceania and North America. To arrive at a scientific understanding of the phenomenon it is necessary to make a wide comparative study. Some material for this now exists in anthropological literature, though by no means all that could be desired, since it is unfortunately still only rarely that such relationships are observed and described as exactly as they might be.

The joking relationship is a peculiar combination of friendliness and antagonism. The behaviour is such that in any other social context it would express and arouse hostility; but it is not meant seriously and must not be taken seriously. There is a pretence of hostility and a real friendliness. To put it in another way, the relationship is one of permitted disrespect. Thus any complete theory of it must be part of, or consistent with, a theory of the place of respect in social relations and in social life generally. But this is a very wide and very important sociological problem; for it is evident that the whole maintenance of a social order depends upon the appropriate kind and degree of respect being shown towards certain persons, things and ideas or symbols.

Examples of joking relationships between relatives by marriage are very commonly found in Africa and in other parts of the world. Thus Mademoiselle Paulme[6] records that among the Dogon a man stands in a joking relationship to his wife's sisters and their daughters. Frequently the relationship holds between a man and both the brothers and sisters of his wife. But in some instances there is a distinction whereby a man is on joking terms with his wife's younger brothers and sisters but not with those who are

Reprinted by permission of the editors from *Structure and Function in Primitive Society*, London: Cohen and West Ltd., 1952, pp. 90-93.

older than she is. This joking with the wife's brothers and sisters is usually associated with a custom requiring extreme respect, often partial or complete avoidance, between a son-in-law and his wife's parents.[7]

The kind of structural situation in which the associated customs of joking and avoidance are found may be described as follows. A marriage involves a readjustment of the social structure whereby the woman's relations with her family are greatly modified and she enters into a new and very close relation with her husband. The latter is at the same time brought into a special relation with his wife's family, to which, however, he is an outsider. For the sake of brevity, though at the risk of over-simplification, we will consider only the husband's relation to his wife's family. The relation can be described as involving both attachment and separation, both social conjunction and social disjunction, if I may use the terms. The man has his own definite position in the social structure, determined for him by his birth into a certain family, lineage or clan. The great body of his rights and duties and the interests and activities that he shares with others are the result of his position. Before the marriage his wife's family are outsiders for him as he is an outsider for them. This constitutes a social disjunction which is not destroyed by the marriage. The social conjunction results from the continuance, though in altered form, of the wife's relation to her family, their continued interest in her and in her children. If the wife were really bought and paid for, as ignorant persons say that she is in Africa, there would be no place for any permanent close relation of a man with his wife's family. But though slaves can be bought, wives cannot.

Social disjunction implies divergence of interests and therefore the possibility of conflict and hostility, while conjunction requires the avoidance of strife. How can a relation which combines the two be given a stable, ordered form? There are two ways of doing this. One is to maintain between two persons so related an extreme mutual respect and a limitation of direct personal contact. This is exhibited in the very formal relations that are, in so many societies, characteristic of the behaviour of a son-in law on the one side and his wife's father and mother on the other. In its most extreme form there is complete avoidance of any social contact between a man and his mother-in-law.

This avoidance must not be mistaken for a sign of hostility. One does, of course, if one is wise, avoid having too much to do with one's enemies, but that is quite a different matter. I once asked an Australian native why he had to avoid his mother-in-law, and his reply was, 'Because she is my best friend in the world; she has given me my wife'. The mutual respect between son-in-law and parents-in-law is a mode of friendship. It prevents conflict that might arise through divergence of interest.

The alternative to this relation of extreme mutual respect and restraint is the joking relationship, one, that is, of mutual disrespect and licence. Any serious hostility is prevented by the playful antagonism of teasing, and this in its regular repetition is a constant expression or reminder of that social disjunction which is one of the essential components of the relation, while the social conjunction is maintained by the friendliness that takes no offence at insult.

The discrimination within the wife's family between those who have to be treated with extreme respect and those with whom it is a duty to be disrespectful is made on the basis of generation and sometimes of seniority within the generation. The usual respected relatives are those of the first ascending generation, the wife's mother and her sisters, the wife's father and his brothers, sometimes the wife's mother's brother. The joking relatives are those of a person's own generation; but very frequently a distinction of seniority within the generation is made; a wife's older sister or brother may be respected while those younger will be teased.

In certain societies a man may be said to have relatives by marriage long before he marries and indeed as soon as he is born into the world. This is provided by the institution of the required or preferential marriage. We will, for the sake of brevity, consider only one kind of such organisations. In many societies it is regarded as preferable that a man should marry the daughter of his mother's brother; this is a form of the custom known as cross-cousin marriage. Thus his female cousins of this kind, or all those women whom by the classificatory system he classifies as such, are potential wives for him, and their brothers are his potential brothers-in-law. Among the Ojibwa Indians of North America, the Chiga of Uganda, and in Fiji and New Caledonia, as well as elsewhere, this form of marriage is found and is accompanied by a joking relationship between a man and the sons and daughters of his mother's brother. To quote one instance of these, the following is recorded for the Ojibwa. 'When cross-cousins meet they must try to embarrass one another. They "joke" one another, making the most vulgar allegations, by their standards as well as ours. But being "kind" relations, no one can take offence. Cross-cousins who do not joke in this way are considered boorish, as not playing the social game.'[8]

The joking relationship here is of fundamentally the same kind as that already discussed. It is established before marriage and is continued, after marriage, with the brothers- and sisters-in-law.

Notes

1 Reprinted from *Africa*, Vol. XIII, No. 3, 1940, pp. 195-210.

2 'Joking Relationships in East Africa', *Africa*, Vol. XIII, p. 170.

3 'La Parenté à Plaisanteries en Afrique Occidentale', *Africa*, Vol. II, p. 244.

4 'Parenté à Plaisanteries et Alliance par le Sang en Afrique Occidentale', *Africa*, Vol. XII, p. 433.

5 Professor Marcel Mauss has published a brief theoretical discussion of the subject in the *Annuaire de l'École Pratique des Hautes Études, Section des Sciences religieuses*, 1927-8. It is also dealt with by Dr. F. Eggan in *Social Anthropology of North American Tribes*, 1937, pp. 75-81.

6 *Africa*, Vol. XII, p. 438.

7 Those who are not familiar with these widespread customs will find descriptions in Junod, *Life of a South African Tribe*, Neuchâtel, Vol. I, pp. 229-37, and in *Social Anthropology of North American Tribes*, edited by F. Eggan, Chicago, 1937, pp. 55-7.

8 Ruth Landes in Mead, *Co-operation and Competition among Primitive Peoples*, 1937, p. 103.

Section II

SEXUALITY

All human societies are composed of women and men, and in addition, all societies include adults as well as children. For every generation then there are reproductive contexts and socializing agents assuring patterning of behavior and social continuity. All human societies also show a decided preference for heterosexuality and coitus. Were this not the case our species would soon face extinction. As Ford and Beach point out: "Along with other members of his society each person finds certain opportunities and restrictions provided by his culture which tend to mold his sexual behavior into a particular pattern" (1951: 17).

Human sexuality can be expressed in numerous ways and in diverse contexts constituting a variety of cultural patterns. Some societies permit, or even expect, premarital sexual encounters and Robert Suggs (1966: 99) suggests that Marquesan girls may have experienced their first intercourse by age ten and boys between seven and twelve after their circumcision.

Societies may also permit extra-marital sexual relations which may coincide with polygynous unions. Most societies world wide ascribe a restrictive element to marriage which not only pertains to sexual access but also the legitimization of offspring. One such restriction involves rights acquired during the marriage by the husband and his family over the wife and her reproductive potential. This may involve the transfer of bride-wealth, but irrespective of the latter's presence, marriage involves obligation of a reciprocal nature.

The first reading, delving back into Judeo-Christian traditions, illustrates the practice of levirate (from Latin levir, meaning husband's brother). According to this practice, which is encountered among many patrilineal peoples throughout the world, a deceased man's brothers retain sexual rights over the widow and may raise children in the name of the deceased. Essentially they are assuring the continuity of the male line and patrilineal descent principle.

In this reading we find an account in which Onan was acting in accordance with tradition when he slept with the widow of his deceased brother. However, we do not learn whether Onan practiced masturbation (to which his name has been linked in the form of Onanism) or withdrawal. Though practiced as a natural method of birth control coitus interruptus (withdrawal) is quite unpredictable.

The sexual behavior of people is as much a part of their culture as is eating, sleeping, or working. Sexual relations then have accepted or sanctioned times, places, and ways for expression. This assures a degree of predictability and allows one person to expect with a fair degree of accuracy how another person of the same group—and the same or opposite gender—will react in a given context. We may then speak of that complex of beliefs, values, actions, and relationships—thus attitudes and behavior—as sexuality, a subject studied by the science of sexology. John Money, in his book *Love and*

Love Sickness (1981:xi), states that "Sexology is very much concerned, in the final analysis, with the interconnectedness of what goes on between the groins and between the ears relative to the procreation of the species." What goes on between the ears is of course heavily influenced by culture and this in turn influences what goes on between the groins. We will then be able to speak of cultural patterns of sexuality. Davenport describes a puritanical Christian community in Ireland (pseudonymously called Inis Baeg by Messenger who conducted the study) where the ethos negates sexuality, and so there is hardly any mention of sexual subjects and "all forms of sexual behavior are apparently infrequent" (1978:123). By contrast African societies, marked by polygynous unions, suggest much greater openness about the subject and much more intense expression. Thus Ford and Beach suggest that a Thonga man may copulate with three or four of his wives in a single night. Chagga men are reported to have "intercourse ten times in a single night...however, one must consider the possibility that the male orgasm does not occur with every act..." (1951:79).

The final two readings in this section deal with ways of expressing sexuality. Karl Heider discusses the Dani who live in Irian Jaya (western New Guinea) and describes the exceptionally low level of sexuality among the Dani men as having ecological and cultural explanations. Arlo Nimmo, who conducted research among the Bajau of the southern Philippines, describes a very open system in which sexual topics are freely discussed and sexual gratification is seen as normal.

References

Davenport, William A. 1978. Sex in Cross-Cultural Perspective, Pp 115-163. Frank A Beach (ed) *Human Sexuality in Four Perspectives*. Baltimore: Johns Hopkins Press.

Ford, Clellan S. and Frank A. Beach. 1951. *Patterns of Sexual Behavior*. New York: Harper Torchbooks.

Money, John. 1981. *Love and Love Sickness*. Baltimore: Johns Hopkins University Press.

Suggs, Robert C. 1966. *Marquesan sexual behavior*. New York: Harcourt, Brace and World.

GENESIS 38: 1 - 10

ABOUT THAT TIME JUDAH LEFT HIS BROTHERS and went south and pitched his tent in company with an Adullamite named Hirah. There he saw Bathshua the daughter of a Canaanite and married her. He slept with her and she conceived and bore a son, whom she called Er. She conceived again and bore a son whom she called Onan. Once more she conceived and bore a son whom she called Shelah, and she ceased to bear children when she had given birth to him. Judah found a wife for his eldest son Er; her name was Tamar. But Judah's eldest son Er was wicked in the LORD's sight, and the LORD took his life. Then Judah told Onan to sleep with his brother's wife, to do his duty as the husband's brother and raise up issue for his brother. But Onan knew that the issue would not be his; so whenever he slept with his brother's wife, he spilled his seed on the ground so as not to raise up issue for his brother. What he did was wicked in the LORD's sight, and the LORD took his life. Judah said to his daughter-in-law Tamar, 'Remain as a widow in your father's house until my son Shelah grows up'; for he was afraid that he too would die like his brothers. So Tamar went and stayed in her father's house.

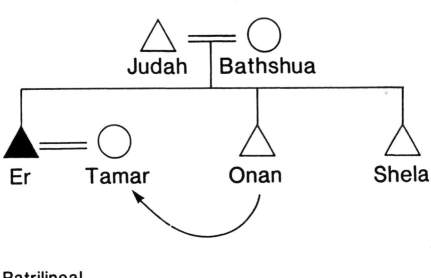

Patrilineal
Onanism
Levirate

Reprinted from *The New English Bible,* New York: Cambridge University Press, 1971. Genesis 38:1-10.

DANI SEXUALITY: A LOW ENERGY SYSTEM

Karl G. Heider
University of South Carolina

I

The Grand Valley Dani have a four-to-six year postpartum sexual abstinence.

The period of abstinence is invariably observed.

The norm of a long postpartum sexual abstinence is neither supported by powerful explanations nor enforced by strong sanctions.

Most people have no alternative sexual outlets.

No one shows signs of unhappiness or stress during their abstinence (cf. Heider 1970:74).

Most people find these five statements difficult to accept. Even an anthropological audience, which is accustomed to hearing the most exotic facts about different cultures, feels somehow that these statements stretch their credulity. Anthropologists, together with most other social scientists, hold Freudian assumptions about a high pan-cultural level of sexuality. These assumptions make the description of the Dani behaviour extremely improbable. A fair example of conventional thinking is found in a recent (1972) cross-cultural study of the postpartum sexual abstinence by Saucier, who was trained in both psychoanalysis and anthropology. Saucier considers that a long postpartum sexual abstinence is one of more than one year, and says that such a long abstinence places a great burden on the women and those men who are monogamous. Therefore, he concludes,

> to explain such a taboo we must postulate serious reasons for its introduction and a strong social organization for its maintenance (1972:238).

This is a strong position, one which Saucier feels is self-evident, based on indisputable assumptions, and so not necessary to elaborate on. His paper was published as part of a symposium on population in *Current Anthropology*. The symposium papers were sent to fifty scholars for comment, and eight comments were published, but no one challenged Saucier. So it is fair to say that Saucier accurately represented anthropological thinking on sexuality and the postpartum sexual abstinence. In fact, the Freudian ideas about sexuality have permeated our intellectual atmosphere. They are often passed off as an unchallenged part of general knowledge. Anthropologists, who are culturally relativistic in many matters, are quite comfortable with assumptions of an innate sexual drive, or quotient of sexual energy which must be expressed somehow, directly or indirectly. Certainly anthropologists

Reprinted by permission of the editors from *Man (NS)*, Vol. 11, 1976, pp. 188-201.

have long been interested in the performance ethnography of sex, but even this is based on covert Freudian assumptions of pan-cultural or biologically-innate levels of sexuality.

But my problem, as the anthropologist reporting these statements about the Dani postpartum sexual abstinence, is compound. In the first place, since the statements are unlikely, or go against expectation, a special degree of proof is required: a proof far more rigorous than that demanded of claims which, however strange they may be, fall within an expectable range of variation. What compounds the problem is that these statements refer to sexual behaviour and to internal psychic states, both of which are extremely difficult to document. And, further, they are negative statements. They claim an absence of expected occurrences, and nothing is more difficult to demonstrate than that people *never* do or feel a certain thing.

Yet, if this is a true description of the Dani, as I think it is, the subject is worth pursuing. It has important implications for the understanding of a few thousand people in the mountains of Irian Jaya, Indonesia. And it has more general implications for our understanding of the range of human sexual behaviour. Particularly it speaks to the issue of whether the level of sexuality is culturally learned, or is more innate. As we shall see, the Dani data provide a strong argument for the importance of cultural conditioning.

It seems best to broaden the scope of the discussion from a consideration of just the Dani postpartum abstinence to a consideration of Dani sexuality in general. There are two reasons for this, one theoretical, and the other more practical. In theoretical terms, the Dani postpartum sexual abstinence is mainly significant as an indication, or manifestation, of a remarkably low level of sexuality. So, rather than just examine a single trait, we can look at a number of traits which contribute to a complex pattern or tendency, which runs throughout Dani life.

The more practical reason is simply one of strategy. It would be virtually impossible to prove the postpartum sexual abstinence case. It is hard to imagine any anthropologist being able to obtain the sort of data which could conclusively prove that a couple does not have sexual intercourse for a five year period. Certainly I do not have such data. But if the very suggestive data on the postpartum sexual abstinence are put together with other, related data on sexuality, a strong circumstantial case can be made.

The proposition to be shown in this article, then, is: The Grand Valley Dani have an extraordinarily low level of sexuality.

For convenience, I will use the term 'Dani'. In fact, I am discussing only Grand Valley Dani men. (For a general ethnographic description of the Dani, see Heider 1970.) There is reason to believe that other Dani—especially the Western Dani—are quite different in this respect from the Grand Valley Dani. And my data come mainly from men. I observed Grand Valley Dani women, but rarely discussed anything with them.

By 'sexuality' I mean both sexual behaviour and sexual attitudes. I mean to say I that Dani do not often behave sexually nor does sex have much interest for them.

Although the proposition will demonstrate 'an extraordinarily low level' of sexuality, it does not support a general proposition that the sexuality of cultures can be calibrated on a scale. Rather, I would suggest that most cultures have fairly similar levels of sexuality (expressed, of course, in a myriad of ways) and that it would serve no purpose to try to rank them in terms of precise levels of sexuality. But the Dani level of sexuality is so clearly beyond the general range that we will have no trouble in saying that it is 'extraordinarily low'.

This is an unorthodox essay, more than description and less than explanation. By drawing together the various behaviours which are relevant to sexuality, I shall present an interrelated contextualised behavioural and cognitive pattern, one which forms a major theme in Dani life: namely, the low level of psychical or emotional energy which the Dani invest in sexuality and, indeed, in many other sorts of behaviour. My own understanding of the Dani pattern began with noticing negatives, or absences: the lack of theatrical climax in ceremonies, the casual attitudes toward death, the unconcern about sex. But this article is not merely a list of what the Dani lack. It tries to build an understanding of what a low energy cultural system implies.

II

The place to begin a description of Dani sexuality is with the postpartum sexual abstinence. Let us take up, one by one, the statements at the beginning of the article.

1. The Grand Valley Dani have a four- to six-year postpartum sexual abstinence.

There is no question that the Dani claim this. In many circumstances many different Dani men have told me that the parents of a child refrain from sexual intercourse with each other from the time when the child is born until the child is about five years old.

The time period is only approximate. The Dani do not reckon time units like months or years. They have little interest in quantification (in contrast to the neighbouring Kapauku, who are similar in many respects to the Dani, but are avid quantifiers—cf. Pospisil 1958). Indeed, the Dani have no words for four, five, or six, although they can be pushed into expressing these as a combination of 'one' or 'two'. When I asked the length of the postpartum sexual abstinence, my informant would express it in relation to the age of some child we both knew, or he would simply indicate it by holding his hand at the height of a child of the appropriate age. Since the Dani do not reckon people's ages in years even these data are only approximate. But it seems very safe to say that when the Dani describe the length of the postpartum sexual abstinence, they are referring to a period of between four and six years.

It is worth noting that a similarly long period of postpartum sexual abstinence was reported, independently, from the Jalé, who are a neighbouring Dani-speaking group (Koch 1968: 90). There seem to be no reports of any society which has a longer postpartum sexual abstinence as a general norm. The Cheyenne are often cited as having a ten-year postpartum sexual abstinence, but this was apparently a very unusual and virtuous undertaking, and not a general Cheyenne practice (cf. Grinnell 1924:149).

2. The period of the postpartum sexual abstinence is invariably observed.

This is a broad claim, but I have no reason to doubt it. There are two sets of evidence in favour of it. First, there is the fact that the Dani say that the postpartum sexual abstinence is invariably observed. Although I was often told quite scurrilous things about people, no one ever told me that someone else had prematurely broken their abstinence. I assume that if such an explicit norm were casually violated, I would have learned about it casually. And I did not. On the other hand, if the violation of the norm were of great consequence, I would have heard about it as a serious accusation. And I did not. It is worth adding that Dani life is generally quite public. Neither the landscape nor the architecture provides much privacy, so it would be extremely difficult to do anything in secret.

The second kind of evidence is biological. No full siblings are closer in age than about five years. This conclusion is based on those siblings whom I knew or saw, and, since the Dani do not reckon ages in years, on my estimate of their age differences. But the genealogical data were quite good, and the estimates of age were fairly good, at least for those under age 25 or so.

Since the norm only prohibits sexual intercourse between the parents of a child, and is not a general prohibition on intercourse for them as individuals, there were several men and one woman who were parents of half-siblings only a couple of years apart in age.

Of course, the pattern of siblings five or more years apart in age is one which could be produced by other means than a long postpartum sexual abstinence. Contraception, coitus interruptus, abortion, or infanticide could be used singly or in combination to produce such a pattern. But all my data suggest that none of these is actually practised and that the pattern of widely-spaced siblings is indeed due to the observance of the postpartum sexual abstinence.

3. The norm of a long postpartum sexual abstinence is neither supported by powerful explanation nor enforced by strong sanctions.

I was never able to learn a reason for the long postpartum sexual abstinence. When I pushed the line of questioning, people would say that violations of the abstinence would cause trouble with the ghosts, who might hurt or even kill the adults involved, and might cripple a child conceived during a violation of the abstinence. But it is important to realise that this ghostly sanction is neither very salient nor very powerful. Elsewhere I have described at some length the casual attitude which the Dani have toward their ghosts (1970: 37 sqq). Briefly, the Dani explain much of their ritual, including warfare, in terms of the need to placate the ghosts of their own dead. But in fact they were extremely casual in discussing the ghosts, and in performing the supposedly-necessary placatory behaviour. So while it is literally correct to say that this postpartum sexual abstinence has a supernatural sanction, it must be understood as a fairly casual, pro forma sanction.

Of course, it would be possible to enforce a five-year postpartum sexual abstinence in any society, given a powerful enough external control system. I found no evidence of such a system in Dani society. I think that it is fair to say that in most societies the control system would have to be very powerful and obvious. So obvious, in fact, that no anthropologist could miss it—certainly not after staying for some 30 months, as I did amongst the Dani.

4. Most people have no alternative sexual outlets.

An obvious 'solution' to the deprivation of a long postpartum sexual abstinence would be polygyny. But although the Dani practise polygyny, it is not very effective in this way. None of the women and a minority of the men have more than one spouse. The figures for the 148 males in the neighbourhood which I studied are:

Dogum neighbourhood males: marital status		
Status		N
Not yet married		53
Never married (permanent bachelors)		3
One wife		49
More than one wife		43
2 wives	23	
3 wives	14	
4 wives	5	
9 wives	1	
	Total	148

(from Heider 1970: 72, table 2.2)

But even these figures are misleading, since not all the 47 per cent. of married men (29 per cent. of all males) with multiple wives would actually have free access to another wife throughout the five years of their postpartum sexual abstinence with one wife. Two wives may have borne children within a few years of each other; and often co-wives do not get along well together, and live in different compounds. During the first year or so of a child's life, a man is likely to stay in the compound with the infant, and not with the wife to whom he has sexual access.

Other possible sexual outlets for a couple would be coitus interruptus with each other, extramarital sexual intercourse, masturbation, homosexuality, or bestiality. To the best of my knowledge, none of these is practised by any Dani, whether or not subject to a postpartum sexual abstinence.

5. No one shows any signs of unhappiness or stress during the period of abstinence.

The strongest evidence for a lack of concern, or anxiety, during the long postpartum sexual abstinence is my own ethnographic authority, based on more than two years' work with the Dani, in the course of which I explicitly probed into these matters. The information about the postpartum sexual abstinence was always given me in a quite matter-of-fact manner, and no man even hinted that he or anyone else might be in the least unhappy or stressed by such a long deprivation.

In order to investigate this point more systematically, I designed an elicitation experiment, utilising a Facial Expression Reaction Test. The experiment attempted to find some difference in sexual anxiety between men who were deep into their postpartum sexual abstinence and men who had sexual access to one or more wives. I have described the experiment in some detail elsewhere (Heider ms.). Although it has some general methodological interest, the results were not very conclusive. Certainly it did not turn up any overwhelming evidence for anxiety caused by celibacy.

III

Other data

The birth rate. There are no hard data for frequency of sexual intercourse among the Dani other than that absolute minimal figure represented by the birth rate. Even though the Dani have low interest in sex, they do perform it frequently enough to maintain the population. However, the apparent birth rate is rather low. The following table shows the number of children per married woman.

Number of children per woman in the Dugum neighbourhood.		
Married Women having borne	N	
No children	13	(all young married women who have not yet begun to have children)
1 child	86	
2 children	57	
3 children	13	(inlcudes two women with twins)
4 children	1	(woman with two children by each of two husbands)

(Heider 1970: 73, table 2.4)

These data come from genealogical data supplied in most cases by someone other than the woman involved, and so they represent remembered children—not total births, and certainly not total conceptions. Nevertheless, they do indicate the relatively low birth rate of the Dani. And, in turn, they indicate the low frequency of sexual intercourse for the Dani, since there is no good evidence of anything other than abstinence to account for the low birth rate. Dani men do talk about abortion. They are certainly aware of the possibility and they say that it is common, but I was never able to get convincing evidence that it is actually practised. Some Dani women have told me of a plant which they claim is contraceptive, but I have no convincing data on that either. I cannot completely rule out the possibility that the Dani use abortion or contraception rather than abstinence to keep down the birth rate, but it seems reasonable that if they were major factors I would have been able to learn more about them. Infanticide seems completely out of the question; no Dani ever hinted that it was ever practised, and I have no data to suggest that inadvertent infanticide occurred.

Extramarital sexual intercourse

There seems to be remarkably little extra-marital or premarital sexual activity. This conclusion is based on lack of evidence but it is a significant lack. If such affairs occurred, I should have learned about them through either casual gossip or serious accusation, and I did not. In the two years when I lived in the Dugum neighbourhood, I came to know of only one adulterous affair, and it precipitated a serious fight within the neighbourhood.

Even courting does not involve sexual intercourse. In fact, the Dani say that a couple do not begin to have sexual intercourse until a specific ceremony is held, two years after the major wedding exchange ceremony and thus two years after the couple has established a common residence (cf. Heider 1972: 182).

The wedding ceremonies themselves are very much group affairs. Weddings take place only at the major Pig Feast, held every four to six years, and never during the intervals. Although the marriage matches themselves are generally arranged by the two principals, marital sex is very much subject to the slow pace of the ceremonial cycle. This is further strong evidence for the unimportance of sex in Dani life.

Homosexuality

Another obvious possible locus for expression of sexuality would be homosexuality. But apparently the Dani do not practise it. Although most married men in a compound sleep most nights in the sleeping loft of the one men's house, this seems to involve no erotic homosexual behaviour.

Child-rearing. Infant eroticism is another obvious locus for sexuality, but the Dani infants receive remarkably little erotic input. This had been my general impression during my earlier research in 1961-1963. In 1970, Eleanor Rosch and I carried out systematic one-day (6 to 10 hours) observations on ten mother-preverbal infant pairs in the Grand Valley, and for comparative purposes we replicated those observations with another ten closely matched mother-infant pairs in the Western Dani region around Karubaga (the site of Denise O'Brien's research in 1961- 1963.) The observations were recorded on audio- and videotape. Although we have not yet analysed the data, it became obvious to us during the observations that although we were seeing among the Western Dani an expectable amount of mothers erotically manipulating their infants, there was virtually none of this among the Grand Valley Dani.

Initiation. Boys' initiation ceremonies often emphasise the sexual aspect of manhood, but the comparable Dani ceremony (which may not even be properly called 'initiation') emphasises moiety membership and not any masculine coming of age. In fact, only half the boys ever go through the ceremony, and in the one which I observed in 1970, the ages of the initiates ranged from about four to eighteen (cf. Heider 1970). There is one event with erotic symbolism, where the initiates throw reed spears into a tree as an explicit metaphor of the sexual intercourse they will later engage in. This is a rare and fleeting evidence of sexuality in Dani life.

The penis gourd. The penis gourd would seem to be as obvious a focus for sexuality as the post-partum sexual abstinence. Dani males from about the age of six wear a long upright penis gourd at virtually all times except when they are urinating or having sexual intercourse. Penis gourds, or other similar phallo-crypts which exaggerate the size and erection of the penis, have been used in many re-gions of the world, including late medieval and early Renaissance Europe. But the Dani penis gourd does not have any explicit sexual connotations for the Dani (this is not so true for non-Dani) nor do the different sizes and shapes of the penis gourd have apparent sexual connotations (cf. Heider 1969: 386-8; 1970: 244-7).

Teenagers' play. One of the very few areas of Dani life where there is any significant level of sexuality is in the songs, drawings, and string figures done by teenage boys and girls.

The songs, called *silon*, have a standard tune with regular form. Some are merely about natural phenomena, but others are quite explicitly sexual. They are sung by one or more boys, accompanied by laughter and nudging, in full recognition of their improper humour (cf. Heider 1970: 305-9).

The same teenage boys are responsible for crude charcoal drawings on rock overhangs through-out the neighbourhood. One common design, a short-stemmed down-pointing arrow, is called 'vulva'. The same symbol is scratched in sand or, after the introduction of machetes, chopped in tree bark (cf. Heider 1970: 181-4).

Also, one of the standard string figures performed by either a boy or a girl is called 'copulation' and involves moving loops together to represent a man and a woman copulating (Heider 1970: 205).

These three areas of sexual reference are extremely mild, and are remarkable only because they represent the most explicit sexuality—indeed, practically the only explicit sexuality—in Dani culture.

IV

Associated cultural phenomena

There are a number of other factors which seem relevant to this discussion of Dani sexuality, and which support the general picture of the Dani drawn so far.

On the whole, Dani interpersonal interaction is marked by low affect. The Dani are congenial and even-tempered, with few emotional peaks. Anger is rarely expressed, and confrontations are simply avoided through early withdrawal. There are rarely brawls, fights, or even shouting matches in a compound. An experiment designed to elicit facial expressions of affects confirmed this, showing that the Dani tended to express disgust expressions when given situations that might have been ex-pected to arouse anger (cf. Heider ms.).

Low intellectuality. One of the essential features of Freudian thought is that each person has a certain innate fixed amount of sexual energy which must be expressed in some fashion (cf. the excellent discussion in Gagnon and Simon 1973 : 11 sqq). Freud himself, in *Civilization and its discontents*, wrote

> Since a man does not have unlimited quantities of psychical energy at his disposal, he has to accomplish his tasks by making an expedient distribution of his libido. What he employs for cultural aims he to a great extent withdraws from women and sexual life (Freud 1930; English translation 1961: 103-4).

If this is true, then one might expect that the Dani, who do not use their energy in sexual directions, would have made notable achievements in intellectual or aesthetic directions. In fact, there is no sign of such achievements.

In most areas the Dani show very little intellectual elaboration (cf. Heider 1970). The Dani counting system, already described above, is a good example of this. The Dani have numbers 'one', 'two', (a rarely used) 'three', if necessary a 'twotwo', and 'many'. Certainly Dani men are not stupid (whatever that might mean). But they do not live in an intellectualised, abstract world.

Likewise, the Dani have very little that one could call art (I have discussed Dani art and the difficult problem of defining art in the Dani case in 1970: 180-193). This is especially true if one excludes ornamenting the body with feathers and grease, and the fine craftsmanship of a five-metre spear. The Dani are a direct, practical, pragmatic people.

Conservatism. It seems logical to mention here the extraordinary resistance of the Grand Valley Dani to change. Elsewhere I have attempted to explain this conservatism as the result of deep satisfaction with their traditional culture (Heider 1975). Whatever the causes, there is no question that the Dani show little adventurous innovation, despite a good deal of microflexibility. That is, the norms of behaviour allow considerable variation of behaviour, but the norms themselves do not change.

Finally I must emphasise that the Dani are a healthy, vigorous, strong people. Certainly through the early 1960's there was no malaria or other apparent debilitating endemic disease. As well as I could judge by the people's appearance and activity level, their diet was quite adequate. The various Dutch and Indonesian doctors who worked in the Grand Valley had found no serious diseases. It seems very unlikely that some undiscovered physical factor could be responsible for the Dani pattern which I have described.

V

Sexuality and relativism

The Dani data speak directly to a fundamental controversy about the nature of human sexuality, a controversy which is succinctly described in Gagnon and Simon (1973): namely, do all humans have an innate high level of sexual energy which must be expressed directly or indirectly (the Freudian view); or is the level of sexual energy determined by the cultural and social circumstances (the relativistic position)? The low level of Dani sexuality gives clear support to the relativistic position. Even the loophole of rechannelled, indirect expression of sexual energy, postulated by Freudian theorists, is of no avail. The Dani are a clear case of a culture with low sexuality. It is not necessary to explain why this occurs, although causal explanations are desirable in the long run. For now it is sufficient to have established the ethnographic facts.

The apparent uniqueness of the Dani case makes it especially important. Although Gagnon and Simon have argued strongly for the relativistic position, their data are primarily from groups within U.S. society—e.g., prison populations—which demonstrate (to use the subtitle of their book) 'the social sources of human sexuality' (1973). But even they, in what is admittedly only a very cursory glance at cross-cultural data, do not even postulate an entire society with low sexuality (cf. 1973: 306-7). They use the term 'sexuality' in much the same way as I do, to refer to both activity and affect. They refer to cultures with high affect, or concern about sex, but little activity (e.g. the Irish community studied by Messenger [1971]); and, at the opposite extreme, cultures with high sexual activity levels but low affect, or concern about sex (e.g., the Polynesian community studies by Marshall [1971]). This is an ironic situation indeed. These sociological champions of the relativistic position have challenged the Freudian assumptions when applied to individuals and groups. Yet, when they think of entire societies they implicitly (and intuitively?) utilise Freudian assumptions about pan-cultural levels of activity. It would be hard to find better testimony to the powers of these assumptions. This is also a strong testimony to the importance of the Dani data which so directly contradict the pan-cultural validity of these assumptions.

VI

Dani sexuality as a low-energy system

The goal of this article has been to bring together many diverse features of Dani culture and present them as manifestations of a single basic pattern. The features on which we have been focusing are the postpartum sexual abstinence and other aspects of sexual expression. At the beginning it seemed reasonable to speak of the Dani's low level of sexuality. As a first-level descriptive label for the Dani sexuality pattern, this is acceptable, but we can now move a step further.

The low level of sexuality seems to be consistent with the low level of intellectual elaboration, and the low level of affect. All these are part of a larger pattern of Dani behaviour which can be thought of as a set of low energy systems.

To term Dani sexuality a low energy system is merely to say that the Dani put little energy into sexual activities and into thinking about sexual activities. Much of Dani behaviour and thought is characterised by low energy expenditure. This concept of a low energy culture is a very imprecise one, difficult to define, and impossible to calibrate. But it is one way of looking at a great deal of Dani behaviour, and making sense of it.

The Dani do not invest much energy in their activities. They have little sustained, systematic, elaborated achievement. Certainly they live comfortably, and even well. No Dani ever goes hungry. They procreate, feed and shelter themselves, have ceremonies—and they do all these things quite adequately. They are not a deprived, broken down, or unhealthy society. But in none of these realms do the Dani act intensively, elaborately, or with great dramatic peaks of intellectual or emotional achievement.

This is not simply physical energy. If so, it would be fairly easy to describe and measure. And, to anticipate a bit, it would probably be fairly easy to explain low physical activity in purely physical terms. This energy is as much psychic or emotional as it is purely physical. There are situations in which Dani act strenuously and energetically. A good example of this is Dani behaviour in battle, which has been well-documented in Robert Gardner's film, *Dead birds* (1963). A battle lasts for part of a day, and exertion is very sporadic. Men spend most of the time relaxing behind the lines, talking, watching, and only occasionally moving forward to engage the enemy for an hour or so, before falling back to the rear again. But most significant in this context is the marked absence of aggression, hatred for the enemy, or even much at all in the way of sustained excitement (cf. Heider 1970: 127-8). Dani men reach an even more intense peak in the secular phase of war, a concentrated two or three days of ambushes and battles. However, this occurs only every decade or so. In fact, the overwhelming majority of the time which Dani spend in warfare and warfare associated activity is devoted to casual, low-energy activity.

VII

Energy and steady states

In a famous exploratory essay (1949), Gregory Bateson had grappled with a somewhat analogous problem in trying to understand the Balinese value system. In particular, he wrote about a set of attitudes and activities which were characterised by non-climaxing, balanced, plateaux of behaviour. Bateson used the term 'steady state' to describe the Balinese system. Bateson had been concerned with what he called 'schismogenic sequences'—competitive opposition which culminates in climax, followed by a lowered state. This had been one subject of *Naven*, his book on the New Guinea Iatmül. But he did not find the same pattern among the Balinese. This was surprising, and contrary to the expectations which he held, based on 'so many theories of social opposition and Marxian determinism' (1949: 39) and, in particular, the earlier formulations of game theory.

In the Dani case, it is a high level of sexuality, which was predicted by Freudian and Freudian-derived theories, which was found to be lacking.

The analogy goes a step further, for in some respects the Balinese culture resembles Dani culture. Particularly, Bateson's metaphor of plateau, or steady state lacking cumulative climaxing, seems very appropriate for the Dani. However the differences are even more striking than the similarity. In Bateson's work there is the sense that this Balinese plateau is one of high intensity. I understand the Dani plateau to be one of very low intensity. The Balinese maintain a steady state at a high energy level, the Dani a steady state at a low energy level. To use a culturally-apt metaphor, the difference is between a person balancing on a high wire and a person sitting on the ground. Both may appear nearly motionless, but the difference in energy level is considerable.

VIII

Causality

This all raises the question of causality. Of course, I am assuming that there is something to be explained: that we have established that Dani sexuality is a low-energy system—and indeed, that much of Dani life can be called a low-energy system; and I am assuming that the Dani are quite exceptional in this respect, and are not merely towards the low end of some normal curve of cultural energy.

The question can be phrased, then, either as 'Why are the Dani the way they are?' or 'Why are the Dani so different from other cultures?' The answers might be biological, or they might be cultural. However, it seems to me thoroughly unlikely that the Dani situation can be accounted for by some unique genetic, nutritional, or medical circumstances. My own predilection as an anthropologist is to look for a cultural factor as cause. I would think somewhat along the lines which Bateson took when he suggested that an explanation for the Balinese 'steady state' could be seen as the outcome of Balinese childhood experiences which resulted in 'some sort of modification, deconditioning, or inhibition' of a basic tendency of human beings to 'involve themselves in sequences of cumulative interactions' (1949: 42). In the Dani case, we can assume that something has happened to impede 'a basic tendency' of human beings to develop a high level of sexual energy which may be expressed in a variety of ways.

But what factors could account for the Dani situation? Better yet: what sorts of factors should we look for? It would be easy to fit some biological factors into our explanatory scheme: a unique gene pool, a debilitating disease, or a major nutritional deficiency could easily account for low energy level. But, alas for easy explanation, there are no apparent biological candidates. (We must be somewhat tentative here, for a thoroughgoing physiological investigation of the Dani could possibly turn up something which has so far escaped notice.)

But there are two factors, one environmental and the other more cultural, which might have some relevant causal status on the grounds that they involve a low input of stress into Dani life.

The first factor is the environment of the Grand Valley itself. It is remarkably benign. Flora, fauna, climate, and topography combine to create optimal comfort and minimal stimulation for human life (cf. Heider 1970: 212 sqq). All is mild, and there are no excesses: no dangerous plants or animals, moderate rainfall (around 78.5 inches per year) with no excessive floods or drought; mild temperature, with extremes of 29.5$C (85$F) and 6$C (42$F). Perhaps even more important, the Dani recognise no regular yearly rhythm of hot and cold or wet and dry. Indeed, even non-Dani who live in Grand Valley but come from Europe and North America, and are looking for seasonal cycles, have the greatest difficulty in satisfying their need for climatic order. Now, if it is true that the Dani experience no seasons, this may have powerful cognitive implications. For most cultures, the seasonal cycle forces a long-term organisation of subsistence activities and thereby promotes the development of an associated ceremonial cycle and a set of time units with which to handle it all. One can imagine that out of the cognitive demands of this periodicity grow intellectual opportunities for an even wider range of cognitive and intellectual elaborations. But the Dani lack the demands and therefore, perhaps, the opportunities. Instead, they plant and harvest the year round, and their ceremonies are either triggered by the accidents of birth or death, or, like the great Pig Feast, are held irregularly every few years. And the Dani do not use temporal units like day, month, or year to order their life. Obviously, the Dani do act with reference to the future, as when they plant sweet potato cuttings, or taboo the killing of pigs in order to build up the herds in anticipation of a ceremony a few months in the future. But they do not act in terms of a timetable of future demands as people must do to a certain extent if their environment has seasons.

Elsewhere I have suggested that the Dani lack 'the cognitive pacing that a strong yearly seasonal round might provide' (1970: 296). I had also argued that the absence of seasons is a contributory factor to the low level of sexuality. But now I think that both propositions, however ingenious they might seem, are vastly overstated. They are based on the assumption that regular seasonal changes of climate (like those found in the temperate zone) make certain cognitive demands on a people, and are themselves a sort of energising force. For the purposes of this present discussion of Dani sexuality, there are two important considerations: first, although the Dani themselves do not recognise seasons, and have no activities geared to a regular seasonal cycle, a Western scientist looking at the rainfall charts for the Grand Valley can talk of 'a short season of heavy rain and cloud' (Brookfield 1964: 36). Both Peters (1965: 15) and I (1970: 212) have emphasised the great variability in the occurrence of the rainy period, and the rainfall itself does vary in the Grand Valley from about 60 mm to about 350 mm a month (cf. Heider 1970: 213 Diagram 7.1). So there is variation in rainfall, even though its regularity is minimal and goes unnoticed by the Dani. (This is not the place to go into the question of how much variation it takes to invalidate a concept of regularity like 'seasons' [but cf. Brookfield & Brown 1963: 20-4].)

And second, although the Dani pattern of sexuality is unique, their climate is not. It is still fair to say that the climate of the Grand Valley is remarkably equable. But the attempt to link this causally with Dani sexuality is seriously compromised as soon as one looks at data from elsewhere in the New Guinea Highlands. Pospisil described an almost identical climate for the temperamentally very different Kapauku to the West (1963: 81), as did Glasse for the Huli to the East (1968: 19). At best we are left with a weak causal statement: the relatively benign natural environment of the Grand Valley is consistent with (and perhaps even contributory to) the low level of Dani sexuality.

The social environment of the Grand Valley Dani, like their natural environment, is fairly blank and uniform. Although the peoples of the New Guinea Highlands are known for their cultural (or at least linguistic) diversity, in fact the Grand Valley Dani are quite effectively isolated from other peoples by high uninhabited mountain ranges. Until regular European contact began in 1954, few Grand Valley Dani had experienced—or even seen—people with cultures and languages different from their own. Anthropologists and historians have long thought that the interaction between different cultures was an important stimulation for the evolution of culture. It is also reasonable to assume the converse: that extreme cultural isolation would have some effects. And certainly the Grand Valley Dani receive comparatively little stress or stimulation from either natural or cultural environment.

The second factor which seems suggestive here is the extremely low stress which Dani infants receive. For the first year or so, a Grand Valley Dani infant spends much of its time in the warm, shaded, softly-padded carrying net against its mother's back. This became especially apparent only when Eleanor Rosch and I carried out systematic observations of mother-infant pairs among both Grand Valley Dani and the Western Dani. The Western Dani infant was often taken out of the carrying net and held or carried in the open, exposed to massive stimulation even when this hampered the mother's work. Thus, during the several hours a day which the mothers spend working in their gardens, the Western Dani infants are squirming, clinging, seeing, and hearing, while the Grand Valley Dani are snugly snoozing.

Toilet training—and, indeed all training—is remarkably gentle and non-coercive for the Grand Valley Dani child. In short, Dani childhood is a period of little stress or stimulation.

Certainly I can make no conclusive causal claim for either environmental factors or childrearing practices. Both are further evidence of low level stress, and so they are at least significant as further aspects of the entire complex of low energy, whatever their causal status. In any case, for the moment at least it is not possible to demonstrate that the level of sexuality varies significantly with climate and child care, even within the New Guinea Highlands.

Conclusions

I began this essay by advancing a problematic ethnographic fact about a small group of Dani in the central highlands of Irian Jaya. In attempting to account for this fact, I used the strategy of holistic accumulation. More and more ethnographic facts were brought together, and were shown to constitute ever more inclusive patterns of behaviour. The extremely long postpartum sexual abstinence was shown to be part of a generally low level of sexuality; the low level of sexuality is consistent with generally low energy levels in much of Dani life; and the low energy levels are found in demands or inputs, as well as performance, or output for Dani individually and as a group, from infancy onwards. There are suggestive causal threads, but no single satisfactory conclusive causal chain emerges. The concept of energy levels is an effective one for understanding Dani behaviour. It remains to be seen whether it will have a comparative, cross-cultural use. Certainly the most important finding of general interest is that the Dani do have a low level of sexuality. This constitutes solid support for a relativistic view of sexuality.

Note

This article is based on research carried out among the Grand Valley Dani of Irian Jaya, Indonesia (West New Guinea), during two and a half years between 1961 and 1970. The research was supported by grants from the Foundations' Fund for Research in Psychiatry, the Cross-Cultural Study of Ethnocentrism Project, and others. So many people have helped me to think about these problems during the last fifteen years that it would be hopeless to try to name them all, but at least I would like to acknowledge Eleanor Rosch, my collaborator in research among the Dani in 1968 and 1970. While preparing the final version of this article I was a Fellow at the Center for Advanced Study in the Behavioral Sciences.

References

Bateson, Gregory 1936. *Naven*. Cambridge: Univ. Press.

_____ 1949. Bali: the value system of a steady state. In *Social structure: studies presented to A. R. Radcliffe-Brown* (ed.) Meyer Fortes. Oxford: Clarendon Press.

Brookfield, H. C. 1964. The ecology of highland settlement: some suggestions. *Am. Anthrop.* **66**, 20-38.

_____ & P. Brown 1963. *Struggle for land: agricultural and group territories among the Chimbu of the New Guinea Highlands*. Melbourne: Oxford Univ. Press.

Freud, Sigmund 1961. Civilization and its discontents. In *The Standard Edition of the complete psychological works of Sigmund Freud* (ed.) J. Strachey, vol. **21**. London: Hogarth.

Gagnon, John H. & William Simon 1973. *Sexual conduct: the social sources of human sexuality*. Chicago: Aldine.

Gardner, Robert 1963. *Dead birds* [film]. Film Study Center, Harvard University. New York: McGraw-Hill/Contemporary Films (distributors).

Glasse, Robert M. 1968. *Huli of Papua: a cognatic descent system* (Cah. Homme N.S. **8**). Paris: Mouton.

Grinnell, George Bird 1924. *The Cheyenne Indians: their history and ways of life*, vol. I. New Haven: Yale Univ. Press.

Heider, Karl G. 1969. Attributes and categories in the study of material culture: New Guinea Dani attire. *Man* (N.S.) **4**, 379-91.

_____ 1970. *The Dugum Dani: a Papuan culture in the highlands of west New Guinea*. Chicago: Aldine.

_____ 1972. The Grand Valley Dani pig feast: a ritual of passage and intensification. *Oceania* **42**,169-87.

_____ 1975. Societal intensification and cultural stress as determining factors in the innovation and conservatism of two Dani groups. *Oceania* **46**, 53-67.

_____ ms. Nonverbal studies of Dani anger and sexual expression: experimental method in videotape ethnography. Paper presented to the American Anthropological Association meetings, Nov. 1973, New Orleans.

Koch, Klaus-Friedrich 1968. Marriage in Jalémo. *Oceania* **39**, 85-109.

Marshall, Donald S. 1971. Sexual behavior on Magaia. In *Human sexual behavior* (eds) Donald S. Marshall & Robert C. Suggs. New York: Basic Books.

Messenger, John C. 1971. Sex and repression in an Irish folk community. In *Human sexual behavior* (eds) Donald S. Marshall & Robert C. Suggs. New York: Basic Books.

Peter, H. L. 1965. *Enkele hoofdstuukken uit het sociaal-religieuze leven van een Dani-groep*. Venlo: Dagblad voor Noord-Limburg.

Pospisil, Leopold 1958. *Kapauku Papuans and their law* (Yale Univ. Publ. Anthrop. **54**). New Haven: Yale Univ. Press.

_____ 1963. *Kapauku Papuan economy* (Yale Univ. Publ. Anthrop. **67**). New Haven: Yale Univ. Press.

Saucier, Jean-François 1972. Correlates of the long postpartum taboo: a cross-cultural study. *Curr. Anthrop.* **13**, 238-49.

BAJAU SEX AND REPRODUCTION[1]

H. Arlo Nimmo
California State College at Los Angeles

This paper is a description of Bajau beliefs and practices regarding sexual intercourse, reproduction, and childbirth. The data were collected incidentally to a field investigation of social change among the boat-dwelling Bajau of the southern Philippines, and therefore are not intended to be complete or final. However, since so few ethnographic accounts of the boat-dwelling Bajau are available, it seems wise to publish anthropologically collected data on these people—especially in light of the fact that the traditional culture of the Bajau is rapidly changing as they are currently abandoning their nomadic boat-dwelling habits to become sedentary house-dwellers.[2]

The Bajau are traditionally known as a nomadic, boat-dwelling people who inhabit the Sulu Islands of the southern Philippines. The Sulu Bajau are only one of several boat-dwelling groups scattered throughout Southeast Asia; others have been reported in parts of the Celebes, southern Malaya, and the Mergui Islands of Burma. Although the historical relationship of these different groups is still unknown, little doubt exists concerning the close relationship of the several groups of Bajau within the Sulu Islands; these groups all speak a single language, share many common cultural features, and were until recent times predominantly boat-dwellers. Today, most of the Sulu Bajau have abandoned their boats as living quarters for land- or reef-based dwellings. The most confirmed boat-dwellers are found in the Tawi-Tawi Islands of Sulu, where they number some 1600 individuals, while the most confirmed house-dwellers live in the Sibutu Islands, especially in Sitangkai, and comprise a population of about 2400. Wherever the Bajau are found, they represent a small minority of the total population. For example, they constitute only 3.1 per cent of the population of the Tawi-Tawi Islands, and in Sibutu they form about 23 per cent of the total Sibutu Islands' population. Within Sulu, the Bajau have always been viewed as an outcaste group by the land-dwelling Muslims, but in recent years as many of these sea folk have abandoned boat-dwelling and embraced Islam, they have become incorporated into the Islamic community of Sulu. Those of Tawi-Tawi, however, are still predominantly boat-dwelling subsistence fishermen who continue to follow their traditional life styles (Nimmo 1968).

Although extremely mobile, the Tawi-Tawi Bajau limit their movements to a fairly well-defined sea area, about 250 square miles, southeast of the large island of Tawi-Tawi. Within this area are located the five main Bajau moorages, or villages, and the two small cemetery islands where the sea people bury their dead. These seas are characterized by extensive coral reefs as well as numerous small islands which are farmed by the land-dwelling Muslim peoples upon whom most Bajau are dependent for the vegetable portion of their diet.

Reprinted by permission of the editors from *Ethnology*, Vol. IX, 1970, pp. 251-262.

The Bajau houseboat typically houses a single nuclear family. Although this family does a great deal of traveling among the various houseboat moorages, it always identifies one moorage as its home; or, if the husband and wife are from two different moorages, the family divides its allegiances and time between these two moorages. Frequently, the nuclear family fishes and travels with married siblings of either the husband or wife to form the second important social unit in Bajau society, the sibling alliance unit. This unit reveals great structural variation and is very ephemeral since house-boats regularly join and leave the unit. Its primary function is that of mutual aid for fishing, ceremonies, and any other activities which require group effort. Each moorage consists of several of these sibling alliance units to comprise a group of cognatically related persons, or a localized kindred, with an older man acting as headman. At the larger moorages, several such localized kindreds may be found, and the headman of the kindred which first began mooring there serves as headman for the entire village. No formal political organization exists beyond the village level to unite the several moorages, but because of the many kin ties and frequent movements among them, the moorages constitute a single, albeit dispersed, Tawi-Tawi community (Nimmo 1969).

Sexual Behavior

Although the intimacies of one's sexual behavior are never discussed openly among the Bajau, sex is not a hushed topic of conversation. Nor does it loom large in the conversations of the Bajau. To the Bajau, the sexual urge and need is almost as natural as any of the other bodily functions, and is nothing to become overly concerned about, an attitude obviously related to the fact that sexual gratification is always available. Premarital sexual relationships are common and expected; consequently, when the Bajau youth begins to feel the stirrings of his sexuality, he need only find a willing partner, which is rarely a problem, to satisfy his urges.[3] Upon marriage, of course, his spouse more conveniently satisfies his sexual desires.

Bajau discuss sexual matters quite frankly in the presence of members of the opposite sex, regardless of age or marital status. Once I heard two women speak with some detail, in the presence of their children and a neighboring man, about the adulterous amours of a village man. On another occasion, two women and a man, affines to one another, discussed rather clinically the probable size of my penis and the possible nature of my sex life. Bajau also joke freely about sex in mixed company and among children. Once, when I was discussing the nature of the Bajau bride-price with a group of adults and children, one of the men told me jokingly that the bride-price was actually paid for the bride's vagina since that was the greatest asset a bride has to offer her husband. The household laughed heartily at the joke, after which we continued our discussion. On another interview occasion with several women, the nature of twins entered the discussion. One of the older women jokingly asked me if I knew how to make twins, and, if so, she wanted me to make some for her. All laughed without embarrassment and thought it a good joke.

Bajau sometimes use euphemisms to refer to sexual matters—not in order to disguise the topic, but rather for the humorous misunderstandings which often result. Once two Bajau girls asked my assistant the price of mangoes in the nearby port town. He told them that they were selling for about ten centavos a bunch. The girls expressed disbelief at the price and said they were much more expensive among the Bajau—at least a peso, and often more than two pesos. My assistant was surprised at the inordinately high price and asked why. They responded that Bajau mangoes were bigger, sweeter, and lasted longer. The girls then began giggling and my assistant finally realized that they were actually referring to the sexual favors of Bajau girls and not to mangoes. Sometimes a man's penis is referred to as his sail or mast, and reference to either of these structures may lead to a joking conversation filled with sexual metaphors. A young man who is known to be having a rather active sex life is said to be out "laying his eggs." These examples serve to illustrate the freedom with which sex is discussed as well as the lack of embarrassment associated with the topic. However, I do not wish to convey that sex is a constant topic of conversation, for such is certainly not the case.

Although it is a voiced ideal among the Bajau that young people should wait until marriage before engaging in sexual intercourse, it is well known that very few Bajau youth reach marriage without having had sexual experiences. In reality, it is expected that young people will engage in such behavior, which is for the most part condoned by Bajau society. Children early become aware of the nature of the human genitals. They wear no clothes until the age of eight or ten, and commonly explore one another's genitals during these early years. Parents do not become upset with such behavior unless the child displays undue curiosity, when he may be scolded, or more likely teased, until his attention is diverted to something else. Women normally expose their breasts after the birth of their first child, but always wear a sarong to cover their genitals. On the other hand, the loose nature of men's clothing often exposes their genitals—not to mention their common practice of diving in the nude for certain types of fishing. Consequently, the Bajau child matures with little notion of mystery surrounding the human genitalia.

Bajau youth make themselves attractive to members of the opposite sex through the use of numerous beauty aids. Young girls rarely wash their hair, but frequently comb coconut oil into it, the smell of which has a strong feminine association in the Bajau olfactory. Commercially made face powders are sometimes rubbed on the female face to lighten the complexion, or may be caked on heavily in traditional Sulu style so that the face appears masked in white powder. Lipstick is widely used by young girls, and sometimes a really made-up lass may place a spot of it on either cheek. Girls also use fingernail polish and perfumes whenever these are available. To complete her costume, the properly attired young Bajau girl wears jewelry which may include various combinations of earrings, rings, bracelets, necklaces, and brooches. Boys always use heavily scented wax on their hair, and also occasionally use face powder to lighten their complexions. They often let the little fingernail or the thumbnail grow extra long, and may even apply fingernail polish. Those who have whiskers sometimes cultivate mustaches, but such hirsute displays are not widespread owing to the sparsity of facial hair among the Bajau. Both sexes, of course, enjoy dressing in their finest clothes.

A well-filled body is considered beautiful by both sexes; a wiry, muscular body is not considered particularly attractive, nor is an overweight body. Black, oiled hair is preferred over the reddish, sun-bleached shades characteristic of most Bajau. Certain female movements are sexually arousing to the

Bajau male. Especially erotic are the slow, languid hip and arm movements of the traditional dances as well as the walking sway of slender female hips.

Love magic, though known in Sulu, is not widely used among the Bajau. Most Bajau men claim to have heard of such magic, but I encountered none who admitted using it. One man, however, claimed that the following formula never fails: If a man gathers sand upon which a girl has stepped, wraps it in a white cloth, and ties it in his boat, the young girl will develop an itching on the soles of her feet which will not stop until she enters the boat, at which time she is very vulnerable to seduction. The informant claimed that a non-Bajau had told him the formula, but he denied ever having tried it himself. Amulets can be worn by females to protect themselves from the love magic of males, but I met only one girl who wore an amulet for this specific purpose—a string necklace which had been made by her grandfather. Since finding a sexual partner is not difficult for the Bajau, it is not surprising to find that love magic is poorly developed among them.

The amours of most Bajau youth take place in the early hours of the evening, shortly after sunset. The unmarried teenagers of the village usually congregate on the nearby beach or exposed reef during the hours of dusk for games and conversation. During this time, romances begin and rendezvous are planned. After dark young people commonly congregate in one of the larger houseboats to play music and sing songs. Here, too, affairs may begin. Many Bajau youth make new contacts during ceremonies. At certain phases of the moon, which complement fishing cycles and insure that many Bajau houseboats are in the nearby waters, Bajau ceremonies of healing, circumcision, and marriage are held. Boats from all the nearby waters come to attend the festivities, and the size of the host village is consequently greatly expanded. The early part of the evening celebration is attended by all the community and consists primarily of music and dancing, but as the evening wears on the adults and children retire to the houseboats and leave the rest of the night to the unmarried teenagers, who continue to play music, sing, and size up prospective mates. Quite often a young couple infatuated with one another may call upon a third person, boy or girl, to act as go-between in arranging a rendezvous between them. Girls are often as forward as boys in initiating such a meeting. A boy is expected to give the girl a small gift for her sexual favors, and this practice continues as long as the girl is amenable to the boy's propositions.

According to Bajau tradition, if a boy and girl are caught in sex relations the boy may be fined or forced to marry the girl. The boy is always assumed responsible for the act, while the girl is never fined even though she may have initiated the rendezvous. If the couple and their families are agreeable to a marriage between the two, this course is usually taken; otherwise, the fine is paid by the boy and is divided between the headman who mediates the settlement with the girl's parents. Fines vary but are usually no more than twenty pesos, a sizable amount for the Bajau. However, there is often much bickering, and the fine may never be paid. If a young girl becomes pregnant, she is married immediately. If she has been having sexual relationships regularly with a particular boy, he is the one who marries her; but if she is not sure of the paternity of her child, she picks the most desirable possibility and points the accusing finger at him. Consequently, illegitimate births are almost unknown. Although it is common knowledge that most girls engage in sexual intercourse before their marriage, it is nonetheless considered improper for a girl to be too free with her sexual favors. A girl with such a reputation is unable to command a high bride-price and may have to settle for a less desirable mate. This is supported by the belief that if a girl has sexual relationships with many different men, her fertility is diminished. Since children are highly desired by the Bajau, such a girl is unattractive as a prospective wife.

Unmarried couples have sexual intercourse at any convenient private place, e.g., a vacated houseboat or a lonely part of the beach or reef. For the married couple, the sex act always takes place in their houseboat after the other members of the household are asleep. This is essential for privacy since the houseboats are small and single-roomed. The regularity with which married persons have sex relations varies: young newlyweds are said to indulge every night, or perhaps several times during a single night, for the first few weeks of marriage, but as the marriage wears on the frequency drops and eventually ceases in old age.

Bajau engage in very little sexual foreplay, and this is usually initiated by the man. He may embrace his mate, fondle her breasts, or manipulate her clitoris. Apparently only among some of the acculturated youth is kissing occasionally practiced; adults express repulsion at the notion of mouth-to-mouth contact. Inquiries regarding any type of oral sexuality were also met with repulsion and with expressions of disbelief that such behavior is practiced by anyone. After arousing his wife, the husband crawls into the sarong which she uses for sleeping. The most common position is the normal one, i.e., the woman lays on her back with spread legs to receive the man, but if there is danger of detection the couple may perform the act on their sides facing one another. If a man's penis is large or if he is entering a virgin, he sometimes finds it necessary to use a lubricant; most commonly his own saliva serves the purpose, but many men claim the white of an egg is even more effective. This apparently has been learned from the land people, however, since the Bajau rarely have eggs to use for any purpose. The sexual act is very brief, partly because of the crowded nature of most households; one must take advantage of the moment before a sleeping household member awakens to ruin the opportunity. The Bajau claim that males reach climax more easily than the females, but most females nonetheless have an orgasm during intercourse, since the male who allows himself to reach climax before his mate is an undesirable lover.

Most Bajau do not recognize any times when sexual intercourse is universally tabued. If one is willing to put up with the uncleanliness of menstruation, sex is legitimate even at that time. A pregnant woman receives her husband throughout her pregnancy until it is uncomfortable for her to do so. In fact, it is widely believed that frequent intercourse during pregnancy tends to strengthen the fetus. On the other hand, caul births are believed to result from sexual intercourse during the last month of pregnancy, and it is consequently considered best to refrain from sexual intercourse during the final stages of pregnancy.

Bajau identify and name the external reproductive organs, but they have little detailed knowledge of the internal organs. *Puki* is a generic term used for the female genitalia, while the vagina is called *ke puki*, "hole of the puki." The clitoris is called *sellit*, and the fluid emitted when it is stimulated is called *angomohe*. The only internal female organ identified by the Bajau is the womb, which is called *patulian onde-onde*, "sleeping place of the infant." The female ejaculation is called *boheh puki,* "water of the puki." The generic term for the male genitalia is *botok* which, when used specifically, means penis. The glans penis is called *kok botok,* "head of the penis," whereas the prepuce is *kulit botok,* "skin of the penis." *Buyun* is the scrotum, and the testicles within are called *big'gih buyun,* "seeds of the scrotum." The external urethral orifice of the penis is called *boah botok,* "mouth of the penis," and the sperm is referred to as *boheh botok,* "water of the penis." The expression for a male orgasm is *angontah boheh botok,* which means literally "to vomit the water of the penis." Pubic hair is called *bu botok* for men or *bu puki* for women, "hair of the penis" or "hair of the vagina." The Bajau claim ignorance of the physiological functioning of the sexual organs.

It is widely believed throughout Sulu that sexual intercourse is more enjoyable to both the man and the woman if the man is circumcised. This is occasionally voiced also among the Bajau, but it is not a widespread belief, doubtlessly because the Bajau do not practice true circumcision. The Tausug and some land-dwelling Samal of Sulu practice true circumcision, that is, an operation which removes the entire foreskin of the penis. This is quite unlike the operation which is practiced by the Bajau and certain land-dwelling Samal groups. At the appropriate age, usually around thirteen or fourteen, the circumcision ceremony is held for the Bajau boy. Much celebration surrounds the event, but the operation itself is very simple. The older man who performs the operation simply stretches the foreskin over the glans penis and makes a small nick in the foreskin with a knife or piece of split bamboo. Ashes are then rubbed into the wound, the foreskin is pushed back to expose the glans, around which a white cloth is tied. Sometimes if the foreskin is too tight, it must be slit in order to push it back beyond the glans. In most cases, the foreskin is apparently tight enough and short enough so that it remains beyond the glans to give the appearance of true circumcision. Occasionally, the foreskin nevertheless does return to cover the glans, but there is no subsequent operation to remedy this. The Bajau do not presently practice any female genital operation, although some informants claim that a type of clitoridectomy was performed in the past. I could, however, learn nothing of the operation. Apparently such a female operation was also formerly performed by the land people, and is rumored to be still practiced by some of the more traditional inland Tausug.

Adultery occurs among the Bajau, but it is difficult to determine its frequency since it is, of course, always clandestine. Adultery is a ground for divorce if the offended spouse cares to push the issue, but more often it causes merely an initial flurry of emotions, and perhaps a brief separation of husband and wife, followed by an eventual reconciliation. A man guilty of adultery must pay a fine, which is divided between the headman and the offended husband. A woman is never fined for her role in an adulterous affair. Only three cases of adultery came to my attention during my sixteen months of research among the Tawi-Tawi boat-dwellers. The cases never emerged as issues for the headman, but everyone in the villages knew of them. All three of the offended spouses were aware of the adulterous affairs of their mates, but for various reasons were content to not interfere; one was an old woman married to a much younger man, another was a somewhat feeble-minded man, and the third was a man married to a young girl with such a long history of extramarital affairs that he apparently no longer took an active concern in her intrigues.

The Bajau claim that masturbation is rarely practiced among them, and such would seemingly be the case since sexual partners are normally available to satisfy any sexual urges that may arise.

Certain herbs found in the Sulu forests may allegedly be mixed into a concoction and drunk by a female to prevent conception. However, I found no informants who could identify the actual herbs, or who had ever used the potion. Bajau also claim that certain herbs can be consumed to bring about miscarriage, but again none professed ever to have used them. The infant mortality rate is so high among the boat-dwellers that no woman would willingly try to prevent conception or destroy her unborn child. Even if she has many children, more are desired since it is likely that some will die before reaching adulthood. For these reasons, the thought of infanticide arouses horror in the Tawi-Tawi Bajau.

Childbirth

Children are greatly valued by the Bajau, and the young wife who becomes pregnant shortly after her marriage is considered fortunate. Children are desired for very practical reasons, namely, to provide assistance to their parents during their childhood and later to care for their aged parents. So highly valued are children that barrenness is a ground for divorce. The blame for barrenness, however, rests upon neither the husband nor the wife, but rather is usually attributed to fate—an explanation which the Bajau call upon to explain most events they do not understand. Village gossipers occasionally blame a woman's barrenness on some personal misbehavior in her past or that of her husband, but most often the afflicted persons are not considered responsible for their misfortune. Such childless couples sometimes adopt children from kinsmen who have more than they can support, or they may simply go through life childless and depend upon nephews or nieces to care for them in their old age. It is unimaginable to a Bajau that a woman should want to prevent pregnancy. Even if she has many children, other kinsmen are always available to adopt her child. Thus, as noted, contraceptives are unknown.

The Bajau have little understanding of the actual physiological process of pregnancy. They are well aware that conception is dependent upon sexual intercourse, but as to the relation of the two there is little certainty. The most common explanation is that when the semen enters the vaginal tract it brings about a cessation in the menstrual flow which coagulates to form the fetus. The semen must be thick and milky in color to bring about conception; if it is clear and watery, conception will not occur. Most informants claim that sheer chance brings about conception at some times and not at others. There appears to be no knowledge of fertile periods in the menstrual cycle.

Although the Bajau are aware that conception involves the participation of both male and female, it is an unstated assumption that the male has a greater role in conception and the development of the fetus than the female. Several childless women, or women with only one or two children, told me they could not become pregnant because their husbands' semen was not strong enough to penetrate them. Further substantiation of the more important role of the male is the belief that a man should have frequent intercourse with his wife during her pregnancy lest the infant be born very weak or with parts of his limbs missing. The prevailing tabu against patrilateral parallel cousin marriage is also enlightening. Such marriages are believed to be incestuous because cousins in this relationship are considered as closely related as siblings. However, matrilateral parallel cousins and all other cousins are free to marry. The implication seems to be that children created by the semen of brothers are sibling-like, whereas children born of two sisters are less closely related because females are more passive in conception and merely provide a receptacle for the development of the fetus which is implanted by the male. If asked, the Bajau deny that one parent is more important than the other, but the above beliefs attribute a greater significance to the male role.

After a woman becomes pregnant, little change occurs in her daily routine until the final stages, when it may be necessary for her to refrain from some of her more strenuous activities. She observes few if any dietary restrictions; the only one mentioned to me was abstinence from sweets, which are believed to harden the fetus and make delivery difficult. But even this belief is not widespread. Pregnant women experience food cravings, and the Bajau husband occasionally seeks scarce foods to satisfy his wife's cravings. An infant who slobbers a great deal while nursing is believed to do so because his mother's food cravings were not satisfied. A pregnant woman should refrain from ridiculing a person suffering from a physical or mental deformity lest her child suffer the same affliction. Various other superstitions surround pregnancy, e.g., a woman should bathe immediately if she observes clouds passing over a full moon. For the most part, however, pregnancy is not surrounded by many tabus. A woman continues to have regular sexual intercourse with her husband; in fact, as noted, frequent intercourse is believed essential for the proper development of the fetus, except during the final month when it may result in a caul birth.

Some Bajau believe that there are ways to determine the sex of the unborn child. If during the moment of the ejaculation which impregnates his mate, a man breathes inward, the child will be a girl. However, if at this moment he breathes outward, the child will be a boy. Several men claimed faith in the explanation, but all denied ever having tested it since most are never certain which ejaculation brings about conception, and, more importantly, few are concerned at that crucial moment with the direction of their breathing. Women believe that a male fetus makes much more prenatal movement than a female. No Bajau, however, claimed any foolproof method for predicting the sex of the unborn child.

Morning sickness appears to be fairly common among Bajau women during the early months of pregnancy. Sometimes a woman suffering from such illness is given an herbal concoction to drink, but most believe that little can be done for the malady since it is considered a natural incident of pregnancy. If a pregnant woman suffers considerable illness or discomfort, certain ceremonies may be conducted to placate the spirits believed to be causing it. Miscarriages are so common that all the women I interviewed had experienced at least two, and most had had so many they could not even remember the exact number. All agreed that miscarriage occurs most commonly during the early months of pregnancy, and is normally caused by overexertion.

The Bajau woman is able to predict with a fair degree of accuracy the time of her delivery by keeping count of the number of months since the cessation of her menstrual flow. Ten lunar months are considered the normal length of pregnancy. When she begins to feel labor pains, the Bajau woman calls upon her female kinsmen to assist her; if they happen to be in the vicinity, her mother and sisters are almost always present. Usually some older woman, locally known as a midwife, delivers the child, while a shaman, male or female, is always present to chant and ward off evil spirits to insure the safe birth of the infant. In addition, a host of other people, children and adults, are usually present to witness the birth. The pain of childbirth, of course, varies among individual women, but all my informants agreed that childbirth was the most painful experience they had ever undergone. Furthermore, all claimed to approach each of their deliveries with the fear of death, a fear easily understood in light of the high mortality of women during childbirth.

When a Bajau mother is ready to deliver, she is propped on cushions or bundles in the boat. Often a rope is tied to the roof for her to pull in order to help the delivery and ease the birth pains. As labor increases and delivery is imminent, the shaman bends over the woman, chanting prayers to insure easy delivery as well as good health and fortune for the mother and child. The midwife assists the delivery by pushing on the woman's abdomen to help expel the child, and once the head emerges, she extricates the rest of the body. Bajau mothers claim that often their children are born feet first, and several maintained that birth was less painful this way. The Bajau do not cut the vaginal opening in the event of a difficult birth but rather rely exclusively upon magical remedies.

After the infant has been expelled from the womb, the midwife cleans the mucus from its nose and mouth. If the child is not breathing normally at birth, the midwife may give it mouth-to-mouth resuscitation to instill breathing. However, the infant is never slapped in any way to initiate breathing; most Bajau could not imagine such cruel behavior toward an infant. The midwife holds the umbilical cord between two fingers at the child's stomach and squeezes the liquid from the cord, which is then cut about three inches from the stomach with a piece of split bamboo and tied with any available string. The child is then bathed in usually unheated water—fresh water if it is available, otherwise sea water. The afterbirth is normally expelled shortly after delivery, but, if not, magical chants are used, and sometimes the abdomen is massaged to bring about expulsion.

The placenta and afterbirth are variously disposed of. Among the Tawi-Tawi Bajau, they are normally placed in a coconut shell and buried on the nearby island by the father. However, the Sitangkai Bajau prefer to bury them in the sea beneath the house of birth to guarantee that the child will become a good swimmer. When carrying the afterbirth away for disposal, the father should look to neither the left nor right, but straight ahead, lest his newly born child become cross-eyed. After the stub of the umbilical cord falls off, it is tied to the cradle. When the stub falls from the cradle of a boy child, it is taken to the deep sea and thrown overboard to insure that the child will become a good fisherman; if the child is a girl, the stub is placed in a tree, the leaves of which are used for mat-making, to insure that the girl will become a good mat-maker.

Shortly after the birth, boughs from citrus trees, cut in the forest by the father and his male relatives, are placed on the top and sides of the boat. These are believed to prevent the entrance of certain evil spirits which may cause harm to the newly born child. For the same reason, during the first few weeks after birth, a black spot of charcoal, called *sinagan*, is placed on the forehead of the baby, and various amulets are tied around his neck and arms.

For several days after delivery, the mother is given a rice mush to eat, but she begins immediately to pursue as many of her normal household tasks as she can. During the one or two days following birth, before the mother's milk begins to flow, the child is nursed by the mother's sister or some other close relative. Within the first week of birth, solid foods are given to the child in the form of a rice or cassava gruel, and certain bananas which are believed to have medicinal value.

Stillbirths are not uncommon among the Bajau and are usually attributed to some serious illness of the mother during pregnancy. Infants born dead are simply buried on any nearby island rather than taken to the cemetery islands where all other Bajau are buried. The Bajau have no knowledge of any special care to administer to premature babies except to increase the number of protective amulets on their persons. Caul births are apparently fairly common and, as noted earlier, are attributed to sexual intercourse during the final month of pregnancy, when the caul is believed to be formed from the father's semen. In the event of a caul birth, the sack is simply removed from the infant. One woman told me this was as easy as removing the cellophane from a package of cigarettes. Informants claim that deformed births are very rare, and attributed their occurrence to fate or to misbehavior on the part of the mother. The Bajau consistently denied any knowledge of multiple births beyond twins and were amazed to hear of triplets, quadruplets, and quintuplets. One old woman claimed that only animals had such births in Sulu, not people. No special explanations are offered for the occurrence of twins except fate. When twins are born, it is almost always assumed that one or both of them will die owing to their smaller size and more delicate constitution. Such an assumption is grounded in experience since I learned of only two sets of living adult twins among the Tawi-Tawi Bajau, and of none among the Sitangkai Bajau.

Because it is considered bad luck to name a child too soon, a baby usually does not receive a name until he is several months old. A boy's name generally takes the suffix of his father's name; for instance, the five sons of Masarani are Mastarani, Sugarani, Armisani, Motorhani, and Honorhani. Much less frequently the suffix of a girl's name follows the suffix of her mother's name. The name itself usually identifies the sex of the child. In addition to his given name, a Bajau often has a nickname, which sometimes replaces his original name.

If a Bajau baby survives his first two years of life, his chances of living to maturity are good. However, the infant mortality rate is extremely high, and it is not uncommon to encounter a family with more deceased than living children. In fact, infant mortality is so high that some parents cannot even recall the number of their deceased children. Common causes of infant death include dysentery and various respiratory diseases. It appears, however, that the infant mortality rate has dropped among the house-dwelling Bajau at Sitangkai. Census data and geneologies reveal a considerable reduction in infant mortality within the present generation of house-dwellers as compared to the preceding generations who lived in boats. This drop is due not only to the more healthful nature of house-living, but also to the partial adoption of modern medicine. If the mortality rate continues to decrease, Sitangkai will soon begin to feel the pressures of overpopulation which other parts of the Philippines already experience.

Notes

1 This paper is based on two years of field research in Sulu Province, Philippines, sponsored by the East-West Center, Honolulu; the National Science Foundation, Washington, D.C.; the Wenner-Gren Foundation for Anthropological Research, New York; and the Carnegie Corporation of New York. The author gratefully acknowledges the support of these foundations.

2 Any paper which proposes to deal with the sexual behavior of a society can rarely be complete for several reasons. In most societies, sex is a delicate subject, the intimacies of which are not normally openly discussed—especially with a note-taking outsider. Consequently, the data of the researcher are biased by the fact that he has obtained them from individuals who are willing to talk about such matters and who may consequently be atypical of their group. Second, the lone investigator must be content to receive a one-sided view of sexual attitudes and behavior. If he is a man, he will come to understand sex as understood by the men of the society and will learn very little about female attitudes except as these are perceived by men. If the investigator is a female, she will have comparable problems with male informants. Third, one must often be content to learn about what people say they do rather than what they actually do. Much anthropological data may be verified through observation to test whether the subject actually does what he says he does. However, since most sexual behavior occurs in extreme privacy, observation is normally excluded. Participant observation may yield additional insights, but these again are one-sided. A final problem may be that of finding a time and place where sex may be discussed with persons who are willing to talk about it. In most societies, certain aspects of sex are not mentioned before members of the opposite sex, certain kinsmen, or children. The intimacy of living, characteristic of most communities studied by anthropologists, sometimes make it difficult to find the proper privacy for the discussion of sexual matters.

The foregoing is simply a warning to the reader that this discussion of Bajau sexual behavior does not pretend to be complete. Most of the informants were males, although a few females offered views on some of the less intimate aspects of the subject. The fifteen male informants included unmarried, married, divorced, and widowed men, while the three women informants were all married and volunteered their information in the presence of their husbands.

Because of the nature of the subject, the information on childbirth was easier to obtain. The data are based almost entirely upon five interviews with females. These were all mothers, and three of them were renowned as midwives. Most of the women enjoyed discussing the subject, and the three midwives all took pride in displaying their professional knowledge. Perhaps a female anthropologist could have obtained additional insights, but I do not feel that my sex was any great hindrance to my questions on childbirth. To verify some of the data, I was able to observe three births among the Tawi-Tawi Bajau.

Most of the data were collected among the boat-dwelling Bajau of the Tawi-Tawi Islands; a smaller proporation came from interviews conducted among the house-dwelling Bajau of Sitangkai in the Sibutu Islands. Differing views between the two groups have been noted.

3 This is less true among the most acculturated Bajau of Sitangkai who are adopting their Islamic neighbors value of premarital chastity for females.

References

Nimmo, H. A. 1968. Reflections on Bajau History. Philippine Studies 16: 32-59.

_____ 1969. The Structure of Bajau Society. Unpublished Ph.D. dissertation, University of Hawaii.

Section III

CHILDHOOD

The urine of young children is marked by gonadotropin inhibitor. This prevents the hypothalamous from secreting the releasing factors and gonadotropins, ie. follicle stimulating hormone (FSH) and luteinizing hormone (LH), which are virtually absent in the body fluids of infants and young children. By age six or seven the child will have about 2.2 units per liter of FSH and only a trace of LH. (By contrast, adult levels of these hormones are 5.6 and 4.7 units per liter respectively.) During puberty dramatic changes occur in the amounts and ratios of these hormones as they relate to egg maturation and ovulation and sperm production as well as endocrine hormone production.

Sexual thoughts and acts, being as much a part of culture as are other aspects of living, will thus reflect the mores, values, and attitudes of the adults of society. These may permit free exploration of the body and the interaction between partners, or it may be very restrictive. Childhood is a time of physical growth and social learning. It is a phase in the life cycle when parents and other adults must permit the young person to experiment and develop her or his potential, yet must protect against dangers which may be physical or psychological in nature. This learning is referred to in ethnographic studies by different terms such as socialization, enculturation, or education.

Social scientists speak of socialization and enculturation as distinct from education. They use the former term to describe the process (much of which is subconscious and based upon rewarded behavior) by which the young are assisted to assume roles in the social system or to share the ideas, acts, and artifacts of the group among whom they live. The more technical differences between socialization and enculturation need not concern us here. Normally, in traditional societies, these processes differ only slightly from education. From an early age children are presented with the desirable and "right" ways of behaving, and with the right tools to use in specific situations. The result of this education is relative homeostasis in the person and relative continuity in the acts and artifacts of group members. It assures that the new generation will be imbued with the valueorientations, knowledge, and existential premises of the older generation. It assures that the traditional pattern of life will not be disturbed too greatly. Education, socialization and enculturation in traditional societies are almost synonymous, and the French sociologist Emile Durkheim in fact spoke of education as the systematic socialization of the younger generation by adults.

Socialization recognizes the gender of the child and between birth and puberty there is increasing differentiation of roles and conveying rules of sexual modesty. However, the criteria which mark this will differ from society to society and time to time within the same society. Discussing a puritanical island folk community in Ireland, which he glossed as Inis Baeg, Messenger writes: "The seeds of repression are planted early in childhood by parents and kin through instruction supplemented by rewards and punishment, conscious imitation, and unconscious internalization" (1971:29). The socialization process may also be less restrictive as was true in Tahiti. As an example consider the human body and clothing. In many societies small children go completely naked. Among the Gadsup of New Guinea boys go naked up to age seven or eight while girls of three weeks old start wearing little grass skirts and are never again without a grass skirt (du Toit 1975:12). Traditional people normally wear pubic coverings but women do not cover their breasts. In fact, in Mangaia female breasts are not involved in heterosexual activities because they are not considered sexually arousing. On the other hand, the Koran requires that women "Draw their veils over their bosoms and not display their beauty..." (Sura XXIV. 31). Some orthodox groups go so far as to not only wear a veil but cover the whole face. What about the rating system on American television? What is PG-13? How would such programs sell on Saudi Arabian television? Is this part of socialization?

The papers that follow deal with socialization. In the first paper, Alice Schlegel looks at Hopi childhood and follows the young girl into menarche, which marks her transition into adulthood. In the second paper we accompany Ian Hogbin in visiting the traditional people of Wogeo, an island that lies about 30 miles off the coast from Wewak on the north coast of Papua New Guinea. He describes childhood and the awakening of sexual impulses around puberty as well as their expression in various contexts.

References

du Toit, Brian M. 1975. *Akuna, A New Guinea Village Community.* Rotterdam: A.A. Balkema.

Messenger, J.C. 1971. Sex and repression in an Irish folk community, pp.3-37. Marshall, D.S. and R.C. Suggs (eds) *Human Sexual Behavior.* Englewood Cliffs, N.J.: Prentice Hall.

The Holy Quran. 1946. Text, Translation and Commentary by Abdullah Yusuf Ali. Khalil Al-Rawaf: Qatar.

2. A Gadsup Girl

CHILDHOOD

1. A Venda Girl

THE ADOLESCENT SOCIALIZATION OF THE HOPI GIRL[1]

Alice Schlegel
University of Pittsburgh

With few exceptions, notably Mead (1928), anthropologists have displayed little interest in the process of adolescent socialization. The largest body of literature concerning the adolescent period concentrates upon puberty ceremonies, those ritual markers of the social transition from childhood to adulthood that occur sometime during the biological transition we term adolescence. Some, such as Richards (1956) and Turner (1967), have regarded these ceremonies as vehicles for the messages of cultural values, expressed and reinforced through rites and symbols. Others, such as Young (1965), view them as devices to express and legitimize the separation of the young person from the family circle and his or her incorporation into the appropriate adult sex group. Regarding the effects of the ceremony upon the initiate, they may be seen as providing mechanisms for the establishment of the proper sexual identity (Whiting, Kluckhohn, and Anthony 1958) or of personal identity (Cohen 1964). However, for all their importance as socialization devices, we must not forget that puberty ceremonies are not universal, nor are they necessarily held for both sexes in a society that holds them for one. Even where they exist in dramatic form, they can be only part of the process by which the social transformation is made from the child to the sexually, economically, and culturally productive adult.

In this paper, we shall examine the adolescent socialization process of the Hopi girl. We shall see that, for her, this is a time of crisis: a period of strained relations with her mother, moodiness and unpredictability, and fear that she will be rejected by a lover. In examining the adolescence of Samoan girls, Mead (1928) discovered no evidence of unusual moodiness or anxiety reactions and no increase of intergenerational conflict. She concluded that where the life pattern is set and young people do not have to choose between conflicting pathways, there are no dilemmas and no crisis. The Hopi girl follows a set life plan, and she is subjected to no cultural dilemmas; yet she goes through a period of crisis that appears to have the form of the familiar Western adolescent crisis. This is due, I suggest, not to similar socialization pressures, but rather to socialization pressures of quite a different form but of equal intensity. For the Hopi girl, adolescence is the time when socialization for her adult sex role begins in earnest. Although younger boys and girls are taught many of their sex-specific economic tasks at a young age, earlier socialization does not emphasize sex differences to a marked degree. Boys and girls go through the same first initiation together and receive the same ceremonial instruction.[2] It is not uncommon to see mixed-sex play groups of pre-adolescents playing at either structured or unstructured activities. Parents try to treat all of their children, of both sexes, equally, and similar punishments are given to boys and girls.[3] The primary goal of childhood socialization is to inculcate

Reprinted by permission of the editors from *Ethnology,* Vol. XII, 1973, pp. 449-462.

Hopi ethics and values, while the intensive training for sex-specific roles comes later. Children are socialized to be Hopi; it is at adolescence that girls are socialized to become women.

Hopi Socialization Goals

The term *Hopi* has strong ethical connotations, while *kahopi* or "not Hopi," is derogatorily applied to people who deviate from the ideal. The Hopi is defined by the following characteristics:

1. Peaceableness. In his relations with other Hopi and outsiders, the Hopi is peaceful and nonaggressive. Before American pacification of the area, warfare was regarded as a necessary evil and seems never to have received the glorification it did in other American Indian societies. Aggression within the community is deplorable. When physical aggression occurs between men, it takes the relatively nonviolent form of pushing one another, usually until bystanders intervene. The rare violent fight that does take place is remembered and talked about for years. Women are less rigidly socialized in this respect than men; although fights between women are uncommon, they are thought of as happening oftener than fights between men. They take the form of pulling hair and clothing. The ascribed motive is usually jealousy over an adulterous affair that the husband of one is having with the other.

2. Responsibility. The focus of Hopi community life is the elaborate ceremonial cycle, in which clans and lineages have defined roles and duties. For the entire system to work, each person must play his part, and the dereliction of any individual can result in the ineffectiveness of the entire ceremony.

3. Co-operation. Closely related to the need for responsibility is the need for co-operation. The ceremonies are essential for the well-being of the people, both physically and spiritually, there being no rigid division between these spheres. Therefore, people must cooperate and submerge private interests to the good of the group.

4. Humility. The noncompetitiveness of the Hopi is elaborated into an ethic of humility. Not only does the Hopi not strive to be better than anyone else, but he also constantly represents himself as worse—poorer, less clever, a simple man or woman. To be too clever or prosperous is to risk being considered a witch, one who has sold his life—his "heart"— for power and must steal other hearts in order to stay alive. So long as one fulfills one's duties to family and community, one is not encouraged to strive for success.

5. Self-reliance. It should not be assumed that noncompetitiveness entails a lack of self-reliance. A Hopi may be inordinately sensitive, by other standards, to the approval or disapproval of the community, but he is expected to make his own decisions and take responsibility for them. One often hears the phrase *pi um' i*, "it is up to you." While quick to criticize, Hopi are chary about giving advice. If the advice is followed and things turn out badly, the giver shares responsibility for the consequences.

It is to these ends that children of both sexes are socialized. Socialization differences for the sexes, while not as marked as in many other societies, fall in the areas of training for peaceableness and responsibility.[4] As already mentioned, women are not expected to control their aggression as much as men, and some expression of aggression is felt to be natural for women. This accords with the primary social and spiritual role of women, which is to be mothers of the people. As mothers they must protect their young, and the Hopi draw an analogy between the fierceness of the animal mother and the human female. Another factor is that female aggression is not as threatening to community solidarity as is male aggression. With the exception of three rather minor ceremonies, the ceremonial cycle is under the control of men, although women do play necessary but secondary roles in the male ceremonies.

The ultimate load of responsibility training is probably no greater for the female than for the male, but the timing is different. The woman's life revolves around the domestic sphere, and her domestic training begins early and is markedly increased during adolescence. The man's life revolves around two spheres: the domestic, in which he participates principally as provider, performing almost all of the subsistence activity, and the public, in which he takes one or more ceremonial and possibly political roles. The boy begins his training for subsistence activities, farming and herding, as early as the girl begins hers for domestic activities, around age four. He also participates in ceremonies at a young age, after his first initiation at seven or eight. But he is not expected to take on any positions of ceremonial responsibility until after his second initiation, during his late teens or early twenties. Nor is he likely to have full responsibility for a field or herd of sheep or cattle until his marriage, at about the same age or a little later. For girls, the full weight of household responsibility begins at puberty, when she begins to be a full-time household worker.

Female Social Role

The House. In this matrilineal, matrilocal society, houses are owned by women and are usually inherited by ultimogeniture (Udall 1969: 50-51). This is a practical matter: daughters bring their husbands into the house, but after a few children are born these dwellings of two-to-four rooms become too crowded, and pressure is put upon the husband to build a house nearby for his family. The last daughter and her family usually remain with the parents. All household goods and furnishings belong to the wife. Clan land is allocated by household, so that men cultivate fields obtained through their wives. (There are some variations on this, with men having usufruct rights over land belonging to their own or father's clan, if there is land to spare). Once the produce is brought into the house and the wife has formally thanked her husband, it is hers to allocate or dispose of as she wishes.

To some degree, men always think of their natal houses as their true homes. This is where they keep their ceremonial equipment, or that part of it which is not stored in the *kiva* (the ceremonial chamber). It is a duty of the female head to care for the household ceremonial equipment, both house fetishes and the objects used by her clan and lineage male members. She docs this by "feeding" them, through sprinkling them with corn meal. Without such feeding, they lose their power.

The Community. While most of the ceremonies are controlled by men, women play essential roles in them. There is another way in which women contribute to ceremonial activity. In summer, dances are held in the village plaza, and it is often a woman who sponsors the dance. This means that she, with the help of her male and female relatives, provides the food to feed the dancers and much of the food they distribute to the audience. This involves a large expenditure of goods and labor, and her contribution is highly appreciated. On the day of the dance, it is said, "she stands above the *kikmongwi* [village chief]."

There are three women's ceremonies, staged by the three women's societies, that occur in autumn between September and early November. This is the woman's portion of the ceremonial calendar, the male portion extending from late November to late August. These ceremonies seem to be concerned primarily with female fertility and secondarily with hunting.

That portion of the public sphere in which women have no hereditary authority is community politics. (They do, however, have a voice in clan politics, in the settlement of land disputes—see Forde 1931). Women, even Clan Mothers, do not determine which of the possible successors to political and ceremonial office shall be chosen from within the lineage or clan. That is done by the previous incumbent. Whatever power they do have is exercised through influence or the threat of nonco-operation. (I should mention, however, that there is at present a woman who claims title to village chieftainship in Old Oraibi. This is considered unusual, but her claim is not disputed on account of her sex.)

From this brief sketch we can see that the Hopi have divided their spheres of activity into the public, which is controlled by men, and the domestic, controlled by women. The wife brings the husband into her domestic sphere, and she can send him out. Of course, he is free to leave her and go to another woman or return to his mother or sisters; but in any case he resides in a house owned and controlled by women. As the Hopi say: "The man's place is on the outside of the house."

It is in her domestic role that the Hopi woman is socially and spiritually important. She is the very source of life. She gives birth to the people, and she nourishes them with food. She maintains the power of ceremonial objects through feeding them. It is not surprising that, when asked, women claim that they are more important than men, with the qualification that men are necessary, too.

Early Socialization of the Hopi Girl

Even before birth, the sex of a Hopi child is a matter of importance. While parents give the conventional response that boys and girls are equally welcome, and most couples want at least one child of each sex, there is some difference in attitude toward them. Women state plainly that "you raise up a daughter for yourself," whereas "you raise up a son for somebody else." This refers to the fact that the girl will remain with or near her mother, while the boy will transfer his residence, labor, and much of his responsibility to his wife's household. His loyalties will be divided; as the Hopi say, "he moves over to her side." Men want sons who can help them with farming and herding and act as companions, but they want daughters too. When a man grows old, he usually lives with the daughter who inherited her mother's house, even after the mother dies. He has no right to live in the house of his son's wife. An old man without a daughter is in an unenviable position. Frequently couples without a daughter will adopt one, an excess child of the wife's biological or classificatory sister.

Girls, even small ones, are to be respected, in theory at least. They are not to be punished as severely as boys, because "they will grow up and make *piki* [cornmeal wafer bread] for us." Even as small children, they are kept close to home, whereas boys run about freely. The value of the girl, due to her life-giving character, is expressed in one of the beliefs concerning witchcraft. While anyone's heart can be stolen, it is believed that children, whose hearts are stronger because they are young and pure, are the most frequent victims. A boy's heart gives the witch four more years of life, whereas the girl's gives him eight.

While the infant is tiny, it is the center of attraction for the family. It is constantly attended by mother, mother's sisters, or grandmother. The father, too, looks after the baby and sings lullabies to it. This idyllic picture may change in a couple of years, when a new sibling arrives. The older child is then ousted from its central position and seems to wander about, eager for attention from anyone who will give it. Children of this age are often the charges of older sisters. It may not be coincidental that this age, from about two to six, is seen by mothers as the age of most frequent temper tantrums.

At four or five, socialization patterns start to diverge for boys and girls. Girls begin to grind corn, and their earlier attempts may be fed to the chickens (Udall 1969: 7). From this age, girls also accompany their mothers to the spring for water. Thus they learn the two most time-consuming tasks for the Hopi woman, corn-grinding and water-fetching.

The great delight of the child from two to six or seven is the appearance of the kachinas at dances. These are, in reality, masked men from the village impersonating the supernatural figures, but the children are told that these are the real kachinas. The kachinas know one's thoughts and actions. If the child has been good, they reward with rattles or bows and arrows, for boys, and kachina dolls, for girls. If he or she has been naughty, a gift is withheld, or given toward the end of the dance when the child has despaired of receiving anything. (The gift, of course, has been prepared by the father or other male relative.) The kachina dolls are more or less realistic painted wooden figures, eight to fourteen inches high, of the kachinas. They are not sacred, but they are not toys, and the girl must take good care of them. They are usually hung on the inside walls of the house. Like other personal property, the dolls belong to the girl, and only she can decide whether to keep, sell, or give them away. The gift of the kachina doll is a means by which the girl is trained to care for ceremonial objects.

The kachinas are generally benevolent, although mothers threaten children that the kachinas will not bring them anything if they misbehave. There are some kachinas, however, that are malevolent, the ogre kachinas. Soyoko, the monster who eats children, is the worst, and children tremble at the thought of being taken by her.

A more prosaic punishment for children at this age is to have water poured over them. After a time or two, a threat is enough. Children are punished when they disobey, or if they damage someone else's property deliberately. Unintentional damage is not likely to be punished.

At six or seven, life becomes a more serious matter for the child. Both boys and girls are expected to help their parents more. Girls are given the onerous task of caring for the younger siblings. They drag them about on their errands or take them along when they play with other little girls close to the houses. One of the worst things a girl can do is to neglect an infant charge. This can result in ostracism for days, shaming the child deeply (Eggan 1956). A contemporary but traditional mother says that children get stubborn at this age, girls becoming particularly so.

The major discontinuity in Hopi socialization occurs at this time for both sexes. This is at the first initiation, which allows people to participate, according to sex role, in the kachina ceremonies. The initiation takes places in one of the kivas, and a central feature is that some of the initiates are whipped, the boys more severely than the girls. It is at this time that the children learn that the kachinas are really their own fathers and uncles, in costume. According to several accounts (Simmons 1942: 84; Eggan 1956), this can result in anger, disillusionment, and severe depression. It is in this atmosphere of bewilderment, fear, and pain that the children must unlearn in a few hours what they had believed up to this time and what was a source of great happiness to them. Community support is evidently not enough to prevent disillusionment and unhappiness in many children.

It is also at this time that the child goes to school and learns that the *bahana* (white person) world differs from the Hopi. During the time under examination here, most Hopi seem to have extracted from their school experience the knowledge useful to Hopi life. They have learned to read and write and operate within the *bahana* world, and they have benefited from teachings about hygiene, home economics, livestock improvement and other such practical matters. Few have attempted to establish a permanent role in the *bahana* world or to bring *bahana* life-style into the village. (For an exception to this, see Qoyawayma 1964).

By the time she is eight or ten, the Hopi girl has become a competent and generally cheerful young person. According to one elderly lady, this is the happiest period in a young girl's life. Her explanation was that "you know what Hopi life is," meaning that the child is now taking part in a small way in adult social and ceremonial life. It is also during this period that there is some respite from control by the mother, as the girl is able to get around by herself, with younger siblings in tow if necessary, and spend time with her girl friends. Mixed age and sex play groups do form, but girls seem to prefer the company of other girls their own age. Dennis (1940) gives descriptions of girls' games, and Udall (1969: 15-16) tells of the favorite diversion, playing house with bone dolls.

Girls can express aggression more freely at this age than they could earlier. They are sometimes impertinent to their mothers and have even been known to slap them. Mothers tend to ignore this or laugh it off, accepting it as the natural thoughtlessness of childhood.

It is also at this time that girls can move about more freely than at any other time in their childhood. One elderly lady recalled to me somewhat fondly the raids that groups of boys and girls would make on the ripening peaches and pears in their neighbors' orchards. One man placed thorny branches on the ground, covering them with sand, so that when the young predators came their feet were pricked by the thorns.

Adolescence

The appearance of menstruation, or arrival at the age when menstruation is expected, marks the change from relative freedom to restriction for the Hopi girl. She is about twelve or thirteen and ready to be thoroughly inducted into her female social role. Her mother begins to restrict her movements, keeping her close to home. She is encouraged to spend more time with her sisters, and running about the village is criticized as unseemly. One mother told her daughters, now in their fifties and sixties, to stay out of other people's houses, i.e., those of nonrelatives, because "you might hear bad things there." Since evil thoughts and words are as dangerous to the purity of heart as are evil actions, this was a warning for her spiritual safety as well as her social reputation.

The girl is prepared for menstruation by her mother, who tells her that this is a sign that she is ready to bear children. No feeling of shame is connected with menstruation; and if some of the blood should appear on her clothing, it does not cause embarrassment to the woman: "the menfolk know that this is something women do."

Sometime during her adolescent years, the girl goes through a corn-grinding ceremony for three days. Titiev (1944: 203) speaks of Third Mesa girls going through this during late adolescence. It seems not to be connected with puberty (although a similar ceremony on First Mesa is). It is after this ceremony that the girl's paternal grandmother or aunt puts her hair into the distinctive "butterfly whorl" style.

The burgeoning sexual interest in the girl and her male age-mates puts the girl in rather a difficult position. Chastity is the ideal, and parents do watch their daughters; but it is expected that there will be attempts at youthful experimentation. A rather ambivalent attitude toward sexuality is expressed here. On the one hand, sex is good because it is through sexual intercourse that human life comes into being. On the other hand, sexuality outside of marriage is regarded as having a predatory nature, and jokes are made about men "going hunting for two-legged deer." It is expected that boys will make advances to any women, outside the prohibited categories, that are available. The emphasis upon premarital chastity, or at least nonpromiscuity, varies from family to family. It seems to be more important in girls from important families, those whose fathers, mothers' brothers, and brothers take leading roles in the political-ceremonial system. (For a further discussion on premarital sexual behavior see Titiev 1944: 30-31.) However, if an illegitimate child should be born, it is accepted by the girl's family and lineage as a fully recognized member. The father's family should perform the social recognition rituals shortly after birth just as if the parents were married. If the father is unknown or refuses to recognize the child, the mother's father's family performs them. When the girl marries, her husband is expected to assume the social role of father to her child, whether or not he is its genitor, except for clan matters, in which the genitor's clan takes responsibility. In actuality, however, some men are reluctant to do this, and then there is tension between husband and wife.

The girl must be wary of boys' advances and do nothing that will attract their sexual interest, if she is to remain chaste. This is particularly true at menstruation, when the smell of menstrual blood is believed to make the woman more sexually attractive to men as they are made aware of her sexual readiness.[5]

When girls do leave the house, they should go about their errands quickly and unobtrusively. If they leave the village, they should be chaperoned by younger siblings, who will report any misbehavior to the parents. Now is the time when younger siblings can avenge themselves for any grievances accumulated while their older sister carried them about as toddlers. Girls counteract this with bribes or threats.

The girl is expected to relieve her mother in many of the routine matters of household care. Girls now begin grinding corn in earnest and learning the complicated corn dishes that characterize the Hopi cuisine. The ability to grind well is a matter of pride to a girl and makes her attractive to a boy's family as a future daughter-in-law. Mothers sweeten the burdensome task by telling their daughters that grinding brings the blood to their cheeks and makes them pretty. Small groups of girls, friends or relatives, sometimes grind together, singing grinding songs and chatting.

This restriction on activity leads to some conflict with the mother (on this point see Goldfrank 1947: 535). Women in their 50s and 60s recall that they sometimes accused their mothers of being "mean," which for the Hopi has a more pejorative loading than it does in Standard English. Pert remarks are no longer tolerated as they sometimes are in ten-year-olds. A disobedient adolescent girl finds herself restricted to the house, and if she is really rebellious, her uncle (mother's brother) is called in to talk to her. No legal or religious sanctions are applied to the rebellious girl, but she realizes that her family is all she has to turn to. When tensions arise she may spend more of her free time in the homes of her mother's sister or father's sister, where she is always welcome; but ultimately she has to accept her mother's authority.

The life of the adolescent girl is by no means one of unremitting toil. After grinding is done, in the early evening, girls may get together to go to the spring for water. However, this is a somewhat dangerous activity, as the spirit of the Water Serpent, who lives in springs, may impregnate her with a snake child if she is not careful. From her early years, a girl is taught to keep away from the spring unless it is necessary to get water, and then to keep the skirt of her dress between her legs. Only women past menopause, or women known to be barren, can clean out the spring, a job usually assigned to men and boys.

One of the most enjoyable activities for the girl is the early evening picnic, held after a kachina dance or ceremony. Girls and boys dress carefully and make every attempt to appear at their best. Girls prepare dishes which they bring to the picnic spot. The boys arrive with rabbits they have caught, and the girls cook them. The boys and girls feast together under the ever-watchful eyes of the little chaperones. (For a more detailed description, see Titiev 1944: 31-32.)

The goal of the girl's work, and even of her amusements, is to prepare her to be a wife and mother. Every family wants its daughters to bring in young men who are strong, able, and come from respected families. A lazy or promiscuous girl is not likely to be considered a proper wife by such a boy or his family. As part of the wedding ritual, the girl goes to the groom's house for three days and grinds corn for his mother. It would be shameful if she were not to do a good job at this. She is, furthermore, expected to live in his household and cook for his family during the time that his male relatives are weaving her wedding robes, and her mother reminds her of this as she teaches her daughter to cook.

The choice of a spouse is, in theory, up to the young people, outside of the prohibited categories of own clan, father's clan, and "any close relative," i.e., anyone with a common grandparent. However, the girl's mother or mother's brother can refuse to allow the marriage. The boy, also, should consult his family before making his wedding plans.

In initiating the marriage, it is the girl who takes the active part. She makes the proposal, in the traditional manner, by presenting the boy of her choice with a loaf of *qömi*, a special cornmeal cake.

There are several occasions at which this is generally done (Titiev 1944: 32-33). The boy is obligated to receive it, so as not to offend the girl. Whether or not the proposal is accepted is up to him and his family. If accepted, it is arranged for the girl to come to his household to begin her bridal grinding. In one story—whether fact or legend I do not know—a bride had begun her grinding. A second girl, determined to have the boy, came a day later, set up her grinding stone next to the first girl, and began to grind. The boy's family was appalled and did not know what to do; since a bride is always treated with respect and deference, they could tell neither one to go home. The first girl was so humiliated that she left and, in keeping with Hopi beliefs about rejection by a lover, died soon afterward. The second stuck it out, and the marriage was completed. However, the boy had wanted the first girl, so after the wedding he simply refused to leave home and join his wife.

This tale points out several features of Hopi courtship and marriage. First, it is up to the girl to get the groom. In writing about Second Mesa, Nequatewa (1933: 42) says that the girl goes to the boy's house "to set her trap." This attitude characterizes Third Mesa as well. Second, even if the wedding is performed, there is no guarantee that the groom will follow the bride to her home. Even willing boys may stay at their mother's house from several days to several weeks, and an unwilling groom may decide not to go at all. One elderly lady, who has had a long and apparently happy marriage, told me that her husband delayed a few days before joining her; and when he did, he left some clothes at his mother's house so he could stay there if he wished. His father finally brought him to his wife, saying: "Don't go back home anymore, your place is here now." Her comment about new husbands was: "It's hard for them to get adjusted."

This can be understood when we realize what is in store for the boy. He must leave the comforts of his mother's house for the hard work, responsibilities, and few initial rewards of his wife's house. For girls, however, marriage is a necessity. It is in this way that they fulfill their social role. Marriage is also necessary to insure a woman her place in the afterlife. The wedding robe is used as the woman's shroud, and on this her spirit floats into the Spirit World.[6] A girl is thus under considerable pressure to find a husband, while a boy is under no such pressure to find a wife and, in fact, looks upon marriage as restricting his freedom and imposing upon him the arduous responsibility of providing for a family. (The male attitude is documented in Simmons 1942).

A girl, finally, may become so depressed over rejection by a lover that she dies. The Hopi believe that a healthy body depends upon a healthy mind. Sorrowful and depressing thoughts suppress the life force and, if allowed, result in death. Up to the moment of his last breath, a sick person is urged to think of happy things so that he or she will recover. Rejection by a lover is only one of the sad events that can lead to a depressed state, but it is one to which girls are particularly susceptible. I know of no stories about boys dying of rejection; they usually get the aid of a supernatural helper and win the girl, or avenge themselves in some way upon the girl for being so "proud." This suggests that boys are perceived as being less vulnerable to rejection; and, in fact, the Hopi maintain that this is true.

Once the girl has married, and especially after she has borne a child, the pressures are off. She is socially recognized as a woman, or *wuhti*, rather than a girl, or *mana*. (A male changes his status from *tiyo*, "boy," to *taka*, "man," after his second initiation.) Her status change is marked by a change in hair style. She is more free to express aggression than she was during adolescence, although now it is directed toward women outside the household rather than at her mother. If she has her own house, she is owner and household head. If she lives with her mother, she begins to see herself as co-head. There is no ceremony or other marker for the assumption of headship; rather, it is assumed gradually as the mother ages and takes on fewer responsibilities. I have no evidence that this presents a problem for either generation.

Once her wedding robes have been woven, the requirement for the woman's passage into the spirit world has been met. Even if the marriage dissolves, she keeps them: she "paid for them" by the groom service she performs while they were being woven.

Why the Crisis?

I have pointed to two sources for the adolescent crisis of the Hopi girl: the restrictions her mother imposes upon her, and the need to find a husband.

At puberty, the brief spell of relative freedom from control by the mother is over for the girl. Her early socialization trained her to be a Hopi; at puberty the specialized training for her sex role is increased. She is drawn back, both literally and figuratively, into the house, and from now on most of her contacts will be with members of her own clan and lineage or with other female relatives. This contrasts with the socialization of the adolescent boy, who is participating more in the ceremonial activities that unite the men of the village. While her brothers spend their days in the fields and their evenings with age-mates in the kiva or roaming about the village, the girl is kept home, or limited to the company of one or two other girls. Her mother is her authority figure and disciplinarian, and it is toward her mother that her resentment is expressed. But mother-daughter conflicts are shameful as they break the unity of the household and the lineage, so the girl is punished if her resentment develops into rebellion.

The immediate goal of the girl's adolescent training is to become a wife and mother. In the face of it, it seems strange that the girl should be so anxious about rejection by a lover. Every woman, except the insane or severely deformed, does get married. Even if her husband should leave her, it is not difficult to find an acceptable second husband. This must be as apparent to the girl as it is to the observer. Hence, an explanation is needed for this irrational fear.

We can find it in the type of relationship being sought, a love relationship with a man: the Hopi, for all their practicality, believe that love is a prerequisite to a good marriage and necessary for the marriage to last. A woman expects to be taken care of by her husband "as the farmer takes care of his corn plants," lovingly and dutifully.

The affective model for this type of relationship is the father-daughter relationship. Her father's attitude toward her should be one of tenderness and concern. He is not a disciplinarian; after early childhood, she is disciplined by her mother and, if necessary, her mother's brother. The father, then, is an affectionate figure, who should always support and protect his young daughter.

In reality, the father-daughter relationship depends to a great extent upon the relationship between the girl's parents (Eggan 1950: 32). If there is trouble and the father goes home to his mother or sister, the girl has few opportunities to see him. She may visit him there, when he is at home, but, as the Hopi have virtually no street life, casual encounters or public meetings are likely to be rare. Her brother, on the other hand, sees his father in the fields or the kiva. Older boys may even go with their fathers in case of separation, although the Hopi acknowledge that this is seldom done. Thus, while her brothers can continue the close and affectionate relationship if the parents separate, it is difficult for the girl to do so. In any event, the solidarity among the females of the household would predispose the girl to side with her mother.

The potentially tenuous nature of the father-daughter bond and the difficulties this can cause the girl are illustrated by three stories given me by an elderly man in response to TAT cards. I had showed some of the cards to informants to elicit themes related to interpersonal relationships, particularly those dealing with the family. To Card 18GF, showing two figures he interpreted as mother and daughter, he told a story dealing with the despair of a young girl because her father did not weave her a new dress. This made her ashamed in front of the villagers, and she took this as a sign he did not love her. She wanted to die, and only her father's reassurance and promise of a dress saved her. To Card 18BM, on which is depicted a man with hands reaching from behind and touching him, he told of two girls who went to the house where their father was living after separating from their mother. They begged him to return with them, and they put their hands on him to pull him home. To Card 12M, showing a man leaning over a figure on a bed, he gave a story dealing with a young girl who became sick because her mother expelled her father from the house. This man's relationship with his own wife and grown daughters is close, and he denies that any separation occurred during his marriage. While admittedly these stories are idiosyncratic, they do illustrate one Hopi's assessment of the difficulties that girls can encounter when their fathers leave home or appear to be unreliable.

Even when the marriage is stable, the girl sees much less of her father than do her brothers. The father is a tender but remote figure to his daughter, whereas he is close to his sons. It is also possible that the trauma of the initiation ceremony has a different effect upon girls than upon boys. Both can be disillusioned, but boys at least can use their masculine identification as a means of conquering distrust of the adult men. Girls have no such possibility.

I suggest that the attitude toward the father acts as a model for the attitude with which the girl approaches her lover or would-be husband. She hopes for tenderness but fears that her wishes will not be gratified. She is aware, and fearful of, the pain of rejection. Particularly at this time, when her relationship with her mother is strained, she is more vulnerable to disappointments in other areas of her emotional life.

Conclusions

A number of authorities have given their reasons for the genesis of the adolescent crisis among American youth. Mead (1928) speaks of conflicting pathways. Pearson (1958: 23), a psychoanalyst, emphasizes the pressure on the adolescent to "learn himself as an individual—not as a member of a group, or as a member of his family, but as he, himself." Erikson (1971: 260) discusses the balance that must be struck between some freedom of role choice and the paralyzing effect of too much freedom. Others (e.g., Smith, 1969) point to such factors as rapid social change, social mobility, and taboos on premarital sexual experience.

None of these hold true for the Hopi girl. There are no conflicting standards or alternative choices leading to dilemmas: there is one Hopi road for everyone. Even less must the Hopi girl learn herself as an individual: it is during adolescence that she is drawn even more into her household group. Other factors isolated as leading to the adolescent crisis in Western youth are simply not applicable to the Hopi situation.

The similarities—moodiness, intergenerational conflict, and anxiety over sex and love—rise from different sources. We must conclude, then, that the adolescent crisis is not a product of modern Western culture, but rather one that can occur wherever heavy social and psychological pressures are put upon young people. The Samoan girls studied by Mead evidently had no such pressures put upon them at adolescence. The Hopi girl, on the other hand, is undergoing what is probably the most difficult period of her life. Her crisis, then, is comprehensible within the context of the socialization process.

Notes

1 The ethnographic data were collected from Third Mesa. The time period under consideration is circa 1890-1920, although Thompson and Joseph (1945), found corroborating evidence in the psychological tests they administered to Hopi school children in 1942-43. I wish to thank Helen and Edward Kennard for their observations on young children in the two-to-six age range.

2 Children can enter sex-specific ceremonial societies before adolescence, such as the Snake Society for men or the Mamzrau Society for women, but not all enter, nor do those who do so all enter before adolescence.

3 There is one punishment that is restricted to boys, namely, for bedwetting, which is ignored in girls. It is of a ritual nature involving visits to the Water Clan and the singing of water songs. Why bedwetting should be treated in this manner, and why only boys should be thus treated, has not been satisfactorily explained.

4 For a cross-cultural study of sex differences in socialization, see Barry, Bacon, and Child (1957).

5 There is no taboo on sexual relations during menstruation; in fact, it is believed that sexual intercourse during or around the time of menstruation increases chances of conception, probably because the fetus is regarded as being formed through coalescence of mother's blood and father's semen (Simmons 1942: 259). One woman told me that people do not have sexual relations during the woman's heavy flow, as this might be harmful to the woman.

6 On the Second Mesa, it is believed that the plaque a man receives at the wedding serves the same purpose as the woman's robe in the voyage into the Spirit World (Nequatewa 1933). However, this belief does not seem to have the same strength as the one about the wedding robe, and certainly bachelors outnumber spinsters.

References

Barry, H. III, K. Bacon, and L. Child. 1957. Cross-Cultural Survey of Some Sex Differences in Socialization. *Journal of Abnormal and Social Psychology* 55: 327-332.

Cohen, Y. A. 1964. *The Transition from Childhood to Adolescence.* Chicago.

Dennis, W. 1940. *The Hopi Child.* New York.

Eggan, D. 1956. *Instruction and Affect in Hopi Cultural Conditioning.* Southwestern Journal of Anthropology 12: 347-70.

Eggan F. 1950. *Social Organization of the Western Pueblos.* Chicago.

Erikson, E. H. 1971. *Youth and the Life Cycle. Adolescent Behavior and Society: A Book of Readings,* ed. R. E. Muuss, pp. 253-264. New York.

Forde, C. 1931. Hopi Agriculture and Land Ownership. *Journal of the Royal Anthropological Institute* 61: 357-405.

Goldfrank, E. 1945. Socialization, Personality, and the Structure of Pueblo Society. *American Anthropologist* 47: 516-40.

Mead, M. 1928. *Coming of Age in Samoa.* New York.

Nequatewa, E. 1933. *Hopi Courtship and Marriage.* Museum Notes, Museum of Northern Arizona 5: 42-48.

Pearson, G. 1958. *Adolescence and the Conflict of Generations.* New York.

Qoyawayma, P. (Elizabeth White). 1964. *No Turning Back.* Albuquerque.

Richards, A. I. 1956. *Chisungu: A Girls Initiation Ceremony Among the Bemba of Northern Rhodesia.* London.

Simmons, L. 1942. *Sun Chief: The Autobiography of a Hopi Indian.* New Haven.

Smith, E. 1969. Youth-Adult Conflict in American Society. *Issues in Adolescent Psychology,* ed., D. Rogers, pp. 477-495. New York.

Thompson, L., and A. Joseph. 1945. *The Hopi Way.* Chicago.

Titiev, M. 1944. Old Oraibi. Papers of the Peabody Museum of American Archaeology and Ethnology, Harvard University 22: 1. Cambridge.

Turner, V. 1967. *The Forest of Symbols.* Ithaca.

Udall, L. 1969. *Me and Mine: The Life Story of Helen Sekaquaptewa.* Tucson.

Whiting, J. W. M., R. Kluckhohn, and A. Anthony. 1958. The Function of Male Initiation Ceremonies at Puberty. *Readings in Social Psychology,* ed. E. E. Maccoby, T. M. Newcomb, and E. L. Hartley, pp. 359-70. New York.

Young, F. 1965. *Initiation Ceremonies: A Cross-Cultural Study of Status Dramatization.* Indianapolis.

PUBERTY TO MARRIAGE: A STUDY OF THE SEXUAL LIFE
OF THE NATIVES OF WOGEO, NEW GUINEA

H. Ian Hogbin

Children, accustomed to running about during their early years without clothing, are soon aware of the more superficial anatomical differences between boys and girls. I once overhead a little boy aged five tell his sister, who was eighteen months younger, that, possessed of a penis and testes, he was a man, whereas she, with a vulva, was a woman. "I'm a woman with my vulva; woman with my vulva; vulva, vulva, vulva," the little girl shrieked, much to the amusement of the bystanders, who made no effort to silence her or to divert her attention. One woman, indeed, told her that she would have breasts also when she grew up.

The natives are by no means prim in speech, as this incident proves, and, although lewd jesting is indulged in only when contemporaries are alone together, the sexual organs and excretory functions are freely mentioned whenever the necessity arises. I often heard Sabuk, who possessed potent magic for curing swollen testes, asked quite openly to come and attend to a sufferer, and the photograph of a wax anatomical model in one of my books was much asked for by both men and women, who used to grin together and comment on the smallness of the penis. Again, the men withdraw only a yard or two to urinate no matter who is sitting close by, and one is liable to hear a blunt announcement at any time that someone is going into the bush to empty his bowels. For sexual intercourse alone euphemisms are usual, the crude word *kakalok* being uttered only by the men. In mixed company and before certain relatives the couple are said to have "done a little something" or to have "made the thing [i.e. the penis] wrinkled."[1]

References to sexual functions are avoided in the presence of the very young, however, who are told that babies are picked by the mother off certain trees, where they grow like fruit. This information is before long corrected by playmates, and by the time the child has reached its eighth or ninth year the adults, taking its acquaintance with the more fundamental facts of conception for granted, discuss such matters as intercourse and pregnancy in its hearing. The assumption, to judge from personal impressions, is well founded. "The man and woman copulate—he puts his penis in her vulva—and by and by she has an infant in her belly," one lad explained in response to a question. Yet his knowledge was dependent entirely upon hearsay, for the youngsters do not carry out experiments for themselves, and the grown-ups take precautions against observation while in their more intimate embraces—even young married couples refrain from sharing the same bed unless spending the night alone.

In spite of much outspokenness, the adults, and eventually the children also, are always liable to burst out laughing if sex is mentioned. The subject seems to be looked upon as amusing because

Reprinted by permission of the Editors from *Oceania*, Vol. 16, No. 3, 1946, pp. 185-209.

vaguely indelicate, though why this should be so I am unable to say. I could find no evidence that the present generation is throwing off the repressions of a Victorian past, nor did anyone appear to be finding relief in nervous laughter for his embarrassment at having been under the necessity of giving overt proof of his emancipation. No one is straight-laced, not even the oldest, and I did not see a single person display signs of being scandalized.

The general attitude may be judged from an item of gossip which gave food for mirth over a period of weeks—indeed, I overheard a group of men guffawing over it six months after the incident had occurred. Wiap's wife, it appeared, had seized his waist belt during a family quarrel and twisted it so tightly that he had been forced to yell in agony that his testes were being squashed.

Again, the most popular myths, apart from those well known to all dealing with the fundamentals of the culture, are those which we would describe as thoroughly obscene. Three of these I heard repeated more than a dozen times, and on each occasion the children present joined in the laughter at appropriate intervals.

The first, which explained why the penis is its present length, told of how in the days of long ago the culture-hero Kofa had a penis so long that he was compelled to roll it up and carry it in a coil on his shoulder. While looking for a lost pig on the mountain top he one day saw his sweetheart at work below, and, unwrapping the penis, he projected it through the air to her feet. But as he was so far away she could not hear his warning, and, thinking that she was being attacked by a snake, she defended herself with a digging stick. Poor Kofa fainted with the pain, and, on coming to his senses, found that all save a few inches of the organ were lost to him.

The second tale was about a woman who had two snakes in her vulva. Every time a man had intercourse with her one of these bit him, until in the end only the young headman Wura remained. One snake he managed to kill by hoodwinking it with a model penis made of wood, and, cutting off the head, he threw the carcase into the sea. The second was more cunning, but, after various adventures, all of them bawdy, he at last succeeded in catching it in a slip-knot. Unfortunately, it escaped and wriggled off into the bush, where its descendants are to be found to this day, still bent on vengeance against men. Sea snakes, on the other hand, descended from the headless carcase, are incapable of doing harm.[2]

The hero Maiaf, according to the third story, had a feud with a girl named Wal after she refused his offers of marriage. Seeing her by chance when she was digging a pit in the garden, he determined to have his revenge then and there. Seizing her from behind, he forced her head into the mud till she could neither see who her attacker was nor call for help, and then committed rape. But before making his escape he had the bad luck to drop a feather ornament, which Wal picked up. Some days later, having pretended to find it in the village near the men's house, she enquired who was the owner. Maiaf, unsuspicious, alone put forward a claim, and she thus knew that he must be the culprit. All the women agreed to help her punish him, and a plan was rapidly concocted. She was to make an assignation with him but to put on an under-petticoat and tie it firmly between her legs. While he was fumbling with this the women sprang upon him and made him submit to every possible indignity. He was ill for several months, during which time she married someone else, a fact which made him more angry than ever. On his recovery, he killed a frog, which, when it was half rotten and stinking, he put inside a bamboo. That night he crawled under the house where Wal and her husband lived, and, holding the bamboo just below the spot where they were eating their meal, took out the stopper. The husband, thinking that she had emitted wind, was most indignant and beat her soundly. She ran out of the door, where Maiaf was waiting with a stick to hit her over the head. The blow killed her, but, as no one knew of his presence, people thought she must have bumped her brains out on the rafters in her haste.

Even the more solemn myths often include indelicate incidents, apparently for the sole purpose of providing comic relief by way of dramatic contrast. In the middle of a serious account of how two children killed a giant, one is suddenly informed that, to make certain of his death, they applied hot stones to his genitals "until his testes burst with a noise like the firing of a gun," and of another highly important culture hero it was said by way of an irrelevant aside that "his breath stank because he had no anus."

The Awakening of the Sexual Impulses

The first glimmering of a true appreciation of sex seems to come to the boys, at least, during pubescence, when, although no attention is as yet paid to girls, self-consciousness about the genitals makes an appearance. Hitherto many reminders have been necessary to ensure tolerable decency in the adjustment of the clothing, but all at once extreme modesty becomes noticeable even when they are in the company of the men, who are themselves, if alone with the members of their own sex, by no means so scrupulous. (I did not come across any exhibitionism, but few men hesitated to strip openly if no woman was present when they wished to bathe or change into another garment.)

Interest in the genitals soon leads to masturbation, which is said to be common also amongst the girls. The practice, so long as an adolescent and not an adult is involved, is looked upon as perfectly normal. "They are trying out their organs," say the elders with a grin, though some of them may suggest half seriously that urination may be difficult afterwards. The youths usually go off in couples to a secluded nook in the bush, but on one occasion four of them were discovered in an empty house, to the intense amusement of the whole island, women as well as men. The thought of them all so absorbed in their orgy as to be oblivious of the sound of an approaching footstep struck everyone as extremely funny.

At about this time, or perhaps a little later, in the fifteenth or sixteenth year, the boys begin to add gusto to the coarse jests with which conversation is frequently salted. Such talk is considered to be harmless in itself, but inappropriate if members of a different generation are present, especially those classified as parents or children. Decorum ought also to be preserved, it is said, in the company of the grandparents, but I often found them encouraging the lads in lewdness. "Here comes itching penis" and "Where are big testes going?" are accepted as more or less conventional phrases of greeting by persons who are of the same age, and I have many times heard not only the youths, but fathers of families and even greybeards playfully accuse one another of adultery. "I hear that the men of Dap have to watch their wives so carefully that they never have a wink of sleep," decrepit Ibwara called out as the aged Bagasal walked through Kinaba village. "That's what they tell me about Kinaba," was the reply. "Why don't you come to Dap with me to give your women here a rest?" Abnormalities of the genitals are also referred to with monotonous regularity, and a youth who had been circumcised while in hospital on the mainland was teased unmercifully by his associates and accused of being forced into the operation on account of his lust.

I know nothing of any instructions given by mothers to their daughters—the men insisted that, as sexual intercourse is in normal circumstances harmless to the girls, lectures are unnecessary—but, as soon as the boys show signs of approaching maturity, the elders, far from telling them how best to approach the women, begin solemnly warning them to keep their distance. The vulva, they claim, is the most disgusting part of the human anatomy, male or female, unpleasant to look at and loathsome to smell. So repellent is it, in fact, that even an imbecile would be instantly aware of the danger and refrain from going near. Fully-grown men have constantly to take precautions after marriage, and an immature youth who took risks would be foolish indeed. "Cut one of those creepers, and what happens to it? It shrivels up and dies," the headman Marigum remarked to his son Dal one day when the three of us were out together in the forest. "If a boy has sexual intercourse before he is fully grown the same thing happens to him—copulation makes his sinews wither, and he remains stunted and half formed. Mark what I say, son, keep away from women till you're old enough to marry. Think well of your cousin Igaru—he chased girls and is now dead. And you know what a little runt of a man Wager is—that's girls for you again!"

Such warnings are not without effect, and several youths of sixteen or seventeen for whose word I can vouch with some degree of certainty assured me that they intended to take their father's advice. My own two servants, Dal and Gris, aged sixteen, with whom I was especially intimate, both claimed to be still virgin and denied any wish to experience as yet the pleasures of dalliance. Like other boys of the same age, they appeared to be really at home only with persons of their own sex, though their conduct when in mixed company was friendly and free from embarrassment.

The inevitable fate of every youth, however, seems to be seduction by a woman older than himself. Two attempts had been made already on Gris's virtue, one by Mango, the wife of a close relative of his mother, and one by Waramwein, a girl of twenty-one. Mango, so he told me, suggested when he met her one day coming from the garden that, as her husband was out fishing for the day, they might retire together into the bush, and Waramwein on another occasion actually put her hands on his genitals, urging him to put them with hers and "make the two of them feel good." His excuse to both was that he was still too young.

Fearing the worst, the men admonish their sons to be careful, above all, not to listen to the women of their own moiety. Supernatural penalties are never invoked, and the only explanation spontaneously offered is that the culture-heroes of long ago prohibited sexual relations between members of the same group. On my pressing for a reason for so arbitrary a regulation, most informants had nothing further to add, though one or two sought to justify it somewhat lamely on the grounds of expediency. Disregarding for the time being their statements that early affairs have nothing whatever to do with marriage, they now pointed out that alliances sometimes breed a desire for marriage. If both parties are from the one moiety, they continued, trouble is inevitable, for the relatives will refuse to recognize the match.

No mention is ever made of the women who, though of the correct moiety, are forbidden on account of their close relationship. "But they are the same as real sisters," Jaua exclaimed in astonishment when I asked him why. "And only a madman would lie with his sister. You'll be wanting to ask next, I suppose, why boys aren't informed that they musn't copulate with their mothers. They don't have to be told; they know."

Of the ten or a dozen first affairs which I recorded in my notebooks, Waru's is best worth quoting here, for, although all are concerned with incidents of the same type, he was much more candid, as usual, about his hopes and fears. He was a little bigger than Dal—probably about seventeen—when his friend Kaunara told him that a young woman named Kimarol had sent a message asking him to meet her on a certain hilltop behind her father's garden. "She wishes the two of you to do a little something together," Kaunara explained. Waru replied that he was totally lacking in experience and would have no notion of what to do. Ignorance was no excuse for refusing the invitation, he was told, for Kimarol would soon remedy the deficiency; besides, did he have no wish to learn? Yes, he said, but he did not like the girl well enough to have her for a teacher.

"Yes, yes; of course I wanted to go," he remarked at this point in the recital. "But I was also afraid. Certainly I was unwilling to have Kimarol laughing at my clumsiness, yet more important than that was the fear of never growing tall and strong. My father was always telling me how dangerous intercourse with a woman before I grew up would be, and his words were loud in my ears. I didn't say anything about that to Kaunara, for he'd have scoffed—he often used to say that the elders were making fools of us youngsters. I wasn't so sure, and I just said I didn't like Kimarol."

The girl went on sending messages, and at last, when he and Kaunara were out in the bush, he found that arrangements had been made for the two of them to meet her. He admitted that at the first mention of the plan he was glad that his hand was being forced, for he had been dreaming of her nightly and was burning with desire. But on catching sight of her his courage failed him, and he fled. Finding that she was in hot pursuit, he climbed a tree and refused to budge, though for a time she stood underneath and made the most enticing offers, telling him that she had had enough experience for both. That night he was angry with himself for letting such an opportunity slip, though he was also relieved at his escape from danger.

Kaunara waited a month and then arranged another meeting. Again Waru turned to run away, but Kimarol seized the end of his loincloth and threatened to pull it off and leave him naked. "She's got you now," said Kaunara, "I'll go off to my garden."

"I was terrified," Waru told me; "I thought both of my ignorance and of my father's warnings—she'd soon be laughing at me, and then within a few days perhaps I'd be ill. But she embraced me and pulled me on top of her, and then I forgot. I was very stupid though and didn't at all know what to do. Just think—I lay there like a block of stone, as though I were asleep! 'Wriggle your behind,' she said. I tried but was so embarrassed that she had to do it all. And when we'd finished I ran away. For days I was frightened—I used to wake up at night and wonder how long before I'd die. Yet in another month I was with her again, and, after that, although I sometimes remembered what my father had told me, desire kept on making me forget."

The girls seem to begin their sexual life earlier, often, perhaps usually, a little before their first menstruation, which takes place much later than among persons of European race. The average age is probably sixteen, though one or two girls whose menarche celebrations I attended were over seventeen. The seducer is always older and in some cases a married man, extramarital intercourse being of common occurrence. To lie with a virgin is the ambition of many, and most young girls find themselves pursued by a dozen or more.

Bond Friendship

The concern of the elders is genuine, for they are convinced that contact with females always involves risk. The peril is supposed to be really grave after copulation has taken place, when the fluids from each partner enter the body of the other. The woman is automatically cleansed by the natural process of menstruation, which rids her of the fluids which have been absorbed, but for the man positive action is necessary—he has to incise his penis and induce an artificial menstruation (the same word, *baras*, is frequently used for both). Serious as is the danger for adults, it is still worse for the immature, "whose bones and sinews are soft and pliable"; moreover, as the youths are not taught the male-menstruation ritual until the final stage of their initiation, in the nineteenth year at the earliest, and often very much later, they are as yet unable to purify themselves. To give them instruction at an earlier age, according to the unanimous opinion of the parents, would invite disaster, for condoning their conduct would make indulgence even more frequent.[3]

Most young men are prepared in their rational moments to acknowledge the wisdom of abstinence; sexual intercourse, they agree, is best avoided until the threshold of manhood has been passed. But a number complained at different times that the motives of their tutors were not above suspicion, being inspired in part by jealousy. "They want to keep the girls for themselves and don't want us as rivals," Baj, a handsome youth of eighteen, once told me bitterly.

Such charges are heard most frequently if one of the senior men is thought to be conducting an intrigue, or if a youth has been rejected in favour of a man older than himself. "Copulation dangerous? Of course it isn't," Wiari snarled in anger on hearing the name of his uncle linked with that of the girl whom he was himself courting. "I tell you truly, Obin, that this talk of peril is a tale that the old men tell to keep us quiet. They know that the women prefer our smooth skins and straight limbs, and they're afraid of us." Talking the matter over a couple of months later, he admitted that his judgment had been somewhat hasty, though his uncle and many others, he added, were probably glad that their juniors were so vulnerable.

I am inclined to accept this last remark of Wiari's as an adequate summary of the situation. The elders, though sincere, would scarcely be human if they did not rejoice inwardly in the possession of a weapon which helps to eliminate a number of potential rivals more attractive than themselves. This opinion is confirmed by the explanation consistently put forward for the hostility of headmen and certain others towards their eldest son. "They hate him looking at the girls with whom they wish to lie," informants stated.[4]

None of the elder men admitted that he was himself jealous, but, although many confided in private accounts of intrigues conducted long before the last stage of their initiation, all were continually complaining in the youngsters' hearing that sexual intercourse is begun at a much earlier age nowadays than in the time of their own youth. I taxed one or two with being humbugs but was put in my place with the self-righteous reply that the young had to be lectured for their own good. "We have to hand on to our sons the advice which our fathers gave to us," they said complacently.

Well aware that any mention of the subject would give rise to disapproval and resentment, a youth keeps silent about his escapades when in the presence of his elder relatives. Fearful of gossip, he is discreet also with most of his contemporaries and contents himself as a rule with taking only one of them into his confidence, a companion whom he knows from experience that he can trust. The two share all their secrets and announce before long that they have become bond-friends.

In parts of Africa men wishing to become blood-brothers carry out a ceremony invoking supernatural penalties on whoever shall afterwards break his faith. Wogeo bond-friends are not as careful as this, but betrayal is rare, for each knows so much about the other. If the pair decide that a mistake has been made, however, and separation follows, they at once begin avoiding each other. Everyone was pleased when I engaged Dal and Gris as my personal servants and predicted a strong friendship between them. They seemed to be ideally matched, for not only was each the son of a headman, but they were born in the same month. Unfortunately, a difference of opinion took place during the first week of their service, and from that time onwards, though they had to work together, they never spoke except through an intermediary, and then only for the purpose of transmitting my orders. The inconvenience of having two servants who practised mutual avoidance can be imagined.

Bond-friends are always, for obvious reasons, of approximately the same age and residents in the same district. Meetings are therefore easily arranged, and they spend a good deal of their time together, often sharing a bed even when they belong to different villages. They usually walk about arm in arm and address one another fondly as "Foroman" or "Wanein," pidgin-English terms which have practically replaced the local expression, *wasabwai*.[5] Such demonstrations of affection are the more remarkable since other persons, including spouses, shun bodily contact in public.

The convention is that members of the same moiety, being "like brothers," are too shy to discuss their love affairs with one another. As the chief requirement demanded from a bond-friend—in the years of late adolescence and early manhood, at least—are sympathy during the recital of accounts of past intrigues and facility in organizing new ones, the pair always belong to different groups. Such an arrangement also serves to minimize rivalry and simplify the planning of assignations. Moiety incest being forbidden, suspicion would at once be roused if a youth of one group were seen talking to a girl of the other. She is not his "sister," and the onlookers would presume that he was bent on having an affair with her. But the girls of his own moiety may be approached freely, and he can put the claims of his friend forward whenever a convenient opportunity offers.

Bond-friendship continues to be of importance till marriage, when many men—possibly the majority—sacrifice it on the altar of domestic peace. The wives object to the husband's intimacy with his partner, claiming that intrigues are still being planned, and the tie is in general not considered to be worth putting up with their disapproval. "My wife made such a fuss every time she saw me with my bond-friend Kaunara that at last I took to avoiding him," Waru told me. "We speak nowadays if we meet but rarely enter one another's houses."

Where relations still remain cordial, gifts of food and all sorts of services are exchanged, but the two do not call for assistance in planning extramarital affairs. Wiawia and Kaurom, for example, both married men with families, were frequently at work in one another's gardens, and when Kaurom built a new canoe he asked his partner to recite additional magic over the hull to enhance its seaworthiness. Both denied any interest at present in girls—were they not fathers with family responsibilities?—but Wiawia agreed when pressed that had anyone attracted him he would have preferred to make his own arrangements about meeting her. "I'd be ashamed now that we're so old to talk about such things with Kaurom," he added.

My own bond-friendship with the youth Kalabai revealed clearly that a distinction is drawn between the obligations of partners before and after marriage. He suggested the relationship between us largely in the first instance as a joke, but, on discovering that I was serious about accepting the proposal, at once intimated willingness to abide by his responsibilities. Did I wish to take any of the girls into the forest? was his first question. "Very well, then, we'll be friends like married men," he continued on my denying any such intention. "You can give me rice and tea when I come to your village and I'll have coconuts, taro and betel-nut for you when you're in mine. And if you want anyone to carry a box when you go visiting on the other side of the island, well then, ask me, and I'll carry it." He was as good as his word and from that day onwards became my baggage-carrier-in-chief. Moreover, when I was ill with malaria he brought his father along and insisted on my drinking a nauseous magical potion which the old man prepared. "You gave me white man's medicine when I was ill; now you are laid up I, your bond-friend, bring you ours," he said.

My last night on the island was spent in the company of my particular cronies, with Kalabai sitting on my right, my hand held firmly in his. "From to-night I put a taboo (vae) on this house," he declared solemnly. "The timber may rot, and the trees grow up where the hearth stood, but I shall never come to this spot again as long as I live." He thus paid me a rare compliment, for only when a much-beloved bond-friend dies does a man publicly announce that he will never enter the dwelling in future nor accept food from the dead man's children.

Care of the Person

A marked change is noticeable in a youth's appearance as soon as he starts taking an interest in girls. "Look, he's letting his hair grow and wearing flowers," the adults remark. "His penis must be beginning to itch." Boys who still prefer to associate with companions of their own sex are invariably untidy: their hair is long and unkempt, their clothing—the bare minimum—frequently in tatters, and, although often in the water, they swim more for the pleasure of the exercise than for the sake of washing. The older youths, however, besides growing the hair; are careful both of their dress and the cleanliness of their bodies. They prefer a full-skirted loincloth to the costume of former times, the G-string, which is worn by the older men, choosing bright colours for day wear and plain white, if possible, for the evenings, "when patterns cannot be seen and red looks dull and black"; and each day, unless the weather is cold, they take a protracted bath, scrubbing themselves with handfuls of sand, rubbing their teeth with leaves or a charred stick, and rinsing their mouths thoroughly with salt water. Afterwards, as they sit on the shore drying in the sun, they massage their muscles until the skin shines like burnished copper.

The lengthening hair was in former times dragged back to be confined in a wicker-work cone—a style still popular with the older generation—the forehead being then shaved to increase its apparent height.[6] (The regular use for the beard, which is at best thin and straggly, of the piece of obsidian or bottle glass which serves as a razor is unnecessary until early manhood.) Nowadays the locks are teased instead into a fuzzy mop with the aid of a coarse bamboo comb. Watching a pair of youths carrying out their toilet on the trunk of an overhanging Callophyllum tree in front of my house, I found that they spent eleven minutes combing their hair in the morning and seventeen minutes after a bathe in the late afternoon. Their thoughts may perhaps be guessed from the fact that on both occasions each was crooning mildly erotic songs.

Decorations are most lavish at dances, when the whole of the family jewellery is produced, and the menfolk strut about in feather headdresses, turtle-shell forehead plates, and woven wristbands, armlets, collars, and headbands, all of them encrusted with cowries, shell rings, and dogs' teeth. On such occasions everyone wears something, including the children and the elders, but at other times the only persons who use ornaments and cosmetics to any considerable extent are the boys and the younger men. Youths in their late teens and early twenties, in fact, are rarely seen without some kind of adornment, if only a flower, which may be fixed either in the hair or in the hole in the lobe of the ear. Kalabai, when we were out walking together, on one occasion plucked a flower and offered it to me. Suddenly realizing, however, that my ears were not pierced, he asked in puzzled tones, "where, then, do white men wear flowers?" Looking glasses are to-day much in demand, but in olden days each person had to request his friends to adjust his ornaments, for forest pools and the water in the bottoms of canoes, the only mirrors then available, were not very satisfactory.

The natives' keen eye for decorative effect is at no time more in evidence than when they are choosing which cosmetics and hair dye to use with the ornaments they have decided to wear. Kalabai one afternoon produced the crest of a ground-pigeon (*Goura victoriæ*), a magnificent fan nearly as large as a dinner plate, made up of black feathers, each one tipped with flecks of blue and white. "I haven't been able to wear this because I can't get any white powder," he remarked. "I've got red and yellow ochre, but you wouldn't use either of them with feathers like this." I promised him as much as he wanted, and the next afternoon he turned up with the crest stuck in one side of his specially blackened hair to ask for just one small dab to put on the opposite cheek. Any more, he said, would spoil the effect.

On another occasion Baj asked for the loan of a looking glass to see whether, as someone had said, his cockade of red Cordyline leaves and white cockatoo feathers clashed with his hair, which he had smeared with a henna-coloured vegetable paste. The cockade being found to strike a jarring note, he removed it and pinned a large black and yellow butterfly in its place. Then, after rubbing the red paint from his cheeks, he took a packet of yellow ochre and a stick of charcoal from his handbag. "Black and yellow in the hair demand black and yellow on the face," he explained.

Again, Bunia, when given the skin of a bird-of-paradise by his father, took off every other ornament and scrubbed his face. "The bird-of-paradise is enough; don't you agree that to wear anything else would be silly?" he asked. It was a superb skin, quite the finest I had seen, verging from deep sulphur on the breast to the purest white at the tail, and I could only congratulate him on his good taste. Unfortunately, a misguided friend persuaded him to replace his armbands.

As most people are acutely sensitive to smells, care is also taken to counteract the stench of perspiration. (The body odour of a person suffering from ringworm is felt to be so offensive that he has to remain on the leeward side when working with a group.) The usual method is to keep the armbands stuffed with fragrant herbs, though, in addition, the younger folk smear their shoulders either with coconut oil in which flowers have been steeped or cheap European perfumes.

The final aid to beauty is magic, which is held to be so important that, if a dance is being performed the whole village combines to carry out the necessary rites. On less formal occasions, however, each person recites a spell for himself. "Make me so beautiful," a characteristic specimen concluded, "that when my sweetheart sees me she will forsake her kinsfolk and follow."

Standards of Beauty

The women bathe themselves with care and carry out magical rites to enhance their attractiveness but, except on very special occasions, such as at certain dances in which the men take no part and the ceremonies connected with first menstruation, do not decorate themselves to nearly the same extent as the men. Face painting, for example, is considered to be quite out of place, and no woman would ever consider dying her hair which, in any case, is cropped short. Again, although flowers are sometimes attached to the ears, and armlets and simple necklaces occasionally put on, the more elaborate cockades and headdresses are held to be far too mannish for female wear.[7]

The difference between men and women in this respect is clearly revealed by an analysis of popular songs, dozens of which appear every year, ninety per cent. of them dealing with sexual longings.[8] Those about youths are concerned solely with the appeal of their ornaments; those about girls, on the other hand, dwell rather on personal charms, such as the sheen of the skin, the shape of the nose, or the firmness of the breasts. I quote two characteristic examples, the first of which, composed by one of his friends, was said to be about Kalabai:

> "He has two ear-rings,
> Two ear-rings which shine like two suns.
> He gazes at himself in the looking glass.
> Yes, his sweetheart likes him."

The contrast between this and the following song, an effort of Jaua's younger days about a girl whom he was at the time pursuing, is striking:

"My sweetheart has a soft skin,
Skin soft and smooth.
Her skin glows like sunset on the waters,
Like the sunbeams through the palm leaves."

The loveliness of firm unblemished skin or flesh—the same word is used for both—is celebrated in song after song. The phrase "bright and clear as the petals of a flower" appeared in several, and one contained a somewhat curious comparison with the radiance of my newly polished shoes. The importance of bloom is indicated also by the number of different magical rites concerned with achieving it, and by the fact that its loss is supposed to be one of the penalties for failing to observe so many of the taboos. Further, the spirits which in folk tales lure men to destruction, though age-old, are customarily described as "having the appearance of a young girl with clear, unwrinkled skin shining as if it had been oiled" (the supernatural origin of these beings is revealed by their concave eyes and inverted nipples).

This preoccupation with skin is readily understood when the prevalence of ringworm, tropical ulcers, and sores is taken into consideration. Such complaints are regarded as repellent on account of the stench to which they give rise, and sufferers are said to be passed over when affairs are being planned. Most of them marry in the end, but one young man of my acquaintance refused to accept the girl of his father's choice on the ground that, being subject to sores, she offended his nose, and another sent his new wife back to her parents when she developed an ulcer on her cheek.

Freedom from the odour of perspiration and a sweet breath are also insisted upon, and the girls are as punctilious as the boys in rubbing their armpits with wet sand and rinsing their mouths. The reason sometimes given by the men for repulsing the advances of older women is the "stinking wind" arising from their decayed teeth.

Without youth, it is claimed, there can be no allure, and husbands who are jealous after their wives have borne a couple of children are a stock subject for laughter. On hearing that Wiap had reprimanded his middle-aged spouse for working in the garden without a chaperon, the whole village hooted with mirth, each man playfully accusing the others of a preference for women with wrinkles. "Come, come," Jaua called out to Waru, "We know you like tying their breasts around your back when you lie with them, smelling their foul breath, and rubbing your hands on their withered flanks."

Casual alliances sometimes take place, nevertheless, and one toothless old crone used to solicit the youths with a certain amount of success. "Desire doesn't disappear with the teeth," she protested, "and so long as a woman can still dig she wants to do a little something now and then." The physically repulsive are also not entirely lacking in attraction, for a deaf mute who suffered from goitre, though unsought in marriage, had borne not less than six children.

The petite has apparently less æsthetic appeal than the massive, for girls pointed out to me for commendation were all somewhat large—indeed, I venture to say over-large—with broad hips and powerful limbs. The knock-knees with which most of them were disfigured were certainly deplored, and it was admitted that a narrower pelvis gave a better hang to a petticoat. "But knees aren't really important," I was told, "and a big woman is stronger than a little one."

Of the features, high foreheads and narrow noses are singled out for special praise, though the noses of Europeans, "sharp as an axe," are said to be too thin. Fat cheeks, on the other hand, give rise to derisive laughter and unflattering comparisons with the full moon. A young girl with pendulous breasts, "like a grandmother," is also held to be unfortunate—they should be firm with the nipples still facing outwards, not turning to the ground.

Dark men seem for the most part to prefer brunettes, and those who are themselves light select partners of the same hue. Europeans are most emphatically not envied for their blonde colouring, which is regarded as far too reminiscent of albinos. Condolences were offered to me on two occasions on account of my pallor, and Jaua was probably expressing the opinion of the majority when he said that if he were white he supposed that he, too, would be ashamed and cover his body with as many clothes as possible.

Early Affairs with Girls from the Same District

A boy has ample opportunity to meet the girls from neighbouring villages and to judge their attractions, for no one expects females to be shy or retiring. They mingle freely with their own menfolk, exchanging gossip and advice, and at once come forward to help in entertaining guests. Occasionally, when a youth had brought visitors to the house while some special task was in progress, I heard apologies offered for his sister's absence. She would be along later, he explained; and, sure enough, on the completion of the work she brought her lime pot and betel pepper and sat alongside.

Casual visits of this kind are made during the late afternoons, when gardening has been finished for the day, and on moonlit nights. In the period from 4.30 to 6 p.m., it was no uncommon thing to have ten or twelve youths from other places making their appearance in Dap, some to deliver messages from their parents, some ostensibly to pay a call on an uncle or aunt, and some for no other reason than that they wanted to go for a walk. Still larger crowds assemble when from time to time on the nights of the full moon word goes out that some of the men are organizing a set of games. Many of these bear a strong resemblance to those of our own childhood—so much so that I had no difficulty in introducing Twos and Threes and Oranges and Lemons. One, called "Pigs," is very like Prisoners' Base; another, "The Fishhawk and the Fish," like the Cat and the Mouse; and a third almost identical with Sir Roger de Coverly. Only the youths and young married men take part, but the womenfolk watch from the side and, if need be, sing the accompanying ditties, which usually have about as much meaning as "Here we go gathering nuts and may."

It appears that in the majority of cases the boy, having been attracted by one of the girls, sends his bond-friend to ask her to arrange a meeting. If she is reluctant, as sometimes, for modesty's sake, she pretends to be—or definitely unwilling, perhaps on account of a preference for someone else—recourse is had to magic to make her change her mind. A present of areca nut or tobacco which has previously been bespelled is offered, or else the leaves from her armbands are stolen, charmed, and hung up behind the boy's bed. Sometimes she does the choosing herself, and boldly seeks out the friend to carry her invitation. Once both parties are agreed, a convenient spot is picked out for a rendezvous, usually near a distinctive tree to prevent mistakes, and each sets out as unobtrusively as possible to keep the appointment. If the girl has a companion, the two boys may go together, but love-making is felt to be too private for the presence of even closest intimates, and the couples separate as soon as the meeting place is reached. Without clocks, time cannot be accurately gauged, and the first arrival may have to hide in the undergrowth to escape the notice of passers-by. A broken bough is left on the ground, and the other party, recognizing the signal, emits a low crooning noise to indicate his presence.

If the time is short or the risk of discovery considerable, intercourse takes place standing up, the man penetrating from the rear, for in this position separation is easy. But lovers who expect to be alone for some time go deep into the forest seeking a soft bank for their embraces. They nestle close together and, though kissing is apparently unknown, stroke one another's flanks with tender fingers. Men are said to avoid touching a woman's genitals, and doubtless many do, but her hand gradually descends lower and lower and finally grasps the boy's penis, which, after a certain amount of fondling, she inserts in her vagina. Penilinctus is often mentioned, though how honest the people are when expressing disgust I do not know.

The two favourite attitudes for sexual congress are described respectively as "the stretched out" and "the sitting." In the first, the woman is on her back with legs apart, and the man rests on top, "wriggling his buttocks," but supporting some of his weight on his extended arms; in the second she sits on his knees and twines her legs around his back. There are also a number of individual preferences and variations, one only of which, with the woman on top, is disapproved on account of its impropriety.

After orgasm, the woman wipes both herself and the boy with her skirt, and they lie chatting for a short time. "They feel like a person who has had a good meal—lazy and as yet disinclined to move," said one informant. But, fearing that their absence may have been noticed, they arise at last and discreetly make their way by separate paths either to a forest pool or to the shore, where each has a good bathe "to remove the smell of intercourse."

The boy is under no obligation to hand over a present, but usually does so. A little tobacco or betel pepper is normally considered to be sufficient, though, if he has recently returned from overseas, cash or some object bought in a European store may be expected. Persons short of money when the District Officer was collecting head tax were jokingly advised by their friends to go to the girls rather than to the men for help. "Here in Wogeo the women serve us as banks," a sophisticated youth remarked.

A single encounter is sometimes sufficient, but arrangements are often made for future meetings, and a date not-too-far-distant fixed for the first. Marriage is at this early stage not even hinted at, but, if a more or less serious attachment comes into being, each party usually endeavours to make the other agree for the time being to abandon promiscuity. Their anxiety is based not on fear of venereal infection, a risk which seems to occur to no one, but on considerations of vanity.

"You ask me why it is the boy wants to keep the girl to himself? Because he likes to believe that she thinks him good looking and all the other boys ugly," was Jaua's comment when we were discussing the matter. "You see, if she goes with this one and that one he knows that she doesn't have a high regard for him—that she doesn't consider him to be important. Besides, he doesn't want them lying with her and then laughing at him afterwards for believing that she's still set aside for himself." Lovers' promises are of little value, however, for not only did several youths go out of their way to tell me that they were conducting two or three intrigues simultaneously, but those I knew best openly boasted of having fooled each girl into believing that she alone mattered.

Jealousy

Secrets are apt in a small village to become common property, and, in spite of the young man's efforts to avoid publicity, most people soon have a shrewd suspicion of what he is about. So far as contemporaries are concerned, general indignation is apparent only if he is outstandingly successful, when all begin to murmur against him. From this conversation one would gather that they were solely concerned with the debauching of the girls, but it seems that the real explanation for their annoyance is once again to be sought rather in wounded self-pride.

A spectacular success can usually be achieved only after the completion of a term of service on an overseas plantation, when, clean and healthy, the boy also possesses a number of presents with which to bribe his way into favours. Of the three or four cases which came to my notice, Kanakula, who for a short time was in my employment, was undoubtedly the most revealing.[9] He was under contract to a European, for whom he worked as cook-boy, but at the time of my arrival had been allowed to take a holiday and was living with his relatives at Maluk, in the Bwanag District, at the opposite end of the island from Dap, where I was staying. Hearing of my difficulties in the kitchen, he came over and suggested that I might care to avail myself for a couple of months of his services, an offer which I gladly accepted.

By native standards Kanakula was exceptionally handsome, as even his enemies admitted.[10] Broad of shoulder and narrow of hip, he had muscles which rippled under a glossy skin of golden brown, and, as was perhaps to be expected, most of his idle moments were before long taken up with intrigues. The local youths began complaining angrily about his treatment of our girls—"He's behaving as though they were sows" was the comment of one—and, when three weeks after he joined me I missed several cakes of toilet soap, no time was lost in reporting that he was the thief. "He took it to give to the girls. Of course, they didn't want to lie with him—they've been doing so only for the sake of the soap," several of the boys explained to me. "Why don't you send him back to Maluk, where he belongs? If he stays he'll only take something else and make you angry. Besides, you don't want to pay him money for working for you when Dal and Gris can cook your meals quite well." Two of them even begged me to give him a good hiding in addition, or else to stop his wages. I informed them that I would have been more impressed by such touching concern for my property if they had displayed the same willingness to identify the thief on previous occasions when my belongings had been taken.

A month after this incident occurred two youths came back from an evening ramble in the forest and the news that they had stumbled on Kanakula and Magar, the headman Marigum's second daughter, who had not long completed the ceremonies associated with her first menstruation, in an ardent embrace. Kabub, the man to whom she had been promised, though the betrothal had not been formally announced, was furious at the news, especially when it transpired that she had till that day been a virgin. A wordy argument took place between him and Kanakula, and they finally agreed to settle the matter with a football match, the modern substitute for a fight, in which each was to be supported by his kinsmen and friends.

Most of Kanakula's relatives were out of reach in Maluk, but it so happened that four or five of them were at the time staying in Dap, where they had just been landed by a schooner from one of the mainland plantations. On the appointed day, however, to everyone's astonishment, these men decided to support Kabub. They were angry with Kanakula, they said, because he had also been lying with the girls of Bwanag District during his visit home before his departure from Dap. Kabub was accordingly able to take the field with a small army of supporters, whereas Kanakula could muster only two, his fellow servants, of whom one, Dal, was present out of pity, he and Kabub being closely related. The match was necessarily a farce, and Kanakula received a drubbing which would certainly have been more severe had he not been under my protection.

The defection of the returned labourers called forth much criticism, for, being single, they had no real claim on any of the girls. "They hate Kanakula just because the women like him—that's all it is," Jaua insisted. "He was copulating while they were away working, and now they're angry. But are they married? No! Or betrothed? No! Why should it matter to them what Kanakula does, then? I tell you, they're jealous of him, and jealousy has made them forget that he's their kinsman. Yes, they certainly ought to have supported him. You're right about that. I *have* told you, over and over, as you say, that relatives must help one another. A fight between them in Maluk, when no outsiders were present, wouldn't have mattered so much, but here in Dap the boy is a stranger with no one else to depend on. Yes, it's indeed a bad business."

The most upsetting part of the whole episode was the effect of their conduct on Kanakula. After making his escape he bathed, put on a new white loin-cloth, and, seating himself on a bench in front of my kitchen, gave way to a prolonged fit of weeping. The gesture, in true Wogeo style, was unashamedly theatrical—his lamentations followed one another in a rhythmical flow—but I have no reason to suppose that his grief was on that account assumed. Dal and Gris embraced him, and the Dap housewives brought platters of food to tempt his appetite, but for upwards of an hour he refused to be pacified. As a final rhetorical flourish he stated solemnly for all to hear that, being now without relatives, he would return to the mainland for good.

Sweethearts from Distant Places

Long-continued affairs seldom take place between persons of different districts, for the settlements are so far apart that regular meetings can only be held with difficulty. A certain amount of social intercourse occurs from time to time, however, especially at the conclusion of a festival, when the population of the whole island is concentrated in one place. Marigum once remarked when we were watching a dance together that such entertainments were in some respects to be regretted. He agreed that they were a pleasant form of entertainment but pointed out that, although there is no organized licence afterwards as in some places on the mainland, the youths are thinking all the time about impressing some girl and making an assignation.

Opportunities for renewing an acquaintance made in circumstances of this kind occur when small groups of women are engaged at a distance from the village in some such feminine activity as weeding the headman's garden, gathering shell-fish, or collecting reef coral for making lime. Visitors from another district can on such occasions be entertained without risk, for the local menfolk are usually busy elsewhere. Messages in the form of a Cordyline leaf in which two knots have been tied are accordingly sent to the lovers, who arrive with a present at about midday for an hour or two's dalliance. The arrangements are initiated by the younger married women, who, according to informants, are even more eager than the single girls. "They want to even things up with their husbands," Kalabai told me in explanation.

With so many persons involved, sometimes as many as a dozen, the news leaks out more quickly than usual. The men of the district to which the women belong, construing what has taken place as an insult to themselves, send a challenge to the lovers, and the matter is settled by an appeal to force. In olden days a fight took place, each party being backed up by relatives and friends. A day was fixed, and, spears in hand, all adjourned to a level area near the boundary between the two districts where such combats regularly took place. The headmen stood close at hand ready to intervene if blood was shed, though, as everyone was trained from childhood in dodging missiles, their services were seldom required.

To-day, with fighting forbidden, the battlegrounds have been turned into what are politely called playing fields, and amorous expeditions are now followed by a football match, or "kick cross," as it is termed. No careful selection of sides is made, and, as anything from thirty to fifty men take part, the game not infrequently develops into something of a brawl. The residents of Wonevaro district, in which Dap is situated, were involved four times during my year's visit, twice with the Takul district to the north and twice with Bagiau to the west, and on each occasion I was called in to attend to broken heads or bruises. Formal peace-making ceremonies do not take place, but ordinary social relations are resumed a few days later.

Incest

Moiety distinctions are regarded as more or less irrelevant when the two young people are resident in different districts. They meet so rarely that the fact that they may belong to the same group is usually ignored. "We know whether persons from different places are of the bat or hawk moiety, but, if we don't see them constantly, a thing like that doesn't matter," Kalabai remarked. "Only if you talk to people every day, eat and work with them, is it important. When I meet folk of my group, the hawk, from over in Takul, I certainly say to them that we're all one flesh; but you must understand that they're really only the shadows of the true brothers and sisters. How can they be anything else when I only see them occasionally? And if a girl isn't my sister we're allowed to do things together." Baj, feeling less need for self-justification, stated simply that, if he had to walk so far to keep an appointment that he was tired on arrival, he did not care what moiety the girl belonged to.

Even within the district boundaries the prohibition on sexual relations between members of the same group is not as rigidly observed as the natives sometimes pretend, and many freely confessed without much pressure that they had periodically disregarded it. Extra special precautions are considered to be advisable in order to minimize the chance of scandal, and the couple therefore take no one, not even the bond-friend, into their confidence. "The elders tell us to avoid the women of our own moiety, but is it possible for anyone to ignore half of all those on the island?" one youth asked. "Mind you, we usually select women from the other moiety, for only a madman would copulate all the time with those who are forbidden. Yet every now and then we all of us like to do so. Nobody must know, of course; and if they don't, who can complain?"

Concealment becomes increasingly difficult if the meetings continue, and, in the end, everyone begins to have suspicions. Yet the misdemeanour is for the most part overlooked so long as the outward conventions are preserved, and, although there is much gossip, the wagging tongues are at once silent at the approach of either of the guilty parties. Kabub and Kasule, of the bat moiety, were rumoured to be lovers very early in my visit, but nobody took them to task till the woman became pregnant, and at one stage I was warned not to refer to the subject in Kabub's presence lest he should be ashamed. The person who caught Kagilia red-handed with the girl Daden broadcast the news, however, thus forcing the culprit to run away to relatives in another district, where he remained till a schooner requiring an extra deck-hand called in and took him away. There was much talk for a short period amongst the elder men of how in former times he would have been put to death, but enquiry failed to reveal a single case where this had occurred. So far as I could discover, the guilty youth merely absented himself for a few weeks or months until his disgrace was forgotten. Nowadays, as formerly, the girl is severely reprimanded and beaten by her mother, but in no way ostracized by the rest of the community. Daden, for example, was married before Kagilia's departure.

The regulation forbidding cohabitation between close blood kin appears to be more strictly adhered to; I collected the names of only about half a dozen living persons who had flouted it. All informants without exception denied having themselves been so much as tempted to do so, a statement which, considering their habitual frankness—Jaua admitted an adultrous union with the wife of one of his uncles—I am inclined to accept at its face value. "How could anyone lie with the daughter of his father's and mother's brothers and sisters?" Kalabai asked. "Why, they're like the real sisters—one talks to them about the same things, works with them, and accepts food daily from their hands." Reminded that, as a marriage between cross-cousins had taken place in his own village, some persons must have been able to overcome their scruples, he insisted that these had something wrong with them. None of the sensible people, such as those who were regular visitors to my house, would be capable of such conduct.

True incest is so rare as to be practically unknown, the only two cases on record having occurred so long ago that details are now forgotten. One concerned a brother and sister who were so infatuated that they set up an establishment together, and the other a father and daughter. All four were said to have been slain at the request of the headman of the group to which they belonged "to prevent other persons from following this evil example."

The custom of interpreting such expressions as "Your mother is your spouse" and "Your sister is your spouse" as serious insults suggests, nevertheless, the possibility of a repressed desire for intercourse with these persons. I could find no confirmation for this surmise with respect to mother and son, but it is probably no accident that many myths are concerned with the doings of men and their sisters. Copulation is admittedly never hinted at openly, but the natives may well have their symbols just as we do. Dreams of lying with the sister must also occur, for I once overheard a man warning his three grandsons to do their best on waking to banish such visions from their minds. "A good way of forgetting is to relate what has happened to the bond-friend," he advised. "If you keep it to yourself you'll go on thinking about it, and that would be wrong."

This conversation came as a surprise, for, when a few days before I had told Jaua that I had had a nightmare in which I believed myself to have been bewitched, he instructed me not to worry, since this was simply the result of our discussion of sorcery during the afternoon. "If a man dreams of something," he said, "he's probably been thinking about it recently." I accordingly sought him out now to ask whether dreams of the sister were the result of incestuous thoughts. No, was the reply; the person must have been thinking of copulation in general terms and, in some other connection, of his sister and confused the two. The experience was nothing to be ashamed of, he continued, but, as it was unpleasant, one naturally tried to forget about it. Other informants gave the same answer when later on, after seeing a youth ridiculed for claiming that his dream of a certain girl was proof that she was carrying out love magic, I made the same enquiry. His own desire was sufficient in itself to account for the fantasy, I was told.

Perversions

The natives discuss pederasty with frankness and humour, using the word *yakamul*, from the name of a village between Wewak and Aitape, spelt Jakamul on most maps, where the men are said to have been accustomed to engage in it from the earliest times. Such behaviour, though sometimes condemned as foolish, calls forth no moral indignation, for the local opinion is that everyone is entitled to the kind of pleasure which he prefers, and many persons freely admit personal acquaintance with similar practices while away working for Europeans. Women are seldom available on the larger plantations and in the towns, and the older labourers, already accustomed to indulgence, are forced to take youths as lovers instead. A boy's behind is said to be a not unsatisfactory substitute, though everyone from Wogeo prefers the real thing and is thankful on his return to go back to it. "It is like the tinned meat they give us on the goldfields," said one informant. "We like it quite well, but once home again we gladly eat pork and fish once more and never think of buying it from visiting schooners." Even bond-friends, who wander about together with arms entwined, are said to have no wish to make homosexual experiments. They may engage in mutual masturbation for a short time, it was agreed, but not after the greater attractions of normal intercourse are fully appreciated.

One or two folk tales mention women who had sexual relations with dogs, but all forms of bestiality appear in real life to be unknown. I also failed to discover a single case of a child having been interfered with, and, although rape is occasionally attempted, the woman seems invariably to make her escape unharmed. One young man who during my visit succeeded only in having a piece of flesh bitten from his arm became something of a laughing stock. His offence was never mentioned in his presence, not even by the girl's relatives, but behind his back everyone ridiculed him for having had to make the attack, thereby admitting his failure to persuade her to accept him.

The Unmarried Mother

Readers will perhaps be surprised to learn, in view of the circumstances, that illegitimate children are rare. Recent research in the biological sciences has established, however, that, contrary to popular belief, a normal girl is not capable of conception immediately after her first menstruation, but that a longish period usually elapses before ovulation begins.[11] The natives, better informed in this respect than ourselves, have worked out the rule that at least four taro harvests—between two-and-a-half and three years—separate the coming-of-age ceremonies and pregnancy. Guri, the first wife of Gwaramun, headman of Job village, was one of the few exceptions. Married almost immediately after she had begun to menstruate, she gave birth to an infant in less than a couple of years. So astonished were the villagers at this achievement that they used to refer to her as the coconut which had put forth shoots before falling to the ground from the parent tree.

Young girls accordingly take no precautions against pregnancy: confident as yet of their inability to conceive, they leave contraceptive measures to mature women who are either still single or else, though married, for some reason anxious to restrict the number of their children. Almost the only two persons in the Wonevaro district pointed out as having taken steps to safeguard themselves were Mor, a spinster aged twenty-four, and one of the wives of the headman Kauni, Boda by name, who had nearly died on each of the four occasions that she had given birth to a stillborn infant.[12]

Native contraceptives cannot, in any case, be in the least effective—Boda began using them long before the third pregnancy, and Mor had had three miscarriages. According to local theory, conception takes place when the menstrual blood has been damned up in the womb by a considerable quantity of semen. Preventive measures consist therefore of endowing this blood with such potency that it breaks through the blocked passage, an object achieved by means of magic. Either of two kinds of leaves has to be chewed, those of the bamboo—selected because in former days knives were made from the stem of the plant—and those of a particular kind of creeper with sharp thorns. Opinion was divided as to the frequency of the dosage, some maintaining that a bundle of leaves every day for a week would be permanently effective, and others that a quantity had to be taken every month or two.

If a single girl is sufficiently unfortunate as to become pregnant she hastily endeavours first to persuade one of her lovers to marry her before the condition becomes noticeable. Met with a refusal, she eats a special kind of bark chosen as an abortifacient on account of its oily—and hence slippery—surface. Illness follows and, in some cases, probably on account of the general poisoning of the system, miscarriage.

Yet, although the unmarried mother is condemned, she is never looked upon as a social outcast to be repudiated and scorned. Persons not closely related behave when in her company as far as possible as though nothing untoward had occurred, and even behind her back most of their criticisms are levelled against her ineptitude at having failed to secure a husband. The members of her family may be less reticent with their strictures, but most of them are still anxious to do their best for her and for the infant.

The sisters are usually the most bitter, though their own chances of marriage are in no wise affected. Two of Sanamuk's sisters beat her severely as soon as they realized that her attempts to procure an abortion had failed. The third, Yam, came to the rescue but did not hesitate on that account to speak her mind. "You with a bastard in your belly, aren't you ashamed?" she was reputed to have asked. "What about this child? Who'll be its father? Or are you going to be mother and father both? Do you know what everyone will be saying about you?—that you couldn't persuade a single one of your lovers to marry you, not one. You're all right to lie with—that's clear—but no good to marry."

The parents seldom, if ever, make open reproaches, preferring to indicate their displeasure with an icy silence. Offering as excuse their unwillingness to have a grandchild reared without a father's guiding hand, they generally insist that it shall be handed over after weaning to one of the childless couples who are anxious to adopt it.[13]

The brothers always construct the birth house, but their behaviour otherwise is somewhat unpredictable. A number have been known to beat an erring sister, but others, probably the majority, are sympathetic. Gwaramun, Sanamuk's only brother, is reputed to have expressed his pleasure at the birth of her infant. As no one would seek her hand in marriage for a long period, he said she would now be able to remain at his side. The villagers were rather sceptical of his good faith at the time, but agreed later, when, at her request, he refused to permit the baby to be sent away, that he was certainly very fond of her and might have been speaking the truth.

No effort is made to force the child's father to contribute towards its upkeep; in the native view a bastard has no father, as is implied by the word used, *tama-tabwa*, literally, "father-not."[14] Frequent intercourse either with one man or with several is supposed to be essential for conception; moreover, if a number are involved, as is said to be always the case when the woman is unmarried, each makes a contribution to the child's physical make-up. People accordingly discovered that the forehead of Sanamuk's baby resembled Wakalu's, its eyes Kabub's, its lower jaw Sawang's, and its ears Labim's. To approach all these was felt to be impossible, and to confine the demands to one absurd. It occasionally happens that a girl claims to have been faithful, but nobody believes her, and her brother does not risk the ridicule with which a request for compensation would be greeted.

The reason for the lover rejecting the suggestion of marriage will now be obvious: he dislikes fathering a child for which he believes himself to be only partly responsible. (If later he finds that he cannot beget an offspring he may be forced to adopt one, but young people have no wish at this stage to anticipate such difficulties.) The girl may swear that she has been true to him, but, convinced that he has not lain with her sufficiently often to be the sole cause of her condition, he affirms that she must of necessity be lying. The pregnancy is regarded, in fact, as proof of her lack of discrimination, and the young and attractive men now look elsewhere, leaving her to be ultimately claimed by a widower, or perhaps by someone suffering from a minor physical disability.

Bastards entrusted to a foster parent do not appear to be treated any differently from other adopted children. Now regarded as legitimate, they are no longer at a social disadvantage. I can make no generalization about those reared in the household of a mother's brother, for I was familiar with only two, a couple of small boys aged between six and seven. Yet it was probably no accident that they were both shy and lacking in assurance. Their uncles did not appear to display the affection which might have been expected from a father, and, though I never heard of anyone either being unkind or taunting them, they already knew that they were "the children of all the men in general" and thus without paternal kin. A comment made during an initiation ceremony at Gol village gave a hint of the sort of treatment to which they had to accustom themselves. The arrangements had been made by the headman Kawang on behalf of his young nephew aged six, but two or three men with sons not much older collaborated with him, and at the last minute the uncle of the village bastard, a lad of ten, sent him along also. "The boy is far too old and ought to have been initiated long ago," my host remarked. "But, you see, he has no father to care for him."

Notes

1 Still another polite expression for intercourse is *yafyaf*, from yaf, the loop of rope which a man puts round his ankles when climging a coconut palm.

2 In actual fact snakes from New Guinea waters are at least as poisonous as those found on land. The natives' faulty observation is possibly to be accounted for by the reluctance of the sea snakes to attack.

3 Cf. the disapproval expressed by many persons when the United States Army authorities, to prevent the spread of verereal infection, made contraceptives available and operated prophylactic stations. "The psychological effect on the young soldier of this elaborate set-up," wrote the Rev. Paul L. Blakely, S.J., "conveys, almost irresistibly, the impression that the Government expects him to indulge in riotous courses." (*America,* August 1941).

4 *Vide* H. I. Hogbin, "The Father Chooses his Heir," *Oceania,* Vol. IX, pp. 1-39.

5 I do not know the derivation of "foroman," but "wanein" is a corruption of "one name" (i.e., namesake).

6 *Vide* illustrations in H. I. Hogbin, "Sorcery and Administration," *Oceania,* Vol. VI, pp. 1-39, and "Social Reaction to Crime," *Journal of the Royal Anthropological Institute,* Vol. LXVIII, pp. 223-262.

7 Petticoats, which when new are either creamy white or else a mass of coloured flounces, are, however, far gayer than the drab bark cloth from which the men's garments of former days were made. The convention that women should avoid further decoration therefore may well be another example of good taste.

8 The remainder commemorate passing events. My own visit led to the appearance of three, of which the favourite was:
> Obin sits in his chair;
> Obin rings the bell;

Gris cooks Obin's dinner;
Dal puts the dinner on the table.
The scale of notes is very limited, and the rhythm, the same as in dance tunes, extremely monotonous.

9 The case is discussed more fully in "The Father Chooses his Heir" and "Social Reaction to Crime," *op. cit.*

10 *Vide* the portrait of him painting his face in "Social Reaction to Crime," *op. cit.*

11 *Vide* M. F. Ashley-Montagu, "Infertility of the Unmarried in Primitive Societies," *Oceania,* Vol. VIII, pp. 15-26; and also *Oceania*, Vol. XII, p. 96.

12 *Vide* H. I. Hogbin, "Adloption in Wogeo," *Journal of the Polynesian Society,* Vols. XLIV, XLV.

13 As its origins are then concealed, I was unable to make a census of illegitimate children.

14 A less common term is *niang-daradi,* "father-nothing."

Section IV

PUBERTY

The English word puberty is derived from the Latin *pubes*, which refers to body hair, groin, and adult. It therefore implies the bodily changes that take place during late childhood and adolescence. These changes of physical maturation that are recognized during puberty, must be distinguished from female menarche and male sexual maturation. Puberty is due to a gradual change in hormonal secretions and their maturing influence. The actual transition markers, menstrual flow (and ovulation some time later) in females and sexual maturity in males, mark the end of a process of change started during childhood and the beginning of a new life phase of adulthood.

Among girls aged 8 to 11, adrenal and gonadal secretion of hormones stimulate physical maturation. This involves development of the internal sex organs as well as secondary sexual characteristics. During this period there is a gradual but significant increase in gonadotrophins, namely a doubling of FSH (Follicle Stimulating Hormone) and a much greater increase in LH (Luteinizing Hormone). This also implies an increase in estrogen production which stimulates the development of target organs. Usually breast development is the first visible sign of maturation with full development reached by ages 13 to 18. Pubic hair usually appears next and the adult pattern coincides with physical maturation at about age 18. Glandular development and water content of the breast will change monthly as the young woman starts to menstruate regularly.

Among boys puberty occurs about two years later. Serum gonadotrophins increase gradually after age 6 or 7 in the form of FSH which will be responsible for sperm production and ICSH (Interstitial Cell Stimulating Hormone) responsible for testosterone production. The latter is primarily responsible for enlargement of the testes, the development of public hair (between ages 12 and 16), and later facial and axillary hair. At this time an increase of penis size also occurs. While ejaculation may start at age 11, mature sperm will usually not be present for a number of years.

For both girls and boys puberty is a potentiating stage, placing them at the beginning of adulthood. In the United States girls will normally experience menarche around age 12 or 13, but in societies where nutrition, hygiene, and socioeconomic factors are less favorable this event may be delayed. In New Guinea it may be as late as age 18. Regular ovulation usually follows the onset of menstruation by a year or two. Accompanying sexual maturation in boys there is not only mature sexual organs but also continuous sperm production.

Most societies the world over recognize these maturational changes which take place in girls and boys. It is in fact a status change as the person leaves childhood and is capable of assuming the adult reproductive role. Anthropologists have followed the lead of Arnold van Gennep in recognizing these changes as *rites de passage* or rites of transition. Such a rite is marked by three phases: separation, margin (or *limen*), and aggregation, enabling the individual "to pass from one defined position to another which is equally well defined" (1960:3). For our purposes it involves the separation of the child from the world of the prepubertal and uninitiated, a period of liminality during which education and other specialized information transfer occurs, and a ritual of incorporation into the adult gender specific community. It should be pointed out that for girls this ceremony is usually measured by chronological age (marked by the physical event of first menses) and usually is an individual ceremony. Boys are normally initiated as a group based on sociological age, an appropriate time in the annual cycle, or availability of time and money.

Young women may undergo physical tests or psychological trauma at this time (Lincoln 1991), and they may also be subjected to genital circumcision (see Dorkenoo 1994; Hicks 1993; Lightfoot-Klein 1989). In some cases these operations are performed during childhood but normally they are performed after the physical growth, which accompanies puberty, has taken place. This operation may involve circumcision (the cutting of the prepuce or hood of the clitoris—an operation known among Muslims as Sunna), excision or clitoridectomy (the amputation of the clitoris and frequently also the removal of the labia minora and the labia majora), introcision (cutting into the vagina and/or splitting the perineum), or infibulation (known also as Pharaonic circumcision) which involves excising the clitoris, labia minora and at least two thirds or the whole of the medial section of the labia majora. "The two sides of the vulva are then pinned together by silk or catgut sutures, or with thorns thus obliterating the vaginal introitus except for a very small opening..." (McLean and Graham 1980:3). After marriage this process has to be painfully reversed to allow sexual intercourse.

Normally boys are exposed to a longer period of separation involving puberty rituals, frequently accompanied by initiation into secret societies, and Allen (1967) suggests that we differentiate between puberty and initiation rituals. At puberty we may find the separation of a group of boys based on their relative ages into a circumcision school or something similar. This event may be marked by a genital operation, such as circumcision (the removal of the prepuce), subincision (the slitting of the urethra), or superincision (making a longitudinal slit in the upper surface of the prepuce). In some societies puberty and initiation may be marked by the knocking out of a front tooth, removal of a finger joint, plucking of hair, or by tattooing or scarification. Such physical alterations serve both to mark pubertal status as well as membership in a brotherhood.

In the first of the readings that follow, John Kennedy describes male and female circumcision in Nubia. But lest we believe this to be something of the past, Amna Badri reports on a survey she performed in the Sudan which shows this practice still quite common. See also the references discussed above. The last report in this section recounts the experience of little Batou Doucara. With her parents, migrant workers from Mali in West Africa, she lived in Paris. Her father wanted to assure that she would be "proper" and fit back into Malian society when they return.

References

Allen M.R. 1967. *Male Cults and Secret Initiations in Melanesia.* Melbourne: Melbourne University Press.

Dorkenoo, E. 1994. *Cutting the Rose.* London: Minority Rights Publications.

Hicks, E.K. 1993. *Infibulation.* New Brunswick: Transaction Publishers.

Lightfoot-Klein, H. 1989. *Prisoners of Ritual.* Binghampton: The Haworth Press.

Lincoln, B. 1991. *Emerging from the Chrysalis.* New York: Oxford University Press.

McLean, S. and S.E. Graham (eds). 1980. Female Circumcision, Excision and Infibulation: The facts and proposals for change. *Minority Rights Report,* No.47, London.

Van Gennep, A. 1960. *The Rites of Passage.* London: Routledge and Kegan Paul.

3. Plains Indian — assuming adulthood

PUBERTY

4. Zulu — puberty initiation

6. Xhosa — *a mkweta* during
puberty

INITIATION

5. Istanbul, Turkey — *sünnet*, circumcision
confirmation

CIRCUMCISION AND EXCISION IN EGYPTIAN NUBIA

John G. Kennedy
University of California, Los Angeles

Herodotus found the Egyptians practising circumcision when he visited their country around the middle of the fifth century B.C., and stated that either they or the Ethiopians invented the custom. This conclusion reflects nothing more than the great antiquity of record keeping in this part of the world, but paintings do attest that in Egypt circumcision was practised at least as far back as the VI Dynasty, 2340-2180 B.C. (Ghalioungui 1962: 95-7). Female excision was also a custom of ancient Egyptians as reported by Strabo (Ghalioungui 1963: 96). The evidence for this is less clear, but we know that it was customary among several tribes of the Arabian peninsula in pre-Islamic times (Levy 1962: 252).

Circumcision of males is still nearly universal in the Middle East. Though not mentioned in the Koran, it is an essential feature of the Islamic faith, as it is of the Jewish and Coptic religions. Female excision is also still widespread in Islamic communities from India to Morocco (Levy 1962: 252; Smith 1903: 16 f.n.). Both customs are practised by the Nubian peoples who have traditionally inhabited that strip of the Nile between Aswan, Egypt, and Dungola, Sudan.

In spite of the persisting vitality of circumcision and excision in the Middle East, most scholars attempting to account for genital operations or to test 'initiation' hypotheses, have tended to exclude this area from their samples.[1] Undoubtedly an important reason for this neglect is that there are few detailed data from the area.[2] A more significant reason is perhaps that the ceremonies do not easily fit the theories. For example, most theories are based upon a 'rites of passage' model—implicitly assuming that puberty, being the time of transition to adulthood, is naturally marked by such a ritual. As the causal basis underlying the rites, these functional theories postulate society's 'needs' for altering the child's personality. Whatever their differences, they rest on the assumption that children are somehow inadequately socialised for their adult roles, and that the ceremonies are designed to correct these socialisation failures (e.g. Cohen 1964; Freud 1939; Whiting *et al.* 1958; Young 1965). Middle Eastern ritual operations which are performed on prepubertal children who are undergoing no transition to adulthood do not easily fit such formulations.

Rather than making a critical analysis of theories of initiation, I wish to provide contrastive data and interpretation which may assist in illuminating the general problem. I shall begin by describing the circumcision rites for Egyptian Nubian boys as they were practised in some parts of Nubia (e.g. Diwan and Abu Hor) as late as 1933, and excision rituals for girls as they are still frequently performed (see below for discussion of changes). This account will add data to the meagre ethnographic base of rituals of this type in the Islamic culture area. The interpretative comments indicate how the

Reprinted by permission of the editors from *Man (NS)*, Vol. 5, 1970, pp. 175-191.

complexity of factors involved in Nubian circumcision and excision rituals raises serious questions concerning present theories.

The data presented here were in the main gathered during a field study carried out in 1963-4 in Kanuba (pseudonym), a village of Nubians which had resettled near Kom Ombo after being displaced from Nubia proper by the third raising of the Aswan Dam in 1933. The village, of some 450 people, is a conglomerate of families from several parts of Nubia, though the majority are from the *Omidiyas* of Abu Hor (Kenuz speaking) and Diwan (Mahass speaking). Additional information concerning circumcision and excision was obtained from the villages of Dahmit, Abu Hor (Kenuz), Diwan and Ballana (Mahass), on three trips to Nubia of several weeks each between 1962 and 1964.

Nubians

Prior to their total relocation at Kom Ombo (1963-4), which was required by the high dam at Aswan, most of the Egyptian Nubians lived in isolated villages strung along both banks of the Nile between Aswan and Wadi Halfa. They were divided into three linguistic and subcultural zones (Kenuz, Arabic and Mahass). The traditional economic base was subsistence agriculture of *dhurra*—a sorghum grain—and date palms, supplemented by animal husbandry.

Historically its meagre resources and consequently low population density have kept Nubia politically marginal to the powerful states to its north and south. For centuries the region was periodically disrupted by military turmoil, and both Egypt and the Sudan have historically influenced Nubian culture continuously through trade, participation in slave traffic, labour-migration and travel. Economic and political instability, coupled with limited economic capacity, thus resulted in a Nubian labour migration pattern. This centuries-old accommodation in the cities of Egypt and Sudan was intensified by the building of the Aswan Dam in 1902, and by its heightenings in 1912 and 1933. Each of these flooded more of the already inadequate productive land of Nubia (Geiser 1967; Scudder 1967). The present dam at Aswan is only the culmination of the progressive displacement process suffered by these people.

The Nubians have been Muslims since the fourteenth century, when Arab penetration completely displaced Jacobite Coptic Christianity. They adhere to the Maliki School of Islamic Law, like most of the Muslims of the northern Sudan. Nubian religion also contained many elements which are now considered 'pagan', or non-Islamic by educated urban Nubians. Life cycle events of birth, circumcision, marriage and death were marked by elaborate ceremony and pageantry embodying a syncretism of popular Islamic and these 'pagan' customs.

*   *   *   *   *

Boys' circumcision ceremonies

The Nubians allowed circumcision[3] to be carried out at any time from forty days after birth to ten years after, but they strongly preferred it to occur between the ages of three and five. Older informants insist that boys' circumcision ceremonies called *baláy dawí* ('big wedding') were the largest of all Nubian rituals. Though sometimes more costly in complexity, time, and organisation, circumcisions were, however, actually subordinate to weddings. Circumcisions and weddings were occasionally held simultaneously, so that the costs could be minimised, and poorer families might also economise by having several boys circumcised in a single co-operative ceremony. When this happened, or when a wealthy man's child underwent the operation, the elaborateness of the communal celebration transcended any other type of Nubian ritual.

A good show was an important indicator of the wealth and prestige of the family, and arrangements for the ceremony were usually begun long in advance. Members of the patrilineage aided the father in defraying initial expenses, and some of the costs were made up during the ceremony through the *nokout* (small gifts). The major expense was the provision of sacrificial animals, and the required numbers of these varied among the sub-regions of Nubia. In the Diwan-Derr area the slaughter of four cattle was considered ideal, but this could only be realised by wealthier families. Costs were sometimes reduced by eliminating certain parts of the celebration where sacrifices were necessary, and poorer families might substitute sheep for cattle. Other expenses were the large amounts of grain necessary to provide bread for the guests, the many baskets of dates offered, and the bottles of perfume frequently sprinkled upon the celebrants. New and special clothing had to be provided for the immediate family of the child, and the securing of a camel and donkey for the ceremony was often a considerable financial burden.

A circumcision was officially inaugurated on the day called *gáwi nahar*. The invitation was signalled by a slave who made the rounds in the village and adjacent villages announcing the event and the schedule of activities. The following day women began gathering at the child's house to help the preparing of special clothing and the preparation of food for the guests—*shareya, durra* bread, dates, and *abreek*.[4] The period of preparation lasted from fifteen to twenty days, and when all was completed the slave again made his rounds of invitation. Soon after, festively adorned guests began arriving by boat, donkey, or on foot.

The first day of the actual circumcision ceremony was called the *baseem*. Music and dancing began that afternoon which was to continue almost unceasingly for four days. A cow was killed in the afternoon of the *baseem* and by evening a feast was ready.

The place of honour was occupied by the five year old *arees* (groom) wearing his new clothes. If the family could afford it, he wore a red or white *jalabeya* (a loose, long sleeved gown), a green *kuftan* (loose overgarment), and a red fez decorated with beads and coins of gold and silver.[5] His adult female relatives were dressed in blue *jarjars* (overdresses of sheer material) over white dresses; with their gauzy blue veils, they stood out from the other women who wore their newest and brightest coloured clothes and their treasured gold jewellery. The boy's father wore a new *zabout* (dark brown woolen handwoven cloak) over his white *jalabeya*.

The operation was usually performed on the morning following the first day of dancing and feasting. The boy was dressed in a white *jalabeya* of a very light material to prevent irritation to the wound. He was often unaware that he was to undergo the painful genital operation. Very early in the morning he was bathed, and gold necklaces belonging to his mother or grandmother and called *bandoki* or *farajala* were placed round his neck. Henna (a red dye used cosmetically and ritually) was applied to his hands and feet by an elderly female of the family, and *kohl* (black female eye cosmetic) to his eyelids. A woman's veil was put over his head after the henna had been applied. Such ritual precautions were taken against the bloodthirsty *jinns* who are believed to attack fertility and are more aggressive towards males. Other hovering Nile spirits (*dogri*) are pleased and distracted by the symbols of bridal beauty. Women were dancing, and musicians playing in the courtyard, while the ritual preparations proceeded within.

During this part of the ceremony the customary *nokout* were presented to the family. Money was rare in Old Nubia, and in the nineteenth century *nokout* usually consisted of dates, sugar cones, wheat, and dhurra. Each man's donation to the father, and each woman's gift to the mother was loudly announced by a slave and then carefully recorded in writing. Informants from the Kenuz area of Abu Hor stated that while the *nokout* was being recorded another slave (or a relative) stood by brandishing a sword shouting 'May God give him children'.[6] Other *nokout*, usually in the form of coins, were given to the 'barber' who performed the ritual surgery. *Nokout* coins were placed in a pan of Nile water so that they might be decontaminated from the dangerous *jinns* who hover around money.

Several informants recounted variations of the following rituals for the circumcision operation. The boy in ceremonial dress was seated on a mat, his mother and father on his left and right sides. A plate of henna was placed on the mat in front of his mother, and a bowl of water was set before the boy. The ritual commenced with the mother sticking a lump of henna to the boy's forehead. The father affixed a gold coin in this henna, preferably a gold pound. The boy then sat quietly as more *nokout* was presented by the guests; the name of each donor was again loudly proclaimed to the gathering. After this, water from the bowl was used to remove the henna from his forehead, and the mother's sister or some elder female relative came forward to hold him for the knife.

As he chanted the powerful Muslim incantation—'In the name of Allah, the compassionate, the merciful', the 'barber' severed the foreskin. Having been admonished not to act like a girl, the boy restrained his tears. His mother had been holding his face away so that he would not look at his wound and thereby become sterile. She now cracked three eggs into a small bowl and held it to his nose to prevent fainting. Some of the raw egg she applied to the wound.

The women meanwhile intensified their dancing and drumming uttering long cries of joy (*zahgareet*) and, at intervals, shouting out 'congratulations to the groom'. Accompanied by the singing and drumming crowd, his mother (or an adult sister) then carried the boy to the Nile. There he was bathed, and the barber or midwife ritually threw his foreskin with an old coin out into the water. This offering was believed to pacify the spirits of the river.

After the operation, the entire crowd of villagers and guests began a procession (*zeffa*) to one of the saints' tombs in the vicinity. In Diwan, Tongala, and other nearby districts, the tomb of Sheikh

Shebeyka was visited. The boy's father, carrying a sword, headed the procession followed by the be-decked boy riding on a donkey. A slave riding a camel and beating a huge Sudanese drum came next. This camel also transported two huge sacks of *asleeg*[7] and *abreek* which were to be used for the cere-monial meal at the saint's tomb. The cow which would be slaughtered for the main dish of this feast followed behind the camel. Following the animals came the boy's mother with the rest of the family. The large crowd of singing and dancing people was spread out along the path.

The dances were essentially the same as those used at weddings. Several lines of men with locked arms danced backwards. They were separated from the opposing lines of women by a dance master. Waving a staff and swaying in rhythm between them, the dance master kept the groups of men and women apart, and controlled the progress of the procession. Grouped beside the rows of dancers were five or six musicians beating their *tars* and leading the singing. These drummers were either women dressed in white, or slaves. The procession sometimes had to travel as far as ten kilometres, so it was several hours before the group reached the shrine.

Arriving some time in the afternoon, the dancing and singing crowd was greeted by the caretaker of the shrine (*nakeeb*). The cow was handed over to him to be slaughtered with the help of some of the older men, while the people relaxed and socialised. Under the direction of the *nakeeb*, men immedi-ately began cooking the ceremonial feast. The *abreek*, which had been carried by the camel, was used with the cooked beef to prepare a dish called *fatta*. The animal's head, neck, skin, stomach, and legs were donated to the *nakeeb* as an offering to the saint.

The singing and dancing were resumed by the crowd and continued uninterruptedly, and while the feast was being prepared the boy and his father and some of the close relatives ritually circled the saint's tomb seven times. On each circuit, they petitioned the spirit for such favours as health, fertil-ity, and wealth. An important part of the ceremonies at the shrine were *zikr* rituals in which the men chanted Sufistic praises to God, swaying their bodies in ecstatic rhythmic unison.

By the time the ceremonial meal was eaten, it was necessary to commence the return procession to the village. The people sang and danced their way back, and, after reaching the boy's home, contin-ued to celebrate far into the morning.[8]

On the following afternoon the ceremonies commenced again. The boy again received visitors and accepted *nokout*. He sat on his *baranda* wearing a white *jalabeya* and the gold of his female rela-tives. It was obligatory for the father to serve dates and *asleeg* to all visitors who came to congratulate the boy. Again, the dancing and singing continued unabatedly through the day and into the following morning. This joyous but exhausting pattern of celebration was repeated for two more days, making a total of four.

On the evening of each day a *zikr* ritual was held by the men. Thus, while women were dancing to the tambourine drums (*tars*), men chanted ecstatic praise to Allah. The event reached its climax when two cows were slaughtered, and the culminating feast was served.

Following the celebration, the boy was kept in the house for ten days. Unless infection had set in he was then considered recovered. Native herbs were applied to the cut to facilitate healing and a small bag of salt was tied to his wrist for the same purpose. On recovery, this bag was removed and thrown into the Nile as an offering to the female river spirits. While he was secluded the boy ate alone, served by women of the family. He was given special 'strengthening' foods (pigeons, chickens, and eggs), the same foods which are eaten by brides and grooms to promote fertility and virility.

For the circumcision, and for forty days thereafter, the boy was required to observe many precautions concerned with *mushahara*: this refers to Nubian beliefs that a person undergoing a crisis such as giving birth, marriage or death, is in grave supernatural danger for a period of forty days, or for the period until the new moon. This danger is activated by the actions of other people. For example, if one crosses the Nile, sees blood at the market, or sees a dead body within the period of sacred vulnerability, by entering the room he endangers the health, fertility and life of the person undergoing the life crisis. Thus a number of taboos are enjoined upon all in the vicinity by the *mushahara* conditions (see Kennedy 1967*a*). Being also considered vulnerable to the evil eye and to *jinns* he wore *hegabs* (charms) to prevent attacks which could endanger his procreative potential.

Girls' excision ceremonies

The Nubian excision operation removes a girl's clitoris and closes her vulva with scar tissue and is much more extreme and radical than circumcision. It is referred to as the 'pharaonic' or 'Sudanese' style,[9] and is actually an infibulation.

Though her operation is more severe, the girls' ceremony is comparatively abbreviated and private. It might be scheduled to coincide with a boy's circumcision, but more usually it is conducted privately by women of the neighbourhood with no protracted preparations.

On the night before the operation, the small 'bride' (*aroosa*) is adorned with gold and dressed in new clothes. In the manner of a real bride, her eyes are made up with *kohl*, and her hands and feet are dyed with henna. The following morning neighbourhood women gather at the house. With little fanfare or preparation, the midwife quickly performs the operation. As several women spread her legs, a bowl is placed beneath the girl to catch the blood and the clitoris, the labia minora and part of the labia majora are excised with a razor or knife. The women meanwhile chant 'Come, you are now a woman.' 'You became a bride.' 'Bring her the groom now.' 'Bring her a penis, she is ready for intercourse', etc. These cries are interspersed with protective Koranic incantations, punctuated at intervals by cries of joy (*zahgareet*). According to some informants, this chanting and shouting serves partially to drown the screams of the child. Incense is kept burning during the operation to scare away the *jinns* and the evil eye. Raw egg and green henna are then applied, and the child's legs are tied together.

After the ordeal, the mother and nearest female relatives serve dates, candy, popcorn, and tea to the visiting women, and the hostess sprinkles them with perfume. Everyone congratulates the girl and some women give her small gifts. The neighbourhood women each give 'small' *nokout* to the mother.

Sometimes the child's legs remain tied together for forty days. More typically she is regarded as healed seven to fifteen days after the operation. This healing process generally provides the scar tissue for the complete closure of the vulva, except for a small urination orifice which is kept open by a match or a reed tube. To give her strength and to promote her fertility the girl is fed with lentil soup, chickens, and broth of pigeons. Throughout the healing period she is treated like a bride, or a woman giving birth.[10]

Meaning of the ceremonies

The Nubians consider that the genital operation is necessary for all normal children, and they readily give several reasons for it. Almost invariably, the immediate explanation offered is that circumcision is a religious obligation prescribed in the *hadith* of the Prophet Mohammed.[11] *Tahari*, the name of the operation, is a variant of the Arabic for ritual purification, and the Nubians believe that it symbolically purifies the child—making possible his future participation in prayers. The operation is also claimed by informants to be a prophylactic measure promoting cleanliness. This is often implied when they say: 'When the child begins to scratch himself that is the time to arrange for his circumcision.'[12]

The operation is also believed magically to promote fertility, and to maintain general body health. Although the idea is vaguely articulated, there is a belief that without circumcision a degree of completeness of manhood or womanhood would be missing. This is also implied in the notion that the operation prepares the person to enter marriage.

Besides excision of her clitoris, the female operation involves an infibulation which closes the vulva with scar tissue. This severe measure is said to have the aim of preventing the loss of virginity and eliminating the possibility of a shameful pregnancy. Such reasons are direct expressions of the belief that women have an inherently wanton character which is physiologically centred in the clitoris. The Nubians argue that the only way to blunt the inherent sexual wildness of girls and to preserve their chastity is through this means, though there is no medical evidence that any diminishing effect on desire is actually produced (Barclay 1964: 238; Bonapart 1952: 68-73).

A final Nubian rationale for circumcision and excision is an aesthetic one. Without the operation, the sex organs are disgusting to the marriage partner both visually and to the touch.

Circumcision and weddings

Nubian circumcision ceremonies strongly resembled weddings, and I do not believe they can be understood apart from their connexion with marriage. Marriage symbolism was everywhere present. This can be seen in the name of the event—the 'big wedding', the names for the participants—bride and groom, and the form of the ceremony—with its joyful processions (*zeffas*), songs, dances, feastings, visits to saints' tombs, etc. In much detail, these ritual patterns duplicate the marriage rituals.[13] Since the form and symbolism of the two rituals resemble each other so closely, a brief consideration of the wedding will help us to understand the meaning of circumcision ceremonies.

Of the two ritual events, weddings are the more complex. A wedding might last fifteen days instead of four, and there are ritual exchanges of food between the families and an extended series of symbolic customs to bring bride and groom together. Informants report that families felt the need to

The male is also traumatised to some extent by the marriage situation. On the wedding night he is honour-bound to perform intercourse with his often hysterical and terrified young bride. In addition to the interpersonal trauma, his fertility, virility, and health are also endangered by the attraction of dangerous spirits to the contaminating blood. Several male informants privately admitted impotence and confusion on their wedding mornings. They described feelings of revulsion by what they felt was a cruel act, and emotions of fear of the contaminating potency of female genital blood. Several weeks were often needed before intercourse afforded any satisfaction.[14]

The Nubian circumcision and excision ceremonies represented preliminary stages to the marriage complex. Both were community events with social functions relating to community solidarity and identity. They indicate to us, as they dramatised to the Nubians, the importance of marriage and of the particular set of beliefs, motivations, and social principles which were to be activated at the person's entrance into full adult status. In some ways, the male circumcision ceremonial suggests a village 'coming out party'. The family announced a proud possession to the community—a healthy son, who in a few years would be ready to marry. The entire community joyfully lauded this announcement, showed its respects to his family, and took numerous ritual precautions to insure his fertility. The girls' ceremony, though more muted in keeping with the lesser status of women and their lack of importance in perpetuating family lines, still possesses many of the same elements and social emphases.

Group solidarity at the level of family, lineage, and community is activated and reinforced by the great focus of activity and concern upon the individual child. Besides the cluster of attitudes and values surrounding the family, kin group, and community, the Nubian social principles of sex separation, male dominance, and age-generation dominance were all overtly delineated and thus reinforced by the roles of the participants, their spatial alignments and verbal behaviour during these ceremonies. The identical symbolism, functions, and patterning of these ceremonies indicate their close association in people's minds. Such facts show that circumcision, excision, and marriage were components of a single ceremonial complex with multiple meanings for individuals and for the community. They cannot be adequately treated as separate ritual entities. Neither can the genital operations be abstracted and explained apart from the total ritual complex, as is so often done in cross-cultural comparisons.

*   *   *   *   *

Psychological effects

In the Upper Egyptian village of Silwa, circumcision ceremonies show many similarities in meaning and content to those I have described for the nearby Nubians; and Ammar (1954) has interpreted them psycho-functionally as means for 'aligning the child with its sex group'. He also proposes the supplementary psychological hypothesis that the operation and ritual help the child to identify with the parent of the same sex, while the drama makes him aware of the social implications and responsi-

display generosity and wealth, and the marriage and circumcision both afforded the opportunities to demonstrate this.

Marriage ceremonies usually took place at the time of the date harvest; a time of family unity when the men returned from the cities, and a time of abundance. In Old Nubia, weddings were thus intensively symbolic of family and community solidarity. Circumcisions, with their parallel symbolism and spirit, functioned similarly in this respect. In addition, the custom of giving *nokout* and help at weddings and circumcisions concretely dramatised the network of reciprocal ties of obligation which formed an important aspect of the social organisation of the community.

Marriage had extreme importance in the life-cycles of individuals by validating adult status and ushering each person into full social standing. Islamic sanction backs this notion in the saying that 'marriage completes one's religion'. Until marriage, a Nubian is not considered fully Muslim, and thus in a real sense is not a complete social being. Men have no vote in community affairs, and women cannot validate their maturity and social worth by bearing children until they have crossed this all-important threshold. Being prerequisite to marriage, and in many ways rehearsing it, circumcision and excision are implicated in this validation of full adult standing and community membership.

Besides the manifold specific meanings and functions associated with marriage, other related and more general associations with sexuality and fertility were extremely important in Nubian circumcision ceremonies. Elsewhere I have discussed the great significance of fertility to Nubians—the tremendous degree of concern, and the symbolism which surrounds everything related to reproduction (Kennedy 1967b). The life-cycle crises of birth, circumcision, and marriage all follow a pattern in which the flowing of blood from the genital region entails a forty-day period of 'sacred vulnerability'. During this time the person is considered particularly susceptible to spirit attack which might cause loss of fertility and potency, sickness, etc. 'Fertility' thus symbolises a most important and emotionally loaded cluster of Nubian values.

Sexuality *per se* is also an important focus in Nubian life-cycle rituals. In the excision and circumcision operations as they relate to marriage, sexuality is given a dramatic focus. The anxieties surrounding it and its general importance are highly intensified. A painful consequence of the excision is that at marriage another operation must be performed to open the vagina. Though it is considered preferable that the groom deflower the bride, this reopening operation is generally performed by a midwife with a knife or razor. Usually being only ten to fourteen years of age at the time of her marriage, the girl vividly remembers her excision, but is still largely ignorant of what to expect from intercourse. She is also unsure as to the kind of behaviour to anticipate from her mate during private moments. She is conditioned to feel shame about sexual matters and often is frightened at the prospect of intimate contact. The fear surrounding the initial consummation of marriage is magnified by the belief that spirits are strongly attracted to genital blood. Nubian tradition has taught her that those most treasured values—health, fertility, and the welfare of eventual children—are especially threatened at such critical times as birth, circumcision, marriage, and menstruation. Many of my informants attested that the consummation of marriage was fraught with terror and anxiety, though fears are slightly counteracted, at an intellectual level, by rumours that the sex act will eventually be pleasurable.

bilities of his sex role (1954: 121, 124). Honigmann, commenting on the Silwa ceremonies as reported by Ammar, noticed that their timing coincides with the period of the first oedipal crisis, and also that during everyday socialisation, children are threatened with circumcision to induce obedience. He concludes that: 'By this theory (i.e. oedipal complex notions) threatening young children with genital mutilations and then carrying them out, could be construed as taking advantage of a developmental state to intensify and exploit such worries in order to enforce docility' (1967: 218).

Informants reported that this ritual complex often had a significant impact upon the attitudes and personalities of Nubian children, but enforcement of conformity seems a minor aspect of a complex set of influences. Most circumcisions in Old Nubia were performed between the ages of three and six, and as Honigmann noted, this is the 'oedipal' period—a stage of increased interest in the genitals, masturbation, exhibitionism, and aggression. Children frequently have fears concerning damage to the valued sex organ, guilty fantasies about the mother, etc. It is during this period too that much of the superego (conscience) formation is completed.

This is a critical period of sexual awakening, when the child is also mastering language, locomotion, and learning his potentialities for manipulating the environment. It is just at this time that the Nubians chose to traumatise him with a genital operation. The operation forcefully and painfully draws his genital area to his attention. Particularly the male child could not help but be impressed by the great ceremonial drama centred upon him, and specifically upon his sex organ. The numerous ritual precautions against *mushahara* and evil *jinns* maintained awareness at a high level, as did the congratulations and constant jokes concerning the operation.

The Nubian girl's drama was more limited but she was subjected to much more severe genital pain and a much longer confinement. As she lay with her legs bound together from fifteen to forty days, her mind was continuously on her genital area. Old women vividly remembered this period of misery even fifty to sixty years later. Genital awareness and the fearful ramifications of sexuality were verbally reinforced by continuous admonitions concerning chastity and marriage. Even more affect and meaning were instilled by a myriad of taboos and ritual precautions having the purpose of repelling danger from hovering *jinns*, who were believed ready to attack her genitals. A sense of the mystery and importance of sex, a vivid fear of the evils of unchaste behaviour, the great responsibility of child rearing, and an intense awareness of his or her genitals were all powerfully impressed upon the consciousness of the circumcised or excised child.

These ceremonies thus had an ambivalent psychological impact. They were ego-supporting and future-oriented on the one hand; and punitive, painful, and fear-instilling on the other. Such a situation might be interpreted as ideal for intimidating the child, suppressing sexual and aggressive oedipal desires, and inculcating docility—thus reinforcing superego development. The behaviour of the actors during the circumcision operation itself, however, suggests other considerations. It will be remembered that the mother and father are both present in supportive roles throughout the boy's operation. The mother, or a surrogate, gives him support by holding him, applying herbs to his wounds, etc.

Also, it is the barber, not the father, who inflicts the pain. Contrary to Freudian interpretations, the principal effect here is not the suppression of aggressive drives towards the father, nor the enforcement of docility. In view of the fact that the Nubian father typically has been away working in the city for long periods of his life, it is particularly difficult to presume strong oedipal hostilities towards him. Neither is there anything to imply that incest desires are directed away from the mother. If anything, her physically supportive role in the ceremony would tend to increase the boy's dependency on her.

The evidence suggests that a principal effect was to create in the child an intense awareness of his sexuality and anxiety concerning its social significance. He was subjected to pain, surrounded by taboos and precautions against damage to his genitals, and imbued with fear of the mysterious 'life-force' fertility—the symbolic and social implication of which he could not possibly understand. Marriage loomed ahead as a dimly comprehended though joyful event. Yet it was also vaguely foreboding, dangerous, and somehow related to his sex organ.

Ammar is of course correct in one sense when he states (1954) that the Silwa child was being 'initiated' into a sex role. However, the uncritical application of van Gennep's passage-rite model in the Nubian case would mislead by over-simplification and preconceptions of function. By physiological criteria, the Nubian child is actually considered a member of a sex category from birth. There is never any question of feminine characteristics which must be eliminated (as suggested by van Gennep 1960, and Whiting *et al.* 1958; 1961). The birth of a boy is a time of rejoicing and congratulations, and from that time forward continual references to his gender along with behaviour patterns relating to it are made in his presence. In the ceremonial operation his already unequivocally assigned sex-identity was publicly recognised and celebrated. The ritual was a part of the social process by which a family asserted its social presence and ranking, and reaffirmed its solidarity. At the individual level, the boy was symbolically given a collective stamp of approval and a vote of acceptance by the community, He was simultaneously identified on at least four levels: 1) as a member of a sex category; 2) as a member of a familistic group; 3) as a legitimate community member; and 4) as a member of the vast Islamic religious system. This dramatic demonstration that especially *he* was important to the group, was an effective means of helping to establish the strong and confident self-image and sex identity which are so marked among older Nubians.

But it must be emphasised that while group membership was recognised, there was no role transition or 'passage' in the sense usually assumed by analysts of such rituals. The uncircumcised child was laughed at and mildly teased by the already circumcised children, yet afterwards he assumed no new role behaviour. He was still looked upon as a child and treated by adults in accordance with his chronological age. The ritual was a preparation for the really significant role-change to come later—marriage.

The feminine wedding symbolism in which the boys' eyes are blackened with *kohl*, his hands dyed with henna, and a bridal veil ritually removed, might superficially appear to be matters of symbolic 'passage' to male status. Ammar makes such an inference for identical practices at nearby Silwa, and states that his inference was stimulated by the following comment by the circumcising 'barber': 'Let us put this female cloth around you, and by making you look like a girl tonight, you will be able to avert the evil eye' (1954: 122). I do not see how this inference of a change from female status may be made from such evidence. The Nubians explicitly deny such a meaning. They do not regard the boy as being in any way feminine prior to his operation. Rather, the symbolism conveys a temporary assumption of female attributes in order that his maleness can be recognised and celebrated. The removal of the veil, by dramatic contrast, reaffirms his well-known masculinity, at the same time underscoring the general value of maleness in Nubian culture.

There are complicating factors for any easy interpretations of the symbolism here. As in the Silwa barber's statement, the stated Nubian motivation for this part of the ritual is simply protection against hostile spirits. Since these creatures are believed to be more threatening to boys, it is safer to disguise the male child. But why is he dressed as a bride and not simply as a girl? Actually girls also wear the costume of the bride at their own excision ceremonies. Women giving birth dress in this same costume to please the river spirits, and males are similarly decked out on the ocassions of their marriage and participation in *zar* ceremonies (Kennedy 1967*a*; 1967*b*). It thus becomes clear that to interpret this ritual behaviour as having the purpose of divesting the child of female identity would be grossly to misunderstand the situation. Females undergoing the same ritual actions as males obviously do not want to change their sex identity, and if they did they would not go about it in this way.

Contrary then, to such hypotheses as those of Whiting *et al.* (1958) and Young (1965) which postulate masculine socialisation as the basic function of such rituals, the Nubians have no notion of erasing opposite sex attributes in the children. The child is to them an incomplete human being, and it devolves upon the adult community magically and symbolically to complete him as a person. It is incomplete masculine personality and incomplete feminine personality which require ritual attention. The notion that such practices imply changes from prior membership in the opposite sex category is unwarranted here. When the child is circumcised he is surgically purified. His nascently existing sexuality is thus magically perfected, and he is ritually endorsed as a social person belonging to the appropriate sex category.

From the child's point of view, it seems clear that his developing ego was bolstered by this circumcision or excision ritual. Much of the cultural value system which had been previously absorbed without awareness was now crystallised for him by the ceremony. At the same time, his own sex identity was forcefully impressed upon his consciousness. He was clearly shown that he was a male with masculine prerogatives, and it was powerfully dramatised how he fitted into the scheme of both cosmos and community. However, together with these character structuring impacts were the anxieties aroused by intense pain and fear of supernatural threats. The ritual expressed a structural ambivalence through the simultaneous association of good and evil, pleasure and pain.

A clear social status difference between the sexes which reflects prevailing cultural attitudes is evident in these Nubian rituals. In the male ceremony, positive ego-reinforcing elements predominate over the anxiety-producing ones. The female rite also possesses some elements of positive reinforcement, but its emphasis is primarily upon punishment and social control. The ceremony makes it plain to the girl that she bears a tremendous responsibility to bear children. There is also a clear implication of woman's natural lack of self-control in regard to sexuality. It becomes very clear to her that she possesses an organ which is attractive to men, with potentially dangerous social consequences. All through her early socialisation she learns that women are sensual creatures lacking in intellect and moral control; in effect second-class Muslims who are generally excluded from the mosque and not permitted in at all while menstruating. She finds out that because of her 'weakness' and sexual propensities she is a threat to the family honour. There is no doubt that what Antoun (1968: 672) calls the 'modesty code' has great importance in motivating girls' excision rituals. Honour and social validation are secondary to punishment and pain. Sexual fears, anxieties concerning fertility responsibility, and a clearcut impression of her social subordination to men are forcefully stamped into a young girl's consciousness.

There are some ego-supporting ritual elements too in the emphasis upon the female role in procreation, and the focus upon sexual attractiveness. On the other hand, the importance of the attractiveness of the sexual organ in feminine self-esteem shows the considerable cultural anxiety in the area of sexuality. Other evidence of this can be seen in the fact that if the husband were leaving the village to work in the city, even when this was long after marriage, women would often gladly submit again to an infibulation operation. They might prove their faithfulness in this way two or three times. Several cases were also reported to us in which young unmarried girls were subjected to a second operation when an older female relative judged that the first excision was not complete enough aesthetically to please a potential husband, or to give complete assurance of chastity.

These differences between the sexes in ceremonial emphases reflect the principles of sex-separation and sex-dominance which are so important in Nubian social organisation. Perhaps few places in the world have more rigid norms than the Middle East regarding the separation of the sexes. Nowhere is sex differentiation based upon a more clear assumption that men and women are two different orders of human beings. Nubians share these general Islamic ideas and practices. Nubian men and women live the greater parts of their lives within groups of their own sex, and the differences between the sexes are dramatised by numerous behaviour patterns and symbolic markers. The distance between the social and experiential worlds of the sexes has also been widened by the Nubians' long pattern of labour migration which took most of the men to cities for much of their adult lives. It was thus a rigidly dichotomised and hierarchical adult social world into which the Nubian child was moving. For the community the circumcision and excision ceremonies dramatised and reaffirmed the importance of this structure. For the child they emphatically inculcated its form and meaning, while placing him clearly at a certain point within it.

Changes in the rituals

Of all Nubian ceremonies, those concerned with male circumcision have probably changed most in recent years. The operation has become a simple religious necessity, and as in other parts of Egypt, is privately performed by a 'barber'. In boys' ceremonies there has been a massive reduction of the rituals and they are no longer the occasion of great ceremonial feasts. On the day of his operation he is still given a few gifts by relatives, and the parents offer dates to guests. A few protective precautions against the evil eye and muchahara have been retained. The reason given for these changes is that the costs of the ceremonies became too great in the face of the diminishing resources of Nubia.

Girls' excision ceremonies have continued much in the form described. This is probably related to women's greater isolation from acculturating influences, as well as to the fact that their ceremonialism was much more meagre in the first place. The trend of change in the girls' ritual has been towards a lessening of the severity of the operation. There is an increasing tendency to substitute the 'Egyptian method', a simple excision of the clitoris, for the infibulation. This eliminates the necessity for a special 'opening' operation at marriage. This change towards moderation is justified by a *hadith* of the Prophet Mohammed: 'It is a *sunna* to cut a small part but not all' (Trimingham 1965). Changing attitudes are also reflected in the frequent comment that the Egyptian method permits the wife greater pleasure in sexual intercourse.

In support of the argument I have made, there is evidence that these ceremonial changes are consistent with other changes in Nubian culture. As Nubian men have been progressively forced away from their villages, they have been more consistently in contact with urban values—values which have been rapidly changing in the direction of those characteristics of the urban variant of Egyptian national culture. With the loss of their palm trees and agricultural resources, and with rising dependency upon monetarily recompensed labour, land has decreased in importance as a focal Nubian value. This change has been accompanied by a corresponding decrease in emphasis upon lineage continuity and its accompanying values and attitudes. These changes were most pronounced in the southern part of Egyptian Nubia. Studies there just prior to the recent resettlement showed that the social structure was based almost entirely upon nuclear family households and their individually developed reciprocal relationships, rather than upon the lineage and tribal structures of the past (Fernea 1967: 260-86).

Such changes, along with increased education and accelerated communication with the outside world (e.g. through transistor radios, magazines, newspapers, and transportational mobility) have produced alterations in the meaning of marriage and in the status of women. In spite of conscious attempts to preserve traditional custom, it is no longer as meaningful to marry a cousin or to have a great many children. There is evidence that many of these customs are weakening or breaking down. As would be expected in such a case, the multiple supports underlying the intense emphasis on fertility have been undermined. Though still of considerable importance to the Nubians, this value is losing its previous importance and meaning. The hierarchical principle of male dominance is also diminishing in the face of 'western' egalitarian ideas which are spreading in the cities. These ideas are becoming much more widespread and dominant through the increasing proportion of men who take their families to live with them in the urban areas (Geiser 1967). Such changes have also decreased the pattern of extreme sex separation in daily life.

Since all these social principles and social values were obviously supportive of and linked to, the complex system of circumcision, excision and marriage rituals, it is not surprising that the social changes have tended to empty them of their emotional content and meaning. Such an interpretation is reinforced by evidence of sex differentials in change. Men's ceremonies have all but disappeared. They remain largely as token markers of religious identification, but women's customs have continued relatively unchanged, though they too show signs of responding to changing female roles.

* * * * *

On reflection, the grossness and inadequacy of the present state of theory about such rites as have been discussed in this article are apparent. Nubian circumcision ceremonies cannot be simply categorised as 'rites of passage', or as 'initiation rites'. They embody a complex constellation of interrelated beliefs, values, and principles of social structure—all of which must be examined in order to comprehend their form and existence. Furthermore, though the rituals had important effects on the social awareness and identity formation of children, they had no obvious relationship to gaps or failures in the socialisation process—such as are assumed in the modern theories of Whiting *et al.* (1958), Cohen (1964), and Young (1965).

The emphasis is not upon a present passage or initiation, but upon the *future* (marriage and procreation) with all its social implications. For the child, the manifest stress is upon social preparation and spiritual protection. He is prepared for later participation in religion, marriage, and procreation. He has taken a large and necessary step prerequisite to an adult life which will not be activated for a number of years.

In the circumcision and excision rituals for individuals, the community celebrates and thus reaffirms many of its vital anxiety-laden concerns and values. Communal solidarity and continuity, family prestige and continuity, sex separation, male dominance, and male superiority are all expressed, as are the most specific fears related to fertility, sexuality, and gender identity. With such a complex of concerns and anxieties, and under conditions of a supernatural world view, the genital area of the body is a natural point of ritual focus. There appears to be no need or reason for invoking such Freudian notions as that circumcision represents a castration threat by the father which is designed to quell reawakening oedipal desires in their sons. Nor is there any justification for Bettelheimian ideas of opposite-sex imitation (1954).

My interpretation and the widespread structural similarities of such rituals, suggest that these same values and principles may well be at work, in the same fashion, in societies where the operation actually does take place at puberty, and where it does mark a status transition to adult life. Such factors are not limited to a stage of life. Therefore the same complex of concerns could produce such rituals in societies with infant circumcision and in those groups which circumcise long after puberty.

The analysis suggests that the relationships of genital operations to the larger marriage complexes of such societies requires more investigation It also leads to the inference that those older theories emphasising fertility, sexuality, and gender perfection, should not be discarded, and are probably more useful in understanding such practices than are some of the newer ideas which give great explanatory weight to concepts of identity and personality change. A more general implication is that the interrelation of psychological and social processes in these rites is much more complex than these theorists have assumed.

Attempts to formulate a theory which can account for all customs of genital operations seem doomed to failure. Many kinds of motivation and social forces might have the same end result. The common categorisations which assimilate all these customs under the wider rubrics 'rites of passage' or 'initiation', bear re-examination. The wide variations in timing, as well as the great diversity of customs which theorists assume to be psychologically and functionally 'equivalent', vitiate our confidence in the validity of all cross-cultural studies so far undertaken. It is now appropriate to abandon the search for a simple one-factor theory, and to seek multiple explanations which deal with larger complexes of determinants.

Notes

Directed by the author, the Kanuba study was part of the Nubian Ethnological Survey of the Social Research Center, American University in Cairo. The Nubian Ethnological Survey was directed by Dr Robert Fernea and was supported by the Ford Foundation. In addition to the Kanuba study, it included field studies in Nubia proper (Callendar, Fernea, Scudder) and in Cairo and Alexandria (Geiser, Callendar—see references). An important role in planning and execution of the Survey was performed by Dr Laila Shukry El Hamamsy, director of the Social Research Center. In the Kanuba project, my field assistants were Dr Hussein Fahim, Omar Abdel Hamid, Samiha El Katsha and Sohair Mehanna.

Since the ceremonies connected with boys' circumcisions no longer have the traditional form described here, data concerning them are from informants' memories. Reports of varying lengths were gathered individually from sixteen older informants (eleven males, five females), who had participated in the ceremonies as children. Additional checking of details was carried out in tape-recorded groups sessions with older men in Kanuba. Most of the information concerning boys' ceremonies refer to the Diwan Omodiyya (Mahass speaking). Other details are from the Kenuz-speaking Omoduyyas of Abu Hor and Dahmit. Girls' ceremonies survive almost intact to the present, and two of these were witnessed by Sohair Mehanna (Kanuba), and Fadwa El Guindi (Dahmit).

For further information on Nubian culture see Burkhardt 1822; Fernea 1966; Fernea & Kennedy 1966; Geiser 1967a; 1967b; Herzog 1957; Kennedy 1967a; 1967b. Earlier drafts of this article benefited from comments by Walter Goldschmidt and Robert Edgerton, neither of whom can be held responsible for defects in the present version.

1 For example, Cohen (1964) and Whiting *et al.* (1958) do not include the area in the samples. Young (1965) and Brown (1963) each use one Middle Eastern monograph (Ammar 1954). Young spends most of his discussion of this example in trying to account for its apparently anomalous data for his hypotheses (e.g. 1965: 74-5; 82-3, 102, 143). Brown's inclusion of Silwa is also dubious because the case does not fit her age criteria (1963: 838). In any event the coding of it is completely wrong. See tables on pp. 840, 844 and 846, in which she codes Silwa as not having female rites. Freud (1946) and Bettelheim (1954) do not mention the Middle East except for reference to Jewish infantile circumcision.

2 Some information exists, e.g. Lane 1908: 58-60, 511-15; Ammar 1954: 116-24; Barclay 1964: 237, 243.

3 In most other parts of the Islamic world the classical Arabic word *khitan* is used (Ghalioungui 1963: 96).

4 *Sharaya* is a spaghetti-like ceremonial food, eaten with sugar and milk. *Abreek* is a paper-thin bread made of *durra*. Among other uses, it is an ingredient in *fatta*, the typical main dish of all Nubian ceremonial occasions.

5 This costume is very similar to that described by Lane (1908: 58) for Cairo in the early nineteenth century.

6 The sword apparently wards off evil spirits which are threatening to fertility and health at this time (see Kennedy 1967b). Similar customs are reported for the Diwan area (Mahass speaking) weddings at an earlier period. I presume they were found in circumcisions there as well.

7 *Asleeg* is cracked roasted wheat, or popped corn.

8 In the Diwan area, a second such procession was made on the following day to another saint—Sheikh Saad. His shrine was across the Nile, making it necessary to collect a fleet of boats from surrounding villages.

9 There appears to be no evidence that infibulation of this type was practised by the pharaonic Egyptians (Barclay 1964: 238).

10 The present tense is used in this description because the customs regarding girls' excision appear relatively unchanged.

11 'To be a Moslem, it is believed, is to be circumcized . . . . However, there is no text in the Koran that enjoins circumcision upon Moslems, and it is only mentioned in the prophetic tradition . . . . Another prophetic tradition says "Circumcision is my way for men, but is only enobling for women" '(Ammar 1954: 120).

12 '. . . they (the Egyptians) circumcize themselves for the sake of cleanliness, preferring to be clean rather than comely' (Herodotus describing the custom about 430 B.C.).

13 Similarities between circumcisions and weddings are not restricted to the Nubians. They have been remarked for other groups in the Sudan and Egypt (e.g. Ammar 1954; Barclay 1964; Lane 1908; Trimingham 1965).

14 The adjustment process of the partners was facilitated by the Nubian custom of confining the bride and groom to the bridal chamber for forty days, where they were served by a slave, ate special foods, and were under many taboos. This was a period when all other activities were suspended, and all attention devoted to learning about the new life partner.

References

Ammar, Hammed 1954. *Growing up in an Egyptian Village*. London: Routledge & Kegan Paul.

Antoun, Richard T. 1968. On the modesty of women in Arab Muslim villages: a study in the accommodation of traditions. *Am. Anthrop.* **70**, 671-97.

Barclay, Harold B. 1964. *Buurri al Lamaab*. Ithaca, N.Y.: Cornell Univ. Press.

Bettelheim, Bruno 1954. *Symbolic wounds*. Glencoe, Ill.: Free Press.

Blum, Gerald S. 1964. *Psychoanalytic theories of personality*. New York: McGraw-Hill.

Bonaparte, Marie 1952. Notes on excision. In *Psychoanalysis and social science* (ed.) Geza Roheim. New York: International Univ. Press.

Brown, Judith K. 1963. A cross-cultural study of female initiation rites. *Am. Anthrop.* **65**, 837-53.

Burkhardt, J. L. 1822. *Travels in Nubia*. London: John Murray.

Callendar, Charles 1967. The Mehannab: a Kenuz tribe. In *Contemporary Egyptian Nubia* (ed.) R. Fernea. New Haven: HRAF Press.

Cohen, Yehudi 1964. The establishment of identity in a social nexus: the special case of initiation ceremonies and their relation to value and legal systems. *Am. Anthrop.* **66**, 529-52.

Fernea, Robert A. 1967. Integrating factors in a non-corporate community. In *Contemporary Egyptian Nubia*. New Haven: HRAF Press.

_____ & John G. Kennedy 1966. Initial adaptations to resettlement: a new life for Egyptian Nubians. *Curr. Anthrop.* **7**, 349-54.

Freud, S. 1939. *Moses and monotheism*. New York: Alfred A. Knopf.

_____ 1946. *Totem and taboo*. New York: Random House.

Geiser, Peter 1967*a*. Some differential factors affecting population movement: the Nubian case. *Hum. Org.* **26**, 164-77.

_____ 1967*b*. Some impressions concerning the nature and extent of urbanisation and stabilisation in Nubian society. In *Contemporary Egyptian Nubia* (ed.) R. Fernea. New Haven: HRAF Press.

Gennep, A. van 1960. *The rites of passage*. Chicago: Univ. Press.

Ghalioungui, Paul 1963. *Magic and medical science in ancient Egypt*. London: Hodder & Stoughton.

Herzog, Rolf 1957. *Die Nubier*. Berlin: Akademie-Verlag.

Honigmann, John J. 1967. *Personality in culture*. New York: Harper & Row.

Kennedy, John G. 1967*a*. Nubian *zar* ceremonies as psychotherapy. *Hum. Org.* **26**, 185-94.

_____ 1967*b*. Mushahara: a Nubian concept of supernatural danger and the theory of taboo. *Am. Anthrop.* **69**, 685-702.

Lane, Edward 1908. *The manners and customs of the modern Egyptians*. London: Dutton.

Levy, Reuben 1962. *The social structure of Islam*. London: Cambridge Univ. Press.

Scudder, Thayer 1967. The economic basis of Egyptian Nubian labor migration. In *Contemporary Egyptian Nubia* (ed.) R. Fernea. New Haven: HRAF Press.

Smith, W. Robertson 1903. *Kinship and marriage in early Arabia*. Boston: Beacon Press.

Trimingham, J. 1965. *Islam in the Sudan*. London: Frank Cass.

Whiting, J. W. M., Richard Kluckhohn & Albert Anthony 1958. The function of male initiation ceremonies at puberty. In *Readings in social psychology*. (eds) E. Maccoby *et al*. New York: Holt, Rinehart & Winston.

Young, Frank W. 1965. *Initiation ceremonies: a cross-cultural study of status dramatization*. New York: Bobbs-Merrill.

FEMALE CIRCUMCISION IN THE SUDAN

Amna el Sadik Badri

Introduction

This paper presents a literature review of research on female circumcision in the Sudan from 1979 to April, 1983.

Origins of female circumcision

The origins of female circumcision are unknown. In 1969, Niebuhr, the German traveller reported that, in Oman, on the shores of the Persian Gulf, among the Christians of Abyssinia, and in Egypt among the Arabs and Copts, this custom was prevalent (Baasher, 1979). Baasher also notes that "Ghalioungui seems to be right when he pointed out that the state of preservation of mummies does not permit firm conclusions as regards the presence of this practice." However, El Dareer (1979, 1983) pointed out that circumcision of women was practiced in Ancient Egypt, as the evidence of female mummies from 200 B.C. had demonstrated.

In the Sudan female circumcision goes back to antiquity and has been passed from one generation to the next. It has not only become part of the bribal customs and traditions, but also was associated with religion. Hence, it is deeply entrenched in society (Badri, 1979).

Background

There are three types of female circumcision practiced in the Sudan.

1. Sunna, which entails the excision of the tip of prepuce of the clitoris;

2. Intermediate type, which involves the removal of the entire clitoris with some parts of the labia minora intact, or the removal of the clitoris, the whole of the labia minora, parts of the labia majora and the stitching of the two sides together, leaving an opening;

3. Infibulation (Pharaonic circumcision), which involves removal of the entire clitoris, the labia minora, and the labia majora, leaving the two raw edges to adhere, which produces a lengthwise scar.

Reprinted by permission of the author and editors of *The Ahfad Journal,* Vol. 1, 1984, pp. 10-20.

Prevalence of the practice

Gasim Badri (1979) distributed a questionnaire to 68 Sudanese gynaecologists in 12 towns covering all the regions except the southern region of Sudan to get their opinions about the prevalence of the practice of female circumcision. Of the 48 gynaecologists who responded, 77% believed that there had been a slight decrease, while the remaining believed there had been a moderate decrease. Sixty-seven percent (67%) observed that infibulation was the most common form of female circumcision; 23% believed that the intermediate type was the most prevalent; while about 10% thought that the Sunna form was the most common form.

Results of six surveys of prevalence by type are listed in Table 1.

Table 1

| | | Type of Circumcision | | | | |
Researcher	Year	Infibulated	Intermediate	Sunna	Uncircumcised	Total
G. Badri	79	60%	1%	33%	6%	100%
S. Abel Hadi	79	86%	0%	12%	2%	100%
Sudan Fertility Survey	79	79%	0%	17%	4%	100%
A. Badri	81	100%	0%	0%	0%	100%
A. El Dareer	83	83%	12%	2%	1%	98%*
B. Badri	83	25%	55%	11%	6%	100%

*The remaining 2% represents subjects who could not be classified by type.

Table 1. Survey results on the prevalence of female circumcision in percentages by type of circumcision.

The Sudan fertility survey (Democratic Republic of the Sudan, 1979) was based on a sample of 3114 evermarried women from northern Sudan. Of this sample 63.1% of the women were younger than 35 years old, with the majority of them between age 25-34 years old. Of this sample 27% of the women came from urban areas, whereas 72% came from rural areas. With this high percentage of representation from rural areas, it is not surprising to find that 51.6% of these women had never been to school. The prevalence of female circumcision according to the results of this survey was 95.9%. There was no significant difference between these results and the results obtained by El Dareer's (1983) survey in the degree of prevalence. This last survey was conducted during the period 1978-1981. The El Dareer survey covered four regions: Darfour, Kordofan, Central and Eastern regions, and Khartoum Province. El Dareer found that female circumcision is practiced all over the areas studied with a prevalence of 98%. The survey was done among a sample of 3210 women of whom 2244 were evermarried women and 934 were either single or engaged. Of these 3210, 1390 (43.3%) were illiterate and 49.8% came from rural areas whereas 50.2% were from urban areas. The majority of these women (68.9%) were between age 15-34 years old.

In 1979, a study was done among 100 female patients in three hospitals in Khartoum Province (S. Abdel Hadi. 1979). The prevalence of female circumcision among this sample was 98%. It is interesting to notice that these women represent different Sudanese tribes (Table 2).

Table 2

Type of Circumcision	Tribe							
	Galien	Shaygia	Danagla	Shukria	Hussania	Gumuaia	Kawahla	Dinka
Infibulation	88%	100%	95%	79%	100%	83%	100%	0%
Sunna	12%	0%	5%	21%	0%	17%	0%	0%
Uncircumcised	0%	0%	0%	0%	0%	0%	0%	100%
Total	100%	100%	100%	100%	100%	100%	100%	0%

Table 2. Percentages for type of circumcision by tribal affiliation, reported by Hadi (1979).

These women ranged in age between 15-50 with 86% between 18-35 years and 66% between 15-30 years old. Of this sample 43% were illiterate.

Apart from seeking the opinions of gynaecologists, Badri (1979) also sought the opinion of female college students in Omdurman, Sudan. In a survey of 190 female university students ranging in age between 19 to 41 with a modal age of 23 years, and with 90% of them in their twenties, he found that 94.2% of the students were circumcised. Results for the university students, however, differed in one important way from the other survey results: whereas 79% or more of the older women in the other surveys had been infibulated, only 60% of the college students reported such circumcision.

Reports of a Health-Education project in rural White Nile Province indicated that 100% of the total female population aged over 15 years were infibulated. The degree of illiteracy among this age group of females was 97% (Badri, 1981).

In a recent study among 150 high school students in Khartoum City, Badria Badri (1983) found that 94% were circumcised. Of these, 58.9% had an intermediate circumcision, whereas 29.8% were infibulated and 11.3% had the Sunna form.

The results suggest that there has been no significant decline in the practice of female circumcision. However, there probably has been a gradual decline in the infibulation type among educated women who are inhabitants of the Khartoum (three towns) area.

Age of Circumcision

The most common age for performing the operation of female circumcision is between 5-9 years.

According to the Sudan Fertility Survey (1979), 86% of the women studied were circumcised before they were 10 years old, with 74% between 5-9 years. Similar results were obtained by El Dareer (1983) who found that 81.4% of the women in his sample were circumcised by the time they were 9 years old, with 63.3% having been circumcised between 5-9 years of age.

Badri (1983) found that almost 81% of the girls who were circumcised had the operation prior to their eighth birthday, with 76.6% having had the operation when they were 4-7 years of age. Among girls who were less than 5 years of age at the time of circumcision, the minimum age—seven to forty days is found only among Eastern Sudan tribes such as the Beja and Beni Amir (El Dareer 1983).

Complications of female circumcision

All (48) of the gynaecologists who responded in the Badri study (1979) saw female circumcision as harmful. Although they pointed out that infibulation leads to more severe complications, they argued that any form of female circumcision is bound to create serious complications, such as infections, urinary complications, shock, tetanus, haemorrhage and retention cysts. Other complications cited were difficulty during and lack of satisfaction from coitus, infertility arising from the failure of the husband to achieve penetration or from infections stemming from the operation, and difficulty in delivery.

The reports of the gynaecologists may overstate the prevalence of complications. Their views reflected their experiences in treating women who had problems. In another study of patients in hospitals in Khartoum Province, Abdel Hadi (1979) found that only 30% of the women questioned reported complications. These were divided about equally among shock, bleeding, and subsequent difficulty during coitus.

Physical complications were reported by 14.2% of the high school girls in Khartoum (Badri, 1983): another 27.7% reported some form of psychological shock, and 9.9% reported having experienced both physical and psychological shock, making a total of 51.8% who reported some form of complication.

El Dareer (1983) provides the most comprehensive data on complications. Table 3 shows percentages of women who reported either immediate or longterm complications by the type of circumcision they experienced. Sunna circumcision resulted in the fewest complications while Pharaonic and intermediate gave rise to the greatest percentages of complications. Specific forms of immediate and longterm complications by type of circumcision are shown in Tables 4 and 5, respectively. For most complications, frequency of occurrence was greatest for women who had Pharaonic circumcision and least for those who had Sunna circumcision.

Table 3

Complications	Sunna		Intermediate		Pharaonic	
	%	N	%	N	%	N
Intermediate	8.6%	81	26.1%	399	25.6%	2695
Longterm	19.8%	81	31.4%	452	32.8%	2645

Table 3. Percentages for intermediate and longterm complications from female circumcision, as reported by El Dareer (1983).

Table 4

Type of Circumcision	Bleeding	Shock	Swelling	Fever	Failure to heal	Difficulty passing urine	Urine retention	%	N
Sunna	71.4%	-	-	-	-	-	28.6%	100%	7
Intermediate	34.7%	-	7.6%	15.4%	12.5%	13.5%	16.3%	100%	104
Pharaonic	18.4%	4.5%	6.2%	17.0%	20.0%	23.0%	10.9%	100%	689

Table 4. Percentages for forms of immediate complications by type of circumcision, as reported by El Dareer (1983).

Table 5

Type of Circumcision	Painful scar	Vulvar abcess	Inclusion cyst	Urinary tract infection	Pelvic infection	Difficulty in penetration	Pain during coitus	Difficulty in passing menses	Total %	N
Sunna	-	-	-	58.3%	42.7%	-	-	-	100%	12
Intermediate	1.4%	10.6%	2.1%	35.9%	19.7%	24.7%	3.5%	2.1%	100%	142
Pharaonic	1.0%	14.7%	1.8%	26.0%	23.9%	22.6%	5.9%	4.1%	100%	869

Table 5. Percentages for forms of long term complications by type of circumcision, as reported by Dareer (1983).

Why female circumcision is practiced

Although medical opinion is against female circumcision and although research shows that at least 30% of those who are circumcised face one or more complications, female circumcision is still widely practiced in the Sudan. Why?

Four reasons were advanced by the gynaecologists included in the Badri study (1979). The first is the ignorance of the public, especially the mothers and grandmothers, as to the immediate and later dangers of female circumcision. This view is supported by the fact that 83.7% of the mothers whose daughters were circumcised were illiterate, and 71.9% of these mothers had pharaonic circumcision performed on their daughters (El Dareer, 1983). The second reason is the lack of health education. The third reason is that there is a widespread but false belief that female circumcision is endorsed by religion. The fourth and main reason for continuation of the practice is based on a set of social values. Virginity at marriage for women is a requirement in Sudanese society. As part of this traditional value system, female circumcision is believed to prevent promiscuity and ensure virginity at marriage. Girls accept this view and ridicule those who are not circumcised, calling them ghalfa, uncircumcised, or nigsa, unclean. Badri (1983) found this phenomenon and reported: "An unexpected finding was that some high school girls indicated that they forced their parents to have them circumcised mainly because they were called names like ghalfa or nigsa by classmates who had been circumcised". Another reason given for continuing the practice is the belief that men prefer women to be circumcised and hence uncircumcised women will not be married. Finally, there is the attitude of men that female circumcision is a women's concern or a mother's decision and therefore men assume a passive role in decisions concerning circumcision of their daughters.

El Dareer (1983) reported that fear of social criticism and ignorance of consequences were seen by men and women as the main reasons for continuation of the practice of female circumcision (Table 6). Among high school girls, Badri (1983) found that protecting virginity was the most frequently given reason for continuation of the practice, given by 21% of the girls, followed by, reduces sexual desire (17%), promotes cleanliness (10%), for beauty (7%), increases chances of marriage (7%), and other reasons (18%), while the rest (20%) gave no response.

Future of the practice

There is some evidence that attitudes toward the practice are changing. Medical authorities are against the practice (Badri, 1979). However, this belief is not shared by other groups, including some within the health profession. Ten percent of the sample of 40 midwives in Khartoum and Port Sudan, expressed the view that female circumcision of the Sunna type should be continued (Badri, 1979). It is worth mentioning here that the results of the Sudan Fertility Survey show that 98% of the operations were done by midwives. El Dareer reported a percentage of 92.5%. Most midwives are trained for delivery and are not trained to perform female circumcision. Moreover, Pharaonic circumcision is illegal. When questioned, midwives give social and religious reasons for performing female circumcision and not the obvious reason that they also benefit financially (Badri, 1979).

Table 6

Reasons	Percentage	
	Women	Men
Fear of social criticism	35.8%	30.6%
Ignorance of consequences	23.3%	34.8%
Ignorance of parents	19.1%	5.0%
Influence of grandmothers	15.5%	5.6%
Insufficient health education	40.0%	13.9%
Other	59.0%	10.1%
Total	100%	100%

Table 6. Percentage for reasons given by women and men for continuation of female circumcision, as reported by El Dareer (1983).

Attitudes toward female circumcision appear to be changing, however. El Dareer (1983) found that only 17% of the respondents in his sample of adults were opposed to the practice, whereas Badri (1979) reported that 80% of a sample of college girls indicated they would not circumcise their daughters. Attitudes reported for high school girls (Badri, 1983) also showed declining support for the practice: 69% said the practice should be stopped.

Price (1979) has reported data on women whose families had decided against circumcision. Parents differed from the population at large in being better educated, the mothers had an average of 8.1 years of schooling and fathers had 17.7 years of schooling; and were primarily urban residents. 65% of the families had lived in Khartoum for at least 15 years. The women themselves were young, 16 to 29 years of age, with a mean of 21; 70% were single; and 90% had either completed a university degree or had completed the maximum years of education appropriate for their ages.

In 78% of the families the decision not to circumcise the daughter was made by both parents, though both parents were opposed to circumcision in only 56% of the families, childbirth complications was the main reason for opposing the custom, listed by 67% of families. Some families listed more than one reason. Such reasons included hazards to the health of the girl or woman (56%), problems associated with sexual relations in marriage (34%), deprivation of the women's sexual pleasure (34%), and the pain involved (34%). When asked what single factor most influenced her decision against female circumcision 57% of mothers responded that it deprived women of their sexual pleasure as opposed to 29% who cited complications at childbirth. Thirty percent of the families were persuaded female circumcision was an undesirable practice by a husband or father who was a doctor, 20% of the families reported being persuaded by a relative who was an active member of the 1940's campaign against female circumcision.

The only data about the effects of being uncircumcised on the lives of women come from the exploratory investigation by Price (1979) based on 10 families in Khartoum. All the women interviewed expressed positive feeling about not being circumcised and all of the mothers and daughters continue to approve of the decision. None had encountered problems because of being uncircumcised other than teasing by friends as suggesting that the woman was unclean or hypersexual. One respondent reported having felt worried and feared that she being uncircumcised might cause problems for her marriage from possible objections by the inlaws. Others were certain that they would marry educated men and that these men would approve of their not being circumcised. For the three who had married, their husbands were reported to strongly approve of their not being circumcised. Married women expressed the opinion that they found sexual relations with their husbands much more pleasurable than did their circumcised friends.

Approximately 45 % of the respondents felt that the majority of people who knew about their being uncircumcised had mixed feelings of approval and disapproval, approximately one third felt that most people who knew approved, and about 22% felt that most who knew disapproved. However, none of the families had reported social rejection.

Next steps

Over 90% of the women in both urban and rural areas continue to be circumcised; however, there appears to be a decline in pharaonic circumcisions, especially among girls from families with above average levels of education.

Although pharaonic circumcision is illegal, it is still widely practiced. On the basis of current information, increasing knowledge of the complications arising from the practice would appear to be the best way of reducing the practice. Another way to address the problem will be to correct the false religious beliefs offered in support of the practice. Also it will be necessary to reduce the social pressure on girls and their families to have the operation performed. The issue of female circumcision should continue to be discussed openly and through all educational and social means, not only by health, religious and other specialists, but also by families who have stopped circumcising their daughters.

References

1. Amna El Sadik Badri. A new approach to abolish female circumcision in the Sudan. Paper presented at the NGO Forum, Copenhagen, Denmark, 1980.

2. Amna El Sadik Badri. Report on programme children health through mothers education. Omdurman, Sudan: Babikr Badri Scientific Association for Women's Studies, Jan., 1982.

3. Badria Suleiman Badri. Knowledge and attitude towards female circumcision among high school girls. Omdurman, Sudan: Ahfad University College for Women, 1983.

4. Gasim Badri. The views of gynaecologists, midwives and college students on female circumcision. In: *Proceedings of the Symposium on the Changing Status of Sudanese Women.* Omdurman, Sudan: Ahfad University College for Women, 1979.

5. Taha A. Baasher Psychosocial aspects of female circumcision. In: *Proceedings of the WHO Seminar on Traditional Practices Affecting the Health of Women and Children*. Khartoum, Sudan: World Health Organization, 1979.

6. Asma El Dareer. *Woman, Why Do You Weep?: Circumcision and its Consequences*. London: Zed Press, 1983.

7. Salwa Abdel Hadi. Female circumcision in the Sudan. Omdurman, Sudan: Ahfad University College for Women, 1979.

8. Democratic Republic of the Sudan. *Sudan Fertility Survey*. Vol. 1. Khartoum, Sudan: Ministry of National Planning, 1982.

9. Gail Price. Factors related to Sudanese families deciding against female circumcision. In: *Proceedings of the Symposium on the Changing Status of Sudanese Women*. Omdurman, Sudan: Ahfad University College for Women, 1979.

A SEXUAL RITE ON TRIAL

Newsweek

The infant had been bleeding sporadically for two days before her parents finally bundled her to a Paris emergency room. First the doctors managed to save little Batou Doucara's life. Then they called the police. Batou's father, a sanitation worker from Mali, had removed his three-month-old daughter's clitoris with a pocketknife. He explained that he had simply carried out his people's ancient custom of female excision. But French prosecutors called the clumsy operation criminal and took him to court. Beyond the issue of guilt or innocence, the case has posed a fundamental conflict between atavistic but very powerful non-Western sexual values and contemporary Western ideas of women's rights.

Excision persists principally in Africa and the Middle East. In its simplest form, the rite nicks the clitoris and can be compared to male circumcision, widely sanctioned by custom and religion in the West. The more radical forms remove the entire clitoris and labia, apparently to enforce chastity by depriving women of the organs of sexual pleasure. World Health Organization officials estimate that as many as 75 million women have undergone excision in one form or another. As Europe has imported cheap labor from Africa, it has imported excision as well. The clash of cultures has not been easy to reconcile. In Paris last week the judge postponed a verdict in the Doucara case, asking for more medical evidence. "This just shows how impotent our laws are to deal with excision," complained one angry French feminist.

The Batou Doucara case was only the first to reach the French courts. Last July another Malian infant, Bobo Traouré, died after a botched excision. The professional *exciseuse* escaped prosecution by fleeing to Mali, but the dead girl's parents now face trial on charges of criminal negligence. Reports from hospital worked who have witnessed the results of crude, amateur surgery have prompted legislation banning excision in Norway, Sweden and Denmark. But there is no law against the operation in Great Britain, and some nursing homes and private doctors on London's Harley Street acknowledge that they perform clitoridectomies for immigrant women at fees as high as $1,700. The Royal College of Obstetricians calls the procedure "barbaric, futile and illogical."

'Walls of Silence': Such comments strike some Third World women as cultural chauvinism. At the world conference of the United Nations Decade for Women in 1980, the delegation from Upper Volta stormed out rather than debate a resolution condemning sexual mutilation. Other African delegates advised their American and Western European sisters to confine their concern to problems like illiteracy, hunger and disease. Protesting the Doucara trial in Paris, a Malian laborers' group demanded that the French government "guarantee our rights to live according to our customs," and some experts warned that banning the practice would only drive it further underground. Doucara's defense attorney urged the judge to rule that no Western law applied. "My client should be acquitted," he said.

The controversy over excision won't just disappear. In Kenya recently, President Daniel Arap Moi banned the custom after 14 excised girls had died. The French Ministry for Women's Rights has announced a new tack "in solidarity with African women, to break down the walls of silence"—a policy recognizing that excision will persist as long as the attitudes about women and sex that it exemplifies remain. "The more we talk about it the better," said a United Nations official. "As soon as you name an evil, you go a long way toward putting an end to it.

Section V

MENSTRUAL CYCLE

All normal physically healthy adult women experience a monthly cycle which involves menstruation and ovulation. This cycle is the result of hypothalamic action which secretes gonadotropin-releasing factor (or hormone) which in turn stimulates the anterior pituitary gland to secrete follicle stimulating hormone (FSH) and luteinizing hormone (LH). Under influence of the former of these hormones the follicular cells increase the amount of estrogen issued during the first half of the menstrual cycle. The result is the thickening of the endometrium as it prepares a favorable and nourishing environment in case the egg cell is fertilized. On about the fourteenth day as the follicle has matured there is a surge of luteinizing hormone and a rise in follicle stimulating hormone causing the follicle to swell and rupture, releasing the egg cell. If this egg cell is not fertilized, estrogen and progesterone concentrations decline, resulting in reduced oxygen and nutrients and the resultant shedding of the endometrial lining along with blood and other tissue. Flow, occurring normally about every twenty-eight days, is a normal biological phenomenon called menstruation. This biological function, however, is rich in superstition and folklore.

A girl's first menstrual experience referred to as menarche is, among many peoples the world over, ritually marked because of its potentiating significance. The girl now will be physically capable of conception and reproduction, socially capable of assuming the wifely role, and economically capable of growing and preparing food for a husband and family. As the woman menstruates every month it is seen as a sign of her potential in the marriage relationship. In some parts of the world women fear the termination of this cycle since it would mark them as old, no longer able to conceive, and thus no longer of prime interest and value to their husbands. Wisdon recounts that among the Chorti Indians in Guatemala a certain plant is used in large doses to induce menstrual flow. "They are often drunk by older women to induce the flow after menopause" (1940:289) and to extend youth just one more time. The regular flow is also considered healthy and cleansing as it represents the shedding of "old, impure" blood and the production of new fresh blood. Therefore Indian women (du Toit 1990:105) in their reproductive years are considered healthier than menopausal women who no longer experience this monthly shedding of what they consider to be the old impure blood.

Numerous societies throughout the world continue to recognize the menstrual period on a monthly basis as a time of danger, contamination or pollution. When a woman menstruates, it is believed, her womb is open allowing for flow but simultaneously placing her in danger of being invaded by drafts, winds, or contaminants. Women who menstruate are also potential sources of contamination or pollution to others. Among pastoral peoples menstruating women must avoid the animals, while agriculturalists deny a menstruating woman access to the gardens.

When our parents and grand-parents were young, and in many parts of the world this is true even today, menstruation was never mentioned in company—especially mixed company! The most a woman would venture, and this was in intimate personal relationships, was that she "had the curse", her "friend was visiting", it was "that time of the month", it was her "time of the moon", or that she was experiencing her "period". That phase of our history marked a very clear distinction between female and male realms, distinctions which have faded with a greater openness in relationships. Other cultures retain these separate gender realms.

Restrictions on sexual intercourse during this time are common. These restrictions may be based on beliefs about the dangers associated with a woman during a state of impurity—a belief widely shared by women and men. Restrictions may also derive from practical beliefs such as that held by the men on Aoriki in the eastern Solomon Islands. Prior to major fishing expeditions sexual intercourse is avoided because, it is believed, intercourse leaves an odor on a man and the bonito and tuna can sense this.

Women who are experiencing flow may be obligated to avoid the kitchen or contact with food preparation. Frequently there is a separate hut where women are isolated for the duration of the period. Women in this condition are also said to be dangerous to men. However, among the Wogeo, a Papua New-Guinea society, men ritually create the same state by imitating menstruation. In the process they become ritually unclean, subject to taboos, and a danger to themselves and society (Hogbin 1970). Avoidance behavior which results from this condition is not unique to traditional societies. French perfumeries excluded women who were menstruating, and such women were not allowed to pick mushrooms, tend silkworms, or be involved with fermenting grapes for fear they would spoil the wine.

Such rules of avoidance, derive from and give rise to a wealth of folklore. The two readings which follow illustrate this from different parts of the world. In the first Snow and Johnson show how attitudes toward menstruation can affect a wide range of beliefs and actions. These authors report on information gathered in a Michigan-based study but also present a number of folk beliefs from other parts of the United States. The second paper reports on research among women in South Africa who are of Indian origin. These women represent and give continuity to beliefs representing the rich cultural tradition of the Indian sub-continent.

References

du Toit, Brian M. 1990. *Aging and Menopause among Indian South African Women*. Albany: State University of New York Press.

Hogbin, Ian. 1970. *The Island of Menstruating Men: Religion in Wogeo, New Guinea*. Scranton: Chandler Publishing Company.

Wisdon, C. 1940. *The Chorti Indians of Guatemala*. Chicago: University of Chicago Press.

MYTHS ABOUT MENSTRUATION: VICTIMS OF OUR OWN FOLKLORE

Loudell F. Snow and Shirley M. Johnson

> There's somethin' about a girl gets a disease quicker than a boy. On account of her different sex. She's easy to catch or she's eager to catch ever'thing. Because she'll get it in her breast. Different things come through the breast, through your vagina too, you know. There are two things you have a man don't have, than make you easily [get sick]. (1)

The speaker of the above words was a 49-year old black woman living in Arizona. The concern she expresses, however, that women—*because* they are women—are at risk health-wise is found all around the world. It is believed by women in "primitive" tribes and in technologically advanced societies, in rural areas and modern cities, by illiterates and college graduates alike. Folk beliefs have been aptly described as drawn " ...from a common pool of knowledge about specific situations or things," and that they "..serve as the basis for judgments and consequent coping behavior." (2) When they concern health they are instrumental in shaping patient practices. The information to be presented here will demonstrate that women's attitudes toward menstruation may adversely affect their own body image, perceptions of disease causation, diet, contraceptive use, and the ability to plan pregnancies.

The data are part of a larger study in which forty women enrolled at a public clinic in Ingham County, Michigan were interviewed about the female reproductive cycle. The health facility serves a low-income, multi-ethnic and relatively poorly educated clientele, and communication problems are often exacerbated by a language barrier as well (42% of the women interviewed spoke languages other than English as children, mainly Spanish). A questionnaire covering knowledge and attitudes toward menstruation, childbearing, contraception, pregnancy and birth, venereal disease, the menopause, and personal health care experiences was developed and administered to the women; it took approximately two hours to complete. Both of the investigators are women and either they or three research assistants, also women, did the interviewing.

Knowledge and Attitudes Concerning Menstruation

It might be expected that modern young women, exposed to a good deal of factual information about the menstrual cycle would be knowledgeable about it, but this is not necessarily the case. In one recent study of thirty-five white middle-class girls, for example, all, had had access to a good deal of information about menstruation and they considered themselves to be quite knowledgeable on the

Reprinted by permission of the authors from *International Journal of Women's Studies*. Vol. 1, 1978, pp. 64-72.

subject. When questioned, however, it was evident that they had little understanding of the internal female organs and how they function; they seemed "...unable to assimilate the education material about anatomy and physiology. They were best informed about the hygienic aspects of the process [reinforced, the authors believed, by advertisements from companies manufacturing feminine products], and seemed mainly concerned about what to do when a menstrual period occurred." (3) Significantly, the majority of the girls described menstruation as "like a sickness," and strongly associated it with excretory soiling. Mexican-American women in Southern Arizona echo the same feeling when they describe the menstruating woman as one *esta enferma*, "she is sick." (4)

Cultural background may play an important part in shaping attitudes toward menstruation as a multi-ethnic study has shown. (5) Investigators from the University of Miami School of Medicine interviewed women from the five largest ethnic populations in Miami, Florida; Bahamians, Cubans, Haitians, Puerto Ricans and Southern U.S. Blacks, asking a series of questions to determine their understanding of and feelings about the menses. The first question, "Why do women menstruate?" brought a response from a majority of Bahamians, Cubans, Haitians and Puerto Ricans that it was to rid the body of "unclean" or waste or "unnecessary" blood; the majority of the Southern black women said that they did not know.

The results of our study also showed that the women interviewed were generally unaware of the real function of the menstrual cycle. We asked three questions, 1. Where does menstrual blood come from?, 2. Why do menstrual periods begin when they do?, and 3. Why do menstrual periods stop when they do? Just over half of the women even mentioned the uterus in their reply to the first question: instead they gave vague answers ("up there somewhere"), incorrect ones ("from the ovaries," "from the tubes") or stated that they did not know. Even fewer women were able to correctly answer questions about the onset (25%) or cessation (35%) of menstrual flow; only 5 women mentioned the shedding of the uterine lining.

Their lack of knowledge was not surprising considering that most of them (63%) had no knowledge of menarche prior to the event. One young patient brought up in the hills of West Virginia was horrified at her first menstruation and spent an afternoon in an outdoor privy reciting a "bloodstopping" verse from the Bible, (7) when that did not work she shamefacedly went to her aunt to tell her that she was "hurt down there." This patient also exemplified the belief of many of the women that menstruation is a topic not discussed by nice people, to the point that she felt it is "a sin and a shame" for a menstruating woman to go out in public. The women's shame and embarrassment at being expected to discuss such an intimate topic with male physicians was considerable. A year after the event, the same young woman mentioned a number of times her mortification at having had to go to the Emergency Room of a local hospital when she suffered a vaginal hemorrhage; " ... I just couldn't help it."

Menstruation and Uncleanliness

The association made by the young girls of menstruation and excretion has already been mentioned, as has the feeling of many of the Miami women that the purpose of menstruation is to rid the body of unclean matter. This view of menstruation as a process whose main purpose is to rid the body of impurities was a major theme in our study as well. Many of the women viewed the uterus as a hollow or-gan which is tightly closed between periods as it fills with tainted blood and then opens to allow the blood to be released as menstrual flow. A statement by one woman shows the belief that the uterus opens and closes to let substances in (semen) and out (menstrual blood, babies): she felt that a preg-nant woman could not contract a venereal disease during pregnancy because at that time "the uterus is closed and germs cannot enter."

It seems clear that many women associate menstruating with a process of systemic cleansing, and further correlate bodily cleanliness with good health. The corollary, that bodily *uncleanliness* is associ-ated with disease was also demonstrated by beliefs about the causes of venereal disease. This proved to be quite a taboo topic, one which many women said they usually did not discuss; two women, in fact, re-fused to answer any questions about it at all. One third of those who did, however, gave "dirt" as a cause of venereal disease; wearing dirty undergarments, living in a dirty house, or failing to bathe after a men-strual period. In their efforts to keep the body clean both externally and internally, then, many of the women reported what most health professionals would see as an over-dependence on douching. Thirty of the forty women do douche, and of these, nineteen (63%) do so one or more times a week. Such vig-orous douching may actually contribute to health problems, not prevent them. (7)

Menstruation and Female Weakness

The majority of the women interviewed believed that uterine blood loss contributes to a state of vul-nerability for a woman, whether this is menstrual flow or the bleeding associated with a miscarriage, an abortion or childbirth. They therefore practiced a number of avoidances which they believed would promote better health. Most of the respondents, for example, said that a woman should avoid climbing or strenuous household tasks at such times, for, as one woman put it, "Your female organs are working hard enough, why work 'em to death? "

There was a strong association between health problems and the uterus being "open": if it is open to let the blood *out*, that is, it might be possible for some unwanted agent, cold air, water or disease, to come *in*. One young Mexican-American woman went so far as to say that during menstruation "the uterus is open, so don't go to a funeral or you can catch cancer". She believed that the "germs" of whatever caused the death of the individual might enter the open uterus and produce disease.

Illnesses due to evil magic were also mentioned; several black women expressed their fear that their own menstrual blood could be used against them by witchcraft at a time when they were espe-cially vulnerable. One woman interviewed during a preliminary phase of the study went so far as to burn all her used menstrual pads, sincerely believing that they could be used by an enemy to turn her into a snake! During a study in a black neighborhood in another part of the country, in fact, one of the authors was constantly admonished to take precautions in disposing of menstrual pads or tampons, lest she be "cut down" by her own menstrual blood in the hands of a sorcerer. (8)

Intercourse During Menstruation

The women were asked if they thought it all right to engage in intercourse during menstruation and most (63%) vehemently said that it was not: "Even an animal won't do that!" This informant said that in the Appalachian neighborhood where she was raised, such a practice was used to characterize the most "low-down trashy kind" of people: "They probably do it while she's on her period!"

Only one woman we interviewed gave messiness as a reason for the proscription. Five others believed that it is the time when a woman is most likely to become pregnant, believing that as the uterus is open the sperm are free to enter. Most women, however, cited health problems as the reason for their avoidance, blaming such a practice for promoting cramps, increased menstrual flow, hemorrhage, infections, or even uterine cancer. The theme of uncleanliness was again apparent; as one woman put it, "You're supposed to be cleaning yourself *out*, not getting dirty!"

No matter what the rationales given, however, the avoidance of intercourse during the menses has important implications for family planning. The woman who mistakenly believes she is most likely to become pregnant at that time and therefore believes that she is "safe" at midcycle is a prime candidate for an unwanted pregnancy. The woman who strongly feels that it is wrong to have intercourse during menstruation may avoid or stop using effective methods such as oral contraceptives or the IUD which may alter the menstrual cycle by breakthrough bleeding, spotting, or increased flow.

Menstruation and "Cold"

Most health problems mentioned, however, had to do with the fear of "cold" entering the body, either cold air or cold water, and causing the flow to stop. The same woman who feared that she might be turned into a snake, in fact, reported the death of a girlhood friend foolhardy enough to bathe during the menses:

> No, I don't think you should bathe. When I was growin' up my girlfriend she died from bathin' during her menstruating period. They say it stops you, stops your womb up or some-thin' up there, the water does. She was taking a bath during her menstruating period and she died in the tub. Another reason I don't think you should be in too much water is you'll catch cold. You'll catch cold because your veins are open. (9)

The belief that cold will stop menstrual flow is a remnant of the classical humoral pathology of Galen and Hippocrates, where the body was thought to be composed of four "humors;" blood, phlegm, black and yellow bile, each humor associated with heat or cold, wetness or dryness. Blood, seen as hot and wet, was thought opposed to and therefore coagulated by anything cold. Such cold was found in air, water, certain herbs and medicines, and in various foodstuffs. This Hot/Cold theory of disease is still found in many parts of the world, especially in Latin-American cultures. (10) More than a third of our informants (38%) believed that some form of cold may stop up menstrual flow and result in life-threatening health problems. They believed that if the normal menstrual flow did not take place it would "back up" in the body to cause a stroke, insanity, or the much-feared "quick TB," a malady especially common in Southern folk belief. (11) All of these things are believed possible to occur if the menstruating woman bathes, shampoos her hair, gets caught in the rain or goes barefoot in wet grass; as one of our informants put it "When you're on your period you're not supposed to wash your hair, take a bath—that'll cause quick TB. You're not supposed to run around barefooted; there again the dampness, quick TB...And goin' out in the rain, that's a death sign right there, quick TB. And you'll get cold so quick in your female organs; they're weak and you get cold in 'em." (12) The association between tuberculosis and impeded menstruation has a long background in the history of medicine, and it should be recalled that the menstrual periods *may* stop in advanced cases of untreated tuberculosis, so the observation may be correct even if the interpretation is not. (13) A correlation between tuberculosis and cold and diseases of women is even made explicit in a 1977 almanac:

> *February's Diseases.* In the North, February is the coldest month of the Winter. It offers new opportunities for catching cold and starting pneumonia and consumption. Rheumatism, sleeplessness, constipation and female troubles begin this month. (14)

The young woman mentioned as so horrified because she had had to consult a physician while hemorrhaging vaginally (and whose symptoms eventuated in a hysterectomy at age 28) blamed her health problems on, as a teenager, ignoring the advice of her grandmother and going out in the rain while menstruating.

The fear that cold may halt menstrual flow and impair the health of the woman is responsible for a number of dietary changes for some women as well. Many Latin-American women, for example, classify certain foods as "cold" (irrespective of actual temperature) and believe that they must not be eaten during menstruation. (15) Unfortunately, these foods usually include citrus fruits, melons, tomatoes, and green, leafy vegetables; all important vitamin sources in the traditional Latin diet, already deficient in vitamins. Black and Southern white women may also avoid citrus fruits, vinegar, pickles and other astringent foods in the belief that they are "drying" and may therefore clot menstrual blood.

The belief that health is jeopardized if the menstrual flow is impeded may also cause anxiety if, as commonly happens, use of oral contraceptives results in lessened flow, or even amenorrhea. "I guess I get nervous because I wonder where the flow is going. It might back up," said one of the women in the Florida study; "Where is the bad blood going to be stored?" asked another. (16) Such a belief ultimately resulted in an unwanted pregnancy for one of the women in our study, and her case illustrates what too often happens when a woman and her physician do not really communicate. Mrs. L., the young woman who blamed her hysterectomy on failure to observe menstrual taboos as a youngster, initially came to the clinic because she was so dissatisfied with the care given her by her private physician. She had been brought up to believe that discussion of bodily functions is not nice, and she was particularly ashamed at discussing sexual matters with her male gynecologist. She was given an oral contraceptive after the birth of her second child, but became alarmed when her periods ceased:

... he put me on birth control pills and I couldn't take 'em, and I really got worried when he took me off 'em. They made me a nervous wreck, they made me scream and yell, I wasn't content, I was grumpy, I was just a mess. My periods stopped, completely stopped; in three months time I wasn't even havin' a period. And that right there in itself will just about make a woman go insane! Well, I was always told and heard that if a woman doesn't have a period and isn't pregnant that really drives 'em nuts, it gets on their nerves real bad. Makes 'em just lose their mind. And I *think* that's just about what I was ready to *do*! And I went in and he took me off of those pills.

She was too embarrassed to tell the doctor that she wanted another method of contraception, believing that he should "know" it because she "tried so hard to take those pills!" On her own she began using contraceptive foam as it was available without a prescription; unfortunately, she thought that its action was as a sticky substance "to catch the sperm," and she douched it out immediately after intercourse. Of course, she was soon pregnant again, a fact which she blamed on her unknowing doctor.

Miscellaneous Folk Beliefs About Menstruation

Some women also voiced beliefs about menstruation which serve to identify the process as a negative one. What should be viewed as a perfectly normal female function is still seen as something placing the woman herself in a dangerous situation or exerting a negative effect on her immediate environment. The first of these beliefs has distinctly Freudian overtones; it is that certain reptiles are attracted by the smell of menstrual blood and may chase menstruating women foolish enough to be outdoors. One study of Mexican American women in West Texas describes their fear of snakes (*chirrioneros*) and lizards (*axolotls*) which can invade the body of the woman to simulate a pregnancy and cause her to give birth to litters of the creatures. (17) Although pronounced slightly differently, several of our Mexican-American patients similarly expressed fear of the *chirrionera*, which "whistles as it jumps from tree to tree" following the menstruating woman, or the *ajolote*, which may impregnate the woman or "eat the woman up on the inside and cause her to die." One black patient also stated that a menstruating woman should stay out of the fields lest a male "whip snake" chase her and "whip her to death."

The idea that the menstruating woman is a vile creature whose very presence will wilt flowers, kill crops, render cattle barren and generally pollute anything and everything she comes in contact with has, of course, been around for centuries. (18) Still, it is startling to read in a recent publication that "A swarm of bees will die at once if even looked upon by a menstrous woman." (19) It is sadder still to hear women report that *they themselves*, while menstruating, feel that they cannot can tomatoes (the jars will explode), work in the garden (the cucumber vines will die), or pick up a newborn baby (it will cause the baby to have cramps).

Several recent studies, in fact, have demonstrated that premenstrual and menstrual symptoms, both emotional and physical, are at least in part brought about by women's (and society's) expectations that they will occur. Paige has pointed out, for example, that Protestant, Catholic and Jewish women differ "...considerably in their attitudes toward menstruation and sex and in their levels of anxiety during their periods." (20) A University of Illinois study of twenty-four middle class *couples*, however, demonstrated that changes in mood were *not* correlated with the menstrual cycle for the women and that their husbands showed just as much variation in affect as their wives; we do not, of course, look for signs of premenstrual tension in men. (21) Finally, an experiment has shown that symptoms can actually be brought on by expectations; "...women who were led to believe that they were premenstrual [when they were not] reported experiencing a significantly higher degree of several physical symptoms, such as water retention, than did women who were led to believe they were intermenstrual." (22) We are, it seems, victims of our own folklore.

Summary and Conclusions

The responses of a group of forty Michigan women interviewed about their knowledge of the female reproductive cycle has revealed that they were naive and misinformed about the true function of menstruation. They were unable to identify the origin of menstrual blood, or to state why menstrual periods start or stop. They identified the menstrual function with cleaning out the body, and seemed to have little awareness of its connection with female fertility. They were in the main concerned that sexual intercourse not take place during the menses, mistakenly believing that they were more likely to get pregnant at that time, or that it would result in health problems for them. They were greatly concerned about the supposed effect of "cold" upon menstruation, believing that a bath, a shampoo, a walk in the dew or in the rain might "back up" menstrual flow to result in a stroke, insanity, or "quick TB." They often believed that eating "cold" or "drying" foods during menstruation would have the same effect, thereby depriving themselves of important nutrients. They seemed to see themselves in a very negative light, agreeing with ancient and traditional views of menstruating women as dirty, vile and polluting creatures whose very presence is a blight.

The majority of these beliefs, of course, are simply not true. Cold air, water or food will *not* stop a menstrual period; lessened menstrual flow is *not* a stopped-up sink, it will *not* "back up" to appear as a tubercular hemorrhage. Intercourse during menstruation should be strictly a matter of preference between the two partners, and should not be viewed as a hazard to either. The menstruating woman will *not* cause a new baby to cramp, ruin the canning, spoil the cooking, or lay waste an entire garden. She is *not* the prey of snakes and lizards, lying in wait in their burrows for her to pass by. She will *not* cause the death of a swarm of bees, nor do the "germs" of cancer wait to fly from a coffin into her open uterus. Her menstrual blood cannot be used by a witch to harm her.

She is, of course, merely expressing a particular phase in a hormonal cycle, and should be viewed only in that light. It is up to all of us to teach our daughters—after we believe it ourselves—that they are not dirty, weak, vile or vulnerable, they are women. We cannot make the next generation comfortable with menstruation, however, until we are comfortable with it ourselves.

Notes

(1) Loudell F. Snow, "Folk Medical Beliefs and their Implications for Care of Patients," *Annals of Internal Medicine*, 81 (1974), 82-96.

(2) Alice H. Murphree, "Folk Beliefs," in *The Health of a Rural County*, eds. Richard C. Reynolds, Sam A. Banks, and Alice H. Murphree (Gainesville: The University Presses of Florida, 1976), pp. 111- 123.

(3) Lynn Whisnant and Leonard Zegans, "A Study of Attitudes Toward Menarche in White Middle-Class American Adolescent Girls," *American Journal of Psychiatry*, 132, 8 (1975), 809-814.

(4) Margarita A. Kay, "Health and Illness in a Mexican American Barrio," in *Ethnic Medicine in the Southwest*, ed. Edward H. Spicer (Tucson: University of Arizona Press, 1977), pp. 96-150.

(5) Clarissa Scott, "The Relationship between Beliefs about the Menstrual Cycle and Choice of Fertility Regulating Methods within Five Ethnic Groups," *International Journal of Gynaecology and Obstetrics*, 13 (1975), 105-109.

(6) Loudell F. Snow, "Folk Medical Beliefs," pp. 82-96: and Alice H. Murphree, pp. 111-123.

(7) H.H. Neuman and A. Decherney, "Douching and Pelvic Inflammatory Disease," *New England Journal of Medicine*, 195 (1976), 789.

(8) Loudell F. Snow, "Popular Medicine in a Black Neighborhood," in *Ethnic Medicine in the Southwest*, pp. 19-95.

(9) Loudell F. Snow, "Folk Medical Beliefs," pp. 82-96.

(10) Margaret Clark, *Health in the Mexican-American Culture*, 2nd ed., (Berkeley: University of California Press, 1970); and Alan Harwood, "The Hot-Cold Theory of Disease. Implications for Treatment of Puerto Rican Patients," *Journal of the American Medical Association*, 216 (1971), 1153-1158.

(11) Vance Randolph, *Ozark Superstitions*, (New York: Columbia University Press, 1947), p. 195; and Ellen Stekert, "Focus for Conflict: Southern Mountain Medical Beliefs in Detroit," in *The Urban Experience and Folk Tradition*, eds. Americo Paredes and Ellen Stekert (Austin: University of Texas Press, 1971), pp. 95-127

(12) Loudell F. Snow and Shirley M. Johnson, "Modern Day Menstrual Folklore," *Journal of the American Medical Association*, 237 (1977), 2736-2739.

(13) Loudell F. Snow, "Old-Fashioned Medicine is Still With Us," *The Osteopathic Physician*, 43 (1976), 51-64.

(14) *MacDonald's Farmers Almanac 1977*, (Binghamton: Atlas Printing Company, 1976).

(15) Margarita A. Kay, pp. 96-150; Margaret Clark,; and Alan Harwood, pp. 1153-1158.

(16) Clarissa Scott, pp. 105-109.

(17) Rosan Jordan, "A Note About Folklore and Literature (The Bosom Serpent Revisited)," *Journal of American Folklore*, 86 (1973), 62-65.

(18) Karen Paige, "Women Learn to Sing the Menstrual Blues," *Psychology Today*, 7 (1973), 41-46.

(19) *MacDonald's Astrological Dream Book*, (Binghampton: Atlas Printing Company, 1972).

(20) Karen Paige, pp. 41-46.

(21) Alice J. Dan, "Behavioral Variability and the Menstrual Cycle," paper presented at the annual convention, American Psychological Association, 1976.

(22) Diane N. Ruble, "Premenstrual Symptoms: a Reinterpretation," *Science*, 197 (1977), 291-292.

MENSTRUATION:
ATTITUDES AND EXPERIENCE OF INDIAN SOUTH AFRICANS

Brian M. du Toit
University of Florida

With few exceptions, studies in the climacteric and research on menopause have been clinical in nature and frequently pertained to endocrinological imbalances. However, a growing number of studies by trained social scientists are appearing. In some cases these are ethnographic studies (e.g., Maoz 1973; Flint 1974; Davis 1983; Beyene 1984; and Lock 1986) while others are survey and/or theoretical in nature (e.g., Bart 1979; Datan et al. 1981; Brown 1982; Kaufert 1982; du Toit and Suggs 1983; Lock 1985; McKinlay and McKinlay 1985; du Toit 1986; Beyene 1986). Valuable groundwork for these latter studies were done by others, frequently psychologists. Researchers and writers have benefitted from the work of Neugarten et al. (1963), Bart (1972), Gutmann (1977), Maoz and Durst (1979), Cooke and Greene (1981), and the continued questions and contributions of these and other scholars. Currently the most exciting work is done when persons representing different disciplines and working together, frequently in a cross-cultural context, share information and data analysis. It is rewarding to ask sociological and anthropological questions about the social aspects of aging and the climacteric specifically. It is also informative to get the social significance of physiological events and changes as these frequently underlie changes in the social status of persons.

The data for this paper were collected during a year's fieldwork in southern Africa and form part of a team project. During 1984-85, five communities were simultaneously studied.[1] Each member of the research team administered the use of identical interview schedules developed for this project, following the same temporal and topical sequence in the process. For each research population a total of 60 women were selected, of whom 30 were premenopausal and 30 were postmenopausal (the latter category being definitionally limited to a condition resulting from natural aging and ovarian failure, rather than resulting from surgery). While the research samples are relatively small, they provide tremendous depth due to the nature and scope of the topics covered in the structured interviews. The product, then, consists of quantitative and qualitative material containing specific data on each of the particular sites, and comparative data on rural, urban, and ethnic communities situated in the southern tier of Africa.

This paper pertains to only one of the five communities studied namely the Indian women, predominantly resident in Laudium on the outskirts of Pretoria, Transvaal. [The reader will find good general discussions of Indian South Africans in Kuper (1960) and Meer (1969)].

Reprinted by permission of the editors from *Ethnology*, Vol. XXVII, 1988, pp. 391-406.

The project under discussion attempted to move away from the biomedical model in the clinical setting to a cultural-behavioral model in the home and social setting. The project furthermore envisioned comparing data from third world situations while contrasting variables such as rural-urban, religion, language, etc. It had recently been emphasized that "information from developing countries in particular is scanty; there are virtually no data on such basic matters as the age distribution of the menopause; and little is known about the socio-cultural significance of the menopause in different settings" (The Lancet 1982). In a different context Utian (1980:114-115) points out that "the response to menopause is modified by many factors, one important one being the socio-cultural environment... Certainly, far more attention needs to be directed at the socio-cultural aspects of menopause and much more recognition given to its role in the overall mechanism of symptom production."

Some of the questions addressed by the research, but not dealt with in this discussion, are the extent to which variations in family (of orientation and procreation) and household have an affect on the menopausal experience. Are postmenopausal women recognized as a distinct category in the society? What is the importance of socialization by parents, siblings or cultural surrogates regarding menopause? To what extent are menopausal symptoms the result of socio-cultural influences; and what are these influences? Do women experience the "hot flash" and other common symptoms in African societies (cf. Moore 1981)?

The Sample

In order to arrive at a research sample, the writer contacted a social worker who had an office attached to the local hospital. She explained the nature of the research to women who came to her as well as to many women she knew in the community. In time they introduced the writer to friends and in this way networks were used to select case studies. Due to the religious, linguistic, and economic heterogeneity of the Indian population, a conscious effort was made to select women who were representative of these categories. However the major criteria forced a selection of younger women who were married (this is a normal and expected status in the Indian community) and were menstruating regularly, as well as a group who were postmenopausal. This group included women who had not been subject to surgical menopause. These women should have reached natural menopause and not menstruated for at least twelve months prior to being interviewed.

On this basis 30 women in each category were selected but for a variety of reasons some of these women did not complete the year-long study. The final sample contained 29 pre- and 27 postmenopausal women. General information was available on many more. The women included in this phase of the project included 42 married, 13 widowed, and one divorced woman. The majority, 39 women, had been born in Transvaal but four came from India. Among the premenopausal category the oldest is 48 and the youngest is 34. The mean age is 41.8 while the median is 43. In the postmenopausal category the range is quite extensive, the oldest being 75 and the youngest 42. However, the next youngest is 50. The mean age of the postmenopausal category is 60 while the median is 61. Formal education, especially for the previous generation represented by most postmenopausal women, was limited for girls and most girls were taken out of school (especially if these were co-educational) on experiencing menarche. The result is that among the premenopausal women all had some schooling but only five (17 per cent) had more than twelve years of schooling. Among the postmenopausal women only one (3.7 per cent) had more than twelve years of schooling and seven had no schooling at all.

Many Indian South Africans now use English or Afrikaans, the two official languages of the country, as the home language, the latter particularly in the Transvaal where this study was conducted. The home languages of the 56 informants represent the linguistic universe, namely Tamil (13), Gujerati (11), English (11), Maemen (10), Afrikaans (8), and Hindi (3).

While Christianity, especially in the form of Pentecostalism, has made some inroads, particularly among lower socio-economic groups, most Indians are Hindu or Muslim (Oosthuizen 1975). Religiosity varies and some women indicated they were nominal members of some religion while others were more committed and active. This sample consists of 26 Hindu, 25 Muslims, and five Christians. It is of interest that four of the five Christians are Roman Catholic or Anglican and only one belongs to a Pentecostal church.

Method of Research

The interview schedules used in this cross-cultural research project were divided into four sets of structured questions, some yielding quantitative data, others qualitative information. The first dealt essentially with family background and socialization; the second with being a woman and coping networks; the third interview explored life style and life course; the final interview dealt with the women's medical history, climacteric beliefs, menopausal symptoms and sexuality. These interviews were done sequentially. Thus each woman was interviewed at least four times during the course of a year. This increased acquaintance between subject and researcher and facilitated communication and trust.

In dealing with certain questions there obviously was greater need for recall than in others. This pertained to family history, socialization, and menarche. In other questions, such as those regarding menstruation and associational conditions, women in the premenopausal category could recount experience while those in the postmenopausal category had to rely on memory. Women were always interviewed in their homes where they felt comfortable and confident. They were always interviewed alone and if some other person entered, the interview was temporarily halted.

In an attempt at maximizing the comparative value of these research results, findings are here compared with data presented by Marcha Flint (1974) in her study of Rajput Indian women. However, Flint dealt extensively with menarche and also compared menopause as it occurs in two categories of women, those living at middle altitude in Himachal Pradesh as compared to those living at low altitude in Rajasthan. Comparative data (e.g., in Tables 1 and 2 below) will not differentiate these ecological variables. Further comparative data come from Sharma and Saxena (1981) who deal specifically with climacteric symptoms, a topic to be explored elsewhere. These authors, however, correctly point out that "almost no research on this subject has been carried out in the third-world countries" (Sharma and Saxena 1981:11).

Table 1
Duration of Menstrual Periods in Days

Category of Subjects	Under 3 Days		3-5 Days		6-7 Days		>7 Days		N.R.		Total
	#	%	#	%	#	%	#	%	#	%	
Premenopausal	2	6.9	16	55.1	6	20.6	2	6.8	3	10.3	26
Postmenopausal	-	-	18	66.6	6	22.2	1	3.7	2	7.4	25
All Subjects* (du Toit)	2	3.6	34	60.7	12	21.4	3	5.4	5	8.9	51
All Subjects (Flint)	67	13.9	294	61.5	107	22.3	11	2.3	-	-	479

*There were 2 (7.4 per cent) postmenopausal and 3 (10.3 per cent) premenopausal women who did not respond.

Table 2
Menstruation Cycle Length of Subjects

Category of Subjects	27 Days & Under		28-30 Days		31 Days & Over		N.R.		Total
	#	%	#	%	#	%	#	%	
Premenopausal	5	17.1	23	79.3	-	-	1	3.4	29
Postmenopausal	4	14.8	17	62.9	-	-	6	22.2	27
All Subjects* (du Toit)	9	16.2	40	71.4	-	-	7	12.5	56
All Subjects (Flint)	46	9.6	412	85.8	22	4.6	-	-	480

The Menstrual Event

Traditional societies have long recognized the significance of menstruation and have isolated women during flow either by limiting their activities or restricting them through isolation. This has also been true in the history of Western culture. The reasons for these taboos are based on diverse interpretations of cause and effect. These interpretations are based on biogenic, psychogenic, and sociogenic explanations.

Biogenic Explanations

Sir James George Frazer, in *The Golden Bough* (1945:606), refers to the Roman naturalist Pliny who warned about the effect a menstruous woman had in turning wine to vinegar, blighting crops, killing seedlings, bringing down fruit from trees, and causing other misfortunes. Frazer points out that at the time he was writing people in many parts of Europe held much the same beliefs and a menstruating woman would never be allowed to assist in making jam, brewing beer, making wine, or engaging in a range of such activities. Menstruating women were expected to withdraw from the kitchen and related household roles due to the contaminating nature of their condition.

Ashley-Montagu (1940:218) surveys a wide range of experimental evidence available at the time of his writing and concludes: "It would appear that menstruous women are capable of exerting noxious effects upon living tissues. The indications are that a substance excreted through the hands during menstruation, is the agent responsible. The evidence points to an alkylamine, probably trimethylamine."

According to Ashley-Montagu, earlier traditional societies would have recognized the correlation between the secretion of this substance and certain deleterious effects on plants and gardens, thus creating the menstrual taboos which required isolation of women during menstruation. How pastoralists came to associate menstruation and the need for isolation is not answered by this argument. However, hunters and pastoralists may be classified together by Kitahara's (1982) discussion, below.

A closely related theory is that developed by Clellan Ford (1945). His is one of the first studies utilizing the Human Relations Area Files, and he based his conclusions on evidence derived from 64 randomly selected societies. Ford (1945) states that the taboo on sexual intercourse during menstruation is nearly universal, as is the belief that the woman is unable to control the flow of blood by muscular tension. For this reason she cannot prevent the discharge from coming into contact with various objects. This latter problem is dealt with by three major solutions:

> First, such contact can be automatically avoided by secluding the woman herself during her period. Second, even if the woman is not strictly isolated, contact with her discharge can be greatly minimized by severely restricting her activities through the imposition of specific taboos. Third, the problem can be solved by providing the woman with an efficient means of collecting, concealing, and disposing of the menstrual fluid... the more efficient the methods available to a woman for collecting, concealing, and disposing of her menstrual discharge, the less necessary it will be to isolate her or to paralyze her activities with severe restrictions (Ford 1945:17-18).

Psychogenic Explanations

Stephens (1961:391) tests the hypothesis he framed as follows: "The extensiveness of menstrual taboos observed in a primitive society is determined (to a significant extent) by the average intensity of castration anxiety felt by men in that society." He immediately admits that there is, of course, no way of directly measuring the intensity of this anxiety, so he derives several ways of testing the hypothesis with related measures derived from psychoanalytic theory.

Based on a test of this hypothesis Stephens (1961) concludes that the dominant belief in a majority of societies is that menstruating women are dangerous to men, though they are never dangerous to other women. In this conclusion Stephens, along with most earlier anthropologists, errs, assuming that women were secluded during menstruation and the postpartum period because they were dangerous to men. Faithorn (1975:132), discussing the Kafe of the Papua New Guinea highlands, points out that men and women are taught the dangers of pollution and that "they may also threaten or contaminate others of the same sex, or even themselves." Her point, which is well taken, is that earlier researchers emphasized the woman as the polluting agent instead of recognizing that substances "out of proper context, can be polluting" (Faithorn 1975:138). (See also, in a different contextual discussion, Douglas 1966.)

In a psychoanalytic argument, Stephens (1961) suggests that the menstrual taboo continuum is really a range of the intensity of the fear men experience in regard to women who experience menstrual bleeding. The sight or knowledge of the menstruous woman would, according to Stephens, awaken in the male a castration anxiety. The major aim of Stephens' study is to prove the universal presence of the Oedipus complex. The author suggests that the greater the intensity of castration anxiety felt by men, the more elaborate would be the menstrual taboos. Total isolation of women in menstrual huts and accompanying taboos on contact would then be matched by the greater intensity of castration anxiety. This total isolation coincides with Ford's (1945) idea according to which the greater the fear of blood and infection, the lower the status of women would be.

Montgomery (1974) also employs a psychogenic approach to explain menstrual taboos. Using Bettelheim's hypothesis of vagina envy as a point of departure, she (Montgomery 1974:149) suggests "that the degree to which a man is regarded and regards himself to be integral to the processes of procreation and to the sexual functions of women will modify the ambivalence and jealousy he feels toward those functions." Using this hypothesis, she expects to find that the greater the amount of participation (ideologically and behaviorally) by men in procreation, the lower the number and intensity of menstrual taboos. A point she does not mention is that empirical data on the male role in procreation is a product of scientific education. Furthermore, a shift from the traditional orientation both of individuals and societies tends to be coincident with a rise in the status of women.

Montgomery also uses the Human Relations Area Files to survey the number and kinds of menstrual taboos observed by 44 societies. She develops a series of six menstrual taboos that are seen as cumulative and therefore arranged sequentially. These are:

1.   Menstrual fluid is unpleasant, contaminating, or dangerous.

2.   Menstruants may not have sexual intercourse.

3.   Personal restrictions are imposed upon the menstruants, such as food taboos, restriction of movement, talking, etc.

4. Restrictions are imposed upon contact made by menstruants with men's things; i.e., personal articles, weapons, implements used in agriculture and fishing, craft tools, men's crops, and religious emblems and shrines, where men are the guardians.

5. Menstruants may not cook for men.

6. Menstruants are confined to menstrual huts for the duration of their periods (Montgomery 1974:152).

The result of her survey confirms the cumulative pattern of the taboos. Thus, when a certain category number was scored as being present in a certain society (provided that all the information was available) none of the lower categories were ever absent.

Sociogenic Explanations

A theoretical approach that has much in common with the psychogenic explanation, but avoids the psychoanalytical bases and places heavier emphasis on the social component, was employed by Young and Bacdayan (1965). These authors correlated menstrual taboos and male solidarity; i.e., the maintenance by all males in a society of a unified definition of their situation expressed through such institutions as men's houses, male secret societies, age-grades, and the like. When such positive correlations are present, these authors see it as part of the structural characteristic they designate as rigidity. The rigidity of a society will vary depending on other social conditions.

> If social rigidity is defined as the relative lack of intercommunication among the parts of the system, then a group wherein men and women are sharply separated, as measured either by male solidarity or by menstrual taboos, is clearly rigid. Perhaps the extreme pole of this dimension would be a community where all families are isolated and there is no communication even within sex or generation groups. At the other end we can imagine a community that is highly solidary with free intercommunication among all subgroups. In the midst of revolutionary fervor, high-status groups may accept the Indian or the untouchable as "brothers," and for a time status boundaries may be overridden. Women frequently benefit from such solidarity movements, as events in underdeveloped countries attest (Young and Bacdayan (1965:230-231).

Rigidity, then, is both effect and cause of the status of women. As the women gain status due to a variety of factors, communication increases and rigidity decreases. If such causal factors disappear, communication can break down, segregation can be reinstated, and rigidity will increase. Whether menstrual taboos, once abandoned, can be reinstated is questionable.

Recently Kitahara (1982) has suggested that there might be a correlation between menstrual taboos and hunting. As the importance of hunting as a subsistence base increases so will the taboos to exclude women because the menstrual odor will negatively affect hunting. The author refers here to the odor of menstrual blood not in the way Ashley-Montagu (1940) discussed it but as being equivalent to the odor of venous blood (Nunley 1981) which produced an avoidance response by white-tailed deer. In his statistical analysis, Kitahara finds an association between menstrual taboos and hunting but is quick to point out that this does not suggest any causal relationship. Instead he (Kita-hara 1982:903) argues for a combination of variables that are causally related, "For example, if the importance of hunting can really explain a portion of menstrual taboos, the degree of male solidarity is also a conceivable variable to be included in the model."

All of the authors discussed above dealt with the presence and causes of menstrual taboos in nu-merous societies. The origins may be bio-, psycho-, or sociogenic but they all assume the regular is-sue of blood. These taboos are present and influence the activities of women, though the taboos may be more or less rigid.

Obviously not every set of research data contains sufficient ethnographic detail to consider the varying theoretical approaches and explanations. The material in this study for instance does not con-tain a great deal on male solidarity, but we will return to this topic. This paper explores the experience of menstruation as an event, and the attitudes which surround this event, among a sample of Indian South African women.

The Menstrual Experience

The monthly flow of blood, frequently accompanied by physiological conditions of pain or tension and psychological conditions of stress or relief, is something many women experience on a regular basis. But the exact physiological and psychological states associated with premenstrual stress and menstruation, as well as the specifics about the event, may vary from woman to woman. It is well known that factors such as activity (Dale et al. 1979; Mathus et al. 1982), diet (e.g., nutritional defi-ciencies and anorexia nervosa), and life style influence the experience of menstruation. This paper explores how the experience (among premenopausal women) versus retrospect (among postmeno-pausal women) differed; i.e., how premenopausal women experience and view menstruation when they are compared with the recall of postmenopausal women in the same community. Since the regu-larity and duration of flow will vary through time, especially during the young years and again during the climacteric, research concentrated on the "regular" length of menstruation and the "normal" time interval between periods. When a woman indicated that she now was experiencing irregular flow, she was asked about the normal and regular experience.

The first question pertains to the number of days that the women experience bleeding. Table 1 shows that for most women, both the pre- and postmenopausal category, menstruation lasts between three and five days, yet there is some range and the range is greater among the younger women. The median and the mode is five.

Some women had comments on the number of days their menstruation lasts. Those who experi-ence flow for only two or three days believed they obviously have less blood than those for whom flow lasts seven or eight days, and the latter can thus anticipate greater suffering later when the blood exists no longer; i.e., menopause (see below). Most premenopausal women look forward to menopause when they will not have this monthly "bother," and yet, experiencing it now on a regular basis is reassuring that at least they are not pregnant.

Days between menstrual periods refer to the number of days between the onset of the menstrual flow and next time this event will occur. Table 2 lists this time interval. Here the median and the mode is 28.

Due to reasons of health, level of activity, diet, or other factors, a woman may experience associational conditions and other syndromes. One of the most common reported by subjects involves symptoms or complaints, usually referred to as the Pre-Menstrual Syndrome (Abraham 1980:170). Indian women complain of a heaviness, a bloated feeling, irritability, general crabbiness or tension frequently associated with headaches. This P.M.S. is more frequently reported by the premenopausal women where 75.9 per cent describe some form of irritability or discomfort. Only 51.9 per cent of the postmenopausal women described earlier experienced similar symptoms. (It needs to be repeated here that postmenopausal women were asked whether they had experienced these conditions while they were still menstruating.)

When asked about irregular menstrual periods, the postmenopausal women once again indicated that they had experienced them less than the younger ones. It is possible (though the research design attempted to avoid bias) that the figure for the older women is a product of selective memory. This same association may explain the experience of painful periods. Fewer young women indicate that this is a problem for them.

Heavy bleeding is seen to be quite evenly distributed among pre- and (upon recall) postmenopausal women and equally experienced. Bleeding between periods, either in the form of spotting or due to medical reasons is not common and, while a few of the postmenopausal women indicate that they had experienced it, this form of bleeding is not found among 83.9 per cent of the total sample.

One would expect infections of the reproductive organs to be a condition more common to the older generation. In part at least, this might be due to the living conditions many of them experienced. Prior to present arrangements, in which most persons live in private homes or apartments, either as owner or renting part of a very large structure, things were different. Many Indians lived in racial ghettos where overcrowding and lack of hygienic conditions were common. Antibiotics for treatment were either too costly or simply not available and many of the older women told of the pain and discomfort they had experienced and of a wealth of folk-cures they employed. Overall their social and economic conditions are much improved over what they were two or three decades ago. Table 3, however presents a different picture. Three of every four postmenopausal women denied having experienced infections of the reproductive tract, while more than half of the younger category of women indicated experiencing some infections. The fact that the postmenopausal women responded negatively to five of the six associational conditions suggests that they were healthier or that we are dealing with selective remembering and reporting. Table 3 presents the occurrence of associated conditions among the pre- and postmenopausal sample of women.

Table 3
Conditions Associated with Menstruation

	Premenopausal Women				Postmenopausal Women				All Women in Study			
	Yes		No		Yes		No		Yes		No	
Condition	#	%	#	%	#	%	#	%	#	%	#	Yes
PMS	22	75.9	7	24.1	14	51.9	13	48.1	36	64.3	20	35.7
Irregular Periods	10	34.5	19	65.5	5	18.5	22	81.5	15	26.8	41	73.2
Painful Periods	17	58.6	12	41.4	10	37.0	17	63.0	27	48.2	29	51.8
Heavy bleeding	13	44.8	16	55.2	12	44.4	15	55.6	25	44.6	31	55.4
In-between bleeding	7	24.1	22	75.9	2	7.4	25	92.6	9	16.1	47	83.9
Infections	17	58.6	12	41.4	6	22.6	21	77.8	23	41.1	33	58.9

Attitudes About Menstruation

The structured interview schedules included questions that dealt with aspects of menstruation as it relates to gender role and status (du Toit 1987a), birth control and sexuality (du Toit 1987b), aging, health, and so forth. In addition to quantitative data these questions generated valuable descriptive information.

One issue of interest was whether a woman has an advantage because she menstruates. Table 4 indicates that the majority of women do think so, with 81 per cent of the women in the postmenopausal category seeing menstruation as an advantage. The reasons given are that she can have children, that it is a cleansing process leaving the system healthy, that it indicates her youthfulness, and two younger women said it gives them a break from religious ritual because they were unclean. This reason, by the way, is identical to that held by postmenopausal women who gave a negative response to this question. They explained that it prevented them from praying, from lighting the (Hindu) lamp, from going to the (Muslim) mosque, or from assisting in washing the deceased in funerary preparations. It is interesting that when the same women were asked whether men had an advantage because they did not menstruate, 48 (85.7 per cent) replied in the affirmative. Men can go where they want, they are free to do anything, they are not restricted in the practices of religion or sex, and they do not have the monthly "bother."

Table 4
Does Wife Have an Advantage Because She Menstruates?

Population Category	Yes		No	
	#	%	#	%
Premenopausal women	19	65.5	10	34.5
Postmenopausal women	22	81.5	5	18.5
All women in sample	41	73.2	15	26.8

A further question in this context asked whether the physical signs of old age were caused by the fact that women no longer menstruated. As indicated in Table 5, there was a positive association between the cessation of menstruation and the onset of ailments and signs of old age, but the reasoning (see below) was of interest. As was the case in the earlier question, the postmenopausal women responded affirmatively to this question with greater frequency. This response was documented by the problems that befell women who no longer "lost blood" either by monthly bleeding or in "forming a fetus." The blood which now had to remain in the system caused the problems in health. Respondents also believed that postmenopausal women no longer "feel for a man" and most postmenopausal women either had their own beds or their own rooms.

Table 5
Sign of Age Caused by Cessation of Menstruation?

Population Category	Yes		No	
	#	%	#	%
Premenopausal women	16	55.2	13	44.8
Postmenopausal women	18	66.7	9	33.3
All women in sample	34	60.7	22	39.3

Since there were concerns about health, we expected that women who were in the menstrual period would be viewed as less healthy. This did not materialize as about a third saw them as less healthy and a third saw no difference, but this does not imply that they are not more susceptible to illness during this time of the month. Almost two-thirds of the total sample (this is also a direct reflection of both the pre- and postmenopausal categories) indicated they thought women were physically more susceptible while they were menstruating because they were losing blood or because the uterus was "open." Only seven (12.5 per cent) women thought that at this time women were less susceptible to illness.

Women who are menstruating are not supposed to participate in religious and ritual activities, but there was no stated taboo on them engaging in kitchen work (see Flint 1974:116 who found such a taboo among almost three-fourths of her Rajput subjects in India). When the research subjects were asked whether there are certain times when a woman should not have sexual intercourse, without exception all stated that sexual intercourse should be avoided during flow. The older women explained they had learned it was dangerous for a man or that venereal disease could be contracted or passed on. Younger women explained that it was "messy" or it "just doesn't seem clean." These findings confirm Flint's (Flint 1974:116) statement that the "most frequent taboo during the subjects' menstrual cycle is that of no sexual relations." In fact, about 94 per cent of Flint's subjects mentioned this taboo.

Why Do Women Menstruate?

In addition to questions exploring the stated reasons why women menstruate and why they stopped menstruating, a further question sought the cause of the permanent stopping of menstruation. Questions were phrased in such a way that respondents could give "scientific" or popular folk-derived responses without feeling intimidated. Most women saw menstruation as somehow related to a cleansing of the body ("system") as "old blood," impurities, or surplus blood leave the body. No fewer than twelve (44.4 per cent) post- and fourteen (48.2 per cent) premenopausal women offered this category of explanation. A common, related explanation is that the body is preparing for its natural condition of pregnancy. Five post- and four premenopausal women explained that it was God's doing, the way He made women, or as explained by Muslim women, "Allah told Eve not to eat from the tree but she did and that is why women are punished." One person explained old women used to use herbs to assist in the normal flow of menstruation and that her own generation bled normally. "Nowadays girls go to a doctor or to a clinic."

The reason for a woman to stop menstruating was invariably explained as due to pregnancy. Neither the mechanism nor the relationship to blood is clearly understood. There is a widely held suggestion that the blood goes to forming the fetus through clotting (and thus there is no more flow) subsequent to fertilization by the man. Menstruation is clearly identified with not being pregnant. The cessation of menstruation first raises the question of pregnancy and depending on the age of the woman, pride and joy or fear and shame. Age in this context of course implies status. The woman will have adult children and may even have a daughter-in-law living with her. Depending on the family and the particular woman, it will also imply position, marital status and economic security. Should such a woman become pregnant, the shame will be overwhelming. As a number of women explained, "you can't have a child the age of your grandchildren!" For the young woman who must satisfy her in-laws and her husband, pregnancy assures her status and security in the marriage. Most of the women in this research sample were in the first category and did not desire more children.

When menstruation has stopped and a doctor has confirmed that a woman is not pregnant, there is really a single emotion. Relief. When asked how women feel about not having their periods any more (in the case of women in the premenopausal category we phrased the question to refer to a future condition) twenty (69.0 per cent) of the 29 premenopausal and 21 (77.7 per cent) of the 27 postmenopausal women said, "relief." For some it is the end of an unpredictable period of heavy bleeding, for some it removes the danger of pregnancy, and for some it is proof to their husbands that they are now old and should no longer be expected to engage in sexual intercourse. There is a slight concern among premenopausal women that she now is "just a shell of a woman," or that she now will become bloated, overweight, or saddled with the diseases of old age (see below). Many of the older women are relieved because they now can participate more fully in the religion and ritual (both at home and in the temple or mosque). One younger woman said she would be "immensely relieved. On a recent pilgrimage to Mecca I had to take tablets so I wouldn't menstruate because you can't pray if you have your period."

The reason why women permanently stop menstruating is variously conceived and explained. Since Allah does not want Muslims to become pregnant at that age, they no longer experience menstruation. Since women as they age produce less and less blood, they finally produce the same amount as men and thus there is no surplus to shed. Since a woman has done her duty of having the children, the "eggs dry up," or the "sex organs lose their elasticity," or "the tubes become congested" (the latter explanation was given by a woman who had five D & Cs), or "the womb becomes weak and tired of bleeding every month." A postmenopausal woman explained that "after age 40 the womb becomes small and then closes. Now she can't have her periods nor feel for a man."

Folk Explanations Concerning Menstruation

A very interesting side effect of menstruation was mentioned by a large number of women, both pre- and postmenopausal. In spite of the relief that menopause brings and the bother caused by menstruation, the regular flow of blood is seen as healthy. It is only logical if a young woman loses blood, and a pregnant woman produces a child which utilized that blood, an old woman is somehow going to suffer because the blood does not come out in either of the previous two ways. As an older woman explained, "Bad blood needs to come out. Some have their period for six or seven days, others like me for only two. Most of these others later suffer with high blood [pressure] because they have too much blood."

Among the postmenopausal women only six (22.2 per cent) call menopause a natural, normal event that does not necessarily affect health. Among the premenopausal women sixteen (55.2 per cent) do not necessarily see a causal relation between menstruation and aging or ill health. Some referred to friends who were naturally menopausal at a younger age or surgically menopausal and who "still look young" or "look even lovelier." Two of the latter category of respondents, both nurses, explained that estrogen production stops and a third said aging is caused by hormones and sexual activity. "One who is sexually very active will look radiant and young."

But the majority of the research sample of 56 Indian women explained the kinds of ill health caused by old blood or the impurities that remained in the body. These include overweight with big breasts and a bloated stomach, frequently accompanied by breathlessness. Because the "blood doesn't flow," older women get varicose veins, because the "blood goes up" they get "high blood" (pressure), and because they have too much blood they have hot flashes. In fact twelve (44.4 per cent) of the postmenopausal sample indicate that they did experience hot flashes, some quite discomforting. Of these twelve women, five (41.7 per cent) experienced the flash particularly in the face (see Voda 1981). Other associational problems are "sugar" (diabetes), one person mentioned cancer,[2] another skin itch, and a third thought that such women get smaller. Very often women admit to feeling dizzy, sleepy, or sloppy.

Conclusion

In overview I would not attempt either a biogenic explanation, even though there is a taboo on kitchen activity during flow, or a psychogenic explanation, even though sexual intercourse is avoided during flow. This meets, in varying degrees, the first three taboos discussed by Montgomery (1974). Socio-genic explanations are perhaps easier to test and were convincing in confirmation. Indian society is characterized by male dominance and the domesticity subordination of women. This social rigidity, relative lack of communication between men and women, limited communication between different generations with resultant absence of anticipatory socialization at either menarche or menopause, created clear categories along age and gender lines. Menstruation is thus a clear social marker associated with womanhood, adulthood, reproduction, and health. Its cessation marks the absence of one or more of these. It is appropriate to say that as secularization and education increases, rigidity is decreasing, and formerly taboo subjects are now discussed not only among different age categories of the same gender, but also between members of different genders.

That a large number of Indian South African women included in this study made a rather logical connection between the flow of blood and health without the explanation of bio-scientific medical theory is interesting. Diseases normally more frequent in aging (particularly in persons who are not physically active) are related to blood and/or impurities that do not escape the body in the form of menstrual flow. However, looking back at the history of Western medicine, such logic should not seem strange. Early medical writers in Europe saw "menopause as a critical time, particularly for urban women, judging hysteria and cancer extremely common, both the result of the reflux of humors that could no longer escape through menstruation..." Slightly later it was advised that "women should combine resignation with frequent visits to a doctor, who would perform small bleedings against the possibility of hemorrhage" (Sterns 1976:88 and 89).

Notes

1 The project team consisted of the following members: Brian M. du Toit, who studied urban Indian women and served as director; David N. Suggs, who studied the Tswana women of Mochudi, Botswana and served as computer consultant; Thea de Wet who studied rural Afrikaner women; and Sona du Toit, who studied urban Afrikaner women. The urban Tswana component of this project was, unfortunately, never completed. We wish to express our deep-felt appreciation to each of the women who co-operated with us, as well as all those who assisted us.

2 Diabetes is very common among Indian South Africans. I am not aware of data regarding cancer among Indian women. The mean age for cancer of the cervix among Black women in this region is in fact 36.0 years (Fragoyannis et al. 1977:493).

References

Abraham, G. E. 1980. The Pre-Menstrual Tension Syndrome. *Contemporary Obstetric and Gynecologic Nursing,* ed. L. K. McNall Vol. III: pp. 5-39. New York.

Ashley-Montagu, M. F. 1940. Physiology and the Origins of the Menstrual Prohibitions. *The Quarterly Review of Biology* Vol. 15: pp. 211-220.

Bart, P. B. 1972. Depression in Middle-aged Women. *Readings on the Psychology of Women,* ed. J. M. Bardwick, pp. 134-142. New York.

Bart, P. 1979. Why Women's Status Change in Middle Age: The Turns of the Social Ferris Wheel. *Sociological Symposium:* 1, Fall.

Beyene, Y. 1984. An Ethnography of Menopause: Menopausal Experience of Mayan Women in a Yucatan Village. Unpublished Ph.D. dissertation. Case Western Reserve University, Cleveland, Ohio.

_____ 1986. Cultural Significance and Physiological Manifestations of Menopause: A Biocultural Analysis. *Culture, Medicine, and Psychiatry* 10:47-71.

Brown, J. K. 1982. Cross-Cultural Perspectives on Middle-Aged Women. *Current Anthropology* 23:143-148.

Cooke, J. D., and J. G. Greene. 1981. Types of Life Events in Relation to Symptoms of the Climacterium. *Journal of Psychosomatic Research* 25:5-11.

Dale, E., D. H. Gerlach, and A. L. Wilhite. 1979. Menstrual Dysfunction in Distance Runners. *Obstetrics and Gynecology* 54:47-53.

Datan, N., A. Antonovsky, and B. Maoz. 1981. A Time to Reap. *The Middle Age of Women in Five Israeli Subcultures.* Baltimore.

Davis, D. L. 1983. *Blood and Nerves: An Ethnographic Focus on Menopause.* Institute of Social and Economic Research, Memorial University of Newfoundland, St. John's.

Douglas, M. 1966. *Purity and Danger: An Analysis of the Concepts of Pollution and Taboo.* New York.

du Toit, B. M. 1986. The Cultural Climacteric in Cross-Cultural Perspective. *The Climacteric in Perspective,* eds. M. Notelovitz and P. van Keep, pp. 177-190. Lancaster.

_____ 1987a. Mothers and Grandmothers - Role Stability among Indian South Africans. Paper presented at the annual meetings of the Southern Anthropological Society, Atlanta, Georgia.

_____ 1987b. Sexuality and Family Planning among Indian South Africans. Paper presented at the annual meetings of the Society for Applied Anthropology, Oaxaca, Mexico.

du Toit, B. M., and D. Suggs. 1983. Menopause: A Sociocultural Definition. Florida *Journal of Anthropology* 8:1-23.

Faithorn, E. 1975. The Concept of Pollution among the Kafe of the Papua New Guinea Highlands. *Toward an Anthropology of Women,* ed. R. R. Reiter, pp. 127-140. New York.

Flint, M. P. 1974. Menarche and Menopause of Rajput Women. Unpublished Ph.D. dissertation, the City University of New York Graduate Center.

Ford, C. S. 1945. A Comparative Study of Human Reproduction. *Yale University Publications in Anthropology,* Number 32. New Haven.

Fragoyannis, S., C. Brits, and P. Griessel. 1977. Age Patterns of Tswana Women with Carcinoma of the Cervix. *S. A. Medical Journal* 52:493-494.

Frazer, J. G. 1954. *The Golden Bough*. (Abridged Edition). London.

Gutmann, D. 1977. The Cross-Cultural Perspective: Notes toward a Comparative Psychology of Aging. *Handbook of the Psychology of Aging*, ed. J. Birren and K. W. Schaie. New York.

Kaufert, P. 1982. Anthropology and the Menopause: The Development of a Theoretical Framework. *Maturitas* 4:181-193.

Kitahara, M. 1982. Menstrual Taboos and the Importance of Hunting. *American Anthropologists* 84:901-903.

Kuper, H. 1960. *Indian People in Natal*. Durban.

Lock, M. 1985. Models and Practice in Medicine: Menopause as Syndrome of Life Transition. *Physicians of Western Medicine*, eds. R. A. Hahn and A. D. Gaines, pp. 115-139. Boston.

_____ 1986. Ambiguities of Aging: Japanese Experience and Perceptions of Menopause. *Culture, Medicine and Psychiatry* 10:23-46.

Maoz, B. 1973. The Perception of Menopause in Five Ethnic Groups in Israel. Thesis, Leyden University.

Maoz, B., and N. Durst. 1979. Psychology of the Menopause. *Female and Male Climacteric*, eds. P. A. van Keep, D. M. Serr, and R. B. Greenblatt, pp. 9-16. New Baltimore.

Mathus, D. N., and A. L. Toriola. 1982. Age at Menarche in Nigerian Athletes. *British Journal of Sports Medicine* 16:250-252.

McKinlay, S., and J. McKinlay. 1985. Health Status and Health Care Utilization by Menopausal Women. *Aging, Reproduction and the Climacteric*. New York.

Meer, F. 1969. *A Portrait of Indian South Africans*. Durban.

Montgomery, R. E. 1974. A Cross-Cultural Study of Menstruation, Menstrual Taboos, and Related Social Variables. *Ethos* 2:137-170.

Moore, B. 1981. Climacteric Symptoms in an African Community. *Maturitas* 3:25-29.

Neugarten, B. L., V. Wood, R. Kraines, and B. Loomis. 1963. Women's Attitude toward the Menopause. *Vita Humana* 6:140-151.

Nunley, M. C. 1981. Response of Deer to Human Blood Odor. *American Anthropologist* 83:630-634.

Oosthuizen, G. C. 1975. Pentecostal Penetration into the Indian Community in Metropolitan Durban, South Africa. Human Sciences Research Council, Publ. Series No. 52. Durban.

Sharma, V. K and M. S. L. Saxena. 1981. Climacteric Symptoms: A Study in the Indian Context. *Maturitas* 3:11-20.

Stearns, P. N. 1976. *Old Age in European Society*. New York.

Stephens, W. N. 1961. A Cross-Cultural Study of Menstrual Taboos. *Genetic Psychology Monographs* 64:385-416.

The Lancet. July 17, 1982.

Utian, W. H. 1980. *Menopause in Modern Perspective*. New York.

Voda, A.M. 1981. Climacteric Hot Flashes. *Maturitas* 3:73-90.

Young, F. W., and A. Bacdayan. 1965. Menstrual Taboos and Social Rigidity. *Ethnology* 4:225-240.

Section VI

SEX ROLES

For most people, gender is determined by their chromosome pattern. Thus when chromosomes, gonads, and genitalia agree, gender identity normally follows the same pattern. When gender identity does not agree with physical appearance and gender role we might be dealing with hermaphroditism, homosexuality, transvestism or transsexuality.

Gender identity refers to the personal and private perception of being female or male, thus a psychosocial awareness and identification. Normally there is a congruity between genetic sex, anatomical sex, and gender identity. The reason for this is explained by cognitive-development, biosocial interaction, or learning theories; gender identity usually is expressed in gender roles. Gender roles normally derive from the members of the family and the community reinforcing identity and behavior which coincide with their expectations in accordance with male or female genitalia. Thus girls and boys are expected to behave in culturally sanctioned ways.

Gender classification and therefore gender role assignment usually falls to the parents. When a baby is born in an African village, a New Guinea hamlet, or a Latin American peasant farm the parents will first notice the external genitalia (phenotypic identification) and on that basis identify the neonate as a girl or a boy. "The structure of an infant's genitals plays an extremely important role in channeling its future development...More important than the physical structures are the social and cultural interpretations of the sex assigned to the child. Genital dimorphism provides the biological baseline for the roles of society and culture in sexual differentiaion" (Frayser 1985:85). The crucial years for the development of gender identity are from eighteen months to three or four years. Social-learning theory emphasizes the role of a gender model and the continuous reinforcement of gender role. Most societies recognise only males and females, lacking recognition of gender conflict or its expressions. Thus they expect every adult member of the group ultimately to get married and to assume the marital role (whether homosexuality is recognised or not), eg. southern Nguni (see Laubscher 1951). Reference in most cases is to the "woman as wife" or "woman as mother", and so too for the man.

Gender roles are cultural and their content will vary from one society to another; gender identity on the other hand is normally quite clearly that of being a man or a woman. Thus being a man in New Guinea will differ from being a man in France but each will have expected roles and ways of expressing these. For as yet unexplained reasons, some individuals are not comfortable with their genital organs and their culturally assigned gender. Such persons who suffer persistent discomfort and desire to live as members of the opposite gender are referred to as transsexuals. In a number of societies transsexuals are culturally recognized and given a role in society. Some of the better known examples are the Mohave Indian **alyha** (male transvestite homosexuals) and **hwame** (female homosexuals) described by George Devereux (1937), the Tahitian **mahu** discussed by Robert Levy (1973), the **hijras** of India written about by Serena Nanda (1990), and the **xanth** in Omani society. Martin and Voorhies (1975) speak of this recognition of more than the usual two genders as supernumerary sexes. As an example they discuss the widespread recognition of **berdache** in North America. Usually the berdache dresses in female attire and behaves like a woman. Following a vision the person transforms his gender identity from male to female. Such persons in fact constitute a third category of gender roles.

In the paper that follows Unni Wikan places the **xanth** in the context of gender roles. Wikan was intrigued "by the Omani triad of gender roles" and describes the cultural recognition of transsexuals as it contrasts with the male and female roles in this Muslim country. In contrast to most societies the world over, there is here a social recognition of a third gender category.

Turning to very clearcut female roles we join Molly Dougherty in visiting the young African American women in Edge Crossing, a north-central Florida community. Socialization, as employed in this study "is the interplay of the child and his environment resulting in his learning behaviors acceptable to the group" (Dougherty 1978:59). The transition from girl to young woman follows steps which are acceptable to the group—including pregnancy and childbirth. This brings the discussion to women's reproductive rights, and human rights in general, as discussed by Robin Cook.

References

Devereux, George. 1937. Homosexuality among the Mohave Indians. *Biology,* Vol.9: 498-597.

Dougherty, Molly C. 1978. *Becoming a Woman in Rural Black Culture.* New York: Holt, Rinehart and Winston.

Laubscher, B.J.F. 1951. *Sex, Custom and Psychopathology.* London: Routledge & Kegan Paul.

Levy, Robert. 1973. *Tahitians: Mind and Experience in the Society Islands.* Chicago: University of Chicago Press.

Martin, M. Kay and Barbara Voorhies. 1975. *Female of the Species.* New York: Columbia University Press.

Nanda, Serena. 1990. *Neither Man nor Women: The Hijras of India.* Belmont, Calif.: Wadsworth.

8. Mother and daughter in
Bucharest, Romania

SEX ROLES

7. Mother and daughter in Akuna,
New Guinea

MAN BECOMES WOMAN: TRANSSEXUALISM IN OMAN AS A KEY TO GENDER ROLES

Unni Wikan
University of Oslo

I

During social anthropological fieldwork in Oman I discovered that this society sustains a complex system of gender roles: not merely women and men, but also male transsexuals. An analysis of this role system may serve to illuminate both the general question of the bases of sexual identity, and the dynamics of gender role formation. In the following I address myself to such sociological themes, rather than the equally interesting questions of psychological origins of transsexualism, and hypotheses about its historical origins. I seek to develop a role analysis which does not see the transsexual in artificial isolation, but confronts the role in the context of the reciprocal roles of man and woman, and the basic constitution of social persons and relationships in this society.

Such an analysis requires that I explicate both conceptualisation and interaction: I shall try to show how the conceptualisation of each role in the triad reflects the existence of thee other two, and that the realisation of any one role in behaviour presupposes characteristic behavioural components of the other roles. In this manner I mean to use the role of the transsexual as a key to answer the following questions: What is the basis for the Omani conceptualisations of sex and gender identity? What insight does this provide into the construction of male and female roles in Oman, and into fundamental values and premises in Omani society? And finally, what light do these facts shed on us and our own conceptualisations of male and female identity?

Transsexualism, as I choose to define it, is a socially acknowledged role pattern whereby a person acts and is classified as if he/she were a person of the opposite sex for a number of crucial purposes.[1] The classic anthropological case is the *berdache* the Plains Indians—men who dressed like women, performed women's work and married men. But the last reported surviving *berdache* was already fifty years old when Lowie did his fieldwork among the Crow in 1907 (Lowie 1935). In this older literature such a role has generally been referred to as a transvestite, but it is not easy to assess its crosscultural distribution. The Human Relations Area Files, for example, classify transvestites with homosexuals—an entirely different phenomenon. Ford and Beach (1951) report sporadic cases of transvestites in the anthropological record, particularly among the Koniag of Alaska, Tanala of Madagascar, Lango of Uganda and Chuckchee of Siberia. In all these societies their numbers were

Reprinted by permission of the editors of *Man (NS)*, Vol. 12, 1977, pp. 304-319.

small, and except for the last case the role is poorly described. We can probably assume them to have disappeared today.

On the Oman coast, on the contrary, transsexualism occurs frequently so that in town of *c.* 3,000 adult males, about sixty transsexuals (sing. *xanth*) are found—in other words, one in every fifty acts and is reacted to by others as if he were a woman. To exemplify some of the concrete behaviour which 'as if he were a woman' implies, let me describe the process by which I myself discovered the phenomenon:

I had completed four months of fieldwork in the small coastal town of Sohar, reputed home of Sindbad the Sailor, when one day a friend of mine asked me to go visiting with her. Observing the rules of decency we made our way through the back streets away from the market, where we met a man, dressed in a pink *dishdasha* (long tunic), with whom my friend stopped to talk. I was highly astonished, as no decent woman, and I had every reason to believe my friend was one, stops to talk with a man in the street. So I reasoned he must be her very close male relative. But their interaction did not follow the pattern I had learnt to expect across sex lines, she was too lively and informal, their interaction too intimate, I began to suspect my friend's virtue. Could the man be her secret lover? No sooner had we left him than she identified him. 'He is a *xanth*' (effeminate, impotent, soft), she said. In the course of the next twenty minutes' walk she pointed out four more. They all wore pastel-coloured *dishdashas*, walked with a swaying gait and reeked of perfume. I recognised one as a man who had been singing with the women at a wedding I had recently attended. And my friend explained that all men who join women singing at weddings are *xanth*. Another was identified as the brother of a man who had offered to be our servant—an offer we turned down precisely because of this man's disturbingly effeminate manners. And my friend explained that all male servants (slaves apart) are *xanth*, that all *xanth* are homosexual prostitutes, and that it is quite common for several brothers to partake of such an identity. Another bizarre experience now became intelligible: at a wedding celebration, on the wedding night, when no male other than the bridegroom himself may see the bride's face, I was witness to a man casually making his way into the bride's seclusion chamber and peeping behind her veil! But no one in the audience took offence. Later that night the same man ate with the women at the wedding meal where men and women are strictly segregated. At the time I took him to be a halfwit: that was the only reason I could find for such deviant behaviour to be accepted. The man's strangely effeminate manners and high-pitched voice, giving him a rather clownish appearance, lent further credence to my interpretation. Now I realised that he, and the five men we had met today, were transsexuals.

This incident highlights problems of discovery and interpretation in fieldwork made acute in a strictly sex-segregated society like Oman. It leads me to pose the question whether male transsexuals, who have not previously been reported in the anthropological literature on the Middle East, may have escaped notice because the vast majority of fieldworkers have been men. Barred from informal contact with the women, the male anthropologist might miss the crucial clues to the transsexual phenomenon. He is likely to meet some effeminate men whom he will recognise as homosexuals (like our would-be servant), and others who will strike him as halfwits (like some Omani male singers). The fact that Omani transsexuals do not assume full female clothing will also give credence to the above interpretations. But the essential feature of the phenomenon: persons who are anatomically male but act effeminately and move freely amongst women behind purdah, this will escape him since the arenas where this interaction takes place are inaccessible to him.

Intrigued by the Omani triad of gender roles I devoted two further months in 1975/76 to collecting data on this theme. These new data revealed that the number of transsexuals was higher than I had at first assumed, since the remaining forty-nine men were found to include former transsexuals in an unknown number; a career as a 'woman' may have several alternative terminations: a) The man may be a woman for some years, whereupon he reverts to being a man for the rest of his life. b) He may live as a woman until old age. c) He may become a woman, return to being a man, again become a woman, etc.... To us it would appear obvious that the decisive criterion by which men and women are distinguished is anatomical, and that it is only through hormone changes and surgical modification that one's sex and gender role are changed. Omanis apparently hold a fundamentally different view. But it should be emphasised that this potential for change is a characteristic of males only. Omani females, on the contrary, retain female identity throughout life. I shall return below to the reasons for this contrast between the possible careers of men and women.

II

Let me now turn to a description of the role which we seek to analyse. Its character as an intermediate role is most clearly shown in counterpoint to male and female roles. But first some brief cultural and social background.

Oman shows an extreme pattern of sexual segregation, with practice largely conforming to the rules codified by the Prophet Mohammed some 1400 years ago. One reason for this is the fact that Oman till November 1971 was a closed country, a kind of Tibet of the Middle East, governed by an absolute Sultan of eccentric fanaticism, who rejected all modernisation. He feared the demoralising effects of change to the extent that the whole secular educational system of the country consisted of two elementary schools for an estimated population of 750,000. Persons seeking further education had to flee the country, and remain in exile. These conditions were completely changed when Sultan Qabus bin Said overthrew his father. The new ruler is as absolute, and as admired, as his father was, but has taken the reverse position and cultivates progress in all its forms—with one exception: women should be honoured and protected as enjoined by Islam. So while he, in his struggle to transform Oman into a developed nation, provides elementary schooling for girls and married women, he retains the traditional patterns of segregation and their symbolic expressions. Indeed, his own marriage last year followed these traditions, and none of the wedding guests was allowed to see the bride's face (only himself and her closest relatives).

Traditional Omani gender roles show the following characteristics:

Around the age of three, girls start observing sexual modesty. They cover all parts of the body other than hands, feet and face. The face comes next, around the age of 13, when black masks (*burqa*) are assumed which screen forehead, cheeks, nose and upper lips. This mask is the essential sign of modesty and is removed before men only in the most intimate relationships: before husband, father, brother and son, and before God in prayer. But the transsexual is no man—and women bare their faces freely before him.

The transsexual himself, on the other hand, is not allowed to wear the mask, or other female clothing. His clothes are intermediate between male and female: he wears the ankle-length tunic of the male, but with the tight waist of the female dress. Male clothing is white, females wear patterned cloth in bright colours, and transsexuals wear unpatterned coloured clothes. Men cut their hair short, women wear theirs long, the transsexuals medium long. Men comb their hair backward away from the face, women comb theirs diagonally forward from a central parting, transsexuals comb theirs forward from a sideparting, and they oil it heavily in the style of women. Both men and women cover their head, transsexuals go bare-headed. Perfume is used by both sexes, especially at festive occasions and during intercourse. The transsexual is generally heavily perfumed, and uses much make-up to draw attention to himself. This is also achieved by his affected swaying gait, emphasised by the close-fitting garments. His sweet falsetto voice and facial expressions and movements also closely mimic those of women. If transsexuals wore female clothes I doubt that it would in many instances be possible to see that they are, anatomically speaking, male and not female.

The transsexual's appearance is judged by the standards of female beauty: white skin, shiny black hair, large eyes and full cheeks. Some transsexuals fulfil these ideals so well that women may express great admiration for their physical beauty.

Eating cooked food together represents a degree of intimacy second only to intercourse and physical fondling. Only in the privacy of the elementary family do men and women eat together; and Omanis are so shy (*yistihi, yitxayil*) about eating that host and guest normally do not eat major meals (as contrasted to coffee, sweets and fruit) together even when they are of the same sex. Whenever food is offered in public, as e.g. at weddings, transsexuals eat with the women.

Omani women are secluded in their homes. They do not visit public arenas, such as the market, and must have the husband's permission to go visiting family or friends. The transsexual, in contrast, moves about freely; but like women, he stays at home in the evenings, whereas men may spend their time in clubs and cafés.

Division of labour follows sex lines. Housework is women's work. The transsexual does housework in his own home, and is often complimented and flattered for excelling women in his cooking, home decoration and neatness. He may also take employment as a domestic servant, which no woman or freeman can be induced to do.[2] By this employment he supports himself, as a man must. But wherever tasks are allocated by sex, the transsexual goes with the women. At weddings women sing, while the men are musicians; transsexuals are praised as the best singers. By appearing together with the women singers at weddings the transsexual broadcasts his status to a wide public. These performances characteristically serve as occasions to announce in public a change of identity from man to transsexual.

Women are jurally minors and must be represented by a ward. Transsexuals represent themselves, as do all sane men. Legally speaking, they retain male status.

What then does the transsexual mean by saying, as he explicitly does, that he is a woman, and why is he socially classified and treated as a woman in situations where sex differences are important? He was born as an ordinary boy, and was treated as a boy until he started his career as a prostitute. Why then is he classified as a *xanth*—a person with a distinctive gender identity—and not merely as a male homosexual prostitute?

Let us observe closely the process by which the transsexual returns to a male identity in order to search for an answer to this question. The change from transsexual *to* man takes place in connexion with marriage. But the critical criterion is more explicit than this: the transsexual must, like every normal bridegroom, demonstrate that he can perform intercourse in the male role. Among Omani Arabs marriage celebration has a customary form so that consummation is publicly verified. Intercourse takes place between the spouses in private; but next morning the groom must document his potency in one of two ways: by handing over a bloodstained handkerchief, which also serves as a proof of the bride's honour, to the bride's attendant (*mikbra*), or by raising an outcry which spreads like wild fire, and lodging a complaint to the bride's father and maybe also the district governor (*wali*), because the bride was not a virgin, and he has been deceived.

If neither of these events takes place, the impotence of the groom is revealed by default. This will cause grave concern among the bride's family and nervous suspense among the wedding guests. The groom will claim that he is not feeling well, and the bride's family will give him the chance to restitute himself, but rarely more than a week's time. (Twenty days was the maximum informants had heard of being granted to a close paternal relative). If he does not succeed within such a period of grace, they demand their daughter back and return the brideprice.[3]

An impotent groom suffers great shame and loses much money.[4] His adequacy as a man is in doubt; he rarely dares marry an Omani *maiden* again, but will choose a local widow or divorcée, or a foreigner (Egyptian, Indian etc.) in which case the marriage rites have a form that does not entail public proof of consummation. According to informants, grooms for this reason dread the wedding night as much as do brides. And the transsexual who passes the test becomes, like every other successful bridegroom, a *man*.

From this moment, all women must observe the rules of modesty and segregation before him:[5] always wear the mask, never speak to him, never let him step into the compound when the husband is absent. The transsexual is transformed from a harmless friend to a compromising potential sexual partner. There is now no difference between him and other men as social persons.[6]

But in all his demeanour—facial expressions, voice, laughter, movements—a transsexual will reveal his past: his femininity remains conspicuous. To some Omani female friends I consequently expressed pity for the poor woman who has such a 'woman' for a husband—she could not possibly respect him, I felt.[7] No No! they corrected me-*of course* she would respect him and love him. He had proved his potency; so he is a *man*.

Here then may be the key to an understanding of transsexualism in Oman. It is the sexual *act*, not the sexual organs, which is fundamentally constitutive of gender. A man who acts as a woman sexually, *is* a woman, socially. And there is no confusion possible in this culture between the male and female role in intercourse. The man 'enters' (*yidxil*), the woman receives, the man is active, the woman is passive. Behaviour, and not anatomy, is the basis for the Omani conceptualisation of gender identity.

Consequently, the man who enters into a homosexual relationship in the active role, in no way endangers his male identity, whereas the passive, receiving homosexual partner cannot possibly be conceptualised as a man. Therefore, in Oman, all homosexual prostitutes are ascribed the status of *xanth*.

Such conceptualisations also imply that a person with female sexual organs is a maiden (*bint*) until she has intercourse. At that moment she becomes a *woman* (*horma*). A spinster, no matter how old, remains a girl, a maiden. In the hypothetical case of a woman entering into a lesbian relation whereby she publicly emerged as the active partner I imagine that she would be classified as a man.

Yet Omanis recognise, as do all other peoples in the world, the fundamental, undeniable character of anatomical sex. Girls and boys, female and male, are identities ascribed at birth. This is one reason why the Omani homosexual prostitute becomes a transsexual, treated *as if* he were a woman. Yet he is referred to in the masculine grammatical gender, nor is he allowed to dress in women's clothes, for reasons we shall return to shortly: attempts by transsexuals to appear dressed as women have taken place, but were punished by imprisonment and flogging. But since the transsexual must be fitted in somewhere in a society based on a fundamental dichotomisation of the sexes, he is placed with those whom he resembles most: in this society, with women.

It is consistent with these conceptualisations that in the absence of sexual activity anatomical sex reasserts itself as the basis for classification. When in old age a transsexual loses his attractions and stops his trade, he is assimilated to the old man (*agz*) category. From the few cases I came across my impression is that such men tend to avoid large public occasions where the issue of their gender identity would arise.

Most societies regard sexual organs as the ultimate criterion for gender identity. It is fascinating to speculate over the origin of the transsexual status in Oman. Did it emerge through a clarification of the male role, whereby Omani men declared 'you act like a woman—you do not belong among us'? Or was it the transsexual himself who wished to be a woman and progressively transgressed the gender boundary? The fact that transsexuals cluster in groups of brothers suggests the existence of developmental causes for their motivation. Or the motive may be, as I have suggested elsewhere (Wikan 1975), a desire to escape from the exacting demands of the Omani male role. But in either case why is the transsexual not seen as a threat to the virtue of women, and constrained by the men? Physically, there is no denying that he has male organs. Yet, considering the lack of safeguards observed, it is true to say that he is treated as a eunuch. And as far as I know no documentary sources are available that might illuminate the origin of the Omani transsexual status.

However, every role has a sociological origin, which may be identified in synchronic data. That a role once was created does not explain its continued existence: it must be perpetuated, recreated anew every day in the sense that some persons must choose to realise it, and others acknowledge it as part of their daily life—whether in admiration, disgust, contempt, or indifference. In how they relate to the role incumbent, they also reveal something of themselves and their values. The institutionalised role of the transsexual in Oman 1976 is therefore a clear expression of basic premisses and values in that culture today.

III

In a few places in the world, a transvestite transsexual role (it is not clear as to which one) has been crystallised, but disappeared again with the advent of modernisation and Western values. But the essence of Omani *xanth* behaviour—homosexual relations—is practised in most societies, without people there regarding it as evidence of transsexual gender identity. Thus, homosexuality is a common and recognised phenomenon in many Middle Eastern cultures, often in an institutionalised practice whereby older men seek sexual satisfaction with younger boys. But this homosexual relationship generally has two qualities which make it fundamentally different from that practised in Oman:

1.   It is part of a deep friendship or love relationship between two men, which has qualities, it is often claimed, of being purer and more beautiful than love between man and woman.

2.   Both parties play both the active and the passive sexual role—either simultaneously or through time. In contrast, there is nothing in the Omani transsexual's behaviour which is represented as pure or beautiful; and he does not seek sexual release for himself. Indeed, till he has proved otherwise (most?) people doubt that he is capable of having an erection.[8] Like a fallen woman, he simply sells his body to men in return for money: he is a common prostitute.

And here lies the other component, I will argue, of the explanation why the transsexual emerges as an intermediate gender role, rather than representing an irregular pattern of recruitment to the female role. The transsexual is treated *as if* he were a woman; for many critical purposes he is classified with women; but he is not allowed to become completely assimilated to the category by wearing female dress. This is not because he is anatomically a male, but because he is sociologically something which no Omani woman should be: a prostitute. For such a person to dress like women would be to dishonour womanhood. The woman's purity and virtue are an axiom. Officially, there is no such thing as female prostitution. (In practice, its frequency is not at all low; and how this can be in a small, transparent community is a question to which I shall return below). By his mere existence the transsexual defines the essence of womanhood, he moves as an ugly duckling among the beautiful and throws them into relief. Through him, the pure and virtuous character of women may be conceptualised. One may speculate whether this aspect of the female role would be so clarified, were it not for him.

According to this hypothesis it would be difficult to maintain a conception of women as simultaneously pure and sexually active, if they were publicly acknowledged also to serve as prostitutes. If the public view, however, is that prostitution is an act of transsexuals, whereas women are not associated with the moral decay that prostitution represents, then women may be conceptualised as pure and virtuous *in* their sexual role. *Womanhood* is thereby left uncontaminated by such vices, even though individual women may be involved.[9]

The transsexual thus illuminates major components of the female role in Oman. But he can also serve us in a broader purpose, as a key to the understanding of basic features of Omani culture and society, and the fundamental premisses on which interaction in this society is based.

Homosexual prostitution is regarded as shameful in Oman; and all forms of sexual aberration and deviance are sinful according to religion. Young boys who show homosexual tendencies in their early teens are severely punished by anguished parents, and threatened with eviction from the home. So far, reactions in Oman are as one might expect in our society. But the further course of development is so distinctly Omani that any feeling of similarity disappears.

If the deviant will not conform in our society, we tend to respond with moral indignation, but no organisational adjustments. He is disgusting and despicable, a violation of our sense of modesty and a threat to public morality. Strong sanctions force him to disguise his deviance and practise it covertly. But because we do not wish to face up to him, we also fail to take cognisance of his distinctive character. As a result, we construct a social order where men and women who are sexually attracted by their *own* sex, none the less are enjoined to mix freely with them in situations where *we* observe rules of sexual modesty, such as public baths and toilets.

Omanis on the other hand draw the consequences of the fact that the sexual deviant cannot be suppressed. He is acknowledged and reclassified as a *xanth*—transsexual, and left in peace to practise his deviance. The condition is simply that he establishes his little brothel under a separate roof; he must rent a date-palm hut for himself. But this may be located anywhere in town, and it is not shameful to sublet to him.

This reaction to the sexual deviant is a natural consequence of the basic Omani view of life: the world is imperfect; people are created with dissimilar natures, and are likewise imperfect. It is up to every person to behave as correctly—i.e. tactfully, politely, hospitably, morally and amicably—as possible in all the different encounters in which he engages, rather than to demand such things of others. To blame, criticise, or sanction those who fall short of such ideals is to be tactless and leads to loss of esteem. The world contains mothers who do not love their children, children who do not honour their parents, wives who deceive their husbands, men who act sexually like women.... and it is not for me to judge or sanction them, unless the person has offended me in the particular relationship I have to him. It is up to the husband to control and punish his wife, the parents their children, the state, if it so chooses, the sexual deviant. The rest of us are not involved—on the contrary, we are under an obligation always to be tactful and hospitable to people.

And even the party who has been offended will have difficulties imposing compliance to his rights. For human nature is strong and unbending, and not easily broken. A wife who is unfaithful—the husband may lock her up, but she will break out, he may beat her, but she will persist. Coercion is no answer. A marriage between two who do not love each other can never succeed. Desires, drives, longings and propensities force their way to the surface despite all constraints. The best way for man is to accept others as they are, while training himself to virtue and gracefulness. That is the way to win esteem.

Such interactional premises provide the preconditions for *xanth*—as well as female prostitutes (*qahba*)—to operate as they do, despite a unanimous agreement that their activities are immensely wrong and sinful. A woman who prostitutes herself deceives her husband, but harms no one else but him and herself. And unless he surprises her in the act, he will never have proof. Neighbours will not inform, for that would be embarrassing, and the matter does not concern them. Thus the most bizarre situations are created—as for example friendships where flagrant prostitutes and the most virtuous and innocent women interact and intervisit. Let a personal experience illustrate this live-and-let-live attitude of Omanis: Within my circle of friends was indeed one prostitute. She pursued her activities so blatantly that no one could be in doubt. When she came home from her escapades, her friends could sometimes not resist the temptation to ask where she had been—and she would answer 'visiting relatives'. Always the same question, and the same answer. Once in a while it might also happen that our conversation in her presence turned to the theme of prostitution and prostitutes—other, socially distant prostitutes. They would burn in hell, said my friends, for there is no greater sin than that. And our prostitute friend participated in such conversations without any reference even of the most oblique kind being made to her own activities, though we knew that she knew that we knew....But to mention this with a single word would be bad taste, and create a scandal. However, as time passed our prostitute friend's behaviour developed in a fashion which we all found increasingly evident and shameless and I developed a corresponding need to react negatively to her and sanction her within our circle of friends. But in this, it was I and not she that was sanctioned by our common friends: What wrong had she done towards me? Was she not always hospitable, friendly, and helpful?

Their own 'sanctions' consisted merely in never going alone with her by taxi anywhere, e.g. to the hospital. The taxi would pass through neighbourhoods where the prostitute was well known, since she moved about everywhere, while they did not, and so she might affect their spotless reputations.

In other words, we are dealing with a society where the conceptualisation of the person is subtle and differentiated. One act or activity is only *one* aspect of the person, and only one facet of a complex personality. No person is branded by any single act committed, and mistakes in the past can be corrected and ignored. It is bad taste to harp on them later. Perhaps this attitude is the prerequisite for the transsexual's ability to restitute himself as a man and become a fully respected member of society. Never in my discussion with men or women could I find an attitude reminiscent of the 'once a criminal—always a criminal' assumption. It was only by persisting in asking that I was ever able to confirm my identification of former transsexuals. People did not bring up the fact, even when speaking of biographical matters, and when I finally did ascertain such facts, they were categorical in their view that 'Yes, N. N. once was a *xanth*, but now he is a man'.

The fact that persons are not prepared to sanction each other for their behaviour towards third persons does not mean that they are uninterested in observing and judging such behaviour. Particularly Omani men are concerned about their own and each other's integrity as whole persons. They have an image of themselves which they cultivate and seek to perfect, and an honour and public renown which they carefully build and protect. They also observe,others closely so as to develop an understanding of their character and qualities—in part so as to know whether to cultivate or avoid relations with them, depending on what their judgment on these matters might be. In a complex society with many arenas and subcultures, rich and poor, freeman and slave, religious diversity, and where performance is judged by demanding standards of grace and dignity, it is important to be able to anticipate what alternative relations and companionships may entail honourable or compromising potentialities.

The premisses that human nature is unbending and that rights to sanction are restrictively allocated might be thought to provide the basis for a system of social relations where the most unyielding will always triumph. Realities in Oman are very different from this for three important reasons:

a. Both men and women always try to project an honourable and graceful presence—to embody beautiful manners.

b. Persons do have real sanctions over each other in their direct relationships. Thus a wife who wants to remain married to her husband and yet desires to be unfaithful may be constrained to behave honourably by the threat of divorce on his part.

c. The state underwrites all social relations and obligations. This last point requires some elaboration.

Every Omani has a court of appeal in the district governor (*wli*). He presides daily in the central fort of the town, assisted by judges (*qzi*) who are knowledgeable in Islamic law; and they hear cases and settle conflicts; and the *wali*'s word is law. No matter is felt to be so personal or intimate that it cannot be brought before the *wali*. A husband whose wife denies him intercourse, a groom who finds his bride to be a 'woman' (i.e. not a virgin)—they may, and often will, complain to the *wali*. And the *wali* will call the parties in the case, together with whatever witnesses can be brought; he will have as many aspects of the case clarified as possible, and then make his sovereign decision public. Anyone who does not submit to the verdict is thrown in jail. And that will also happen sometimes, since the Omani's nature is so unyielding that not even their deep respect for authority is always sufficient to constrain them.[10] But this whole procedure is subject to one very significant limitation: Only the concerned party can make the complaint. Thus, for example, parents may not take action on their daughter's behalf if her husband refuses her permission to visit them. Then he has committed an injustice against her, not them, and only she can lodge a complaint. And in this same principle of restricted rights to sanction lies also the explanation of why the *wali* does not act against female prostitution, even though such behaviour is a sin according to the State religion,[11] and he is well aware of its existence. But when a woman deceives her husband, it is he and no one else who suffers an injustice. He has sovereignty over her sexuality, and so has the right to punish her.[12] But no one else has cause for complaint. For the *wali* to intervene in the matter would be to encroach on the husband's sovereignty; as long as the woman pursues her unfaithfulness with discretion, the State is not concerned. But if she were to step forth in public and proclaim herself a prostitute—as the *xanth* does—then the state would be the offended party, for prostitution practised by women in public is unlawful.

Male prostitution in public, i.e. the Omani pattern of transsexualism, on the contrary, is only sinful and not unlawful. What fundamental differences between male and female roles are revealed through these differential constraints on men and women? In an earlier part of this article I used the transsexual as a way to uncover basic features of the role of women. Let us now investigate what insights he provides into the role of men.

IV

The State has sovereignty over men, and is responsible for upholding law and morality. In view of this it is remarkable that the absolute Sultan of Oman should choose to allow male prostitution to flourish, and I believe the explanation to lie in two circumstances:

a.   The State practises a *laissez-faire* policy towards persons who are not seen as harming others, while at the same time

b.   the State acknowledges that transsexuals have utility: they act as a safety valve on the sexual activity of men, and thus as a protection for the virtue of women.

The Omani view clearly sees the sexual drive as a component of man's nature—perhaps that component which of all his nature is most difficult to control. This is consistent with basic Muslim conceptions that the availability of licit sexual release is vital to the man's protection against *zina*—illicit intercourse (cfr. Mernissi 1975). Omani women explain that an adult man needs frequent sexual release.[13] Both men and women argue that satisfaction of this need should be sought with a woman, who should be his wife. But what then should an adult, unmarried man do, or a married man who is absent on labour migration?[14] He should not covet his neighbour's wife, much less seduce her. Prostitute women should not exist, and to the extent that they do exist, they are difficult to find. Transsexuals, on the other hand, are everywhere conspicuous. It is highly plausible that they serve to relieve the pressure on more or less faithful women from frustrated single men, and that the Sultan is aware of their function in this respect. I, therefore, assume that he will continue to allow the transsexuals to practise their trade, despite the blemish they represent on the facade that he may wish Oman to present to the world. They are, after all, a lesser evil than female prostitutes would be by Omani standards.

No stigma attaches to the man who seeks the company of a transsexual for sexual purposes, though both men and women agree that the act itself is shameful. But the world is imperfect, and shameful acts an inherent part of life.

The Omani emphasis on the man's persistent need for sexual assertion may seem reminiscent of the Mediterranean Don Juan complex. But the similarity is superficial, and a brief comparison may be useful to throw into relief some fundamental features of the relationship between man and woman in Oman.

Don Juan seeks to conquer as many women as possible. He brags of his seductions as proof of his virility. Women are prey which can be made into trophies of his self-assertion. But because Mediterranean societies likewise observe sexual shame, there arises a genuine discrepancy between the consequences of the sexual act for man and woman respectively. Where Don Juan wins honour, the woman loses it. Yet Don Juan persists in humiliating women so as to enhance himself. The sexual act is principally a mode of self-assertion and a source of social esteem, and may be only secondarily a way to satisfy a biological need. To use another male partner would presumably be below Don Juan's dignity, for only women can give the desired aggrandisement and glory.

What do we learn about the man in Oman from the fact that he seems content to go to a transsexual? Quite clearly it cannot be crucial to him to demonstrate his power over women. In that case he would presumably search till he found a woman who could be tempted to be unfaithful to her husband, with or without payment.

The answer must be that the man primarily seeks to satisfy a biological drive. He needs sexual release because this is part of man's nature, and not to demonstrate his power over women. But why does he choose to go to a transsexual, rather than to masturbate in private? Part of the explanation may be the Muslim fear of polluting the right hand, part of it may be a feeling that masturbation is an immature act, whereas mature sexuality involves penetration. Of course it is possible that the Omani man does both; but folk opinion clearly sees the *xanth* and not masturbation, as the alternative to a woman. Perhaps this is a measure of the extent to which the *xanth* is indeed thought of as a—albeit prostituted—*woman*?[15] Granted that the man prefers to obtain his sexual satisfaction in a relationship with an alter, economic considerations may contribute to making the transsexual preferable to a prostitute woman. A transsexual costs only 1 Rial Omani (*c. £2*) while a woman costs five times as much. But I am inclined to favour another interpretation.

A transsexual is preferable to a woman because he is his own master, whereas she is another man's property. By means of the transsexual a man can achieve his purpose without detriment to others. This interpretation would seem contradicted by the Omani statement that it is greater shame for a man to seek a transsexual than a female prostitute. But this statement, I believe, addresses a conundrum that has been abstracted from its context, and is answered by the basic logic that sexual relations are between man and woman and not between man and man. In its real context, judged by Omani values, it seems to me more valid to argue that the favoured solution should be the one where a man can satisfy his needs without infringing on the rights of others.

This is in harmony with basic Omani values. 'The ornament of a man is beautiful manners, but the ornament of a woman is gold,' says an Omani proverb. A man should not commit injustices, nor cause strife, nor seek honour for himself by dishonouring others. To deceive and seduce brings disrepute; bragging about one's virility, or any other aspect of one's person, is vulgar. To brag at all is incompatible with beautiful manners. An Omani Don Juan is unheard of, and this is not because the Omani does not, like Don Juan, seek self-assertion and social esteem. But he does this in a society which admires and values very different qualities in a man. Virility and manliness are minimally associated with the callous conquest of women, and maximally associated with being in command of oneself and one's situation, and acting with grace and integrity towards all—women and men, slaves and sultans.

With this insight into the constitution of the male role we gain a new perspective on the opportunities for realising the female role. Different from our expectations of the position of women in Muslim countries—that they are oppressed, subjugated and unhappy—and in contrast to the stark realities in some such countries, the Omani woman has an honoured and respected place in her society. She derives confidence from her knowledge that the man wins honour by treating her gracefully. This does not necessarily mean that he can or will give her what she most desires. Men do not value the ornaments of women—golden jewellery, clothes, and luxury foods for hospitality—as highly as they do. But it does mean that a husband will always strive to act correctly and respectfully towards his wife, if he values his own honour at all. To humiliate and illtreat her brings disrepute.

Though a few men seem content to disregard their honour as well as their wives, the majority are praised by their wives for their correct and beautiful manners. Indeed, I very rarely heard complaints about a husband's role performance. No doubt one may question the reliability of negative evidence in this matter since Omani wives pride themselves on displaying absolute loyalty to their husbands, making them reluctant to confide even in their best friends. However, there were occasions when criticism was voiced, and it is significant that the substance of such discontent was always a wish that the husband would give the wife greater resources for hospitality. But I never heard an Omani woman express dissatisfaction with the basic duties and rights she has by virtue of her status, even though change and modernisation are occasionally discussed, and rather exaggerated stories of the new freedoms of women in other Gulf states circulate among them. Indeed many of the constraints and limitations imposed on women—like facial masks, restrictions of movement and sexual segregation—are seen by them as aspects of that very concern and respect on the part of the men which provide the basis for their own feeling of assurance and value. Rather than reflecting subjugation, these constraints and limitations are perceived by women as a source of pride and a confirmation of esteem.

The stark differences which obtain between wife and husband with regard to sexual autonomy are likewise perceived by Omani women as an unquestionable part of the moral and social order. Women are much preoccupied with sexuality, and constantly tease each other with how desired they are by their respective husbands, and how much these other women enjoy the sexual act. Yet no one admits to enjoying it herself. None the less, no one complains of lack of consideration when the husband demands sexual intercourse when the wife is tired or otherwise disinclined. As far as I could understand the Omani wife experiences her obligation as a kind of right or privilege, similar to her right and duty to serve her husband food when he comes home hungry. A husband's undeniable right to intercourse thus entails the wife's reciprocal right to receive him, and she herself values her position and defends it. If she suspects her husband of seeking the company of a prostitute (while living at home with the wife), she will refuse him, saying 'A whore is good enough for you'—and he will not be accepted again till he promises to reform himself and abstain from such connexions. Omani women even hold the view that proven infidelity on the part of the husband gives the wife grounds for divorce. Whether the *wali* would support them in this or not is beside the point. The belief is a measure of the kind of recognition to which the women themselves feel they are entitled.

This attitude to the husband's sexual rights is also related, I believe, to what women perceive men's sexual needs to be: a biological urge which demands satisfaction. Because the man in such a relationship is not seeking dominance or achieving self-aggrandisement, it is not humiliating for the woman to serve him. Marriage implies unequal duties and unequal powers for each of the parties, and this is experienced by both wife and husband as meaningful and proper. In other connexions it will be the husband who has to discipline himself and perform acts which may be inconveniences or hardships, but serve *her* needs—as when working to provide her with ornaments literally by the sweat of his brow in the fierce heat of an Omani summer's day. And so it must be in a culture which acknowledges fundamentally different needs for man and woman: each must on occasion be prepared to satisfy some needs in the other which they never feel themselves, if there is to be a reciprocal relationship.

Another reflection of this same respect for the woman in Oman can be seen in attitudes to sterility. It is a common view in Muslim countries that an infertile woman is a fundamental failure as a human being. She stands in danger of divorce, for a wife justifies her existence by producing children. But not so in Oman: here many qualities of her total person are prominent in her husband's evaluation of her: loyalty and faithfulness, tact and hospitality, love and consideration, etc. Fertility is desired, but it is not a condition, and as shown above the whole person is not stigmatised by failure in any one particular respect. If the husband is fond of her for her other qualities, the most that an infertile woman risks is that the husband will also take a second wife to provide him with issue—despite a generally high rate of divorce in the society.

There can hardly be any other contemporary society where law and customary rules combine to define so powerless a position for women as in Oman. They have no say in the choice of spouse, cannot leave their house without the husband's permission, are debarred from going to the market to make a single purchase, may often not choose their own clothes, must wear masks before all males who are not first-order relatives, etc., yet I have never met women who to the same degree seem in control of themselves and their situation. Omani women impress with their self-assurance and poise. They comport themselves with beauty and dignity, as if confident of themselves and their position. This is no doubt partly because their tasks and responsibilities are clearly defined and they command the resources to perform them with honour and grace. But above all, it is so because of the fundamental respect which men accord them in the pursuit of their 'ornament', namely, beautiful manners, and the preconditions that are thereby created for conceptualising and realising a valued identity.

V

Conclusion

An analysis of the role of the transsexual in Oman entails a presentation also of the reciprocal roles as will be true in any role analysis. The system in this case consists basically of the triad: woman, man and transsexual. Such a set of gender roles provides an unusually productive opportunity to explore more thoroughly the basic properties and preconditions of male and female roles. The discussion has particularly addressed the question of how the role of the transsexual affects the role of woman directly, both by providing a buffer for her virtue, but even more by supporting the very conceptualisation of womanhood as pure and virtuous, in harmony with Muslim ideals. The relationship between man and transsexual reveals important aspects of Omani conceptualisa-tions of male and female sexuality, and shows some important prerequisites for the respectful mutuality that seems to characterise traditional Omani gender roles, despite extreme inequalities in authority and freedom. Finally, the responses to the activities of the transsexual, and to other sexual deviations, demonstrate basic features of the Omani conceptualisation of the person, and the constraints on mutual sanctioning and interference which characterise their social system. The various interconnexions uncovered in this discussion may also be illuminating for the understanding of other gender role systems.

Notes

Fieldwork was done in the period March-August 1974, December 1975 and January 1976 in the coastal town of Sohar, jointly with my husband Fredrik Barth. This town seems to be representative of a culture area stretching from Kaborah (some miles north of Muscat) to the northern boundary of the Sultanate of Oman. When I refer to Oman, this should be understood as the coastline, whereas Omani is a shorthand abbreviation for the numerically predominant Arab population of this coastline. This fieldwork was supported by a grant from the Norwegian Research Council for Science and the Humanities, which I gratefully acknowledge.

1 By the usage recently established in psychiatric and sociological literature (e.g. Benjamin 1966; Stoller 1968, 1971; Taylor Bucker 1970); it is probable that the Omani xanith is best classifed as a transsexual rather than a transvestite, in that his subjectively cherished identity seems to be that of female, not male, whereas he has no fetishistic attitude to the clothing of women. However, the status of xanith is clearly an example of the type of phenomenon frequently described as transvestism in anthropological literature, and should be seen in this comparative perspective.

2 In Oman domestic employment is taken only by young boys, transsexuals or ex-slaves—before all of whom women may discard their masks.

3 The reader may wonder why the couple do not in such circumstances deceive the public by producing a bloodstain by other means. But such collusion has no meaning since the couple have in fact never met before, there is no loyalty between them, and indeed theydo not *become* a couple until consummation takes place. A bride divorced due to the impotence of the groom may later be remarried as a virgin bride, with no reduction in brideprice.

4 Though the official brideprice, limited by government decree to 300 Rial Omani (*c. £600*), is returned, a groom has normally paid considerable sums above and beyond this, in part to cover wedding expenses, in part as illegal consideration to the bride's father. This money can not normally be retrieved.

5 Normally a transsexual groom-to-be will stop his prostitute activities a few weeks prior to marriage.

6 As their motive for an eventual marriage, transsexuals give the desire for security in sickness and old age. Only a wife can be expected to be a faithful nurse and companion. Significantly, however, our best transsexual informant, a femininely beautiful seventeen-year-old boy, did not realise the full implications of marriage for his gender identity. He was definite that he would be able to continue his informal relationship with women after

marriage, arguing that he was to women like both a father and a mother. This is out of the question in Omani society, but may serve as a significant measure of the transsexual's own confused identity.

7 Transsexuals fetch their brides from far away, and marriages are negotiated by intgermediaries, so the bride's family will be uninformed about the groom's irregular background.

8 Women were definite that transsexuals who were prostitutes on a large scale (*woegid xanith*) were incapable of performing intercourse in the male role. However, one popular transsexual whom we interviewed was equally definite that he could, though he had never tried, arguing that he knew several men who had practised on an even larger scale than himself, yet been potent. When I reported this view to some female friends, they categorically rejected it. To their understanding there is an antithesis between performance in the male and the female sexual role—true bisexuality cannot be imagined. Therefore, if an ex-transsexual proved potent, the modest extent of his activities would thus be proved *ex post facto.*

9 Indeed, the term by which women refer to the activities of prostitute women (i.e. women who are not merely unfaithful for love, but have sexual relations with several men) is *yixannith,* the active verbal form of *xanith.*

10 In these court sessions, we have witnessed wild protests from the sentenced, who was taken away by the guards, but later released after intercession by friends and family.

11 The link between religion and state in Oman is indeed even stronger than this expression indicates, and more nearly approaches the close identity found in early Islam.

12 But not *too* severely, for then the woman will appeal to the *wali* who, according to my female informants, would command the husband: 'Be gentle to her if you wish to remain married to her. If you cannot do that, then divorce her.'

13 Age is unspecified—maybe 'adult' means sexually mature, maybe *c.* age 20—I do not know whether men would express themselves so categorically.

14 Average age at marriage is *c.* 25 years for men. Nearly one quarter of all employed men in Sohar are labour migrants.

15 It is remarkable that women regard transsexuals as so similar to themselves that they assume them to *feel* like women, and be 'ashamed' *(yistihi)* before men, as are ordinary women.

References

Benjamin, H. 1966. *The transsexual phenomenon*. New York: Julian Press.

Ford, C. S. & F. A. Beach 1951. *Patterns of sexual behaviour*. New York: Harper.

Lowie, R. H. 1935. *The Crow Indians*. New York: Rinehart & Co.

Mernissi, F. 1975. *Beyond the veil: male-female dynamics in a modern Muslim society*. Cambridge, Mass.: Schenkman.

Stoller, R. J. 1968. *Sex and gender*. London: The Hogarth Press.

_____ 1971. The term 'transvestism'. *Arch. Gen. Psychiatry* **24**, 230-7.

Taylor Buckner, H. 1970. The transvestic career path. *Psychiatry* **33**, 381-9.

Wikan, U. 1975. Hustyrann eller kanarifugl—kvinnerollen i to arabiske samfunn (Domestic tyrant or pet canary—women's roles in two Arab societies) *Tidsskr. Samfunnsforsk.* **16**, 299-321.

BECOMING A WOMAN IN RURAL BLACK CULTURE

Molly C. Dougherty

Pregnancy—One Subphase

The transition from childhood to adulthood is a rite of passage with a long transitional phase. The transition is a period of learning the feminine role and lore, courtship, and household responsibility. In rites of passage where the transitional phase is elaborate and constitutes an independent state, as in adolescence, the arrangement of the three phases is reduplicated. The analysis of pregnancy, delivery, and acceptance of motherhood reveals a reduplication of the process seen in adolescence.

In pregnancy, and more dramatically in childbirth, the girl is dependent, helpless, held in suspense and dread only to be elevated to a higher status for having endured the process. Turner (1969:201) states that when liminality appears in rites of passage the neophyte is humbled precisely because he is to be structurally exalted at the end of the rites. Status elevation for females occurs some time after delivery in the post-liminal phase. Incorporation into adulthood occurs only after she demonstrates to the satisfaction of adult women that the process of pregnancy and childbirth have had their proper effect. Humbled by the discomforts and sacrifices required by childbirth, women deserving adult status assume full responsibility for their infants in relation to physical needs, and to the kin group.

With the pattern of rites of passage as a model, the processes of pregnancy and childbirth are examined. Then, the final rite of passage—acceptance into motherhood, admitting the female to adult status—is analyzed. The discussion focuses on girls who deliver infants surviving the first year of life. Adult status is achieved through procreation. Although education, employment, religious endeavors, and the care role can ultimately produce adult status without procreation they are less frequently seen in Edge Crossing. Through such endeavors adulthood is achieved much later and the transitional phase between childhood and adulthood is terminated more gradually.

Among adolescents who infrequently utilize birth control, pregnancy is not an unanticipated outcome of courtship. When pregnancy occurs it is often met with ambivalence because various social relationships necessarily undergo alteration and produce disequilibrium requiring unfamiliar interactions. Girls perceive that pregnancy can strengthen, formalize, and validate courtship bonds. Even though pregnancy may not be "planned" in the current usage of the term it is a fortuitous event with relatively predictable results.

Girls usually become pregnant in the middle or late teenage years, after they have acquired a body of female lore relating to courtship, feminine behavior, and sexuality. The first awareness of pregnancy usually marks interactional shifts in courtships, adult-adolescent interactions, and peer-

Reprinted by permission of the author and publishers from *Becoming a Woman in Rural Black Culture,* New York: Rinehart & Co., 1978, pp. 88-100.

group activities which become more obvious as the pregnancy develops. In the first trimester of pregnancy most girls divulge their condition to very few persons because these early months are uncertain ones. They are not positive that they are pregnant and have not become comfortable with the possibility. Cessation of menstruation is not regarded as a positive sign of pregnancy because they often have menstrual irregularities that include amenorrhea. Nausea, pica, and "brightening" of the skin are considered early symptoms of pregnancy. Breast enlargement, usually occurring in pregnancy, is not seriously regarded because many girls are still experiencing developmental growth at their first conception. The physical signs of early pregnancy are often easy to disregard. Sometimes girls feeling ambivalent about pregnancy pass the symptoms off and avoid serious consideration of the consequences until later.

When young women look back on their first pregnancy many of them recall that cessation of menstruation was a signal to them but that other symptoms were more important. Some girls "know" from the moment of conception that they are pregnant. One recalled that she got a "chill" after having sexual intercourse and a twitch in her eye later in the evening. The chill indicated that she was pregnant and the twitch in her eye was a sign of good luck. Some youths who "know" that they are pregnant minutes or hours after sexual relations say that they "just feel funny" in the region between the sternum and pubic bone and know that the feeling can mean only that they are pregnant.

While some girls are sure of pregnancy right from the start, others are unaware of their condition until they are told by someone else. Often it is through customary interactional sets that pregnancy is realized. Males have a special ability to detect pregnancy. It is sometimes a girl's sexual partner who tells her that she is pregnant. Because women "be more quarrelish" from the onset of pregnancy, some men know from a woman's attitude that she is pregnant. It is also said that a woman "feels different on the inside" during intercourse and men detect pregnancy in this way. Adult women in the household often keep a careful eye on girls despite a lack of verbal communication. When a girl experiences amenorrhea the adult asks, "How come I ain't seen nothing?" The girl responds, "You just ain't been paying attention, I been coming around." As time passes the facts inevitably become known, but girls are relatively successful in keeping pregnancy a secret until they are ready to cope with the alterations in social interactions it brings.

A girl's relations with her boyfriend necessarily undergo change as a result of pregnancy. For most, it is an event creating a bond of common interest between them for life. The pregnancy and forthcoming child symbolize a union between them of greater significance than courtship offered. Procreation is a serious matter; it brings together not only the prospective parents but their descent groups as well.

It is difficult for girls to anticipate how males will respond to their pregnancy. Most males are said to want children and feel "proud" when they know that they are the parent of an unborn child. Even so, the timing, their feeling for the expectant mother, or other courtship and family relationships may cause the event to be less than warmly welcomed.

Clearly, both males and females are aware that pregnancy is a distinct possibility in courtship, but males often respond in what females describe as unexpected ways. A girl aims toward eliciting from the male acknowledgement of paternity and symbolic or tangible evidence of continuing interest in his child and thereby the mother. Girls normally approach the subject of pregnancy before it occurs and have some idea of how the male feels about her "having a baby for him." After conception girls often do not tell the prospective father that they are pregnant. Their behavior, including pica and appetite and mood changes, is empirical evidence that eventually reveals to him that pregnancy has occurred. They may continue the relationship for three or four months while the male tells the girl that she is pregnant and she either denies or ignores his statements.

Even after the girl is sure that she is pregnant she may not openly admit it to the prospective father. Instead, she hints, remarks on how she feels and dodges his direct questions. The indirect approach to such matters is in consonance with the practice of keeping males in suspense.

When a girl is pregnant her status relative to all others is changed. Ideally, the prospective father becomes more solicitous of her. The usual reciprocity that flows between courting couples continues but the male increases his contribution because of "the baby." In early pregnancy both parties are cautious in requesting or providing further commitments. A girl usually reduces or terminates other courtship relationships while she is adjusting to pregnancy and formalizing her relationships with the baby's father and his family. Interactions in her household affect the approach a girl makes to the prospective father. If girls are "dogged" too much at home they tend to increase pressure on the father to "take care" of them, marry, or form a separate household. On the other hand, if the prospective father is too reticent in assisting her in the expected ways, her family supports her more actively and verbalizes disapproval of the male who "messed her up." The interrelations between the two are reciprocal and the girl is influenced in her decisions in one by the interactions in the other. Youths tend to achieve a balance between the two, but it is more often the girl's family that is primarily responsible for her support, especially during the first pregnancy.

Many girls and adult women state that a girl is entitled to one pregnancy before marriage but that she had better marry before the second child is born or risk being "put out" of the house. When girls have a first child they are socially not adults but usually have assumed adult roles when they become pregnant a second time. The stress placed on having a male support them after the first child expresses the responsibility adult women are expected to assume regarding their offspring. Despite adults' expectations of young women they do not usually insist that they leave home. The composition of households in the community indicates that few girls are "put out" even if they do not gain support of males after first pregnancies.

A closer examination of male-female relations during pregnancy clarifies why girls usually maintain strong ties with their families. Sometimes a girl is unsure who is the father of her unborn child, and certain problems ensue. It is considered foolish and slightly immoral for a girl to be uncertain about the paternity of her child, who will need to know his kin so that he will not unwittingly marry a relative. When the paternity of the unborn child is uncertain, the girl usually assigns a father to him; the male designated as father can accept or refute his involvement. It is said that a girl may be "liking one boy" and "going with" another. When she becomes pregnant she "puts it" on the one she likes and hopes he'll "do right by her." The alleged father may disclaim any involvement. In other cases, the father does not want to "settle down," so that the girl's most reasonable alternative is to remain with her own family. Sometimes the man has heard or believes that the young woman has been unfaithful and he refuses to accept responsibility for the pregnancy even though he, and everyone else, "knows" the baby is his. On rare occasions the girl refuses to divulge the identity of the father; he may be married to a local resident or related to her by blood or marriage. Pregnancy is one way that females gain adult status and achieve an identification with a descent group other than their own. These changes are sufficiently important that girls are willing to undergo the process even if there is no assurance that males will accept paternity.

The response of males is more unpredictable than that of adult women, who usually support and assist girls through their first experience in womanly endeavor. Adult women are verbally uncommunicative with girls about courtship but often make careful observation of their behavior, know when they are pregnant, and behave as if they are very displeased about the event. In early pregnancy girls are subjected to leveling to a low status position and are separated from their former status. They are accused of being "messed up" and of having behaved disgracefully. They are indicted for having "gotten the baby in the streets" and for persistently "laying up under some man." They may have thought they were "smart" but they will find out what all that "running" leads to when they have the baby and they will surely "pay" for all that fun. The girl is said to be personally responsible for bringing an innocent soul into the world who could have "stayed in heaven" where he belonged. The financial worries and other problems children bring are paraded in front of the girl and the most dramatic example of how troublesome children are is personified in the girl's pregnant condition. The tirades of adult women are frequent and merciless against girls suspected of being pregnant or who have recently been diagnosed as pregnant. Girls endure the abuse with downcast heads as if properly ashamed of their actions and of the result.

The initial displeasure of adult women toward a girl's pregnancy is anticipated. If the adult continues to "dog" her more than a month or so she becomes anxious to persuade the prospective father to help her escape the situation. This is rarely necessary because after the girl has been made to feel her low status and insecure position, the accusations subside.

Eventually the physical and emotional load the girl is carrying is acknowledged by adult women and they share with her their own experiences with pregnancy and childbirth. The support offered by adult women helps to "lighten the burden" she bears. She is relieved of some household tasks and permitted to sleep and rest as much as she needs. The sharing of experiences with women who have experienced pregnancy and childbirth draws the girl closer to them, helps her adjust to the process, and prepares her for childbirth. Remedies for common complaints of pregnancy, proper behavior, and other knowledge are transmitted to her. Many of the beliefs and practices she learns during pregnancy have been documented by Murphree (1968), who worked in a north-central Florida community but did not restrict her research to blacks.

Pregnancy demonstrates the power of the weak (Turner 1969) because in pregnancy girls are simultaneously separated from their former status and drawn into knowledge and behavior reserved for adults. The growth and continuity of the kin group is dependent on procreation so the pregnant girl contributes to the strength of the group. After pregnancy occurs, the prospective father is measured not as a fanciful boyfriend but as a potential family member. He is permitted more familiarity with the girl at home and spends more time in interactions with family members.

The girl's mother has an interest in formalizing the relationship between the prospective mother and father, but there is a strong reluctance by either party to act impulsively. While a few men deny paternity or refuse to support a child in some way, both males and females are reluctant to become legally bound in marriage.

Most women agree that girls should not he pushed into marriage or any permanent relationship if they are not ready or do not feel that they have found "the right man." It is better for a girl to have a child who is wholly dependent on her family than to force her into a relationship with a man with whom she is not happy. Loosely structured relationships in which the male acknowledges paternity and does "what he can" for the mother and her family seem to prevail. Often prospective parents do marry while the girl is pregnant, but there is little familial pressure for them to do so.

During pregnancy the male usually financially and emotionally supports his girlfriend as well as possible. He is drawn more closely into her home and establishes reciprocal relationships with her kin. One dimension of his behavior by which his potential is measured is the amount of time he spends with the pregnant girl and the lengths to which he goes to attend to her desires and needs. Many prospective fathers pay the hospital and physician's fees connected with the birth. The baby often carries the surname of his father even though his parents are not married. The father's behavior symbolizes his involvement in the procreative process and his claim to the offspring.

Girls often develop strong ties with the prospective father's female kin. In early pregnancy the paternal kin behave similarly to the girl's own kin. They deny their concern over the pregnancy and say that it is up to the girl and her mother to keep her "out of trouble." As the pregnancy progresses they demonstrate concern for her and are solicitous of her needs, share their pregnancy and childbirth experiences with her, and ask how "their" unborn baby is doing.

The more intense interactions of the girl with adult female kin, the prospective father, and his kin alter her interactions in the peer group. By the fifth month of pregnancy she withdraws from school, reducing even further her peer-group interactions. The important business of learning feminine lore about pregnancy, altering courtship relationships, and coping with the emotional and physical demands of pregnancy removes her from former entertainment activities. In addition she is separated from peers because she has gained an altered status. Former close friends think she is acting "grown" and "too smart" for them. The camaraderie of the peer group is never regained. Later, when other peers are also mothers, close friendships are renewed, but the sharing of activities, feelings, and experiences is not as open and the common adult enemy has vanished.

Pregnancy involves several novel interactional sets that reflect the altered status of the pregnant girl. Introduction to the health-care process during pregnancy usually occurs between the third and sixth month. Girls have little or no experience in the health-care system before pregnancy. They are prepared for the event by women who describe the process or are told that they will find out what it is like soon enough. They are always left with the impression that no matter how disturbing the initial examination is, it is nothing in comparison to the labor experience.

Girls are usually accompanied to prenatal visits by an adult woman who knows the clinic or office procedure. The adult takes care of all contact with health personnel up to the entry of the girl into the examining room. The adult provides support and guidance for her in securing care and in coping with the system, but during the most anxiety-provoking part of the process she is left unsupported. The girl enters the examining room in the presence of strange medical personnel, is stripped of her clothing, and offered a skimpy gown to cover her nakedness. She provides the answers to questions on her medical history with the meager information she has garnered about her own and her family's health. Then she is directed to lay on a narrow, hard table while she is quizzed, palpated, and examined verbally and physically. The pelvic exam, reserved for the end of the examination, is more threatening than the rest and it is often perceived as painful.

The girl endures the whole procedure with a minimum of comment and complaint. This is a moment in and out of time (Turner 1969); she is utterly separated from the normal social life, ground down to the lowest level, and deprived of the normal attributes of her status. The anxiety generated is great but she emerges more confident than before. All has been revealed and seemingly, nothing lost. The anxiety gives way to success and an off-handed attitude. In retrospect it was nothing in comparison to her expectations; having endured the process she is better equipped to cope with the trials and dangers that lie ahead in the path toward womanhood.

Girls become fairly well-adjusted to the fact of pregnancy and the alterations in interactions it produces by the seventh month. Having withdrawn from school, they spend their days at home, engaging in housework, talking with women, and courting. The expected behavior, practices, and beliefs associated with pregnancy have become part of their knowledge. The pregnancy, obvious to all, is publicly acknowledged and the courtship relationship is relatively stable. The prospective father "sits with" the girl at home rather than engaging in normal courtship behavior for fear that dancing, drinking, and excitement will harm the mother or the baby. Some girls express a desire to get out, dance, drink, and have sexual relations toward the end of pregnancy, but they are usually protected from these desires by solicitous females or the prospective father.

It is in the latter months of pregnancy that the suggestion of incorporation into the status of pregnancy is present. Girls spend most of their time resting, waiting, and sleeping. Their interactions in all sets diminish and they await the completion of the process. The physiology of pregnancy with strain on the various bodily systems explains some of their lethargy but the time spent in quiet reflection is something more. Having heard the lore of pregnancy and childbirth from others, they are vaguely anxious about childbirth, but it lies too far in the future to actively worry. The "fullness" they feel, backaches, constipation, leg cramps, and swelling in the feet are problems to be treated and endured.

Incorporation into the status of pregnancy is never complete because the patient waiting gives way to anxious anticipation of the baby's birth. Relief from the physical burden and the desire to know whether the baby is male or female and healthy or not contribute to restlessness near term. Girls are caught in a double bind, wanting to be relieved of pregnancy but dreading the ordeal of childbirth. Most of them are ready to be through with pregnancy when they begin labor.

Before proceeding to a discussion of childbirth in Edge Crossing it is helpful to discuss the ideology of childbirth among middle-class Americans during the past 25 years. Dick-Read (1956) popularized the concept that knowledge about and relaxation during labor resulted in women experiencing less discomfort during birth. Dick-Read proposed that fear of pain during birth led to the muscular tension that caused pain; breathing exercises to enhance relaxation and prevent pain were described. Other volumes (Karmel 1959) based on similar principles but not claiming complete absence of pain during birth were introduced. Women using prepared childbirth principles during their own childbirth experiences formed organizations to disseminate childbirth information. Later, classes were organized throughout the United States to teach childbirth information and breathing techniques (Bing 1969).

The philosophy of prepared childbirth involves understanding and emotional support. Understanding the physiology of pregnancy, proper muscle preparation, and emotional support, primarily by the woman's mate, are stressed. During the past decade, prepared childbirth has gained great popularity among American women.

The participation of women's mates seems to be an extension of the family system of post World War II America. The middle class is mobile, separating women from their own mothers who traditionally assisted them during pregnancy. Shared conjugal roles in which male and female support and assist one another with most endeavors occurs. These characteristics contrast with male-female relationships in Edge Crossing, where there is customarily a separation of males and females in most activities.

There are probably very few middle-class women in the United States who have not heard of prepared childbirth. Most of them deal with pregnancy by learning about the physical and emotional aspects of the experience. Prepared childbirth classes are available in every major city in the United States and most smaller towns have organizations designed to assist women and men through their early parenting experiences. But it is largely the middle-class population which is attracted to the classes, suggesting that they are based on a strong middle-class orientation to parenting and childbirth.

Prepared childbirth classes and other materials available to the public suggest that sedation and anesthesia during labor and delivery are not necessarily beneficial to women and probably detrimental to infants. Many pregnant middle-class women seek the care of physicians who permit them some control over their labors and in the medications they receive. Hospitals are often described as unnatural locations for an uncomplicated birth (The Boston Women's Health Book Collective 1973). There is growing support for the availability of home delivery by parents who wish to avoid the hospital milieu (Lang 1972) and growing numbers of pregnant women seek the support of their friends and mates to assist them at home births. Relatively few physicians in the U.S. are warmly receptive to this extension of prepared childbirth principles and usually will not assist at a home birth or supervise midwives who wish to participate. There are, in fact, relatively few certified nurse-midwives in the U.S. to work in newly opening roles for them. A lay midwife lives in Edge Crossing. She is one of a diminishing number of women in the rural South who are not formally educated as nurse-midwives but are licensed by the state to deliver babies in areas where medical care is not readily accessible.

It is increasingly common for middle-class women to have sophisticated knowledge about their own bodies and to be prepared for the muscular contractions and discomforts of childbirth. They find childbirth a physically laborious and emotionally gratifying experience. Such women have different ideas and beliefs about the birth process, the responsibility of their mates, and the potential hazards of childbirth than do women in Edge Crossing. Middle-class women usually have children in their twenties, after they have had a variety of educational and employment experiences. In Edge Crossing, many girls experience their first pregnancy in adolescence, often before finishing high school or having employment experience.

To women in Edge Crossing, birth is painful and dangerous. They feel that it is proper for women to bring forth children, and for them to do so, as the Bible dictates, "in pain." The segregation of male and female roles in all areas of social life is redefined in childbirth. Women who have experienced childbirth are considered knowledgeable about it. Men are not expected to understand pregnancy and birth; it is not their responsibility to be actively involved in the process. Most women in Edge Crossing know women who have died in childbirth and all of them have known more than one infant who has died. In comparison, middle-class women tend to view pregnancy and birth as a normal part of their adult experience, and one without unusual danger to their lives. Statistically, low-income women die during childbirth and lose infants in their early years more frequently than do middle-income women. The experiences, values, and beliefs of middle-class women and women in Edge Crossing result in differing behaviors in childbirth. The next section describes childbirth among young women in Edge Crossing.

Childbirth—A Second Subphase

The labor and delivery experience, second subphase in the rite of passage, differs in its social manifestations from pregnancy in many ways. The childbirth experience is of fairly short duration; socially it lasts a day or so and medically it is usually of shorter duration. Birth normally takes place in a health-care institution separated physically and socially from the community. Childbirth is a crisis for all concerned and is perceived as an intense, critical experience.

The enactment of the rite of passage associated with labor and delivery is discussed below. Before girls are ready to "get down" in labor they are treated more kindly than during earlier months. They are frequently asked, "How you feeling, honey?" by adult women who closely observe their behavior and reactions to detect the onset of labor. Usually girls are not sure exactly what signs are going to herald the beginning of labor but know that most women say that they will know when it happens. Most women consider the best indicator of labor to be the frequency and "sharpness" of labor pains. Usually expectant females have "little naggers" for days or weeks before the birth but when a woman is "really in labor them pains be eating her up."

The intensity of pain in labor and the way women "bear with" their pains is one aspect of labor all pregnant girls have heard about repeatedly. Adults often relate to girls their own experiences with birth. Most women say that they hurt very badly during labor but were determined not to make a sound. A few admit that they screamed, hollered, squirmed around in bed, and made "real fools" of themselves. The ideal behavior is to endure the "suffering" in silence and to pray to God for a safe delivery. There is little that anyone can do to relieve the pain of childbirth because it is a matter between them and God. In childbirth women are cast adrift from society and controlled by supernatural forces.

Girls, responding to the mandate to communicate with God, accept the "burden to bring forth fruit in pain" in a consistent fashion. They are very quiet about their expectations, the symptoms they experience, and about their own feelings. When contractions start they stoically endure them without comment and often do not report them to anyone because they may be told that they are not in labor. The onset of labor is usually recognized by other women who note behavioral changes in the girl, who may be up in the night to the bathroom or moodily changing position every few minutes. Adults question the girl to determine whether "it be her time." They want to know if she's "seen a sign" (the bloody, mucous discharge that often occurs in early labor) and whether her "water's broke" (amniotic sac has ruptured). Pains, the "sign," and water breaking are the three symptoms of labor most seriously considered by adult women. Of these, the pains are the most important because they ultimately push the baby "out of his bed."

Girls are not expected to be responsible for detecting the onset of labor, or for arrangements to get to the hospital. These are taken care of by adult women, who may recruit a man to drive. In the process of birth the role of males is minimal; the passage of the girl from pregnancy to biological motherhood is in the hands of women who know the process and its distinctive patterns. When it is decided by two or more females that the girl is in labor, a car is secured and she is assisted into it. Word is sent to the prospective father and a small cluster of critical personnel deliver her to the hospital. The prospective mother, the passenger in the process, is totally relieved of ordinary responsibility, interacting with no one, totally introspective, and coping with the involved physiological process taking place within her.

Socially separated from society, she is transported to an institution which removes her physically from the normal spatial, temporal, and interpersonal indicators of her status. The critical personnel accompany her to the door of the labor room, where she is whisked through a series of procedures designed to cleanse her of the physical remains of her former position. In the company of strangers, her clothes, hair curlers, and jewelry are removed. An enema and perineal shave cleanse her of impurities in the area of focus for the coming birth.

The phase of separation is clearly marked, and the break from the former position is abrupt. The short rite of passage of childbirth is indelibly etched on her mind. She can never return to the status of the uninitiated. The girl, utterly alone, stripped totally of her possessions, endures periodic contractions demanding her concentration. She is placed in bed in a small, sparsely furnished room and forbidden to get up; she calls on inner reserves of strength to sustain her.

After the initial, dramatic separation she is permitted minimal contact with social ties. She is allowed only one visitor because additional personnel increase the risk of contaminating the purified, ritual passenger with worldly pollutants. The visitor, her only link with previous life, and she have limited interactions because the contractions and physical process of labor require nearly all her attention.

The visitor, leaving the labor room regularly, reports to the critical personnel who wait outside the door. The number of waiting persons varies but the nucleus is those most closely involved in the girl's passage into adulthood. Most of them are female and include the mother, grandmother, sister, and prospective father. Those not physically in attendance are drawn into the process when they are telephoned and given reports on the girl's condition.

Analysis of the interactions and behaviors of personnel in the transitional phase reveals three distinct sets of persona. The focus of the ceremony is on the girl, who interacts minimally with the other two. The critical personnel who wait in the wings represent the skeletal structure of society awaiting the return of the ritual passenger in an altered status. The medical personnel are ritual specialists who supervise the birth process and assume total responsibility for her safe passage. Their interactions and expectations explicate their significance to the process.

The girl, relinquished by her family and friends, is socially in a limbo between life and death. Devoid of status, she endures the suffering she has known would be hers in the attainment of motherhood. She is neutral, dependent, unable to undertake the simplest tasks and barely in control of her physical activities. She is immediately dependent on unusually powerful strangers who perform complicated procedures and have medications mitigating her physical and emotional distress. In the limbo between life and death the girl is uncertain what is to be her fate. If continuing in pain is all there is to life she would rather be dead, yet death may be more dreadful still. The paradox of her predicament results in her joining the forces controlling her destiny. As the physical discomforts of labor increase she turns to the medical personnel and to God for relief and solace. Her cry, "Oh, nurse, help me, doctor, help me, Jesus, help me, Oh God, help me, please help me," is like a litany, each incantation pleading to a higher power to hear her case and have mercy. The drama acted out between the girl, medical personnel, and supernatural powers is divorced completely from ongoing social life.

The critical personnel outside the labor room wait, worry, and pray for a safe delivery or, if that is denied, her safe passage into the world beyond. Having only the power of prayer to influence the situation, they commit her to the hands of experts and to God. They seize every shred of information about the girl and examine it from every angle to evaluate its meaning. The wait, which may be an hour or so, seems endless. They too are drawn into limbo, humbled by the proportions of the crisis and immobilized until it is resolved.

Eventually the girl reaches the limit of her endurance. Fatigued by the force of the contractions and irritated by the length of the labor, she is discouraged because she may never escape the situation to live once more. She pleads for help and insists that she can do no more. She complains, "Somebody do something," surrendering any remnant of self-control. Agitation, discomfort, and loss of control noted by medical personnel are expected toward the end of the first stage of labor. The passenger, completely conquered by her physiology, has lost the measure of control she grasped so dearly. Simple instructions receive the response, "I can't do it." Medical personnel try to renew her courage, assist her with every move, demand nothing from her and insist that she is enduring the worst, that she will "feel better soon." Unbelieving, the girl is sure she will never feel better and that the end is near.

Some women do experience a measure of relief as the cervix becomes fully dilated and the baby presses outward. The pushing response is a natural one but a medical professional usually stays with the girl, encourages, and supports her. Often anxiety and exhaustion allow no relief after full dilation and she continues to feel out of control until the birth.

The procedure of moving into the delivery room, positioning on the table, the examinations, and further cleansings contribute to further confusion and anxiety. The most frustrating and difficult part of labor lasts an hour or two but during this period the girl experiences the reality of possible death.

The moment of birth brings relief to her and the medical personnel responsible for her. She experiences immediate relief of discomfort and much of her anxiety. Within a minute or two she asks "What is it?" and is told "It's a boy," or "It's a girl. Do you want to see?" The baby is held up, head down, cord cut and clamped, for visual examination. She smiles and is visibly pleased.

The girl, medical personnel, and supernatural forces have cooperated; she lives again and is proud of her accomplishment. She remains fully separated from the social world, her accomplishment unannounced to the persons who await news of her safe passage. Within half an hour after the crisis is past, the baby is transported to the nursery via the waiting room. Family and friends learn that the crisis is past by seeing the baby. The meeting is a brief one because medical personnel rarely linger long among contaminated outsiders. The critical personnel are pleased that their prayers have been answered and that the girl will be returned to them, elevated in status by her ordeal and successful completion of the test.

An hour or so after delivery the girl is transported to the recovery room, her condition still monitored by medical personnel. The visitor, expelled from the area during the delivery, is invited to return and they talk in subdued tones. She smiles and says that she is feeling fine. The visitor comments on the baby and asks whether she needs anything, but doesn't linger because medical personnel insist that the girl must rest. The visitor is satisfied that she is out of danger.

The interaction between the visitor and the mother is the initial sequence in the phase of incorporation into a new status. The incorporation phase occurs gradually as the physical condition of the mother approaches normal and she is integrated into the social behavior expected of mothers.

The interactions of mother and infant [previously discussed] are not repeated here; the focus is on the articulation of space, time, and the social realities of parturient women. The girl, considered out of danger when the delivery is past, is still in a delicate condition. Remaining in the hospital for two or three days after delivery she submits to the demands of the institution. Most of her time is spent in bed engaging in the procedures and routines required by medical personnel. She is presented with three meals each day, symbolically returning her to one aspect of normalcy. Regular interactions with her infant, scheduled between other routines, periodically remind her of the fruits of her efforts. She is permitted visitors at very restricted intervals so that her needs for rest, nutrition, and therapy are not interrupted by outside stimuli. The girl begins to realize the magnitude of her accomplishment by the behavior of the medical personnel and visitors. She has never received so much attention or been catered to so extensively.

Usually girls are presented with another indication of incorporation into adult society before release from the hospital. Medical personnel discuss with them their plans for future pregnancies and offer to provide them with the knowledge and techniques to accurately predict their next child. The panorama of birth control techniques are displayed and girls are permitted to choose, with minimal guidance, the most attractive alternative. Most of them prefer the contraceptive pill and are given a three-months supply to take home with them.

Most girls look back on their postpartum hospitalization experience as a "good time" with good food, "laying up in the bed," and few demands on them. But they develop a longing to return to social life. The critical personnel who delivered them to the institution return to recover them and the new addition to the descent group. The identical persons may not all return but appointed representatives are among them. The mother, her worldly possessions, and the baby are released by the institution and returned to society.

The girl returns home triumphant; everyone is impressed with the baby. She is required to remain in the house, keep warm, and wear shoes so that she does not get chilled and become sick. The baby is her major responsibility and she is forbidden to "stir around too much" for a week or so because it is thought to cause "female trouble," excessive postpartum bleeding and, later, loss of muscle tone. Other knowledge and lore associated with the puerperium is transmitted to her during this period. Engorgement of the breasts with milk is treated with applications of camphorated oil and by expression of the milk. Fish is avoided, as it is during all periods of uterine bleeding. A diet and medications encouraging regular evacuation of the bowels are administered. The girl is permitted to rest as much as necessary to regain her strength.

The childbirth process drains the youth physically and socially but she is restored to society in a different status. The baby and mother are as one. The baby, important in the continuation of society and in joining of two kin groups, is the substance of the mother's elevated position. The status elevation occurring when girls become mothers is dramatic after the humility of early pregnancy and childbirth. The father, visiting baby and mother as often as possible, sits with her and proudly holds the baby. The importance of the baby is demonstrated by the gifts, visits, and comments visitors make.

After a week or so girls are not considered so delicate and are permitted outdoors. They begin to assume some household responsibility and permit the baby to be held and fed by others. It is after the mother has regained her strength and is permitted to leave the house that she becomes involved in the final rite of passage between childhood and adulthood. This rite, enacted wholly within the social context, is less dramatic than that of childbirth, but is ultimately more significant. It permits the girl to choose between adulthood demonstrated by motherhood, or a return to adolescent behaviors.

Most girls choose the role of motherhood and adult roles without equivocation. The importance of the baby to the descent group is demonstrated by the vigilance of adult women. They do not permit the infant to be neglected. If the biological mother does not conform to their expectations she is relieved of the responsibility for her baby. All young mothers are observed for behaviors indicating a lack of interest in the baby and omissions are brought to their attention. The acceptance or rejection of motherhood is determined by the biological mother and women in the descent group. This process constitutes the final subphase into the rite of passage between childhood and adulthood.

INTERNATIONAL HUMAN RIGHTS AND WOMEN'S REPRODUCTIVE HEALTH

Rebecca J. Cook

Neglect of women's reproductive health, perpetuated by law, is part of a larger systematic discrimination against women. Laws obstruct women's access to reproductive health services. Laws protective of women's reproductive health are rarely or inadequately implemented. Moreover, few laws or policies facilitate women's reproductive health services. Epidemiological evidence and feminist legal methods provide insight into the law's neglect of women's reproductive health and expose long-held beliefs in the law's neutrality that harm women fundamentally. Empirical evidence can be used to evaluate how effectively laws are implemented and whether alternative legal approaches exist that would provide greater protection of individual rights. International human rights treaties, including those discussed in this article, are being applied increasingly to expose how laws that obstruct women's access to reproductive health services violate their basic rights. (STUDIES IN FAMILY PLANNING 1993; 24, 2: 73-86)

Protection of women's reproductive health has not been a priority for governments, as reflected by the laws they have created. Historically, the principal duty of women has been viewed as bearing children, particularly sons, and as serving as the foundation of families. The cost to women's health of discharging this duty went unrecognized. Poor health, influenced by early and excessive childbearing, and premature death during labor or from weakness or exhaustion due to pregnancy and close birth spacing, were explained as destiny and divine will. Maternal mortality and morbidity were, therefore, not considered amenable to control through health services, education, and law.

Women's reproductive health raises sensitive issues for many legal traditions because the subject is related to sexuality and morality. If women could enjoy sexual relations while preventing pregnancy and avoiding sexually transmitted diseases, then, many believed, sexual morality and family security would be in jeopardy. Such traditional morality is reflected in laws that attempt to control women's behavior by limiting or denying women's access to reproductive health services.

Many women die or are chronically disabled from complications of pregnancy. Maternal deaths are defined as deaths among women who are pregnant or who have been pregnant during the previous 42 days.[1] The World Health Organization has estimated that each year 500,000 women die from pregnancy-related causes and that unsafe abortion "causes some 25 to 50 percent of [maternal] deaths, simply because women do not have access to family planning services they want and need, or

Reprinted from *Studies in Family Planning*, Vol. 24, number 2, March/April 1993, pp. 73-86.

have no access to safe procedures or to humane treatment for the complications of abortion."[2] These statistics are only one indication of the neglect of women's reproductive health and well-being.

Epidemiological studies can be used to indicate which women have limited access to care and are therefore at higher risk than others of maternal mortality and morbidity. The universal risk factor is the fact of being female. Maternal sickness and death may be triggered by pregnancy, but frequently result from cultural, medical, and socioeconomic factors that devalue the status and health of women and girls. Maternal mortality

> often has some of its roots in a woman's life before the pregnancy. It may lie in infancy, or even before her birth, when deficiencies of calcium, vitamin D, or iron begin. Continued throughout childhood and adolescence, these faults may result in a contracted pelvis and eventually in death from obstructed labor or in chronic iron-deficiency anaemia and often death from haemorrhage. The train of negative factors goes on throughout the woman's life: the special risks of adolescent pregnancy; the maternal depletion from pregnancies too closely spaced; the burdens of heavy physical labor in the reproductive period; the renewed high risk of childbearing after 35 and, worse, after 40; the compounding risks of grand multiparity; and, running through all this, the ghastly dangers of illegal abortion to which sheer desperation may drive her. All these are links in a chain from which only the grave or menopause offer hope of escape.[3]

There are, therefore, many causes that contribute to maternal death, and some combine with others to compound the risk of death.[4] For example, pregnant women whose blood is infected with human immunodeficiency virus (HIV) face aggravating factors that can lead to early death.[5]

Paternalistic control of women's sexual and reproductive behavior manifests itself in laws and policies. For example, access to voluntary sterilization services in some countries is contingent on the number of cesarian sections that a woman has undergone.[6] Laws and policies stereotype and punish women because of their role in reproduction, denying them equal opportunities with men. For example, laws that prescribe younger ages for women to marry than for men maintain the stereotype of women as restricted to childbearing and service roles, while denying them the years of education, preparation, and experience made available to men.[7]

Laws protective of women s health may be lacking; where they exist, they are rarely or inadequately enforced. In countries with no legal age of marriage, or where that age is low, or where the law is not enforced, adolescent pregnancy is common. Such pregnancies are associated with high obstetric risk and maternal mortality.[8]

In Nigeria, where there is no legal minimum age of marriage, 25 percent of all women are married by age 14, 50 percent by 16, and 75 percent by 18.[9] Kelsey Harrison and others have indicated the human cost of adolescent pregnancy in Zaria, Nigeria. Girls younger than age 15 constituted 30 percent of reported maternal deaths. A high proportion of teenage pregnancies ended in fetal loss, induced abortion, or infant death, as well as death or harmful consequences to the girl. Consequences included vesicovaginal fistulas (VVF), an injury to the bladder, urethra, and lower end of the bowel causing constant leakage of urine and, sometimes, vaginal excretion of feces. The adolescent VVF victims suffer infection and may be made infertile, becoming social outcasts as a result of divorce or of being forced into prostitution.[10]

Women's dignity and autonomy are abused during the delivery of reproductive health services, because the doctrine of informed consent is not enforced or is misapplied.[11] For example, the rate of cesarian sections is unnecessarily high in both developed and developing countries, in part because women are pressured to undergo the procedure without being given adequate information to make an informed choice between cesarian or vaginal delivery.[12]

In contrast to this traditional neglect, a humane view is emerging that women's reproductive health is defined as:

> a condition in which the reproductive process is accomplished in a state of complete physical, mental and social well-being and is not merely the absence of disease or disorders of the reproductive process. Reproductive health, therefore, implies that people have the *ability* to reproduce, to regulate their fertility and to practice and enjoy sexual relationships. It further implies that reproduction is carried to a *successful outcome* through infant and child survival, growth, and healthy development. It finally implies that women can go *safely* through pregnancy and childbirth, that fertility regulation can be achieved without health hazards and that people are safe in having sex.[13]

Services to promote and maximize reproductive health include providing appropriate sex education and counseling, and the means to prevent unintended pregnancy, to treat unwanted pregnancy, and to prevent sexually transmitted diseases and other manifestations of sexual and reproductive dysfunctions, including infertility.[14] Epidemiological and related data show how reproductive health services can reduce maternal mortality and morbidity and contribute substantially to women's reproductive health.[15] Epidemiological data demonstrate life and health risks from pregnancies that come too early, too late, too often, or too close together in a woman's reproductive years.[16]

Laws that deny, obstruct, or limit availability of and access to reproductive health services are being challenged as violating basic human rights that are protected by international human rights conventions. The primary modern human rights treaty referred to in this article is the 1979 Convention on the Elimination of All Forms of Discrimination Against Women (the Women's Convention).[17] This treaty gives expression to the values implicit in the Universal Declaration of Human Rights,[18] and reinforces the Declaration's two initial implementing covenants, the International Covenant on Civil and Political Rights (the Political Covenant),[19] and the International Covenant on Economic, Social, and Cultural Rights (the Economic Covenant).[20] Similarly derived from the Universal Declaration are regional human rights conventions, including the European Convention for the Protection of Human Rights and Fundamental Freedoms (the European Convention),[21] the American Convention on Human Rights (the American Convention),[22] and the African Charter on Human and Peoples' Rights (the African Charter).[23] Other specialized conventions exist, such as the International Convention on the Elimination of All Forms of Racial Discrimination (the Race Convention),[24] which prevents discrimination against women of all racial groups, and the Convention on the Rights of the Child (the Children's Convention),[25] which protects the rights of girl children.

The Women's Convention obliges countries that have ratified it, known as states parties, in general "to pursue by all appropriate means and without delay a policy of eliminating discrimination against women,"[26] and in particular "to eliminate discrimination against women in the field of health care in order to ensure ... access to health care services, including those related to family planning."[27] States parties assume obligations to determine risks to women's reproductive health. The means chosen by states parties to address dangers to reproductive health are to be determined by national considerations, such as patterns of reproductive health-service delivery and the epidemiology of reproductive disability. The goal is the reduction of maternal mortality and morbidity and enhancement of the dignity of women and their reproductive self-determination.

If international human rights law is to be truly universal, it has to require states to take effective preventive and curative measures to protect women's reproductive health and to afford women the capacity for reproductive self-determination. International human rights treaties require international and national law to secure women's rights to: (1) freedom from all forms of discrimination; (2) liberty and security, marriage and the foundation of families, private and family life, and information and education; and (3) access to health care and the benefits of scientific progress.[28]

Treaty Interpretation

Empirical evidence and feminist legal methods can be used to reveal the law's neglect of women's reproductive health and expose legal bias that damages women. Empirical surveys and epidemiological studies, including those developed by the United Nations (UN) and its specialized agencies,[29] demonstrate how governmental neglect of reproductive health results in high levels of avoidable maternal and infant death and sickness, and in the exclusion of women from educational, economic, and social opportunities.

Empirical data show inequities in access to reproductive health services. Governments need to weigh evidence of how laws endanger the rights of women. Data are widely available showing that maternal and infant mortality and morbidity are associated with a dearth of family planning services.[30]

Rachel Pine has commented on evidence of the harmful consequences of laws requiring parental notification of their daughters' intended abortions, laws that are contrary to mentally competent minors' rights to confidential abortion services. Her observation is relevant both to national and international protection of human rights:

> At times it seems that the law's ignorance of its actual impact is one of the most severe threats to basic civil liberties. When justice is blind to the fruits of scientific and social research, and to the demonstrable effects of a statute in operation, rules of law are divorced from the empirical world. Courts are thus rendered impotent in the exercise of their duty to safeguard fundamental, constitutional guarantees, for rights may be violated in innumerable ways not apparent by speculation.[31]

Some national courts have taken account of data that demonstrate how applications of national laws do violence to international human rights values. In Canada, for instance, the Supreme Court struck down restrictive abortion provisions of the Criminal Code in 1988 for violating women's rights to security of the person protected by the Canadian Charter of Rights and Freedoms. The Court acted primarily on evidence from a government-sponsored report, which the government had failed to act upon, demonstrating that the law operated inequitably and delayed necessary health care.[32]

A modern development in the formulation of rights has been the emergence of feminist legal theories.[33] These theories, particularly those that are evolving from third world contexts,[34] recognize pluralism in feminist understanding of law and of legal institutions. Feminist theories provide a basis for the formulation and interpretation of laws designed to prevent and provide redress for violations of women's rights.

Feminist legal approaches start with the conviction of women's unjust subordination, and they evaluate law in terms of how it contributes to the dismantling of such injustice.[35] According to Bartlett, varying methods of evaluation "though not unique to feminists, attempt to reveal features of a legal issue which more traditional methods tend to overlook or suppress."[36] The challenge to feminists is to apply their methods of analysis to international human rights law[37] in order to remedy the legal neglect of women's reproductive health. Bartlett begins her analysis of feminist legal methods by explaining that:

> In law, asking the woman question means examining how the law fails to take into account the experiences and values that seem more typical of women than of men, for whatever reason, or how existing legal standards and concepts might disadvantage women. The question assumes that some features of the law may be not only non-neutral in a general sense, but also "male" in a specific sense. The purpose of the woman question is to expose those features and how they operate, and to suggest how they might be corrected.[38]

Bartlett points out that this question challenges the assumption of the law's gender neutrality. She observes that:

> Without the woman question, differences associated with women are taken for granted and, unexamined, may serve as a justification for laws that disadvantage women.... In exposing the hidden effect of laws that do not explicitly discriminate on the basis of sex, the woman question helps to demonstrate how social structures embody norms that implicitly render women different and thereby subordinate.[39]

Feminist analysts try both to expose the negative effects of law on women's reproductive health and to make government more accountable for these effects. Bartlett notes that:

> For feminists ... asking the woman question may make more facts relevant or "essential" to the resolution of a legal case than would more non-feminist legal analysis.[40]

Feminist thinking challenges the accuracy of prevailing presumptions about women's reality, and has "begun to expose the deeply flawed factual assumptions about women that have pervaded many disciplines, and has changed, in profound ways, the perception of women in . . . society."[41]

Epidemiological studies can help lawyers better understand and explain the impact that the neglect of reproductive health has had on women and their families. However, lawyers are not generally trained in the use of statistical data, and epidemiologists often lack understanding of legal process and reasoning, including the rules of evidence, the operation of burdens and standards of proof, and the adversarial use of analogies and hypotheses. The difficulties of interdisciplinary work can be overcome by understanding the limitations of each discipline. Some feminists have stressed

both the indeterminacy of law and the extent to which law, despite its claim to neutrality and objectivity, masks particular hierarchies and distributions of power. These feminists have engaged in deconstructive projects that have revealed the hidden gender bias of a wide range of laws and legal assumptions. Basic to these projects has been the critical insight that not only law itself, but also the criteria for legal validity and legitimacy, are social constructs rather than universal givens.[42]

Feminists have also offered the cautionary insight that empirical evidence

tends to limit attention to matters of factual rather than normative accuracy, and thus fails to take account of the social construction of reality through which factual or rational propositions mask normative constructions.[43]

The International Protection of Women's Reproductive Rights

International protection of women's reproductive rights ranges from limited judicial or quasi judicial processes to the application of broader means of furthering accountability of states parties to human rights treaties. By their terms, such treaties establish committees to monitor compliance with their requirements. The Committee on the Elimination of Discrimination against Women (CEDAW), for example, is the treaty body established to monitor compliance with the Women's Convention. Other treaty-based bodies, such as the Human Rights Committee and the Economic Committee, are established to monitor compliance with the Political Covenant and the Economic Covenant, respectively.

All major human rights treaties provide for a system of reporting. Some of the treaties' bodies, such as the Human Rights Committee, also have the authority to receive petitions from individuals claiming that their governments violate the treaty. States parties are required to make regular reports to the responsible supervisory committees on the steps they have taken to implement their obligations and the difficulties they have experienced in doing so. Reports are examined by the relevant treaty bodies in the presence of representatives of the reporting states.

Treaty bodies have the power to make general comments or recommendations to indicate ways in which states parties should interpret and apply the respective treaties. These comments can be particularly useful for elaborating the specific content of broadly worded treaty guarantees. For example, the CEDAW General Recommendations indicate how states parties might formulate their practices under the convention and report periodically to CEDAW. They set goals by which to measure governments' observance of their international duties to put the rights of women into effect. Ratifying states are given latitude to choose the means to achieve those goals.

To date, the International Labour Organization (ILO) is the only specialized agency that has provided expert advice to CEDAW on the substance and working of the General Recommendations relating to women and work.[44] The ILO, unlike most of the UN specialized agencies, integrates its development work with its human rights activities and provides assistance to most human rights committees on setting standards and making them operational. The World Health Organization (WHO), together with the United Nations Population Fund (UNFPA), might consider providing the same kind of assistance to CEDAW, the Human Rights Committee, and the Economic Committee to ensure that states parties address women's reproductive rights adequately through, for example, general recommendations for reporting states. International nongovernmental organizations (NGOs), such as the International Women's Rights Action Watch, are constantly working to maximize state compliance with the treaties.

National methods designed to protect women's reproductive rights will be more effective in the long run than international methods of protection, because the latter are too limited in number and scope to deal with the particular complexities of violations in different community contexts. National protection of human rights as defined by international treaties derives its legal force from the incorporation of those treaties into domestic law.

Application of international human rights at both levels is explored here in terms of discrete and legally distinguishable categories of rights. Women's reproductive health interests often cross the boundaries that separate one legally described right from another. Advocates tend to invoke several rights that are alleged to have been jointly violated. They identify specific articles of conventions that they claim have been violated; tribunals will distinguish one right from another in their judgments, but cases referring to reproductive health include all of the different rights implicated in particular grievances.

The following analysis proceeds from women's right to be free from all forms of discrimination through women's rights as enumerated in international treaties: rights to life, liberty, and security of the person, the right to marry and found a family, the right to private and family life, rights of access to information and education, the right to reproductive health and health care, and the right to the benefits of scientific progress. Explanations of how each of these rights has been or could be applied to reproductive health problems are given as examples. How these rights are applied differs depending on the patterns of reproductive health problems in individual countries and how these patterns are understood.

The Prohibition of All Forms of Discrimination

The Women's Convention characterizes women's inferior status and their oppression not just as a problem of inequality between men and women, but also as one of specific discrimination against women. The convention goes beyond the goal of sexual nondiscrimination (as required by the UN

Charter,[45] the Universal Declaration[46] and its two implementing covenants,[47] and the three regional human rights treaties[48]), to address the disadvantaged positions of women.

In contrast to previous human rights treaties, the Women's Convention frames its objective as the prohibition of all forms of discrimination against women, as distinct from the norm of sexual nondiscrimination. The convention develops the legal norm from a sex-neutral norm that requires equal treatment of men and women, usually measured by the scale of how men are treated, to recognize that the particular nature of discrimination against women and their distinctive characteristics is worthy of a legal response. The definition in article 1 of the Women's Convention reads:

> ... the term "discrimination against women" shall mean any distinction, exclusion or restriction made on the basis of sex which has the effect or purpose of impairing or nullifying the recognition, enjoyment or exercise by women, irrespective of their marital status, on a basis of equality of men and women, of human rights and fundamental freedoms in the political, economic, social, cultural, civil or any other field.

When a law makes a distinction that has the effect or purpose of impairing women's rights, it violates this convention's definition of discrimination, and must accordingly be changed by the state party.

The inclusion in the title of the Women's Convention of the phrase "all forms" emphasizes the determination to adopt a treaty to eliminate "such discrimination in all its forms and manifestations" described in paragraph 15 of its preamble. The convention's preamble expresses concern in paragraph 8 "that in situations of poverty women have the least access to food, health, education, training and opportunities for employment and other needs." As a result, the convention entitles women to equal enjoyment with men not only of the so-called "first generation" of civil and political rights, such as the right to marry and found a family, but also of the "second generation" of economic, social, and cultural rights, such as the right to health care.

The Women's Convention, in prohibiting all forms of discrimination, including private discrimination, is intended to be comprehensive. It recognizes that women are not only subject to specific inequalities but that they are also subject to pervasive forms of discrimination that are woven into the political, cultural and religious fabric of societies. In addressing all the forms of discrimination that women suffer, the Women's Convention requires states to confront the social causes of women's inequality. Article 5(a) requires states parties to take all appropriate measures:

> to modify the social and cultural patterns of conduct of men and women, with a view to achieving the elimination of prejudices and customary and all other practices which are based on the idea of the inferiority or the superiority of either of the sexes or on stereotyped roles for men and women.

Female circumcision, for instance, arises from the stereotypical perception that women are the principal guardians of a community's sexual morality, and also the primary initiators of unchastity. Article 5 (a) points to the need to examine such customary practices, and might be used to require states to educate those condoning and practicing female circumcision about its harmful effects[49] and to use legal sanctions where appropriate.[50]

Included in the goal of eliminating all forms of discrimination is the elimination of marital status discrimination. This objective is shown in the provision in the article 1 definition that offensive conduct is that which distinguishes on the basis of sex, and which has the effect or purpose of denying women "irrespective of their marital status" their human rights and fundamental freedoms in the "civil or any other field." For example, a practice of health clinics to require a wife, but not an unmarried adult woman, to obtain the authorization of a man, namely her husband, in order to receive health care constitutes marital status discrimination that violates the convention and would, accordingly, have to be changed.

UN documentation draws on extensive worldwide evidence to reach the conclusion that "the ability to regulate the timing and number of births is one central means of freeing women to exercise the full range of human rights to which they are entitled."[51] Women's right to control their fertility through invoking the prohibition of all forms of discrimination against women may be considered a fundamental key to women's entitlement to other human rights. Article 12 of the Women's Convention prohibits all forms of discrimination against women in the delivery of health care:

1   States Parties shall take all appropriate measures to eliminate discrimination against women in the field of health care in order to ensure, on a basis of equality of men and women, access to health care services, including those related to family planning.

2   Notwithstanding the provisions of paragraph 1 of this article, States Parties shall ensure to women appropriate services in connection with pregnancy, confinement and the post-natal period, granting free services where necessary, as well as adequate nutrition during pregnancy and lactation.

In considering whether a restrictive abortion law offends this article, the question must be asked:[52] Does the law have a significant impact in perpetuating either the oppression of women or culturally imposed sex-role constraints on individual freedom?

A restrictive abortion law exacerbates the inequality resulting from the biological fact that women carry the exclusive health burden of contraceptive failure. Contraceptive failure is defined as "counts of unintended pregnancies occurring during the practice of contraception and the number of months spent at risk." The estimated rates of contraceptive failure in the United States range from 6 percent of women who use the pill and experience failure during the first 12 months of use, to 14 to 16 percent for the condom, diaphragm, and rhythm method, and 26 percent for spermicides.[53] Moreover, a restrictive abortion law requires a woman with an unwanted pregnancy to carry that pregnancy to term with all the consequent moral, social, and legal responsibilities of gestation and parenthood.

Since such a law has this impact, is it justified as the best means of serving a compelling state purpose? The purpose of such a law is to serve the state's interest in the protection of prenatal life, which becomes more compelling as the pregnancy advances. A restrictive abortion law is only one means of protecting prenatal life, and the question has to be asked whether it is the *best* means. Other means include sex and reproductive health education and making contraceptive services widely available so that women will have only pregnancies that they desire, reducing the need for abortion services and the overall abortion rate.

In 1987 legal abortion rates "ranged from a high of at least 112 per 1,000 women of reproductive age in the Soviet Union to a low of 5 per 1,000 in the Netherlands."[54] The Netherlands has a liberal abortion law, but also public funding of sex education and accessible contraceptive information and services, resulting in low and declining abortion rates. The Dutch law enables postcoital treatment in the event of contraceptive failure. This law characterizes interceptive methods used before the pre-embryo has become implanted in the uterus as contraception and not as abortion. This description is consistent with the medical definition of pregnancy.[55] The Dutch approach presents the best means of serving a compelling state purpose in the protection of prenatal life that is consistent with the right to be free from all forms of discrimination.

The Rights to Life, Liberty, and Security

The Right to Life and Survival

The most obvious human right violated by avoidable death in pregnancy or childbirth is a woman's right to life itself. Article 6.1 of the Political Covenant provides that "every human being has the inherent right to life. This right shall be protected by law. No one shall be arbitrarily deprived of his life."[56] The right to life is traditionally referred to in the context of the obligation of states parties to ensure that courts observe due process of law before capital punishment is imposed.[57] This understanding of the right to life is essentially male-oriented, since men consider state execution more immediate to them than death from pregnancy or labor. The feminist legal view suggests that this interpretation ignores women's reality. The Human Rights Committee has noted that "the right to life has been too often narrowly interpreted. The expression 'inherent right to life' cannot be properly understood in a restrictive manner, and the protection of this right requires that States adopt positive measures."[58]

The Committee considers it desirable that states parties to the Political Covenant take all possible measures to reduce infant mortality and to increase life expectancy. A compatible goal is reduction of maternal mortality, accomplished, for example, by the promotion of methods of birth spacing that would increase the likelihood of infant and maternal survival.

The argument that a woman's right to life entitles her to access to basic reproductive health services, and that legislation obstructing such access violates international human rights provisions, can be made on behalf of an individual woman. The argument must be expanded, however, where the threat to a pregnant woman's survival comes not from her medical condition, but from her membership in a group at high risk of maternal mortality or morbidity due to pregnancy. The collective right to life of women in groups at risk raises the question of whether states have a positive obligation to offer appropriate reproductive health services to such women, or at least provide education and counseling services that alert them to risks and to the means to minimize risks. The African Charter emphasizes collective rights in its preamble and might well be invoked to impose such obligations on African governments.

The Right to Liberty and Security

The strongest defense of individual integrity under the Political Covenant exists in article 9 (1), which provides that "everyone has the right to liberty and security of the person.... No one shall be deprived of his liberty except on such grounds and in accordance with such procedures as are established by law."[59] This right would seem to prohibit interference by the state in individual pursuit of means to limit, or to promote, fertility. A woman's right to liberty transcends her right to protect her life and health, and recognizes her right to reproductive choice as an element of her personal integrity and autonomy that is not dependent on health justifications.

Under international human rights law, states cannot compel women to conceive children against their will, nor force men to impregnate women. A violation of liberty and security occurs when the state denies women access to means of fertility control, leaving them to risk unintended pregnancy. For example, in El Salvador, where contraceptives are not widely available, women have about twice as many children as they want.[60] Further, a violation occurs when a state's laws allow husbands or partners to veto wives' or girlfriends' use of birth control. Courts in at least eight countries and a regional human rights tribunal have rejected applications by husbands or partners to prohibit abortions.[61] Parental veto laws may be condemned when they obstruct personal choices by mature or emancipated minors who are able to make their own sexual decisions, and to bear the consequences of their choices.[62]

The application of international human rights instruments to laws restricting women's choices has not been explored adequately. A special case for the protection of liberty and security concerns women who are imprisoned for terminating their own pregnancies. In Nepal women are often convicted for self-induced abortion, which is punishable by life imprisonment.[63] The offense, by definition, applies only to women, and may, therefore, constitute discrimination on the basis of sex. Article 2 (g) of the Women's Convention requires states parties "to repeal all national penal provisions which constitute discrimination against women." Women may be inappropriately charged for this offense, particularly if they had no access to contraceptive services, and be denied access to legal representation in court proceedings.

A barrier to the application of the right to liberty and security has been uncertainty about the interaction of free choice and wise or good decisions. Those with experience of life may well be able to make better choices than those without experience, but wisdom and experience are not legal conditions of freedom. Individuals may reach legal capacity for autonomous choice before they may appear trustworthy to exercise their freedom wisely. The tendency of the state to protect mature individuals against their poor choices, and to place them under the control of others whose judgment is deemed to be reliable, does violence to internationally legally protected rights to individual liberty.

Article 7 of the Political Covenant provides that "no one shall be subjected to torture or to cruel, inhuman or degrading treatment or punishment." The applicability of this provision to medical interventions, and to denial of desired medical care, is evidenced in the sentence of article 7 that provides: "in particular no one shall be subjected without his free consent to medical or scientific experimentation." Article 19 of the Children's Convention requires states "to protect the child from all forms of physical or mental violence, injury or abuse, neglect or negligent treatment, maltreatment or exploitation, including sexual abuse." These articles furnish grounds to oppose the cruelty, inhumanity, or degradation of compelling an adolescent to continue a pregnancy that endangers her life or health, and such treatment of children as female circumcision.

States ignoring the consequences for adolescents of the unavailability of contraceptives, the lack of services for unintended pregnancy, and the practice of female circumcision would be found in violation of the Political Covenant's article 7, as well as of article 19 of the Children's Convention.

The Right to Marry and Found a Family

In its origins, the recognition of the right to marry and found a family is a reaction to Nazi racial and reproductive policies that began with forced sterilization and culminated in genocide.[64] Article 23 of the Political Covenant and article 10 of the Economic Covenant both recognize the family as the "natural and fundamental group unit of society." The former states that "the right of men and women of marriageable age to marry and found a family shall be recognized."[65] The latter recognizes that "special protection should be accorded to mothers during a reasonable period before and after childbirth. During such period working mothers should be accorded paid leave or leave with adequate social security benefits."[66]

The Human Rights Committee's General Comments to article 23 of the Political Covenant explain that:

the right to found a family implies, in principle, the possibility to procreate and live together. When States Parties adopt family planning policies, they should be compatible with the provisions of the Covenant and should, in particular, not be discriminatory or compulsory.[67]

The right to found a family is inadequately observed if it amounts to no more than the right to conceive, gestate, and deliver a child. An act of "foundation" goes beyond a passive submission to biology; it involves the right of a woman to plan, time, and space the births of children to protect their health and her own. Accordingly, article 16 (1) (e) of the Women's Convention requires states parties to ensure that women enjoy "rights to decide freely and responsibly on the number and spacing of their children and to have access to the information, education and means to enable them to exercise these rights."[68]

Maria Isabel Plata explained[69] that adopting the Women's Convention into Colombian law[70] made this article part of the 1991 Constitution of Colombia.[71] The Colombian Ministry of Public Health has interpreted the Women's Convention to establish a gender perspective in national health policies that considers "the social discrimination of women as an element which contributes to the ill-health of women."[72] A new ministerial resolution orders all health institutions to ensure women the right to decide on all issues that affect their health, their life, and their sexuality, and guarantees rights "to information and orientation to allow the exercise of free, gratifying, responsible sexuality which cannot be tied to maternity."[73] The new policy requires provision of a full range of reproductive health services, including infertility services, safe and effective contraception, integrated treatment for incomplete abortion, and treatment for menopausal women. The policy emphasizes the need for special attention to women at high risk, such as adolescents and victims of violence.

In some parts of the world, the right to found a family is threatened primarily by reproductive tract infections. In Africa, for example, such infections cause as much as 50 percent of infertility.[74] Government inaction that violates this right constitutes a basis for state political accountability, whether or not the law classifies the right as one that governments must protect through positive action. If the right is negative, in that a state must not obstruct its exercise, the state might still be liable, not because of the infertility itself, but because of the differential impact infertility has on the lives of women.[75]

The right to found a family incorporates the right to enhance the survival prospects of a conceived or existing child through birth spacing by contraception or abortion. This right is complementary to the right of a woman to survive pregnancy. The right to marry and to found a family can be limited by laws that are reasonably related to a family-based objective, such as laws requiring a minimum age for marriage. An objection to many age-of-marriage laws is that the age they set is too low for the welfare of women, and therefore of their families, and that they set lower ages for women than for men. Women are frequently induced to marry at the minimum legal age or a lower age through nonenforcement of the law or exceptions to the law, because they lack alternative opportunities.

Parental support obligations may terminate legally at the age of marriage, an age when most women have no means to support themselves through paid employment and no opportunities to pursue education or careers. They marry and bear children early because their societies recognize no function or worth for women except that defined by biology. Women need legal protection against being conditioned to serve prematurely in the founding of families. Human rights provisions that no one shall be obliged involuntarily to enter marriage fail to recognize that many women "volunteer" for marriage because they lack an alternative.

The Right to Private and Family Life

The right to private and family life is distinguishable from the right to found a family, although for some purposes the latter right may be considered to be part of the former. Article 17 of the Political Covenant provides that "no one shall be subjected to arbitrary or unlawful interference with his privacy, family, home or correspondence, nor to unlawful attacks on his honour and reputation."[76]

The European Convention specifies conditions under which private and family life may be compromised or sacrificed to interests of the state. Article 8 provides that:

1   Everyone has the right to respect for his private and family life, his home and his correspondence.

2   There shall be no interference by a public authority with the exercise of this right except such as
        is in accordance with the law and is necessary in a democratic society in the interests of national
        security, public safety or the economic well-being of the country, for the prevention of disorder
        or crime, for the protection of health or morals, or for the protection of the rights and freedoms
        of others.

This article was held not to have been violated in the case of *Bruggemann & Scheuten v. Federal Republic of Germany.*[77] Two West German women claimed that a 1976 restrictive abortion law interfered with respect for their private lives contrary to this article in that they were not permitted privately and alone to decide to terminate their unwanted pregnancies. The majority of the European Commission of Human Rights rejected the women's claims and found that the restrictive laws did not constitute an interference with private life.

Greater scope was given to a woman's right to private life in the case of *Paton v. United Kingdom.*[78] The European Commission upheld a British decision preventing a woman from being coerced to continue an unwanted pregnancy through her husband's veto of her abortion. The commission gave priority to respect for the wife's private life in her decision on childbearing over her husband's right to respect for his family life in the birth of his child, and found that the husband's right could not be interpreted to embrace even a right to be consulted on his wife's decision. The commission explained that a state's interest in an unborn life is not greater than that of the biological father's, so that preclusion of his right necessarily precludes the state's right to prevail.

Rights Regarding Information and Education

Rights to seek, receive, and impart information are protected by all the basic human rights conventions[79] and are essential to the realization of reproductive health. The Women's Convention explicitly requires that women have the right to information and counseling on health and family planning.[80]

Article 10 (1) of the European Convention protects "the right to freedom of expression [which] shall include freedom . . . to receive and impart information and ideas without interference by public authority and regardless of frontiers." The European Court of Human Rights in the recent case of *Open Door and Dublin Well Women v. Ireland*[81] found that the Irish government's ban on counseling women about where to find abortions abroad violates this article. In order to comply with this decision, the Irish government can no longer ban this counseling. This decision also applies to other countries that are members of the European Convention in the event that they try to restrict the counseling of women seeking services in other countries.

The right to education[82] serves the goal of individual and reproductive health. Women have greater access to contraceptives when they can read and understand the risks to their health and the health of their children caused by close birth spacing.[83] Education affecting sexual matters can raise issues, however, of rights to freedom of thought and religion.[84] Conflicts have arisen when public school systems have introduced health-oriented programs of instruction on sexual matters to which parents have objected on grounds of their religious convictions.

In the Danish Sex Education case,[85] some Danish parents objected to compulsory sex education in state schools. They complained that it violated the state's duty to respect "the right of parents to ensure such education and teaching in conformity with their own religious and philosophical convictions,"[86] and either jointly or alternatively it violated their right to religious nondiscrimination, rights to private and family life, and the right to freedom of thought, conscience, and religion as set out in the European Convention. The European Court held that compulsory sex-education classes in Danish schools violated none of these duties or rights because they were primarily intended to convey useful and corrective information which, though unavoidably concerned with considerations of a moral nature, did not exceed "the bounds of what a democratic state may regard as in the public interest."[87] The Court recognized, however, that

> the State . . . must take care that information or knowledge included in the curriculum is conveyed in an objective, critical and pluralistic manner. The State is forbidden to pursue an aim of indoctrination that might be considered as not respecting parents' religious and philosophical convictions.[88]

The Right to Reproductive Health and Health Care

By article 12 (1) of the Economic Covenant, states parties "recognize the right of everyone to the enjoyment of the highest attainable standard of physical and mental health." Article 12 (2) provides that the steps to achieve the full realization of this right

> shall include those necessary for: a) The provision for the reduction of the stillbirth-rate and of infant mortality and for the healthy development of the child . . . d) The creation of conditions which would assure to all medical service and medical attention in the event of sickness.[89]

Article 12 addresses reproductive health services indirectly, in that multiple pregnancies and short birth intervals endanger infant survival and health. This article is reinforced by article 24 (f) of the Children's Convention, which requires that states parties "develop preventive health care, guidance for parents and family planning education and services." Epidemiological evidence demonstrates the significance of birth spacing to this goal.

The breadth of the concept of "health" is apparent in the preamble to the Constitution of the World Health Organization, which describes health as "a state of complete physical, mental and social well-being and not merely the absence of disease or infirmity."[90] In this sense, idealistic and ambitious though it may appear, the right to seek the highest attainable standard of health is inherent in every human being. Because mental and social well-being are components of health, unwanted pregnancy that endangers mental or social well-being is as much a threat to women's health as is pregnancy that endangers survival, longevity, or physical health.

States parties may be called upon to explain their failures to protect to such bodies as the Economic Committee.[91] The Economic Committee may want to seek assistance from WHO and UNFPA in the development of a general recommendation for reporting on the progress made in improving women's reproductive health, according to the WHO Indicators for Health for All by the Year

2000.[92] WHO indicators now include the reduction of maternal mortality by half by the year 2000.[93] Countries that are not moving progressively to meet this goal can clearly be found in breach of their human rights responsibilities to protect the lives and well-being of women. If, for instance, epidemiological or other evidence indicates that rates of maternal mortality or morbidity are rising without justified cause, the country may be asked to give promises of improved performance. Enforcement of promises will not be effected by such means as economic sanctions in most cases, but through, for example, international embarrassment generated by condemnation by nongovernmental organizations.

A general recommendation could explain that the right to reproductive health is part of the right to health care. This right includes the negative right of recourse to contraception and sterilization without legal obstruction, and also the positive right to be afforded access to related counseling and services. Similarly, women may claim a right to arrange an abortion, particularly when their personal history raises the medical risks of pregnancy above those faced by other women in their communities. Abortion is the practice of medicine, and women may claim access to physicians capable of undertaking the procedure safely. That is, the right to an abortion to preserve health may be claimed as a positive right where women are compelled to seek unqualified practitioners whose procedures are themselves a risk to women's health.

The Right to the Benefits of Scientific Progress

Article 15 (1) (b) of the Economic Covenant recognizes the right of everyone "to enjoy the benefits of scientific progress and its applications." Further, according to article 15 (3), states parties "undertake to respect the freedom indispensable for scientific research . . ."[94] Freedom of research requires states parties to tolerate and accommodate research on new techniques of fertility control and enhancement, and may require states to facilitate such research and development, particularly from women's perspectives.[95] The right to access to scientific advances is important, since so many of the modern techniques of fertility control and promotion, and of assisted reproduction, are the results of recent scientific research. Women's freedom from unwanted pregnancy by means of safe, effective, and convenient contraceptives has been achieved by scientific investigation.[96] These new means include male fertility regulating methods,[97] contraceptive implants,[98] nonsurgical abortion,[99] and contraceptive vaccines.[100]

The right to the benefits of scientific progress requires states parties to facilitate the use of birth-control methods proved to be safe and effective, and to favor interpretations of existing law that would facilitate their use. For example, some Islamic teachings allow abortion for up to 120 days of pregnancy, but abortion laws in some Islamic countries are not implemented accordingly.[101] Where abortion is already lawful, the right to the benefits of scientific progress and its applications requires governments to facilitate the availability of nonsurgical abortion, as was recently done in the United Kingdom by an amendment to the British Abortion Act of 1967.[102] Laws and practices obstructing drug approval and the importation of safe and effective drugs and other methods violate this right.[103]

States parties to the Economic Covenant are obliged to ensure that health professionals apply appropriate scientific knowledge according to the wishes and interests of their patients. When states delegate legal control of health professionals to self-regulating authorities that fail in this responsibility, the state may be held responsible in international law for treaty violation. A high rate of abortion performed by methods that are less than the safest available is one example of such failed responsibility. Suction abortion is safer than dilatation and evacuation, but in many parts of the world physicians' retraining in the safer method is not required.[104] State responsibility might require the passage of such laws as one passed in Italy that requires "the use of modern techniques of pregnancy termination, which are physically and mentally less damaging to the woman and are less hazardous."[105]

To protect access to the benefits of scientific progress states might enact what are called "use it or lose it" patent provisions governing therapeutic, diagnostic, and preventive health-care products.[106] When such product patents have been granted to sponsors that subsequently fail or decline to market them, governmental authorities in several countries, including France,[107] have the legal power to transfer the patents to a new holder that will undertake or approve the marketing of the products. In conferring a patent on a drug manufacturer, a government is giving the manufacturer a monopoly to market a therapeutic product. In return for giving this monopoly, the government expects a health benefit for its population. The potential for involuntary transfer acknowledges that a drug patent serves not only the commercial interests of the holder, but also the interest of the government in the health of potential users. When the French patent holder indicated an intention to withhold RU 486 from the market, the then Minister of Health, Claude Evin, threatened to use this transfer power, describing the drug as "the moral property of women."[108]

Conclusion

The widespread disadvantage that women suffer through neglect of their reproductive rights, under laws and practices perpetuated by states, denies them more than their enjoyment of health. Women's reproductive functions have been used to control women themselves. States have advanced their chosen social, economic, and population agendas by implementing laws and employing practices that control women's reproduction. To gain autonomy, women must attain reproductive self-determination, their path to many of life's opportunities.

Respect for the human right of reproductive self-determination includes the prohibition of all forms of discrimination against women, and the changing of laws and of practices that are the instruments of such discrimination. Governments must be made accountable not only for their acts of discrimination and their failure to eliminate the discriminatory laws and practices that they have inherited, but also for the effects of their conduct on the status of women within their countries.

International governmental agencies and NGOs can monitor states' conduct. The Committee on the Elimination of Discrimination Against Women can be a catalyst for the advancement of women's reproductive rights by developing general recommendations on standards against which country performance can be measured. Such recommendations might include reducing maternal mortality, establishing minimum legal ages of marriage, and promoting healthy birth spacing. CEDAW can also hold states parties to strict account by scrutinizing national reports with help from international agencies and NGOs.

Family planning and women's associations are beginning to provide legal services to women in order to help them protect their reproductive rights.[109] Rights are worth little to women where there are no corresponding duties on the part of governments, organizations, and individuals to respect those rights. Violations of rights will go unrecognized and unremedied where there is no understanding of those rights or no legal services to advocate remedies.

Great potential exists to enforce state responsibility for the observance of women's reproductive rights by employing the resources of international law. These include mechanisms of account under the Women's Convention, the Political and Economic Covenants, and the regional human rights treaties. Of the human rights of particular concern to women, that which frequently exists as the precondition to the enjoyment of others is the right to reproductive self-determination. This right expresses the fundamental principle of respect for "the inherent dignity and . . . the equal and inalienable rights of members of the human family," which the Universal Declaration of Human Rights observes to be the foundation of freedom, justice, and peace.[110]

References and Notes

1 World Health Organization. 1985. *Prevention of Maternal Mortality: A Report of a WHO Interregional Meeting.* Geneva: WHO. P.5.

2 Safe Motherhood Conference Conclusions.1987. *Lancet* i: 670.

3 Mahler, Halfdan. 1987. "The safe motherhood initiative: A call to action!" *Lancet* i: 668-670.

4 Fathalla, Mahmoud. 1987. "The long road to maternal death." *People* (IPPF) 14:8.

5 Melica, F. (ed.).1992. *AIDS and Human Reproduction.* Basel: Karger.

6 Brazilian Medical Code of Ethics, chapter VI. Article 52 (1965), cited in T. Merrick, "Fertility and family planning in Brazil." 1983. *International Family Planning Perspectives* 9: 110.

7 Cook, Rebecca and Jeanne Haws. 1986. "The United Nations Convention on the rights of women: Opportunities for family planning providers." International Family Planning Perspectives 12: 49-53.

8 Population Information Program. 1985. "Youth in the 1980s: Social and Health Concerns." *Population Reports*, Series M, No.9.

9 See Digest, *International Family Planning Perspectives.* 1985. 11:98, summarizing National Population Bureau, The Nigeria Fertility Survey 1981/82, Principal Report, 1984.

10 Hamson, Kelsey et al. 1985. "The influence of maternal age and parity on child-bearing with special reference to primigravidae aged 15 and under." *British Journal of Obstetrics and Gynaecology,* Supplement 5: 23-31.

11 Dickens, B. 1985. "Reproduction law and medical consent." *University of Toronto Law Journal* 35: 255-286.

12 Norzon, C. et al. 1987. "Comparisons of national cesarian-section rates." *New England Journal of Medicine* 316, 7: 386; Barros, F. et al. 1991. "Epidemic of caesarean sections in Brazil." The Lancet 338: 167-169.

13 Fathalla, Mahmoud. 1991. "Reproductive health: A global overview." *Annals of the New York Academy of Sciences* 626: 1-10.

14 Sai, Fred and J. Nassim.1989. "The need for a reproductive health approach." *International Journal of Gynecology and Obstetrics,* Supplement 3: 103-114.

15 Maine, Deborah. 1991. *Safe Motherhood Programs: Options and Issues.* New York: Columbia University Center for Population and Family Health.

16 Royston, Erica and S. Armstrong (eds.). 1989. *Preventing Maternal Deaths.* Geneva: WHO.

17 18 December 1979, 34 United Nations (UN) GAOR Supplement (No.21) (A/34/46) at 193, UN Doc. A/Res/34/180.

18 GA Res. 217 A (III), UN Doc. A/810 (1948).

19 GA Res. 2200 (XXI), 21 UN GAOR Supplement (No. 16) at 52, UN Doc. A/6316 (1966).

20 *Id.* at 49.

21 213 U.N.T.S.221 (1959).

22 OASTS at 1 (1969).

23 OAU Doc. CAB/Leg/67/3/ Rev. 5 (1981).

24 660 U.N.T.S.195 (1965).

25 G.A. Res. 44/25, 44 UN GAOR, Supplement No. 49, UN Doc. A/ 44/ 736 (1989).

26 Article 2 of the Women's Convention.

27 Article 12 (1) of the Women's Convention.

28 Cook, Rebecca. 1992. "International protection of women's reproductive rights." *New York University Journal of International Law and Politics* 24: 645-727.

29 AbouZahr, C. and E. Royston. 1991. *Maternal Mortality: A Global Factbook.* Geneva: WHO; Law, M., Deborah Maine, and M. Feuerstein. 1991. *Safe Motherhood: Priorities and Next Steps.* New York: United Nations Development Program.

30 Winikoff, Beverly and Maureen Sullivan.1987. "Assessing the role of family planning in reducing maternal mortality." *Studies in Family Planning* 18,3: 128-142.

31 Pine, Rachel. 1988. "Speculation and reality: The role of facts in judicial protection of fundamental rights." *University of Pennsylvania Law Review* 136: 655-727.

32 *R. v. Morgentaler* (1988), 44 D.L.R. (4th) 385 (S.C. Can).

33 MacKinnon, Catherine. 1989. *Toward a Feminist Theory of the State.* Cambridge, MA: Harvard University Press; West, R. 1988. "Jurisprudence and Gender." *University of Chicago Law Review* 55: 1-72.

34 See, generally, An-Na'im, A. 1987. "The rights of women and international law in the Muslim context." *Whittier Law Review* 9: 491-516; Plata, M. and M. Yanusova. 1988. *Los Derechos Humanos y La Convención Sobre la Eliminación de Todas las Formas de Discriminación Contra la Mujer 1979* (Human Rights and the 1979 Convention on the Elimination of All Forms of Discrimination Against Women). Bogotá, Colombia: Printex Impresores; Rahman, A.1990. "Religious rights versus women's rights in India: A test case for international human rights law." *Columbia Journal of Transnational Law* 28: 473-98.

35 Lacey, N.1987. "Legislation against sex discrimination: Questions from a feminist perspective." *Journal of Law and Society* 14: 411-420.

36 Bartlett, Katherine. 1990. "Feminist legal methods." *Harvard Law Review* 103: 829-888.

37 Bunch, C. 1990. 'Women's rights as human rights: Toward a revision of human rights." *Human Rights Quarterly* 12: 486-498; Byrnes, A. 1992. "Women, feminism and international human rights law—methodological myopia, fundamental flaws or meaningful marginalization?" *Australian Year Book of International Law* 12: 205-240; Charlesworth, H., C. Chinkin, and S. Wright. 1990. "Feminist approaches to international law." *American Journal of International Law* 85: 613-645.

38 Bartlett, p. 837.

39 *Id.*, p. 843.

40 *Id.*, p. 856.

41 *Id.*, p. 871.

42 *Id.*, p. 878.

43 *Id.*, p. 871.

44 Byrnes, A. 1991. "CEDAW's tenth session." *Netherlands Quarterly of Human Rights* 3: 332-358.

45 Articles 13 (1),55 (c) and 56.

46 Article 2.

47 Political Covenant: articles 2 (1),3,4,14, 23, and 24; Economic Covenant: articles 2 (2) and 3.

48 European Convention: article 14; American Convention: article 1; African Charter: article 2.

49 Inter-African Committee on Traditional Practices Affecting the Health of Women and Children. 1987. *Report on the Regional Seminar on Traditional Practices Affecting the Health of Women and Children in Africa*; United Nations. 1991. *Report of the Working Group on Traditional Practices Affecting the Health of Women and Children,* E/ CN.4/Sub.2 /1991/6.

50 Judgment of 10 July 1987, Case of Fofana Dala Traore, Cour d'Appel (convicted of circumcising her daughter contrary to French law). Le Monde, 13 July 1987; *Annual Review of Law and Population*, 1987, p. 205.

51 *Status of Women and Family Planning.* 1975. UN Doc. E/CN.6/575/Rev.1.

52 Law, S. 1984. "Rethinking sex and the constitution." *University of Pennsylvania Law Review* 132: 955-1,040; *Andrews v. Law Society of British Columbia* (1989) 1 S.C.R.143 (S.C. Can).

53 Jones, E. and J. Forrest. 1989. "Contraceptive failure in the United States: Revised estimates from the 1982 National Survey of Family Growth." *Family Planning Perspectives* 21: 103-109.

54 Henshaw, S. 1990, "Induced abortion: A world review." *Family Planning Perspectives* 22: 76-89.

55 Hughes, E.C. (ed.). Committee on Terminology of the American College of Obstetrics and Gynecology. 1972. *Obstetric-Gynecologic Terminology,* pp.299 and 327; The Committee on Medical Aspects of Human Reproduction of the International Federation of Gynecology and Obstetrics unanimously agreed that "pregnancy is only established with the implantation of the fertilized ovum." Fathalla, Mahmoud, Committee on Medical Aspects of Human Reproduction, International Federation of Gynecology and Obstetrics, personal communication,14 November 1985.

56 This article reflects article 3 of the Universal Declaration and is given further effect in, for instance, article 2 of the European Convention, article 4 of the American Convention, and article 4 of the African Charter.

57 Sieghart, P. 1983. *The International Law of Human Rights.* Oxford: Oxford University Press. Pp.128-134.

58 CCPR/C/21 /rev. 1 at para. 5, 19 May 1989.

59 This article reflects article 3 of the Universal Declaration and is given further effect in, for instance, article 2 of the European Convention, article 4 of the American Convention, and article 4 of the African Charter. This right, protected in article 7 of the Canadian Charter of Rights and Freedoms, was held to be violated by the restrictive criminal abortion law by the Supreme Court of Canada in *R. v. Morgentaler* (1988),44 D.L.R. (4th) 385 (S.C. Can).

60 Garcia, A. 1. 1991. "Situacion general de las mujeres en Centro America y Panama." In *Las Juezas en Centro America y Panama.* Ed. T. Rivera Bustamente. Center for the Administration of Justice, Florida International University, San Jose, Costa Rica, pp. 15-40, cited in C. Medina, "Towards a more effective guarantee of the enjoyment of human rights by women in the Inter-American system." In *Women's International Human Rights.* Ed. Rebecca Cook. Forthcoming. P. 344.

61 Cook, Rebecca and Deborah Maine. 1987. "Spousal veto over family planning services." *American Journal of Public Health* 77: 339-344.

62 Knoppers, B. et al.1990. "Abortion law in francophone countries." *American Journal of Comparative Law* 38: 889-922; Paxman, J. and J. Zuckerman 1987. *Laws and Policies Affecting Adolescent Health.* Geneva: WHO.

63 Women's Legal Service Project. 1989. *Female Inmates of Prisons in Nepal.* Kathmandu, Nepal: Women's Legal Service Project. P.13.

64 Eriksson, M. K. 1990. *The Right to Marry and to Found a Family: A World-Wide Human Right.* Uppsala, Sweden: Justus Forlag.

65 This article reflects article 16 of the Universal Declaration and is given further effect in article 12 of the European Convention, article 17 of the American Convention, and article 18 of the African Charter.

66 Article 10 (2).

67 CCPR/C/21/Rev. 1/Add.2, 19 Sept.1990.

68 This right was first established in international law at the Women's Convention. The origins of the right date from a 1966 UN General Assembly Resolution on Population Growth and Economic Development [xxii] that recognized that "the size of the family should be the free choice of each individual family." This principle was proclaimed as a right in article 16 of the 1968 Teheran Proclamation on Human Rights, stating that ". . . parents have a basic human right to determine freely and responsibly the number and spacing of their children," and in article 4 of the Declaration on Social Progress and Development, stating that "parents have the exclusive right to determine freely and responsibly the number and spacing of their children." Article 22 of the same declaration obligates the state to provide families with "the knowledge and means necessary to enable them to exercise this right." (UNGA Res.2545 [XXIV], 1969).

69 Plata, Maria. "New challenges for the Women's Convention: Reproductive rights in Colombia." In *Women's International Human Rights.* Ed. Rebecca Cook. Forthcoming.

70 The Colombian Presidential Decree No. 1398 of 3 July 1990; Colombian Law 51 of 1981.

71 1991 Colombian Constitution, article 42.

72 Ministry of Public Health. 1992. *Salud para la mujer, mujer para la salud.* Bogotá: Ministry of Public Health.

73 Colombian Ministry of Public Health Resolution 1531 of 6 March 1992.

74 Wasserheit, J. 1989. "The significance and scope of reproductive tract infections among third world women." International Journal of Gynecology and Obstetrics, Supplement 3: 145-168; Germain, Adrienne et al. (eds.).1992. *Reproductive Tract Infections: Global Impact and Priorities for Women's Reproductive Health.* New York: Plenum Press.

75 International Women's Health Coalition. 1991. *Reproductive Tract Infections in Women in the Third World.* New York: International Women's Health Coalition. Pp.3-6.

76 This article reflects article 12 of the Universal Declaration and is given further effect in, for instance, article 11 of the American Convention and articles 4 and 5 of the African Charter.

77 3 Eur. H.R.244 (1977).

78 Eur. H.R. Rep.408 (1980).

79 Article 19 of the Universal Declaration, article 19 of the Political Covenant, article 10 of the European Convention, article 13 of the American Convention, and article 9 of the African Charter.

80 See articles 14 (b) and 16 (e).

81 64/1991/316/387-388, 29 October 1992.

82 Article 26 of the Universal Declaration, article 13 of the Economic Covenant, article 2 of protocol 1 of the European Convention, article 26 of the American Convention, article 17 of the African Charter, and article 10 (e) of the Women's Convention.

83 Casterline, John, Susheela Singh, John Cleland, and H. Ashurst. 1984. "The proximate determinants of fertility. In *World Fertility Survey Comparative Studies* No. 39. London: World Fertility Survey.

84 Article 18 of the Universal Declaration, article 18 of the Political Covenant, article 9 of the European Convention, articles 12 and 13 of the American Convention, and article 8 of the African Charter.

85 *Kjeldsen, Busk Madsen, and Pedersen v. Denmark*, 1 Eur. H. R. Rep. 711 (1976), referred to here as the Danish Sex Education case.

86 Article 2 of protocol No. 1 of the European Convention.

87 Paragraph 54 of the Danish Sex Education case.

88 *Id.*, paragraph 53.

89 This article reflects article 25 of the Universal Declaration and is given further effect in, for instance, article 13 of the European Social Charter, article 26 of the American Convention, and article 10 of its Additional Protocol in the Area of Economic, Social, and Cultural Rights (signed in San Salvador, El Salvador, "Protocol of San Salvador," *OEA Documentos Oficiales* OEA-Ser. A-44 [SEPF], 28 I.L.M.156, 1989), article 16 of the African Charter, and article 24 of the Children's Convention.

90 The Preamble to the Constitution of the World Health Organization. In *Two Official Records of the World Health Organization*, 1948. Geneva: WHO. P.100.

91 Leckie, S. 1991. "An overview and appraisal of the fifth session of the UN Committee on Economic, Social and Cultural Rights." *Human Rights Quarterly* 13: 545-572.

92 WHO.1981. "Global Strategy for Health for All by the Year 2000." *Health for All* Series No.4. Geneva: WHO.

93 Starrs, A. 1987. *Preventing the Tragedy of Maternal Deaths: A Report on the International Safe Motherhood Conference*. Nairobi, Kenya. Washington, DC: World Bank, p. 8.

This article reflects article 27 (2) of the Universal Declaration.

95 WHO and International Women's Health Coalition. 1991. *Creating Common Ground: Women's Perspectives on the Selection and Introduction of Fertility Regulation Technologies*. Geneva: WHO/HAP/ITT/ 91.

96 WHO. 1992. *Annual Technical Report 1991 of the Special Programme of Research, Development and Research Training in Human Reproduction*. Geneva: WHO/HRP/ATR/91 /92.

97 *Id.*, pp. 59-76.

98 Dorig, B. and F. Greenslade (eds.). 1990. *Norplant Contraceptive Subdermal Implants*. Geneva: WHO.

99 Van Look, P. and M. Bygdeman. 1989. "Andgestational steroids: A new dimension in human fertility regulation." In *Oxford Review of Reproductive Biology*, vol. 11. Ed. S.R. Milligan. Oxford: Oxford University Press. Pp.1-61.

100 Ada, G.L. and P.D. Griffin (eds.).1991. *Vaccines for Fertility Regulation: The Assessment of Their Safety and Efficacy*. Cambridge, England: Cambridge University Press.

101 Sachedina, Z. 1990. "Islam, procreation and the law." *International Family Planning Perspectives* 16: 107-110.

102 The United Kingdom Human Fertilisation and Embryology Act of 1990, U.K. Stats.1990, c.37.

103 Pine, Rachel. 1997. "Benten v. Kessler: The RU 486 import case." *Law, Medicine and Health Care* 20: 238-242.

104 McLaurin, K. et al. 1991 "Health systems' role in abortion care: The need for a pro-active approach." *Issues in Abortion Care* 1: 1-34.

105 Sec.15 of Law 194 of 22 May 1978 (Italy).

106 Boland, R. 1992. "RU 486 in France and England: Corporate ethics and compulsory licensing." *Law, Medicine and Health Care* 20: 226-234

107 Code de Commerce, Brevets d'Invention, articles. 37-40, 2 January 1968.

108 Cook, Rebecca. 1989. "Antiprogestin drugs: Medical and legal issues." *Family Planning Perspectives* 21: 267-272.

109 Plata, Maria. 1988. "Family law and family planning in Colombia." *International Family Planning Perspectives* 14: 109-111.

110 Paragraph I of preamble.

Section VII

BIRTH CONTROL

Under the general heading of birth control one can take the limited focus of discussing only those practices preventing conception and fetal development, and thus practices which limit the birth of viable offspring. One may, however, take a wider view—as we will do here—and see this in the context of family planning. In the latter case we will include discussion of continence and contraception, but also of abortion and infanticide.

Birth control in some fashion has been practiced for most of human history though two of the major world religions Roman Catholicism and Islam (Maududi 1974) prohibit it. The two most widespread methods of birth control are abstinence and coitus interruptus. "It is not surprising that these two methods are commonly found, for either can be arrived at from the simple awareness that conception results from the injection of ejaculate, and, except for a few questionable instances, all societies possess this knowledge" (Davenport 1978:151).

The natural way of sexual abstinence was frequently associated with a variety of sexual taboos observed during certain phases of a woman's menstrual cycle, a couple's reproductive cycle, or times in the community's ritual cycle, e.g., warfare, harvesting of the first fruits, etc. Sexual continence may also be required of hunters or fishermen. In the process of breaking a taboo or performing a prohibited act, the whole community might be placed at risk. Many traditional societies have prolonged postpartum sex taboos. Generally speaking "societies with long periods of postpartum abstinence have generally low fertility" (Nag 1962:79). Other persons avoided pregnancy by practicing coitus interruptus—something like playing Russian roulette with a loaded six-shooter.

Vaginal douching with water or herbal mixtures was described by Lucretius, the Latin poet and philosopher, around 90 B.C. Very early on, camel pastoralists noticed that if they inserted a round stone into the vagina of the female camel the animal would not become pregnant during a safari and thus was born the idea of intrauterine contraception. Two Egyptian mummies have been found with semiprecious stones in their uteri. More than one hundred and fifty years ago, when rubber was discovered, the first barriers were prepared both to cover the cervix and as a more effective condom. Prior to this, condoms had been fashioned from sheep's gut or fine satin. Birth control could also be achieved naturally by prolonged lactation (which prevents ovulation), or by an extended postpartum sex taboo. Sexual operations, both ovariectomies and removal of penis or testes were described by the Greek historian Strabo. Operations could also be used for other purposes such as to prevent involuntary nocturnal emission or to assure continence. The former was considered a waste of nervous energy and controlled by spermatorrhea rings. Continence was assured by chastity belts. George Baggerley was found quilty in a court of law in 1737 in Leicester, England. It seems Mr. Baggerley was going to be away from home for some time and "he had cruelly with needle and thread sewn up his wife's vagina".

If pregnancy did occur, ethnoscience the world over discovered a variety of herbal or chemical abortifacients which prevented fetal development. The anthropologist George Devereux (1955) studied abortion in 400 preindustrial societies. He arrived at sixteen different techniques used by women. These include killing the fetus by mechanical means from outside eg. massage, squeeze, or strenuous activity, or by direct action internally on the fetus. This includes inserting objects or fluids into the uterus. Women may also ingest drugs or other preparation which may result in harming the fetus or dislodging it from the uterus.

Based on her use of a large cross-cultural sample Frayser concludes that "Where abortion is allowed, infanticide is also likely to be permitted. When abortion is disapproved, so, too, is infanticide" (1985:297). Abortion is more like to be acceptable in South American societies and unacceptable in African societies. Infanticide is disapproved of in North American, Eurasian, and Circum-Mediteranean societies. Infanticide may of course be selective as when one twin is killed or have a gender preference. Female infanticide is the more common form. In modern India there is a growing business for technicians who can produce a sonogram for a pregnant woman confirming fetal sex. Female fetuses are frequently aborted. As drastic a measure as infanticide involves infant neglect and ultimate death. These methods may all be employed in family planning and child-spacing.

Modern science has presented family planners with a variety of hormonal preparations to control ovulation, sperm production, or maturation of the blastocyst. Science has also brought it home to most communities throughout the world that family planning, access to and utilization of resources, health, and education are all interrelated. Along with insight and technical knowledge, researchers can also conduct studies and share this knowledge.

In the first paper du Toit illustrates how culture and language go together and the degree to which cultural traditions persist in a modern urban community. The next three papers discuss contraception and family planning in Mexico, Bolivia, and Peru. All three of these papers emphasize the importance for family planning programs to address both the woman and the man. While the practice of birth control may be an individual act, family planning is practiced by both sexual partners. It is based on communication and reason, and requires respect and trust . . . and honesty.

References

Davenport, William H. 1978. Sex in Cross-Cultural Perspective, pp. 115-163. Frank A. Beach (ed) *Human Sexuality in Four Perspectives*. Baltimore: Johns Hopkins University Press.

Devereux, George. 1955. *A Study of Abortion in Primitive Societies*. New York: Julian Press.

Frayser, Suzanne G. 1985. *Varieties of Sexual Experience*. New Haven: Human Relations Area Files Press.

Maududi, Abul A'la. 1974. *Birth Control*. Lahore: Islamic Publications Lim.

Nag, Moni. 1962. Factors affecting human fertility in nonindustrial societies. *Yale University Publications in Anthropology* 66. New Haven: Human Relations Area Files Press.

MENARCHE AND SEXUALITY AMONG A SAMPLE OF BLACK SOUTH AFRICAN SCHOOLGIRLS

Brian M. du Toit
Department of Anthropology,
University of Florida, Gainesville, FL 32611, U.S.A.

Increasingly the sexual involvement of teenagers is becoming a subject of concern for parents and health administrators, and a subject of interest for researchers. As sexually transmitted diseases spread and teenage pregnancies increase there is concern regarding the lack of knowledge on the part of sexually active youngsters. But unplanned and unwanted pregnancies are too often a product of secondary causes such as neglect, lack of concern or interest, absence of supervision or related socio-psychological or socio-economic factors. Frequently we may be dealing with youngsters raised by urban migrants or persons who were socialized by such older persons who had been reared in a rural tradition. These invariably involve a different set of morals and different expectations. A study of teenage sexuality should form the baseline for understanding decisions regarding sexual activity as well as planning for family health, family planning, and the use of birth control methods.

The study reported here was conducted during April 1985 in Atteridgeville, a Black residential area in Pretoria.[1] With permission from the Department of Education and Training, the author arranged with the local inspector and school principals to administer a questionnaire to students at two Black schools. One of these was a primary school where all the girls in the sixth and seventh grade (i.e. standard four and five in the local education system) were incorporated; the other was a secondary school where we administered the questionnaire to all eighth and ninth grade girls (i.e. standard six and seven). The ages of respondents range from 10 to 20 while the four grades were represented by 23, 55, 47 and 41 girls respectively. The great age distribution is typical of a rapidly urbanizing population and also the socioeconomic conditions in urban ghettos.

On the day we administered the questionnaire I was accompanied by my research assistant. She is a young woman in her twenties who is from a typical urban Black family, the father speaking Zulu, the mother Sotho, but the normal home language was English. After I explained the nature of the research, it was once again presented in Zulu and Sotho. In the same way each question was explained in the three languages. Sotho and Tswana are very close to each other and in this way we spoke to most persons in the study in their home language while everybody understood at least two of the languages we used. There were no boys or school officials present. Table 1 gives the home language of respondents.

Reprinted by permission of the editors from *Social Science and Medicine,* Vol. 24, 1987, pp. 561–571. Pergamon Press PLC.

Table 1. Home language of respondents		
Language	Number	Percentage
Afrikaans	2	1.2%
Tswana	34	20.5%
Zulu	32	19.3%
Sotho	88	53.0%
Other	10	6.0%

In this paper I will discuss the traditional background from which many of these girls or most of their parents come. It is essential to understand traditional beliefs and institutions if we are to understand and explain (but not necessarily solve) current problems. Following this general discussion the data from the questionnaires will be presented. In the last two sections we compare this material with previous studies on menarche and physical maturation, and finally look at the implications of our data for family planning and birth control programs.

The Traditional Picture

Krige, many years ago, pointed out that the "problems involved in illegitimacy have two aspects which it is necessary for us clearly to distinguish, the one moral, the other social. Illegitimacy as a moral problem is part of the far wider problem of sex morality in general including adultery, and illegitimacy is not necessarily an indication of the extent of immorality" [1, p. 23]. The social aspects must be seen against historical factors and current living conditions. It is important, paraphrasing de Jager [2, p. 237] that in the traditional Black communities pre-marital sexual relations were socially recognized and controlled while being regarded as moral as long as the parties conformed to the rules and norms which regulated such behavior. This institutionalized sex involved teenagers, i.e. pubertal youth who had been instructed in the effects and implications of pregnancies. Participation in this form of sexual activities was expected of teenagers and a girl who did not practice sex as it was allowed, or a boy who did not have a lover, were thought odd. But, says Schapera, "all the Southern Bantu agree in demanding that an unmarried girl must not become pregnant" [3, p. 60].

Since sexual activity normally involves two persons, and we are speaking of heterosexual activities, one or both persons might be married to third parties. It is then necessary in this overview to deal both with pre- and extramarital sexual relations. The traditional picture to be sketched applies to the various ethnic-linguistic groups in southern Africa represented in our school sample.

As is true in most traditional societies, there was a clearly defined realm for young men as contrasted with young women. This does not imply that children, i.e. prepubertal youths, did not have contact. Krige [4, p. 78] explains the playful courtship for 'sexual purposes' between girls and boys, and also points out that pubertal boys were warned that they could cause pregnancy, "he should keep as far as possible from the sexual organ of a girl and confine himself, in any intercourse, to the thighs"

[4, p. 93]. This form of external intercourse, known as *ukuHlobonga*, was recognized and clearly regulated, as were the implications for transgression.

> UkuHlobonga, then, is, what *we* should call, a 'regulated' vice, bound by many 'rules'. It occurs only between the unmarried; with those married, such intercourse would be termed ukuPinga (adultery). It must be confined, by the male, only to those whom he may legitimately marry, that is, must be exogamous—no intermarriage, no Hlobonga (properly so called). A transgression in this last respect, though, of course, not punishable, would still be regarded as a serious impropriety, if not disgrace [5, p. 569].

The Swazi, also ethnically Nguni like the Zulu, recognized a similar practice of premarital sexual relations. They referred to it as *ukujuma*. Part of the normal sex education of children was to explain this form of 'sexual indulgence.' The girl is taught to keep her legs tightly together thus preventing penetration [6, p. 87]. Also at puberty when specific guidance and instruction is given, children are "taught that the correct behavior is to *juma* and not to fornicate" [6, p. 151].

Further south among the Xhosa much the same pattern was found as girls aged 8-12 and boys between 9 and 14 started to meet in gatherings for 'sweethearting' or *ukumetsha* [7, p. 180]. Sexual matters are openly discussed by adults and the young are therefore not ignorant of such matters. They are permitted to gather in the veld or an isolated hut where they dance and sing and then pair off to sleep. "The couple lie in each other's arms, but the hymen of the girl must not be ruptured" [7, p. 180]. If the girl is deflowered the young man will be scolded and punished, most likely in the form of a fine which will be paid to the girl's parents.

If we turn our attention to the Sotho-speaking peoples on the plateau, a similar pattern can be found. Among the southern Sotho informants told Ashton that the youth used to be so pure that youths and maidens bathed naked together and yet remained chaste. We should however keep in mind that 'youth' was shortlived in earlier times. Casalis [8, p. 197] states that "When the young people have scarcely attained their fourteenth year their parents begin to think of their marriage. This is an all absorbing affair..." However, in reality in modern times almost everyone is said to have premarital love affairs, "there is good evidence that some children's sexual experience begins even before puberty" [9, p. 40].

Among the Western Sotho-speakers, better known as the Tswana, Schapera has very extensively documented attitudes regarding pre- and extramarital sexual relations. In earlier times girls, he states, "were generally married soon after they came out of the initiation 'school'" [10, p. 64], and it was regarded as a disgrace if she became pregnant before she was married. In fact the child, if not aborted, would be killed. This implies sexual involvement before or just after the puberty initiation.

Dealing, however, with modern times, he states that "few of the BaKxatla, whether men or women, are still virgins at marriage" [10, p. 68]. Sexual experience is acquired from the age of seven or eight, and small boys and girls play a game called *mantlwane* in which a miniature hut is constructed of branches and leaves. In this they imitate the married life of parents as they assume the role of 'husband' and 'wife.' There is a more modern angle which is quite novel, namely the belief that if a woman is a virgin, "she will hurt the back and thighs of her husband when he has intercourse with her," and for this reason parents are willing to see a daughter deflowered [10, p. 71]. Much the same picture applies to the Bafokeng, a different Tswana group. Because of the greater freedom among modern youth and due to a much later age at marriage, sexual involvement and unwanted pregnancies are common [11, pp. 200-201].

If we turn to the north, much the same picture as that among the Tswana emerges. The Pedi were said in early times not to have practiced external intercourse [12, p. 7 and 13, p. 99] but it seems that contact with the Nguni brought a change in this regard. Mönnig [14, p. 110] states that "boys are taught how to have sexual relations with girls, without penetration." These activities would follow social gatherings by youths who conclude 'pretended marriages' and assume many of the normal relations between husband and wife. Should a girl become pregnant the boy who is responsible will be punished very severely [14, p. 119]. Almost an identical picture is sketched for the Thonga by Junod [13, pp. 97-98] where the *gangisa* custom is practiced in almost the exact way as it is described for the Pedi.

However, it was essential that no pregnancies should result. Comparative statements made by Junod half a century earlier confirm much of this. On the day of marriage the Pedi bride was submitted to a physical examination by old women representing both families [13, p. 297]. This picture was almost the exact opposite of the Thonga custom in this regard, where "girls are absolutely prohibited from having any sexual relations before marriage and, on the contrary, after marriage a woman who has had children can have intercourse with other men than her husband" [13, p. 99]. This latter practice would obviously be interpreted as adultery, and in fact among the Pedi "while it is expected that extramarital relations will occur, these still have to be conducted with the necessary decorum" [14, p. 326]. This applies equally to the man and the woman.

In summary, almost every traditional Black community in southern Africa permitted, and expected, some form of sex play or external sexual intercourse among young people. It was always subject to social control, and was not supposed to lead to pregnancy. The men and women who were raised in these traditions frequently became urban migrants or residents. What occurs when these traditions must adapt to urban conditions of overcrowding, lack of space and privacy, lack of social control and discipline as parents both work away from home?

Modern Urban Conditions

There is no need, nor do we have the space, to expand on conditions created by urban migration and urban living. The conditions created by this process are, however, of central concern to us especially when they are linked to South Africa's laws of population control. We will here deal briefly with the effects rather than the process or the government policy.

In order to limit the number of urban residents, housing administration issues a house to an adult male household head, and ideally individual family units reside in individual houses. However, any residential survey proves that in many cases the male may reside there while the wife works the rural land holding; that boarders and renters share space; that the members of extended families visit for extended periods or reside permanently; or that couples live together while the union has not yet been legalized and frequently had not yet been traditionally sanctioned. A related complication is the decreasing significance of the extended family resulting in the young people, particularly in single parent families, growing up without family control or support.

This problem is particularly acute when the economic conditions necessitate that the parents both work. Young children and teenagers alike return home after school, or skip school, and spend long hours alone before a mother or father return home to supervise and discipline. Some years ago, Karen Shelly, a graduate student of mine worked with teens in a residential neighborhood in Durban. She discovered that the 'pretended marriages' we discussed above for the Pedi, were also present among Zulu youths in the city.[2] They took on the form of 'fictive kinship relations' with actual kinship terms (both consanguineal and affinal) being employed. "Through the fictive kinship game, teen-girls and teen-boys assume some of the roles which they anticipate having in the future" [15, p. 128]. She goes on to state that older teenage girls do admit to having sexual relations.

As is true in many Third World communities. the mother-child relation is the most important one as many households turn out to be matrifocal. Thus a mother and children may live alone, rent part of a house, or squat. The man, husband or boyfriend, may be away temporarily or permanently associated with finding or keeping a job.

As part of the influx control and population administration with the help of South Africa's pass laws, all cities have single male hostels. The wives or girl friends of these urban-living men are resident in farming, rural, or homeland, areas while the men work in factories, steel mills, or mines. The result is that a large number of these men visit in urban Black neighborhoods and befriend schoolgirls. The condition is complicated when teens spend long hours alone in a room or house while parents are at work. It should be kept in mind that these 'dormitory cities' lack decent leisure time activities, e.g. parks, organized support, movies, youth clubs and the like.

When we turn to the more serious relationships between men and young women we must recognize the dominant role of the man. Craig and Richter-Strydom state that "Strong peer pressure to prove adult status, fruitfulness and manliness through pregnancy exists" [16, p. 452]. It is generally accepted nowadays that a woman must first prove that she can in fact have a child before serious marriage negotiations will develop. This view is held also by parents, particularly women/mothers strangely enough, since they frequently get saddled with caring for children born to a school age or working daughter. Some years ago Rip and Schmidt [17, pp. 17-18] reported on a survey regarding the attitude of males and females on the sexual behavior of teenage girls. Table 2 reflects the difference made by *lobola* negotiations, particularly for women. *Lobola* (a word used in the Nguni languages) or bogadi (used in the Sotho languages) refers of course to bride wealth.

Table 2. Attitude of male and female respondents (parents) in respect of the sexual behavior of an unmarried girl of 16 years of age.

Approve that their 16-year old daughter	Men (%)						Women (%)					
	Def. Yes	Yes	No	Def. No	Total	N	Def. Yes	Yes	No	Def. No	Total	N
Sleeps with a man who has already begun lobola negotiations and who is engaged to him	4	7	14	75	100	244	27	15	10	47	100	254
Expects a child from the above man	4	9	15	73	100	244	27	15	11	48	100	254
Sleeps with a man who has only promised to marry her	0	2	10	87	100	244	0	0	20	79	100	254
Expects a child from the above man	0	2	11	86	100	244	0	0	19	80	100	254
Sleeps with a man with whom she has only a casual relationship	-	-	9	91	100	244	0	0	12	87	100	254
Expects a child from the above man	-	0	8	91	100	244	-	-	12	88	100	254
Sleeps with a total stranger	-	-	5	95	100	244	-	-	7	93	100	254
Expects a child from the above man	-	-	5	95	100	244	-	-	7	93	100	254

0 = Percentage is less than 0.5.   Def. = Definitely

Traditionally this would have involved cattle transferred from the male during and after marriage negotiations to the father (and mother) of the bride. In earlier days there also was the institution of sororate by which a woman who proved to be sterile or for some reason unable to conceive, would have 'sister' substituted to satisfy the marriage contract.

Presently the sororate has fallen into disuse and bridewealth involves money and other goods such as household needs. One example of how things have changed comes from an earlier discussion by Krige, but numerous variations are present. She reports here on a case listed as 'illegitimate' in the social workers casebook:

A woman had been living with a man for twelve years, during which time four children had been born, all registered as illegitimate. Her mother, a widow, rather than insist on lobola which might have had to pass to a male relative, required instead 'support' for herself and lived in the house of her daughter. No church rites had been undergone because, in common with almost all urban dwellers, the family regarded such ceremony without accompanying feasts as incomplete and derogatory and they had no money to meet this expense. Yet, during the period of my investigations, the couple, having accumulated sufficient savings, celebrated a church ceremony which I attended (this after the birth of four children!) and in this manner legalized according to European standards a marriage which had in reality been proper all along [1, pp. 21-22].

But family matters are changing as people settle in cities. Men still see children as a form of wealth,[3] the male is still essentially the one who opposes the use of birth control devices, coitus interruptus may still be the best known and most frequently practiced technique of birth control [18, p. 5], but there are also natural conditions which protect some of the young girls. While girls in the city are exposed at an earlier age and are at a greater risk for premarital pregnancy, they are protected from pregnancy due to lower fecundity levels for considerable period after first menstruation [19, p. 173; 20, pp. 253-256]. Add to these the cultural and socio-economic conditions and there is the likelihood of a decline in fertility[4] but it does not really touch the teenager who has very little knowledge and a great deal of pressure.

With this background information, firstly concerning the traditional cultural values and institutions, and secondly, concerning the urban living conditions, let us look at the research findings.

Research Data

The age composition and language affiliation of our research sample has already been mentioned in the introduction. This discussion will deal with physical aspects of maturation; sexual knowledge; and sexual activity.

Physical aspects of maturation

Half of the responding girls stated that they had noticed breast sensitivity, 143 (86.1%) had noticed a change in the size of their breasts and 23 (13.9%) had not. As regards the growth of pubic hair, 134 girls (80.7%) had noticed growth, while 32 girls (19.3%) indicated that they had not yet recognized it.

When we inquired as to the *degree* of breast development and the *amount* of pubic hair growth, we received fairly comparable responses. We are dealing here with self-reporting and the girls' subjective evaluation of the degree of change (see also the discussion which accompany Tables 8 and 9 below). Table 3 summarizes these responses.

Table 3. Breast development and pubic hair growth among a sample of Black South African schoolgirls

	Breast development		Growth of pubic hair	
	Number	Percentage	Number	Percentage
Slight	78	52.3	75	55.6
Moderate	64	43.0	53	39.3
Large/pronounced	7	4.7	7	5.2
No reply	17		31	

The next question asked: 'Have you experienced your first menstrual period?' An affirmative response was given by 110 girls (66.3%) and 56 girls (33.7%) indicated that they had not experienced menarche. On the question regarding regularity of menstrual periods, 56 (50.9%) indicated that they experienced their periods on a regular basis, and 54 (49.1%) did not. In the light of a high incidence of sexual activity (see below) and a number of the students who had already experienced pregnancies and live births (as indicated by my research assistant), irregularity of menstrual periods should be recognized as due either to immaturity (i.e. anovulation); or interruption (i.e. fertilization which may or may not result in pregnancy); or medical reasons.

Sexual knowledge

The research reported on in this paper formed part of a much wider project involving the climacteric in cross-cultural perspective. With this in mind, I was interested in the knowledge menarcheal girls had regarding the climacteric and the menopause in particular. We presented them with a set of questions of which the responses can best be presented in tabular form. Our reasoning was that since these young women were just entering the reproductive age, it would be important to see what they knew about reproduction, aging and changes in fecundity.

Two questions were aimed at their general knowledge regarding the age at which a girl can first become pregnant and the age at which a boy/man can first cause pregnancy. This knowledge, it would seem, is basic to any sexual education course and certainly underlies any family planning program. Table 4 presents these two sets of data side by side. It is obvious that there is a general lack of empirical knowledge, e.g. the belief that only adult men can cause pregnancy. It is interesting that the age of 21, which is the age of legal maturity in South Africa, is also recognized in both categories as the most important age of sexual maturity.

	Earliest age at which girl can become pregnant		Earliest age at which boy/man can make girl pregnant	
Age	Number	Percentage	Number	Percentage
12 or younger	36	21.6	11	6.6
13	13	7.8	1	0.6
14	12	7.2	7	4.2
15	19	11.6	23	13.9
16	5	3.0	19	11.4
17	3	1.8	9	5.4
18	10	6.0	13	7.8
19	3	1.8	15	9.0
20	9	5.4	9	5.4
21	37	22.2	27	16.4
22 or older	19	11.6	32	19.2

Table 4. Earliest age for female and male fertility

With particular reference to matters regarding menopause, we asked whether a woman was ever too old to become pregnant? A majority of 117 (70.5%) said yes, while 48 (28.9%) answered negatively (there was one girl who did not respond). When they were asked in the very next question whether a woman ever stops menstruating, they apparently did not see a connection. Most of the girls, i.e. 138 (83.1%), recognized that menstruation stopped sometime in the life cycle, while 28% (16.9%) did not think it ever stopped.

When we asked the girls at what age the changes occurred, we got the same lack of specificity. When asked to indicate the age at which a woman was too old to become pregnant, if in fact that occurred (see previous paragraph), we were given ages which ranged from 30 to 99 years old. One-third of the respondents admitted that they did not know. We should recognize, however, as Table 5 illustrates, that age 45 and age 50 were the two specific ages most frequently selected, and that 46 girls (27.7%) indicated the range between 45 and 50 when fecundity in fact decreases and when most women cease child bearing. They may even have heard an aunt or grandmother exclaiming 'No I'm too old to have another baby.'

Table 5. Age when a woman can no longer become pregnant and when she stops menstruating

Age	Age when woman is considered too old to become pregnant		Age when woman is thought to stop menstruating	
	Number	Percentage	Number	Percentage
Below 34	7	4.2	6	3.6
35-39	4	2.4	5	3.0
40-44	13	7.8	22	13.2
45-49	21	12.6	29	17.5
50-54	28	16.9	32	19.3
55-59	5	3.0	7	4.2
60-64	16	9.6	19	11.4
65-69	2	1.2	3	1.8
70 Plus	14	8.4	11	6.6
D/K	56	33.7	32	19.3

D/K = don't know

Whether any of them saw the connection between menstruation and fertility is not clear. However, when asked at what age (if at all) a woman stops menstruating, we once again find a tremendous range suggesting a lack of knowledge. One fact must be granted and that is that our question did not differentiate between natural cessation of menstruation due to ovarian failure as contrasted with a possible hysterectomy. Nevertheless, ages indicated by respondents range from age 21-99. Once again, we had 32 girls (19.3%) who admitted that they simply did not know. As was true in the previous discussion, the ages of 45 and 50, with respectively 26 (15.7%) and 29 (17.5%) respondents, were selected as the age at which a woman stops menstruating. The range of 45-50 years of age, when menopause is common, was in fact selected by 58 girls, that is by 35% of the total sample or 43.2% of those who responded to this question. One would expect that in the absence of formal education on the subject, young girls form their own subjective information based on information from female kinsman or overhearing discussions at home. Such lack of specific knowledge about the upper limits of the reproductive age may in fact be more widespread, including other societies such as our own in the U.S.

Sexual activity

Having asked the previous questions. and thus having received responses regarding knowledge essential to responsible sexual activity, we then went one step further by asking how many times a woman must engage in sexual intercourse before she becomes pregnant. Amazingly, see Table 6, we received the same range of responses indicating the same lack of knowledge. Responses range from 1 to 50 while nine students admitted they did not know by not responding.

Table 6. Number of times engage in sexual intercourse to cause pregnancy

Number of times engage in sexual intercourse to cause pregnancy	Selected by students	
	Number	Percentage
1	47	29.9
2	17	10.8
3	18	11.5
4	12	7.6
5	25	15.9
6 or more	47	24.2
No reply	9	-

Having received this information we next asked: 'Have you ever engaged in sexual intercourse?' With only one student not responding, 71 (42.8%) answered 'yes' and 94 (56.6%) answered 'no.' When we followed this up with a question regarding their age at first intercourse the youngest was nine years old, and 66.7% of them had engaged in intercourse by age 15. Two-thirds of those who had engaged in sexual intercourse had done so five or fewer times. This can be interpreted either as experimentation or as the early phase of regular sexual activity (Table 7).

The Comparative Picture

It is always important to place research findings in context. This is the only way in which they will be useful and allow for a comparative perspective. The first part of this paper dealt with the traditional picture. This permitted us to view our findings against a traditional system of beliefs and institutions which sanctioned certain behavioral forms but gave a negative reaction to premarital pregnancy. In this section I would like to place the maturational data in the context of the limited number of studies already conducted on this topic.

Table 7. Girls who menstruate by age compared to girls who have engaged in sexual intercourse by age

Age category	Total number in sample	Girls who have commenced menstruation		Girls who have engaged in sexual intercourse	
		Number	Percentage	Number	Percentage
11	15	1	0.91	0	0.00
12	10	0	0.00	1	1.41
13	18	5	4.54	1	1.41
14	15	11	10.00	4	5.63
15	45	38	34.55	18	25.35
16	23	23	20.90	18	25.35
17	13	13	11.83	13	18.31
18	11	11	10.00	8	11.27
19	6	6	5.45	6	8.45
20	2	2	1.82	2	2.82
		110	100.00	71.1	100.00

The earliest systematic survey of menarche in southern Africa was conducted in 1943 among four samples of rural Africans, two in Transvaal (plateau and very hot) and two in Natal-Transkei (mountains and temperate). The study included 1038 girls. Emily Kark found that among the girls 409 girls who had experienced menarche only one was aged 13, all the rest were 14 or older. "At 15 years, 40.5% of the girls were having menses; at 16 the majority (80%) had started, while it was only at 19 years of age that all the girls were menstruating" [21, p. 39]. She attempted to show the influence of altitude and climate but these were of only slight significance. (Kark also conducted a survey of menarche among Indian South African girls. This is being included in a different report, see [22].)

A second study on this subject is that of Oettle and Higginson [23]. Their study deals with 1002 girls in Alexandra, a black satellite city adjoining Johannesburg. The survey was conducted during a routine diptheria immunization program. While relating diet and general nutrition as factors which affect the onset of menarche, they merely conclude that "nutrition is somehow important" [23, p. 187]. They find too that the mean menarchal age is 14.89 years.

In the same year Burrell carried out a survey of menarche at the suggestion of A. G. Oettle, among African schoolgirls in the Transkei. Attempting to follow up on the economic status as a factor, a question on the survey permitted the researchers to classify a girl as coming from a 'poor' or a 'not poor' family. These were rural schoolgirls and the criterion employed to decide on 'poor' vs 'not poor' was one in which the school principal and the teacher together made the classification. "The not-poor girls benefit by receiving plenty of amasi (fermented milk) daily and a weekly ration of beef and poultry" [24, p. 259]. The age at which 50% of all the girls were menstruating differed slightly between the two groups (15.42 years for the 'poor,' versus 15.02 years for the 'not-poor'). The mean menarchal age was 15.22 years.

In 1969 Leary reported the data he collected during a research project in 1965 among Pedi (northern Transvaal) schoolchildren. The sample included 145 girls. It is significant that "menarche had not occurred in a single girl under 15 years of age, but 50% of the 15-year-old group were menstruating" [25, p. 324]. Our data allowed for a greater comparison with the research findings of Leary. Some years ago Tanner [26] had developed criteria which permitted him to classify physical development at puberty into five stages. These, along with other secondary sex changes, are discussed by Rauh and Brookman [27]. Leary narrowed the stages in breast development down to a three stage development and in his research he made (routine) clinical examinations. Following Leary we simply asked whether there has been breast development and in self-reporting students were asked to decide whether it was slight, moderate or large. While such evaluations are subjective they are specific relative to each respondent's size, weight and stage of development. Table 8 compares our findings with those of Leary.

Table 8. Breast development *

Age (years)	Stage 1		Stage 2		Stage 3	
	Leary	du Toit	Leary	du Toit	Leary	du Toit
11	6.7	46.6	-	-	6.7	-
12	52.3	40.0	-	30.0	4.8	10.0
13	47.1	55.5	5.9	38.9	11.8	5.6
14	57.9	60.0	15.8	33.3	15.8	6.6
15	33.3	55.6	8.3	37.8	50.0	6.6
16	-		-		-	

* Findings expressed as percentages of the number of girls in each age-group (see Table 9).

When we look at the relationship between age and secondary sexual characteristics, it is obvious that the urban residents report earlier maturation. Once again we are using self-reporting on a subjective basis. The four stages of pubic hair growth discussed by Rauh and Brookman [24] may be prejudicial since it is based on a Caucasian prototype. However, the age when all have experienced these characteristics is very similar to the age given by Leary. Table 9 presents this information.

Table 9. Secondary sexual characteristics *

Age group	Breast development		Pubic hair		Menstruation	
	Leary	du Toit	Leary	du Toit	Leary	du Toit
11	13.0	46.6	-	20.0	-	1.1
12	57.1	80.0	23.8	70.0	-	-
13	64.7	100.0	29.4	55.5	-	5.4
14	78.9	100.0	68.4	86.7	-	12.0
15	91.7	100.0	83.3	100.0	50.0	41.3

* Findings expressed as percentages of girls in each age-group

It is important to recognize that there are 113 girls who are 15 years of age or younger. Of these 56 (49.6%) had not yet experienced menarche. However, there are 53 girls who are 16 or older of whom not a single one has not experienced her first menstrual period. This data compares well with that of previous researchers in southern Africa. Kark [21, p. 37] indicates that in her study 40.5% of all 15-year-olds had experienced menarche, but it is only at age 19 that all the girls had reached this stage of maturity. Our data show that in the urban school population 84.44% of 15 year old girls had experienced menstruation and no 16 year old had not started menstruation. Oettle and Higgins [23, p. 183] list 14.89 years as the mean age for their subjects. while Burrell *et al.* [24, p. 261] list 15.22 years.[5]

The data for present day urban schoolgirls show a slightly earlier date for the onset of menarche, but certainly an earlier date for all girls to attain menses. Table 10 presents a comparison of Emily Kark's data collected in the early 1940s in rural areas in South Africa.

Birth Control

The Family Planning Association of South Africa originated in the 1930s. Its focus was to provide information on family planning and maternal care. "The clinics that were run by the Family Planning Association, with the exception of the present clinic in Johannesburg, were handed over to the State in about 1974 for financial reasons..." [28, p. 7]. Perhaps more significantly, 1974 marked the inception of the National Family Planning Programme undertaken by the Department of Health, Welfare and Pensions. Guidance is given through the mass media as well as personally by nurses in clinics and hospitals and also by family-planning workers who visit the homes of couples.

Table 10. Comparison of the number of girls in each category who experienced menarche

Age group	Kark (1943)			du Toit (1985)		
	Number of girls	Number having menses	Percent-age	Number of girls*	Number having menses	Percentage
11	78	0	0	15	1	6.66
12	76	0	0	10	0	0
13	82	1	1.22	18	5	27.78
14	112	21	18.75	15	11	73.33
15	121	49	40.50	45	38	84.44
16	98	79	80.61	23	23	100.00
17	91	87	95.61	13	13	100.00
18	68	67	98.54	11	11	100.00
19	49	49	100.00	6	6	100.00

* This sample includes eight girls who are 10 years old and two who are 20 years old. The total sample is 166.

The aims of the Family Planning Programme are:

(a) to publicize, within the next five years, the idea of family planning among all adults and to endeavour to involve in family planning service 50% of all women who are exposed to the risk of conception;

(b) to establish effective family planning services in all health organizations so that the service will be within easy reach of all persons.

In the educational programme, person to person guidance is of primary importance to ensure personal conviction, decision making and the practice of family planning [29].

At the beginning of 1978 the Department of Health, Welfare and Pensions, whose task involves implementing the National Family Planning Programme requested the Human Sciences Research Council to conduct extensive research in this field [30, p. 1]. The result is a large number of systematic surveys which give good baseline data for empirical studies and also studies of changing attitudes and practices. In addition, in depth studies have been made in Daveyton, a Black city, concerning familiarity with and use of various birth control methods.

Unfortunately family planning is directed at the mothers and mature women. Teens who are first exposed to sexual intercourse have little or no knowledge about pregnancy. Our research findings underline this clearly, while Craig and Richter-Strydom state that "82% of the pregnant girls had not known anything about menstruation at the time of its onset" [16, p. 453]. This same group reported that none of the girls had wanted to become pregnant, "yet only 12% had been using contraceptives (which obviously failed)" [16, p. 454]. No school system in South Africa has sex education and the girls are left to learn from concerned parents, peer group members or not at all. In a few cases the more mature or daring might visit a clinic. Information about birth control methods is readily available at clinics and through workers. For this reason, and because we anticipated sexual involvement by the older respondents in our sample, we included a number of questions dealing with birth control.

It should also be mentioned in this context that youths, girls and boys, received sexual education in traditional times. Krige [45, pp. 105-106] describes the Zulu custom and the supervision by the girl's age mates and her mother. Junod [13, p. 177] speaks of "instruction in sexual matters" among the Thonga: Stayt [31, pp. 113-114] gives the same for the Venda; while Marwick [6, p. 151 and 88] describes how young persons receive instruction in the familial context and that "marriage is an essential prelude to the birth of legitimate children." In fact, the Zulu made a clear distinction between a girl who had a lover and practiced *hlobonga* in the prescribed way and an *isigalagala* (an immoral woman). In the same way they distinguished between the child born to a married woman from an adultarous relationship (called *ivezandlebe* lit. illegitimate child) and a child born to an unmarried young woman (called *ingane yesihlahla*, lit. child of the forest).

We should also be reminded that many young persons today are socialized by a grandparental or parental generation that holds many of the traditional values. This is particularly true when children are sent from the city for shorter or longer periods to visit relatives in the rural areas or when a grandmother or aunt lives with the family. In her study of township teens, Shelley refers to the traditional Zulu practice of external intercourse. She then states: "Today, however, teen-girls say that it is seldom practiced among schoolgirls. Although they learn about this practice from older sisters or grandmothers, few young women find that their boyfriends will agree to external intercourse" [15, p. 132].

It is clear then, that both from traditional sources, e.g. the socializing influences of grandparents or other older persons, as well as information generally available to urban residents, there was an emphasis on knowing how to avoid pregnancy if not to abstain from sexual intercourse. Against this background, it is interesting to discuss the responses of our teenage respondents.

The first question in this section asked whether the respondent had 'ever heard about birth control methods?' A large number, 40 girls (24.1%), indicated that they had not. Among those who indicated they had heard of birth control the pill was by far the best known and the most highly preferred. The second was the intra-uterine device, referred to by some women as *shongololo* (the centipede). Another popular method is the injection. In South Africa the injection of Depo-provera, still unavailable in the United States, is common and its use was found among women in all ethnic groups.

It is a well known fact that in male dominated societies the man is of critical importance in family planning [32,33]. Frequently the woman must give proof of fecundity before a man will marry her, and in the community under discussion such proof often precedes any negotiation to transfer the *lobola/bogadi* (bride wealth). There is a question whether the man is even involved in birth control. We asked the sample of schoolgirls whether 'a man (can) practice birth control'. The responses, presented in Table 11, are telling.

Table 11. Can a man practice birth control?		
	Number	Percentage
Yes	59	35.5
No	51	30.7
Don't know	56	33.7

The very next question asked whether the girls had ever heard about condoms. A staggering 147 girls (91.3%) said 'no,' and only 13 girls (8.1%) responded affirmatively.[6] When we explored their information concerning the male's role, we found even less knowledge. Asked about 'surgical or sterilization', 92% indicated they had never heard of it, and when 'withdrawal' was mentioned, 95% denied any knowledge of this form of male birth control. The latter figure is interesting since Mostert and du Plessis [18, p. 70] indicate that coitus interruptus is the best known and most frequently practiced form of birth control. I want to repeat here that the questions were all asked one at a time and explained in English, Zulu and Sotho.

Findings regarding specific kinds of birth control devices and their knowledge concerning and preference for these, will be discussed elsewhere. It is sufficient to emphasize that Black South African teenage girls simply do not have enough information about birth control methods. This is particularly true if we keep in mind the lack of general sexual knowledge (e.g. the number of times intercourse should take place, age at which girl can become pregnant, age at which boy/man is able to cause pregnancy, and related basic information), and the number who are sexually active.

Attitudes

A final set of questions pertain to the attitudes which schoolgirls hold regarding sexuality and a woman's control over her own sexuality. It was argued that these attitudes are at once a product of the socialization they received as well as the conditions under which they live. Their attitudes will reflect the patrilineal society from which all of them come but also the educated urban conditions where the realities of earning an income must be balanced against the effects of family size, family composition and living conditions.

Above we already discussed the age at which these schoolgirls have become sexually active and the number who claim to have engaged in sexual intercourse (see Table 7 above). However, the ideal differs quite markedly from the actual behavior. When respondents were asked how old a girl should be before she first engages in sexual intercourse, 64 (58.18%) of all those who had reached menarche, and 36 (64.29%) of the pre-menarcheal students, indicated age 20 or above.

The ethnographic information we discussed contrasted the traditional life in a strong kinship based community with the modern household based life in the city. With traditional external intercourse something of the past, our next question whether a woman should wait until marriage before engaging in sexual intercourse, implied intercourse with penetration. It is interesting that a larger percentage of menarcheal girls (52.34%) said 'no' than pre-menarcheal ones (35.71%). A major factor here is the age variation. Since all 16 year old girls have experienced menarche, those in the pre-menarche category are below this age. When 64.29% of them indicated that a woman should wait for marriage before engaging in sexual intercourse we are most likely dealing with the younger, less experienced and less sexually active group in the study sample.

Given the status of males and their traditional role of dominance we asked two related questions the responses to which are presented in Tables 12 and 13. The first the question asked whether a girl had the right to refuse a boy/man who wanted to have sexual intercourse. In the second the question pertained to the right of a wife to refuse her husband who wanted to have sexual intercourse. When a boy/man was under discussion 101 or 61.59% of the total sample felt that the girl had the right to refuse sexual advances. However, only 46 or 28.04% of the girls felt that when the husband made advances, a wife could refuse sexual intercourse.

Table 12. Should a girl have the right to refuse a boy/man?

Status of girl responding	Yes		No	
	Number	Percentage	Number	Percentage
Menarcheal	71	65.74	37	34.26
Pre-menarcheal	31	53.57	26	46.43

Table 13. Should a wife have the right to refuse her husband?

Status of girl responding	Yes		No	
	Number	Percentage	Number	Percentage
Menarcheal	23	21.10	86	78.90
Pre-menarcheal	23	41.82	32	58.18

The last two questions dealt with the attitudes of these schoolgirls concerning sexual intercourse and family planning. While the discussion referred to in the previous section pertained to the use of birth control methods and devices, these questions specifically mentioned sexual intercourse in the planning of pregnancies. Thus we asked whether parents could decide exactly how many children they wanted and plan this specifically? Almost 80% of the total sample indicated that this was possible and the totals of pre- and post-menarcheal girls was less than half a percentage point apart. In the last question we asked whether a woman should limit having sexual intercourse to when she wants to have a baby? While the connection was not specifically made, the respondents should have remembered the previous questions which dealt with methods of birth control. Nevertheless, the total responses are quite interesting. Almost half (49.4%) of all the school girls indicated 'yes', that intercourse should be restricted to reproduction.

51.82% of the post-menarcheal girls elected this response as compared to 44.64% of the girls who had not yet experienced menstruation.

Table 14. Present use of modern contraceptive devices according to education

| | Level of education | | |
Contraceptive use	Standard 5 or lower	Standard 6 or higher	All women
Users	32.6	44.8	39.6
Non-users	67.4	55.2	60.4
Total	100.0	100.0	100.0
N	239	324	563
Device used:			
Pill	11.7	34.5	35.0
I.U.D.	28.2	48.3	41.3
Injection	29.5	15.8	20.6
Condom	-	-	-
Sterilization	6.4	1.4	3.1
Total	100.0	100.0	100.0
N	78	145	223

Conclusion

This paper presented the results of a survey concerning secondary sexual maturation, sexuality and knowledge concerning birth control. Rather than present the data in a sterile form, devoid of historical and cultural context, I have attempted to sketch the traditions from which these girls come. In other words, what are the values, accepted behaviors, institutions and levels of information which influence their decisions and give direction to their actions. I have also, where such information exists, compared our interethnic sample of urban schoolgirls with other research samples.

One of the aspects which makes this information unique is that it can be projected against a cultural tradition, participated in by many grandparents and parents, of institutionalized sexual play. While a young Zulu male had to get permission from the girls *intanga* (age set), and while such play could only occur between potential marriage partners, the important fact is that it always involved external intercourse. This was true for most of the linguistic-ethnic groups in southern Africa.

Urban demographic factors created new problems. Residential patterns changed from extended residences to that of a nuclear family or even more than one family per house. Such separate households were not necessarily based on kinship and frequently created conditions for pre- or extramarital relations. Because of the economic conditions young people spend long periods in each other's company or alone. Moreover, friendships frequently develop between schoolgirls and married men, living alone in bachelor quarters or so-called hostels.

Research findings show a general lack of empirical knowledge or understanding as regards sexual matters. This applies to the relationship between age and fertility, as well as sexual intercourse and pregnancy. When all of these matters are considered together and we find that almost half of these teenage girls have engaged in sexual intercourse, the picture must change to one of concern. This is particularly true when we notice the limited knowledge they have concerning birth control and especially the males (joint) responsibility.

In a later part of the discussion we noticed that these urban residents, where living conditions and nutrition compare favorably with the previous study groups, show comparable secondary sexual maturation. The age of menarche in our subjects had in fact decreased, suggesting improved living conditions.

Notes

1 Grateful acknowledgement is made to the Human Sciences Research Council in Pretoria for financial assistance which made this study possible. The analysis, interpretation, and conclusions are the sole responsibility of the author.

2 John Blacking found such fictive kinship groups among Venda schoolgirls in the northern Transvaal, adjacent to the Pedi whom we discussed above [34].

3 In a survey of urban Pedi men, 75% of the group relied in the affirmative to a question whether many children make a man rich [35].

4 "Factors and social conditions which are usually associated with a decline in fertility (or which are regarded as a prerequisite for a decline), can be distinguished among the Bantu in South Africa. The structures based on kinship are weakening in the cities; the social, political, economic and religious value of children becomes more vague as the individual orients himself towards more specialised institutions; the male-dominant family is making way for more equal relationships (it has been averred that especially women are more motivated towards small families) and a marked shift in emphasis from ascribed to acquired status is in evidence together with greater possibilities for social mobility. Add to this the gain in the proportion of literate persons in the population, urbanization, exposure to media of mass communication, female labour, greater prosperity, the growing insistence that children be educated and the availability of modern contraception [36, p. 24].

5 These figures were arrived at by probit analysis. Our own data do not permit this method to be used.

6 A recent study of the use of birth control devices, found not one case of the use of the condom. Table 14, translated from the original report, presents the findings of Van der Merwe [37, p. 12].

References

1. Krige E. J. The disintegration of family life. Illegitimacy. Paper Presented to Conference on African Family Life. Christian Council of South Africa, Pretoria, 1940.

2. Jager E. J. de Die tradisionele seksuele sedelikheid van die Suid-Afrikaanse Bantoe: N Kruis-kulturele onder-soek. *Nederduit. Gereform. Teol. Tydsk.* **5**, 1964.

3. Schapera I. Premarital pregnancy and native opinion. *Africa* **VI**, 1, 1933.

4. Krige E. J. *The Social system of the Zulus.* Shuter & Shooter, Pietermaritzburg, 1950.

5. Bryant A. T. *The Zulu People.* Shuter & Shooter, Pietermaritzburg, 1949.

6. Marwick B. A. *The Swazi.* The University Press, Cambridge, 1940.

7. Hunter M. *Reaction to Conquest.* The University Press, Oxford, 1964 (first published 1936).

8. Casalis E. *The Basuto.* Nisbett, London, 1861.

9. Ashton H. *The Basuto.* The University Press, Oxford, 1952.

10. Schapera I. Premarital pregnancy and native opinion. *Africa* **VI**, 1, 1933.

11. Coertze R. D. *Die Familie-, erf-en opvolgingsreg van die Bafokeng van Rusten-burg.* H.S.R.C. Publications Series No. 8, Pretoria, 1971.

12. Harries C. H. L. *The Laws and Customs of the Bapedi and Cognate Tribes of the Transvaal.* Hortors, Johannes-burg, 1929.

13. Junod P. *The Life of a South African Tribe*, Vol. 1, 2nd edn. Macmillan, London, 1927.

14. Mönnig H. O. *The Pedi* van Schaik, Pretoria, 1967.

15. Shelley K. Township teens: A study of socialization processes among urban Black schoolgirls in South Af-rica. M.A. thesis. University of Florida, 1975.

16. Craig A. P. and Richter-Strydom L. M. Unplanned pregnancies among urban Zulu schoolgirls. *S. Afr. med. J.* **63**, 1983.

17. Rip M. and Schmidt J. J. *Black Pre-Marital Illegitimacy in Pretoria*, H.S.R.C. Research Findings No. S-N-100. Pretoria, 1977.

18. Mostert W. P. and Plessis J. L. du *Die Gesinsbouproses by Bantoes in die Munisipale Gebied Pretoria.* Re-search Report No. S-17. H.S.R.C., Pretoria, 1972.

19. Longmore L. *The Dispossessed.* Jonathan Cape, London, 1959.

20. Mayer P. *Townsmen and Tribesmen* Oxford University Press, Cape Town, 1971.

21. Kark E. Menarche in South African Bantu girls. *S. Afr. J. med. Sci.* **8**, 1943.

22. du Toit B. M. Menarche among Indian South African girls. Unpublished manuscript.

23. Oettle A. G. and Higginson J. The age at menarche in South African Bantu (Negro) girls. *Hum. Biol.* **33**, 1961.

24. Burrell R. J. W., Healey M. J. R. and Tanner J. M. Age at menarche in South African Bantu schoolgirls living in the Transkei Reserve. *Hum. Biol.* **33**, 1961.

25. Leary P. M. Nutrition and the menarche. *S. Afr. med. J.* **5**, 1969.

26. Tanner J. M. *Growth of Adolescence.* Blackwell, Oxford, 1962.

27. Rauh J. L. and Brookman R. R. Adolescent developmental stages. In *Children are Different: Developmental Physiology* (Edited by Johnson R., Moore W. M. and Jeffries J. E.). Ross Laboratories, Columbus, Ohio, 1978.

28. Jardine A. F. Endlovini: a case study of a South African squatter community. Internship report for M.A. degree. University of Florida, 1984.

29. Department of Health. *The National Family Planning Programme.* Government Printer, Pretoria, 1974.

30. Erasmus G. *Users of the Intra-Uterine Device in Daveyton*, Research Findings No. S.N. 212. H.S.R.C. Pretoria, 1981.

31. Stayt H. A. *The Bavenda.* Oxford University Press, London, 1931.

32. Stycos J. M. *Human Fertility in Latin America.* Cornell University Press, Ithaca, N.Y., 1968.

33. Kirk D. Factors affecting Moslem nationality In *Population and Society* (Edited by Nam C. B.). Houghton Mifflin, Boston, Mass., 1968.

34. Blacking J. Fictive kinship amongst girls of the Venda of the Northern Transvaal. *Man* **59**, 1959.

35. Lötter J. M. and Schmidt J. J. Attitudes with regard to size of family and knowledge about use of and attitude toward contraception in a group of Pedi males. *Humanitas* **2**, 2, 1973.

36. Lötter J. M. and Tonder J. L. van. *Fertility and Family Planning among Blacks in South Africa, 1974.* Human Sciences Research Council, Report No. S-39, Pretoria, 1976.

37. Van der Merwe R. B. *Fertiliteit en gesinsbeplanning in Daveyton: Opname onder vroue*, Research Findings, No S-N-219. H.S.R.C., Pretoria, 1982.

SEX, CONTRACEPTION, AND PREGNANCY AMONG ADOLESCENTS IN MEXICO CITY

Susan Pick de Weiss, Lucille C. Atkin, James N. Gribble, and Patricia Andrade-Palos

This article presents the development and results of a study that analyzed the psychosocial determinants of abstaining from sexual intercourse, practicing contraception, and avoiding pregnancy. It was carried out with a representative household and a clinic sample of 12-19-year-old females of lower-middle and lower socioeconomic levels in Mexico City. Among the implications of the results for program design are: (1) the need for clarifying erroneous beliefs and providing detailed, practical knowledge concerning sexuality, pregnancy, use of and access to contraceptives; (2) a broad definition of sex education that emphasizes family communication, values clarification, provision of alternative role options for women other than motherhood, and both the goals and the skills needed to achieve them—for example, independent decision-making. Attention to male attitudes and communication skills as well as ways of improving communication and support networks among peers was also found to be essential. (STUDIES IN FAMILY PLANNING 1991; 22, 2: 74-82)

Psychosocial variables have been shown to be related to adolescent sexual and contraceptive behavior (Atkin and Pick de Weiss, 1989). However, it is clear that these factors vary to some degree across different cultures. The present study compares such variables between female Mexican adolescents who have not initiated sexual relations and those who have; between sexually active adolescents who have used contraceptives and those who have not; and between adolescents who are pregnant and those who have never been pregnant.

In Mexico it has been calculated that, in 1990, 25.1 percent of the population (85.7 million) is between 10 and 19 years of age (CONAPO, 1982). In 1986 the group of 15-19-year-old women had a specific fertility rate of 84 per 1,000 (Secretaría de Salud et al., 1989). It has also been calculated that 17 percent of live births occur in the group under 20 years of age (Secretaría Gobernación, 1990).

The specific characteristics of urban Mexican sociocultural patterns most likely modify some of the relationships found in other countries. It is especially important to consider that abortion is highly restricted in Mexico and generally disapproved of (see, for example, Pick de Weiss et al., 1990), though practiced on a clandestine level. Traditional attitudes and "machismo" still largely determine a woman's role in general, particularly with regard to sexual relations (Díaz-Guerrero,1982; Pick de Weiss,1980a,1980b). Furthermore, the socioeconomic conditions in which the majority of the population lives are more precarious than is true for the population of more developed countries, such as the US.

Reprinted from *Studies in Family Planning*, Vol. 22, Number 2, March/April 1991, pp. 74-82.

The Mexican family structure and interpersonal relation patterns differ in important ways from those of other cultures (Holtzman et al., 1975). The extended family system is very salient to the great majority of Mexicans who, in general terms, tend to favor very close relations and dependence between parents and adult children. However, within the Mexican culture, communication both in general and with respect to sex is often not direct (Nina Estrella, 1989).

In Mexico general knowledge concerning the existence of a variety of contraceptive methods appears to be relatively widespread. Eighty-two percent of the female adolescents interviewed in the representative household survey of Mexico City, which forms part of the sample used for the study reported here, had heard of contraceptives. When it comes to more specific knowledge—such as use of the different contraceptives, how one becomes pregnant, and the menstrual cycle—only two-fifths of the population could provide correct answers (Pick de Weiss et al., 1988b and 1988d). Family planning services are often perceived (sometimes realistically) as inaccessible to the unmarried teenager (Pick de Weiss et al., 1988c).

The present study is aimed at analyzing sexual, contraceptive, and reproductive behavior among female adolescents in Mexico City in relation to a series of psychosocial determinants.

Methodology

The sampling frame used assured that the females in all groups were from similar socioeconomic backgrounds. For the first group, a random household sample of the lower-middle and lower socioeconomic levels was developed, based on a Mercadological Map (BIMSA, 1982), the electoral map of the Federal Electoral Commission (Comisión Federal Electoral, 1978), and personal visits.

The households were selected through a self-weighted, multistage scheme, which included the selection of conglomerates proportional to size. Up to seven visits were carried out in order to find an interviewee. Data were collected simultaneously in all areas of the city.

A total of 3,505 households were visited. All female teenagers between 12 and 19 years of age were listed. Of the 927 females who were eligible, 865 (93.3 percent) were interviewed. Fifty-six (6 percent) could not be located at home and six (.7 percent) refused to participate.

Since the number of adolescents who had had sexual intercourse was not large enough to make comparisons, 200 nonpregnant teenagers who were referred by girls in the probabilistic household sample as probably having had initiated sexual intercourse were visited in their homes and invited to participate in the interview. No mention was made of information given by the previously interviewed girlfriend, so that these adolescents were free to respond to the interview as they wished.

The pregnant adolescents were contacted at two public maternity hospitals in Mexico City, which serve women from principally lower-middle and lower socioeconomic levels. Three hundred and fifty-five pregnant teenagers were included in the study. All pregnant adolescents were primagravida, were from five to nine months pregnant, and, when contacted, said that they had not wanted the pregnancy at the time of conception.

Each respondent was interviewed for about 50 minutes, using an instrument comprising mainly close-ended questions developed for this study (Pick de Weiss et al., 1988d), and in some cases taken from scales that had been previously developed and validated with Mexico City adolescents from lower and middle socioeconomic levels. The content covered psychosocial areas that had been found to be related to adolescent sexual and contraceptive behavior in the literature. The interview was pilot-tested before beginning data collection. Based on distribution analysis, factor analyses, and Cronbach's alphas, the following final scales were developed and used in the analyses:

1   *Use of affect to achieve ends*: Sense of control over one's surroundings is based on affective handling (for example, "being nice" or "getting along with people") rather than through one's abilities and achievements.

2   *Acceptance of sociocultural and parental norms and rules*: This variable refers to compliance with the demands and decisions of other people, particularly with regard to a daughter's acceptance of parental authority.

3   *School aspirations*: Level of scholastic aspirations that the adolescent has for herself.

4   *Perception of father's attitudes*: Perceived attitude of the father as liberal versus conservative regarding sexuality, pregnancy, abortion, and premarital contraceptive use.

5   *Perception of girlfriends' attitudes*: Perceived attitude of the peers as liberal or conservative regarding sexuality, pregnancy, and premarital contraceptive use.

6   *Having talked with mother about sex*: Extent to which the adolescent perceives that she had talked with her mother about sex and boys.

7   *Having talked with girlfriends about sex*: Extent to which the adolescent reported having talked with her friends about premarital sexual intercourse, contraceptive use, pregnancy, and ideal family size.

8   *Sister pregnant*: Presence of sisters who became pregnant during adolescence.

9   *Mother single at time of first pregnancy*: The adolescent reported that her mother became pregnant premaritally.

10 *Acceptance of erroneous beliefs*: Degree to which a group of incorrect myths concerning pregnancy and contraception are believed.

11 *Knowledge of contraception*: Knowledge regarding use of contraceptives.

12   *Future orientation*: Refers to the planning and organization of future goals and activities.

13   *Assertiveness*: Assertiveness is defined as the tendency to stand up for one's rights; and express-
      ing what one believes, feels, and wants in a direct form, while respecting the rights of others.

14   *Control over life events*: An individual's sense that he (she) may control his (her) life.

15   *Perception of mother's personality*: Degree to which the mother was perceived as open to inter-
      action and communication.

16   *Concept of sexual partner*: Positive versus negative concept of the boyfriend.

17   *Perception of partner's attitudes*: Perceived attitude of the boyfriend as liberal or conservative
      regarding sexuality, pregnancy, and premarital contraceptive use.

Results and Discussion

The analysis presented here revolves around three basic questions couched in terms of behavior that
programs might try to encourage: (1) What psychosocial factors are related to a girl postponing sexual intercourse? (2) Which are related to her using contraceptives once having initiated sexual intercourse? and finally, (3) Which factors are associated with her not becoming pregnant? Based on
earlier results that showed differences in sexual and contraceptive behavior of 12-15- and 16-19-
year-olds (Díaz-Loving and Pick de Weiss, 1988), separate analyses were conducted for these
groups. Since very few of the younger girls had practiced contraception and very few were pregnant,
analyses for this group refer only to having versus not having had sexual intercourse.

The results of the logistic regression analyses are given separately for each dependent variable.
First, the results of the significant bivariate analyses are presented, followed by the variables that remain in the best fitting multivariate model. The odds ratios shown in the tables indicate the relative
likelihood of occurrence of the dependent variable when the independent variable changes by one
unit in the direction indicated in the column "coding categories."

The results show that different groups of variables are related to each one of the criterion behaviors in a conceptually congruent manner. The results and discussion are presented separately for each
of the basic questions, concluding with the overall policy implications of the findings.

Not Engaging in Sexual Intercourse

Ten variables were significant in bivariate analyses, of which seven (shown in italics) remained significant when controlling for the effects of the others: use of affect to achieve ends, *acceptance of sociocultural and parental norms and rules, school aspirations,* perception of father's attitudes,

perception of girlfriends' attitudes, having talked with mother about sex, having talked with girl-friends about sex, sister pregnant, mother single at time of first pregnancy, and acceptance of errone-ous beliefs (Table 1).

TABLE 1: Variables that describe adolescents (16-19-year-olds) who have not had sexual intercourse

Variable	Coding categories	Bivariate solution odds ratio	Multivariate solution odds ratio
Use of affect to achieve ends	Low = 1, High = 2	1.62	--
Acceptance of sociocultural and parental norms and rules	Low = 1 High = 2	2.88	2.77
School aspirations	Elementary school or does not know = 1 University = 4	1.27	1.37
Perception of father's attitudes	Conservative = 1, Liberal = 2	1.78	--
Perception of girlfriends' attitudes	Conservative = 1, Liberal = 2	2.33	1.81
Having talked with mother about sex	None or little = 1 Moderate or much = 2	1.48	1.68
Having talked with girlfriends about sex	Not at all = 1 A great deal = 3	2.05	2.41
Sister pregnant	None = 1, One or more = 2	2.26	1.69
Mother single at time of first pregnancy	Mother married at first pregnancy = 1 Mother single = 2	2.25	2.24
Acceptance of erroneous beliefs	Acceptance = 1, Rejection = 2	2.08	--
Knowledge of contraception	Incorrect = 1, Correct = 2	--	--
Future orientation	Low = 1, High = 2	--	--
Assertiveness	Low = 1, High = 2	--	--
Control over life events	Low = 1, High = 2	--	--
Perception of mother's personality	Very withdrawn, closed = 1 Very interactive, open = 4	--	--
Concept of sexual partner	Very negative = 1 Very positive = 4	--	--
Perception of partner's attitudes	Conservative = 1, Liberal = 2	--	--

NOTE: $\pi^2 = 176.45$, df = 7.

The overall image that emerges from these results describes the 16-19-year-old adolescent who does not engage in sexual intercourse as one who accepts traditional family and societal norms but at the same time has open communication with her mother concerning sexual matters. She lives in a peer and family milieu of which adolescent pregnancy and sexual intercourse are not salient aspects, neither as topics of conversation nor as models of behavior. Furthermore, she is a young woman who expects to continue her education to a higher level than the girl who has engaged in sexual intercourse.

The combination of acceptance of sociocultural and parental norms and rules with open communication with one's mother about sex suggests that the girls who have not had sexual intercourse come from families in which strong parental authority coexists with an openness to discuss intimate matters between daughter and mother. Within the Mexican context this combination, in conjunction with the absence of pregnancies in adolescence in the family and low prevalence of communication regarding sex with peers, may provide the necessary support and models to help the girl pursue goals in life other than the culturally prescribed role of motherhood (Díaz-Guerrero, 1982). The high academic aspirations held by these adolescents is congruent with this image. The combination of open communication and strong parental authority might lead to strong ego development and self-confidence (Nunn, 1987), which is related both to academic achievement and avoidance of unwanted pregnancies during adolescence (Mindick, 1978; Slavin, 1975)

The variables that were significant in the bivariate analyses, but no longer in the final multivariate solution, are highly consistent with this overall picture and add specific details that are important to mention. The finding that adolescents who do not engage in sexual intercourse were less likely to use affect to achieve ends is congruent with their greater academic aspirations insofar as they tend to base their achievement expectations on their instrumental efforts (La Rosa, 1986). That these girls also perceived their father's attitudes toward sexuality and contraception as conservative is consistent with the cultural patterns of more traditional families. Finally, the finding that adolescents who did not engage in sexual relations have fewer erroneous beliefs about pregnancy and contraception may reflect a more positive overall attitude toward communication and information within the context in which these adolescents have grown up.

It is important to note that no variables related to the boyfriend and the adolescent's relationship with him were included in this part of the analysis because too many values were missing among the group who had not had sexual intercourse. It is, therefore, not possible to say to what extent such variables play a role in this context.

With respect to the 12-15-year-olds, eight significant predictors emerged, of which five (in italics) remained significant when controlling for the others: *acceptance of sociocultural and parental norms and rules, school aspirations*, perception of girlfriends' attitudes, having talked with mother about sex, *having talked with girlfriends about sex, sister pregnant, mother single at time of first pregnancy,* and acceptance of erroneous beliefs (Table 2).

The finding that basically the same variables, with few exceptions, were predictive of not having had sexual relations among the 12-15-year-old group, suggests that despite their maturational differences (Diaz-Loving and Pick de Weiss, 1988; Pick de Weiss et al., 1988d), the same processes are operating.

TABLE 2: Variables that describe adolescents (12-15-year-olds) who have not had sexual intercourse

Variable	Coding categories	Bivariate solution odds ratio	Multivariate solution odds ratio
Use of affect to achieve ends	Low = 1, High = 2	--	--
Acceptance of sociocultural and parental norms and rules	Low = 1 High = 2	2.17	2.90
School aspirations	Elementary school or does not know = 1 University = 4	1.83	2.10
Perception of father's attitudes	Conservative = 1, Liberal = 2	--	--
Perception of girlfriends' attitudes	Conservative = 1, Liberal = 2	2.04	--
Having talked with mother about sex	None or little = 1 Moderate or much = 2	1.53	--
Having talked with girlfriends about sex	Not at all = 1 A great deal = 3	2.34	3.31
Sister pregnant	None = 1, One or more = 2	2.50	2.79
Mother single at time of first pregnancy	Mother married at first pregnancy = 1 Mother single = 2	2.73	2.02
Acceptance of erroneous beliefs	Acceptance = 1, Rejection = 2	2.04	--
Knowledge of contraception	Incorrect = 1, Correct = 2	--	--
Future orientation	Low = 1, High = 2	--	--
Assertiveness	Low = 1, High = 2	--	--
Control over life events	Low = 1, High = 2	--	--
Perception of mother's personality	Very withdrawn, closed = 1 Very interactive, open = 4	--	--
Concept of sexual partner	Very negative = 1 Very positive = 4	--	--
Perception of partner's attitudes	Conservative = 1, Liberal = 2	--	--

NOTE: $\pi^2 = 62.14$, df = 5.

Practice of Contraception

Once having initiated sexual intercourse, the adolescents may decide to use or not use contraceptives to avoid becoming pregnant. The second set of analyses of the 16-19-year-old adolescents who have had sexual intercourse found that 14 variables were significant predictors of contraceptive use. The six, which are shown in italics, remained significant when controlling for the others: use of affect to achieve ends, *acceptance of sociocultural and parental norns and rules*, school aspirations, perception of father's attitudes, *perception of girlfriends' attitudes,* having talked with mother about sex, *having talked with girlfriends about sex,* mother single at time of first pregnancy, *acceptance of erroneous beliefs, knowledge of contraception, future orientation,* assertiveness, perception of mother's personality, and perception of partner's attitudes.

The girls who use contraceptives are contradicting the prevalent cultural norms against premarital sex for pleasure, that is, without the risk of pregnancy (Paz, 1959). In such a context it is not surprising to find that they have less acceptance of sociocultural and parental norms and rules. Furthermore, they appear to be more mature in terms of the developmental continuum of future planning and orientation. Both the perception of peers' attitudes as liberal and communication with them regarding sexual and contraceptive issues provide a basis for pregnancy prevention. This, together with greater knowledge of possible methods and their use as well as rejection of commonly held erroneous beliefs, and the ability to plan for their future, translates motivation to avoid pregnancy into contraceptive use (Table 3).

In sum, in order to practice contraception, teenagers must have knowledge about available methods, be free of commonly held misbeliefs, feel supported by their friends, and be sufficiently free of traditional authority to do something as taboo as using contraceptives without being married.

Results of the bivariate analyses lend support to this composite image. Among the variables that tapped aspects of the couple relationship, only the adolescent girl's perception of her boyfriend's attitudes toward sexuality and contraception was significant. Furthermore, fathers were also perceived as liberal, suggesting that it is also necessary for the girl to perceive a supportive attitude in such matters from her boyfriend and her father in order to use contraceptives. Others have found, in a similar vein, that encouragement on the part of the male to practice contraception is important for contraceptive use among adolescents (Pick de Weiss, 1980 a,b).

Adolescents who practiced contraception also had a positive image of their mother, with whom they communicated frequently about intimate subjects. Better relations with parents have been shown, in other studies, to be related to better contraception among adolescents (Ball, 1973; Jessor and Jessor, 197a). The fact that their mothers had not been single when first pregnant provided a positive role model for avoiding pregnancy before marriage. Theoretically, such a positive relationship with the mother is also associated with more optimal personality development and positive self-image (Canalizo and Shabot, 1990), such as that found among these adolescents who, according to the bivariate results, were also more assertive, had higher academic aspirations and were more instrumentally motivated, and used less affective manipulation. This is consistent with the greater maturation and ability to plan already noted in these girls.

TABLE 3: Variables that describe adolescents (16-19-year-olds) who have practiced contraception

Variable	Coding categories	Bivariate solution odds ratio	Multivariate solution odds ratio
Use of affect to achieve ends	Low = 1, High = 2	1.89	--
Acceptance of sociocultural and parental norms and rules	Low = 1 High = 2	5.85	3.10
School aspirations	Elementary school or does not know = 1 University = 4	1.50	--
Perception of father's attitudes	Conservative = 1, Liberal = 2	1.97	--
Perception of girlfriends' attitudes	Conservative = 1, Liberal = 2	2.08	2.23
Having talked with mother about sex	None or little = 1 Moderate or much = 2	2.30	--
Having talked with girlfriends about sex	Not at all = 1 A great deal = 3	3.01	1.99
Sister pregnant	None = 1, One or more = 2	--	--
Mother single at time of first pregnancy	Mother married at first pregnancy = 1 Mother single = 2	1.32	--
Acceptance of erroneous beliefs	Acceptance = 1, Rejection = 2	2.06	2.43
Knowledge of contraception	Incorrect = 1, Correct = 2	1.37	7.30
Future orientation	Low = 1, High = 2	2.32	1.70
Assertiveness	Low = 1, High = 2	4.37	--
Control over life events	Low = 1, High = 2	--	--
Perception of mother's personality	Very withdrawn, closed = 1 Very interactive, open = 4	1.53	--
Concept of sexual partner	Very negative = 1 Very positive = 4	--	--
Perception of partner's attitudes	Conservative = 1, Liberal = 2	1.65	--

NOTE: π^2 = 157.41, df = 6.

Not Being Pregnant

Eleven variables were significantly associated with not being pregnant, of which the six italicized ones remained significant in the multivariate solution: use of affect to achieve ends, *acceptance of sociocultural and parental norms and rules, school aspirations,* having talked to mother about sex, *having talked to girlfriends about sex,* mother single at time of first pregnancy, *knowledge of contraception, future orientation,* assertiveness, perception of mother's personality, and *concept of sexual partner* (Table 4).

TABLE 4: Variables that describe adolescents (16-19-year-olds) who have not been pregnant

Variable	Coding categories	Bivariate solution odds ratio	Multivariate solution odds ratio
Use of affect to achieve ends	Low = 1, High = 2	1.62	--
Acceptance of sociocultural and parental norms and rules	Low = 1 High = 2	7.15	2.52
School aspirations	Elementary school or does not know = 1 University = 4	1.94	1.46
Perception of father's attitudes	Conservative = 1, Liberal = 2	--	--
Perception of girlfriends' attitudes	Conservative = 1, Liberal = 2	--	--
Having talked with mother about sex	None or little = 1 Moderate or much = 2	3.20	--
Having talked with girlfriends about sex	Not at all = 1 A great deal = 3	5.07	3.16
Sister pregnant	None = 1, One or more = 2	--	--
Mother single at time of first pregnancy	Mother married at first pregnancy = 1 Mother single = 2	1.37	--
Acceptance of erroneous beliefs	Acceptance = 1, Rejection = 2	--	--
Knowledge of contraception	Incorrect = 1, Correct = 2	72.89	13.63
Future orientation	Low = 1, High = 2	3.00	1.75
Assertiveness	Low = 1, High = 2	4.90	--
Control over life events	Low = 1, High = 2	--	--
Perception of mother's personality	Very withdrawn, closed = 1 Very interactive, open = 4	1.71	--
Concept of sexual partner	Very negative = 1 Very positive = 4	1.42	1.59
Perception of partner's attitudes	Conservative = 1, Liberal = 2	--	--

NOTE: $\pi^2 = 256.26$, df = 4.

More knowledge concerning contraceptives and how to use them was associated with greater likelihood of not being pregnant. These results emphasize the importance, among other things, of providing information about contraceptive use in order to prevent adolescent pregnancy. The fear on the part of parents and educators that increased information concerning the specifics of contraceptive methods will lead to greater interest in sexual intercourse and greater risk of pregnancy is refuted by these findings. Other studies (Zelnik and Kim, 1982) found no relation between sex education and sexual intercourse. They also found that those who had sexual intercourse were more likely to practice contraception if they had obtained sex education.

However, knowledge is not the whole story. Higher levels of communication with friends about sexuality, pregnancy, and contraception was associated with a lower likelihood of becoming pregnant. Such communication may provide useful information and advice for avoiding pregnancy as well as perhaps reflecting greater overall sociability and better peer support at an age at which a strong need exists for stability and external support (Elkind, 1970). This suggestion is tentatively confirmed by the fact that the pregnant girls had fewer girlfriends overall with whom to talk (Pick de Weiss et al., 1988b), suggesting that they were more isolated and in need of company than the nonpregnant adolescents. They may perceive the baby as a means of fulfilling affective needs (Fisher and Ktsanes, 1971).

Among the girls who have initiated sexual relations, those who have less traditional acceptance of sociocultural and parental norms and rules were less likely to be pregnant. This finding means that the pregnant adolescents conformed more to traditional expectations. This somewhat surprising finding is actually quite consistent with cultural messages. Pregnancy, to some extent, exonerates the girls from the shame of having engaged in premarital sexual relations. Sex for procreation is more acceptable than sex for pleasure. By becoming a mother, she is also fulfilling a highly valued cultural role (Diaz-Guerrero, 1982; Paz, 1959). Based on anthropological data from rural Mexico and Peru, it has been suggested that having children is a way of maintaining or improving the social status of the family (Shedlin and Hollerbach, 1981; Tucker, 1986). Even among Mexican-Americans in the US, a positive attitude toward childbearing has been reported (Bradshaw and Bean, 1972). Furthermore, in this regard, it is important to remember that the girls studied did not choose to seek a clandestine abortion as do some unknown proportion of their peers. This may increase the proportion of traditional families in the sample studied.

The nonpregnant adolescents also reported having higher school aspirations and orientation toward the future than their pregnant peers. This finding is highly consistent with those from other studies (Abrahamse et al., 1985; Cobliner et al., 1975; Mindick, 1978; Oskamp and Mindick, 1983) which suggest that the adolescent's life goals are intimately involved with her risk of becoming pregnant or not. In line with this finding it is important to mention that a considerable proportion of pregnant adolescents in this and other studies in Mexico City (Atkin and Givaudan, 1989; Pick de Weiss et al., 1988b) had left school before getting pregnant. It is also possible that once faced with the unplanned pregnancy, girls with lower school aspirations and shorter time perspectives in relation to life goals may accommodate more easily to the prospect of early motherhood than do girls who wish to pursue such long-range goals as a university career. Moore et al. (1984) report some evidence of a positive relation between level of aspirations and delayed childbearing in adolescence. Such adolescents with higher aspirations and long-term goals, if they become pregnant, might be more likely to seek a clandestine abortion. Although no data on this possibility are available from Mexico in this regard, evidence from Colombia suggests that it might be true (Arevalo et al., 1987).

Within the context of the couple relationship, the finding that the adolescent's negative image of her boyfriend was predictive of her avoidance of pregnancy suggests an important motivational aspect within the relationship. One may speculate that, among sexually active adolescents, those who perceive their boyfriends more negatively are less motivated to engage in frequent sexual relations or to accept a pregnancy if it occurs as a way of maintaining the relationship. In Mexico, it is common that single women may become pregnant with the expectation that the boyfriend will marry them. Among Mexican adolescents who were single when they first became pregnant, this expectation became a reality in many cases: 56.7 percent were living with the boyfriend by the third trimester of pregnancy (Atkin and Givaudan, 1989).

Additional information is provided by a look at the bivariate results. The finding that greater assertiveness was associated with becoming pregnant and deciding to continue with the pregnancy was unexpected and merits a brief comment. It may be an indication that girls who are more able to express their own desires were better able to resist suggestions from others to obtain an abortion and more willing to confront the difficulties involved in rearing a child at such a young age. Studies of Mexican adolescents who decide to abort, which could confirm this possibility, are unavailable at the present time.

Another significant personality variable, low use of affect to achieve ends, is consistent with other findings. The adolescent who primarily uses means other than affect (for example, efficacy, competence, instrumentality) to obtain her goals is more likely to invest more effort in planning her future and having higher academic aspirations (Esqueda, 1989), and to be more motivated to avoid pregnancy.

The importance of the adolescent's relationship with her mother for avoiding pregnancy was also apparent in the bivariate analyses. Greater communication about sex, with a mother perceived as active and communicative and who had herself been married when first pregnant, provided an interpersonal context that facilitates pregnancy avoidance. These results reiterate the impact of sexual education within the family, both implicit in role models as well as explicit through communication.

Program Implications

The results of the present study have far-reaching implications for program design both directed at postponing age of first sexual intercourse and at improving contraceptive use and pregnancy prevention. Clarifying commonly held erroneous beliefs and providing detailed, practical knowledge concerning sexuality, pregnancy, and use of and access to contraceptive methods is essential. Studies in Latin America have shown that there is a particularly high prevalence of common misbeliefs related to the menstrual cycle, correct use of contraceptives, and health risks associated with them. For example, in a previous descriptive analysis of the sample, it was found that 35 percent of adolescents thought a woman cannot get pregnant the first time she has sexual intercourse, 60 percent did not know when the fertile period was within the menstrual cycle, and 60 percent thought a condom could be used more than once (Pick de Weiss et al., 1 988b). Programs should be careful to identify the prevalent beliefs in the population to which they are addressed and ensure that they are corrected. Information about contraception should be geared very specifically at ways to obtain and to practice contraception appropriately.

However, sex education should be even more broadly defined and requires an important emphasis to be placed on the family if prevention is to be effective. Strategies should be designed to foster open and clear communication between parents and their children, including intimate topics and values clarification. Considering that such intrafamilial patterns are only beginning to be accepted among the general population, multifocal efforts through mass media, education, and health sectors should be encouraged. Families in which adolescent pregnancies have occurred should be targeted for special attention.

It is clear from these findings that one of the central issues underlying adolescent pregnancy is the lack of alternative role options for women other than motherhood as well as their subordinate role in the society (Zeidenstein, 1989). For programs to really be effective they must address these issues. Strategies should be directed at helping youngsters develop alternative, realistic life goals so that they do not see pregnancy as their only possibility of gaining status and couple commitment. Programs should emphasize not only the goals but also the skills involved in achieving them. These could include training to increase assertiveness, constructive decision-making, and providing the necessary steps for future planning. In order to achieve this it is particularly effective to work in small groups with participatory technology such as group dynamics, role playing, and focus groups.

Attention to male attitudes and communication skills is also essential. It is very common to find that both male and female adolescents are afraid to talk about sex and contraception with their sexual partner. The females perceive it as too risky for the ongoing relationship. Males' attitudes in Latin America reinforce these expectations. Much of female sexual and contraceptive behavior is indirectly determined by the woman's perceptions of the male's attitudes and desires or her expectations within the relationship. Qualitative data have shown that pregnant adolescents prefer to risk pregnancy rather than appear too knowledgeable about sex and contraception, and perceive their partners as being unwilling to discuss the topic (Vargas-Trujillo and Atkin, 1988). Little research has been carried out in Latin America regarding the male's position in this respect and is urgently needed in order to plan more effective programs that optimize interventions for adolescents in Latin America.

The importance of peer influence should be contemplated within preventive strategies. Ways to improve such informal communication and support networks and to assure that the information they provide is accurate should be developed. Such networks should be seen as complementary, rather than opposed, to the strengthening of family communication skills.

Acknowledgment

The authors wish to thank the Panamerican Health Organization, the Population Council, and the United Nations Population Fund for the support provided to carry out the study reported in this article.

References

Abrahamse, A F., P.A. Morrison, and L. Waite. 1985. "How family characteristics deter early unwed parenthood." Paper presented at the Annual Meeting of the Population Association of America, Boston, Mar. 28-30, 1985.

Arévalo, A., A. Castillo, and E. Vargas. 1987. "Aborto, entrega en adopción o conservación de un hijo: tres opciones légitimas ante el embarazo indeseado." In Sexualidad y Planificación Familiar. Eds. A. Giraldo and Maria Consuelo de Santamaría. Bogotá: UniAndes.

Atkin, L. and M. Givaudan. 1989. "Perfil psicosocial de la adolescente embarazada mexicana." In *Temas Selectos en Reproducción Humana*. Ed.S. Karchmer.MexicoCity: Instituto Nacional de Perinatologia.

Atkin, L. and S. Pick de Weiss.1989. "Antecedentes psicosociales del embarazo en la adolescencia." *Perinatología y Reproducción Humana* 3, 3:152-157.

Ball, G.V.1973. "A method of identifying the potential unwed adolescent." Unpublished doctoral dissertation, University of California at Los Angeles.

Buro de Investigacion de Mercados (BIMSA). 1982. "Mapa mercadológico de la Ciudad de México." Mexico City: Buro de Investigación de Mercados.

Bradshaw, B.S. and F.D. Bean. 1972. "Some aspects of the fertility of Mexican Americans." In *Demographic and Social Aspects of Population Growth*, Volume I, Research Reports of the US Commission on Population Growth and the American Future. Eds. C.F. Westoff and R. Parke, Jr. Washington, D.C.: US Government Printing Office.

Canalizo, P. and E. Shabot. 1990. "Autoconcepto y percepción que la adolescente tiene de la relación con sus padres." B.A. thesis, Universidad Anahuac, Mexico City.

Cobliner, W.G., H. Schulman, and V. Smith. 1975. "Patterns of contraceptive failures: The role of motivation reexamined." *Journal of Biosocial Science* 7:307-318.

Comisión Federal Electoral. 1978. *Mapa de la Comisión Federal Electoral*. Mexico City: Comisión Federal Electoral.

Consejo Nacional de Poblacion (CONAPO). 1982. *México Demografico*. Mexico City: Consejo Nacional de Poblacion.

Díaz-Guerrero, R. 1982. *Psicología del mexicano*. Mexico City: Editorial Trillas.

Díaz-Loving, R. and S. Pick de Weiss. 1988. "Relationship of personality to teenage pregnancy, sexual relations, and contraceptive practices: The case of Mexico." Report presented to the Population Council, New York.

Elkind, D. 1970. *Children and Adolescents*. New York: Oxford University Press.

Esqueda, L. 1989. *Necesidad de logro, interrupción de la tarea y energización de la conducta*. Bogota: Centro de Investigaciones Psicológicas de la Universidad de Los Andes.

Fisher, A. and V. Ktsanes. 1971. "Pregnant teenagers: A study of some who married and some who did not." Unpublished paper. New Orleans: Louisiana Family Planning Program.

Holtzman,W., R. Díaz-Guerrero, and J.D. Swartz.1975. *Personality Development in Two Cultures*. Austin: University of Texas Press.

Jessor, S.L. and R. Jessor 1975. "Transition from virginity to nonvirginity among youth: A social-psychological study over time." *Developmental Psychology* 11:473-484.

La Rosa, J. 1986. "Escalas de locus de control y autoconcepto: Construcción y validación." Ph.D. dissertation, Faculty of Psychology, National University of Mexico, Mexico City.

Mindick,B.1978. "Personality and social psychological correlates of success or failure in contraception: A longitudinal predictive view." Unpublished doctoral dissertation, Claremont Graduate School, Claremont, California.

Moore, K.A., C.L. Betsey, and M.C. Simms. 1984. *Information, Services and Aspirations: Race Differences in Adolescent Fertility*. Washington, D.C: Urban Institute.

Nina Estrella, R.1989. "Autodivulgación y satisfacción marital en matrimonios en México y Puerto Rico." M.A. thesis, Faculty of Psychology, National University of Mexico, Mexico City.

Nunn, G. 1987. "An investigation of the relationship between children's self-concept and evaluation of parent figures: Do they vary as a function of family structure?" *Journal of Psychology* 121:563-566.

Oskamp, S. and B. Mindick. 1983. "Personality and attitudinal barriers to contraception." In *Adolescents, Sex and Contraception*. Eds. D. Byrne and W.A. Fisher. Hillsdale: Lawrence Erlbaum Associates.

Paz, O. 1959. *Laberinto de la soledad*. Mexico City: Fondo de Cultural Económica.

Pick de Weiss, S. 1980a. *Estudio social psicológico de la planificación familiar*. Mexico City: Siglo XXI Editores.

Pick de Weiss, S. 1980b. "Hacia un modelo predictivo de la planificación familiar." *Revista Latinoamericana de Psicología* 12,2:119-125.

Pick de Weiss, S., L.C. Atkin, and S.K. Karchmer.1988b. "Existen diferencias entre adolescentes embarazadas y la poblacion en general?" In *La psicología en el ambito prenatal*. Mexico City: Instituto Nacional de Perinatologia.

Pick de Weiss, S., M. Flores, and M.E. Montero. 1988c. "Development and longitudinal evaluation of comparative sex education courses." Report presented to the Agency for International Development, Mexico City.

Pick de Weiss, S., P. Andrade-Palos, L. Atkin, and R. Díaz-Loving. 1988d. "Adolescentes en la Ciudad de México: Estudio socio-psicológico de practicas anticonceptivas y de embarazo no deseado." Report presented to the Panamerican Health Organization, Washington, D.C.

Pick de Weiss, S., R. Díaz-Loving, and P. Andrade-Palos.1990. "Actitudes y norma subjetiva de adolescentes de la Ciudad de México hacia la sexualidad, anticoncepcion y aborto." *Revista Intercontinental de Psicología y Educación* 3, 1 -2:87-98.

Secretaría de Salud, Subsecretaría de Servicios de Salud, Dirección General de Planificación Familiar and Demographic and Health Surveys.1989. *Encuesta Nacional sobre Fecundidad y Salud 1987*. Washington, D.C.: Institute for Resource Development/Macro Systems, Inc.

Secretaría de Gobernación, Consejo Nacional de Población. 1990. "Programa Nacional 1989-1994." Mexico City: Consejo Nacional de Población.

Shedlin, M. and P. Hollerbach. 1981. "Modern and traditional fertility regulation in a Mexican community: The process of decision-making." *Studies in Family Planning* 12, 6/7:278-296.

Slavin, M.E. 1975. "Ego functioning in women who use birth control effectively and ineffectively." Unpublished doctoral dissertation, Boston University School of Education, Boston.

Tucker, G.M. 1986. "Barriers to modern contraceptive use in rural Peru." *Studies in Family Planning* 17, 6:308-316.

Vargas-Trujillo, E. and L.C. Atkin. 1988. "Grupos educativos con metodología participative para adolescentes embarazadas." In *La psicología social en Mexico* 2:343-349. Mexico City: Asociación Mexicana de Psicología Social (AMEPSO).

Zelnik, M. and Y.K. Kim.1982. "Sex education and its association with teenage sexual activity and contraceptive use." *Family Planning Perspectives* 14:117-126.

Zeidenstein, G. 1989. "Adolescent fertility and the health and status of women." Paper presented at the International Conference on Adolescent Fertility in Latin America and the Caribbean, Oaxaca, Mexico, November 6-19, 1989.

MISINFORMATION, MISTRUST, AND MISTREATMENT: FAMILY PLANNING AMONG BOLIVIAN MARKET WOMEN

Sidney Ruth Schuler, Maria Eugenia Choque, and Susanna Rance

Results of an ethnographic study suggest that, despite stereotypes to the contrary, urban Aymara women in Bolivia want to regulate their fertility, and sociocultural norms support fertility regulation. However, the norms also make such regulation difficult to achieve. One barrier is a deep suspicion of modern medicine and medical practitioners, who are not seen as reliable sources of information. This suspicion is reinforced when the quality of health services is inadequate. Among urban Aymara, the level of acceptability of most modern methods of contraception is low. Many would prefer to use traditional methods, even when use of these methods entails considerable sacrifice and risk of conflict with their partners, unwanted pregnancies, and recourse to unsafe abortion. (STUDIES IN FAMILY PLANNING 1994; 25,4: 211 - 221)

A 1993 survey of Aymara women who work in urban markets of Bolivia shows a surprisingly high level of contraceptive use, but a low level of use of modern contraceptives. The survey included 686 Aymara women aged 15-49, living with a partner, and working in small-scale commerce and production activities in La Paz and El Alto. While 74 percent of the women were using some form of contraception, only about 25 percent were using modern methods, mainly the intrauterine device (IUD) (11 percent), oral contraceptives (7 percent), and condoms (4 percent). Of the 49 percent using traditional methods, most were using some form of the rhythm method.[1] Ethnographic data from the same communities confirm that, in general, urban Aymara women want to regulate their fertility and that norms and beliefs about women's roles and reproduction for the most part support fertility regulation. However, fertility regulation is difficult to achieve for most of these women. In-depth interview data are used here to examine some of the social processes that affect Aymara women's perceptions of family planning methods and services, and their propensity to use them. The data were collected as part of a collaborative study concerned with credit and women's economic, social, and reproductive roles and status, undertaken by the JSI Research and Training Institute (JSI), the Taller de Historia Oral Andina (THOA), and The Population Council.

Bolivia is one of the poorest countries in Latin America, where limited access to basic health services is reflected in persistently high levels of morbidity and mortality, particularly among infants, children, and women of childbearing age, and in low levels of modern contraceptive use. In 1989, according to the Demographic and Health Survey (DHS) (Republica de Bolivia, 1990), only 12

Reprinted from *Studies in Family Planning*, Vol. 25, Number 4, July/August 1994, pp. 211-221.

percent of women in union were using modern methods of contraception. Fifty-eight percent were fecund, wanted no more children, or wanted to wait at least two years before having another child, and were not using any contraceptive method (Remez, 1991). Until a few years ago, Bolivian government policy was considered pronatalist, but recently policy has changed. In 1990, the Bolivian government established its first National Reproductive Health Program, and now access to modern contraceptives is officially perceived as an essential part of reproductive health services and as an important determinant of infant and child health. Although still limited in many rural areas, family planning services are now available from a variety of private and public sources in La Paz and El Alto, where the study took place.

The majority of Bolivia's population is classified as indigenous, primarily Aymara and Quechua. More than half of the population is now urban. Bolivia's political and administrative capital, La Paz, a city of about three-quarters of a million people, is an ancient Andean market center, with a large Aymara population. El Alto is a newer city of about 400,000 people on the Altiplano directly above La Paz and is inhabited primarily by recent migrants.[2] Among the Aymara and other indigenous populations of the Andes, commerce traditionally has been recognized as a female activity, and, perhaps because of this tradition, Aymara women, more often than men, work as small producers and street vendors. As in much of Latin America, the economic decline of the 1980s was accompanied by a massive increase in migration from rural areas to towns and cities, and by rapid growth of the informal sector. In La Paz at the end of the 1980s, 75 percent of the women who were economically active were working in the informal sector, and eight out of 10 women in the informal sector were vendors (Coordinadora de la Mujer, 1990).

Despite the historical roots of La Paz as a market center, urban Aymara society in La Paz and El Alto is clearly a society in transition. In particular, with chronic unemployment among men, and families increasingly dependent for their survival on women's incomes, the essentially patriarchal structure of the rural Aymara family and community is eroding. Problems of alcoholism and male violence against women, while certainly not unknown in rural contexts, appear to be intensifying with this erosion. Conflict between spouses or partners, related to this crisis of patriarchy, is an integral part of life for many of the men and women interviewed in this study, and it often influences reproductive strategies and behavior. Mistrust and apprehension related to social and political disparities between the Aymara and the providers of family planning services, who are mainly *mestizo* or of European descent, are also important influences.

Data, Methods, and Study Sample

The data presented below come primarily from three sources. The first is in-depth interviews with 30 women of reproductive age in union. The interviews trace the women's evolving awareness, attitudes, and expectations associated with children and family planning, their sources of contraceptive information and experiences with reproductive health services, the attitudes and roles of their partner(s) in decision making, and adoption and use of contraceptives. The second source is similar interviews with eight men, using a modified version of the semistructured interview guide that was developed for the women (several of these men are husbands of female respondents). The third source is a a set of descriptions from clients' perspectives of women's experiences in family planning service facilities, based on visits by simulated clients (women in traditional Aymara dress) to eight clinics and health centers that provide family planning services in La Paz and El Alto.[3]

The analysis also draws on ethnographic data collected over a one-year period. The 38 in-depth interviews were conducted within a subsample of the 60 households initially included in the ethnographic study by a five-member team of Aymara field researchers, building on the rapport that had been developed over the course of the year-long study.[4] The interviews were conducted in Spanish. They were tape recorded and then transcribed and translated.

Of the 30 women whose reproductive autobiographies form the core of this study, almost half were born in La Paz and El Alto, and just over half are migrants from rural areas and small towns. Half of them dress in the traditional *pollera* (full skirts worn over petticoats) and the rest wear *vestido* (meaning, in this context, modern urban styles of dress). All 30 of the women are bilingual in Aymara and Spanish. Women were eligible to be interviewed if they were younger than 40, living with a partner, and had at least one living child. Our intention was to focus on women in their reproductive years who had at least one child and might, therefore, have begun to think about regulating their fertility. The selection criteria were followed, with the exception of a few women who had recently been separated from their partners.

The women's ages ranged from 23 to 38, and they had an average of three living children. Almost half had given birth to one or more children who died. All of the women knew something about modern contraceptive methods, which have only become widely available in urban areas in the past few years. Eight of them were using modern methods at the time of the interview (six had IUDs and two were using pills), 18 were using rhythm (mainly the calendar method—with varying degrees of accuracy and consistency), and in four cases, the women were relying on combinations of prolonged breastfeeding, long periods of abstinence, herbal infusions to bring on menstruation, and abortion. In three cases, the rhythm method was combined with withdrawal, and three of the couples reported occasional use of condoms, but this was not a regular method for any of them. Six of the women reported prolonged periods of infertility. Two-thirds of the women either directly stated or implied that they had intentionally aborted one or more pregnancies or tried unsuccessfully to provoke a miscarriage. Some implied that they had resorted to passive or active infanticide.

Cultural and Social Norms Affecting Fertility Regulation

The in-depth interviews suggest that most urban Aymara women working in the informal sector want to regulate their fertility. The motivation they express is mainly economic and is often associated as well with a preference for market work over household work. Small children are perceived as a serious impediment to working in the market. As one woman explained:

With a baby, I could not go to the market to sell. I would have to stay at home, boring myself with all the trouble of baby care, doing all of the laundry. At the market, the people I sell to want to be attended quickly. They don't want to listen to a baby crying, and the baby does not let you work.

Another said:

I suffered . . . I used to cry all the time when I had to go to work with both babies. You can't work-you have to carry around a big load of goods and you have to carry two babies. And it was worse when it rained. . . .

Contrary to the common stereotype, cultural norms and beliefs about women's roles and reproduction among the urban Aymara generally support fertility regulation. Women are expected to "take care of themselves," which means somehow avoiding pregnancy, generally by using the rhythm method or some other form of abstinence. Women who cannot manage this are criticized. Women are criticized not only for not having any children, but also for having too many children or having them too early or too close together. Such women are described as breeding like bunnies or like hens laying eggs, or having children that look like *zamponas* (musical instruments made of a row of bamboo stalks that diminish in size) or *saltenas* (little meat pies) coming out of the oven. One woman observed:

People always criticize you. It seems like everything [you do] is wrong. They criticize you if you have no children, they criticize you if you have lots of childre—neverything [you do] is bad.

But cultural and social norms also make fertility control difficult to achieve. One of the most significant barriers to effective use of traditional as well as modern methods of fertility control is a reluctance to discuss sexual matters and contraception openly—reticence between spouses, family members, and friends and acquaintances, as well as with health-care providers. This reticence made it difficult to interview women about contraceptive use and other fertility-control strategies, even though the interviewers were Aymara women whom the respondents had known for some time through the larger ethnographic study. Most of the interviews were long and rambling. Since it was not acceptable to probe when the respondent did not give a clear answer, the interviewer would move on to a new topic instead, and only later follow up with additional questions. The interviews contain many statements that appear vague and contradictory when extracted from the overall context of the interview, and from their cultural context.

The interviews make clear that the women's reticence to speak of sexuality and reproduction is something that most of them learned at an early age. They grew up in households where sexuality was not discussed, and they soon learned that it behooved them not to ask questions or appear to take any interest in such matters. Many scolded their own children, as their mothers had scolded them, or gave preposterous explanations when confronted with questions about reproduction. Two-thirds of the 30 women received no clear information about menstruation or reproduction when they were growing up. Many had no clear idea about how pregnancy occurs nor how to avoid it. They learned that sexuality was shameful and dangerous, and they were told that they needed to "take care of themselves" and avoid pregnancy, but they were not told how.

Nearly one-third of the women in the study first started living with a sexual partner when they were 14 to 16 years old, and most of the rest did so at the ages of 17 to 20 years. Cohabitation was apparently voluntary in only half of the cases. The normal form of marriage appears neither to be arranged by intermediaries nor to be mutually agreed upon by the couple. More commonly, marriage is the result of a combination of accident and force. Almost a quarter of the cases involved forced sexual contact followed by family pressure on the unwilling woman to stay with the man. The forced contact often took place after a night of drinking at a dance or a party when the woman was not fully aware of what was happening until it was too late. In other cases, no forced sex occurred, but the woman was accidentally made pregnant, or she simply stayed out too late, was afraid to go home, and spent the night with the man. In most cases, parents, having failed through warnings and a repressive home atmosphere to dissuade their teenage children from sexual contact, insisted that they marry, however fleeting or precarious their relationships might have been.

Fertility Regulation Strategies and Impediments

Having begun to live with their sexual partners more or less by accident, many of the women learned only gradually about reproduction through the process of having children. All 30 women interviewed eventually developed contraceptive strategies. (Women who were not interested in controlling their fertility were not purposely excluded from the survey.) Initially, most used the calendar rhythm method or other forms of periodic abstinence. They learned about periodic abstinence from a wide variety of sources, including clinics, mothers' clubs, church groups, books and pamphlets, their husbands, relatives, and friends. In many cases, the method failed, either because they were misinformed about the fertile period, or because of carelessness, the man's lack of cooperation, or his direct opposition. As their desperation increased, the women resorted to more drastic methods of fertility control, ranging from induced abortion to sustained periods of sexual abstinence, which often resulted in considerable conflict between partners, sometimes passive or active infanticide, and the use of such modern contraceptive methods as the IUD.

Because of their fear of contraceptives' side effects and their general dislike of modern medicine, most of these women see modern methods as dangerous, drastic measures. Not all of those using modern methods said that they would recommend them to their children. One woman told the interviewer that she was keeping her use of the IUD a secret. When asked why, she said:

> Others might get the same idea and decide to use the same device. Then if something went wrong, if there was a problem, they would all blame me for it.

Perhaps not surprisingly, the six women who experienced periods of infertility tended to regard these as providential.

Fear of Contraceptive Side Effects

Although all of the women in the study had heard of some form of modern contraception, most of them had limited information. Almost all of the women had heard alarming stories and rumors about the harmful side effects of contraceptive methods that had influenced them. Because contraception, if discussed, tends to be discussed only indirectly, the stories about the side effects of methods are typically sketchy and often fantastic, and clear information is rarely sought. For example:

Why haven't you and your husband ever tried the condom?

They say that they are infected. That's what my husband says. He says that he could die.

Who told him that condoms are infected?

I don't know, but he told me that.

Some of the respondents feared general illness, others mentioned specific illnesses, and others mentioned both. In some cases, side effects were described as consequences of having foreign objects or substances introduced into the body. One of the most frequently mentioned and feared side effects is cancer, particularly in conjunction with the IUD, the most commonly used of modern methods. Less serious side effects mentioned include weight gain, weight loss, and blotches on the face. A woman who was considering using the IUD told the interviewer:

Both the women who get them (IUDs) and the women who don't get them say that they cause cancer. They are objects that we shouldn't have in our bodies, that damage our bodies and give us headaches. . . . . Lots of women say that they make you thinner or fatter, or that they make you want to vomit. But other women say that they're fine, so I wonder what really happens. . . . They say the pills affect the nerves and the liver and the heart, but I don't know because I haven't used them. They say that injections affect the nerves, that the spiral [IUD] can cause cancer. That's what I've heard and I believe it.

Physical changes attributed to contraceptive use are considered undesirable not only for cosmetic reasons, but because they are perceived as a sign that something is going wrong with the body, and also because they may mark the sufferer as a contraceptive user. Most women prefer to avoid being identified as users, both out of a general instinct to maintain privacy, and also because they know that contraceptive use is often associated with promiscuity. Both men and women mentioned that buying condoms embarrassed them.

Some religious groups opposed to the use of contraceptives play on women's fears of side effects and even contribute to the spread of the rumors about side effects. None of the women in the study said directly that she was reluctant to practice modern contraception because it was proscribed by her church. However, one respondent, who had tried to induce a natural abortion on at least one occasion but believed that having an abortion in a clinic was wrong, seemed to have been influenced by her church's version of the mode of action of the IUD:

They told us how the IUD would be placed inside us and it would have a little needle. So every month the woman could be pregnant and the baby would begin to grow-two weeks, three weeks-and then it would get bigger and come down on the little needle and be aborted. Every month the IUD would be responsible for abortions.

Her overall impression was that the IUD was a dangerous method. After the calendar rhythm method failed, she decided to try the pill, even though she had heard that she could be physically harmed by it. Several other women mentioned mothers' clubs or radio programs that apparently were church-sponsored as sources of information about negative health consequences of contraceptive methods.[5]

Fear of Service Providers

Another related barrier to fertility control is a deeply ingrained fear and suspicion of modern medicine and medical practitioners,[6] who are not seen as reliable sources of information about modern contraceptive methods. The expectation of discriminatory treatment based on ethnic differences (most doctors and other health personnel are of European or mixed ancestry) is an important contributing factor. One respondent recounted what happened when she went into labor near a military post. She gave birth at the post and then was sent to the hospital in a military ambulance, but was turned away by the hospital. When the post commander found out, he escorted the woman, the baby, and her husband to the hospital, and made a scene when the admissions clerk tried to send them away again. She explained:

The colonel made a fuss. He made some phone calls and made the doctor stutter. I just laughed at how these people with power could make everybody scared, while we poor people get treated like rags.

Another woman told the interviewer about a difficult pregnancy in which she was advised to have a cesarian section.

Did you have the cesarian section ?

No. The baby was born and it was a normal delivery.

So why did they want you to have a cesarian section?

I don't know. I think it was because they wanted to practice or something, or for the money. I don't know.

One of the respondents suspected that she had been sterilized or perhaps had had an IUD inserted without her knowledge:

When I had the last baby and suffered so much, the doctor told me that I wasn't going to have any more kids. I wonder why he said that. . . . Maybe he 'cured' me [did something so that I wouldn't be able to have children]. They say that right after you have the baby is the best time for the doctor to 'cure' you. I wonder whether that's what he did to me.

Fear and suspicion quickly become reinforced when the quality of health or family planning services is inadequate and when information is withheld. One of the male respondents explained:

When we went to the health center, they offered us the Copper-T right away and said that it was the safest. . . . They didn't tell us what effects it might have on our health. But we already had information that the IUD is only good for four years. If you don't take it out after four years, it can stick inside the womb and the woman can get very sick. That's why we chose the pill. My wife found out, for example, that one of her friends got thinner using the Copper-T. Others say it can make women fatter. But the doctors didn't tell us anything about these effects. That's one of the reasons we decided to switch to the calendar method.

Asked whether the doctor had explained that there were side effects from using contraceptives, one of the women told the interviewer:

No. The first time, I did not know anything about the IUD and the doctor just told me that it wouldn't affect me at all. He said that there was a woman who had done this [had the IUD inserted] 20 times, and she was as strong as ever and didn't have cancer. He didn't tell me anything negative, and I think it was a lie, just so he could get money from me. That's all they're interested in—your money.

The transcripts of the eight simulated-client visits to family planning clinics reveal that a pronounced bias exists among service providers in favor of the IUD. When the simulated clients perceived that a particular method was being pushed, they reacted with suspicion. In two cases, respondents (not simulated clients) who wanted their IUDs removed because of side effects were pressured to continue using them. One of the women reported that when she complained of pain and heavy bleeding and asked to have the IUD removed: "[The doctor told me] 'You're fine, healthy as a girl!' that's all he said, so I just went away."

In several clinics visited by the simulated clients, doctors and other staff were perceived either as rude or as friendly but patronizing. In some cases, staff addressed the woman as *hija* (child) rather than as *señora*. Because they tended to dismiss the client's fears about contraceptive methods quickly rather than to understand them, clinic doctors and staff were unable to counter misinformation and dispel the women's fears. Some women were compelled to endure long waits for service (in one case three hours), and were then given very brief consultations. In a clinic that one simulated client described as the best she had visited, the female doctor came into the waiting room and apologized for the delay, explaining what had caused it. Her addressing the crowd of waiting women as equals transformed the simulated client's perceptions of the clinic and mitigated the long wait. Other positive features of clinics that were noted included clear, simple explanations, the staff's taking adequate time with clients, and the offer of a range of health services.

Many women disliked being physically exposed and feared being touched by health-care providers. For example:

Why didn't you use a method of birth control after having the first abortion?

Because I didn't want to. Like I told you, I don't like those doctors feeling inside me. I'm scared of the doctors, and you have to go back every month, every two or three months for checkups when you use those methods.

Some women were less averse to being examined by a female doctor. Although several of the women who expressed the most extreme fear and suspicion had rarely or never had contact with modern health-care providers, in a number of cases, women's aversions apparently increased as a result of actual contact.

Controlling the Partner

In urban Aymara culture, the level of acceptability of most modern methods of contraception is low relative to that in other cultural settings, and many women (and men) prefer to use traditional methods, particularly calendar rhythm and other forms of periodic abstinence. In addition to the reasons described above, many women fear that they will be suspected of promiscuity if they adopt a modern contraceptive method.

Despite its popularity, the rhythm method entails considerable risk and sacrifice. Its use often precipitates conflict between spouses and results in unwanted pregnancies and, in some cases, unsafe abortion. The rhythm method is difficult to use effectively, in some cases because the couple possesses inaccurate information about the fertile period and in others because the husband refuses to comply with the method. As the interviews show, a woman's ability to control her fertility often clearly depends on her ability to control her partner, or to evade his attempts to control her. A strategy more common than rational discussion between spouses is one in which the woman shares a bed with a young child rather than with her husband, and makes certain that the child wakes up if her husband seeks to have intercourse. However, drunkenness of either or both partners makes maintaining periodic abstinence more difficult. Some women attempt abstinence during their fertile days at the cost of being beaten and verbally abused. One woman admitted to starting fights as a diversion and an excuse to avoid sex. Another woman explained: "We can't always go over the man's head. But if the man does not think, then we must think for him."

Sometimes men refuse to cooperate because they fear that the woman's use of contraceptives would undermine whatever control they have in the relationship. Women are often reluctant to bring up the subject of contraception with their husbands because they are afraid that their husbands will suspect them of wanting to use modern contraceptives in order to have an affair. Jealousy over suspected infidelity is a common source of conflict and a topic that was mentioned in many of the interviews. Many of the men seemed ambivalent about having their wives work in the market. They knew that their families needed the income, but at the same time they felt that there was a danger of promis-

cuity. Women who got involved in labor unions or trade associations seemed to be particularly suspect, since men and women mixed at meetings that often were held at night and followed by
socializing and drinking. One of the men told the interviewer:

> When my wife used to stay home and sew, she was nice and quiet. Now that she goes to the market to
> sell she sometimes comes home in a bad mood, and when I ask what the matter is, we get into a fight.
> Ever since she started selling aprons and having her own money she's no longer nice and won't listen
> to you. When they don't work, they're good. In the market they all give each other advice.

> My wife makes me angry when I see the market women smiling with the union leaders, my wife
> among them. I'm not lying to you. When she's home she's different. I get very jealous.

Another male respondent had similar perceptions. In this case the interviewer explained (this interview was not tape recorded):

> He would like his wife to use the Copper-T, but not as long as she is selling in the market, because, he
> says, she would cheat on him. He does not like her to work, because women in the market go around
> with other men—mainly the city police officers, he says. In general he does not like the way women
> sell in the streets because this is a place where they learn to be unfaithful.

In some cases, women, too, assume that other women use modern contraceptives in order to have
affairs but, more typically, this is viewed as a male preoccupation. For example, the interviewer sum-
marized:

> [A]fter they [she and her husband] had talked about not having any more children . . . her husband just
> got jealous and thought that she must be seeing another man. He got so jealous that he said he was go-
> ing to have a baby with another woman if she did not want to have more babies with him. That is why
> many men leave their wives.

The desire to avoid being the target of suspicion appears to explain, in a number of cases, why
women who were extremely anxious to control their fertility failed to take decisive action in getting
information and adopting a modern method. Some women were reluctant even to raise the subject of
contraception with their male partners, preferring that their husbands take responsibility, even if doing that entailed a much greater risk of pregnancy and unwanted births. For example:

You and your husband have not talked about family planning yet?

No. We have just said that we are only going to have two babies. . . . My husband knows that I get my
period one year after each delivery, so maybe soon he will want to talk about family planning.

Why don't you talk to him about this?

Because I'm too scared.

Why is it scary?

Because some women say that the men don't like to listen. They just think that you have another man. That's why some friends have told me that it is bad to talk to our husbands about this—because they get jealous.

My friends say that their husbands get jealous and just hit them.

Lack of communication between partners about topics related to reproductive health was noted in another recent study (Skibiak, 1993.)7 That study also found that about 10 to 12 percent of the men interviewed believed that use of a modern method would either increase or decrease sexual desire in their partners. In contrast, our findings suggest that men are suspicious of modern methods not because they alter a woman's sexual desire, but because they give women the freedom to act on desires that presumably already exist. However, little evidence of such desires was revealed in the women's interviews.

Avoiding Sex

Although the interviews did not include specific questions on this subject, an aversion to sex was apparent in many of the transcripts. This seems to be another important factor explaining the relative popularity of calendar rhythm and more protracted forms of abstinence for birth control. In many of the interviews, sexual desire is portrayed as predominantly a male characteristic that women are obliged to satisfy to some extent. Several of the women told the interviewer that there were three types of men. As one of them put it:

There are those like pigs who can't wait for the woman; there are others that are just average; and then there are those that are like women—they do not care about sex.

The women interviewed showed a clear tendency to prefer the type of man who was not particularly interested in sex. Several women whose husbands wanted sex infrequently described these men as very good husbands, and themselves as lucky, an assessment that seemed to resonate with at least one of the Aymara interviewers. For example, one of the women explained:

I didn't get pregnant [after the first child] because my husband isn't demanding—he leaves me in peace. . . . He's a good man. . . . He just comes home and goes to sleep. He has his own bed and I have mine, apart. . . . [If I don't want to have sex], he doesn't get annoyed, he just goes to sleep.

The interviewer responded approvingly:

Ah, your husband is an understanding man. I guess you've been lucky with your partner.

The need for regular periods of abstinence is clear from the interview transcripts; such periods are sometimes prolonged for up to three weeks of the cycle, "just to be sure," and are perceived by some of the women as an advantage of the rhythm method. One woman who was unusually well-informed about both modern and traditional methods of fertility regulation told the interviewer:

> My husband knows the calendar method by heart. He marks off the days, and when I'm free [not fertile], he wants to have sex all the time. I can't. You know you get tired of it. . . . Sometimes we fight about it—I don't want to be with him and he gets cross and sulks . . . but he'll get over it . . . . I don't need [modern contraceptives] because I'm fine with this method.

Another woman explained:

> I take care—I don't have relations with him anymore [since the death of their youngest child eight months earlier]. . . . He talks to me about it, but I tell him, I don't want any more children, and I don't want to get cured [have an IUD inserted] or go to the doctor. It's best if I do nothing. . . .

Miscarriage and Abortion

Not surprisingly, the heavy reliance on calendar rhythm and other forms of abstinence often resulted in unwanted pregnancies among the women interviewed. Obtaining reliable information about abortion is notoriously difficult, especially in countries like Bolivia, where the great majority of such procedures are carried out secretly because abortion is illegal under most circumstances. Hospital regulations penalize women through higher charges for a dilatation and curettage (D&C) procedure when it is used to ameliorate a problem that is found to be the result of induced abortion rather than miscarriage (Rance, 1993). The existence of legal and financial sanctions, added to the likelihood of social censure and, in some cases, moral ambivalence, makes talking openly about abortion difficult, even in a private discussion with an interviewer who is known and trusted.

As a result of women's reluctance to talk about abortion, our findings probably underrepresent its incidence, which is obviously very common. As mentioned above, about two-thirds of the 30 women interviewed implied or stated directly that they had had at least one induced abortion or had attempted to induce an abortion. In 13 of the cases, the women apparently succeeded in inducing one or more abortions. In a few cases, the cost of a medical abortion was mentioned as an obstacle that drove the women to other risky or ineffective methods. For example:

> I decided I did not want this baby when I was one and one half months' pregnant, but I did not have the money for an abortion. I saved for the abortion, and when I had the money no doctor wanted to do it—they said the baby was too big. I also took herbal teas and lifted all kinds of heavy things so that I would miscarry, but nothing worked.

Several of those interviewed had used herbal abortifacients obtained from doctors or traditional practitioners, which, in a few cases, had been forcibly administered by their husbands. Their reported success rate was low. Several women had tried pills and injections. Another method, commonly used after the first trimester of pregnancy, was lifting heavy objects; it was often unsuccessful. "Accidental" falls down stairs, and, in one case, off a truck, were also common, often resulting in injury to the woman, but leaving the pregnancy intact. One 35-year-old woman who had been pregnant eight times told the interviewer:

> I cried, especially these last few times. I thought about what people would say about me [if she had yet another child], how they would look at me. I always wanted to miscarry—that's why I carried loads of potatoes, thinking that this would make me lose the pregnancy. I did everything—fell, so that the baby would die. I used to travel to my hometown . . . to bring back potatoes, and I would fall out of the back of the truck, and people would say to me that I was pregnant and now I had hurt myself, I would miscarry. But nothing ever happened.

Many of the interviews reveal a tendency to wish for a "natural miscarriage," free of guilt and the threat of punishment. Fifteen of the women seem to have tried to "give nature a helping hand" in ending an unwanted pregnancy, without explicitly admitting that they had made a conscious decision to abort. One woman, after trying to terminate a pregnancy by lifting heavy weights and having injections, said that she finally had a fall followed by hemorrhaging, and went to a hospital for a D&C. She told the interviewer that she regarded abortion as a sin, explaining, "I wanted to have a natural normal miscarriage, but it didn't happen."

In one sense the attempt to end an unwanted pregnancy expresses a woman's assertion of control over her reproduction. However, as described above, in many of the cases in this study such attempts were construed not as deliberate acts, but merely as a wish for nature to intervene. By maintaining a state of ambiguity about abortion (and also in many cases about sex and fertility regulation), women expose themselves to repeated, self-inflicted damage to their physical and emotional health through a succession of often unsuccessful measures to get rid of unwanted pregnancies. Maintaining this ambiguity may also contribute to the persistence of negative social perceptions of induced abortion, despite its being extremely common.

Infant Death Following Unwanted Births

In cases where abortion was not attempted or had failed, some women took measures to lessen the chances of survival of an unwanted child. The most common of these were systematic neglect, inadequate feeding, and failure to provide medical care. Almost a third of the women interviewed had had unwanted pregnancies that resulted in the birth of infants who subsequently died in unclear circumstances that might be interpreted as passive or active infanticide. In all of these cases, the probable infanticide followed a series of ineffective measures to prevent the birth. In most cases, more than one of the following conditions were present: The pregnancy had been unwanted, the woman did not look after herself during pregnancy nor seek prenatal care, she tried and failed to induce an abortion, she made no preparation for the birth, she took no interest in the birth, she received no assistance during delivery, the child was not of the sex desired by one or both parents, the infant was sickly from birth, the child became ill after being breastfed when the mother was angry, the child was left uncovered or alone for long periods, the child died for no apparent reason, the child had not been vaccinated, or it had been denied medical care because such care seemed pointless or cost too much money. Typically, the death was greeted with resignation or relief. One woman who suspended hospital care for her third son who was dying of pneumonia said (referring to him and her first child who also had died in infancy),

> Sometimes I think it's best that they passed away. God knows why He took them. Because I spent a lot of money on their treatment and, even so, couldn't save them. I say it must have been destiny, testing me and telling me not to have more children.

Conclusions

The study's findings suggest that among urban Aymara women, fertility regulation is perceived as extremely important and that, in general, it is supported by sociocultural norms. The findings also reveal the weight of many of the cultural, social, and practical obstacles that these women face in attempting to achieve fertility regulation. While this study included a relatively small number of respondents, the general problems that it illustrates are widespread, both among urban Aymara in Bolivia and among poor people elsewhere who are socially and politically marginalized. For many of the women in the study, the issue of fertility control is fraught with conflict. Interactions with providers of family planning services are experienced through a lens of social inequality and mistrust.[8] Information from such sources is suspect, and modern family planning methods are thought to be dangerous. In addition, fertility regulation is often a focus of conflict between partners.

In this population, the acceptability of modern contraceptive methods is relatively limited, and, for a variety of reasons, many women and their partners prefer to use the rhythm method. Providers of reproductive health services should accept these preferences as legitimate by focusing on education and information to improve women's ability to use periodic abstinence effectively and, perhaps, by promoting condoms and vaginal methods for use in conjunction with the rhythm method. Counseling regarding the rhythm method should encompass such issues related to its use as reliability, the need for cooperation, and the common problems of male jealousy, alcoholism, and violence. A safe, accessible method of menstrual regulation provided as a backup would prevent many unwanted births and self-inflicted injuries.

Social norms, and cultural beliefs and preferences are not immutable; this is a society in transition. The 25 percent of the women in our survey who are using modern contraceptive methods, like the women in the in-depth study who have practiced modern contraception, probably do so despite considerable obstacles—fear related to pervasive rumors about negative health consequences, the need to depend on health-care providers whom they do not trust, the necessity to communicate private matters, and, often, the opposition and suspicion of their partners. In addition, government policies have only recently begun to endorse contraception as a health measure; modern methods of fertility regulation are only now becoming more accessible to lower-income groups, even in cities. That the rate of modern contraceptive use is even this high, in the face of major cultural and social obstacles, suggests that the potential demand for modern contraceptive methods and services is growing and that it will continue to grow.

The principal strategy for fostering this growth in demand should continue to be an emphasis on improving the quality of medical services and encouraging providers to be more sensitive to cultural differences. The style of interaction between service provider and client, while always important, seems to be particularly important in this society. Clinics should offer a range of methods, avoid promoting a single method at the expense of others, and respect and support the client's right to make her (or his) own decisions. Discrimination in hospitals and clinics against women with complications of induced abortion should be stopped, and postabortion counseling and contraceptive services should be provided.

While the topic of sexual jealousy is a complex one in this culture, and how this topic might be addressed by reproductive health programs is not obvious, an important point to note is that the men in this study did not necessarily want to have large numbers of children. In many cases, men's refusal to cooperate in fertility reguration appeared to be symptomatic of a more general struggle for control. The men interviewed saw impregnation as a way of asserting control over and assuring fidelity from their partners. The common perception that modern contraception fosters promiscuity might be weakened through a skillful use of dramatic presentations on radio and television.

In general, given the high level of mistrust of the medical establishment among this population, alternative channels for dissemination of information and provision of nonclinical methods should be sought. Radio and television are two obvious channels, particularly since radio was frequently cited in the study as a source of misinformation about contraceptive methods. In addition to providing information, media campaigns aimed at desensitizing the topics of sexuality and fertility regulation and presenting family planning as a responsible course of action in the context of the life situations of the urban poor might be effective, as they have been in other countries. Themes such as conflict over sexuality and reproduction, jealousy, violence, alcoholism, unwanted pregnancy, and use of contraceptives could be woven together in dramatic presentations, as they often are in life.

Greater exposure to such themes through the media, along with sex education in schools and youth clubs, workers' associations, unions, and community organizations should eventually bring about greater openness and better access to information about contraception. Media and community organizations could also be used to promote the idea that users of health services have the right to clear, comprehensible information, to respectful treatment, and to health and family planning services of reasonable quality.

Notes

1 For more details, see Schuler et al., 1994. Our survey was done almost four years later than the Demographic and Health Survey (DHS), which may explain in part why the contraceptive prevalence rate (CPR) for all methods is so much higher than the 1989 DHS figure of 39 percent for urban areas (Republica de Bolivia, 1990). Another factor is that 85 percent of the women in our sample (compared with 71 percent in the DHS) were between the ages of 25 and 44 years, and women in this age group have higher levels of contraceptive use than older and younger women. In addition, all of the women in our sample were employed (either as producers or as market sellers). While the difference between the DHS (urban sample) and our sample in the percentage using modern methods (18 percent compared with 25 percent) is small enough that it may simply reflect an increase in contraceptive use over fume, this explanation is unlikely to suffice for the extremely high difference in the prevalence rates for traditional methods—21 percent in the DHS urban sample versus 49 percent in our sample. The DHS did not include information on ethnic identity. However, in the Altiplano region, which is inhabited predominantly by indigenous groups, the CPR for traditional methods (18 percent) is three times higher than that for modern methods (6 percent). The findings presented here would lead us to suspect that sociocultural factors as well as limited access to modern contraceptives are at work in the Altiplano.

2 According to National Census figures, the 1992 populations of La Paz and El Alto were 710,940 and 392,774, respectively.

3 This method is described in detail in Schuler et al., 1985 and Huntington and Schuler, 1993.

4 The 60 women in the ethnographic study were purposively selected after censuses were taken within principal market areas in La Paz and El Alto. This study was initiated before the survey of 800 women, and the samples do not overlap. The sample included a variety of types of small-scale producers and vendors. Half were recipients of formal credit (one of the variables in the study) and half used only informal sources of credit. Ten of the women dropped out during the course of the study because they felt the interviews were too time-consuming or because they felt that they were not being compensated adequately (although they were given occasional monetary gifts in compensation for their time). Among those remaining, 30 women were selected based on their willingness to be interviewed in depth about their reproductive behavior (most were reticent to some degree, but some were extremely so). An attempt was made to include at least 10 women who had some experience with modern contraceptive methods and at least 10 who had used traditional methods. Most of the women did not want their husbands to be interviewed, and most of the men were even more disinclined to be interviewed than their wives. The eight men included in this part of the study were the only ones who would cooperate, among those whose participation had not been ruled out by their wives.

5 The description of the baby-skewering IUD came from an evangelical church. In other cases, the church was not identified.

6 The belief system in which these fears and suspicions are rooted is described in Crandon-Malamud, 1991.

7 Men and their partners were interviewed separately. Of the couples interviewed who said that they were using some form of contraception, 43 percent gave inconsistent information as to which method they were using. Many of the men who reported using the rhythm method seemed unaware that their partners had adopted a modern method (pill, IUD, or sterilization).

8 For a more general discussion of this issue, see Simmons and Elias, 1994.

Acknowledgments

This study is based on research supported by Population Action International, with supplementary support from The Population Council Regional Office for Latin America and the Caribbean. Preparation of this paper was funded through the United States Agency for International Development/Bolivia Buy-in to the Population Council's INOPAL II Program. We are grateful to Rosario Mamani and Mary Marca, who worked with María Eugenia Choque in conducting the interviews, to John Townsend of the Population Council, who collaborated in various aspects of the study, to John Skibiak, Mary McInerney, and Sigrid Anderson for their assistance and for their comments on an earlier draft of the paper, to Marina de Montaño for her role in coordination, and to Ann Hendrix Jenkins for her assistance in data analysis and preparation of the report.

References

Bolivian Ministry of Planning and Coordination, Population Policy Unit. 1989. *La Planificación Familiar entre las Mujeres Nativas y Migrantes.* La Paz: Bolivian Ministry of Planning and Coordination.

Coordinadora de la Mujer.1990. *Politicas para la Incorporación de la Mujer en la Estrategia de Desarrollo.* La Paz: Coordinadora de la Mujer.

Crandon-Malamud, Libbet.1991. *From the Fat of Our Souls: Social Change, Political Process and Medical Pluralism in Bolivia.* Berkeley: University of California Press.

Huntington, Dale and Sidney Ruth Schuler. 1993. "The simulated client method: Evaluating client-provider interactions in family planning clinics." *Studies in Family Planning* 24,3: 187-193.

Rance, Susanna. 1993. "Necesidades de Información sobre el aborto." La Paz: International Projects Assistance Services.

Remez, Lisa. 1991. "Rhythm accounts for half of all contraceptive use in Bolivia, DHS reveals." *International Family Planning Perspectives* 17.1: 36-37.

República de Bolivia, Ministerio de Planeamiento y Coordinación. *Encuesta Nacional de Demographia y Salud, 1989.* La Paz, Bolivia and Columbia, MD: Instituto Nacional de Estadistica and Institute for Resource Development/Macro Systems.

Schuler, Sidney Ruth, E. Noel McIntosh, Melvyn C. Goldstein, and Badri Raj Pande. 1985. "Barriers to effective family planning in Nepal." *Studies in Family Planning* 16,5: 260-270.

Schuler, Sidney Ruth, Ann Hendrix Jenkins, and John W. Townsend. 1994. "Credit, women's status, and fertility regulations in urban market centers of Bolivia." Draft report.

Simmons, Ruth and Christopher Elias. 1994. "The study of client-provider interactions: A review of methodological issues." *Studies in Family Planning* 75,1: 1-17.

Skibiak, John. 1993. "Male barriers to use of reproductive health services: Myth or reality?" Paper presented to the annual meeting of the American Public Health Association, San Francisco, 24-28 October.

INVESTIGATING THE SOCIAL CONTEXT OF FERTILITY AND FAMILY PLANNING: A QUALITATIVE STUDY IN PERU

Alfredo L. Fort

There is a widespread idea, held particularly by Peruvian men, that having many children is a sign of faithfulness in a woman; conversely, the use of family planning is strongly associated with infidelity.

Summary

Focus-group sessions conducted in 1986 and 1987 with Peruvian women living in two cities far from the capital indicated that women's control of their fertility is undermined by their low status in society and their ignorance of reproductive physiology. Contributing factors are their lack of any concept of planning for the future and a weak family planning program. Although there has been some increase in the use modern methods of contraception, nearly half of all current users rely on traditional methods such as rhythm, which is often used in reverse and is therefore ineffective. Previous studies had singled out fear of side effects as the main deterrent to the use of modern contraceptives. However, the focus-group discussions revealed that women who were using modern methods were as fearful of harmful effects as women who were not using such methods. In fact, the women who were using modern methods were doing so because their dread of further pregnancies was even stronger than their fear of illness or death.

Although surveys had shown the preferred family size in Peru to be three, the focus groups revealed conditions that encourage women to have more children than they believe is ideal. Child mortality is still at a high level. Couples rarely discuss family size early in their marriage, if at all. Women would prefer to delay childbearing for 2-3 years after marriage, but feel they must have children immediately to please their husbands. Wives also fear their husbands' disapproval if they use explicit methods of contraception, because family planning is associated with infidelity and having many children, with faithfulness. In this context, family planning is used primarily as a means of limiting, rather than spacing, births.

Background

Peru's birthrate dropped from 46.3 per 1,000 population in 1960-1965 to 36.7 per 1,000 in 1980-1985. The total fertility rate (TFR) declined slightly between 1977-1978 and 1984-1986, from 4.7 to

Reprinted by permission of the Editor from *International Family Planning Perspectives,* Vol. 15, No. 3, 1989, pp. 88-94.

4.1 lifetime births per woman. Nevertheless, as is common in many developing countries, particularly those in Latin America, significant change has occurred primarily in the cities, which are expanding rapidly because of migration from rural areas. As can be seen in Table 1, data from national surveys carried out during the past decade have shown large differences in fertility rates between Peru's various geographical regions and Lima, the capital city. For example, the 1986 Demographic and Health Survey (DHS) revealed that the TFR among women living in Lima was 2.5 births per woman, compared with 5.4 and 6.0 among those living in the mountains and the jungle, respectively.

Table 1. Total fertility rates in Peru, by region, 1977-1978 Peruvian Fertility Study (PFS), 1981 Contraceptive Prevalence Study (CPS) and 1986 Demographic and Health Survey (DHS)

Region	PFS	CPS	DHS
Total	4.7	4.5	4.1
Lima	4.1	3.5	2.5
Coast*	5.2	5.1	3.8
Mountains	7.6	7.3	5.4
Jungle	8.1	8.0	6.0

* Excluding Lima

These surveys have also found a moderate increase in the use of contraceptives-particularly that of modern methods (Table 2).[1] For example, between 1977-1978 and 1986, the proportion of women relying on modern methods of family planning rose from 11 percent to 23 percent. Nevertheless, the so-called traditional methods of contraception still predominate. The 1986 DHS indicated that half of all current users rely on such methods; rhythm, the most prevalent method, is used by nearly as many women as the pill, the IUD and sterilization combined.

Table 2. Percentage of currently married women using a method of contraception, by type of method used, 1977-1978 PFS, 1981 CPS and 1986 DHS

Method	PFS (N=5, 061)	CPS (N=3, 925)	DHS (N=2, 899)
Total	31	41	46
Modern	11	17	23
IUD	1	4	7
Pill	4	5	7
Female Sterilization	3	4	6
Injectables	1	2	1
Vaginal *	1	1	1
Condom	1	1	1
Traditional	20	24	23
Rhythm	11	17	18
Withdrawal	3	4	4
Other ¤	6	3	1

* The diaphragm and spermicides.
¤ Douches and folk methods (such as herbs). In the PFS data, this category includes abstinence as well.

Table 3 shows the relative prevalence of the rhythm method in different geographical regions of Peru as reported in the DHS. For example, rhythm is less widely used than the more effective modern methods in Lima (20.6 percent vs. 33.2 percent) and in the jungle (10.9 percent vs. 16.6 percent), while in the mountains, the proportion of women using rhythm is almost twice that of women using the more effective modern methods (16.2 percent vs. 8.7 percent).

Table 3. Percentage distribution of currently married women, by type of contraceptive used, according to region, 1986 DHS

Type of Method	Total	Lima	Coast *	Mountains	Jungle
Most effective modern **	21.2	33.2	27.2	8.7	16.6
Rhythm	17.7	20.6	19.6	16.2	10.9
Other modern ¤	1.7	2.6	1.4	1.4	0.3
Other traditional §	5.0	6.4	3.8	4.7	5.1
None	54.4	37.2	48.0	69.0	67.1
Total	100.0	100.0	100.0	100.0	100.0

* Excluding Lima
** The IUD, the pill, female sterilization, male sterilization and injectables
¤ The diaphragm, spermicides and the condom
§ Withdrawal, douches and folk methods

However, what respondents meant by "rhythm" is uncertain, because the few surveys carried out in Peru used closed-ended questions that did not describe the methods under consideration. Other traditional methods, such as douches and herbs, although mentioned by small proportions of the DHS sample, are used throughout the country, even on the urbanized coast and in Lima. As with the rhythm method, there is a need for more research on the way these methods are used and the context in which they thrive.

Preliminary research and experimental programs in population planning were carried out in Peru in the mid-1960s. Most of these efforts ended with the advent of military rule, which lasted for 12 years. Since 1981, however, a joint project between the Pan American Health Organization and the Peruvian Ministry of Health, with support from the United Nations Population Fund, has been adding family planning services to the more general maternal and child health (MCH) services offered by state hospitals and health centers throughout the country.

Unfortunately, this program has been undercut by a lack of strong political commitment, reflected in the absence of clear targets for either population growth or contraceptive prevalence. The authority given to the program administration has varied from a low position within the MCH program to the nominally high position of a general directorate of family planning. As a result, the program lacks the stability and organization it needs to make substantial progress. Services remain concentrated in hospitals and urban health centers, and the supply of contraceptives has been irregular. Thus, progress in promoting the use of modern methods has been slow. In a 1982 assessment of family planning efforts in more than 90 developing countries, Peru's program was categorized as "weak." An evaluation carried out by the National Population Council in five health regions of Peru estimated that in 1983, 7.3 percent of women of childbearing age became new acceptors through the program. This estimate may be too high because of the inclusion of Lima, which had a rate of 9.2 percent, and the use of reduced catchment populations as denominators when calculating percentages in the inner health regions. In recent years, articles appearing in national bulletins of Peruvian family planning agencies have referred to the "ambiguity with which [our] population problem is managed" and to the "catalepsy" of the National Committee on Population, which was set up to support population activities in Peru.

One important obstacle to the acceptance of modern contraceptive methods may be that the centrally organized and controlled program administration in Lima does not take Peru's cultural variation into account. Little is known about the beliefs and motivations that influence women in their decisions regarding fertility and childbearing, information that could be very helpful in efforts to improve the delivery of reproductive health services and education.

There are two issues in particular that should be explored further. One is that of "unmet need" for contraception among women who are either married or living in a consensual union. A recent analysis of 1986 DHS data found that of four Latin American countries, Peru had the smallest decrease in unmet need during the last decade, and that the level of need among Peruvian women remains very high. Women commonly attribute their reluctance to use contraceptives to a concern about side effects, but it is possible that other powerful deterrents are also involved. An expressed desire to have no more children could conflict with underlying attitudes about family size and the childbearing process. A second question is why women seem to prefer to use family planning to limit rather than to space births.

Because of the complex nature of these questions, we chose to use qualitative techniques rather than a structured survey. Recent literature has reported the use of focus-group discussions in research related to population policy and family planning. For example, focus groups were used in a study of fertility transition in Thailand and in research on family planning awareness, attitudes and practices in Mexico and Indonesia. More recently, such discussion groups were included in studies on attitudes toward sexual and demographic education in Costa Rica and on the factors responsible for nonuse of contraceptives among couples in Nepal who desired no more children (part of the DHS program). We investigated the issues raised earlier in this article through a series of focus-group discussions in two Peruvian cities as part of a larger study investigating attitudes and values related to reproduction.

Methodology

The study was conducted in Cusco and Iquitos, cities representative of two distinct and understudied regions in Peru—the Andes mountains and the Amazon jungle, respectively. The study samples were selected from the shantytowns surrounding the cities, where poor living standards, unemployment and traditional rural family-formation patterns appear to be more common than elsewhere in Peru.

Women had to have at least three living children to be eligible for the study. They also had to be of reproductive age (15-49), currently married or in a consensual union, fecund, not pregnant and residing in a shantytown. In each city, the women who met these criteria were divided into three contraceptive-use categories: those who used modern methods, those who used traditional methods and those who had actually rejected contraceptive use or had never decided to use contraceptives (never-users). The criterion of having at least three living children was included to ensure that the participating women had had the opportunity to think about limiting the size of their family and to make categorization more accurate. In a society in which large families are the norm, it could be misleading to place a woman who had one or two children and had never used contraceptives in the never-user category. The cut-off point of three children was set according to the average number of children (2.7) preferred by currently married Peruvian women. To identify any variation between younger and older women, we separated the participants in each user category into two age-groups: those younger than 30 and those 30 and over. There were two sessions, each with different participants, for each age-group, user group and region, for a total of 24 separate focus-group sessions, 12 in each region.

The modern-method users were the first group chosen at each location. Women attending the family planning clinic of the state hospital in each region who matched the criteria were asked to participate. Those who agreed were given an invitation sheet with the date, time and meeting place, along with a note indicating the nature of the discussion, its duration and the name of the moderator and stating that a small sum would be paid for transportation. Each focus group was conducted a few days after the invitations had been issued; previous experience had shown that holding a session too long after the invitations had been received resulted in low attendance because the women forgot about the session or lost the information.

The focus groups were held in a small room at the state hospital. At the suggestion of local leaders and community health workers, we scheduled the focus groups to begin in the late afternoon and to finish by early evening. Each session lasted approximately two hours and was conducted by the principal investigator. Although the sessions were conducted by a man, the women discussed a wide range of matters related to sex and reproduction without embarrassment.[2] We made a special effort to create a casual and friendly atmosphere, to reassure participants of the value of each individual opinion, and to stress the importance of a nonjudgmental attitude.

The traditional-method users and never-users were made up of women from two shantytowns chosen at random from those where the modern-method users lived. There were no obvious distinctions among the shantytowns involved. Participants were recruited with the help of a woman from a local mothers' club who was given some training on the selection criteria. Recruitment for these two groups was carried out house to house, and meetings were held near where the women lived, either in the community center or in a participant's home. The sessions were conducted during roughly the same period as those involving the modern-method users.

The study was carried out in December 1986 in Iquitos and in March 1987 in Cusco. All sessions in each region were completed within three weeks. A total of 173 women participated. Of these, 77 were from Iquitos (an average of 6.4 women were in each focus group) and 96 were from Cusco (an average of 8.0 women were in each session). The average age of those in the under-30 group was 24.7 years in Iquitos and 24.1 in Cusco; the average age of those in the 30-and-over group was 33.4 and 36.1, respectively.

The investigator used a discussion guide comprising some 30 questions to direct the focus groups. The first section of the guide explored characteristics of family formation, such as the childbearing process and relationships between husbands and wives. The second part was concerned with attitudes toward and experience with various methods of contraception. The final section dealt with abortion. All sessions were tape recorded, and notes about special characteristics of respondents were taken at the same time to allow matching of answers on the tape with specific participants.

Family Formation

The section of the discussion devoted to family formation explored age at first union, family size, the value placed on children and the husband-wife relationship. Each participant was asked to specify her ideal and actual age of union. The average age at union among all participants was 17.7 years. Women in Iquitos not only expressed a desire for earlier unions, but did in fact enter unions earlier than their counterparts from Cusco. Among women who were under 30, the average age at union in Iquitos was 16.6 years, while in Cusco it was 17.5 years; among those who were 30 and older, the average age at union was 17.6 years in Iquitos and 18.6 years in Cusco. Within each region, however, there were no differences between age-groups and between user groups. The norm of earlier unions in Iquitos could explain the higher fertility rate found by the DHS among women in the jungle, in spite of a rate of contraceptive use slightly higher than that found in the mountains.

The participants acknowledged that early union disrupts adolescent life and education and that it leads to increased fertility. They felt that early marriages could lead to marital failure because of lack of experience; there is a pervasive idea that women should know "how to serve [their husbands] well." The group discussions revealed a very common scenario for the start of family life: that of the young woman who is made pregnant by the first man she goes out with. Adolescent women rarely receive much guidance or sex education from their parents: Their queries about how offspring are born are met with incorrect and evasive answers such as "Babies come from airplanes" or "Baby pigs are born from their mother's mouth."

Ideal intervals between union and first birth were also explored in some of the focus groups, particularly those in Iquitos. Among the participants who discussed this issue, the ideal gap was 2-3 years; these women said, however, that union and pregnancy often occurred almost simultaneously. Delay in having children was thought to be contrary to men's wishes, and women felt their husbands would leave them if they did not bear children soon after union. When age differences were taken into account, the women in each group had a similar number of children. However, the average ideal family size of women in Iquitos was higher than that of the women in Cusco (3.2 vs. 2.3). This difference was reaffirmed by their respective definitions of a large family: six children for the women in Iquitos and four or five for those in Cusco.

During this part of the discussion, several important factors became evident. First, the low status of women in both the family and society makes it difficult for women to exercise control over their own fertility. Some of the modern-method users said that they had gone off with a man to escape parental oppression. As someone in the older group said, however, that was "getting out of one cage to enter another." Moreover, in all the groups, women spoke of childbearing as inevitable. Once they begin having children, they said, "the machine starts" and "from one, one goes into having a lot." A third factor that emerged from these discussions was a lack of any concept of planning. These women live an everyday life in every sense of the word: Most wages are earned and spent daily, and goods and foods are purchased at need. Reproduction follows the same pattern, with pregnancies too being unplanned. The women said that they were "taking care" (practicing some form of contraception) "but [the children] are increasing." The belief that fertility is beyond their control could help explain their lack of interest in contraception for spacing, rather than limiting, births.

The issue of family size is closely tied to the value placed on children. In the shantytowns, children apparently have a better chance of survival than in rural areas. Nevertheless, some 20 percent of the babies born alive to women who participated in the focus groups were dead by the time of the sessions. This high rate of child mortality is one reason why women with at least three children might still want to have more. Companionship and financial security in old age are also important motivations in a country where organized social security plans reach only a small proportion of the population, mainly those living in urban areas. Support for aging parents comes primarily from sons, as most paying jobs in Peru are held by men. Therefore, when the participants were asked what sex distribution they would prefer if they were to have only three children, the majority specified two boys and one girl. Moreover, they said, boys "land on their feet," while girls "suffer more" and have to bear with "children and the home workload." Girls will, nevertheless, later provide company for their mothers, visiting them and helping them with the housework. This role differentiation is an extension of task assignments at home: A boy typically fetches water, runs errands or "helps his father," rarely doing any kind of washing or child-minding; girls, on the other hand, start with kitchen work at three or four years of age and then move on to baby-sitting and laundry.

In a further effort to understand the value of children, the investigator then explored attitudes about childless couples and infertile women. The participants condemned couples who choose not to have children as "irresponsible" and "egoistic." They compared a childless home to "a garden without flowers" or "a nest without birds." To these women, children seal and justify unions ("the reason to get married is to have children"), and marital dissolution is an almost automatic consequence of childlessness. They also frequently mentioned the pressure men exert on their wives to have children. If a wife fails to do so, they said, the husband will "find another [woman] with whom to have that child." Questions about infertile women elicited expressions of deep sorrow and pity. The participants saw such women as persons who were experiencing great frustration and whose marital lives were endangered.

It was clear from the group discussions about husband-wife relationships that couples rarely talk about family-size preferences early in their marriage. Family size is discussed, if at all, "afterwards, when there are four or five, only then." What occurs is that the mother eventually gets "fed up" and seeks help. In this context, family planning is usually seen not as a way of spacing, but as a way of bringing fertility to an abrupt end ("we had enough"). Except for the spouses of modern-method users, husbands usually do not participate in this decision.

The women blamed their husbands for insensitivity to the family's needs ("they do not care about numbers"). Indeed, they felt that men see children as a way of keeping their wives at home. In general, the participants saw children as "enslaving" them. Furthermore, a woman who has many children is seen as a "señora" (married, a lady), an image that is believed to prevent her from being approached by other men when she goes out. This appears to be related to the widespread idea, held particularly by men, that having many children is a sign of faithfulness in a woman.

Conversely, family planning is strongly associated with infidelity. Women themselves sometimes adopted this attitude. As one participant said, "Why should I 'take care' if I am not having children from other men?" But the participants also related family planning to "going out," to "dialogue" between women and to "change." They see mothers' clubs, health centers and other communal institutions as schools of a sort. Men ridicule women's participations in such activities, according to wives, "because it is not agreeable to them."

Other differences in roles revolve around cooperation and conflict at home. Although the women started out by justifying their husbands' refusal to help with family duties, further discussion revealed that they were very frustrated by the excessive amount of work they had to perform at home, an injustice that was not acknowledged by men. The participants emphasized the contrast between their confinement and their husbands' absolute liberty; most of them could not even discuss the matter with their husbands, let alone change their minds. The husbands of some of the younger women who were using modern methods did seem to have a more cooperative attitude, however.

Family finances reflected another facet of the husbands' control. Because the men dole out small amounts of money daily, their wives are not able to save any spare cash for hairdressing or clothes, which they feel they need to "keep" their husbands. However, this system does provide them with a unique opportunity for daily socializing as they shop in the local markets.

The women see the liberty of their partners as providing opportunities for affairs outside the home. A not insignificant number of the participants actually justified this as a reflection of men's "different nature," even saying that if a man is unfaithful, his wife is at fault for harassing him or for not "keeping smart enough." Such notions are part of an ideology that also holds it as basically wrong for a mother to go out freely and that "abandonment of [one's] children" is the ultimate shame. The limited efforts of some women to change their situation had encountered strong opposition from their husbands. A few of the participants said that employment of women was a possible way of improving the situation.

The last topic covered in this section was marital violence. The participants said that wife-beating was common, and that beatings usually occurred when a man had been drinking or when he was having affairs outside the home (which, they said, "alters his mood"). Some of the participants associated drinking with higher fertility, probably because of an increase in unprotected intercourse. Separations and abandonment, more common ways of resolving conflict than divorce, are not infrequent.

Family Planning Services

The second section of the discussion explored experience with the government family planning program, attitudes and knowledge about contraception and experience with contraceptive methods. Only the users of modern and traditional methods had had experience with the family planning program based in the state hospital. Because the two groups of women made similar comments about the program, their remarks were not separated. They criticized the service for delays, disorganization and corruption. They rated the attention they received as generally good, although they had some complaints about being rushed through and being treated with insensitivity and hostility. They resented the lack of privacy in the examination rooms, complaining that "everybody sees us" and "there is not a door closed." In all the groups, the women agreed that they would prefer for women doctors to perform internal examinations because they saw them as "more understanding" and "gentler" than men.

In Cusco, the family planning services were inconveniently combined with prenatal services. There were no structured family planning talks for women admitted to the hospital, and doctors and nurses advised patients personally. This situation was conducive to corruption: In some cases, doctors had refused to insert an IUD at the clinic, saying that such devices did not exist, but later referred the patients to their private practice and charged a fee for insertion.

The participants agreed that there were practically no family planning services available in rural areas. They requested that clinic hours be extended into the afternoon, saying that there was a huge amount of housework to accomplish in the mornings, such as early preparation of breakfasts and packed lunches, daily marketing, baby-minding and cooking. In addition, the women themselves often went to work.

The participants said they received hardly any family planning information through the mass media, and very little through health centers, mothers' clubs or government programs. They found the amount of family planning information available to them sparse in comparison with the profusion of material and messages delivered for immunization campaigns.

Use of Modern Methods

In Iquitos, most users of modern methods participating in the discussions were using the pill, whereas in Cusco, the majority were using the IUD. These findings are similar to those on the relative method preferences found in the few surveys carried out in each area. There were no major differences between the two communities in the amount or content of family planning information provided or in the availability of methods.

The participants were asked how they had first learned about family planning. In both Iquitos and Cusco, the most common way was through contact with government health institutions or personnel (most frequently after childbirth or curettage in a hospital or when attending a children's clinic). This was consistent with results of the DHS, in which government hospitals or health clinics were the most frequently identified source of current methods or information about methods. In Cusco, mothers' clubs, relatives and friends were also important sources. Overall, talks by program officers accounted for less than 10 percent of sources of information, a figure consistent with the limited efforts made to date in public education.

In general, women appeared to be using the modern methods correctly, although when they had first begun to use their method, they clearly had received very little information about it, the mechanism by which it worked and the side effects they might experience. Perhaps in part because of this lack of information, they had a long list of complaints and fears about harmful consequences of contraceptive methods. Women in areas in which a particular method was prevalent mentioned more side effects and fears related to that method than to other methods.

Given so many fears about dangerous side effects, why did these women continue using the modern methods? The women typically responded that pregnancy would have been worse than the side effects, citing the "sacrifice," the "pain" and the "heaviness" of pregnancy. One of the participants created a slogan that expressed the intensity of their feelings: "Better death than to have more!" The under-30 group made it clear that their determination to avoid further pregnancies was overriding their fears of cancer and death. Some said that they continued only because of their husband's support.

Use of Traditional Methods

Women who used traditional methods of contraception were able to name the more common modern methods, and sometimes even acknowledged their effectiveness. Nevertheless, they lacked knowledge about use and mechanism of action. Their fears of side effects were more intense than those of the modern-method users. They believed that if they used modern methods, they would be more prone to illness. According to one woman, their fears were engendered by the comments of dissatisfied users who "leave [the methods] when they are harmed." Some women defined an effective method as one that "doesn't harm me."

Women in both regions used a variety of traditional contraceptive methods. They had confidence in a method if they or someone they knew who used it had achieved an interval of two years without pregnancy. In Iquitos, the four most often mentioned were douches, *la regla* ("the period"), Chloromycetin™ (an antibiotic) and herbal beverages. In Cusco, on the other hand, *la regla* was the most popular method, followed by herbal remedies and douches. Some women preferred to combine two traditional methods rather than relying on one. This could reflect a lack of confidence in the effectiveness of any single method or might simply describe the usual pattern of use of traditional methods. Herbs were consistently found to be more prevalent in Cusco (the mountain town) than in Iquitos (the jungle town). This was an unexpected finding, because native tribes in the Amazon jungle are known to use herbal medicine for fertility. However, in Iquitos, the people are basically *ribereños*, dwellers of the river margins who have migrated to the nearest city, and not actually natives, who live deeper in the jungle.

Women using traditional methods had usually learned about these methods from family members, often their husband or mother, or from friends and neighbors. In the case of *la regla* only a few women had obtained information from a talk at the hospital or the school.

The group sessions indicated that the local population regards *la regla* as being equivalent to what we call the rhythm method. However, further discussion revealed that most users were, in fact, applying it in reverse—that is, they were having intercourse during the high-risk days surrounding ovulation. We found a widespread belief that the uterus "opened" during the menstrual period. This event was associated with fecundity, in the same way that the end of fecundity was signaled by the end of menstrual periods. Thus, this method entailed waiting to have intercourse until the uterus "closed." When these women were taught a simplified version of the method—to restrict intercourse to the periods of eight days before and after the menses—they used the method in reverse, waiting until eight days after the menses to begin having intercourse and avoiding intercourse beginning at about eight days before the menses. Some women would wait 10 or even 12 days after the menses before having intercourse, because they believed closure of the uterus could be delayed.

Other common beliefs seemed to reinforce this idea. In Cusco, women said repeatedly that sexual intercourse during the menstrual period was sure to result in pregnancy. A husband who "took care of" his wife would never "make contact" during the menstrual period. Such views were expressed not only by women who used traditional methods, but also by some current users of modern methods. Women do not bathe during menstruation, not only because they believe that there is an open wound, but also because they believe they could have "accidents" (pregnancies) if they carelessly swim in "bad waters." Another practice that seems to arise from this notion is that most herbs and remedies believed to affect fecundity are taken during, or around the time of, the menstrual period.

Some women did not consider *la regla* a method of family planning at all. In fact, when first asked if they were "taking care to avoid getting pregnant or having more children," a not infrequent response was: "No, only naturally." Further questions revealed that they were using *la regla*. Periodic abstinence could be practiced regularly and in a context lacking specific birth limitation purposes. These alternative meanings must be taken into account when interpreting survey responses. Some respondents categorized as nonusers could, in fact, be practicing this "natural" method. In general, women seemed aware that *la regla* was not very effective and that they might be using the method improperly. They were dissatisfied because their husbands did not respect the period of "danger"; in any case, they believed the method was not adequate when used alone.

The focus-group participants seemed to feel embarrassed to speak about abstinence and withdrawal. Women who did comment said these methods were not much accepted or used by their husbands.

Throughout the sessions, particularly those in Cusco, women referred to a variety of local herbs used to delay pregnancies. Among the most popular were parsley, mallow, and field grass mixed with linseed. Other native plants, such as *allcoquisca, duraznillo, rahuar chunca* and *llampu jarma*, are usually taken as an infusion called *mate*, and are sometimes blended with lemon juice or water. The focus-group participants explained that fresh herbs "cool down the ovary" and "sterilize," whereas "warm things fertilize." This reasoning also explains their habit of drinking these infusions after letting them *reposar*, that is, leaving them out in the open during the night, when temperatures fall to a few degrees above freezing.

If they want to have a child, women stop taking the herbs for several months. Most women are not entirely confident that the herbs delay pregnancy, but they regard them as natural and free from side effects (although, according to one woman, too many fresh herbs can "give a cold, a chill").

The focus-group participants believed that douches act through the same mechanism as herbs. In fact, women use a preparation with mallow water or water with lemon juice for the douches, which are said to "cool down the womb." The women said that they restored fecundity by injecting calcium intravenously, an old custom still practiced in many rural areas. The burning sensation produced by the injection of calcium is associated with strength and healing. Women also take vitamins and honey to "warm up" the womb and restore fecundity.

Lemon taken alone, with infusions or medicines, or in douches is thought to exert a powerful effect on fecundity. Focus-group participants said its "sourness" has a spermicidal effect. It also "heals wounds [by] drying them." Here, the rationale seems to be that by diminishing menstrual bleeding, lemon juice impairs fecundity. The extreme acidity of the juice has given rise to a unique name used in the jungle: When people say a substance is *patco* (sour), as lemon is, they probably mean that its sourness affects fecundity.

In many parts of inner Peru, antibiotics can be purchased without a prescription. Chloromycetin™, a popular brand of chloramphenicol originally intended for the treatment of typhoid fever, is widely used by mothers as a folk remedy for diarrheal diseases, and somehow its use has been extended to family-size limitation. Women in the jungle believe that its "sourness kills the microbe [spermatozoid]."

Liver salts, which are generally used in combination with other "sour" substances like lemon, were said to produce anemia (by "killing red blood cells"). Again, the rationale seems to be that these preparations decrease menstrual flow and thus impair fecundity. Women claimed they needed to "take tonics [ferrous syrups] to return to normal menses."

Use of No Method

One of the goals of the focus groups was to determine why some women chose not to use any method of contraception. In addition to the constraints imposed on women by their status in society and in the family and by their limited knowledge of effective methods, other factors directly related to the methods themselves could be involved.

Women gave a range of reasons for not using contraceptives. For example, in Iquitos, women under 30 who had heard about the family planning program or about contraceptive methods referred to "lack of time" and "lack of transportation," among other problems. According to the older women, their husbands disapproved of their using contraceptives. One mother thought that breastfeeding was an adequate method. Nevertheless, fear of health hazards was the most common reason mentioned for not using a modern method. The never-users gave examples similar to the ones mentioned by the modern-method users.

The never-users expressed mixed feelings when they were asked whether they or their husbands would ever use a method of contraception. In some groups (particularly in Iquitos), women reacted positively. Nevertheless, it seemed to be too soon for them to decide. Those under 30 were more likely to think that their husbands would approve, although there was still much uncertainty among them as a group. There was not one spontaneous mention of a specific method likely to be used. In Cusco, some said they would choose to "take care naturally." Their descriptions about the way they would use this method suffered from the same errors as those of the actual users. They expressed a lack of confidence in this method because of changes in menstrual patterns.

Overall, compared with women in the other groups, the never-users were highly distinctive. They seemed to be uninvolved in most local activities and groups, such as mothers' clubs. The majority were not aware of the existence of a family planning program in the state hospital, although it was close to them. Likewise, they used very few hospital services, had not received any information on family planning from any source and knew even less than the traditional-method users about modern methods. The great majority had either no knowledge or incorrect information: "We don't know, don't understand"; "We have heard many things [about the methods]"; "How are we going to take the pills or have the injections, before or after the periods?" They admitted fearing modern contraceptive methods and said that their fear prevented them from using such methods.

It is interesting that although nonusers were able to name some modern methods of contraception (i.e., they could have been categorized as "knowing" a method in a survey using a closed-ended questionnaire), they knew almost nothing about these methods and were very afraid to try them. Likewise, their knowledge of other health matters—such as the treatment of diarrhea and the care of newborn babies, which had been the subject of recent information, education and communication campaigns—was meager.

Abortion was included in the discussion guide in an attempt to assess its place in women's attitudes toward fertility control. In general, the focus-group participants did not approve of induced abortions (or "extractions," as they were euphemistically known) because of danger to the mother's health and moral or religious constraints. (The latter were not mentioned by any users of modern methods.) Nevertheless, throughout all age-groups, the participants justified abortion on grounds of "desperation" if a woman "had too many children." Furthermore, they felt that it was more acceptable if carried out early, because it was still "pure blood." The participants said abortion was common, especially among adolescents, but also among multiparous women. The methods they mentioned included repetitive intramuscular injections of hormonal preparations, insertion of rubber probes, use of pumps, deliberate falls and injection of liquids into the uterus. Herbs are also commonly used to induce abortions in Iquitos. Private doctors perform most abortions, according to the women, but they charge very high fees (as high as one-third of a lower-middle-class monthly salary). Abortions are also performed by practitioners who are not doctors, at lower cost but at greater risk to the woman's health. The survey participants supported legalization of abortion in exceptional cases only, demonstrating that it remains a sensitive issue. In general they preferred to support family planning rather than encourage abortion.

Discussion

This qualitative study of women in two cities in inner Peru revealed a social context largely unfavorable to the use of explicit methods of contraception. Descriptions of the husband-wife relationship seem to confirm Peruvian women's low status in society, with childbearing and childrearing acting as effective instruments of men's domination. An almost total ignorance of the physiology of reproduction and the lack of a concept of planning in everyday life further complicate women's efforts to control their fertility. Women's experience in reproduction resembles a "flood tide of fertility" in which birthspacing is still an alien concept. Users of modern contraceptives do not necessarily possess greater knowledge than nonusers or users of traditional methods about modern methods, but despite various fears of side effects (the main barrier to use mentioned by traditional-method users and never-users) they are deeply committed to their use.

In the context of Peru's social structure, women have recourse to traditional methods, which are used and promoted by friends and relatives and can be obtained very easily at little or no cost. Their use follows the usual pattern of life, such as the habitual drinking of herb infusions or the free use of antibiotic capsules to treat any ailment, and they are perceived as free from side effects. It can be argued that the use of traditional methods is an effective way of tackling a problem not resolved by the current system of modern contraceptive service delivery, in which corruption, disorganization, lack of privacy and lack of promotion predominate. Users of traditional methods resemble the street vendors of the Peruvian economy; in the same way that these informal merchants avoid the hassle of a disorganized and corrupt system of accounting and taxation, "informal contraceptors" avoid long lines, fears of cancer and male disapproval. Informal contraceptors probably do not achieve substantial fertility reduction, but they satisfy their immediate intentions while avoiding an insufficient and stereotyped family planning program that does not take cultural variation into account. In the end, health officers show pride in the large proportion of traditional-method users in the statistics of all current users.

The richness of descriptions found here reflects only a few of Peru's cultures and ethnic groups. If we believe that the traditional-method users and the never-users are potential users of modern contraceptives, we must improve our understanding of their way of life so that we can design programs that are more acceptable to these women. Informational and educational materials, for example, could use the "hot/cold" or "sourness" notions as a basis for approaching audiences, gradually translating these ideas into the physiological mechanisms of modern contraception. Likewise, by devising ways of convincing women that the unsafe days are those in the middle of the cycle, rather than those during and around menstruation, the effectiveness of the rhythm method could be improved. Local expressions gathered through group discussions could be used in the delivery of messages about methods and their effects, including the negative ones; more acceptance and better understanding could be gained in such a way. In any case, a better understanding of the potential client's perspective would promote the creation of more appropriate family planning programs.

Notes

Alfredo L. Fort was the officer in charge of the Peruvian Ministry of Health's maternal and child health/ family planning program in the Amazon region of Peru from 1983 to 1985. He is currently a research student in the Department of Epidemiology and Population Sciences at the London School of Hygiene and Tropical Medicine, University of London, England. This article is based on a study funded by the World Health Organization's Special Programme on Research, Development and Research Training in Human Reproduction. The author is indebted to John Simons for his valuable assistance during the development of the article.

1 Modern methods are defined as oral contraceptives, the IUD, sterilization, injectables, vaginal methods (such as the diaphragm and spermicides) and the condom.

2 Previous experience had shown that women in these areas of Peru were very enthusiastic about attending meetings at which they might learn something useful. Their eagerness to attend a *charla* (talk) and receive something from it seemed to offset any reservations they may have had.

References

1. L.A. Sobrevilla and N. P. Mostajo, "Los Métodos Naturales en los Programas de Planificación Familiar del Perú," *Cuadernos CNP,* No. 13, Consejo Nacional de Población, Lima, 1985; and L. A. Sobrevilla, E. Alcantara and E. Gartner, *Nacer y Morir en la Pobreza: Salud y Planificación Familiar en los Pueblos Jóvenes de Lima,* Universidad Peruana Cayetano Heredia, Instituto de Estudios de Población, Betaprint S. R. L. Ediciones, Lima, 1987.

2. R.J. Lapham and W. P. Mauldin, "Family Planning Program Effort and Birthrate Decline in Developing Countries," *International Family Planning Perspectives,* **10:**109, 1984.

3. J. L. Herrera Miranda et al., *Evaluación de los Servicios de Salud Materno Infantil y Planificación Familiar en Cinco Regiones de Salud,* Consejo Nacional de Población, Ministerio de Salud, Lima, 1985.

4. "Cinco Preguntas a Dr. Carlos Zuzunaga Florez: Lo Poblacional desde una Perspectiva Humanista," interview in *Lugar de Encuentro,* (bulletin of Apoyo al Sector Privado en Planificación Familiar), Año 2, No. 1, Lima, 1988.

5. "Mensajes y Acción," editorial in *AMIDEP* (bulletin of the Asociación Multidisciplinaria de Investigación y Docencia en Población), No. 53, Lima, 1987.

6. C. F. Westoff, "The Potential Demand for Family Planning: A New Measure of Unmet Need and Estimates for Five Latin American Countries," *International Family Planning Perspectives,* **14:**45, 1988.

7. J. Knodel, N. Havanon and A. Pramualratana, "Fertility Transition in Thailand: A Qualitative Analysis," *Population and Development Review,* **2:**297, 1984.

8. E. Folch-Lyon, L. de la Macorra and S. B. Schearer, "Focus Group and Survey Research on Family Planning in Mexico," *Studies in Family Planning,* **12:**409, 1981 (special issue); and H. Suyono et al., "Family Planning in Urban Indonesia: Findings from Focus Group Research," *Studies in Family Planning,* **12:**409, 1981 (special issue).

9. J. Mayone Stycos, "Actitudes de los Estudiantes y Docentes Costarricenses Frente al Sexo y la Educación Demográfica," *Perspectivas Internacionales en Planificación Familiar,* Número Especial de 1987, p.1.

10. A. Shrestha, J. Stoeckel and J. Man Tuladhar, "Factors Related to Non-use of Contraception Among Couples with an Unmet Need for Family Planning in Nepal," study conducted by New Era, Demographic and Health Surveys and Institute for Research Development/Westinghouse, 1988.

11. Instituto Nacional de Estadística, *Encuesta Demográfica y de Salud Familiar (ENDES 1986), Informe General,* Consejo Nacional de Población, Lima, 1988.

12. A. Fort, "Encuesta sobre Planificación Familiar en la Zona Rural de Loreto," *Cuadernos CNP,* No. 12, Consejo Nacional de Población, Lima, 1985; ——, "Conocimientos y Necesidades de Planificación Familiar en Iquitos," study conducted for the Pan American Health Organization, Lima, 1986; and ——, "Evaluación Preliminar de los Servicios de Planificación Familiar en la Ciudad del Cusco," unpublished document, 1987.

Section VIII

PREGNANCY AND CHILDBIRTH

Nature's preference is for sexual intercourse to result in the fertilization of the egg. Not only has the menstrual cycle prepared the female body for this event, it also satisfies the requirement of perpetuating the species. And so conception is reflected in hormonal and physical changes all aimed at creating a hospitable environment for the developing fetus. A rapid increase in progesterone will be maintained throughout the pregnancy, matched by estrogen production. Placental lactogen will stimulate breast development. Calcium and mineral deficiences will accompany fetal skeletal growth and must be supplemented in the mother's diet. Following childbirth prolactin will stimulate milk production and oxytocin will stimulate its ejection during breast feeding.

Our American society is now emerging from over a century during which birthing had been medicalized, delivery hospitalized, mothers drugged for delivery, and perfectly healthy neonates placed on electronic fetal monitors often resulting in negative longterm effects. Major insurance companies rewarded doctors who performed deliveries by Caesarean section because it reduced the chances of being sued for malpractice and shortened the mother's stay in hospital. A number of years ago Hialeah Hospital (in Florida) was No.1 in the country with 53.1 percent of births delivered by Caesarean. Finally the trend is not to enter the hospital but to attend the birthing clinic or even the "new" trend of having a home delivery. It is interesting to read how our American childbirth practices compare with others crossculturally (see Jordan 1993).

The wonder and uncertainty of reproduction has always clouded events surrounding childbirth with fear, reverence and ritual. The result has been that in different ways pregnant women, unborn children, and neonates have been the subject of protective rituals, supernatural taboos and restrictions, and practical safeguards. Many of these actions or avoidances have beneficial implications, others are based on folk beliefs regarding magical relations, association, and causation.

Such associational beliefs may result in taboos regarding foods or behavior. Thus Allan Holmberg (1969:173) comments on the pregnant woman among the Bolivian Siriono Indians.

> She may not eat coati lest the infant be born with sores and a very long head. The guan, the howler monkey, the macaw and the toucan are taboo on the grounds that if they are eaten the infant will cry a great deal when it is born. Likewise forbidden is the meat of the armadillo. A violation of this taboo will cause the infant to have great fear, like the armadillo, which crosses its arms in its hole when it is caught. Other forbidden foods include the night monkey, whose meat cannot be eaten lest the infant inherit its tendency not to sleep at night; the anteater, porcupine, and honey bear, lest the infant be born clubfooted; the jaguar, lest the infant be stillborn; turtle eggs, lest the mother have a miscarriage or be unable to deliver the infant and die; and the harpy eagle, because it is taboo for all except the aged.

Some of these taboos sound strange but they are meaningful to people in that culture. Look at the beliefs of the Thonga who live in Mozambique. Henri Junod (1927:191) explains:

> However, in view of the impending birth, some special taboos have been added to those which apply to all women.
>
> A pregnant woman must not drink water when standing up. She must kneel down, otherwise the water would fall violently on the head of the child and hurt it!
>
> It is taboo for her to wrap her body in too much clothing. She must keep her belly bare and never throw her dress (kapulane) over her shoulders, lest the baby come to the light with its head covered with membranes, a complication which is very much dreaded by Thonga women.
>
> She must not take the sauce of her porridge too hot. The child might be scalded inside and have black spots when born.
>
> It is also taboo to prepare the ntehe before the birth, as no one knows what will happen. The child might die!
>
> The future mother must not eat pigeon's meat, because pigeons have no blood in the muscles of the breast. She would have no milk herself wherewith to nurse the baby. Nor must she even look at a monkey, lest she "take to herself" (tekela) the form of the animal and the child be like it

In technologically advanced and better educated communities we smile about these taboos, and have developed our own pregnancy taboos. These are of course more scientific: Avoid X-rays, be wary of contracting German measles, avoid alcohol, smoking, and aspirin, and do not drink too much coffee.

As people become better educated some of the traditional folk-taboos may be forgotten, or earlier superstitions may adapted to empirical knowledge. Others, however, continue in folk cultures the world over. Such folk traditions still exist in the United States in ethnic communities and among rural or mountain folk. In the first paper which follows Alice Murphree, an anthropologist attached to a rural health program in a north Florida county, relates some of her research findings. The second paper represents the joint effort of professors of pediatrics and anthropology who employ two complementary approaches to the study of birth. They combine the classic anthropological method of participant observation with the survey of literature dealing with the subject. The authors conclude with a discussion of childbirth in the United States.

We should keep in mind throughout that childbirth, like any other aspect of group living, is a part of culture and therefore subject to mutually influencing beliefs and practices. Thus we cannot have a "natural" childbirth if we mean by this purely the biological and physical part of parturition. Every delivery is unavoidably part and product of a complex set of beliefs, taboos, values, behaviors, technology, and context positioned in a particular cultural matrix.

References

Holmberg, Allan R. 1969. *Nomads of the Long Bow*. Garden City, N.Y.: The Natural History Press.

Jordan, Brigitte. 1993. *Birth in Four Cultures*. Revised and expanded by Robbie Davis-Floyd. Prospect Heights, Ill.: Waveland Press.

Junod, Henri A. 1927. *The Life of a South African Tribe*. Vol. I. London: Macmillan and Co.

A FUNCTIONAL ANALYSIS OF SOUTHERN FOLK BELIEFS CONCERNING BIRTH

Alice H. Murphree
Gainesville, Florida

Childbirth is universally recognized as one crisis period in the life cycle, for all peoples acknowledge the mystery of life and the presence of a new individual in the society and most, if not all, peoples feel this crisis period to be dangerous either for the mother or child or through them for the group.[Refs. 1,2] Although some cultures stress conception or gestation and others emphasize delivery or the postpartum period as the dangerous time, the various phases of the birth process are accorded a relatively high degree of interest and emphasis in folk tradition.

Health beliefs and practices in our culture demonstrate many overlappings between folk and scientific medicine,[3] and the same is true for our southern subculture, although the use of folk medicine and scientific medical sophistication are somewhat inversely related, i.e., the greater the degree of scientific sophistication, the less dependence there is on the practice of folk medicine. Thus, in the South, while not as widely acknowledged perhaps as in other cultures, folk beliefs persist in the rural tradition either contemporaneously with or as substitutes for scientific medicine. Rural residents are aware that scientific medicine denies clinical credence to "old timey" remedies, and are consequently somewhat reluctant to admit knowledge, much less practice, of such beliefs; however, birth lore is among the acceptable, and often dominant, discussion topics for married females, both white and Negro.

Birth practices and beliefs are valid indices not only of attitudes toward birth, but often toward health and life itself. When we consider the emerging patterns of such beliefs and practices in the context of rites of passage, it is pertinent to refer to van Gennep.[1] He contends that birth rites are more than just rites of passage: "... these ceremonies have their individual purposes ... birth ceremonies include protection and divination rites...."[1] He further stresses that illness and birth, and other such rites are periods of movement, of separation from and re-entry into the group. There is little question that the rural southern woman experiences this sense of movement and the very real changes n her self-image and sex roles, nor is there doubt that birth beliefs and practices could be the basis for intensive analysis of the structural dynamics and function of rural social organization. However, such an endeavor would be far beyond the scope of this limited paper; instead, because the concept appears both apt and valid, the primary framework here will stem from a concern for the expressive and instrumental aspects of these beliefs and practices.[4]

Reprinted by permission of the editors from *American Journal of Obstetrics and Gynecology,* Vol. 102, 1968, pp. 125-134.

Much folk medicine qualifies as, or at least suggests, the classic homeopathic magic of Frazer's "law of similarity" or the contagious magic of his "law of contact."[5] In one of the more contemporary analyses of magic, we find the following concerning its definition and function:

> All men strive to control their social and physical environments and to determine, or at least to have prior knowledge of, their own lives. Through manipulation, explanation and prediction, the operations of magic, witchcraft, and divination work toward this vital human end.[6]

Further, the following differentiation is made religion and magic:

> Religion is supplicative: by ritual it conciliates personal powers in order to request their favors. Magic is manipulative; it acts ritually upon impersonal powers in order automatically to make use of them. Magic is a formula or set of formulas....[6]

Frazer's laws obviously apply, but Lessa and Vogt's functional and Beattie's symbolic or expressive frames of reference will place these particular beliefs and practices more accurately in the life ways of this subculture. The endeavor represented in this paper perhaps will also serve to add to our understanding of folk beliefs, in general. Such other health attitudes as the mechanistic interpretation of physiology will also be discussed This mechanistic interpretation apparently stems from a perception of physiology in a direct cause-and-effect relationship—analogous to the presentation of physiology in television advertising for patent medicines. For instance, the nervous system is thought to be like an electrical system and the condition of the "coating on the nerves" determines the presence or absence, and degree, of "nervousness" for any given individual. The following section outlines the cultural situation The birth lore reported here will be grouped into four sequential divisions of conception, gestation and abortion, delivery, and post partum.

The situation

The folk beliefs and practices presented in this paper were collected in one of the smaller rural counties in North Florida. "Waters" County (a pseudonym to protect the privacy of the residents) is one of the 25 counties which, early in this century, were the center of the state's economic, political, and social growth. These counties have experienced lack of economic growth (if not recession), emigration of population, a diminishing political influence, and the concomitant social and cultural results of such phenomena, all of which contrasts sharply with other areas of the state which are experiencing a rapidly expanding technologic and agricultural economy, plus tremendous population growth stemming from both immigration and a rising birth rate.[7]

In relation to most other rural peoples, particularly in the South, the residents of this county are not unique in their problems or solutions, and their attitudes and practices are representative of other comparable rural groups. Although, appropriately, it may be thought of as part of the southern perimeter of Appalachia, "Waters" County differs in two significant ways from some other areas of the

South: (1) because it was never within the southern plantation institution, and as a result of the depressed economy and the emigration of population, the current ratio of whites to Negroes is approximately ten to one and (2) due in part to its agricultural marginality, this area was among those most recently settled and retains a frontierlike essence; many of the older residents are children of the original homesteaders. Despite these variations, the material to be discussed falls well within the cultural patterns of similar rural southern areas and southern subculture generally.

"Waters" County has neither doctor nor hospital, and the nearest orthodox medical care, other than Public Health Services, is approximately 20 to 35 miles away. One study[8] showed a lack of orthodox preventive medical practices, and that when illness occurred, a common tendency was to try various alternative methods of treatment prior to seeking professional medical attention, and sometimes in its stead.[Note] Such self-treatment practices range along a continuum including "TV" medicine (my term for self-diagnosis and treatment based on television commercials), "what the druggist fixes up," patent medicines, and folk medicine.

Rural residents know that the value of folk medicine is minimized, if not discredited, by orthodox medicine; and when both subjects are included in the same context, respondents may be sufficiently uncomfortable to deny much of their folk medicine or folk belief knowledge. In a study of self-treatment practices, 11 per cent of the sample admitted current, but infrequent, use of folk medicine practices, but 70 per cent acknowledged its use in the past and 27 per cent were able to supply at least one detailed folk prescription.[9] These figures have greater significance when we consider the age of a residual population resulting from emigration. Also, because such an aged population generally would be past the childbearing years, birth lore was probably much more frequently discussed in the past than it is now. However, field experiences have shown that interviews focusing solely on folk medicine and couched in non-threatening terms are highly productive of specific esoteric information. Key informants in the area of folk medicine and birth beliefs, including one "retired" and two practicing midwives, were readily identified and contacted. None of these individuals was reluctant to discuss "old timey remedies," rather, problems most often arose in terminating interviews.

Conception

Some of the folk beliefs reported here reflect the wide concern of rural southern people of both sexes with libido. Such common statements by females as, "I lost my zip by stirring around too soon after the baby came" or "I ain't the same since I had everything took out," refering to hysterectomy, have their counterpart in the recommendation to males that Sting Nettle (*Cnidosculus stimulosus*) root tea will give him "courage."[10] The two female statements explain a loss of sexual drive or less specifically act to validate their "puniness" (weakness)—an attribute of the ideal female role—and combine with the mechanistic interpretation of physiology; but the male remedy is difficult to assess. It is widely known that physical contact with that particular plant produces severe and unpleasant tactile stimulation; however, the informants' usual explanation about this and other folk remedies refers only to its efficacy for many generations, which is clearly an empirical rationale. This or any of the other plant remedies present problems in analysis, in that without knowledge of the actual pharmaceutical properties, we tend to judge that use is based on magical manipulation. On the other hand, some plant remedies do have counterparts in orthodox medicine; for instance, tea from cherry tree bark prescribed for coughs has much in common with many commercial cough syrup prescriptions, the bases of which are cherry extract.

Another of the concerns focused on the sex act, or the consequences of it, is the possibility of contracting "bad blood" (venereal disease). Two folk remedies to "clear the blood" are teas, one combining Queen's Delight (*Stillingia sylvatica*) and Prickly Ash (*Zanthoxylum clava-herculis*) plants and the other combining Queen's Delight and Virginia Snake Plant (*Aristolochia serpentaria*).[10] Both remedies are among the few in this collection for which precise recipe and dosage instructions (shown below) were supplied, suggesting that "bad blood" is considered a most serious illness (at least by the male informant who supplied them).

> For a "small batch" the number of roots that can be encircled by the thumb and forefinger are gathered, washed, and pared. The roots are placed in a cooking vessel, covered with water, brought to a boil, and allowed to diminish in volume until the proper consistency is achieved: the "color of coffee" is one criterion. The teas are strained and sweetened with either sugar or cane syrup and taken one tablespoonful three times a day. With the Prickly Ash tea, it is suggested that a "little drop of tar" from a pine tree be taken "about once a week" during treatment in order to "keep the kidneys clear."

Related birth beliefs and practices express a complex interrelationship of three factors. First is the belief that the sex of the child can be determined at conception and second is simply that male offspring are highly desirable, at least among whites. Factors one and two are expressed in the belief that if, during intercourse, the man carries a leather string in his pocket, "It will bring a boy."

The third factor presumes a strong homeopathic bond between the sex of the infant and the direction right or left of the perpendicular midline of the mother's body: to the left for girls and to the right for boys. One informant succinctly stated all three factors in avowing that the side to which the female turns following intercourse will determine the sex of the infant. Whichever magical function this belief performs, and in certain circumstances it may be any of the three, more pertinent, perhaps, is consideration of Hertz' dichotomy of the sacred and the profane,[11] or desirability versus undesirability. The tenets of nineteenth century Protestantism, expressed in most areas of rural southern living, and strongly reflected in matters of health, expressed the superiority of males and the moral frailty of women. This well may be an explanation for the left side being female; it is really thought of as less desirable or even profane. Further, we "know" that the right side, based on handedness, is the stronger, and certainly in a rural subculture (as elsewhere) strength is a masculine attribute; conversely, the ideal female sex role includes passivity, weakness, emotionality, and, implicitly or symbolically, leftsidedness.

Gestation and abortion

With reference now, to the gestation period, in the event that the above ritual practices were either unknown or neglected during conception, the "right or left" formula may still be applied to ascertain the sex of the infant. One such divinatory folk belief states that the predominant direction of fetal movement indicates the sex of the infant, and another involves observing with which foot the pregnant female crosses a threshold or begins to climb stairs.

During the gestation period, also, a phenomenon is said to occur equal in interest to the curiosity surrounding the sex of the infant. This phenomenon, believed to be extremely common, results in "marking the baby," and is clearly a magical explanation. Always caused by some action or emotion of the mother, this belief seems an expression of the widespread rural conviction that "the sins of the parents are visited on the children." A birthmark on the infant is attributed to the mother's "craving" a particular food, being frightened or surprised by some animal or incident, or behaving in some unusual fashion. Some "marks" result from the mothers "craving" and eating a particular food and others are believed to result when the mother resists or is unable to satisfy the craving; incidentally, the husband is occasionally, but not always, involved in satisfying the craving, in which case he is considered to be indulging her. For instance, one woman reported being unable to refrain from eating some of a particular tempting crop on her "grape harbor" (a widespread folk phrase for grape arbor), and the baby was born with a "purplish mark like a bunch of grapes" on his side that "he carried 'til he died." This may imply that she was weak and could not resist the temptation and that the "mark" was punishment for and disclosure of her frailty. Another woman said she "marked her baby" because she saw a neighbor's freshly killed pork and "wanted fresh hog meat so bad I could taste it" (gluttony?) but was too polite to ask for it. Using van Gennep's classification of rites,[1] both instances would be dynamistic, contagious, and direct, with the first positive and the second negative. Relative to a mother's behavior, a negative example would be the saying, "Climb a ladder and the baby will be born with a bald spot." Ladder climbing would be considered unseemly and masculine for a woman—and baldness is a masculine trait. Sometimes this same belief holds that an older child's disposition, dietary preference, or allergies are caused by prenatal "marking," i.e., "Ellie Mae (an eleven-year-old daughter) is scared of being around folks 'cause I got to be that way whilst I was carrying her," or "Watermelon has always made him sick on his stomach because I ate too much of it when I was pregnant."

Also pertinent to the gestation period are the practices and remedies used to terminate unwanted pregnancy, referred to by one informant as "teen-age trouble." The generally accepted abortifacients, such as jumping off a wagon, shed, or porch, and the less common one of stepping over a rail fence, seem more to reflect the mechanistic interpretation of biologic function than to express manipulation but may also be expressions of something akin to "unseemly actions produce unnatural results." Using "a tablespoon of black gunpowder (ingested in a glass of water) to make a woman abort" suggests homeopathic manipulation with reliance on the explosive or expellent property of the gunpowder. Another reported practice is to "carry three whole nutmegs in your pocket and eat a little piece every day until the nutmeg is gone." This particular remedy, analogous to plant remedies, is probably well fixed in folk tradition. Nutmeg is one of the oldest known spices and has a long history in herbal phar-maceuticals in the New World. Kreig[12] has this to say: "The widespread, dangerous, and false belief that nutmeg possesses abortifacient properties has caused serious poisoning and fatty degeneration of the liver in its victims."

A miscarriage, whether spontaneous or induced, may result in suffering for the mother from a condi-tion known as "poisoned blood" (septicemia from incomplete delivery of fetal tissues). A traditional southern rural folk remedy to clear this "blood poison" is a heated poultice made from Red Oak (*Quercus falcata*) bark tea and corn meal which is placed on the abdomen.

Birth

An interesting folk belief concerning the delivery phase of the birth process is that "the baby comes at the same time it is got." In other words, folklore makes a positive correlation between the hour of con-ception, actually coitus, and the hour of birth. This seems to function as a rather fatalistic magical ex-planation for extended periods of labor, i.e., if delivery does not occur at the time of "getting" in one 24 hour period, it will not (or cannot) occur for another 24 hour period. However, the symbolism is unclear.

A well-known popular notion, sometimes applied in the comparison of rural and urban cultures, holds that "primitive" women bear their young with more facility than women of complex societies. In this rural folk collection, ten of the twelve items relating to delivery refer either to the difficulty or to the danger of childbirth, indicating a great concern about this phase of the life cycle and suggesting that the notion indicated above may be erroneous. Three kinds of tea were recommended as "good to keep the labor coming" or to hasten delivery. The first, made from the Low Bush Myrtle (*Myrica cerefera*) plant,[10] is as traditional as other plant remedies and, again the magical implications are ob-scure. The second tea, made from black pepper *may* be considered efficacious because the sneezing paroxysm's expulsive qualities suggest the results desired to expel the fetus or because black pepper is believed to stimulate circulation and to "get the muscles to working." Either rationale demonstrates the mechanistic interpretation of physiology and strongly suggests magical homeopathic manipula-tion. The third tea, made of dirt dauber's nests, although highly recommended by a midwife, was unex-plained. A personal familiarity with these tubular mud nests, affixed by the insect to eaves and walls of buildings, suggests only the homeopathic relationship between the emergence of the insect from the nest ("sliding" down and out the tube) and movement "downward" of the human infant during deliv-ery. Coca-Cola was reported as useful during labor in two complementary ways: "Drinking a Coke will bring on the baby, if it is time, or ease off the pain if the time's not right." No magic seems involved in the Coke remedy; however, Coca-Cola may well be considered to possess medicinal properties. Cokes are "known" to contain "dope" and sometimes this soft drink is actually called "a dope" rather than "a Coke." This is probably a cultural remnant from the nineteenth century; witness an advertisement of the 1880's, "Coca-Cola, The Ideal Brain Tonic, Delightful Beverage, Specific for Headache, Relieves Exhaustion." A distinct manipulative application of the law of similarity is evident in the practice of utilizing a sharp instrument to "cut the labor pains." A knife, razor, scissors, or ax is placed on or under the bed, preferably without the patient's knowledge and allowed to remain until delivery is completed. This practice is also reported from Kentucky,[13] and one of the Floridian informants maintained that "It works just as good in the hospital as at home." While there are fewer home deliveries than even 15 years ago, this seems an excellent example of the tenacity of folk belief and the ease with which it transports to the orthodox medical situation.

Albeit, as far as was reported, there is nothing as exotic as the true couvade in rural southern culture; there are indications that at least the symbolic presence of the male is deliberately incorporated into the birth process. It is unknown whether this is an inclusion of males into a stress situation by the females, or an intrusion into the all important life-producing female domain by the males. Fathers have been known to suffer "morning sickness" and labor pains and it has been suggested that this may be a "sympathy" phenomenon, i.e., when one of two individuals in a close social relationship suffers, the other mirrors some of the same symptoms. Thus the father could be manifesting his interest in, and bond with, his wife and family, but he might also manifest shame of such weak, "womanly" behavior. Manipulative homeopathic or contagious magic is strongly indicated in folk beliefs concerning males and delivery. Either the physical presence of the father or some article of his clothing is often utilized to precipitate birth. One rural southern informant said, "If the father comes into the room and puts his hand on her stomach, it helps the pain." An excellent example of magic is the belief that "when the old man's black hat is the put over the birth place, it brings the baby quick"; and sometimes, during difficult labor, the father's hat is worn by the mother or his shirt is placed across her abdomen. The overt magical transmission of male strength to the female in labor, plus the notion of his symbolic presence, may be widely recognized in folklore, for although specific or cross-cultural references were not sought, similar practices are known to occur within the Brahman caste in India.

Still another belief bearing on the father's relationship, in this instance directly to the child, concerns the child "who never knew its father." This particular belief states that the infant born after its father's death is endowed with the power to see into the future and/or perform "conjures." No explanation was given for this, but it is, perhaps, implied that the father's spirit bestows the power on the child. Perhaps, because power is related to uniqueness, this expresses the extreme "unnaturalness" of a child not only outliving the father, but of the father dying even before the child's birth. Or perhaps such a peculiar child needs special powers to help protect him in his father's absence.

Should excessive bleeding occur during or after delivery, it is very likely that one of several commonly known verbal formulas for "stopping blood" would be used. One widely known practice[14-17] involves the repeating of Ezekiel 16:6:

> And when I passed by thee, and saw thee polluted in thine own blood, I said unto thee when thou wast in thy blood, Live: yea, I said unto thee when thou wast in thy blood, Live.

This should be performed by someone who "has their mind on the Lord." In addition, there is at least one other less commonly known verbal formula:

Stand blood, don't spread, over our land, God the Father, God the Sun (sic), and the Holy Ghost ask it in the name of our Lord Savior, Jesus Christ. Amen.

This is conceded to be a "conjure" and must be performed by one who has "the power." Both formulas incorporate obvious passages from the sacred religious writings of the people who use them; one, the more esoteric, uses the most sacred phrase in Christianity. Referring to the previously quoted passage from Lessa and Vogt[6]; a personal power is being supplicated and a favor is requested, all of which indicates that religious feelings, prominent in the sphere of health in the rural South, and religion itself merges into the area of magical belief, particularly in periods of stress.

Another folk practice pertaining to delivery also has a strongly manipulative magical component with a protective element. In the event of a stillbirth, this belief states that subsequent stillbirths for that particular woman can be prevented by placing the infant corpse face down in the coffin before burial. The rationale, if known, could not be supplied by the informant, but one might conjecture that mobility of the dead infant's spirit is involved as is the suggestion that unnatural events involving death require inverse procedures.

Post partum

After a successful delivery, the umbilical cord may be used to prognosticate the number of future deliveries the mother can expect. A midwife reported, validating her belief by quoting an old country doctor, that "the number of knots or bumps on the cord (counted before cutting) will tell how many babies there will be." Because both physicians and midwives are intimately familiar with the convolutional characteristic of umbilical cords, for them at least, this belief patently presupposes that all women who have had one child will have more. This overlap between folk and orthodox medicine may well express another cultural remnant, i.e., large families had high economic value in rural areas.

The delivery phase of the birth process can be considered terminated with the disposal of the placenta, membranes, and cord. All reported disposal methods are excellent examples of protective contagious magic with the implication that either mother or child may be harmed through the afterbirth. One midwife said she always burned the afterbirth, either in the fireplace or in the yard, making sure nothing remained. Because "salt keeps down infection," one midwife routinely "salted the placenta and buried it very deep or buried it in the salty dirt floor of the smoke house." Both the burning and the burying methods were also cited as protection from molestation by animals, but the belief in magical bonds is clear.

In addition to noting that the postpartum period is the first opportunity for ascertaining whether the infant has been "marked" and for validating prophecies as to sex, we find that the three major concerns are excessive bleeding, "afterbirth pain," and "risin's" or abscess of the breast. Excessive bleeding would be treated by the same means as during delivery while observing such precautions as that cited by a midwife against the use of aspirin for afterbirth pain, because "aspirin thins the blood and causes more flow." Here, again, is an expression of the mechanistic conceptualization of physiology.

As for afterbirth pains, although it is believed that "you have a day and a night of afterbirth pains for every child you already got," it is also believed that these pains can be shortened or completely eliminated. One method, seemingly more empirical than magical, involved administering a "good big drink of whisky" or even a sufficient quantity to "get her drunk" as the best treatment for postpartum discomfort and fatigue. Other, perhaps more singular folk treatments, include utilization of a sharp instrument, believed as effective for afterbirth pains as for "cutting" labor pains. Also, several informants affirmed that "the old man's britches" hung on the bed post or placed across the foot of the bed would remove the possibility of afterbirth pains for the traditional 9 day confinement. Both measures are apparently the same type of reasoning as their counterparts discussed in the section on delivery: again we have the manipulative, sympathetic magic of the sharp instruments and the magical article of the husband's clothing, symbolizing his presence.

The widespread concern with breast "risin's" is reflected in one informant's statement that "I just bore that pain and birthed them and then my breasts riz," implying that women's lot may be excessively painful. Many of the same remedies may be used here as for boils or "risin's" under other conditions, although these presented refer specifically to abscesses of the breast. A poultice made from axle grease was reported as good. to cure a particular "risin" and to prevent future occurrences. Another is to drink a cup of fresh milk in which the "shot from a buckshot" have been allowed to stand for one hour. Both were highly recommended, but somewhat obscure, although the milk in the second seems significant. A tentative explanation is that this is imitative: milk from which lumps, i.e., buckshot, have been removed is drunk to remove lumps from the breast.

A final and particularly potent cure or "conjure" involves gaining the "power to scatter (smooth away) risin's" by smothering a mole in one's hands. The significance of the mole is unclear unless we hypothesize that "risin's" are similar to mole burrows in that both are subsurface formations. It is noteworthy that in this belief, the power accrues to a man, particularly as it concerns abscesses of the breast, always associated with childbirth. The informant proudly reported that her husband had this "power" and that men "from all over the country" brought their wives to him to cure. Is this another incorporation of the male into the predominantly female sphere of activity?

Conclusion

Several folk beliefs and practices concerning birth have been presented and, where possible, their expressive functions within rural southern culture have been commented upon. Certainly, some of the basic values relative to male and female sex roles have emerged, as has the implication that these are based on stereotypic nineteenth century Protestant beliefs. There is the apparent deliberate incorporation of the male into what is usually thought to be an exclusively female sphere: pregnancy and birth, which may again express the feeling that anything so vital to the individual and the group as birth cannot, or should not, exclude men. Tied with this are the values of sacredness and profanity in the right-left dichotomy; and there is also the belief in the natural and the supernatural in an inverse relationship. Areas of overlap between folk and orthodox medicine have been illustrated with the suggested usefulness of the concept "folk-orthodox" for this phenomenon.

The folk remedies that are unexplained other than in terms of tradition may also be subsumed under Beattie's second reason for belief in magic: "...it may provide a way of coping with situations of misfortune or danger with which there are no other means of dealing."[4] It should be noted here that attitudes are mundane concerning remedies involving specific ingredients as compared to the awe for those involving "conjures" or someone "having the Power"—another expression of the natural-supernatural dichotomy.

The omission of identification of racial source for this folklore is purposeful, simply because, thus far, there seems to be little differentiation. Most of these, and other extant conjures, were supplied and practiced by whites and may or may not be specifically known by Negroes; some beliefs were reported by both races, and some by Negroes. This tends to support, and is a partial basis for, the contention (a personal one) that, at the lowest socioeconomic level, cultural differences between the races become narrower. Further research in this and many of the other areas suggested in this paper would add much to our knowledge of contemporary American culture. It should be noted also that folk beliefs exist for all stages and activities of life and, whether placebos or not, they express and are deeply rooted in cultural tradition.

Notes

a Regular family periodic examinations by physicians were reported for 7 per cent of the base families. In 14 per cent, only adults had regular checkups and 79 per cent of the families saw a physician only when there was a specific complaint. Most respondents felt the problem of cost of medical attention and the distance to acquire it were deterrents. The few who reported seeking prompt attention for illness seemed almost apologetic and said, "I'm funny about that" or "We're bad to run to the doctor." The term "bad to" connotes both frequency and deviation from the usual.

b This implies that rural men are either fully dressed (the pocket would be in the trousers) or partially dressed (it would be a shirt pocket) during intercourse, which is not unexpected, as nudity is considered sinful. It is not known at present whether this is done with intent, indicating magical manipulation, of if it is a post factum explanation, but the former seems more logical as the latter would be too great a test of memory. The informant offered no explanation concerning why this would "work."

c This was also reported via personal communication from a woman who formerly lived in Pennsylvania, indicating its widespread occurrence.

d Advertising on a clock, now in the possession of personal friends, and formerly in a store near Knoxville, Tennessee.

e It should be noted that customarily fathers have been permitted in hospital "labor rooms" and, in some more modern hospitals, are currently allowed to accompany the mother to the "delivery room."

f The source for this was a personal communication from a female member of the Brahman caste.

g This is an accurate transcription of the handwritten formula the female informant permitted me to copy. Customarily, such "conjures" cannot be transmitted to one of the same sex, nor to a family member; neither can they be discussed, lest they lose their potency or the "conjurer" lose his or her power.

h Certainly, such prevalent rural "faith healing" religious sects as the Church of God and the Assembly of God demonstrate the merging of religion and magic into magicoreligious belief systems.

i A "risin" is any painful boil, infected mass of tissue, or abscess visible on the surface of the body. In this case, it is mastitis, and it is apparently felt to be a fairly common complaint.

References

1. van Gennep, Arnold: The Rites of Passage, translated by Monika B. Vizedom and Gabrielle L. Caffee, Chicago, 1960, The University of Chicago Press.

2. Gluckman, Max, editor: Essays on the Ritual of Social Relations, New York, 1962, Humanities Press, Inc.

3. Saunders, Lyle, and Hewes, Gordon W.: J. M. Education 28:43, 1953.

4. Beattie, John: Other Cultures, New York, 1964, The Free Press of Glencoe.

5. Frazer, J. G.: The Golden Bough, abridged edition, New York, 1960, The Macmillan Company.

6. Lessa, William A., and Vogt, Evon Z.: Reader in Comparative Religion, White Plains, New York, 1958, Row, Peterson & Company.

7. United States Census of Population, 1960.

8. Murphree, Alice H.: The Health Resources and Practices of a Rural County (a mimeographed report), Gainesville, 1965, Behavioral Sciences Division, Department of Psychiatry, College of Medicine, University of Florida.

9. Murphree, Alice H.: Self-Treatment Practices in a Rural County (a mimeographed report), Gainesville, 1966, Behavioral Sciences Division, Department of Psychiatry, College of Medicine, University of Florida.

10. Murphree, Alice H.: Florida Anthropologist 18: 175, 1965.

11. Hertz, Robert: Death and the Right Hand, translated by R. Needham and C. Needham, New York, 1960, The Free Press of Glencoe.

12. Kreig, Margaret B.: Green Medicine, Chicago, 1964, Rand McNally & Company.

13. Thompson, Lawrence S.: Kentucky Folklore Rec. 3: 95, 1959.

14. Brewster, Paul G.: South. Folklore Quart. 3: 33, 1939.

15. Campbell, Marie: Folks Do Get Born, New York, 1946, Rinehart & Company.

16. Norris, Ruby R.: Kentucky Folklore Rec. 4-5: 101, 1958-59.

17. Randolph, Vance: The Ozarks, New York, 1931, The Vanguard Press.

Additional references

18. Currier, Richard L.: Ethnology 5: 251, 1966.

19. Durkheim, Emile: The Elementary Forms of the Religious Life, translated by Joseph Ward Swain, New York, 1954, The Free Press of Glencoe.

20. Foster, George M.: J. Am. Folklore 66: 201, 1953.

CHILDBIRTH IN CROSS-CULTURAL PERSPECTIVE

Betsy Lozoff, Brigitte Jordan, Stephen Malone

In the United States in recent years disenchantment with standard maternity care has been growing: on occasion, the appropriateness of the medical model for our entire conception of birth has been challenged. Yet there has been little information available concerning the range of alternatives to current obstetric practices and, because each culture tends to consider its way of managing childbirth superior to any other, little opportunity to generate and evaluate such alternatives. A cross-cultural comparison of childbirth systems can yield the information necessary for an understanding of the process of childbirth that is unavailable from within any particular system. Cross-cultural study of childbirth is also important for another, somewhat more complex reason. Traditional birthing systems are beginning to change under the influence of Western medicine. Ironically, however, since Western obstetric practices are themselves under pressure to accommodate to changing views of childbirth, some of the very practices currently exported to developing countries are being questioned at home. Furthermore, since only women give birth, studying the many ways in which childbirth is managed in different cultures can broaden our appreciation of female networks, interests and strategies. There has been a growing recognition that our views of social organization have consistently ignored the place of women in society, a deficiency that has resulted in distorted theory and impoverished ethnography (Rosaldo & Lamphere, 1974).

   The research we will be describing in this paper represents two complementary approaches to the cross-cultural study of birth. One (Jordan, 1983) consists of intensive study of childbirth in different cultures through immersion in the phenomenon, direct observation and, whenever possible, actual participation in births. This type of approach permits a detailed description of the ways in which childbirth is managed in widely differing cultures.

   Anthropological participation in childbirth, we believe, is a particularly useful approach in that it encourages the investigator to see the birth process from the point of view of the people she studies, thus helping her to avoid gratuitously imposing own-society, especially medical, categories for the collection of data about birth. Nevertheless, such approaches have been notably few. Our aim in these investigations has been to broaden the scope of description and analysis by characterizing childbirth practices in relatively general terms, such as how decisions are typically made in different cultures. The second approach (Lozoff, 1982, 1983) consists of analyzing the existing ethnographic record to examine specific hypotheses. Although such analyses depend on the quality and completeness of available reports and are, by nature, somewhat crude and global, they permit one to address specific issues for which anthropological arguments have been made. For instance, criticisms of many stan-

Reprinted by permission of the publishers from *Marriage and Family Review*, Vol. 12, 1988, pp. 35-60.

dard hospital practices in our culture often contain implicit assumptions about childbirth practices in nonindustrial cultures, such as that mother and infant are typically in skin-to-skin contact immediately after birth. We analyzed anthropological data from a large sample of nonindustrial cultures (Murdock & White, 1969) to determine to what extent such assumptions are supported by the available data. In this paper we will treat both approaches in turn, beginning with the more general participant-observational approach.

Cross-Cultural Comparisons of Birthing Items: Towards a Biosocial Analysis of Childbirth

Childbirth is an intimate and complex transaction whose topic is physiological and whose language is cultural. Neither element is available without the other. Childbirth practices are produced jointly by universal biology and particular society; the physiology of birth and its social-interactional context are mutually informing. We have proposed previously (Jordan, 1983) that a biosocial framework, which considers both the universal biological function of birth and the specific sociocultural matrix within which it is embedded, is needed in analyses of the process of parturition. Indeed, the natural childbirth movement in contemporary American obstetrics reflects a growing recognition of the intimate relationship between the physiological aspects of parturition and its social and organizational management.

In most societies birth and the immediate postpartum period are considered a time of vulnerability for mother and child; in fact, this is frequently considered a time of at least ritual danger to the entire family or community. To deal with this danger and with the existential uncertainty associated with childbirth, societies tend to produce a set of internally consistent practices and beliefs about the management of both physiological and social aspects of childbirth. Birth practices tend to be highly uniform and ritualized (and may even be invested with a sense of moral requiredness) *within* any given system. Whatever the nature of a particular birthing system may be, its practitioners will tend to see it as the best way, and perhaps the only way, to bring a child into the world. We implicitly acknowledge such recognizable and culturally specific configurations of practices and beliefs when we speak, for example, of "American obstetrics" or "Yucatecan ethno-obstetrics."

While the range of variation *within* a given culture is restricted, the range of variation *across* different cultures will depend on local history, social structure, ecology, technological development, and the like, and is therefore likely to be quite high. For instance, while in all known societies access to births is restricted to a more or less rigidly specified group of people (Ford, 1964), the identity of those allowed to attend varies across cultures (see below).

It is as yet not at all clear what the appropriate categories for cross-cultural comparison of childbirth systems should be. We would argue, however, that such a comparison will be most fruitful if it includes both the medical-physiological and social-ecological aspects of childbirth. Such a biosocial framework will provide a means of integrating the collection and analysis of data. Toward this end, we have studied four very different birthing systems through intensive fieldwork in the United States, the Netherlands, Sweden, and among the Maya Indians of Yucatan (Jordan, 1983).

The four cultures we studied present interesting contrasts. In the United States the great majority of births take place in hospitals and are attended by physicians. (Although childbirth practices in this country are changing, for the purpose of analysis we are concerned here only with those practices associated with standard hospital obstetrics.) Sweden and Holland are both industrial nations with socialized medical care and infant mortality rates that are among the lowest in the world: 7.2 infant deaths per 1,000 live births in Sweden in 1983 and 8.4 deaths per 1,000 live births in the Netherlands in 1983. In comparison, there were 11.5 infant deaths per 1,000 live births in the U.S. in 1983. (All mortality figures are from the *World Health Statistics Annual 1985*. Although the use of infant mortality rates is limited by variations in how live births are defined and other factors, such figures provide a convenient means of judging the relative safety of childbirth in different countries.) In both European countries all women receive systematic prenatal care, and abortions are available on demand. Births in Sweden occur in hospitals and are managed by highly trained midwives; in Holland about 40% of all births are home births, and delivery by a midwife is common both in the home and in the hospital. Yucatecan culture is technologically less sophisticated than that of the U.S. or the two European countries. Childbirth among Maya Indians is managed by the family, occurs in the home, and is accommodated into the routines of daily life. Women are aided by a traditional midwife, their husbands, and other family members and friends. Infant mortality figures are not available for Yucatan; in Mexico as a whole the mortality rate was 38.5 deaths per 1,000 live births in 1980. (For a detailed account of childbirth in Yucatan, see Jordan, 1983.)

Through extensive involvement in the birth process in these four cultures, we have identified features of these various birthing systems that might be appropriate for a more holistic analysis. The seven dimensions presented here—the local definition of the event; preparation for birth; attendants and support systems; the ecology of birth; the use of medication; the technology of birth; and the locus of decision-making—represent a preliminary step towards a more complete framework for cross-cultural comparison.

Definition of the Event

A society's definition of birth is fundamental; it allows those belonging to the culture to develop a set of internally consistent and mutually dependent birth practices. In the United States birth is predominantly viewed as a medical event and a pregnant woman is accordingly treated as a patient. As such she is expected to fulfill the role of "sick person" (Parsons, 1951): she is considered relatively helpless and exempt to some extent from her normal responsibilities for herself, and she is required to seek technically competent help from medical personnel for treatment of her "condition." In Sweden birth is considered an intensely fulfilling personal experience. The Dutch regard birth as a natural event. The Maya Indians similarly view birth as a difficult but normal part of family life.

The local conception of the birth event determines in large part how the problem of pain will be managed. Pain appears to be a recognized and expected part of birth in all societies. What differs among various cultures is the manner in which pain is treated—whether, for example, it is emphasized or discounted. In the United States, where pain relief is available only at the discretion of the medical attendant, attendants are constrained by medical considerations to withhold medication as long as possible. Consequently, laboring women who desire medication for pain must convince the attendants, whether through outward displays of pain or through other means, that their pain is sufficient to warrant medication. The system thus has a built-in bias for orienting both the woman and her attendants to pain. In Sweden women are informed about what kinds of medication are available, the conditions under which they are not advisable, and any known and possible side effects. Decisions about what medication to take, if anything, and when to take it are theirs. This is consistent with the Swedish treatment of birth as a personal experience. Because the Dutch view birth as a natural event, women neither expect nor receive any sort of medication for pain. It is believed that, given time, nature will take its course. Among Maya Indian women, some pain is also an expected part of birth; indeed, it is an expected part of life processes in general. Pain appears in the stories women tell about their birth experiences; such stories represent a way of indicating that distress in labor is normal and a sign of progress, and that it will eventually pass.

Preparation for Birth

All systems have both formal and informal means of disseminating information about childbirth to pregnant women, although little is known about informal educational processes. In Yucatan instruction occurs while labor is in progress. Maya Indians maintain that neither the woman nor her husband should know about the birth process before their first child is born. Nevertheless, since births take place within the family compound, only minimally separated from the rest of family life, the couple is not completely naive. The other three cultures rely heavily on prenatal care. In the United States prenatal care is variable: the proportion of women receiving prenatal care and education is highest among well-educated women in higher socioeconomic brackets and lowest among indigent women delivering in large urban hospitals. In the Netherlands and in Sweden prenatal care is free, comprehensive and universal. Routine prenatal care is the domain of midwives, and is designed in part to distinguish between normal pregnancies and those which will be potentially complicated. The Dutch and Swedish systems locate responsibility for the course of pregnancy and birth within each individual woman.

Attendants and Support Systems

The identity of birth attendants largely determines the nature of interactions between the woman giving birth and others present, and thereby influences to a significant degree the way in which she experiences the birth event. In particular, nonspecialist participants provide a source of emotional support, and their inclusion permits an interpretation of the event as a normal, albeit difficult, part of life.

For many women in the United States, only medical personnel are present during their labor and delivery. Medical attendants are typically viewed as the physician's assistants rather than as the mother's helpers, and transactions between the woman and attendants are accordingly viewed as medical transactions. Uncertainty, stress, pain, and physiological difficulties are handled by means of medical routines, such as medication, sedation, drugs to regulate contractions, and, often, instruments or surgery to deliver the baby. Yucatecan culture, by contrast, emphasizes patience and noninterference; the attitude of birth participants tends to be that the baby will be born when it is ready. Family and friends constitute a pool of nonspecialist attendants who provide emotional and physical support for the woman. In Sweden the birth team consists of the mother, a midwife and her assistant, and a nonspecialist attendant of the woman's choosing, such as her husband, friend, or relative. Swedish midwives are highly trained, in performing technical procedures. While obstetric technology is readily available, midwives also tend to respect a woman's wish for privacy: a woman can be alone with her nonspecialist attendant for much of her labor if she wishes. In the Netherlands the composition of the birth team is similar. Since no medication is used during labor and delivery, all discomfort is handled through breathing and relaxation techniques, with the birth team providing the necessary encouragement and support. In these countries, much more so than in the U.S., birth is a collaborative affair in which all present participate.

The Ecology of Birth

By virtue of the mere fact that it is located somewhere, birth unavoidably occurs on someone's territory. A woman may give birth in her normal environment, such as in her home or other familiar surroundings, or in a special-purpose facility, such as a hospital or clinic. Of the birthing systems we have studied, the Yucatecan is clearly the most unspecialized with regard to birth location. A Maya woman gives birth at home, where a blanket used as a screen provides a measure of privacy, but does not separate her from familiar household activities. Although hospital deliveries are becoming increasingly common in the Netherlands, Dutch women prefer to give birth at home and will do so unless complications are expected. In Sweden all babies are delivered in hospitals. The hospital ambience, however, offers some of the comforts of home: a woman in the early hours of labor, for example, can pass the time in an early labor lounge, where she can read, watch television, eat a snack, talk to her husband or friend, and otherwise do some of the things she might do at home. In contrast to the European orientation toward minimal disturbance even in a hospital or clinic environment, American obstetric wards have traditionally been designed with a view toward organizational efficiency and the availability of technological resources. In spite of some variations in the standard hospital delivery pattern, particularly in birthing rooms, women are often confined to a hospital bed, an intravenous glucose drip is started, and a fetal monitor attached. Subsequently, laboring women are transferred to a delivery room to give birth on a delivery table. After birth, mothers and infants have customarily been separated, an arrangement required by a hospital organization that treats the mother-child unit as separate patients.

The Use of Medication in Childbirth

For present purposes we regard as medication any substance introduced into the woman's body to affect the course of labor or to provide relief from pain. The use of medication provides a convenient means of gauging the degree to which particular systems justify interference in the birth process. The Dutch system provides no medication during normal births. Even when stimulation of labor is medically indicated, such as for postmaturity, or if rapid delivery is necessary due to a pathological condition, the criteria for what is considered normal are still quite broad. For instance, while in the U.S. ruptured membranes are considered an indication for inducing labor due to the risk of infection, the predominant view in the Netherlands is that ruptured membranes do not warrant any unusual action as long as fetal heart tones are normal and the woman's temperature does not rise. Furthermore, Dutch birth personnel prefer mechanical means, such as digital stripping of the membranes, over pharmacological or surgical means for inducing labor.

The Yucatecan system similarly emphasizes noninterference in normal births. A slow labor is not inherently considered cause for concern. Maya women tend to continue with household activities until contractions become too strong. In the event that contractions should subsequently slow down, they stimulate labor by giving the woman a raw egg to swallow, which causes retching and usually stimulates contractions. In Sweden stimulation of labor, sedation, and pain relief through pharmacological methods are fairly common, although drugs are used moderately. Women have a great degree of control over the kinds and quantities of drug they receive. In contrast, reliance on pharmacological agents is pronounced in the United States, where induction and stimulation of labor and the use of analgesics and anesthetics are widespread.

The Technology of Birth

The instruments and equipment required for culturally proper management of labor and delivery constitute a significant element in a society's birthing system. The collection of objects we group together in this category include all items deemed important in a proper birth and not just "obstetric tools"; the cross of palms used in Yucatan to ward off evil spirits is just as important to the Maya Indians as the birthing stool women use or as the delivery table is in the United States.

The technology of birth offers important clues to the local definition of the birth event. In societies where tools are simple, easily replaceable, general purpose household objects, birth is more likely to remain within the realm of normal family life than it is in societies where the collection of instruments is extensive and highly specialized (Jordan, in press). The degree of technological sophistication of birth tools is also related to the extent of specialization of birth attendants, and the artifacts associated with birth help to define the nature of the relationships among birth participants through the claims to professional expertise they support.

The Yucatecan tool kit is the most unspecialized of those we studied. The majority of Maya birth equipment consists of common household objects: the woman's hammock, the wooden stool on which she sits to give birth, the bowl for washing the baby and the clean rags for swaddling the baby are all everyday items. In contrast, the technology of the American birth system—which comprises the instruments and machinery of the labor and delivery rooms, X-ray and laboratory facilities, operating rooms for Caesarean sections, newborn resuscitation equipment, and so on—is clearly quite sophisticated.

As the technology of birth increases in complexity and sophistication, there thus appear to be concomitant changes in several important aspects of the birth process: its location, the identity of birth attendants, and the distribution of knowledge about birth (Jordan, in press).

The Locus of Decision-Making

The nature of the decision-making process during labor and delivery is intimately tied to the degree of self-management allowed the woman and, ultimately, to the question of who "owns" the birth. In Yucatan decisions about whether the woman should eat, which position she should assume, when she should begin to push, whether she is pushing hard enough, and what should be considered unsatisfactory progress are made jointly by the laboring woman, her helpers and the midwife. This collaborative process implicitly acknowledges the competence of all involved. Although the midwife's opinion carries considerable weight, even such "professional" decisions as whether to call in a doctor are negotiated. Dutch midwives typically work with the assumption that a woman is able to read her own body's cues; in normal births, the woman is treated as someone who is competent to manage what is seen as a natural process. In general, however, there are relatively few decisions to be made, since the Dutch conception of birth is that it is best aided by letting nature take its course. Of those decisions that must be made, moreover, many are institutionally managed: whether birth will occur at home or in the hospital, for instance, is decided on the basis of medical and social indicators; the question of who will accompany the woman is one which, although her decision, is restricted by the policy of allowing only one companion; and decisions about medication for pain are irrelevant, since none is typically used.

Births in Sweden occur in hospitals, but it is clearly the woman who, in an uncomplicated labor, makes what decisions the system allows, such as whether she will receive medication for pain. Although medical decisions are made by the physician on call, midwives are highly trained, and the range of situations considered normal, and therefore manageable by the laboring woman and the midwife staff, is quite broad. In contrast, women giving birth in the U.S. traditionally have almost no part in the decision-making process. The assimilation of childbirth into the medical realm subjects the birth event to medical decision-making criteria: since parturition is defined as a medical event, the woman is considered a patient who is, by definition, incompetent to influence the management of her birth.

Summary and Discussion

A biosocial analysis of childbirth indicates that the U.S. birthing system differs in several respects from that of the Dutch, the Swedish, and the Maya Indians of Yucatan. The Dutch and Maya Indians regard birth as a natural process, in which very little interference is necessary. Although in Sweden births occur in hospitals, medication for pain relief is available and artificial stimulation of labor is sometimes used: Laboring women have a strong voice in the birth process. Birth is defined as a medical/pathological event only in the United States, and, as we have indicated, the medical model of birth has many important ramifications. In recent years the appropriateness of the medical model of childbirth has come into question in many circles. Critics of the medical model sometimes argue in favor of alternative obstetric practices on anthropological grounds. In the following section we will describe research designed to address such arguments.

Childbirth in Nonindustrial Societies

Criticisms of standard hospital routines sometimes imply that they are "unnatural" and that we in this country have lost something important and meaningful that may still exist in other cultures. There is often a tendency to romanticize birthing in traditional cultures, to assume that women slip off into the bush to drop their babies with little effort and pain before returning to their work (Ford, 1964). Discontent with the hospital practice of separating mother and infant immediately after birth has given rise to the notions that this practice is unique to industrial societies and that women in traditional cultures experience close, skin-to-skin contact with their infants immediately after birth and nurse them right away.

To determine whether or not these implicit beliefs are accurate, we (Lozoff, 1982, 1983) analyzed existing ethnographic records, available for a sample of 186 nonindustrial societies, in which the subsistence economy is based on agriculture, herding, hunting and gathering, and fishing (Murdock & White, 1969). These societies comprise a geographically, historically, and linguistically diverse sample that is representative of nonindustrial cultures as a whole. We analyzed ethnographic descriptions of childbirth and the immediate postpartum period in these various cultures to answer such questions as: Who usually attends birth? Is the father of the baby typically present? Are mother and newborn in skin-to-skin contact immediately after birth, as is implied in criticism of standard maternity care in this country, or are they typically separated for some period of time? Do women in nonindustrial cultures breastfeed their infants immediately after birth or do they wait for some period of time? It should be noted that the quality of the ethnographic material is variable and sometimes based on second-hand reports. Nonetheless, the representative nature of the sample makes its analysis a potentially valuable complement to in-depth studies of individual cultures. The data related to labor and delivery will be presented first: data related to the period immediately following birth, and in particular to the extent of contact between parents and infant, will be presented afterward.

Labor and Delivery

We found that virtually all cultures had special methods to avoid painful, difficult births, which implies that even in nonindustrial societies there is some anxiety about the pain and danger associated with childbirth. In the colonial era in this country the Puritans exhorted women to prepare for death as they approached childbirth (Wertz & Wertz, 1979). Pain and potential mortality are recognized and expected as a part of birth in almost all societies. Perhaps as a result, we found that women giving birth had assistance and companionship in almost all societies. Women routinely gave birth alone in only 2% of the societies in Murdock and White's sample; they were permitted to give birth alone in only an additional 2%. In the remaining 96% of the societies in Murdock and White's sample women were expected to have companionship. Birth assistants were almost always women, especially women who had themselves given birth; indeed, men were often categorically excluded, with the possible exception of the father of the baby. The women present during birth were more than simply companions, however. In the 71 societies for which such information was available, the woman's assistants actively tried to influence labor by massage, herbal remedies, manipulation, and even bouncing on the abdomen. In some groups the birth assistant actually dilated the cervix manually to facilitate the birth process in difficult cases. In others, attendants functioned mostly as *doulas*, or supportive companions (Sosa, Klaus, Kennell, & Urrutia, 1976). The husband of the woman giving birth was allowed at the birth in 27% of the 120 societies for which this information was available. We found evidence that men were actually instrumental in assisting in childbirth in only two cultures. That childbirth in U.S. hospitals is typically dominated by men is thus a situation quite unlike that in nonindustrial societies.

Data concerning the presence or absence of children during childbirth were very scanty. Siblings were allowed to attend birth in only 11% of the cultures in this sample, and were specifically excluded in 25%. Sibling presence was not recorded for the remaining cultures.

In 70% of the cultures in Murdock and White's sample, the most common birth position was with the torso upright; in half, the women squatted or kneeled; in the other 20%, they sat or stood. Women delivered using the hands-and-knees position in only four cultures in the sample. Although women delivered recumbent or semi-recumbent in a third of all cultures, there was no society in this sample in which having the mother's feet in the air is the position of choice. Thus there was no analogue in this sample of the lithotomy position used in standard hospital births in this country.

Women in nearly all cultures prefer to give birth in a familiar location (Jordan, 1983). The Kung San Bushmen, for instance, seek out a favorite spot in the bush (Shostak, 1981), while in some parts of New Guinea women give birth in a special women's hut (Schiefenhovel, 1983), and a woman living in colonial America would usually have given birth in her mother's house (Scholten, 1977). Most commonly, women give birth in their own houses or huts.

It is almost universally expected that women will rest after childbirth. This was reported for in 97% of the 186 cultures in Murdock and White's sample. The average period of seclusion in these cultures was one week. In our own colonial past, women from the community took turns helping the mother for three to four weeks, so she could stay in bed and take care of her baby (Wertz & Wertz, 1979). Among the Maya Indians of Yucatan, the mother and baby are thought to be extremely vulnerable to the influence of spirits from the bush immediately after birth. All doors to the house therefore are closed during childbirth and any cracks in the house stuffed with rags to keep such spirits out (Jordan, 1983). In many other cultures, however, it is the mother and baby who are considered dangerous to the rest of society, and it is for this reason that they are secluded. The English word *quarantine* (from the French *quarante*, meaning forty) comes from the tradition of isolating a mother and her new baby for 40 days.

Early Parent-Infant Contact and Breastfeeding

Early Contact

In 1972, Klaus and Kennell reported that allowing mothers and their newborn infants to be together in the early hours after birth resulted in significant increases in the mothers' affection toward their infants. For example, mothers who experienced early contact with their infants maintained more eye contact with them when they were older, vocalized and sang to them more, and kissed them and smiled at them more than mothers who had not experienced early contact. Subsequent studies noted that early contact also had a beneficial effect on later breastfeeding. Klaus and Kennell referred to this phenomenon as mother-infant bonding, and hypothesized that there was a sensitive period for this process; that is, they argued that there was a period of time immediately after birth, when infants tend to be relatively alert, that represents an optimum time for bonding to begin. Klaus and Kennell's pioneering research stimulated additional work in this area, and the concept of bonding has been extended to include fathers (e.g., Greenberg & Morris, 1974).

Despite its controversial nature, research on early parent-infant bonding has motivated changes in the routines of many hospital maternity wards. In addition, early contact studies have fostered a belief that the practices of separating mother and infant and delaying the first nursing represent aberrations of our hospital policies and are absent in traditional cultures. We analyzed the anthropological data to determine if early parent-infant contact would indeed be emphasized in Murdock and White's sample and if such contact might be associated with any differences in later infant care.

There was no special effort to foster *immediate* body contact between mother and infant in 94% of nonindustrial cultures because both mother and newborn were bathed or rubbed. The duration of delay in contact due to bathing was not generally specified but was probably brief. The bathed newborn was given to the mother in approximately half of all societies; the infant was placed in a cradle or basket in the other half. Although the infant commonly remained in his or her mother's sight, *skin-to-skin contact* was quite rare; the infant was given nude to the mother in only 19% of the societies in this sample. Nevertheless, as we noted above, in virtually all societies mother and baby were secluded together in the period following birth and were not a part of the usual daily activities of the community.

General societal ratings of parental involvement and affection, which have been demonstrated to be reasonably reliable and valid, are available for the same 186 societies in Murdock and White's sample (Barry & Paxson, 1971). We dichotomized the following ratings relevant to the effects of postpartum contact: mother's role as caregiver; response to crying; overall quality of infant care; paternal involvement in infancy and early childhood; duration of breastfeeding; and infant's age at introduction of solid food. We compared those societies in which the baby was given to the mother with those societies in which the baby was placed in a cradle or basket. There was no difference between the two groups on any of the following measures: the percent of societies in which the mother was the primary caregiver, in which crying infants received a nurturant response, or in which infants received generally affectionate care. Thus, immediate postpartum contact was not associated with differences in maternal affection and involvement on these global rating scales. It cannot be determined whether differences might have been found if more detailed or sensitive measures had been available.

We performed a similar analysis to determine whether fathers were more involved with their children in societies which allowed them to be present at birth. Societies in which fathers were permitted to attend birth were compared with those in which fathers were prohibited from being at birth on dichotomized ratings of paternal involvement. There was no significant difference between the two groups in the percentage of societies in which fathers were closely involved with their children in infancy or early childhood, although there was a trend toward increased paternal involvement in infancy.

Early Breastfeeding

It has been found in several studies of hospital births that women who breastfeed in the first hour are more likely to be breastfeeding when their infants are two months old than women who breastfeed according to standard hospital routine—i.e., at 4-6 hours or even at 12 hours. This result has been obtained in studies conducted in Brazil (Sousa et al., 1974), Canada (Thomson, Hartsock & Larson, 1979), England (Salariya, Easton & Cater, 1978), Guatemala (Sosa et al., 1976), Jamaica (Ali & Lowry, 1981), Sweden (de Chateau, 1967), and the United States (Hally et al., 1984; Johnson, 1976; Paylor, Maloni, & Brown, 1986; Paylor, Maloni, Taylor, & Campbell, 1985; Wright & Walker, 1983).

Several different mechanisms have been proposed to explain the finding that breastfeeding in the first hour after birth has a significant effect on later breast-feeding. This research originally came under the umbrella of the "early contact" research: it was proposed that there is a sensitive period for breastfeeding as well as for early bonding. An alternative explanation is that babies are in a quiet, alert state more often in the first hour than later on, so they suck more effectively, which in turn stimulates the mother's brain to release the hormones that govern lactation. It may also be that simply by putting babies to their mother's breast, health care professionals convey a message about the importance of breastfeeding, which leads to greater success. Regardless of the mechanism involved, early breastfeeding seems to be a consistently effective intervention, and has in many cases been incorporated into hospital routines.

The research on breastfeeding in the first postpartum hour might suggest that early nursing is crucial for successful breastfeeding in humans. One might reasonably assume, therefore, that virtually all nonindustrial societies would insure that immediate suckling occurs. Our analysis of the data in Murdock and White's sample indicated that this is not in fact the case. Of the 81 societies for which the time of initial breastfeeding could be recorded from ethnographies, infants nursed within the first hour or two in 48%; nursing was delayed more than 24 hours in the majority (52%) and delayed more than 48 hours in 41%. The substantial delay in initial breastfeeding occurs in most cases because these cultures consider colostrum, the milk high in protein and immune body content that is secreted for the first few days after parturition, of no nutritional value or even harmful.

In our own culture women who delay nursing for over 24 hours often have difficulty establishing their milk supply. We analyzed Murdock and White's data to determine if lactation failure was a problem in nonindustrial cultures that delayed the first nursing. There was no difference between those cultures that adhere to a practice of early breastfeeding and those that delay breastfeeding either in the duration of breastfeeding or the age at which solid foods are introduced. Indeed, contrary to common assumptions about primitive cultures, solids were introduced before one month of age in one-third of all cultures, regardless of when infants were first breastfed. Similarly, nursing lasted two years or longer in 81% of the nonindustrial cultures, whether women nursed in the first hour or delayed the first breastfeeding.

Discussion

These anthropological results present something of a puzzle. Few human cultures emphasize skin-to-skin body contact and suckling in the immediate postpartum period, practices associated with longer breastfeeding and increased maternal involvement for individuals in industrial societies. Yet in most nonindustrial groups, mothers are affectionately involved with their infants and breastfeed successfully for two or more years. It may be easier to understand these contradictions if we consider the effect of the early period after birth in the context of the subsequent days and months.

The standard maternity hospital routine in industrial societies of separating mothers and babies is followed by an infant care pattern that commonly comprises frequent separations of mother and infant in the home, minimal body contact, and spaced feeding. In the context of this pattern of infant care, body contact immediately after birth may assume disproportionate significance in enhancing maternal affection. In contrast, in nonindustrial societies separation in the first hour may have less effect on the mother's later involvement with her infant because such separations are not repeated. The brief initial separation of mother and infant is universally followed by postpartum confinement of mother and baby together—a rooming-in period—which is itself followed by extensive mother-infant contact and prolonged and frequent breastfeeding during the baby's early months. In addition, it is likely that many factors—little girls' exposure to breastfeeding throughout their lives, assumptions that breastfeeding will be successful, a supportive environment, frequent nursing, and extensive mother-infant contact—combine to diminish the importance of nursing in the first hour. Thus, the apparent sensitivity of parents in industrial societies to immediate postpartum contact may reflect disruptive influences of our pattern of infant care and our hospital routines rather than a brief sensitive period for parenting, or for developing parental feelings, in the human species.

An appreciation of the embeddedness of perinatal customs in the broader context of infant care patterns and cultural meaning systems provides further insight into the apparent paradox presented by these anthropological data. The task universally faced in all cultures is adequate involvement of caregiver and child, primarily mother and child (Jordan, 1982). This involvement can be conceptualized as a progressive mutual engagement of the senses, which begins with the mother's first sensory contact with the baby and continues with her hearing the infant's first cry, her first sight of the baby, and first holding it and smelling it, and so on, until there is mutual sensory involvement. The culmination of this process is that the mother "owns" the child; the mother feels that this is really *her* baby for which she is prepared to care. The relationship deepens with the mother and baby "talking" to each other, mutual gazing, nipple searching and nipple giving, and so on. It may well be that there is a sensitive period for this process of mutual engagement. Regardless of whether or not a system of this sort is biologically preprogrammed, the anthropological data suggest that culture is stronger than nature. Different cultures facilitate caregiver-infant attachment in different ways: some with immediate contact, some with later contact; some with skin-to-skin contact, some without. Whatever specific means are used, all societies accomplish the task somehow, or babies would not survive.

Childbirth in the United States:
Discontent, Change and Potential Conflict

Judging from the available anthropological data, it would appear that the practices of separating mother, and infant immediately after birth, delaying breastfeeding and excluding fathers from childbirth are not unique to standard maternity care in the United States, common assumptions notwithstanding. Nevertheless, both of the comparative approaches to childbirth that we have described indicate that birthing practices in the U.S. do differ in important respects from those in other cultures. The pathological model of childbirth that pervades our childbirth practices is atypical of the other cultures we studied, even those that are technologically quite sophisticated. Our analysis of the anthropological data from Murdock and White's sample of nonindustrial cultures revealed that, while there is considerable behavioral variability even in so universal a process as childbirth, there are also several birthing practices that are very nearly universal. These near-universal tendencies are predominantly social in nature. In general, all cultures have *rules* governing the process of parturition, although the actual content of such rules may differ among cultures. There are also more specific practices characteristic of virtually all societies: women giving birth almost always receive assistance, usually from other women; women usually prefer to give birth in a familiar setting, most commonly their own home; and virtually all societies prescribe a period of rest and seclusion for mother and infant after birth, a "rooming-in period," during which the pair is separated from community activities and the mother is exempt from her usual responsibilities. In these respects, standard maternity care in the U.S. may not fit the pattern of childbirth practices that seems to characterize nonindustrial cultures.

We have argued that childbirth practices are best understood in the context of the sociocultural matrix in which they are embedded, including the patterns of infant care typical of the culture. One implication of this position is that the relationship between birthing practices and the various phenomena that researchers might examine as outcome variables is likely to be complex. For example, the influence of fathers' birth attendance on their subsequent involvement with their children is liable to depend on many factors, such as cultural notions about the father-child relationship, economic pressures, the division of labor within a family, and the attitudes of fathers and their partners about paternal involvement in infant care (cf. Palkovitz, 1985). As our analysis of the anthropological data from Murdock and White's sample of nonindustrial cultures indicated, whether or not fathers in nonindustrial cultures are allowed to be present at the birth of their babies had no apparent effect on the degree of fathers' later involvement with their children. Indeed, it may well be that whether an expectant father participates in birth has more to do with cultural attitudes about his relationship with his wife than about his relationship with his children. The Maya Indians, for instance, believe that the father must participate in an active capacity at birth so that he can see how his wife suffers; this is expected to prevent him from making sexual demands during the postpartum period (Jordan, 1983).

An additional implication of the view that each culture's system of childbirth is intimately linked to the culture as a whole is that, as changes occur in the larger social and cultural systems with which childbirth systems articulate, there will be corresponding changes in birthing practices. This has quite clearly been the case in the United States in recent years. Those in the feminist health movement have been pressing for the right of women to self-determination in matters regarding their bodies (cf. Jordan, 1977). One outcome of this movement has been the position that women's individual complaints about their birth experiences are not the result of rare circumstances, but are the systematic outcome of standard medical practice. The collectivization of previously individual dissatisfaction has produced powerful pressures on the American obstetric system. At the same time, major segments of the consumer movement as it relates to health care have been engaged in a comprehensive reevaluation of the expanding monopoly of professional medicine. Too, many men have been questioning practices that routinely excluded them from the delivery room and the birth of their own babies, and an increased emphasis on prepared childbirth has resulted in a greater degree of inclusion of fathers in the process of birth. As a result of these and other pressures, childbirth practices in this country are undergoing major changes. This is reflected in the growing visibility of various forms of natural childbirth, in the increasingly common efforts to restructure the physical design of obstetric wards, and in the development of family-centered perinatal care programs.

Such changes would appear to indicate that we as a culture are engaged in a reformulation of the medical definition of birth. It should be noted, however, that hospital birthing rooms make sense only within a system that places the highest premium on medical safety, since the woman's own home would be preferable by most any other criterion. The home birth movement also speaks the language of outcome statistics. At least in the public arena, all of the advantages of home births that one could cite, such as the woman's comfort, financial considerations, the humanization of birth, benefits from taking responsibility for one's life rather than delegating it to professionals and institutions, and the strengthening of the couple's and family relationships that can be obtained from the shared experience, are subordinated to discussions of medical safety. The strongest argument that the home birth movement can, and does, advance is the statistical argument that the outcome of home births is in no way inferior to that of hospital births. That such alternatives to standard hospital births do not represent fundamental changes in the prevailing view of childbirth, then, is apparent.

Regardless of whether the definition of birth in this country has changed in any fundamental respect, obstetric practices in the U.S. nevertheless are clearly changing. Furthermore, it seems quite likely that changes in obstetric practice will produce a significant increase in maternal satisfaction and perhaps infant outcome statistics, too, by reducing the dissonance between women's conceptions of themselves and the treatment they receive in maternity wards (Jordan, 1983). Yet if maternity hospital reform is in fact successful in altering parent-infant relationships' as proponents of early contact have argued, then perhaps families in the U.S. should anticipate new conflicts as this postpartum experience does not fit with the patterns of care during the rest of infancy.

For example, after frequent feeding on demand in the first few days in the hospital, many infants may well be eager to eat every 1-2 hours. There is evidence that this feeding pattern was the norm during much of human history and thus may be particularly suited to human physiology (Lozoff & Brittenham, 1979; Lozoff, 1980). Such frequent breastfeeding is in fact found in most societies, yet in the United States many women find it difficult to sustain and enjoy a "continuous" feeding pattern. In addition, breastfeeding still conflicts with societal norms and expectations. The mother in the U.S. who integrates breastfeeding with her usual activities may still encounter offended righteousness in public situations.

Maternity hospital routines which encourage early body contact between mother and baby also seem congruent with the pattern of care to which humans may be adapted. In the United States many babies, given the opportunity, seem thoroughly delighted to be in constant body contact in their early months, a desire which may stress some mothers. Women in the U.S. generally must provide such contact entirely by themselves without the help of extended family members who in other societies often hold babies while the mother works or rests. In fact, the presence of more than one adult caretaker in a household is, in cross-cultural studies, associated with increased acceptance and indulgence of infants (Rohner, 1975). If the close involvement encouraged in a family-centered childbirth experience is continued into infancy, both mother and father may also experience conflicts about work. Women's work was previously compatible with infant care; women have worked in most human societies, contributing more than 50% of the food for the group during 99% of human history. In contrast, work is generally incompatible with infant care in our culture; conflicts between work and parenthood seem to be created by the structure of work in this society.

Thus, while family-centered changes in maternal hospital practices are certainly needed, such reforms may introduce new dilemmas for parents and infants if not accompanied by transformations in the pattern of subsequent infant care. Cross-cultural study of childbirth provides an important context in which to evaluate and understand changes in hospital routines, including potential conflicts with other infant care practices.

Direction for Further Research

The above review suggests a number of areas in which further cross-cultural research is needed. We need, for example, more ethnographic studies of different birthing systems in order to add to what is known about the range of variability in human behaviors around childbirth. The recent legitimization of "women's topics" in anthropology and related disciplines has already led to the initiation of a number of such studies (Laderman, 1984; MacCormack, 1982; Sargent, 1982), and further results should become available in the next few years. We also need to examine, in more detail, the variation in function of birth attendants in other cultures. Most recent research on traditional midwives has been narrowly confined to assessments of their knowledge and skills (WHO, 1985), with a view to incorporate them in primary health care teams, particularly as village-level dispensers of contraceptive information. Studies of this type all too often do not pay sufficient attention to the cultural meaning of birth and to the social relationships it creates (Jordan, 1986). Little is thus known about continuing family-like ties between birth attendants and the child, nor about the extent to which it is common that grandmothers and other family members lend birth assistance.

Another topic that cross-cultural studies have not yet addressed adequately is the question of father involvement in pregnancy, birth, and the postpartum period. We know that there are many societies where the father of the child is expected to play a significant role during pregnancy and where he has important functions during the postpartum period. For example, a common cross-cultural belief is that the parents together have to "grow" the baby by contributing physical substances: the mother her menstrual blood (which makes the baby's muscle and blood) and the father his semen (which turns into the white parts, such as skin and bone). Fathers, like mothers, may be subject to food taboos and other restrictions on their behavior throughout the pregnancy and into the postpartum period, but information on such practices and what they may mean for the relationship between father and child are only sporadic at this time. Perhaps with the burgeoning of research on fathers in industrial societies, some in-depth studies of fathering in nonindustrial societies will become available.

Cross-cultural studies of birthing have added many valuable insights which can contribute to our understanding of parenthood. Nevertheless, there is still much work to be done.

References

Ali, Z., & Lowry, M. (1981). Early maternal-child contact: Effects on later behavior. Developmental Medicine and Child Neurology, 23, 337-345.

Barry, H., & Paxson, L. M. (1971). Infancy and early childhood: Cross-cultural codes 2. *Ethnology, 10,* 466-508.

de Chateau, P. (1967). *Neonatal care routines: Influences on maternal and infant behavior and on breastfeeding.* Umea: Umea University Medical Dissertations, New Series No. 20.

Ford, C. S. (1964). *A comparative study of human reproduction* (Reprinted from the 1945 edition). Human Relations Area Files, Inc. New Haven: HRAF Press.

Greenberg, M., & Morris, N. (1974). Engrossment: The newborn's impact upon the father. *American Journal of Orthopsychiatry 44,* 520-531.

Hally, M. R., Bond, J., Crawley, J., Gregson, B., Philips, P., & Russell, I. (1984). Factors influencing the feeding of first-born infants. *Acta Paediatrica Scandinavica, 73,* 33-39.

Johnson, N. W. (1976). Breastfeeding at one hour of age. *American Journal of Maternal Child Nursing, 1,* 12-16.

Jordan, B. (1977). The self-diagnosis of early pregnancy: An investigation of lay competence. *Medical Anthropology, 1,* 1-38.

Jordan, B. (1982). Commentary. In M. H. Klaus & M. O. Robertson (Eds.), *Birth, interaction and attachment* (pp. 7-9). Pediatric Round Table Series, no. 6. Johnson & Johnson Baby Products Company.

Jordan, B. (1983). *Birth in four cultures: A cross-cultural investigation of childbirth in Yucatan, Holland, Sweden and the United States* (3rd ed.). Montreal: Eden Press.

Jordan, B. (1986). Technology transfer in obstetrics: Theory and practice in developing countries. *Women in International Development Working Papers*, #126. East Lansing, MI: WID/MSU.

Jordan, B. (in press). The hut and the hospital: Information, power and symbolism in the artifacts of birth. *Birth: Issues in Perinatal Care and Education.*

Ladermann, Carol D. (1984). *Wives and midwives: Childbirth and nutrition in rural Malaysia.* Berkeley: University of California Press.

Lozoff, B. (1980). Reply to Jelliffe, E. F. P. "Infant care: Cache or carry." *Journal of Pediatrics, 96*, 1122-1123.

Lozoff, B. (1982). Birth in non-industrial societies. In M. H. Klaus & M. O. Robertson (Eds.), *Birth, interaction and attachment* (pp. 1-6). Pediatric Round Table Series, no. 6. Johnson & Johnson Baby Products Company.

Lozoff, B. (1983). Birth and "bonding" in non-industrial societies. *Developmental Medicine and Child Neurology 25*, 595-600.

Lozoff, B., & Brittenham, G. M. (1979). Infant care: Cache or carry. *Journal of Pediatrics, 95*, 478-483.

MacCormack, Carol P. (1982). *Ethnography of fertility and birth*. London: Academic Press.

Murdock, G. P., & White, D. R. (1969). Standard cross-cultural sample. *Ethnology, 8*, 329-369.

Palkovitz, R. (1985). Fathers' birth attendance, early contact, and extended contact with their newborns: A critical review. *Child Development 56*, 392-406.

Parsons, T. (1951). *The social system*. Glencoe, Illinois: Free Press.

Paylor, P. M., Maloni, J. A., & Brown, D. R. (1986). Early suckling and prolonged breastfeeding. *American Journal of Diseases in Children, 140*, 151-154.

Paylor, P. M., Maloni, J. A., Taylor, F. H., & Campbell, S. B. (1985). II. Extra early mother-infant contact and duration of breast-feeding. *Acta Paediatrica Scandinavica* (Suppl. 316), 15-22.

Rohner, R. P. (1975). *They love me, they love me not*. Human Relations Area Files, Inc., New Haven: HRAF Press.

Rosaldo, M. Z., & Lamphere, L. (1974). *Woman, culture and society*. Palo Alto, California: Stanford University Press.

Salariya, E. M., Easton, P. M., & Cater, J. E. (1978). Duration of breastfeeding after early initiation and frequent feeding. *Lancet, 2*, 1141-1143.

Sargent, Carolyn F. (1982). *The cultural context of therapeutic choice: Obstetrical care decisions among the Bariba of Benin*. Hingham, MA: D. Reidel.

Schiefenhovel, W. (1983). Geburten bei den Eipo [Birth among the Eipo]. In W. Schiefenhovel & D. Sich (Eds.), *Die Geburt aus ethnomedizinischer Sicht*. Braunschweig, West Germany: Vierweg Verlag.

Scholten, C. (1977). On the importance of the Obstetrick Art. *The William and Mary Quarterly*, 3rd series, *34*, 426-455.

Shostak, M. (1981). *Nisa: The life and words of a Kung woman*. Cambridge,MA: Harvard University Press.

Sosa, R., Klaus, M., Kennell, J. H., & Urrutia, J. J. (1976). The effect of early mother-infant contact on breastfeeding, infection and growth. Ciba Foundation Symposium 45, *Breastfeeding and the mother* (pp. 179-193). Amsterdam, The Netherlands: Elsevier Publishing Co.

Sousa, P. L. R., Barros, F. C., Gazalle, R. V., Bergers, R. M., Pinheiro, G. N., Menezes, S. T., & Arruda, L. A. (1974). Attachment and lactation. Paper presented at XIV Congreso Internacional de Pediatria. Buenos Aires, Argentina.

Thomson, M. E., Hartsock, T., & Larson, C. (1979). The importance of immediate postnatal contact: Its effect on breastfeeding. *Canadian Family Physician, 25*, 1374-1378.

Wertz, R. W., & Wertz, D. C. (1979). *Lying-in: A history of childbirth in America*. New York: Schocken Books.

Wright, H. J., & Walker, P. C. (1983). Prediction of duration of breastfeeding in primaparas. *Journal of Epidemiology and Community Health, 37*, 89-94.

WHO (1985). *Traditional birth practices: An annotated bibliography.* Prepared by Lindsay Edouard and Cecile Li Hoi Foo-Gregory for the Maternal and Child Health Unit, Division of Family Health, WHO, Geneva. (WHO/MC/85.11).

World Health Statistics Annual 1985. Geneva, Switzerland: World Health Organization.

Section IX

PARENTING

Parenting normally is the result of the biological fact of conception and pregnancy followed by childbirth. But many individuals may be voluntarily or involuntarily childless (customarily 10-20% of women are infertile though the figure may be higher among some groups) allowing for adoption. While adoption may satisfy the familial requirements and establish the child as the legal heir to the adopting parents, is the emotional bond the same? Does it depend on the age of the child being adopted? Are the reciprocal bonds the same if the adopting parents already have other children?

Parenting may also involve other members of the kingroup. Not only will such persons—depending on the descent principle recognized and the terminological system followed—be addressed as "father" and "mother", behavior may mimic that of the nuclear family. Williams explains that "An Arunta infant learns very early that the women his mother calls 'sisters' will also care for him, even nurse him...He learns too there are many men . . . (who) will address him as 'son' and will act toward him in the same way as his father does when he cares for him, protects him, or disciplines him" (1972:138). The Arunta child will address such women as "mother" and the men as "father".

The biological fact of birth establishes a unique and special relationship between the infant and certain other persons. These normally include the woman who gave birth to the baby and the man who fathered the child. However, aspects of social organization and social structure must be taken into consideration.

Those societies which trace descent through the father—or those societies which give special status to the father even if descent is traced through both parents—usually combine in one person the role of **pater** (the sociological father) and **genitor** (the biological father). Either through marriage or mutual agreement the father is bonded with the child's **mater** (the sociological mother) who is also the **genetrix** (the biological mother). Since co-residence is normally the rule in these societies we find that the father resides with the mother and infant, either in the same home or very close by, and that there is an ongoing relationship between father and mother, and between father and child. This is a model which is similar to our own family structure and thus is easy to understand.

Many societies world wide, however, trace descent through the mother and her relatives. In these situations the child still spends the early years with the mother but her brother assumes the authority role, i.e., the role of pater. The child's genitor of course assumes the role of pater for his sister's children.

At the core of the whole issue of parenting is the role of the mother and the role of the father. It is argued that since the mother carries the foetus and physically gives birth to the neonate there must perforce be a stronger bond between her, the genetrix, and the child than between the father, the genitor, and the child. If a person accepts this part of the argument then it is logical that the father will have a weaker bond with a child and spend less time and emotion with the child than would the mother.

This approach postulates that there is no such thing as "natural paternal love" though it may be achieved if it is socially required. Paul Bohannan explains that people who support this postulate hold that "paternal love does not have a glandular basis as does maternal love" (1963: 112). Is paternal involvement and commitment determined by glandular action?

Suzanne Frayser conducted a thorough anthropological study of human sexuality using the crosscultural resources of the Human Relations Area Files. She states:

> The fact that humans have longer dependency periods than those of other animals means that an "ardent" male has to do more than inseminate a woman to ensure his reproductive success. He, too, has to become involved in the parenting process, at least to the extent of making sure that the woman he impregnates and her offspring can survive... Paternity is fathering - a social behavior - not merely being a genitor - a physical contributor to conception (1985:357).

The two chapters which follow explore the question of parenting in a cross cultural perspective. In the first Amighi discusses maternal warmth, detachment (neglect), and bonding. In the second Hewlett reports on his research concerning Aka fatherhood and compares this material with father involvement among a selected sample of other societies. While they may not address the question concerning the basis for parental love they certainly explore variations in parenting as illustrated by parental commitment and involvement.

References

Bohannan, Paul. 1963. *Social Anthropology*. New York: Holt, Rinehart and Winston.

Frayser, Suzanne G. 1985. *Varieties of Sexual Experience*. New Haven: Human Relations Area Files Press.

SOME THOUGHTS ON THE CROSS-CULTURAL STUDY OF MATERNAL WARMTH AND DETACHMENT

Janet Kestenberg Amighi, Ph.D.

ABSTRACT: A number of studies have suggested that maternal detachment is common in tropical societies which suffer from high infant mortality. The author's own research revealed evidence of both detachment and positive affect. She suggests that maternal behavior in all societies can be best characterized as exhibiting maternal ambivalence. In order to pursue this thesis, the paper conducts a very brief survey of a) maternality as presented in mythology, folk tales, and rituals, b) cases of direct and indirect infanticide, and c) examples of mother infant relationships in the cross-cultural literature.

John Bowlby hypothesized that there is a universal and instinctive mother-infant bond among humans (quoted in Ainsworth 1967). Inspired by Bowlby, Mary Ainsworth conducted scheduled interviews and observation sessions with mothers of infants among the BuGanda of Uganda. Although she found secure mother-infant bonds in most cases, she found that kissing and cooing to infants occurred rarely and she only observed few instances of face to face mother infant interaction (1967).

Using Ainsworth's data as well as his own, Robert LeVine (sometimes with Sarah LeVine) apparently sought to segregate two aspects of the mother-infant bond-one which involved the mother's concern with the physical survival of her infant and one which involved maternal warmth and/or concern with the emotional well being of her child.

In my own African experience and in the accounts of others from tropical places as diverse as Latin America and Indonesia, there is a general picture of infant care that emerges . . . (1977:23).

Western observers, scientists, and amateurs alike, have tended to conceptualize this pattern as *indulgence* because of the demand feeding, the rapidity of response to crying, the absence of pressure for toilet training, the apparent quiescent contentment of the infants, the inference that the infant's "needs" are being taken care of. But the term *indulgence* as a folk expression in English also connotes an emotional attitude involving "affection," "warmth," and related attributes on the part of the caretaker, whereas the *overt (*my emphasis) behaviors indicating such an attitude are frequently minimal in the non-Western populations being observed (1977:23).

Dr. Janet Kestenberg Amighi received her Ph.D. from the University of Missouri in 1984. Her dissertation, Zoroastrians of Iran Conversion, Assimilation, and Persistence is published by AMS Press, Spring 1990. She has taught anthropology at Tehran University, Cabrini College, and University of West Chester, Penn. She has also taught the Kestenberg Movement {rProfile at the Laban Institute for Movement Study in New York. Address correspondence to her at 763 Denton Hollow Road, West Chester, PA 19382.

In another publication, based on their own observations among the Gusii of Kenya, Ainsworth's study of the BuGanda, and other reports in the literature, the LeVines concluded that an emotionally detached mothering typified agricultural cultures of subsaharan Africa (LeVine and LeVine 1981).

As LeVine suggested, there are many scattered reports in the literature of similarly "aloof" mothers in other areas of the world, e.g. among the Mundurucu of Brazil (Murphy and Murphy 1985), shantytown Brazilians (Scheper-Hughes 1985), mothers of India (Seymour 1983, Minturn and Lambert 1964, cf. Rohner and Chaki-sicar 1983). In fact Robert LeVine went so far as to suggest that maternal aloofness is a typical pattern in agricultural societies of the tropics (1981).

Such a pattern of maternal aloofness develops, according to LeVine, where infant mortality is high. In response to high death rates, mothers are more concerned to protect their infants against threats to their physical survival than meeting emotional needs. Furthermore, to protect themselves from the pain of coping with infant deaths, mothers develop an emotional detachment from their infants (LeVine 1981). Thus in the process of protecting both the survival of the infant and the psyche of the mother, maternal warmth is abandoned or reduced.

However, some researchers, such as Kilbride and Kilbride (1981) and Harkness and Super (1980), report evidence of strong maternal affect in African societies. In my own observations of mother-infant dyads in southern Iran and Bali, I found evidence of both positive and negative affect, of both close bonding and distancing. These observations as well as my reading of the cross-cultural literature, has led me to conclude that the nature of mother-infant relationships, in the Third world and the Western world as well (although varying cross-culturally), is characterized less by maternal detachment than by ambivalence (see Kestenberg, Kestenberg, and Amighi 1988). It is the purpose of this paper to begin an investigation of this thesis.

As the title of this paper suggests, I will not offer a rigorous examination of the cross-cultural data. First of all, data on motherhood cross-culturally is limited. Cross-cultural psychologists and psychologically oriented anthropologists have studied child rearing practices primarily for their effect on the child, rather than focusing on the mother as a topic of investigation herself (e.g. Minturn and Lambert 1964). Those who have studied the lives of women in other cultures have focused primarily on women's roles outside the domestic sphere, women as agricultural workers, women as traders, curers, rebels, etc.

Although it would be worthwhile to investigate maternal affect in specific culture areas, given the limitations of the data, and my own inclinations, I have chosen to conduct a broad and necessarily cursory survey of maternal affect as reflected in: 1) folk tales, mythology and ritual, 2) cases of indirect and direct infanticide, and 3) studies of mother-infant relationships.

Mothers in Mythology, Folktales, and Ritual

Given the difficulty of evaluating maternal affect as evidenced by disagreements in the literature, it might be useful to consider how cultures view maternal affect in the symbolic realm. Are mothers depicted in folk tales and mythology as loving and devoted, or cruel and heartless? Using folk songs of Andalusia, Gilmore demonstrates the ambivalent attitudes toward women in the culture (1988). He suggests that these attitudes derive from the young man's ambivalence towards his mother, the mother who has nurtured him and protected him and the mother who weans him and abandons him. Several European folk tales echo this theme. In "Cinderella," "Snow White," and "Hansel and Gretel," we find this common opposition of the good and the bad mother, often represented as two distinct personalities. Often, the kind gentle mother dies, abandoning her daughter (or daughter and son) to suffer under the hand of the cruel stepmother. It is interesting to note that the good mother is generally the mother of the hero or heroine in infancy, while the cruel stepmother is the mother of the adolescent. Often a fairy god-mother appears whom we can see as either the symbol of the good mother who died and now returns, or as a grandmother or stranger who saves the adolescent. Although these stories focus on the heroine and her feelings of ambivalence towards her mother, as Zipes pointed out, they may also express the jeal-ousy of the aging mother faced with her young and attractive daughter (1988).

Outside of the European culture areas, the good mother- bad mother opposition is rarely found. There is a tale told among the Chaga of Kenya (Parrinder 1967) that roughly parallels this theme, but by and large non-European tales focus on other topics and leave motherhood unscathed.

Motherhood is more often depicted in cross-cultural mythology, particularly in myths of creation. Great Earth Mother Goddesses have existed in almost all cultures. Before Allah in the Middle East was the goddess Allat, and portrayed in the Gilgamesh legends, the goddess Istar: in India there was Kali Maya: in Egypt the Earth Mother, Nut and her daughter Isis, mother of the heavens; in Japan the Sun God-dess Amma-Iorasus et. al. These are goddesses of fertility and procreation, but they are also often respon-sible for death. The goddess Alal of the Ibo of Nigeria is both protector of the harvest and fertility and queen of the underworld. She is depicted with a child on her knee and a sword in her hand. The Mossi of Upper Volta use the same mask of an earth goddess at funerals and to protect their harvest (Parrinder 1967). There are many myths in which the good mother goddess creates life, and then turns evil and tries to destroy it, e.g. the story of Tlamat of Babylonia or the daughter of Re in Egypt (Colum 1930). The good mother and the evil mother of European folktales are often seen to coexist in one unpredictable goddess of birth and death in mythologies throughout much of the world.

Any ambivalence that people of a given culture may feel towards mothers will generally be re-flected in the mythology and rituals concerned with the blood of child birth and menstruation. The blood of the woman, (like woman herself), is commonly seen as both a source of danger and a bless-ing. Menstrual blood can have sacred healing qualities (Walker 1987). The first menstruation is often celebrated as the coming of age of a young girl. However, women who have post partum bleeding or are menstruating are often secluded in huts, or tabooed from touching certain foods or entering sacred places. Their look or their touch was and is widely seen to endanger the lives of men. Yet, women are often told that they are segregated because they have been weakened by child birth or menstruation-segregation is thus both for the health of the woman, so she can be a good mother, and to protect soci-ety from the dangerous mother.

In European culture, it was believed that menstruating women could cause meat to go bad, wine to turn, and bread dough to fall (Martin 1987). Among both the Chaco and the Yanomomo of South America, myths tell of the death of mankind, people sinking into the earth or drowning in floods when a menstruating girl broke the taboo and came out of her hut and was seen by men (Lizot 1985, Osborne 1968). Blood, both the symbol of life and the symbol of death, is often a primary aspect of womanhood. Clearly as Campbell has suggested, those who can give life, are seen as also able to take life away (1988).

It is not only the destructive side of mother which must be feared. Mother love can also be threatening. In American as well as Persian culture, mothers often say, "I love you so much I could eat you up." (In Persian, "Let me eat you," Bokhoramet) is an expression of love. In a Persian creation myth, the first woman and man love their children so much they eat them. Again they bear children and eat them. God, seeing this unseemly beginning of humankind, finds it necessary to reduce parental love for children by 4/5 so that they can survive (Hinnells 1985).

Stories of maternal or parental abandonment of children are very common and found in many cultures. They may express parental ambivalence towards children. When told to children, they also serve as a warning to children concerning parental ambivalence. It is interesting that the parent is rarely portrayed as inequivocably evil, rather the abandonment is usually given a justification based on either problems of starvation or direct threats of the child against the parent. In other words, we are abandoning you, but with good reason. In the various Oedipus tales, it is foretold that the child will kill or replace the parent. In the Old Testament, infants are abandoned when their mothers have no food to offer them. Food is often a central issue. A Central Eskimo myth tells of a child who was abandoned after she seized upon the limbs of her parents to eat them. Instead they cut her up and put her in the ocean to become fish. In other words rather than eat them out of house and home (and limb) she herself was turned into food. In New Zealand and Hawaii, it is told that when the mother goddess bore her fifth son, she saw that there wasn't enough food for him so she tied her hair around him and gave him to the waves. The god of the sea saved him. His mother wasn't forgiven however, for when the boy grew up, he set out to pluck out the heart of the Goblin goddess, his *ancestress* (symbol of his mother?). In other words, (as in the Oedipus tales) retribution was taken against the abandoning father or mother, albeit indirectly.

In conclusion, although we can find myths which tell only of a mother's love for her children, the preponderance of myths and tales depict an ambivalent maternal love, sometimes comforting, sometimes frightening-mother as both savior and destroyer. They seem to reflect the perspective of the grown up child viewing motherhood. Of the fears and feelings of the mother herself, myths tell us little, leaving us to speculate whether the characterization of ambivalent motherhood in mythology reflects the emotions experienced by mothers themselves. It seems likely that the repetition of these myths by mothers and fathers to children are an expression of their ambivalence. However, we now turn to from the symbolic realm to the apparently more concrete realm of behavior.

Child Neglect and Infanticide

Maternal infanticide, rare in nonhuman species, (who are only fertile during certain periods) is quite common among humans (who are fertile year round and must use cultural means of population control). In fact, infanticide has probably been practiced in all culture areas at some point in their history (Devereaux 1967). In an introduction to a collection of articles on infanticide, Hausfater and Hrdy (1981) describe the recurring conditions under which infanticide often takes place. Infants are abandoned or killed when raising them would entail: 1) a risk to the well being of a sibling (as in birth spacing),2) expenditure of resources on an infant unlikely to survive, or 3) "undue" burden on the rest of the family such as the case of female infanticide where dowry payments are high or resources low.

It can be inferred that women are often involved in the abandonment or killing of the baby since most cultures forbid male presence during childbirth. But what are the feelings and attitudes of mothers who kill or abandon their babies? Are their actions undeterred by emotions or bonding? Ethnographies tell us little, perhaps because such data are difficult to obtain.

We might hypothesize that the infanticidal mother is expressing resentment against the new infant who is adding to her burdens or that an emotional detachment is evoked to permit her to abandon or kill her infant. Johnson described cases of native South American mothers who committed infanticide after a difficult birth or difficult pregnancy (1981). We also know that maternal detachment is sometimes facilitated by definition of an infant as nonhuman before a certain event takes place, such as the naming ceremony, the first birth cry, or breast feeding, depending on the culture. However, such data is balanced by reports of mothers deploring the necessity to kill closely spaced infants, as among the !Kung (Shostak 1981) or the joy of an Inuit Eskimo explaining that due to a mild winter they had enough food and would not have to abandon their new daughter (Condon 1987). It is also significant that infanticide is not generally correlated with child abuse. In fact, in Korbin's book on child abuse from a cross cultural perspective, most authors describe the absence of idiosyncratic abuse in pre-western contact conditions even where infanticide was generally practiced (1981). It is difficult to reach any conclusion because the data are so scanty. Even novels by natives, such as the books by Achebe describe maternal pain on the death of an infant, but do not describe feelings associated with "throwing twins into the forest" (e.g. 1959). [1]

We have a little more data on maternal attitudes in the cases of indirect infanticide or selective neglect. Nancy Scheper-Hughes offers some insight in her study of shantytown Brazilian mothers (1985). The group she studied had high rates of infant mortality which Scheper-Hughes attributed to conditions of poverty which in turn she suggested has caused maternal underinvestment. These Brazilian mothers nursed their infants for only a few months, rarely sought medical attention for failing infants and gave up on an infant which they deemed "doomed to die." Other authors describe similar situations among native South Americans (Johnson 1981), Australian Aborigines (Cowlishaw 1978) and Filipinos (Fernandez and Guthrie 1984). Dole describes an Amahuaca mother in Peru dealing with an infant who looked unlikely to survive. The mother ". . . frequently ignored its crying or shoved it impatiently away from her breast (Dole 1974:31 quoted in Johnson 1981:64).

How do these underinvesting mothers feel and how do they behave in less stressed circumstances? Scheper-Hughes interviewed mothers who, malnourished themselves, complained that they were physically drained by nursing, that the infants were sucking out their life blood. Yet, they expressed pity rather than anger for the dying infant whom they did not feel it was possible to save.

Their responses to the infants do not seem to reflect detachment, but rather a combined wish to mother with a wish to personally survive.

Maternal investment in children who do survive and the children's view of motherhood is expressed in a moving story related by Scheper-Hughes. In order to save a dying infant, who was neglected by its mother, Scheper-Hughes took it under her care and gave it food and medical attention. Before leaving Brazil she gave the fairly healthy infant back to his mother who raised him. Years later when Scheper-Hughes returned to her research site, she interviewed the now grown up young man whom she had rescued. Treating him the same as other interviewees, she asked him who was the most important person in his life. He easily responded that it was his mother who was always there to comfort and support him. This case is remarkably parallel to the biblical myths which describe maternal abandonment, miraculous intervention and maternal renewal.

Although the young man's response may have been shaped by a Brazilian ideology of self-sacrificing mothers more than his own experiences, this example and others similar to it, (e.g. Johnson 1981) force us to recognize a more complex picture of motherhood and maternal bonding than the data first suggested. In short we do not find a simple presence of or absence of bonding. A woman who abandons one baby, may lovingly raise another. An infant who is abandoned may be readmitted into the family. There is no easy dichotomy of "cruel stepmother" and "kindly" mother. Rather we see mothers trying to cope with the conflict between raising a child with all the burdens and joys it brings, and abandoning it, preserving resources for herself or her family.

Mother-Infant Bonding and Relationships

There are more data available on the nature of mother-infant relationships in less dramatic circumstances. However, where there are more data, there is also more disagreement. In regards to both African and Asian Indian cultures, quiet controversies have already developed on the evaluation of maternality (Kilbride and Kilbride 1983, Harkness and Super 1980 versus LeVine 1981; and Rohner and Chaki Sircar 1983 versus Seymour 1983). In order to address the disagreements, we can focus on two questions: 1) what is the nature of mother-child relationship (from the child's perspective, the mother's perspective and behaviorally) and 2) how do we measure the relationships?

The methodological question is the one which must be dealt with first. Are the discrepancies in the cross-cultural literature based on a) differences in the nature of maternal affect cross culturally or b) on differences in measurement of affect? Landy (1959) in a statement similar to that of LeVine (1981) suggests that what has passed for indulgence is often really casualness based on maternal indifference. In his study of child rearing in Puerto Rico, he quotes a mother as saying, "I am a woman who works much and I hardly have time for . . . entertaining *myself* with my children (1959:99). Yet his following description is a bevy of somewhat contradictory valuations of maternal nurturance. For example, he says that most mothers are responsive to their infants' crying, however, the responsiveness may be due to fears that crying will make the child sick. Then he says that

... considering their endless round of onerous and time-consuming tasks, these mothers give a fair amount of time to their infants ... though it is often a most cursory kind of attendance. However, a good deal of affection takes place ... but since this is traditional it is not surprising. ... These mothers are fairly warm towards their infants, though not excessively so. (Landy 1959:101).

These ambivalent descriptions continue on. Such data are difficult to evaluate. However, if we seek more methodologically rigorous studies, we find that as reliability goes up, validity does not necessarily do so. Ainsworth's (1967) study of Ugandan infants was described in the beginning of this paper. Although she found low levels of eye contact, nuzzling, or cuddling between mother and infant, she made observations only during formally scheduled interviews in which mothers were probably preoccupied more with the interview than with their infant. We may question even more seriously the validity of the data of those psychologists studying mother-infant bonding cross-culturally who attempt to create laboratory conditions in the field. For example, Dixon et. al. isolated a mother and infant, putting the infant in an unfamiliar infant seat and asked the mother to get her infant's attention for thirty minutes. Then the thirty minutes of mother-infant interaction were videoed and scored for number of predetermined types of interaction (1981).

Not only do we need more naturalistic studies which nevertheless incorporate some methodological rigor, but we also need a reconsideration of variables to be studied. Investigators have focused on mother-infant eye contact because eye contact is an important method of communication in our culture and has been emphasized by such psychologists as Daniel Stern as a fundamental factor in mother-infant bonding. Kissing and cuddling are often selected as behavioral units because they are deemed as indicators of affection in our culture. Few investigators attempt to discover emically defined measures of affect within a studied culture.

In addition to cultural biases, we also suffer from methodological biases. We prefer to use predetermined behavioral units which are easily countable. Yet to what extent are we measuring affect when we count how many times per hour a mother touches or looks at her child? Does our focus on sampling methods lead to a underestimate of types of mother-child interaction which do not occur in regularly spaced units of behavior? Don't we neglect quality time as simply mother and infant falling asleep together?

Alternative modes of mother-infant communication and expression of affect should be considered. Lewis and Ban (1977) in addition to time sampling of the usual six behaviors (hold, look, touch, smile, play, vocalize) studied mother-infant interaction. They counted how often a mother responded to an infant's behavior (smile, vocalization) with some gesture or look, and how often an infant responded to a mother. Although they found considerable frequency differences in behaviors between Zambian, Dutch, Senegalese, American, and Yugoslavian mothers, they found a similar pattern of interaction across these cultures. They wonder whether more similarities would not be found if more "proper" (p. 353) variables were used. (see also Fajardo and Freeman (1981) study of rhythmicity in mother-infant interaction).

If we agree that we must broaden our range of behaviors studied in order to avoid ethnocentric measures (as well as judgments), in what direction should we go? I think the answer is offered to us in the findings of several studies that technological societies focus on distal forms of communication between mother and infant, such as looking, smiling, and vocalizing, while nontechnological societies focus on proximal modes such as holding, touching, and stroking (Brazelton 1977, Goldberg 1977, et. al. though cf. Kohner's study of the !Kung 1977). Because of our own familiarity with distal forms of communication we have neglected communications which occur in the holding, touching, feeling kinesthetic sphere and do not apply the appropriate measures of such types of communication. The awareness of the significance of nonverbal communication is growing much faster than our methods for measuring it. Its importance is signified not only in reports of high degree of holding in nontechnological societies (and a need to understand the affects involved), but also in reports such as the one of an Inuit (Eskimo) boy that although he never shared his fears and hopes with his parents, never discussed with them his life and what he would become, he communicated with them in other ways. Working together, sharing the same room, they developed a sense of each other and belonging that was never communicated verbally (Condon 1987).

It is difficult to redefine affect in a less culture bound way. Our culture influences both the way in which mother-infant bonding takes place as well as the way we perceive it taking place. Since American mothers have relatively low amounts of physical contact with their infants, it is likely that we will be more aware of and focus more on distal forms of interrelating, rather than kinesthetic ones.

Furthermore, our evaluation of kinesthetic relationships is often culture bound. When I showed a film of Ibo mothers of Nigeria bathing infants to an audience of movement therapists in the United States, they almost uniformly judged the mothers low on affect because they handled the young infants without giving any head support and with seeming unconcern for the infant's "obvious" distress (being in almost continual startle reflex, though not crying). However, an Ibo mother who viewed the same film said that she could not judge the mothers' affect from the film because this is how all mothers bathe babies among the Ibo. She did not judge the infants to be in distress-"They're not crying, are they?" she pointed out.

It is difficult to evaluate forms of bonding and separating in other cultures. As Benedict pointed out, members of nonwestern cultures have been horrified by our abrupt separation of mothers and infants at birth and by our isolation of infants in their own beds and own rooms (1932). On the other hand, we tend to condemn the abrupt weaning practiced among such cultures as the Mundurucu of South America. Clearly we cannot discover much about mother-infant bonding and interrelationships in other cultures if we take our measures only from our own cultural repertoires. The central message of anthropology has been that we must not try to understand a behavior in isolation from its culture context. For example, as the Kilbrides pointed out, private sphere behaviors of mothers may differ considerably from their public sphere behaviors (1983). As suggested in the Whiting and Whiting Six Cultures project, behavior should be observed in its natural setting (1975).

The use of multiple measures in the study of mother-infant affect may help reduce the more serious methodological problems. A quantifiable standardized method with a low amount of cultural bias, such as the Kestenberg Movement Profile may be combined with informal interviewing of mothers and children and participation-observation techniques.[2]

Going beyond methodological problems, what can we say about the nature of motherhood within the presently available literature?

1. We find that there is some variation in the course of development of affect. Although Bowlby has suggested the importance of the immediate post partum period for optimal bonding, (1973), it appears that bonding may begin earlier or later depending on cultural and individual circumstances. For example, in many cultures Praise from kin and friends and early fetal movements may serve as early mechanisms for bonding. However in some cultures, e.g. among the Ifaluk, early fetal movements are not recognized and the first movements of the baby are taken as indications of the onset of labor (Lutz 1988). This difference in mother-fetus relations itself is an interesting topic for further investigation.

In some cultures early bonding is postponed and the new infant is not accepted as human until after a specified event has taken place (as we described earlier). Among the Machiguenga of South America, the mother shows "a certain degree" (Johnson 1981:63) of indifference to the baby after birth. After the mother is attended to, then it is decided whether the baby should be raised or not. It is said that only after the mother nurses the child, which may not be until the next day, does she develop an attachment to it. A similar situation exists in several other cultures (e.g. among the Mohave Devereux 1961). The mother's own physical and emotional well-being appears to be a precondition for bonding (Brazelton 1976).

Just as cultural rules may encourage a delay in bonding, they also may facilitate the development of bonding after the child is incorporated into the society. Mothers are often secluded in huts or special rooms with the new infant for a specified period. Although this is generally explained as part of menstrual taboos, it also has the effect of giving the mother undisturbed time with her new infant. This seclusion may last a few days, such as among the Mundurucu (Murphy 1985), or for extended periods, such as among the Kalapalo (Bosso 1973). However extended periods may also emphasize the burdens of child rearing. Among the Ifaluk of Micronesia, mothers often express bad feelings towards their infants during their period of seclusion. They apparently complain about not being able to tend their gardens or other chores. However, the Ifaluk do not blame the mother for her ill temperament, but rather the others who have not offered her sufficient help (Lutz 1988).

2. In ethnographies (in contrast to controlled psychological investigations) where maternal attitudes are considered, there is often indication of mixed emotions towards the role of motherhood. Like the Mundurucu (Murphy 1985), mothers of many cultures express pleasure with having children but dismay with having too many. When mothers are pulled between the needs of child care and of subsistence activities, the latter generally is given preference. For example, Nerlove has found a positive correlation cross-culturally between the early use of supplementary feeding and women's involvement in subsistence agriculture (1974). The conflict between the two important female roles, of food provider and mother can lead to use of alternate caretakers which is sometimes taken as an indication of emotional detachment, but should be seen in terms of resolving the problems of conflicting roles (a problem which rests primarily on women).

Mothers are also heard to voice resentment against the physical burden of pregnancy, breast feeding, and child care as in the case of the impoverished Brazilians (Scheper-Hughes 1983). One

Zoroastrian woman I interviewed in Iran remembered her first experience of motherhood as a coming of age experience. Secluded in a small room with her new infant, she moaned about the cold and the pain of her breasts. "I was so young," she said, "only a child myself, what was I doing with a baby?" Her sister-in-law told her husband of her complaints and he angrily sent her the message that he would bring up the baby without her. She smiled at the memory: "Well," I asked her, "did you give him the baby?" "I was tempted," she told me, "but then my milk came in and no, I did not give up the baby. I was the one who had the milk it wanted."

She had thought of abandonment, but her milk had come in-a miraculous intervention—like in the myths. When she recalled the death of her infant later, she appeared to do so without any emotion. "Weren't you upset?" I asked her.

"I was too young to understand death," she answered, applying to herself a common Iranian view that children are not scarred by early trauma.

In such cases it may be difficult to distinguish between feigned and real indifference, just as it is at times hard to differentiate neglect from permissiveness. A Yanomomo mother threatened her small child who was climbing about on her in their hammock, "Be quiet or the leopard will eat you."

As the author says, "She nevertheless spreads the hammock so that the child can make herself comfortable." (Lizot 1976:74). Her message to the child is an ambivalent though common one. As is frequently the case the verbal message and the kinesthetic one are in conflict. To perceive the whole message, we must be aware of both levels of communication.

I began this paper with an attempt to evaluate the disagreement between the Kilbrides and the LeVines on the nature of early mother-infant relationships. It is easier to reach conclusions concerning methodological problems than to resolve the substantive issues of their dispute. The frequency of reported maternal indifference to infants, particularly in South America and in subsaharan Africa makes it likely that some form of maternal detachment does occur at least in some periods of early mother-infant relationship-though we must keep our methodological reservations in mind. However, case studies, such as that of Scheper-Hughes, Johnson, and my own, offer evidence of recurring ambivalence, or positive attachment counterbalanced by negative withdrawal. It seems that the ambivalent portrait of motherhood conveyed to us in mythology corresponds to the experiences of motherhood in most cultures. It is displayed not only in cases of a mother who may kill one infant and nurture another, or a mother who may neglect an infant who fails to thrive and then devote herself to another, but ambivalence is also expressed in the daily treatment of each infant who experiences the mother's approach and withdrawal in various stages of their relationship.

However, a better understanding of variations in expression of affect or detachment awaits collection of data which does not exclude kinesthetic and other perhaps as yet unknown methods of mother-infant communication.

Notes

1. An unpublished interview by one of my students, with an Ibo woman however, offers considerable insight. The Ibo woman relates that when twins were born, it was (is?) customary for the mother to leave them alone in the

home where they would be found and disposed of by disguised members of the community so that the mother would not know who killed her children. The mother of the interviewee, a strong Christian convert, offered to adopt these children with the mother's permission. She relates that most mothers helped her to run off with the babies before the disguised Ibo arrived. Unfortunately, like most other data the information is anecdotal and in this case third hand.

2. Many authors are aware of the problems with using predefined behavior lists. As Goldberg (1977) says there may be other ways that feelings can be expressed. Lewis and Ban (1977) point out that there can be different kinds of holding. I would like to propose the use of the Kestenberg Movement Profile, a method of movement notation and analysis which breaks up movements into fifty components and also measures the flow of tension changes in muscles. Not relying on culturally defined movements it is relatively culture free. Since most of the movements studied are not consciously produced, it is also less troubled by observer effect. Movement profiles can be made from films of mothers and infants which provide good sampling of the movement day. Although the profile is primarily known among dance therapists, it would be a addition to the anthropological tool kit.

References

Achebe, Chinua (1957). *Thing Fall Apart.* New York: Fawcett Crest.

Ainsworth, M. (1967). *Infancy in Uganda: Infant Care and the Growth of Love.* Baltimore: John Hopkins Press.

Benedict, Ruth (1932). "Configurations of Culture in North America," *American Anthropologist* 34:1-27.

Brazelton, T. (1977). "Implications of infant development among the Mayan Indians of Mexico," in *Culture and Infancy Variations in the Human Experience.* P. Leiderman, S. Tulkin and A. Rosenfeld eds. New York: Academic Press, 151-188.

Bowlby, John (1973). *Attachment and Loss.* 2 vols. New York: Basic Books.

Campbell, J. (1988). *The Power of Myth.* New York: Doubleday.

Colum, P. (1930). *Orpheus: Myths of the World.* New York: McMillan.

Condon, R. (1987). *Inuit Youth: Growth and Change in the Canadian* New Brunswick: Rutgers Univ. Press.

Devereux, George (1961). *Mohave Ethnopsychiatry and Suicide.* Bulletin no. 175, Bureau of American Ethnology, Wash. D.C.

Devereux, George (1967). *From Anxiety to Method in the Behavioral Sciences.* The Hague: Mouton.

Dixon, S. Tronick, E., Keefer, C. and Brazelton, T. (1981). "Mother-Infant Interaction among the Gusii of Kenya," in *Culture and Early Interactions*, eds. T. Field, A. Sostek, P. Vietze and P. Leiderman, Hillsdale, New Jersey Lawrence Erlbaum Assoc.

Draper, P. (1972). *!Kung Bushman Childhood.* Unpubl. Doc. Diss.

Fajardo, B. and Freeman, D. (1981). "Maternal Rhythmicity in Three American Cultures," in *Culture and Early Interactions, op. cit.*

Fernandez, E. and Guthrie, G. (1984). "Belief Systems of and Breast Feeding Among the Filipino Urban Poor," *Social Science and Medicine* 19(9): 991-5.

Gilmore, D. (1986). "Mother-Son Intimacy and the Dual View of Women in Andalusia," *Ethos* 14(2):227-

Goldberg, S. (1977). "Infant Development and Mother-Infant Interaction in Urban Zambia," in *Culture and Infancy: op. cit.* pp. 211-

Harkness, S. and Super, C. (1980). "Child Development Theory in Anthropological Perspective," in *New Directions for Child Development*. C. Super, S. Harkness eds. San Francisco: Jossey-Bass Inc.

Hausfater, C. and Hrdy, S. (1984). *Infanticide. Evolutionary Perspectives,* New York: Aldine Press.

Hinnells, J. (1985). *Persian Mythology*. New York: Peter Bedrick Books.

Johnson, O. (1981). "The Socioeconomic Context of Child Abuse and Neglect in Native South America," in *Child Abuse and Neglect in Cross Cultural Perspectives*. J. Korbin ed. Los Angeles: Calif. Univ. Press, pp. 56-70.

Kestenberg, J., Kestenberg M., and Kestenberg, Amighi (1988). "The Nazis' Quest for Death and the Jewish Quest for Life," *Psychological Perspectiues of the Holocaust and its Aftermath*, R. Brahm ed. New York: Social Science Monographs, pp. 13-44.

Kilbride, P., and Kilbride, J. (1983). "Socialization for High Positive Affect between Mother and Infant Among the Baganda of Uganda," *Ethos* II(4): 232

Konner, Melvin (1977). "Infancy Among the Kalahari Desert San," in *Culture and Infancy op. cit.* pp. 287-328.

Korbin, Jill (1981) *Child Abuse and Neglect Cross Cultural Perspectives*. Los Angeles: Univ. Calif. Press.

Landy, D. (1959) *Tropical Childhood Cultural Transmission and Learning in a Rural Puerto Rican Village*. New York: Univ. N. Carolina Press.

LeVine, Robert (1977) "Child Rearing as Cultural Adaptation," in *Culture and Infancy op. cit* pp. 15-28.

LeVine, S., and LeVine, R. (1981). "Child Abuse and Neglect in Subsaharan Africa," in *Child Abuse and Neglect, op. cit*. pp. 35-56.

Lewis, M. and Ban, P. (1977). "Variance and Invariances in the Mother-Infant Interaction" A Cross Cultural Study," in *Culture and Infancy op. cit*. pp. 329

Lizot, Jacques (1985). *Tales of the Yanomami* New York: Cambridge Univ. Press.

Lutz, C. (1988). *Unnatural Emotions*, Chicago: University Chicago Press.

Martin, E. (1987). *The Woman in the Body: A Cultural Analysis of Reproduction,* Boston: Beacon Press.

Minturn, L. and Lambert, W. (1964). *Mothers of Six Cultures*. New York: Wiley and Sons.

Murphy, Y. and Murphy, R. (1985). *Women of the Forest,* New York: Columbia University Press.

Osborne, H. (1968). *South American Mythology*. Middlesex: Hamyln Publ.

Parrinder, G. (1967). *African Mythology,* London: Paul Hamyln.

Rohner, R. and Chaki-sircar, M. (1983). "Caste Differences in Perceived Maternal Acceptance in West Bengal, India," *Ethos* 15(2): 406-

Scheper-Hughes, Nancy (1985). Culture, Scarcity and Maternal Thinking," *Ethos* 13 (1): 291 -

Seymour, S. (1983). "Household Structure and Status and Expression of Affect In India,"*Ethos* 11(4) 263-

Shostak, M. (1983). *Nisa: The Life and Words of a !Kung Woman*. New York: Vintage Books.

Walker, B. (1968). *The Woman's Encyclopedia of Myths and Secrets,* New York: Harper and Row publ.

Whiting, B. and Whiting, J. (1975). *Children of Six Cultures*. Harvard: Harvard Univ. Press.

Zipes, Jack (1986). *Don't Bet on the Prince,* New York: Methuen.

FATHERHOOD IN CROSS-CULTURAL PERSPECTIVE

Barry S. Hewlett
Washington State University

Despite a steady increase in the quantity and quality of studies of infants, young children and mother-hood in non-Western populations (Munroe and Munroe 1971; Whiting and Whiting 1975; Draper 1976; Konner 1977; Chisholm 1981; Super and Harkness 1982), we know relatively little about the nature of fatherhood in non-Western contexts (see Hewlett 1992 for some exceptions). Theoretical orientations, field methodologies and the nature of father-infant interactions have resulted in an emphasis on mother's role and a lack of data and understanding of men as fathers. Mother-oriented theories of infant and child development have guided cross-cultural research. The child development theories of Ainsworth (1967), Bowlby (1969), Freud (1938), and Harlow (1961) which have generated much of the cross-cultural research, all view the motherinfant relationship as the prototype for subsequent attachments and relationships. According to Freud and Bowlby, for instance, one had to have a trusting, unconditional relationship with his or her mother in order to become a mentally healthy adult. These influential theorists generally believed that the father's role was not a factor in the child's development until the Oedipal stage (three-to-five years old). The field methods to study infancy cross-culturally reflected this theoretical emphasis on mother. Behavioral observations were either infant or mother-focused and conducted only during daylight hours; father-focused and evening observations were not considered. The mother or infant-focused daylight observations thus neglected father's care of other children and father's activities with his own infant in the early evening hours before bed or during the night. Also, standardized questionnaires and psychological tests were generally administered only to mother. One consistent result from the cross-cultural studies was that fathers provided substantially less direct care to infants than mothers. In fact, all cross-cultural studies to date indicate that a number of other female caretakers (older female siblings, aunts, grandmothers) provide more direct care to infants than do fathers. Since fathers are not as conspicuous as mothers and other females during daylight hours researchers tend to emphasize a "deficit" model of fathers (Cole and Bruner 1974). Researchers do not know much about father's role and therefore simply claim that it is minimal. These factors have contributed to the complete absence of systematic studies of fatherhood in non-Western societies.

Given the paucity of systematic research in non-Western societies on father's interactions with children, it is ironic that this variable (i.e., the degree of father vs. mother involvement with children) should be so consistently invoked as an explanatory factor in the literature. It is hypothesized to be related, for example, to universal sexual asymmetry (Rosaldo and Lamphere 1974); variations in sexual dimorphism (Wilson 1975); the origins of the human family (Lancaster and Lancaster 1987);

male and female reproductive strategies (Draper and Harpending 1982); contemporary patterns of gender-activity differentiation (Brown 1970; Burton, Brudner and White 1977); the association of males with culture and females with nature (Ortner 1974); smooth functioning of the family (Zelditch 1955); and proper moral development (Hoffman 1981).

This paper seeks to partially remedy this shortcoming by summarizing a detailed study of fatherhood in one hunter-gatherer population, the Aka of Central Africa, and then placing the Aka study into cross-cultural perspective.

An Overview of Aka Life and Culture

The Aka fatherhood is embedded within a cultural nexus—it influences and is influenced by a cultural system. It is therefore necessary to provide a brief overview of Aka life and culture before describing Aka fatherhood. Greater ethnographic detail on the Aka can be found in Hewlett (1991) and Bahuchet (1985).

The Aka are hunter-gatherers of the tropical rain forests of southern Central African Republic and northern Congo-Brazzaville. They live in camps of 25-35 people and move camp every two weeks to two months. Each nuclear family has a hut, and each camp generally has 5-8 huts arranged in a circle. The circle of huts is about 12 meters in diameter and each hut IS about 1.5 meters in diameter. Each hut has one bed of leaves or logs on which everyone in the family sleeps. The Aka have patriclans and many members of a camp belong to the same patriclan (generally a camp consists of brothers, their wives and children, and unrelated men who are doing bride service for the sisters of the men in camp). The Aka have high fertility and mortality rates: A woman generally has 5-6 children during her lifetime and one-fifth of the infants die before reaching 12 months and a further 23 percent of children die before reaching 15 years.

The physical and social setting of Aka parent-infant relations can be inferred from the above discussion of Aka settlement and demography. The infant lives with a relatively small group of individuals related through his/her father (unless the infant is the first born in which case the family is likely to be in the camp of the wife for the purposes of bride service) and sleeps in the same bed as mother, father and other brothers and sisters. Life in the camp is rather intimate. While the overall population density is quite low (less than one person per square km), living space is quite dense. Three or four people sleep together on the same bed and neighbors are just a few feet away. The 25-35 camp members live in an area about the size of a large Euroamerican living room. The Aka home represents the "public" part of life, while time outside of camp tends to be relatively "private." This is the reverse of the Euroamerican pattern (i.e., home is usually considered private). The camp is relatively young as half of the members of the camp are under fifteen and most women have a nursing child throughout their childbearing years.

The Aka net hunt most of the year. Men, women and children participate in the net hunt. Nets are set up in a semi-circle, men go to the center of the nets and women stay near the net. When a sound is given men in the center of the nets start to shout and pound the ground with logs to flush out and scare the game (primarily antelopes) into the nets. Women have the role of tackling the game in the net and killing the animal. Game captured is eventually shared with everyone in camp. Some parts of the game animal are smoked and eventually traded to Bantu and Sudanic farmers for manioc or other domesticate foods. Aka utilize a diversity of other hunting techniques when the net hunt is not possible (e.g., cross-bow, spear, small traps). Any game captured with these other techniques is shared with everyone in camp. The Aka have strong economic and religious ties to the tropical forest. The forest is perceived as provider and called friend, lover, mother or father.

The high fertility and the nature of the net hunt directly influences parentinfant relations. High fertility means most women carry an infant or young child during their reproductive years. Net hunting entails walking 8-12 km per day which means a woman is unable to rely upon an older sibling to help with infant or child care because older siblings cannot carry infants long distances. Sibling caregivers are common in horticultural societies where child caregiver can sit and watch the infant while mother works in the field. Since most other women have children to carry and siblings are not available, fathers or adult men are generally the only other alternative caregivers on the net hunt.

The Aka are fiercely egalitarian. They have a number of mechanisms to maintain individual, intergenerational and sexual equality. Three of the mechanisms are prestige avoidance, rough joking and demand sharing. Aka try to avoid drawing attention to oneself, even if one has killed an elephant or cured someone's life-threatening illness. If an individual does boast about his/her abilities it is possible that s/he could share less or request more from others in the belief that s/he was better than others. If an individual does start to draw attention to oneself others in the camp will use rough and crude jokes, often about the boastful person's genitals, in order to get the individual to be more modest about their abilities. Demand sharing also helps to maintain egalitarianism; if an individual likes or wants something (cigarettes, necklace, shirt) of another he simply asks for it, and the person generally gives it to him/her. Demand sharing promotes the circulation of scarce material goods (e.g., shoes, shirt, necklaces, spear points) in the camp.

The rough joking mentioned above is also linked to another feature of Aka culture—playfulness. There is no clear separation between "work" and "play" time. Dances, singing, net hunting, male circumcision, sorcery accusations all include humorous mimicking, practical jokes and exaggerated storytelling. Aka life is informal because of egalitarianism and the playful activity that occurs throughout the day by both adults and children. Play is an integral part of both adult and child life and contributes to enhanced parent-child and adult-child communication. Parents and adults have an extensive repertoire of play and can and do communicate cultural knowledge to children through their playful repertoire.

The Aka husband-wife relationship is distinctive by cross-cultural standards and is important for understanding Aka fatherhood. Aka husband-wife relations are exceptional by cross-cultural standards because they spend so much time together cooperating in a number of different activities. Most of the year husband and wife cooperate on the net hunt. The couple sets up the net together, cooperate to get the game into their net, share in the butchering of the animal and rest together between casts of the nets. While there are clearly male and female roles on the net hunt, role reversals take place daily and individuals are not stigmatized for taking the roles of the opposite sex. If one does the task poorly, regardless of whether it is a masculine or feminine task, then one is open to joking and teasing by others (e.g., when the anthropologist chases the game in the wrong direction). When net hunting is not possible due to rain or other social or environmental reasons, husband and wife engage in other cooperative activities (collecting caterpillars, honey, mushrooms, nuts and fruits). Husband and wife also spend considerable leisure time together socializing, dancing and singing. Husband and wife also eat together and sleep in the same small bed. There is not other culture in which husband and wife spend so much time together and regularly engage in cooperative activity (Hewlett 1991 b).

Finally, since the Aka study focuses on Aka fathers and their infants it is important to make a few general comments about Aka infany. Cultural practices during infancy are quite distinct from those found in Euroamerican cultures. Aka parents are indulgent; the infant is held almost constantly, nursed on demand (breast-fed several times per hour), attended to immediately if she/he fusses, and is seldom, if ever, told "no! no!" if they misbehave (e.g., get into food pots, hit others or take things from other children). Older infants (8-12 months) are given considerable freedom to crawl around the hut and camp. They are allowed to use and play with knives, machetes and other "adult" items. They are allowed to crawl into a parent's lap while the parent is engaged in economic (e.g., butchering animal, repairing net, etc.) or leisure (e.g., playing a harp or drum) activity. While older infants are given considerable freedom to explore the house and camp, parents do watch infants to make sure they do not crawl into the fire.

While in the camp there is extensive multiple caregiving of 1-4 month-old infants (Hewlett 1989). Mother holds the infant only 40 percent of the time and the infant is transferred to individuals 7.3 times per hour. Mothers' holding increases to 85 percent and the transfer rate drops to 2 transfers per hour outside of the camp (i.e., on net hunt or in fields).

Aka infants are seldom placed in the care of older siblings. Older siblings or children in the group are not given the responsibility of caring for infants as is found in many non-Western farming communities (Weisner and Gallimore 1977).

Aka infancy is very active and stimulating. Infants are taken on the hunt and are seldom laid down. They are held on the side of the caregiver rather than the back as in many farming communities so there is extensive opportunity for parent-infant face-to-face interaction and communication. The infant can also breast feed by simply grabbing the mother's breast and can breast feed while mother walks. While out on the net hunt the infant will sleep in the infant sling. Aka therefore experience extensive vestibular stimulation as described by Konner (1976) among the !Kung San. Developmental testing of Aka infants indicates that they are mildly precocious in their motor and cognitive development (Neuwelt-Truntzer 1981).

Methods for Aka Study

Both quantitative and qualitative methods were utilized to investigate Aka fatherhood. A quantitative study of 15 Aka families with infants utilized all-day (6 A.M. to 6 P.M.) and partial-day (evening observations) infant and father focal behavioral observational techniques to measure the amount and nature of mothers' and fathers' infant caregiving. In order to elicit Aka conceptions and feelings about fatherhood and motherhood, structured questionnaires and unstructured interviews were conducted with adults, adolescents and young children (see Hewlett 1991a for greater detail on methodology).

The Aka study focused on the following questions:

1.   Degree of father involvement

    a.   How often do fathers actually interact with their infants?

    b.   How often are fathers available to their infants?

    c.   If fathers are not involved with infants what other activities are they involved in?

    d.   How do children characterize the nature of their involvement with their father?

2.   Paternal versus maternal parenting style

    a.   Are there distinctions between the mother's and the father's play behavior with their infants?

    b.   Do mothers and fathers hold their infants for different purposes?

    c.   What do mothers and fathers do while they hold the infant?

d.   Do infants show different types of attachment behavior to mothers and fathers?

e.   How do children view their mother's and father's parenting styles?

General Results

Degree of father involvement

1.   Aka fathers provided more direct care and were proximal to their infants more than fathers in any other human population that has been investigated. Aka fathers were within an arms reach (i.e., holding or within one meter) of their infant more than 50 percent of a 24 hour period and Aka fathers held their very young infants during the day at least five times more than fathers in other human populations. Fathers, on average, held their infants about one hour per 12 hours of daylight observation. Father care increased dramatically in the evening hours. While Aka father care was extensive, it was also highly context dependent—fathers provided at least four

times as much care while they were in the camp setting than they did while out of camp engaged in economic activity (e.g., out on the net hunt or in the villagers' fields).

2. Aka conceptions of good and bad fathers reiterated the importance of father's proximity—a good father showed love (affection) for his children, stayed near them, and assisted mother with caregiving when her workload was heavy. A bad father abandoned his children and did not share food with them.

3. Greater availability was not related to greater father caregiving. Fathers in the village did just as much caregiving as fathers in the forest even though they were much less available during the day.

4. Time allocation data indicated that fathers who did considerable direct caregiving as well as those who did little caregiving spent similar amounts of time in subsistence and manufacturing activities, but fathers who did less caregiving spent more time visiting and talking with other males. Aka fathers less involved in direct caretaking spent more time in "status maintenance."

Father's and Mother's Style of Caregiving

1. Unlike the U.S. fathers, Aka fathers were not the vigorous, rough and tumble playmates of their infants. Only one episode of vigorous play by a father was recorded during all 264 hours of systematic observation.

2. Mothers were most likely to provide nourishment and transport infants while they were holding, while fathers were more likely to hug, kiss, or soothe a fussy infant as they were holding. Mothers were most likely to pick up an infant to feed the infant while fathers were most likely to pick up an infant because the infant crawled or reached for the father (i.e., infant requested to be held by father).

The Aka Results in Cross-Cultural Perspective

Theories Utilized to Explain Cross-Cultural Variability in the Level of Father Involvement

Why do fathers in some cultures do more than fathers in other cultures? Evolutionary ecologists have explained intercultural variation in the level of father involvement by identifying three critical factors: distribution of females (Emlen and Oring 1977), paternal certainty (Hartung 1983), and possible ontogenetic factors (Draper and Harpending 1982). According to Emlen and Oring (1977), when females are in a concentrated area (city or village), the fitness benefits associated with male mating efforts (defending food patches, defending and maintaining a mate, and intrasexual competition) may be high in relation to direct paternal care. In situations where females are widely dispersed (hunter-gatherer camps), Emlen and Oring predict less intrasexual competition and greater paternal care.

Paternity certainty is an important factor for evolutionary ecologists. Malefemale sexual relations in some cultures are relatively permissive. Women may have many lovers, social paternity is important, divorce rates high and extramarital sex common. In such cultures, evolutionary ecologists would predict that direct father involvement would be low because the father would have low paternity certainty. In societies where fathers are relatively certain about paternity, they would predictably invest more time in childcare.

Draper and Harpending (1982) suggest that there is a "sensitive period" at one to five years of age, where boys and girls learn a reproductive and parenting strategy. A boy who sees his mother and father together during this sensitive period would learn that a mate is stable, and therefore would have a reproductive strategy that focused on providing for his mate and offspring. A boy with low father salience during early childhood would learn that mates are not stable and would develop a reproductive strategy to deal with male-male competition for mates (e.g., verbal abilities). Due to this perception of an unstable relationship as an adult he would be less likely to invest time in childcare. Generally, males in matrifocal female farming societies tend to exhibit reproductive strategies that emphasize the male-male competition and de-emphasize childcare.

> Male children born into matrifocal households exhibit at adolescence a complex of aggression, competition, low male parental investment and derogation of females and femininity (while) male children reared in father-present or nuclear household show less interest in competitive dominance with other males and more interest in manipulation of nonhuman aspects of the environment. (1982: 255)

Cultural ecologists have implicated two other factors influencing intercultural variability in the level of father involvement: land availability (Goody 1973) and female contribution to subsistence (Katz and Konner 1981). Goody (1973) compares Eurasian cultures with those of sub-Sahara African and suggests that in Eurasian cultures population density is greater, land availability lower, and social stratification greater than in the sub-Saharan cultures. One consequence of these differences is that Eurasian societies usually practiced dowry which became part of the conjugal fund that the husband controlled. Men in Eurasian societies, Goody suggests, exercised greater control over women's lives, which often meant that men did less childcare.

Katz and Konner's (1981) cross-cultural study found that when women contributed more to subsistence than men, men were more likely to engage in childcare. They suggest that in such cases women would ask them to help with childcare more often.

Social anthropologists have identified three other factors that may predict intercultural variability in the level of father involvement: warfare, level of polygyny in a society (Katz and Konner 1981), and ideology. Katz and Konner found that fathers in societies that practiced warfare were less proximal (physical and emotional proximity) to their children than fathers in societies that did not practice warfare. The level of polygyny is also statistically related to father proximity; fathers in polygynous societies are less proximal to children than fathers in monogamous societies, supposedly because the polygynous father has to divide his time between more children .

Some anthropologists have examined the symbolic nature of fathers within various cultures and have found that certain societies have "earth" fathers in their mythology, while in other societies fathers are more likely to be associated with the "sky" (Coleman 1981). Fathers belonging to the former type are more likely to participate in childcare.

Aka Father's Level of Involvement in Cross-Cultural Perspective

Aka father involvement in infancy is exceptional, if not unique, by crosscultural standards. Tables 1 and 2 place Aka fathers holding and availability in a cross-cultural context. Aka fathers hold their infants and are around their children more than twice as often as fathers in other societies where comparable data exist. Studies of middle class Euroamerican fathers indicate they hold or interact with their infants less than 15 minutes per day during daylight hours (Lamb et al. 1987). Euroamerican fathers also seldom near their infants during the day or sleep with them during the night. Why do Aka fathers do so much more caregiving than fathers in other societies? What factors influence the variability demonstrated in Tables 1 and 2?

Like many other foragers, the Aka have few accumulable resources that are essential for survival. Males essentially inherit a most important resource, brothers. Aka males and females also contribute a similar percentage of calories to the diet. In societies unlike the Aka, where resources essential to survival can be accumulated or where males are the primary contributors to subsistence, evolutionary biologists would predict that fathers would invest more time competing for these resources and, consequently, less time with their children. In contrast, where resources are not accumulable or men are not the primary contributors to subsistence, men generally would spend more time in the direct care of their children. Holocultural and field studies tend to support this hypothesis. Katz and Konner (1981: 174) found that father-infant proximity (degree of emotional warmth and physical proximity) is closest in gatheringhunting populations (gathered foods by females are principal resources, meat is secondary) and most distant in cultures where herding or advanced agriculture is practiced. In the latter cultures, cattle, camels, and land are considered the essential accumulable resources necessary for survival. These findings are consistent with Whiting and Whiting's (1975) holocultural study of husband-wife intimacy. They found husband-wife intimacy to be greatest in cultures without accumulated resources or capital investments. While there are other factors to consider (the protection of resources and polygyny rate), there is a strong tendency for fathers/husbands to devote more time to their children/wives if there are no accumulable resources. Table 2 supports the holocultural findings that fathers in societies with accumulable resources, are less likely to spend time near children than fathers in societies where there are few accumulable resources and where men contribute less to the diet than females.

Table 1. Comparison of father holding in selected foraging populations

Population	Age of infants (months)	Father holding (% of time)	Source
Gidgingali	0-6	3.4	Hamilton (1981)
	6-18	3.1	
!Kung	0-6	1.9	West and Konner (1976)
	6-24	4.0	
Efe Pygmies	1-4	2.6	Winn et al. (1990)
Aka Pygmies	1-4	22.0	Hewlett (1991)
	8-18	14.0	

NOTE: All observations were made in a camp setting (Table from Hewlett 1991)

Table 2. Comparison of father presence with infants or children among selected foraging and farming populations

Population	Location	Subsistence	% time Father Present/In View	Primary setting of observations	Source
Gusil	Kenya	farming	10	house/yard & garden	1
Mixteca	Mexico	farming	9	house/yard	1
Ilocano	Philippines	farming	14	house/yard	1
Okinawan	Japan	farming	3	public places & house/yard	1
Rajput	India	farming	3	house/yard	1
!Kung	Botswana	foraging	30	camp	2
Aka Pygmies	Central African Republic	foraging	88	forest camp	3
Logoli	Kenya	farming	5	house/yard	4
Newars	Nepal	farming	7	house/yard	4
Samoans	Samoa	farming	8	house/yard	4
Carib	Belize	farming	3	house/yard	4
Ifaluk	Micronesia	farm-fish	13	house/yard	5

Sources (Table from Hewlett 1991):
1. Whiting and Whiting 1975
2. West and Konner 1976
3. Hewlett 1991
4. Munroe and Munroe 1990
5. Betzig, Harrigan and Turke 1990

Katz and Konner also found that in societies where hunting by men was the primary mode of subsistence (hunter-gatherers not gatherer-hunters), father-infant proximity was distant. This is consistent with recent field studiesconducted among Ache foragers. Meat and honey collected by Ache men represent the majority of calories consumed (Hill and Kaplan 1988), and Ache fathers hold their children on average only ten minutes per day (Hill et al., 1985). This is the lowest amount of paternal holding recorded for a foraging population that has been quantitatively investigated; no other population where males contribute the majority of subsistence foods has been intensively investigated.

While the above hypothesis correctly predicts differences between intensive farmers and gatherers, and between hunter-gatherers and gatherer-hunters, it is not useful for predicting intercultural variability among foraging populations where females contribute significantly to the diet (gatherer-hunters, such as Efe Pygmies of Zaire and !Kung of the Kalahari). Table 1 demonstrates some of the variability in direct paternal care of infants in societies that have been quantitatively investigated and where females contribute significantly to the diet. Among the Efe and !Kung, females contribute more calories than males (Lee 1979; Peacock 1985), whereas Aka men and women contribute nearly equal amounts. Men in all three societies are not responsible for the majority of the calories consumed and there are no accumulable resources essential for survival. Consequently, these fathers may have more time to invest in the direct care of infants than the Ache fathers. Females in these populations would also benefit by selecting males who would be willing and capable of doing childcare since women are less dependent on men for subsistence. But if the above hypothesis were sensitive to intra-gatherer variation, it would predict that Aka fathers should spend less time with infants than is indicated, since Aka men contribute more to subsistence than Efe or !Kung fathers (Aka males contribute 50% of calories to diet, Efe males 35%, and !Kung males 45%).

The comparative data call into question another factor that is often cited when predicting the level of father involvement: female contribution to subsistence (Katz and Konner 1981). If mothers are busy and contribute the essential resources to the diet this hypothesis predicts that they would call on fathers to help in childcare. Again, if this were so, Efe and !Kung mothers should be getting more infant care from their husbands than Aka mothers.

Other factors often cited as influencing the level of paternal involvement are not useful in explaining intracultural variability among foragers where females contribute the majority of the resources. Paternity certainty, sex-ratio, and level of polygyny are important factors for evolutionary ecologists and cultural anthropologists but they do not help explain why Aka fathers do substantially more direct caretaking than Efe or !Kung fathers. Based on blood analysis, paternity certainty is known to be high for both !Kung and Aka, therefore it is not helpful in explaining differences in paternal care between these two groups. The sex-ratio for individuals over fifteen years of age is 0.86 for !Kung (Lee 1979: 48),1.10 for Efe (Bailey and Peacock 1988), and 0.90 for Aka. Evolutionary biologists might suggest that if there are many more adult males than adult females, such as among the Yanomamo, then male-male competition for females would be greater and males would contribute less to the direct care of infants. But the Efe have the greatest male-to-female ratio, and yet they do just as much infant holding as !Kung. Consequently, sex-ratios are not useful for understanding paternal involvement.

Level of polygyny is also considered an important factor in predicting the level of father involvement. In societies where levels of polygyny are high, direct care by fathers is predicted to be low because male-male competition is expected to be higher, and polygynous fathers must divide their time among more children. But the Efe and !Kung levels of polygyny are much lower than the Aka (3-4 percent among Efe and !Kung versus 15 percent among the Aka); paternal infant care patterns should be just the opposite of those found.

One demographic factor that is related to the level of paternal involvement in these three foraging populations is the total fertility rate (TFR). Efe live in an infertility belt in northeastern Zaire and women average only 2.6 live births during their lifetime (Bailey 1989). !Kung women average 4.7 live births on average (Howell 1979) and Bokoka Aka women average 6.2 live births. The TFR cline follows the paternal involvement cline: The Efe have the lowest fertility and level of paternal involvement, the !Kung are intermediate in both, and the Aka are the highest in both measures. Bailey (1985:185) states that "strong father-child attachments among the Efe were uncommon while fathers took on the responsibility of disciplining their children, they were no more likely to care for their children than most other men in camp." Peacock's (1985) behavioral observations indicate that Efe grandmothers, subadult women, old women and infertile women contribute to infant care, but she does not mention fathers. The low level of Efe paternal involvement may be, in part, due to the availability of other adult females to assist with caregiving. Aka fathers are on the high end, in part, because there are few other adult women without children to help out. But as will be discussed below, fertility is only one contributing factor to high Aka father involvement.

Three factors seem to be especially influential in understanding the extraordinarily high level of Aka paternal care. First the nature of Aka subsistence activity is rather unique cross-culturally. Usually mens' and womens' subsistence activities take place at very different locations. The net hunt and other subsistence activities, such as caterpillar collecting, involve men, women, and children. If men are going to help with infant care on a regular basis they have to be near the infant a good part of the day. The net hunt makes this possible. The net hunt also requires that men and women walk equal distances during the day. In most foraging societies, females do not travel as far from camp as males. Older siblings are not useful for helping their mothers because of the extensive labor involved in walking long distances with an infant. If a mother is to receive help on the net hunt, it needs to come from an adult. Most of the other adult females carry baskets full of food and have their own infants or young children to carry since fertility is high. Fathers are among the few alternative caregivers regularly available on the net hunt to help mothers.

While fathers do carry infants on the net hunt, especially on the return from the hunt when the mothers' baskets are full of meat, collected nuts, and fruit, father-infant caregiving is much more likely to occur in the camp. Aka fathers behavior in camp does not appear to be ecologically "adaptive" as it does on the forest net hunt. Two other factors need to be considered: the husband-wife relationship and father-infant attachment. The net hunt dramatically influences the husband-wife relationship. The net hunt contributes to the time husband and wife spend together and patterns the nature of that time spent together. A husband and wife are together much of the time. Behavioral observations in the forest and village indicated that husbands and wives were within sight of each other 46.5 percent of daylight hours. This is more time together than in any other known society, and it is primarily a result of the net hunt. This percentage of course increases in the evening hours. But, husbands and wives are not only together most of the day, they are actively cooperating on the net hunt. They have to know each other well to communicate and cooperate throughout the day. They work together to set up the family net, chase game into the net, butcher and divide the game, and take care of the children. Husbands and wives help each other out in a number of domains, in part because they spend so much time together. Husband-wife relations are manystranded. Manystranded reciprocity is an important component of the husband-wife relationship. When they return to camp the mother has a number of tasks—she collects firewood and water, and prepares the biggest meal of the day. The father has relatively few tasks to do after returning from the hunt. He may make string or repair the net, but he is available to help with infant care. He is willing to do infant care, in part, because of the manystranded reciprocity between husband and wife. In many societies men have fewer tasks to do at the end of the day, while women have domestic tasks and prepare a meal. Men are available to help out with childcare, but seldom provide much assistance. Ngandu fathers, for instance, are around the house in the evening, but mothers continue to hold the infants as they collect firewood and prepare the meal.

The third important factor in understanding Aka fathers' involvement with infants is father-infant attachment. Father and infant are clearly attached to each other as evidenced by their interaction. Fathers end up holding their infants frequently because the infants crawl to them. Fathers pick up their infants because they intrinsically enjoy infants. The Aka study clearly demonstrates that infants seek out their fathers. Fathers are also attached to their infants. They enjoy being with them and carry them in a number of different contexts (out in the fields drinking palm wine with other males).

While these three factors are especially influential, other factors also play a part: near equal contributions to the diet by males and females; relatively high fertility rates; lack of warfare and violence, especially against women and children; a fierce egalitarian ethic; a mobile foraging lifestyle where it is not useful to accumulate material goods.

Theories Utilized to Explain Cross-Cultural Variability in Father's Style of Interaction

Anthropologists have not paid much attention to the father's style of interaction. Anthropological studies generally assume that if the father is involved with infants and children, he has warm and affectionate interactions with them, while fathers who are not involved in childcare are aloof in their interactions with children. The assumed relationship between involvement and style of interaction can be seen in Barry and Paxson's (1971) cross-cultural code for the "role of father." The father's "proximity" to infants or children is defined as both physical and emotional closeness.

Some British social anthropologists have identified factors that predict intercultural variability in the father's style of interaction with children: inheritance and descent rules. Radcliffe-Brown in his seminal article on mother's brother (1924) initiated the idea that:

> The presence of patrilineal descent groups tends to produce a situation where restraint and authority center about father and the male and female members of his descent group. At the same time, informality and indulgence characterize relations with mother and all of the male and female members of mother's patrilineage (1924:543).

Thus, in a patrilineal society the mother's brother becomes a male mother and the father's sister becomes a female father. Malinowski (1929) went on to describe how just the opposite occurred in matrilineal societies, such as the Trobriand Islanders. Malinowski characterized Trobriand fathers as very indulgent:

> He (father) will fondle and carry a baby, clean and wash it, and give it the mashed vegetable food. The father performs his duties with genuine natural fondness: he will carry an infant about for hours, looking at it with eyes of such love and pride as are seldom seen in those of a European (1929:201).

The closeness between father and children exists, according to Malinowski, because family authority rests with males on the mother's side of the family.

Goody (1959) criticized Radcliffe-Brown's hypothesis, but modified it only slightly by indicating that it was the system of inheritance that was important, not necessarily the rule of descent.

> It is because the father is not vested with jural authority over his son and the son has no title to the inheritance of his father's properties or to succession to his offices and rank, that matrilineal fathers and sons have an affectionate, noncompetitive relationship. Conversely, it is because maternal uncles have jurally sanctioned rights over their nephews and the latter have jurally sanctioned claims on their uncles that there is tension in their relationship. And the pattern is reversed in patrilineal systems because the locus of rights and claims is jurally reversed. Matrilineal fatherhood is defined as primarily a domestic relationship with only a minimal function in the politico-jural domain. Hence its focus is the task of bringing up and educating a child and fathers must rely on moral and affectional sanctions to fulfill it (Fortes 1958:12 in discussing Goody's comparison on the LoDagaba and Lowilli father-son relationship).

Schneider (1961) in his analysis of matrilineal kinship systems also lists an affective father-child relationship as a distinctive feature of matrilineal descent groups. A cross-cultural test of the hypothesis indicated significant differences in father-child proximity between matrilineal and patrilineal societies (Hewlett 1988).

Comparing Aka and American Fathers' Styles of Interaction

Over fifty studies of Euroamerican fathers indicate that father's interactions with infants and young children are clearly distinguished from mother's interactions in that fathers are the vigorous rough and tumble playmates of infants and young children, while mothers are sensitive caregivers. The Euroamerican literature suggests that this rough and tumble play is how infants become attached to fathers and develop social competence (Lamb et al. 1987). Aka father data do not support the contention that fathers are the vigorous, roughand-tumble playmates of the infants as the data for American fathers indicate.

They do suggest that, in comparison to mothers, fathers are slightly more playful: fathers are somewhat more likely to engage in minor physical play with their one- to four-month-old infants than are mothers, and fathers play more frequently with infants while holding than mothers do. But characterizing the Aka father as the infant's playmate would be misleading. Other caretakers holding the infant engage in play with the infant much more frequently than fathers or mothers, and mothers have more episodes of play over the course of a day than fathers or other caretakers because they hold the infant most of the time. The Aka father-infant relationship might be better characterized by its intimate and affective nature. It has already been mentioned that Aka fathers hold their infants more than fathers from any other human population known to anthropologists. Aka fathers also show affection more frequently while holding than mothers, and infants seem to regularly seek father-holding, possibly because of its affective nature.

So how can vigorous play be a significant feature in American studies of father-infant attachment, but not among the Aka? Four factors appear to be important for understanding Aka infant play and attachment: familiarity with the infant; knowledge of caretaking practices (how to hold an infant, how to soothe an infant); the degree of relatedness to the infant; and cultural values and parental goals.

First, due to frequent father-holding and availability, Aka fathers know their infants intimately. Fathers know the early signs of infant hunger, fatigue, and illness as well as the limits in their ability to soothe the infant. They also know how to stimulate responses from the infant without being vigorous. Unlike American fathers, Aka wait for infants to initiate interaction. The Aka mother is even more familiar with the infant's cues; other caretakers are least familiar with them. As indicated earlier, these other caretakers play more frequently with the infant while holding than mothers or fathers and are the most physical in their play, suggesting a relationship between intimate knowledge of the infant's cues and the frequency of play while holding.

Second, knowledge of infant caretaking practices seems to play a role in determining how much play is exhibited in caretaker-infant interactions. Child caretakers were the most physical and the loudest (singing) in their handling of infants. Children were not restricted from holding infants, but they were closely watched by parents. While "other" caretakers were more playful than mothers or fathers, younger fathers and "other" caretakers were more physical than older ones probably because they did not know how to handle and care for infants as well as adult caretakers.

A third factor to consider is the degree of relatedness of the caretaker to the infant. If vigorous play can assist in developing attachment, more closely related individuals may have a greater vested interest in establishing this bond than distantly related individuals. Attachment not only enhances the survival of the infant, but it can potentially increase the related caretaker's inclusive fitness (i.e., if the infant survives to reproductive age, the related caretaker will perpetuate some of his or her own genetic composition [called inclusive fitness by evolutionary biologists]). Aka mothers and fathers establish attachment by their frequent caretaking; vigorous play is not necessary to establish affective saliency. Brothers and sisters on the other hand, might establish this bond through physical play. Aka brothers and sisters, in fact, provided essentially all of the physical play the focal infants received; cousins and unrelated children were more likely to engage in face-to-face play with the infant instead of physical play.

Finally, the general social context of infant development should be considered. American culture encourages individualistic aggressive competition; Aka culture values cooperation, nonaggression, and prestige avoidance (one does not draw attention to oneself even, for instance, if one kills an elephant). Apparently, Americans tolerate—if not actually encourage-aggressive rough-and-tumble types of play with infants. Also, due to the high infant mortality rate, the primary parental goal for Aka is the survival of their infants. The constant holding and immediate attention to fussing reflect this goal. In the United States, infant mortality rates are markedly lower and, as a result, parental concern for survival may not be as great. The Aka infant is taken away from a caretaker who plays roughly with the infant, in part, because it could be seen as aggressive behavior, but also because the pervasive aim of infant care practices is survival of the infant, and rough-and-tumble play could risk the infant's safety.

These factors tentatively clarify why Aka fathers do not engage in vigorous play like American fathers, but do participate in slightly more physical play than Aka mothers (but not more than other caretakers). American fathers seldom participate directly in infant care and consequently are not as familiar with infant cues. To stimulate interaction and (possibly) attachment, they engage in physical play. Aka brothers and sisters are also much less physical in their play with infants than American fathers (Aka never tossed infants in the air or swung them by their arms), again suggesting that Aka children know their infant brother or sister and the necessary infant caregiving skills better than American fathers. These observations are obviously speculative and need further empirical study.

Sociologists LaRossa and LaRossa (1981) describe stylistic differences between American mothers' and fathers' interactions with their infants. They list a number of male-female role dichotomies that reflect different parenting styles. One distinction they make is role distance versus role embracement. Fathers are more likely to distance themselves from the parenting role while mothers are more likely to embrace the parenting role. American women generally want to remain in primary control of the children, and while fathers may show interest in caregiving, they are more likely to distance themselves from caregiving while embracing their roles as the breadwinners. LaRossa and LaRossa also suggest that fathers generally have low intrinsic value and relatively high extrinsic value. while mothers have the reverse.

The intrinsic value of something or someone is the amount of sheer pleasure or enjoyment that one gets from experiencing an object or person. The extrinsic value of something or someone is the amount of social rewards (e.g., money, power, prestige) associated with having or being with the object or person (1981:64).

They use this dichotomy to explain why fathers are more likely to carry or hold an infant in public than in private. Fathers receive extrinsic rewards from those in public settings, while this does not happen in the home. According to LaRossa and LaRossa, fathers

> will roughhouse with their toddlers on the living-room floor, and will blush when hugged or kissed by the one-year-olds, but when you really get down to it. they just do not have that much fun when they are with their children. If they had their druthers, they would be working at the office or drinking at the local pub (1981:65).

These role dichotomies may be useful for understanding American motherfather parenting styles, but they have limited value in characterizing Aka mother-father distinctions. Aka mothers and fathers embrace the parenting role. Generally, mothers and fathers want to hold their infants, and certainly they derive pleasure from infant interactions. As indicated earlier, fathers were in fact more likely to show affection while holding than mothers. Fathers also offered their nipples to infants who wanted to nurse, cleaned mucus from their infants' noses, picked lice from their infants' hair, and cleaned their infants after they urinated or defecated (often on the father). Fathers' caregiving did not appear any more or less perfunctory than mothers'. Aka fathers are not burdened with infant care; if a father does not want to hold or care for the infant he gives the infant to another person. Overall, Aka fathers embrace their parenting role as much as they embrace their hunting role.

The intrinsic-extrinsic role dichotomy does not fit well with Aka mother-father parenting styles either. Again, both Aka mothers and fathers place great intrinsic value and little extrinsic value on parenting. The fathers' intrinsic value is demonstrated above, but the lack of extrinsic value among the Aka can best be seen by comparing Aka and Ngandu fathers (the Ngandu are the horticulturalist trading partners of the Aka). When an Ngandu father holds his infant in public he is "on stage". He goes out of his way to show his infant to those who pass by, and frequently tries to stimulate the infant while holding it. He is much more vigorous in his interactions with the infant than are Aka men. The following experience exemplifies Ngandu fathers' extrinsic value towards their infants. An Ngandu friend showed me a 25 pound fish he had just caught and I asked to take a photograph of him with his fish. He said fine, promptly picked up his nearby infant, and proudly displayed both held his fish and infant for the photograph. His wife was also nearby but was not invited into the photograph. Aka, on the other hand, are matter-of-fact about their holding or transporting of infants in public places. They do not draw attention to their infants. The Aka also hold their infants in all kinds of social and economic contexts.

Conclusion

This paper has examined some of the enormous cross-cultural variability in fatherhood. Dramatic differences were described between American and Aka fathers as well as between fathers in different hunter-gatherer (e.g, !Kung and Aka) and horticultural (Ngandu and Yanomamo) cultures. American fathers are characterized by their vigorous play with children, while Aka fathers are characterized by their affectionate and intimate relations with their children. Several factors were identified as being important for understanding why there is so much diversity in the frequency and nature of father-infant interactions: the nature of husband-wife relations; the workload of men and women in the culture; the availability of infants and children while parents are working (e.g. net hunt versus wage labor); cultural ideologies (e.g., gender egalitarianism or who is best at taking care of infants); and, fertility patterns were all identified as being important forces for understanding fatherhood.

References

Ainsworth, M.D.S.
1967 Infancy in Uganda: *Infant Care and the Growth of Love.* Baltimore: Johns Hopkins Press.
1977 Attachment Theory and Its Utility in Cross-Cultural Research. In *Culture and Infancy: Variation in the Human Experience*, ed. P.H. Leiderman et al. New York: Academic Press.

Bahuchet, S.
1985 *Les Pygmees Aka et la Foret Centrafricaine.* Paris: Selaf

Bailey, R. C.
1985 The Socioecology of Efe Pygmy Men in the Ituri Forest, Zaire. Ph.D. diss. Harvard University.
1989 The Demography of the Efe and Lese of the Ituri Forest, Zaire. Paper presented at the American Anthropological Association Meetings. Washington, D.C.

Bailey, R. C., and N. R. Peacock
1988 Efe Pygmies of Northeast Zaire: Subsistence Strategies in the Ituri Forest. In *Coping with Uncertainty in Food Supply*, ed., I. de Garine and G. A. Harrison. Oxford, England: Oxford University Press.

Bateman, A.J.
1948 Intra-Sexual Selection in Drosophila. *Heredity* 2:349—68.

Barry, H. III, and L. M. Paxson
1971 Infancy and Early Childhood: Cross-Cultural Codes 2. *Ethology* 10:466—508.

Benshoof, L., and R. Thornhill
1979 The Evolution of Monogamy and Concealed Ovulation in Humans. Social and Biological Structures 2:95—106.

Betzig, L., A. Harrigan and P. Turke
1990 Childcare on Ifaluk. *Zeitscrift fur Ethnologie* 114 (in press)

Bowlby, J.
1969 *Attachment and Loss Vol. 1: Attachment.* New York: Basic Books.

Brown, J. K.
1970 A Note on the Division of Labor by Sex. *American Anthropologist* 72:1073—078.

Burton, M., L. A. Brudner and D. R. White
1977 A Model for the Sexual Division of Labor. *American Ethnologist* 4:227—52.

Chisholm, J.
    1983 *Navajo Infancy: An Ethological Study of Child Development.* New York: Aldine.
    1984 A Biosocial View of Prenatal Influences. Paper presented at the Annual Meeting of the American An-
    thropological Association, Denver, Colorado.

Cole, M., and J.S. Bruner
    1974 Cultural Differences and Inferences about Psychological Processes. In *Culture and Cognition*, ed.
    J.W. Berry and P. R. Dasen. London: Methuen.

Coleman, A.D.
    1981 *Earth Father/Sky Father: The Changing Concept of Fathering.* Englewood Cliffs, NJ: Prentice-Hall.

Darwin, C.
    1871 *The Descent of Man, and Selection in Relation to Sex.* New York: Appleton.

Draper, P.
    1976 Social and Economic Constraints on Child Life among the !Kung. In *Kalahari Hunter-Gatherers*, ed.
    Richard B. Leeand Irven DeVore. Cambridge, Mass.: Harvard University Press.

Draper, P., and H. Harpending
    1982 Father Absence and Reproductive Strategy: An Evolutionary Perspective. *Journal of Anthropological
    Research* 38:255—73.

Durkheim, E.
    1933 *The Division of Labor in Society.* Trans. by George Simpson. New York: MacMillan Company.

Emlen, S.T., and L.W. Oring
    1977 Ecology, Sexual Selection, and the Evolution of Mating Systems. *Science* 197 :215—23.

Freud, S.
    1938 An Outline of Psychoanalysis. London: Hogarth

Goody, J.
    1959 The Mother's Brother and the Sister's Son in West Africa. *Journal of the Royal Anthropological Institute*
    89:61 —88.
    1973 Bridewealth and Dowry in Africa and Eurasia. In *Bridewealth and Dowry*, ed. J.R. Goody and S.J.
    Tambiah. Cambridge, England: Cambridge University Press.

Hamilton, A.
    1981 *Nature and Nurture: Aboriginal Child-Rearing in NorthCentral Amhem land.* Canberra: Australian In-
    stitute of Aboriginal Studies.

Harlow, H.F.
    1961 The Development of Affectional Patterns in Infant Monkeys. In *Determinants of Infant Behavior,* Vol.
    1, ed. B.M. Foss. London: Methuen.

Harpending, H.
    1976 Regional Variation in !Kung Populations. In *Kalahari Hunter-Gatherers.*, ed. R.B. Lee and I. DeVore.
    Cambridge, Mass.: Harvard University Press.

Hartung, J.
    1983 Matrilineal Inheritance: New Theory and Analysis. Paper read at the meetings of the American Anthro-
    pological Association.

Hewlett, B. S.
    1989a Multiple Caretaking Among African Pygmies. *American Anthropologist* 91 :186—91.

1989b Husband-Wife Reciprocity and the Aka Father-Infant Relationship. Paper delivered at the American Anthropological Association Meeting, Washington, D.C.

1991 Intimate Fathers: The Nature and Context of Aka Pygmy Paternal Infant Care. Ann Arbor, MI: University of Michigan Press
1992 Father-Child Relations: Cultural and Biosocial Contexts. N.Y.: Aldine

Hill, Kim and Hillard Kaplan
1988 Tradeoffs in Male and Female Reproductive Strategies Among the Ache. In *Human Reproductive Behavior,* ed. L. Betzig, M. Borgerhoff Mulder, and P. Turke. Cambridge, England: Cambridge University Press.

Hill, K., H. Kaplan, K. Hawkes, and A.M. Hurtado
1985 Men's Time Allocation to Subsistence Work Among the Ache of Eastern Parguay. *Human Ecology* 13:29—47.

Hoffman, Martin L.
1981 The Role of the Father in Moral Internalization. In *The Role of Father in Child Development,* ed. Michael E. Lamb. New York: John Wiley.

Howell, Nancy
1979 *Demography of the Dobe !Kung.* New York: Academic Press.

Hurtado, A. M.
1985 Women's Subsistence Strategies among Ache. HunterGatherers of Eastern Paraguay. Ph.D. diss. University of Utah.

Katz, M.M., and Melvin J. Konner
1981 The Role of Father: An Anthropological Perspective. In *The Role of Father in Child Development,* ed. Michael E. Lamb. New York: John Wiley and Sons.

Konner, M.J.
1976 Maternal Care, Infant Behavior and Development among the !Kung. In *Kalahari Hunter-Gatherers,* ed. R.B. Lee and 1. DeVore. Cambridge, MA: Harvard University Press.
1977 Infancy Among the Kalahari Desert San. In *Culture and Infancy: Variations in the Human Experience,* ed. P. H. Leiderman et al. New York Academic Press

Lamb, M.E., ed.
1985 Observational Studies of Father-Child Relationships in Humans. In *Primate Paternalism,* ed. David Milton Taub. New York: Van Nostrand Reinhold Company.

Lamb, M.E., J.H. Pleck, E.L. Charnov, and J.A. LeVine
1987 A Biosocial Perspective on Paternal Behavior and Involvement. In *Parenting Across the Lifespan,* ed. J.B. Lancaster, J. Altmann, A. Rossi, L.R. Sherrod. Hawthorne, N.Y.: Aldine.

Lancaster, J. C.
1983 Evolutionary Perspectives on Sex Differences in the Higher Primates. In *Gender and the Life Course,* ed. Alice S. Rossi. Hawthorne, N.Y.: Aldine

Lancaster, J.B., and C.S. Lancaster
1987 The Watershed: Change in Parental-Investment and Family Formation Strategies in the Course of Human Evolution. In *Parenting Across the Life Span,* ed. J.B. Lancaster, J. Altmann, A.S. Rossi and L.R. Sherrod, eds. New York: Aldine.

LaRossa, R., and M. M. LaRossa
1981 *Transition to Parenthood: How Infants Change Families.* Beverly Hills: Sage Publications.

Lee, R.B.
1979 *The !Kung San: Men, Women, and Work in a Foraging Society.* Cambridge, England: Cambridge University Press.

Malinowski, B.
1929 *The Sexual Life of Savages in Northwestern Melanesia.* London: George Routledge.

Mead, M.
1935 *Sex and Temperment.* New York: William Morrow and Co.

Melancon, T.F.
1981 Marriage and Reproduction Among the Yanomamo Indians of Venezuela. Ph.D. diss. Pennsylvania State University, University Park.

Mukhopadhyay, C. C.
1983 Beyond Babies and Brawn: Rethinking the Sexual Division of Labor in the Family. Unpublished ms.

Munroe, R.H., and R.L. Munroe
1971 Household Density and Infant Care in an East African Society. *Journal of Social Psychology* 83:3—13.
1989 Father's Role in Four Societies. Paper delivered an American Anthropological Association Meeting, Washington, D.C.

Murdock, G. P., and C. Provost
1973 Factors in the Division of Labor by Sex: A Cross-Cultural Analysis. *Ethnology* 12: 203—25.

Neuwelt-Truntzer, S.
1981 Ecological Influences on the Physical, Behavioral and Cognitive Development of Pygmy Children. Ph.D. diss., University of Chicago.

Ortner, S.B.
1974 Is Female to Male as Nature is to Culture? In *Woman, Culture and Society,* ed. M.Z. Rosaldo and L. Lamphere. Stanford, Ca.: Stanford University Press.

Parsons, T., and R.F. Bales
1955 *Family, Socialization and Interaction Process.* Illinois: Free Press.

Peacock, N. R.
1985 Time Allocation, Work and Fertility Among Efe Pygmy Women of Northeast Zaire. Ph.D. diss. Harvard University.

Radcliffe-Brown, A.R.
1924 The Mother's Brother in South Africa. *South African Journal of Science* 21 :542—55.

Radin, N.
1981 The Role of the Father in Cognitive, Academic and Intellectual Development. In *The Role of the Father in Child Development,* ed. Michael E. Lamb. New York: John Wiley and Sons.

Rosaldo, M.Z. and L. Lamphere, eds.
1974 *Woman, Culture and Society.* Stanford, Ca.: Stanford University Press.

Schneider, D.M.
1961 The Distinctive Features of Matrilineal Descent Groups. In *Matrilineal Kinship*. David M. Schneider and Kathleen Gough, eds. Berkeley: University of California Press.

Super, C.M., and S. Harkness
1982 The Development of Affect in Infancy and Early Childhood. In *Cultural Perspectives on Child Development*, ed. D.A. Wanger and H.W. Stevenson. San Francisco, CA: Freeman.

Symons, D.
1978 *Play and Aggression: A Study of Rhesus Monkeys.* New York: Columbia University Press.

Trivers, R.
1972 Parental Investment and Sexual Selection. In *Sexual Selection and the Descent of Man*, ed. B. Campbell. Chicago: Aldine.

Weisner, T.S., and R. Gallimore
1977 My Brother's Keeper: Child and Sibling Caretaking. *Current Anthropology* 18(2):169—90.

West, M. M., and M. J. Konner
1976 The Role of Father in Anthropological Perspective. In *The Role of Father in Child Development*, ed. Michael E. Lamb. New York: John Wiley and Sons.

Whiting, B.B. and J.W.M. Whiting
1975 *Children of Six Cultures.* Cambridge, Mass.: Harvard University Press.

Wilson, E.O.
1975 *Sociobiology: The New Synthesis.* Cambridge, Mass.: Harvard University Press.

Winn, S., G.A. Morelli, and E.Z. Tronick
1990 The Infant in the Group: A look at Efe Caretaking Practices. The *Cultural Context of Infancy,* ed. J.K. Nugent, B.M. Lester and T.B. Brazelton. New Jersey: Ablex.

Zelditch, M.
1955 Role Differentialtion in the Nuclear Family. In *Family, Socialization and Interaction Process*, ed. T. Parsons and R. Bales. New York: Free Press

Section X

THE CLIMACTERIC

The climacteric designates a phase in the life cycle when hormone production slows down and physiological and psychological changes mark accompanying traits of aging. We may thus speak of a male climacteric as well as a female climacteric. For men this change is much less dramatic and does not imply a reproductive transition. In popular use the (female) climacteric marks the transition for a woman from her reproductive to her post-reproductive years. Normally this involves a decade or more which surrounds the menopause—a clinical event when a woman experiences her last menstrual flow.

During these transitional years, starting in her late thirties, there is a general decline in a woman's reproductive ability. Due to the quality of the eggs which remain and their inability to react to circulating hormones this phase is marked by lower fertility, greater frequency of miscarriages, and increased incidence of fetal abnormality. During these years the pituitary gland continues to produce follicle-stimulating hormone (FSH) and luteinizing hormone (LH) and to deposit them in the bloodstream for transportation to the ovaries. However, the aging ovaries fail to respond. The smaller number of follicles which remain are no longer stimulated to mature and ovulation becomes erratic, finally ceasing. The slowdown of ovarian function also results in decreasing amounts of estrogen and progesterone and, finally, the near absence of progesterone. Small amounts of estrogen continue to be produced. The ovarian shutdown is relieved somewhat by the continued production of minute amounts of these hormones by the adrenal glands. The dramatic decrease in estrogen may contribute to the physical sensations referred to as "menopausal symptoms". These include somatic (also called vasomotor) symptoms such as vaginal atrophy, hot flashes and flushing, as well as psycho-somatic and psychological symptoms which may be more culture-specific. Most women are perimenopausal between ages forty-five and fifty-five, experiencing the cessation of menstruation either as one final event, or more frequently as a gradual or infrequent experience of flow. A woman is menopausal, or in our terminology postmenopausal, when she has not menstruated for twelve months. It is now common in industrialized countries for women to receive synthetic hormones as replacement for their own, and Estrogen Replacement Therapy (ERT) is common. An earlier warning about the positive relationship between longterm use of ERT and breast cancer has been revived by recent research.

It is extremely important to document here that the foregoing discussion was a clinical one and therefore may be seen as placing the climacteric in a medical context. It can also be argued, with some confidence, that a major component of the climacteric is cultural (du Toit 1985) and must thus be viewed in the context of status and role, achievement and ascription of such statuses, and, of course, gains or losses as a result of aging. The climacteric, and ultimately the menopause, should thus be viewed within a unique cultural setting which places positive or negative meaning on the aging process. These aspects will differ from one culture to another, but within the same culture there will be an interplay of all these aspects permitting a clear picture.

In contrast to studies dealing with the onset of fertility, there have been relatively few studies which are not of a clinical nature that deal with the termination of fertility. Part of the reason is that life expectancy in traditional societies did not allow this status as a universal. Also, there is no ritual marking the end of the reproductive stage in the life cycle. Women did not advertise the fact that they had lost their status as potential mothers. In fact in some societies they attempted to prolong this as much as possible for fear of losing the husband's attention when they were "old".

While some societies recognise menopause as the end of reproduction and thus a negative experience, most societies see it as a liberating experience. Since they will no longer be polluted every month, women see new roles opening up. This expansion of roles allows Mundurucu women to sit in the meetings of men (Murphy and Murphy 1974), Zapotecan women to go to fiestas alone (Chinas 1973), Gypsy women to be free from the strict 'mokadi' regulations (Trigg 1973), and Ethiopean women mark their age with a Kasa ritual assuming they have reached the age where they "are too old to sin any longer" (Gamst 1969:111).

The three papers which follow deal with aging in general, and specifically with sexuality during the declining years. Meston discusses the physiological and psychological effects of aging. Mary Hotvedt's contribution is from a book on sexuality in the later years, in which her assignment was to look at the topic in cross-cultural perspective. In the third paper Bachmann and Leiblum report on a study of sexual involvement by couples who were in their sixties. The study included only women who were not receiving estrogen replacement therapy. They had to be on normal fluctuating gonadal hormones.

References

du Toit, Brian M. 1985. The Cultural Climacteric in Crosscultural Perspective, pp. 177-190. M. Notelovitz and P. van Keep (eds) *The Climacteric in Perspective*. Lancaster: MTP Press.

Murphy, Y. and R. F. Murphy. 1974. *Women of the Forest*. New York: Columbia University Press.

Chinas, B.L. 1973. *The Isthmus Zapotecs: women's roles in cultural context*. New York: Holt, Rinehart and Winston.

Trigg, E.B. 1973 *Gypsy Demons and Divinities*. Secaucus, N.J.: Citadel Press.

Gamst, F.C. 1969. *The Qemant*. New York: Holt, Rinehart and Winston

10. An old woman in Transkei

CLIMACTERIC

9. An old couple from Canada

AGING AND SEXUALITY

Cindy M. Meston, PhD,
Seattle, Washington

Recent research suggesting that a high proportion of men and women remain sexually active well into later life refutes the prevailing myth that aging and sexual dysfunction are inexorably linked. Age-related physiological changes do not render a meaningful sexual relationship impossible or even necessarily difficult. In men, greater physical stimulation is required to attain and maintain erections, and orgasms are less intense. In women, menopause terminates fertility and produces changes stemming from estrogen deficiency. The extent to which aging affects sexual function depends largely on psychological, pharmacological, and illness-related factors. In this article I review the physiological sexrelated changes that occur as part of the normal aging process in men and women. I also summarize the effects on sexual function of age-related psychological issues, illness factors, and medication use. An understanding of the sexual changes that accompany normal aging may help physicians give patients realistic and encouraging advice on sexuality. Although it is important that older men and women not fall into the psychosocial trap of expecting (or worse, trying to force) the kind and degree of sexual response characteristic of their youth, it is equally as important that they not fall prey to the negative folklore according to which decreased physical intimacy is an inevitable consequence of the passage of time. (Meston CM. Aging and sexuality. In: Successful Aging. *West J Med* 1997; 167:285-290)

> [My] . . . Age is as a lusty winter,
> Frosty, but Kindly.
>
> —WILLIAM SHAKESPEARE
> *As You Like It*[1]

Sexual desire and activity continue well into later life for both men and women but can be affected in various ways by aging. I begin by discussing these effects in men.

Men

Although an age-related decline in sexual activity and desire among men has been reported in numerous studies, maintaining a healthy interest in sexual activity is not uncommon among 70-, 80-, and even 90-year-old men. Pfeiffer and associates[2] reported that 95% of men aged 46 to 50 years and 28% of men aged 66 to 71 years have intercourse on a weekly basis. Diokno and co-workers[3] have reported that nearly 74% of married men older than 60 remain sexually active, and Bretschneider and McCoy[4] found that 63% of men aged 80 to 102 years continue to be sexually active. In view of the fact that sexuality in the literature is often defined exclusively in terms of intercourse, these estimates would probably be even higher if noncoital acts such as touching, caressing, fantasy, and masturbation were taken into account.

The age-related decrease in libido noted among men is most frequently attributed to a decline in testosterone levels and to changes in receptor site sensitivity to androgen. The sex hormone status of a healthy man remains relatively stable from puberty until the fifth decade of life, at which time androgen production gradually declines. The first sign of an alteration in endocrine function is a small increase in pituitary-stimulating hormone levels (gonadotropins), which signals the relative inability of the aging testes to efficiently produce testosterone.[5] Serum testosterone levels gradually decline as a consequence, and by age 80 they may be only a sixth those of a younger man.[6] Although the drop in serum testosterone levels clearly parallels the decline in sexual libido noted with age, there is little evidence to suggest that testosterone replacement therapy augments sexual drive in men with normal baseline testosterone levels. That is, administering massive doses of androgen to an 80-year-old will not restore his libido to what it was when he was 18.[5]

There appears to be a minimal level of testosterone necessary for adequate sexual functioning, above and beyond which additional amounts have no effect. This probably reflects limitations set by the number and sensitivity of functional testosterone receptors. Because most older men apparently have these receptors in numbers above the "critical" level, it is generally assumed that exogenous testosterone would be superfluous and would not restore age-related decreases in sexual drive. Using a placebo-controlled design, Morales and associates[7] examined the effects of exogenously administered adrenal androgen dehydroepiandrosterone (DHEA) on a number of age-related factors in 13 men aged 40 to 70 years. When levels were restored to those of a younger age group, DHEA had no direct effect on sexual interest. Replacement DHEA did, however, have a beneficial effect on general measures of well-being. Such measures may, in turn, have a positive effect on sexual satisfaction and function. Further studies of the effects of DHEA on male sexual function and well-being are required before treatment considerations are warranted.

Women

A decline in sexual interest and desire is frequently reported to be more severe in aging women than aging men. Such assertions are often based on studies that compare the incidence of sexual activity in aging men with that in aging women. For example, recent research indicates that approximately 56% of married women older than 60 (compared with 75% of married men) are sexually active,[3] as are approximately 30% of women aged 80 to 102 years (compared with 63% of men).[4] As noted earlier, sexual interest and activity in studies of this nature are too often measured solely according to frequency of intercourse. Given that by the age of 80 or older there are 39 men for every 100 women,[8] lack of opportunity may well account for a large portion of such gender differences. More importantly, gender differences in the incidence of intercourse and masturbation are apparent in adolescence and throughout adulthood,[9] not only among older people. Hence, age-related changes in sexual activity may best be understood by examining change across a person's total lifespan rather than comparing incidence between genders. To this end, the Janus report[10] indicated surprisingly little change in sexual activity across the average woman's lifespan. In this report, 68% of women aged 39 to 50 engaged in sexual activity at least once a week, as did 65% of women aged 51 to 64 and 74% of women older than 65. As is the case in men, masturbation frequency in women has been noted to decline with age, but it continues to be practiced by approximately half of the healthy female population over the age of 60.[12] In contrast to research indicating that sexual desire declines with age, 9% of women interviewed for a Danish study[13] reported an increase in sexual desire during or after menopause.

One of the primary causes of decreased sexual desire in postmenopausal women is decreased vaginal lubrication or a thinning of the vaginal lining, both of which may lead to pain during vaginal intercourse. In such cases, sexual desire generally returns once some form of treatment (for example, estrogen or lubricants) has relieved the symptoms.[14] A lack of bioavailable testosterone may also reduce sexual desire in women. Although there is no absolute level of testosterone necessary for sexual desire, it has been suggested that there is a threshold level of circulating androgen below which the intensity of desire is affected.[15] It is not clear why some menopausal women experience a sharp decline in testosterone production,[14] nor has it been proved that androgen replacement therapy is of more than marginal therapeutic value in such cases.[15] More importantly, the safety of prescribing testosterone is currently controversial. Testosterone may affect cholesterol and liver protein levels; at high doses, it may also cause masculinizing effects such as facial hair or lowered vocal pitch.[14] Researchers have recently examined the effect of the adrenal androgen DHEA on the sexuality of women aged 40 to 70 years.[7,16] Although neither circulating nor replacement levels of DHEA were directly linked to measures of sexuality in women, DHEA was significantly associated with measures of overall well-being.[7,16] Well-being in turn was shown to be predictive of the quality of sexual relationships.[16] Further studies of this nature are required before suggestions for treatment can be made.

The less frequent reports of increased sexual desire among older women may also be explained by hormonal changes that occur following menopause. When estrogen levels decline, levels of follicle-stimulating hormone and luteinizing hormone increase in an effort to stimulate estrogen production. The increase in these two hormones stimulates certain cells in the ovarian stromal tissue to produce testosterone. Women vary widely with regard to efficiency in producing testosterone in this manner.[14] Women who have an increase in testosterone production during or after menopause may possibly have increased sexual desire. Psychological factors such as elimination of the fear of conception may also play a role in increasing sexual desire after menopause.[14]

Physiologic Aspects of Aging and Sexuality in Men

With regard to actual physiologic changes that occur with age and affect sexual functioning, much individual variation exists. It has been estimated that 55% of men experience impotence by the age of

75.[17] This should not be taken to mean that erectile failure is a normal stage in the aging process. The alterations that lead to decreased sexual functioning, particularly erectile failure, are multifactorial, made up of elements that may be both organic (such as the effects of disease or medication) and psychological (for example, anxiety and guilt). It is clear that all stages of the human sexual response cycle as defined by Masters and Johnson,[18] are influenced by age-related factors, but there is no evidence to suggest that erectile failure is inevitable among aging men who are psychologically and physiologically healthy.

The Sexual Response Cycle

Normal age-related changes that accompany the excitement stage of sexual response in men include a decrease in, or lack of, elevation in testosterone levels; a decrease in scrotal vasocongestion; reduced tensing of the scrotal sac; and delayed erection. Where a young man may achieve a full erection in seconds, an older man may require several minutes to attain a similar response. Age related changes in adrenergic and cholinergic mechanisms may partly explain these changes. The process of erection is a vascular event mediated by the autonomic nervous system. Corporeal smooth-muscle tone plays a primary role in erectile ability; gap junctions and ion channel mechanisms, in turn, are largely responsible for determining the degree of smooth-muscle tone.[19] With advancing age, there is evidence that a decline occurs in the number of β-adrenergic and cholinergic receptors, which may lead to increased dominance of α-adrenergic activity (that is, increased corporeal smooth-muscle tone). This in turn may interfere with the corporeal smooth-muscle relaxation necessary for initiation and maintenance of the erectile response.[19] Age-related cellular changes may also negatively affect the erectile response through an increased deposition of connective tissue, causing a decrease in penile distensibility.[19] This loss of corporeal elasticity may lead to lowered compression among emissary veins, resulting in venous leakage and consequent difficulty achieving erection.

Penile sensitivity also decreases with age.[20] Attaining and maintaining an erection, therefore, becomes more dependent on direct physical stimulation and less dependent on, or responsive to, centrally controlled visual, psychological, or nongenital excitation.[19] As a result, partners may need to facilitate the erectile response by providing manual or oral stimulation before intromission and possibly at periods throughout the sexual act to help sustain erection until orgasm. Penile rigidity declines gradually, beginning in most men at age 60.[19] Generally, rigidity remains adequate for vaginal intercourse, but couples may need to experiment with different coital positions or supplement intercourse with manual stimulation.

The plateau stage of sexual response is prolonged with age, and pre-ejaculatory secretions and emissions are reduced or cease to occur. Prior difficulties with premature ejaculation may be resolved in older men because of the increase in stimulation and time required to reach orgasm. The duration of orgasm decreases with age, there are fewer and less intense spastic prostate and urethral muscle contractions, and there is a decrease in expulsive ejaculatory force. The period of inevitability before ejaculation is reduced from between 2 to 4 seconds in younger men to approximately 1 second in older men and there is a slow but gradual decline in semen volume per ejaculation.[19] Occasionally orgasm may occur without ejaculation. The final postorgasmic or reresolution stage of sexual response is marked by more rapid loss of vasocongestion and an increase in the length of the refractory period. For a man in his 20s the refractory period may last only minutes; for a man in his 80s it may extend to several days—probably the amount of time required for ionic and neurotransmitter concentrations to be restored to normal levels.[19]

Physiologic Aspects of Aging and Sexuality in Women

Effects of Menopause

Menopause, which occurs in most women at about age 50, is associated with substantial reductions in estrogen, progesterone, and androgen levels. Following menopause, estrogen is almost exclusively derived from the peripheral conversion of adrenal androgens. Around age 65, there is a further decrease in adrenal androgen production, often referred to as adrenopause.[15] The decline in estrogen that accompanies menopause leads to a number of normal age-related changes in genital appearance. Such changes include a reduction in pubic hair, loss of fat and subcutaneous tissue from the mons pubis, atrophy of the labia majora, and shortening and loss of elasticity of the vaginal barrel. Vaginal secretions decrease in quantity as a result of both atrophy of the Bartholin glands and a decrease in the number and maturity of vaginal cells. The vaginal epithelium, which is highly estrogen dependent, becomes flattened and loses glycogen; this leads to a decrease in *Lactobacillus* species and lactic acid and an increase in vaginal pH.[21] These alterations affect the vaginal microbial population and put aging women at greater risk for developing bacterial infections.[22] Together with decreased vaginal lubrication, the reduction in thickness of the epithelium from approximately eight to ten cell layers to three to four may lead to postcoital bleeding, mild burning sensations during intercourse, and pain.[22] For such reasons, dyspareunia is the most common sexual complaint among older women seeking gynecologic consultation.[23] With decreased estrogenic stimulation, the uterus is reduced in size and the total collagen and elastic content decreases by 30% to 50%.[24] The uterine cervix also atrophies and loses fibromuscular stroma, and the ovaries, with no remaining follicles, become reduced in size and weight and the ovarian stromal tissue becomes fibrotic and sclerotic.[22] Estrogen replacement therapy, when given systemically at high doses, has a beneficial effect on urogenital tissue[22] but is associated with an increased risk of breast and endometrial cancer.[25] In the absence of other postmenopausal symptoms, vaginal estrogen cream administered a few times per week may be equally effective.

The Sexual Response Cycle

A number of age-related changes affect the female sexual response cycle. During the excitement phase, vaginal blood flow and genital engorgement are less intense than in younger women and take longer to occur. This phenomenon may be less pronounced in women who continue to be sexually active than in those who are celibate, although its mechanism is not well understood.[15] Vaginal lubrication is delayed and reduced in quantity. Whereas in younger women the excitement stage with lubrication may take only 10 to 15 seconds, in postmenopausal women it may take as long as 5 minutes or longer.[26] The decrease in vaginal vasocongestion and lubrication may contribute to dryness of the vagina and may make intercourse painful. A variety of topical lubricants have been used successfully to compensate for insufficient vaginal lubrication. For women who prefer not to use a lubricant during intercourse, nonhormonal preparations such as Replens or oil from a vitamin E capsule, applied vaginally every other day, may greatly alleviate vaginal dryness, as may taking zinc orally.[14] Despite these age-related physiologic changes, several studies have reported that postmenopausal women report little or no change in the subjective experience of sexual arousal.[27]

The plateau phase of sexual response is prolonged in older women, uterine elevation is reduced, the labia majora do not elevate to the same degree as in younger years, the breasts become less vasocongested, and nipple erection is less likely to occur.[1,15] The orgasmic response does not appear to be substantially affected by age. Women retain multiorgasmic capacity, although the number and intensity of vaginal and rectal contractions are reduced.[5] While younger women average five to ten vaginal contractions with orgasm, older women average two or three.[5] As is the case in men, the resolution stage of sexual response in older women is characterized by a rapid loss of vasocongestion.

Illness, Medication Use, and Sexuality Among Older Persons

Physical illness can affect sexual function directly by interfering with endocrine, neural, and vascular processes that mediate the sexual response, indirectly by causing weakness or pain and psychologically by provoking changes in body image and self-esteem. The scope of this article precludes a comprehensive discussion of the effects of medical illness on sexuality; accordingly. only the most prevalent age-related medical illnesses, prescribed medications, and their effects on sexuality will be mentioned here (for a review, see Badeau[28]).

Men

Medical or surgical therapy for a number of age-related diseases can affect erectile function by interfering with the neurologic innervation of the penis. Interventions that may have this effect include lower abdominal surgery, pelvic irradiation, and certain types of prostate surgery.[5] Transurethral resection of the prostate has been reported to cause erectile failure in 4% to 12% of cases.[2] Radical prostatectomy for prostate cancer, cystectomy for bladder cancer, and colorectal surgery may all damage the neuromuscular bundle of the penis. Although increasing attention has been paid to preservation of the neurovascular bundle, men with aberrant cavernous arteries more often than not suffer erectile dysfunction from such procedures.[19] A number of age-related disease states may interfere with erectile function directly. The atherosclerosis associated with cardiovascular disease may involve the penile arteries as well as the coronary arteries. Occlusion of the abdominal aorta or the iliac arteries may also be associated with the failure to attain erection.[5] Because the act of intercourse increases heart rate and blood pressure, fear of chest pain during intercourse may further impede sexual relations. Diabetes mellitus is commonly associated with erectile failure. Within only five years after the onset of type II disease, 60% of male patients have some form of sexual dysfunction.[19] The causes of erectile failure in diabetic men are largely neurogenic and vascular, but also include alterations in corporeal smooth-muscle reactivity and microangiopathy, which may cause arterial insuffficiency.[19] Somatic and autonomic neuropathy may produce neurogenic impotence in older diabetic men. Other endocrine or metabolic disorders associated with erectile problems include hypothyroidism, hyperthyroidism, hypogonadism, hyperprolactinemia, and Cushing's disease. Systemic disorders known to impair erection include renal failure, chronic obstructive pulmonary disease, cirrhosis, and myotonia dystrophica. Among the neurologic disorders that may inhibit erection are spinal cord injury, cerebrovascular accidents, temporal lobe epilepsy, multiple sclerosis, and sensory neuropathy.[1,5]

A wide variety of drugs have been reported to impair erectile ability, particularly among older persons. The aging process influences physiologic drug distribution, metabolism, and excretion and renders older persons more vulnerable to the side effects of medication.[19] Among medications, antihypertensive agents that act either centrally (for example, methyldopa and clonidine) or peripherally (for example, reserpine, guanethidine), β-blockers (such as propranolol or labetalol), α-blockers (including prazocin and terazocin), and diuretics (for example, thiazide and spironolactone) appear to be the primary offenders in causing impaired erection.[19] In addition, cardiovascular drugs (such as disopyramide), cancer chemotherapy agents, anxiolytics (benzodiazepines), antipsychotics (for example, haloperidol, thioridazine, and chlorpromazine), a wide range of antidepressants (such as imipramine, amitriptyline, trazodone, and fluoxetine), lithium, and numerous drugs of abuse (including cocaine, alcohol, narcotics, and amphetamines) have all been linked to impaired erectile function (for reviews, see Schiavi and Rehman[19] and Meston and Gorzalka[30]). With diseases such as depression, hypertension, and atherosclerosis, it is difficult to determine the extent to which the sexual dysfunction is a result of the prescribed medication or the disease per se, given that both may negatively affect the sexual response.

Women

Surgical treatment of gynecologic and breast cancer often has a deleterious effect on sexual function in women by assaulting body image. Although breast or vulvovaginal surgery undoubtedly affects self-esteem in women of all ages, the psychological damage may be further compounded in older women whose body image is perhaps already affected by age-related body changes. Urinary incontinence occurs in up to 25% of older women during intercourse.[31] This disorder commonly leads to dissatisfaction with the sexual relationship or withdrawal from sexual contact because of embarrassment. Renal failure has been reported to cause anorgasmia, decreased libido, and impaired vaginal lubrication in women on dialysis.[1]

Hysterectomy is the most commonly performed operation in women: more than a third of women in the United States have had a hysterectomy by age 60. This procedure has not been shown to have a direct effect on sexual function; some women, however, report a decline in orgasmic pleasure following hysterectomy because of the absence of uterine contractions. For women who view hysterectomy as a further loss of femininity, self-esteem and body image may be damaged by this type of surgery. Conversely, for women who experience relief from pain, abnormal bleeding, or cramping, hysterectomy may result in improved sexual function.[1]

In contrast to an abundance of research on diabetes and male sexual function, there is a paucity of studies examining the effects of diabetes on female sexual function. Decreased sexual desire, anorgasmia, and difficulty obtaining sufficient vaginal lubrication during sexual arousal have been identified in some women with type II diabetes mellitus.[5,15] The duration of diabetes, age, or insulin dosage does not appear to be correlated with sexual function among women with diabetes,[32] and there is no evidence that peripheral or autonomic neuropathies directly affect the female sexual response.[15]

Research into the effects of medication use on sexual function in women has lagged considerably behind that in men. Antidepressant drugs are commonly reported to affect sexual functioning in women. Side effects associated with antidepressant medications include decreased sexual desire, impaired arousal and lubrication, vaginal anesthesia, delayed orgasm, and anorgasmia (for a review, see Meston and Gorzalka[30]). Serotonergic systems are frequently implicated in antidepressant-induced sexual side effects, although data are inconsistent as to whether the role of serotonin in sexual behavior is inhibitory, excitatory, or both.[30] Antipsychotic and neuroleptic medications have also been linked to impaired sexual function in women. Most recently, the antihypertensive drug clonidine has been shown to impair physiologic sexual response in women by decreasing vaginal blood volume and pressure pulse responses.[33] Clearly, there is a need for further research in this area.

Psychological Aspects of Aging and Sexuality

Not surprisingly, a number of psychological factors that influence the sexuality of younger persons also affect older men and women. Of particular importance is the nature of the interpersonal relationship. Marital conflict, relationship imbalances, commitment issues, intimacy and communication problems, lack of trust, mismatches in sexual desire, boredom, and poor sexual technique are just some of the common sources of sexual dissatisfaction noted among couples of all ages.[5,34] In older people these factors may be amplified by anger and resentment that may have built over the years, as well as by feelings of entrapment and resignation if the option to leave the relationship no longer seems viable. As with younger couples, marital satisfaction is closely linked to sexual satisfaction in older couples.[34]

Increases in psychosocial stresses, such as the death of a spouse, loss of a job or social status, deterioration of support networks, and health- and finance-related family problems, are common experiences among the aged. These life changes may contribute to sexual difficulties in older people by increasing the likelihood of depression or anxiety. "Widower's syndrome" refers to the onset of sexual difficulties in older persons who resume sexual interactions after a period of celibacy following the death of a spouse. Sexual difficulties in this situation are generally attributable to unresolved feelings of grief, guilt, anger, or even relief in cases in which the partner had been ill for a long period before death.[5] Performance anxiety related to beginning a new sexual relationship may be a problem for both men and women, but may play a particularly detrimental role in male sexual function because of the wellknown adverse effects of anxiety on erectile function.

Because women generally marry men older than themselves, and are likely to outlive men by an average of seven to eight years, women are more likely than men to experience the death of a spouse in old age. Given the shortage of available older male partners, women are also more likely than men to spend the later years of life alone. Many older women report feeling sexually frustrated at the lack of an available sexual partner. Although masturbation is a viable option, older persons may have been brought up to believe that masturbation is unnatural or even unhealthy. Education and permission from a health care professional may help to alter such misconceptions.[5] Also common among older people are false expectations regarding the effects of aging on sexuality. Self-critical anxieties about one's sexual abilities or physical imperfections can be distracting or even destructive to sexual pleasure and excitement. The societal emphasis that has linked sexuality almost exclusively to young people may lead some older people to feel ashamed of their continued sexual interest and may consequently discourage them from seeking sexual advice. Information from physicians regarding normal age-related changes in sexuality and encouragement, together with advice on how to continue meaningful sexual relations, may play a key role in altering such negative attitudes.

References

1. Kaiser FE. Sexuality in the elderly. Geriiatr Urol 1996; 1:99-109

2. Pfeiffer E., Verwoerdt A., Want HS. Sexual behavior in aged men and women. Arch Gen Psychiatry 1968; 19:735-758

3 Diokno AC, Brown MB, Herzog AR. Sexual function in the elderly. Arch Intern Med 1990; ;50.197-200

4. Bretschneider JG., McCoy NL.. Sexual interest and behavior in healthy 80 to 102 year olds. Arch Sex Behav 1988; 17:109-129

5. Leiblum SR. Rosen RC. editors. Principles and practice of sex therapy. Update for the 1990s. New York: Guilford Press: 1989

6. Schover LR. Prime time: sexual health for men over fifty. New York: Holt, Rinehart & Winston; 1984

7. Morales AJ, Nolan JJ, Nelson JC, Yen SS. Effects of replacement dose of dehydroepiandrosterone in men and women of advancing age. J Clin Endocrinol Metab 1994; 78:1360-1367

8. Current Population Reports Series. US Bureau of the Census 1057:25, 1990

9. Meston CM, Trapnell PD, Gorzalka BB. Ethnic and gender differences in sexuality: Variations in sexual behavior between Asian and non-Asian university students. Arch Sex Behav 1996; 25:33-72

10. Janus SS; Janus CL. The Janus Report on sexual behavior. New York: John Wiley & Sons; 1993

11. Christenson CV, Gagnon JH. Sexual behavior in a group of older women. J Gerontol 1965; 20:351

12. Luderman K. The sexuality of the older person: review of the literature. Gerontologist 1981; 21:203

13. Koster A. Change-of-life anticipations, attitudes, and experiences among middle-aged Danish women. Health Care Women Int 1991; 12:1

14. Barbach L. Sexuality through menopause and beyond. Menopause Management 1996; 5:18-21

15. Roughan PA, Kaiser FE, Morley JE. Sexuality and the older woman. Care Older Woman 1993; 1:87-106.

16. Cawood EHH, Bancroft J.Steroid hormones, the menopause, sexuality and well-being of women. Psychol Med 1996; 26:925-936.

17. Kinsey AC, Pomeroy WB, Martin CE. Sexual behaviour in the human male. Philadelphia (Pa): WB Saunders; 1948

18. Masters WH, Johnson VE. Human sexual response. Boston (Mass: Little, Brown; 1996

19. Schiavi RC. Rehmam. Sexuality and aging. Urol Clin North Am 1995; 22:711-726

20. Edwards AK, Husted J. Penile sensitivity. age and sexual behavior. J Clin Psychol 1976: 32:697-700

21. Semens JF, Wagner G. Estrogen deprivation and hormonal function in postmenopausal women. JAMA 1982; 445:248-253

22. Bachmann GA. Influence of menopause on sexuality. Int J Fertil 1995: 40:16-22

23. Bachmann G, Leiblum S, Grill J. Brief sexual inquiry in gynecologic practice. Obstet Gynecol 1989: 73:425-42:7

24. Woessner JP. Age-related changes of the human uterus: its connective tissue framework. J Gerontol 1963: 18:220-224

25. Dupont WD, Page DL. Menopausal estrogen replacement therapy and breast cancer. Arch Intern Med 1991: 151:67-72

26. Gupta K. Sexual dysfunction in elderly women. Urol Care Elderly 1990; 6:197-203

27. Myers L, Morokoff P. Physiological and subjective sexual arousal in pre and postmenopausal women. Paper presented at the American Psychological Association Meeting, 1985

28. Badeau D. Illness, disability and sex in aging. Sex Dis 1995; 13:219-237

29. Bolt JW, Evans C, Marshall UR. Sexual dysfunction after prostatectomy. Br J Urol 1986; 58:319

30. Meston CM, Gorzalka BB. Psychoactive drugs and human sexual behavior: The role of serotonergic activity. J Psychoactive Drugs 1992; 24:1-40

31. Hilton P. Urinary incontinence during sexual intercourse: a common but rarely volunteered symptom. Br J Obstet Gynaecol 1988; 95:377-381

32. Meston CM, Gorzalka BB, Wright JM. Inhibition of physiological and subjective sexual arousal in women by clonidine. J Psychosom Med 1997; 59:399-407

33. Schreiner-Engel P, Schiavi RC, Vietorisz D, et al. The differential impact of diabetes type on female sexuality. J Psychosom Res 1987; 31:23-33

34. Brecher E. Love, sex and aging: a Consumer's Union survey. Boston (Mass): Little Brown; 1984

SEXUALITY IN THE LATER YEARS:
The Cross-Cultural and Historical Context

Mary Hotvedt

Introduction

Throughout our youth we are given direct and indirect messages about our culture's code of appropriate sexual behavior. The most obvious ones are statements about the right circumstances for beginning sexual experiences with another, the reproductive functions of both sexes, the characteristics of good partners, and the ways in which we can be attractive to potential mates. The opinions, coming from disparate sources such as parents and peer groups, often conflict, but today the sexual concerns of the young are at least discussed. The indirect message is that sexuality is the domain of young adults. It may be an area of interest, anxiety, and experimentation for children and adolescents. For mature adults, sexuality should be a settled matter that declines in importance with the years.

The heavier emphasis on sexuality in the first 25 years of the life cycle, the "formative" years, is poor preparation for the life crises that must be faced by many of us. The man going through a mid-life crisis, the woman leaving a loveless marriage after the children have grown, the older couple whose cherished sexual relationship is disrupted by serious illness, the woman who must decide on hormone treatments after menopause, the widowed and divorced, the mature couple wishing to add more variety to their sex life—all share two common problems. First, they are concerned about their sexuality. Second, they have been told indirectly since childhood that they should not be concerned about sex after youth is past.

In the absence of knowledge, we call upon our folklore about sexuality in the later years. Three repeated themes in these myths stand out:

1. In the later years, we are not sexually desirable.
2. In the later years, we are not sexually desirous.
3. In later life, we are not sexually capable.

The rest of this volume contains information contrary to these three themes. The purposes of this chapter are to delve into the sources of the mythology, to demystify the myths by understanding their cultural and historical roots, to compare several cultures' attitudes and behaviors in order to broaden the perspective of our own culture, and, finally, to suggest the reasons why a book such as this is so timely.

Cross-Cultural Data

Limits of the Data

It is possible that much of the anthropological literature, with some notable exceptions, reflects the cultural biases with which we were raised. Little, if anything, is said about the sexuality of older people, and, often, sexuality itself is not examined much. Furthermore, a researcher who has made a serious attempt to get such information is faced with other difficulties. Much of the most revealing expressions of sexuality take place in private, so that the fieldworker must rely on reported, more than seen, behavior. Thus, informants may state ideal rather than actual behaviors or attitudes (Gebhard, 1971a). Last, the segregation of the sexes is far greater in many other cultures than it is in our own; as a result, a researcher can discuss intimate topics with same-sex informants only, making for useful but uneven ethnographies.

This chapter is not an exhaustive discussion of all the literature available. Examples cited either illustrate commonly seen patterns, supported by other ethnographics done for the same culture, or are unique for their emphasis on sexuality. Research for this chapter involved a search of the Human Relations Areas Files (HRAF), periodicals on gerontology and comparative family studies, and current readings in the social sciences.

A Model for Studying Sexuality

Sexual identity can be seen as having three major components: core morphological identity, sex-role behavior, and sexual orientation (Green, 1974). Core morphological identity, the sense that one is male or female, is the first to form in the individual and the part of sexual identity least likely to change over the life span.

Related to core identity is sex-role (or gender-role) behavior, the individual's conduct that is culturally ascribed to either females or males. While much of the dichotomy of sex roles relates to the reproductive functions and the division of labor in the culture, the exact traits considered desirable for each sex vary among cultures and within the life span for many cultures.

The third component, perhaps the last to develop, is sexual orientation. It embodies not only the sexual experience of the individual but also his/her fantasies, desires, and self-description as a sexual being. Cultures help to channel much of the sexual impulse toward reproductive ends, yet there are great variations between cultures in preferred sexual acts, levels of intimacy between partners, and allowances for homosexual and nonmarital heterosexual experiences.

Much of the data presented here are concerned with continuities and shifts in sex roles as well as sexual activity in the later years. The roles, changing throughout life, are pervasive for almost every aspect of the culture and channel the ways an individual acts or reacts toward others as well as his/her own needs and emotions.

What Are "Later Years?"

There is no cultural universality about the point at which someone passes into the status of "old man" or "old woman." There are trends, however. In many cultures the climacteric in a woman marks a change in her status and roles, as will be discussed in this chapter. No such change is marked in a man, although a man monogamously married to a woman who has experienced menopause may be seen as sharing her status change. In other cases, the marriage of children or the appearance of grandchildren are demarcations of age. Another major change, particularly in extended family situations, is the point at which an adult child and spouse—usually an oldest son and a daughter-in-law—become the practical heads of the household, although the parents may maintain positions of respect. Still another more commonly recognized transition is reached when individuals, usually by this point widowed, are no longer capable of caring for themselves physically and must become dependent on relatives.

The mortality and life expectancy rates for each sex in each culture must be considered. In rural Ireland and France, for example, 18 to 25% of a village's population lives to age 60 or older (Arensberg and Kimball, 1961; Wylie, 1965). Much attention has been given by the press to Eastern European mountain communities whose members live in the range from their 80s to over 100 (Gutmann, 1977). In America, although 11.3% of the total population is 65 or older (Brotman, 1981), only 3.7% of the Mexican American population is over 65 (U.S. Bureau of Census, 1972). The figure for Mexican Americans approximates those reported for several tribal societies (e.g., Murphy and Murphy, 1974) and agricultural societies (e.g., Lewis, 1951; Martin and Voorhies, 1975), reflecting the ravages of disease, the dangers of childbirth, and the perils of warfare and certain occupations.

Thus, the concept of "older" is a relative one, measured against the usual life expectancy of one's sex in the culture and against the perceptible bodily changes that occur sooner in a difficult environment.

Sex Roles and Sexual Behavior

Several researchers have reported shifts in both private and public sex roles for both sexes in later adulthood in many cultures. Factors that affect these shifts for women are the cultural attributions of power to menstruation and the role content of wife, mother, and mother-in-law. For men, sex role changes are related to the father-son and husband-wife reciprocal roles and the seniority system for public power. For both sexes, individual and family economic status, health, religion, and respect are important in determining the exact position of the person.

Whether or not there is a concomitant change in sexual behaviors and attitudes for older people depends on the sex-role content as well as such factors as cultural concepts of beauty, potency, the female orgasm, sexuality in youth, and religious ideals about the nature of sexuality. For men and, to a lesser extent, for women, wealth and power may greatly affect the availability of partners in later years. Thus, partner availability, for both heterosexual and homosexual experiences, should be examined. The economic base of the culture, with which the family is completely intertwined, must be examined for patterning of cultural attitudes toward virtually all aspects of sexual expression.

Tribal, Agrarian, and Industrialized Societies

A lengthy list of variables has been presented, and they must be organized logically for the discussion. A progression from tribal through agrarian to industrialized societies will be used, as it approximates the prehistory and history of the cultures that have contributed to our own.

Tribal Structures

Examples here are drawn from cultures in which all members consider themselves related, at least by mythical ancestry, and in which lineage and family form the basis for the power structure of each community. The economic base may be hunting and gathering, horticulture (simple gardening), herding, or a combination of these elements. Tribal societies dependent on irrigation agriculture and a developed class structure, such as certain Middle Eastern groups, are discussed with other agrarian societies.

Recent research using the HRAF files indicates that overall status of the aged in a society is correlated with the type of subsistence base. Balkwell and Balswick (1981) proposed that the status of older people is low in hunting and gathering societies in which there are great fluctuations in food supply and that their status is high in those economies that have a stable herding and/or agricultural production.

In tribal life, men and women occupy different spheres by division of labor. The tasks that each sex is trained for vary from culture to culture; some are the exclusive responsibility of one gender, whereas others are simply more commonly performed by one group than by another. The division of labor can be visualized as two bell curves overlapping to varying degrees for each tribe. At the median point in each curve are the activities that all or almost all men or women must perform in order to be considered an adequate member of their sex. The nonintersecting tails are the specialized, segregated roles for each sex. The overlapping tails represent the activities shared by adult members, regardless of sex.

The division of labor is bound up with reproduction, particularly on the women's part, and forms the bases of sex roles. In small children, the curves of activities would be far more overlapping, with distance increasing drastically as an Ibibio boy of Nigeria, for example, is drawn away from his mother and is taught traditionally male occupations such as hunting, warfare, and religious rituals in preparation for his initiation into manhood. His sister, at an even earlier age, is being trained in gardening and household tasks that remove her from male playmates and eventually bring her to her own initiation (Andreski, 1970). Marriage, a necessity in most tribes for the true achievement of adulthood, serves the interests of both sexes eventually as they contribute the skills and abilities of each of their spheres to parenthood and householding. The curves begin to move closer together for the more mature adults. In later years, the overlap is significantly greater than it is for young adults, though it is still smaller than the overlap for small children.

The psychological context of sex roles undergoes this melting effect as well, so that women and men could be said to be androgynized with age (Gutmann, 1977). In some cultures, this process is a fairly benign one, based on the recognized respect each sex accords the other. Among the Lepcha of Nepal, studied by Gorer (1967), the sexual division of labor is slight, the major features being that women, the childbearers, are barred from hunting. Sexual antagonism is minimal; both yin and yang are seen as necessary for life.

Despite the complementarity of labor always necessary for a tribe's survival and growth, in many cultures such a deep antagonism exists between the sexes that the sex-role changes of later life signify major power shifts for a man and a woman rather than a solely congenial recognition of common goals and abilities. Andreski (1970) has described this state as a "cold sex-war" in which the power and higher status men consider rightfully theirs is challenged by the women who can make equivalent claims to it. In such cultures, the mythology alludes to a time in which women knew the rituals of power until the men, usually through trickery, stole the knowledge needed for control. The men feel, however, that they must always be vigilant in order to keep women from recapturing their leadership over them. Women view the functioning of the culture quite differently from men, despite their observances of the taboos on them (Murphy and Murphy, 1974), and older women pay only token tribute to men's dominance (Mead, 1950).

The status of an Ibibio man as he ages is dependent on his economic situation and the size of his household, as it is for a woman. Working adult children and a prosperous farm or business allow the man to hold public office, all of which requires resources for financing necessary ceremonies and the arts of hospitality. Until his death he is the paterfamilias, the head of the compound, which includes his wife or wives, his unmarried daughters and sons, his married sons and their wives and children, and often his relatives who are less fortunate. Even a widower or a man with many daughters but no sons can enlarge his family by appointing his youngest child as "home-daughter." Instead of marrying into another family, she remains with her parent and is allowed to have lovers so that her children are of her own rather than their fathers' lineages (Andreski, 1970). Thus, a man of any wealth can fulfill all male sex roles in the later years, freed to do so in part by the death or infirmity of his father, the prior head of the family.

The conflict between an aging father and a maturing son is difficult to resolve when it occurs. In some senses a father is an obstacle to a younger man's own success; in other ways, he is a valuable ally and teacher. Personalities and child-rearing practices of the tribe affect each household, so that warm, nurturing fathers fare better than men who were little more than persons to be feared and respected by their children. Domestic tension may be increased by the technological and educational changes in a society. It is useful and prestigious for a man to send his children to school, his sons to universities, perhaps, in America or Europe. Educated sons have returned with skills their fathers will never have. The aging father's roles as decision maker for the compound and as the oral historian and teacher to children and grandchildren are eroded. Achebe's trilogy of Ibo life in Nigeria (1959, 1960, 1967) is a moving fictional depiction of this process.

A variety of cultural mechanisms handle male intergenerational conflict in the sphere of public power. In many East African tribes, for example, a formal age-grade system assures that at certain points all authority is turned over to a somewhat younger group of men, so that older men assume a passivity in public affairs that Gutmann (1977) sees as paralleling feminine roles. Another mechanism involves moving older men into special public positions that call on them to exercise personality characteristics that are traditionally feminine—nurturing, ameliorating, peaceful traits. For example, among the, Comanche, war chiefs become peace chiefs in later years, trying to constrain the desires of younger men (Gutmann, 1977). Thus, even societies that are gerontocracies have rules by which the oldest members make way, prior to their deaths, for others.

As men age and as their health and householding situation require it—that is, widowhood, dependency on a son or daughter, life along with an aging wife—they may gradually do more "women's work" as part of their daily routine. Older men also may become more nurturing and indulgent with their grandchildren than they are with their own offspring. Gutmann (1977) refers to this as a further androgynization of the male with age.

An older woman is in an enviable position. She has lived through the hazards of childbearing—no small feat. If she has adult children who love and respect her, she has assurance of support for some time and aid with her work. If she is a senior wife, as among the Ibibio of Nigeria, she has the right to respect from her junior cowives and their children and a legal status close to her husband's. She may have a profitable trading business, which her oldest daughter will inherit. Among the Ibibio and several other West African tribes, if she has no living children but does own a flourishing trading business, she may make a "woman-marriage" in which she is the legal "husband" to another women whose children, usually sired by the "husband's" husband or another male relative, will inherit their "father's" business (Bohannon and Middleton, 1968; Andreski, 1970). She also can be involved, due to the wisdom gained from her experiences and her elaborate social network, in a number of special societies with religious, social, and economic prestige. Her daughter-inlaw, particularly the senior wife of her oldest son, is her closest ally, having been raised in her home from late childhood as a kind of adopted daughter. Her son treats her with respect and love. These affectional ties with the younger generation benefit her economically as well as emotionally. If she is fortunate, her husband is still living and they are comrades in their various enterprises. The androngynization process as described earlier possibly contributes to greater husband-wife cooperation at this point.

In sex-antagonistic cultures an older woman assumes an interestingly contradictory position regarding the public and religious rule of men. On the one hand, she is the teacher of women's rituals, the initiator of young girls, and the trainer of younger wives; in these roles she is supportive of the male power structure. Also, as a wife she is deeply involved in the concerns of her husband; she is a guardian of his interests as well as her own. On the other hand, an older women has the knowledge and power within her own spheres, as well as within male spheres, to no longer fear male authority. For an old woman there are many more freedoms. She may sit in on councils of men from which she was once excluded. She may openly criticize or ridicule certain aspects of male roles. In some cases, she may become a ruler over men, as with the Ibibio uncrowned queen known as "Ma" (Andreski, 1970).

Menopause significantly alters women's status and roles in the male sphere. The sexual division of labor and authority is often supported by beliefs in the power of menstrual blood to severely affect the activities of men. No single word can describe that power, because the sense of it differs from culture to culture. Research for this review suggests that in sex-cooperative societies, such as the Lepcha, women's blood can be viewed as detrimental to hunting and that it has an awesome power of a separate sphere, but is not a source of disgust, for men. Sex-antagonistic societies, however, seem fraught with ideas of fear or disgust over pollution by a menstruating woman. In such societies a woman is shunned or placed in seclusion during each cycle until she ritually cleanses herself. In both types of societies a linkage between life and death exists in menstrual blood.

When a woman ceases to menstruate, therefore, she is no longer bound by men's fear of her pollution. She becomes "like a man" (Gutmann, 1977), though not quite, for she has knowledge of the women's sphere, which men cannot have. A woman, therefore, may be able to combine all these factors and become a witch (Gutmann, 1977), the penalty for which is often death if a charge is brought and proved true to the satisfaction of the community.

In a number of societies, men too, in later years, are thought to engage in magic (DeBeauvoir, 1973). Landes (1971) reports several Ojibwa life histories in which older married couples are in league in their sorcery, forcing unwilling families to marry their children to their own for fear of illness or death. The sources of these magical attributes are multiple. First, the older men and women are androgynized; they have knowledge and abilities of both sexes. Second, they have the knowledge of a community through their long experience with it, and that knowledge can be used for their own ends or for their clients' interests. Third, they envy the young who are replacing them, or their success in life, which they lacked (Mead, 1950). Finally, they are closer to death symbolically, if not actually, than are the young, and their energies are attuned to the supernatural world, which they will soon join (DeBeauvoir, 1973; Gutmann, 1977).

The time comes for some people when they become physically unable to care for themselves. This is yet another phase of older life. By their own standards, those who are unable to care for themselves are the least respected. In cultures in which everyone marries and works to ensure life, the infirm person is considered less than a child. Children at least are a resource, but a sick old relative loses much respect and becomes another mouth to feed for no eventual reward. In some cultures, people choose to die before this time in order to avoid rejection or to feel they are contributing something through their death. In other cultures, the children abandoned the parent, as they knew in turn their children would abandon them. Another "solution" is to treat the sick, old persons so poorly that disease or deprivation will quickly take them (DeBeauvoir, 1973). Yet death brings an upward swing in one's status again; the deceased is remembered as an ancestor.

The paucity of data on the sexual lives of older tribal peoples most likely reflects a bias on the part of the researcher. Certain inferences can be drawn from life histories that include descriptions of enduring marital relationships. The more direct data come from cultures that encourage sexual expression throughout the life span, where only partner availability severely alters sexuality in the later years. First, we will examine data from marriages and approved extramarital relationships.

The research found no tribe in which menopause marked the end of sexual relations for couples who are married at the time of the woman's menopause. In Andreski's (1970) accounts of Ibibio women, informants in their 60s who have husbands imply that a sexual relationship exists. These are first to fourth marriages for the subjects, made in some cases after divorce and widowhood. An estimated 40 to 60% of tribes permit a form of extramarital activity for women so that members have the opportunity of leaving arranged unions to find more compatible partners (Gebhard, 1971b). The Canadian Ojibwa, according to Landes (1971), place a high premium on individualism, romantic expression, and compatability. Among the Ojibwa, remarriage and divorce continue until compatible partners are found, and these unions last until death. Among the Eskimo, likewise, such remarriages occur. Additionally, mate sharing (the exchange of sexual partners between visitors and hosts or a husband's loan of his wife to an unmarried male visitor) brings about reciprocal relationships between the households for the rest of life, so that even children may ask favors and hospitality of old mate-sharing partners of their parents (Spencer, 1968). In Lepcha culture, remarriage and sexual expression are continued into a person's 80s, the expected life span, although younger people find such involvement humorous when new lovers are in their 70s (Gorer, 1967).

Menopause in patriarchal, sex-antagonistic societies seems to reduce the marriageability of widows who have no children. In many societies, sterility lowers the status of a woman. In some cases, a widow is remarried to her deceased husband's brother, although, if she is past child bearing and has adult children, she may remain with them.

A man of any wealth and vigor may continue to form marriage alliances as long as other families accept his offer of bride price. Ibibio men of substance who are not Christian may have two or more wives of varying ages. Only one of Andreski's informants had a non-Christian husband who felt he was too old to add another wife to his compound, despite his wife's urging (Andreski, 1970). Polygamy in certain African nations is practiced to varying degrees. Census figures show that 31% of all married men in Benin (1961) and 28% of married Senegalese men (1971) are polygamous (Welch and Glick, 1981).

Few statistics exist to indicate the frequency of marital intercourse. Among the Mangaians, a Polynesian people who have a history of divorce and remarriage similar to the Ojibwa, Marshall (1971) found that men over 48 expect to have at least one orgasm per night, whereas women may have more. Mangaian lovers show virtually no affectional or foreplay gestures in public. Sexual activity, however, is highly enjoyed from an early age, and Marshall (1971) reports that women are always orgasmic.

Among the Lepchas and some Oceanic societies, older women are the sexual teachers of the boys who have been initiated. Malinowski (1929) reported that the Trobiand Islanders, a Melanesian society, place a high value on youth and beauty and, therefore, do not seek out older sexual partners. In one case, however, several young men in the community contracted a venereal disease. No young women were infected. The common partner was a very old woman.

The literature search for data on the other sexual experiences was not a fruitful one. Data on homosexual encounters, extramarital sexuality, and masturbation among the elder generation were not found. What can be surmised is that within tribal cultures, even the sex-antagonistic ones, the continuation or cessation of sexual contact is a matter of individual circumstances for older members. In cultures that encourage female sexuality from youth, women may have more opportunities, despite widowhood, to continue being active. Older men in tribal life, being reproductively capable for a longer time than women, may continue to seek partners until they feel that they are no longer able or interested. Health and wealth, along with status, may be the significant factors here.

Sex Roles and Sexuality in Peasant Societies

Harris (1975 p. 300) defines peasants as "pre-industrial food-producers who pay rent or taxes." They are structurally inferior in the society, whether they are controlled by a nobility (who may in fact be their kin), a state, a conquering army, or a bank. Although the family may be as central to a peasant society as it is to a tribal one, the external pressure on the class as a whole seriously affects the way in which the sex roles and the sexuality of family members are expressed.

It is more common among peasant cultures to find an emphasis on female virginity at marriage, a low regard for female sexuality, and an emphasis on childbearing as the only legitimate reason for marital sex. Among Catholics and Moslems, these attitudes are reinforced by religion. The economic reasons must not be overlooked, however.

A portion of peasants' production and time must go to at least one source that has some punitive control over the family. If payment of whatever kind is not met, aid from other relatives and members cannot be counted on for too long because resources are limited throughout the entire group. Failure to meet payments and to produce can mean loss of land. Marriage and children are essential to the family's continued control of its land. Through marriage, new wealth can be brought into the house as dowry; affines, kin by marriage, can be important allies; the new wife is an additional worker, and children will be both workers and heirs.

Martin and Voorhies (1975) note that in peasant, or agricultural, societies the sexual division of labor seen in tribal economies is extended.

> Agricultural societies, then, generally prefer to keep a woman as isolated from public interaction as possible. Indeed, her value as a potential spouse may depend upon the degree of innocence and mystery she is able to maintain. The social segregation of the sexes accompanying intensive cultivation thus surrounds the woman with a highly charged set of taboos. Perhaps more than any other economic adaptation, the behavioral sets of men and women in agricultural societies are diametrically opposed by culture. Sexuality is certainly one of the most dynamic examples of role complementarity. As the sexual life of women falls under the control of society, no sexual activity for women becomes a social obligation symbolically detached from individual gratification. For females, nonparticipation in extra domestic production, protective spatial isolation, premarital chastity, and institutionalized frigidity go hand in hand [p. 294].

As in sex-antagonistic tribes, peasant men consider themselves to be the rulers of the society. Unlike the tribal men, the peasant men see themselves as having "natural" superior abilities (Martin and Voorhies, 1975) as opposed to being the winners of a past battle between the sexes that could be rekindled if men are not wary.

Whereas the magic of menstrual blood keeps tribal women within their own sphere, the concept of female chastity is used by peasants to keep women under strict familial control until menopause. Women's power to disrupt men's positions lies in their possible sexuality. In a system in which land is at a premium and is desired by others and a few years of misfortune can deplete the resources and work of generations, any challenge to the rightful ownership of the land jeopardizes the family. Any decline in the allegiances between families is a threat. If a man were to die and his son's paternity were in dispute, his family could lose the land to the challenger or to the landlord. If families cannot assure that their daughters are virginal at marriage, no other families will want marriage alliances with them, because of this potential threat. In twelfth century western England, for example, any widow accused of postmarital sex lost her husband's land to the lord. Her only recourse was to ride into court on a black ram, singing:

Here I am,
Riding upon a black ram
Like a whore, as I am....
Therefore, I pray of you, Mr Steward,
Let me have my land again.
        [Bennett, 1969, p. 255]

The most common marriage pattern reported in rural Europe, the Middle East, China, Japan, and Latin America is one in which the bride lives with her husband, particularly if he is the oldest son, in the home of his parents. Eventually, she becomes mistress and her husband becomes master of the house, and, in turn, their son and his wife replace them. The system provides for a waxing and waning of authority for both sexes throughout the life span, with many reports of conflict between husband and wife, father and son, and mother-in-law and daughter-in-law, which have great effects on the later years.

The first major source of stress to look at is antagonism between husband and wife. The initial problem is often sexual in nature. In rural Taiwan, young women enter marriage with no preparation for lovemaking, and they hardly know their husbands. Mothers, remembering their own sad first experiences, say they do not have the heart to tell their daughters what it will really be like (Wolf, 1972). In Tepoztlan, Mexico, Oscar Lewis (1951) reported that a woman avoids sexual relations before marriage and restricts contact after marriage in order to limit pregnancies, and that men discourage their wives' sexual response so that the women will not be unfaithful.

Men are not under the same strictures, although, when they enter into their first marriage, they may not be experienced either. In Tepoztlan, men are expected to have extramarital sex, although wives are angered by the accompanying loss of income and attention to the family (Lewis, 1951). In rural Taiwan, as elsewhere, prostitutes provide safe sexual outlets for men (Wolf, 1972). Rural Ireland and the Aran Islands are among the few reported cultures in which men, as well as women, are expected to be chaste before and during marriage (Arensberg and Kimball, 1961; Messenger, 1971); also, the ages of first marriage are the highest reported. Here too, sex is mainly for procreation, and male orgasm is considered debilitating (Messenger, 1971).

The second major source of stress in the husband-wife relationship is combined male authority and absenteeism. Because young peasant men live more public lives than their wives, and because they may need to accept labor in another area to help the family, they do not have the same degree of contact with their children that women have. Furthermore, the male sex role often, though not always, requires the father to be more authoritarian than affectionate toward both his wife and his children, particularly toward his sons (Kiray, 1976; Lewis, 1951). Also, the home is the woman's sphere, and, in a sense, a husband is there to provide care but not to interfer in her activities (Campbell, 1974).

A daughter-in-law often has a respectful but minimal relationship with her husband's father (Wolf, 1972; Peristiany, 1976). Next to her husband, and the child who will supplant him, her mother-in-law is the most important person in her new household. In Taiwan there is a "honeymoon" period between the new wife and her mother-in-law (Wolf, 1972), but often the "outsider"—as she is called—very quickly becomes the apprentice of the older woman. The birth of a child, particularly a son, improves the new wife's status significantly (Campbell, 1974). The young woman is then on her way to becoming the head of the household and, eventually, a mother-in-law herself.

The third major source of stress comes with the father-son relationship changing drastically with time. In a Greek community, Campbell (1974) reports, fathers, unlike many in peasant societies, are indulgent and affectionate with their sons until the son becomes apprenticed to the father's work. The tension then begins. The son must maintain respect for his father, but he is anxious to be independent. The father knows that soon his son will marry and have a son, which will signify his own time for retirement—not a welcome event. They maintain a delicate balance for the sake of the family.

In rural Ireland the oldest surviving son is kept waiting for his parents' land a long time. He is referred to as "the boy" until he marries, the father and mother being reluctant to be assigned become secondary status in their home. Thus, many "boys" of 45 can be found working their farms with their still dominant fathers (Arensberg and Kimball, 1961). The combined effects of these three sources of stress on sex roles and sexual behavior can now be seen.

As in tribal societies, late adulthood can be divided into two periods. The first is the time in which an individual is still active and in charge of a multigenera-tional household. The second period is retirement, although in peasant society this may occur before illness or neglect force the issue.

In the active phase, men continue much as they have from young adulthood, assuming more authority with age until they are confronted with their sons' maturity and the true nature of their wives' power over the household through the sons as well as through the domestic sphere. In a study of a Turkish community it was found, for example, that mothers were the intermediaries between sons and fathers, helping sons to achieve financial independence from their fathers (Kiray, 1976). Lewis' comments on Tepoztlan men illustrate this point:

> We have seen that frequently husbands are only nominally the heads of household....As men grow older, and as their sexual powers and ability to work decline, their position of dominance is more difficult to maintain. . . . The life cycle of men and women takes an opposite course: Men in early life are in a comparatively favored position, but as they grow older they are weighed down by life situations, women begin with less freedom, lower aspiration levels, and earlier responsibilities, but as they mature after marriage, they slowly gain more freedom and often take a dominating position in the household [Lewis, 1951, pp. 419-420].

Gutmann (1977), in his cross-cultural analysis, notes these patterns in older men; a "feminization" or androgynization occurring that is similar in both tribal and peasant societies accompanied by a "masculinization" of older women as they come to dominate the household and, it should be noted, the social network outside the family.

In peasant societies, then, a woman's heyday occurs fairly late in life, while she is the head of a team of daughters-in-law and faithful sons and is freed of certain restrictions on her mobility and social life. Older women may engage in sexual joking and mimicry, showing less modesty than was required of them in their childbearing years (Arensberg and Kimball, 1971; Lewis, 1951; Wolf, 1972). Arensberg saw this joking by both sexes as in fact a means of reinforcing the strict sexual norms of the community. In rural France, the sexual urge is seen as compelling and natural in both sexes. Everyone jokes and chats about it, finding great hilarity in a younger man's joking pass at a good-natured 99-year-old widow. Nonetheless, actual sexual behavior is very private, and the humorists are careful to choose their subjects discreetly (Wylie, 1964).

Actual sexual behavior between older married partners is difficult to assess. In rural Ireland, menopause may end sexual activity.

> Among the old, if it (sexual interest) exists at all, it is only as a survival of embers that should far better off be long dead. For adults, in adult family life, sex is divested of any awesome, evil character. "God help us," said one woman in this regard, "what is natural can't be wonderful" [Arensberg and Kimball, 1961, p. 208].

In an analysis of Indian Hindu fertility, Nag ascertained that Hindu wives over 44 had an average of about 1 coital experience every 21 days, whereas American white women of the same age group had an average of 1.3 experiences every week (1972). In Tepoztlan, men never encourage their wives to be too sexually interested, for fear they will be unable to satisfy them in later years (Lewis, 1951). Older widows in Tepoztlan often do not remarry, because the children disapprove of a new male being installed in the home (Lewis, 1951). Yet, men's premarital and extramarital relations are often with widows (Lewis, 1951).

Religion encourages older people to turn away from sexual matters as well as from issues of power in the household. In Hinduism, for example, the older householders are encouraged to turn matters over to the next generation in order to spend the remainder of life in religious pursuit (Basham, 1954). In Catholicism, it is thought that the proximity of death should be felt by the old and that they should live a sanctified old age (Arensberg and Kimball, 1961).

A note on the respect accorded older parents in peasant societies: it is traditionally the sons' and daughters'-in-law responsibility to care for older parents, thereby reversing the dependencies of the generations. Parents, however, often do not trust that their children will do so properly (Lewis, 1951). When conflict between mother and daughter-in-law is severe, the older woman is forced out of the home (Arensberg and Kimball, 1961). If fathers' authority has been too keenly felt by sons, the care of aging parents may pass from the uninterested sons' hands to those of daughters, who have had more affectionate ties with the parents. In Moslem communities this is a new pattern, because only recently have some younger married couples lived separately from the husband's family (Kiray, 1976; Peristiany, 1976). In some cases, older parents are abandoned to poorhouses (Tentori, 1976).

As long as one can work and contribute useful advice, one retains some adult status, but respect diminishes with ill health, and the infirm old parent is treated as being worse than a child (Wylie, 1964). In some areas, such as Sicily, an old mother fares much better due to her close relationship with her children (Cronin, 1970), so that some of the achieved higher status of older women stays with them until death.

In summation of sexuality in peasant societies, the rule appears to be that the repression of interest and experience in female children and young women, regardless of its encouragement or discouragement in males, results in less sexual activity in later years. If men are permitted more sexual experience outside marriage, they nonetheless must shoulder the responsibility for sexual initiative and activity within the marriage, in some cases taking care *not* to create desire in women. Under that responsibility, male sexuality appears to become as repressed with age as does its female counterpart.

A Historical Perspective on Our Culture

Trends in both male and female sex roles and sexuality have been delineated for both tribal and peasant groups for two reasons: to impart an idea of patterning and variability in human cultures, and to provide background for understanding the sources of the earlier-mentioned mythology of sexuality and aging that has been a part of our culture.

We are the heirs of these tribal and peasant traditions. The United States has been formed by the incorporation of Dahomeans, Ibibio, Ibo, Ojibwa, Comanche, and Oceanic tribal peoples, to name but a few, and by influxes of European, Asian, and Latin American families from rural backgrounds. Our legal and religious systems share roots with these peasantries. Until recently, we were a rural, agricultural society with a minimal technology, under some of the influences described earlier. Our families of origin often fight to preserve a sense of our original cultural values regarding sexuality and female behavior. With that history in mind, let us now turn to some factors that have created new viewpoints as well as factors that reinforce older viewpoints.

The Development of Competing Norms

Stone (1977) notes three unusual features in the formation of Western society's sexual behavior and attitudes. Referring particularly to the seventeenth and eighteenth centuries, he points out the long gap—10 years or more—between an individual's age of sexual maturity and marriage, with a large percentage of the population never marrying. This is the pattern reported in the twentieth century by Arensberg and Kimball (1961) for rural Ireland. The usual reason for this was the inability of a family to finance all marriageable children (with dowries, land, or a trade) or to find suitable partners, due to limited assets.

Another feature was a religion that looked upon sexuality with hostility, except when the purpose of sex was procreation. Although Protestantism marked a break with the idealization of virginity, it emphasized virginity for women before marriage (Stone, 1977).

Finally, the ideology of romantic love became popularly adopted, Stone theorizes, as the major reason for marriage. In the twelfth century, the cult of romantic love was an upper class preoccupation divorced from the realities of arranged marriage. The fact that the idea was at least appealing to the masses might be indicated by the number of old folk ballads about love affairs that have survived. Love was a popular theme on the stage, in song, and in literature for centuries. In the seventeenth and eighteenth centuries, however, novels became far more accessible to a population that was more literate than ever before, and romantic love became a part of real life—in varying degrees for each class—in the middle 1700s.

In the American colonies, as well as in England, the concept of romantic love as a reason for marriage was gaining strength, although more pragmatic reasons were still important (Queen and Habenstein, 1967). In Massachusetts, for example, marriage was virtually a necessity for survival in the smaller frontier communities of the seventeenth and early eighteenth centuries. Although the single-parent family existed—Boston was once described as a city of "widows and orphans"—the norm was for as many people as possible to marry and to remarry after widowhood. Severe financial penalties were imposed on bachelors, and the early colonial practice of the government giving land to unmarried women as well as men was stopped in some communities. Both practices were meant to ensure the growth of the colony, where land was so plentiful that the European restrictions on inheritance and therefore marriage eligibility, did not hold.

In the same period in English history, and slightly later in America, the extended-family pattern, as described in the discussion of peasants, was breaking down (Queen and Habenstein, 1967; Stone, 1977). With the growing patterns of urban living, wage labor, and a mobile labor force, the rise of the nuclear family was seen. This pattern is replicated today in peasant societies that are being transformed into urban forces (Hotvedt, 1976; Kiray, 1976; Peristiany, 1976). Ireland, although far more agrarian than the U.S. and England, devotes 23.8% of its land to agriculture (Gordon *et al.*, 1981), and a recent study showed that less than 50% of farming parents expected their sons to stay on the farm (Hannon, 1979).

The combined effects of these factors on the sexuality and sex roles of people in their later years are multiple. The structural changes of households and their economics provide the backdrop to the ideational dilemmas. We have noted that, in rural systems, beneath the ideal of male dominance, there exists a pattern of matrifocality; the household is considered mainly the domain of the senior woman, who has the most affectional relationships as well as a good number of authoritative roles. Thus a decline in the extended family that reduces the power of older men also reduces, though perhaps to a lesser degree, that of older women as well. In the early nineteenth century, more older people were forced to retire to almshouses than ever before, reflecting an unwillingness—or an inability—on the part of children in nuclear families to live by the older pattern of caring for infirm parents (Stone, 1977). A hale mother could be welcomed into a daughter's home as an additional helper and friend. She would have the knowledge of childrearing, "women's work," and health care to make a significant contribution (Kiray, 1976; Queen and Habenstein, 1967). Older men who must retire from their own enterprises because of failing strength may find a welcome place in a child's home, but they are at a disadvantage in continuing the fabric of their lives. The admission of their dependency and the loss of their strength and dominance are marks against their masculinity.

Older men today, according to Gutmann (1977), show a coping mechanism marked by a movement away from masculine activities and values in the face of conflict with a younger generation of men; a drift toward a more passive, congenial stance defined as feminine earlier in the life cycle. In another context, in the absorption of the members of some Native American tribes into modern American life, it has been found that women suffered less personality conflict with adaptation, because they could continue the preoccupations of traditional tribal women's roles, whereas men could no longer fulfil their own definitions of masculinity through their work (Georing, 1970).

In England, Stone (1977) argues, the value of the later years changed with the decrease in the extended family. Once it was a period respected as part of the life cycle where one's wisdom compensated for the loss of physical strength. However, it came to be seen as a period of physical and mental decay preceding death. As standards of health improved and people felt less at the mercy of fate, the process of aging was seen as proof of a failure of the individual.

Another erosion of later life was the loss of older people as teachers of the young family members. With the increase of science, literacy, and, finally, the mass media, the young can receive information as swiftly or more so than their elders, greatly reducing the value of the oral tradition and greatly increasing the independence of youth (Mead, 1970). The growth in the number and distribution of romantic novels (Stone, 1977) and their effects on the young can be seen as an early example of this trend.

DeBeauvoir (1973), in "The Coming of Age," sees two coexisting sexual images of older people. On the one hand there is the moralistic, religious ideal of the dignified older man or woman who no longer is interested in sex, the passions having died a natural death. On the other hand, there is the "dirty old man" or the "shameless old lady" (DeBeauvoir, 1973). Neither images stems from what we might now consider a healthy view of sexuality, but the images have long been with us. Indeed, both viewpoints appear in Greek drama and philosophy (DeBeauvoir, 1973).

Within our own history, religion and the older system of arranged marriage and residence with the extended family supported the decline of sexuality with age. For all classes, lust, even within marriage, was inveighed against as being dangerous to psychological and physical wellbeing (Stone, 1977). We know that the actual pattern of premarital sexuality, which in other cultures seems to be related to sexuality in the later years, varied from the ideal under new circumstances. In seventeenth and eighteenth century Massachusetts, cases of premarital sexual violations were extremely common (Queen and Habenstein, 1967). Extramarital and postmarital sexual conduct was far more severely punished and, therefore, less likely to be confessed. And so, again, it is difficult to ascertain the conduct of older people outside or in marriage. Instead, we are left with the ideal of the couple (or widowed person) declining into graceful old age, living a natural celibacy after a family is created, and preparing to meet the Creator by shedding their "earthly desires."

Of the other image, we know a bit more, chiefly through the diaries of famous people who were interested in their sexual selves until death. The appearance of these first intimate diaries coincides with the rise in romantic love. The journals of Tolstoy and Madame Tolstoy, Victor Hugo and his mistress, Trotsky, and many others (DeBeauvoir, 1973) show people grappling with the three myths mentioned earlier: the sexual undesirability, lack of interest, and inability of the later years. Patterns emerge. First, romantic love, perhaps an artificial piece of culture designed to mask the sexual urge (Stone, 1977), figures into the passions of these middle-class and upper-class people in later life. Sometimes the preference is for one's spouse, while at other times it is a heterosexual or homosexual attachment to a new person. Second, the negative effect of aging on women as sex objects as compared to the prospects of older men are seen. If a man had fame as a creative person or wealth and standing, he was capable of attracting and keeping younger partners, although he might still have an involved marital relationship. Women, however, felt keenly the competition with younger women, and sometimes men, who came closer to the romantic ideals of youth and beauty. This jealousy showed, despite the fact that these women received attention from other men. Finally, the journals show that even when coitus became difficult or impossible because of health, sexuality required an outlet and that varieties of expression could be found by both sexes (DeBeauvoir, 1973). It should be noted that these are the accounts of active people to whom the spheres of creativity and work were vital to the self-concept.

Research on older Americans' (average age 68) sexuality and self-esteem was conducted by questionnaire, with 51 men and 99 women responding (Stimson *et al.*, 1981). Both men and women in the study felt that sex was acceptable for older people. Results showed that being sexually active was as critical a variable in self-esteem for older men as it was for younger male samples studied earlier by the same research team. A key difference was that for older men, the quality of sexual performance was related to good feelings of self, whereas the quantity of sexual activity was the important factor for the younger men.

Women in the sample viewed sexual activity as separate from issues of self-esteem, as did younger women in the authors' previous study. The crucial point was that women seem to accept youth as a prerequisite for "desirability" and use youthful standards to judge themselves. When a woman no longer feels attractive, she is no longer sure of her overall worth.

Where We Now Stand

A cross-cultural analysis on sexuality in the later years may be dismaying to the reader as well as to the researcher. Many of us were taught that the strict sexual mores of peasant life are "natural" and correct. The cases of abandonment when ill health occurs—whether in tribal, peasant, or early industrial society—strike uncomfortably close to many of our own fears for our own futures. The scarcity of detailed data on the subject echoes the long tradition we have known in which the personal concerns of older people are supposedly less interesting than those of the young.

It is hoped that this review will give some hope as well as some background through its tentative conclusions. We have seen that great personal and cultural variation exists throughout the life span regarding sexuality. Vital to the continuation of sexual expression in later years, on anything other than an idiosyncratic basis, is a cultural pattern that allows for sexual expression in youth as well. Real sexual and economic domination by men appears to be inimicable to the full expression of female sexuality, which in turn has limiting effects on later male heterosexual expression in traditional societies except, possibly, for the more wealthy, who have the influence necessary to experience new sexual partners. Finally, in tribal and early industrial societies, it is indicated that a sense of vitality and purpose in later years strengthens one's sexuality.

There may have been some gains from the often painful past. Although the demise of the extended family and the rise of romantic love vitiate many of the roles of later years, benefits arise as well. The changes in sex roles that are slowly developing are, in fact, a move to foreshorten the changes (Gutmann 1977) and others see as occurring later in life; that is, an androgynization of both sexes so that the traditional values of masculinity and femininity might be more uniformly expressed by both sexes across the life span (Martin and Voorhies, 1975).

Although the cult of youth and beauty is still deep within our culture, older people are as literate and as verbal (or more so) as the young, and they have begun to influence the media to expand their standards of attractiveness to include a much older age group. In the later years, we may be more free to experience a continued or even new sense of sexuality without the presence of offspring to contradict and remind us of the dignity and asceticism proper to old age. We also feel more entitled to love and compatibility with a partner, regardless of age. Much is possible. To quote Goethe:

> So, lively brisk old man
> Do not let sadness come over you;
> For all your white hairs
> You can still be a lover.
>   [DeBeauvoir, 1973, p. 488]

References

Achebe, C. (1959). "Things Fall Apart." Fawcett, Greenwich, Connecticut.

Achebe, C. (1960). "No Longer at Ease." Fawcett, Greenwich, Connecticut.

Achebe, C. (1967). "Arrow of God." John Day, New York.

Andreski, I. (1970). "Old Wives' Tales: Life-Stories of African Women." Schocken Books, New York.

Arensberg, C., and Kimball, S., eds. (1961). "Family and Community in Ireland." Peter Smith, Gloucester, Massachusetts.

Balkwell, C., and Balswick, J. (1981) *J. Marriage and the Family 43*, 423-429.

Basham, A. L. (1954). "The Wonder That Was India." Grove Press, Inc., New York.

Bennett, H. S. (1969). "Life on the English Manor." Cambridge Univ. Press, London/New York.

Bohannon, P., and Middleton, J., eds. (1968). "Marriage, Family and Residence." Natural History Press, New York.

Brotman, H. (1981). Developments in Aging. "Every Ninth American," prepared for "Special Committee on Aging," U.S. Senate, Washington, D.C.

Campbell, J.K. (1974). "Honor, Family, and Patronage." Oxford Univ. Press, London/New York.

Cronin, C. (1970). "The Sting of Change: Sicilians in Sicily and Australia." Univ. of Chicago Press, Chicago.

DeBeauvoir, S. (1973). "The Coming of Age." Warner Paperback Library, New York.

Gebhard, P. H. (1971a). *In* "Human Sexual Behavior" (D. S. Marshall and R. Suggs, eds.), p. xii. Basic Books, New York.

Gebhard, P. H. (1971b). *In* "Human Sexual Behavior" (D. S. Marshall and R. Suggs, eds.), pp. 207-217. Basic Books, New York.

Gearing, F. O. (1970). "The Face of the Fox." Aldine, Chicago.

Gordon, M., Whelan, B., and Vaughan, R. (1981). *J. Marriage and the Family 43*, 741-747.

Gorer, G., ed. (1967). "Himalayan Village." Basic Books, New York.

Green, R. (1974). "Sexual Identity Conflict in Children and Adults." Penguin, Baltimore.

Gutmann, D. (1977). *In* "Handbook of the Psychology of Aging" (J. E. Birren and K. W. Schaie, eds.), pp. 305-306. Van Nostrand-Reinhold, Princeton, New Jersey.

Hannon, D. F. (1979). "Displacement and Development: Class, Kinship, and Social Change in Irish Rural Communities." Economic and Social Research Inst., Dublin.

Harris, M. (1975). "Culture, People, Nature." T. Y. Crowell, New York.

Hotvedt, M. E. (1976). Dissertation, Department of Anthropology, Indiana University, Bloomington (unpublished).

Kiray, N. (1976). *In* "Mediterranean Family Structures" (J. G. Peristiany, ed.), pp. 266-267. Cambridge Univ. Press, London/New York.

Landes, R. (1971). "The Ojibwa Woman." Norton, New York.

Lewis, O. (1951). "Life in a Mexican Village: Tepoztlan Revisited." Univ. Of Illinois Press, Urbana.

Malinowsky, B. (1929). "The Sexual Life of Savages." Harcourt, Brace & World, New York.

Marshall, D. S. (1971). *In* "Human Sexual Behavior" (D. S. Marshall and R. Suggs, eds.), pp. 103-162. Basic Books, New York.

Martin, M. K., and Voorhies, B. (1975). "Female of the Species." Columbia Univ. Press, New York.

Mead, M., ed. (1950). "Sex and Temperament in Three Primitive Societies." Mentor Books, New York.

Mead, M. (1970). "Culture and Commitment." Doubleday, New York.

Messenger, J. C. (1971). *In* "Human Sexual Behavior" (D. S. Marshall and R. Suggs, eds.), pp. 3-37. Basic Books, New York.

Murphy, Y., and Murphy, R. F. (1974). "Women of the Forest." Columbia Univ. Press, New York.

Nag, M. (1972). *Curr. Anthropol.* **13**, 231-238.

Peristiany, J. G., ed. (1976). "Mediterranean Family Structures." Cambridge Univ. Press, London/New York.

Queen, S. A., and Habenstein, R. N. (1967). "The Family in Various Cultures." Lippincott, Philadelphia.

Spencer, R. F. (1968). *In* "Marriage, Family and Residence" (P. Bohannon and J. Middleton, eds.), p. 142. Natural History Press, New York.

Stimson, A., Wase, J., and Stimson, J. (1981). *Research on Aging* **3**, 228-239.

Stone, L. (1977). "The Family, Sex, and Marriage in England. 1500-1800." Harper & Row, New York.

Tentori, T. (1976). *In* "Mediterranean Family Structures" (J. G. Peristinay, ed.), pp. 273-286. Cambridge Univ. Press, London/New York.

U.S. Bureau of Census (1972). "Statistical Abstracts of the United States: 1972," Table 40. U.S. Govt. Printing Office, Washington, D.C.

Welch, C., and Glick, P. (1981). *J. Marriage and the Family* **43**, 191- 192.

Wolf. M. (1972). "Women and the Family in Rural Taiwan." Stanford Univ. Press; Stanford, California.

Wylie, L. (1964). "Village in the Vaucluse." Harper & Row, New York.

SEXUALITY IN SEXAGENARIAN WOMEN

G.A. Bachmann and S.R. Leiblum

(Received 8 June 1990; revision received 5 July 1990; accepted 31 August 1990)

Sexual behavior was examined in 59 healthy, post-menopausal women between 60 and 70 years of age. Subjects were interviewed by a psychologist, completed medical and sexual questionnaires and had a gynecologic exam and blood drawn for determination of estradiol, luteinizing hormone and total and free testosterone. Partners filled out a mail-back sexual questionnaire. Thirty-nine (66%) of the group were coitally active and twenty (34%) were abstinent. The coitally active group reported higher levels of sexual desire ($P < 0.03$), greater sexual satisfaction ($P < 0.007$), more comfort in expressing sexual preferences ($P < 0.009$) and greater pre-menopausal sexual satisfaction ($P < 0.01$) and on pelvic examination were noted to have less genital atrophy ($P < 0.0005$) than the abstinent group. For the entire sample sexual complaints such as decreased desire and vaginal lubrication in the female and erectile difficulties in the male were reported frequently. Of the hormones studied, higher serum levels of free testosterone were associated with reports of increased sexual desire.

(Key words: Sexual behavior, Menopausal sex, Vaginal health)

Introduction

Factors affecting sexual expression in post-menopausal women are multiple and the relative contribution of and interaction between hormonal, psychosocial and aging determinants are not clearly delineated [1-3]. In relation to genital health, estrogen prevents pelvic atrophy and maintains adequate vaginal lubrication [1,4,5]. In a milieu of low serum estrogen, regular coitus and/or masturbation may have a beneficial effect on retarding atrophic genital changes as well [4,6,7]. Estrogen's role in sexual arousal, desire and frequency is not definitively established although it appears that this hormone probably plays an indirect role in sexual function by eliminating menopausal complaints that often interfere with the older woman's sense of well being and therefore her ability and desire to engage in sexual activity [1,7-10]. Scant data also report that estrogen mediates tactile skin receptors so that some menopausal women may develop touch aversion with estrogen deprivation [11]. Androgens may be essential for stimulating sexual motivational behaviors such as desire, fantasy and arousal, maintaining optimal levels of sexual functioning and possibly contributing to sexual gratification [12-15].

Reprinted from *Maturitas*, 13 (1991) 43-50. Elsevier Scientific Publishers Ireland Ltd.

Psychosocial and aging factors such as the availability of a functional partner, pre-menopausal sexual satisfaction, the cultural and religious meaning of sexuality, chronic illness, etc., rather than gonadal hormone levels, are often reported as more important determinants of sexual interest and expression in all age groups, especially in the subset of women 50 years and older [16-20]. In postmenopausal women not on estrogen therapy hormone levels are significantly decreased from pre-menopausal values and therefore other factors may more accurately predict continued sexual activity [3,6,21].

This research studied the sexual interest and behavior of a population of healthy sexagenarian women not on estrogen replacement therapy or other medications known to affect sexual function. This population was selected for study because gonadal hormone levels are low, the impact of menstrual related hormonal fluctuations are eliminated and because there are scant data on sexual behavior in this age group. Four aspects of sexual functioning were studied.

(1)   Coital activity and sexual desire in sexagenarian women with partners.

(2)   The type and prevalence of sexual complaints in sexagenarian couples.

(3)   The relationship between gonadal hormones and sexual expression.

(4)   The impact of coital activity on genital health.

Materials and Methods

Fifty-nine women between the ages of 60 and 70 years were recruited from a hospital-based private gynecologic practice over a 1-year period. All sexagenarian women seen during this study period were consecutively screened and those who met study entry criteria of currently having a sexual partner, postmenopausal for a minimum of 5 years, not on estrogen replacement therapy, free from major physical or mental disorders, not taking medication known to affect sexual function and not spontaneously offering a sexual complaint as a reason for their gynecologic visit were asked to participate. Of the 72 women who met study criteria, 13 declined either because they did not have the time and/or desire to participate in a sexuality study.

Study participants had an individual psychological interview during which the psychologist ascertained the presence and frequency of dyspareunia, anorgasmia and arousal problems, completed a Locke-Wallace Test of Marital Adjustment and a detailed questionnaire assessing medical, gynecologic and sexual history and had a gynecologic examination [6]. Sexual desire was assessed by interview questioning e.g., current level, past level and, when reported, reasons for change. Vaginal health was determined as described in a previously published report by the gynecologist before the sexual activity status of the subject was known, by subjectively rating six genital dimensions: skin turgor [1-3], pubic hair amount [1-2], labial fullness [1-2], introital size [1-3], vaginal mucosa friability and dryness [1-3] and vaginal depth [1-2] [6]. Lower scores imply more genital atrophy. Forty-nine women consented to having blood drawn for the determination of serum bound and free testosterone, estradiol and luteinizing hormone. At the end of the session, each subject was given a questionnaire assessing male sexual function for their partner to fill out and mail back. The women were instructed not to assist their partners in completing this questionnaire.

Data were analyzed using the Statistical Analysis System (SAS) on an IBM-AT personal computer. Student's t-test and the Pearson correlation were used when the data were normally distributed. The Wilcoxon test and Spearmann correlation were used for ordinal data. Chi-square analysis with Yates correction or Fisher exact test was used to evaluate differences in proportional data.

Results

Sample description

The 59 women were middle class, Caucasian, high school educated, long married and similar on all demographic variables. Subject age was 63.9 (3.3), mean (S.D.) and partner age was 67.6 (5.2). Age at menarche for the group was 13.2 (1.5) and menopause was 49.5 (5.5). When the sample was divided into those that were coitally active ($n = 39$) and those who were abstinent ($n = 20$), there were no significant differences between the two groups.

Sexual behavior and interest

On almost all sexual parameters, the coitally-active group reported greater satisfaction that the inactive group (Table I). The coitally-active women reported a current mean frequency of five coital encounters monthly (S.D. = 4.9, range 1-30), while the abstinent women did not engage in any intercourse. Sixty percent of the abstinent group reported predominately male problems and 40% reported predominately female problems as the reason for their lack of coital activity.

TABLE 1: Comparison of Coitally-Active and Inactive Women

Variable	Active	Inactive	P
N	39	20	0.05
Sexually satisfied	31 (79%)	12 (60%)	0.001
Consider sex important	26 (67%)	8 (40%)	0.001
Comfortable expressing sex needs	31 (79%)	8 (40%)	0.02
Sexual desire (rank 1-5)	3.8	2.9	0.02
Satisfaction with sexual frequency (rank 1-5)	3.8	2.8	0.01

The coitally active women rated their current level of sexual desire as significantly greater than that of the abstinent women ($P < 0.03$), although the two groups did not differ in their report of pre-menopausal sexual interest. For the entire sample, current ratings of sexual desire were significantly lower than premenopausal ratings of sexual desire ($P < 0.0001$).

Sexual and marital satisfaction

The coitally active women reported significantly greater sexual satisfaction currently ($P < 0.007$) as well as over the entire course of their marital relationship ($P < 0.01$) as compared to the abstinent group. In fact, 46% of the active women reported excellent long-term satisfaction with their sexual relationship as opposed to 11% of the abstinent women. Additionally, more coitally-active women (67%) than abstinent women (40%) gave moderate to high ratings of the importance of sexual satis-faction in their lives ($P < 0.005$). Fifty-five percent of the abstinent women vs. only 3% of the active women indicated that sexual satisfaction was not at all important to them. More coitally-active women than abstinent women reported feeling comfortable in expressing their sexual preferences to their partner ($P < 0.009$). Only 3% of the active women vs. 47% of the abstinent women indicated feeling not at all comfortable in making sexual requests and 35% of the abstinent women as com-pared to 13% of the coitally-active women indicated never initiating sexual activity with their partner during the entire length of their marriage.

Coitally-active women reported greater marital satisfaction on the Locke-Wallace Marital Ad-justment Test than abstinent women ($P < 0.05$).

Hormones and sexual behavior

Mean serum hormone levels determined on the 49 samples were; estradiol 8.2 (9.7) pg/ml, LH 62.2 (23.0) mI.U./ml, free testosterone 1.3 (0.9) ng/dl and bound testosterone 24.4 (19.5) ng/dl (Table II). For the entire group, serum hormone levels were not related to coital frequency, sexual arousal, dys-pareunia, touch aversion or genital health as subjectively assessed by the genital health score. There was no significant difference in mean serum levels of estradiol, luteinizing hormone and free or bound testosterone between the coitally active and abstinent group. There was a significant relation-ship between free testosterone and ratings of sexual desire, such that higher serum levels of this hor-mone were associated with reports of increased sexual desire ($P < 0.005$).

Genital health

By the use of the genital health score, coitally active women were noted to have less genital atrophy than abstinent women ($P < 0.0005$). Of a total possible score of 15, coitally active women had a mean score of 12 and abstinent women had a mean score of 10.

TABLE II: Hormone Values in Coitally-Active and Inactive Women			
Variable	Active	Inactive	P
N	31	18	NS
Estradiol (pg/ml)	7.6	9.4	NS
LH (mIU/ml)	59	68	NS
Testosterone (ng/dl) (bound)	268	203	NS
Testosterone (ng/dl) (free)	1.42	1.19	NS

Sexual complaints

This sample of sexagenarian women noted a substantial number of sexual problems for both themselves and their partners. Sixty-one percent of the entire sample of women experienced difficulty with vaginal lubrication and 56% reported diminished sexual interest; other common sexual complaints the women noted were decreased sexual arousal (44%), anorgasmia (32%), decreased vaginal sensation (25%) and dyspareunia (17%). The women reported that 51% of their partners had decreased sexual interest, 49% had difficulty achieving an erection and 44% had difficulty maintaining an erection. Other male problems as reported by the women included premature ejaculation (24%) and delayed ejaculation (17%).

Of the 59 questionnaires assessing male sexual function that women were to give their partners, 36 were mailed back; of these 33 were completed. Of the group that returned the questionnaires, 48% reported difficulty achieving an erection, 48% noted difficulty maintaining an erection, 40% complained of premature ejaculation and 24% complained of delayed ejaculation. Other complaints included lack of privacy (12%) and boredom with partner (3%). It is interesting that the complaint of decreased male sexual interest as reported by the women was not cited as a problem by the men

Comment

From the study of this small group of middle-class, Caucasian, sexagenarian couples, it appears that although there are widespread sexual problems in both men and women, the majority of couples continue to be sexually interested and remain coitally active. Data should be generated to study sexual behavior in women of lower social strata and those without an available partner. In addition, a detailed psychological examination was not performed in our study and only 56% of the males returned a valid questionnaire. As a group, common sexual problems for women are lubrication inadequacy and decreased sexual desire; for men erectile and ejaculatory difficulties are most often reported.

As other studies have reported, there appears to be a lessening of sexual interest in the decades following fifty for both women and men [3,19,22-25]. Although this data is retrospective, both the coitally-active and the abstinent women reported a reduction in sexual desire in the years following menopause; this reduction was greater for the abstinent than active women. The drop in sexual desire for the entire group may be partly attributable to the reduction in gonadal hormone levels, especially androgens. There appears to be a correlation between androgens and sexual desire as this data as well as other data suggest [12, 13, 26].

Although gonadal hormonal levels may play a role in other sexual functions in addition to sexual desire, in this group of sexagenarian women with low, steady state levels of gonadal hormones no correlation could be found between coital frequency, touch aversion, sexual arousal, dyspareunia or genital health and estradiol, luteinizing hormone and free and bound testosterone levels. Evidence is offered by this study that ongoing sexual activity in a milieu of low gonadal hormones is beneficial in maintaining genital health.

Interpersonal, rather than hormonal factors appear to play a greater role in determining the sexual lives of older women [20,27]. In this study, abstinent women not only reported significantly less sexual satisfaction with their current sexual activity, but over the entire course of their marital relationship they recalled less sexual satisfaction and less comfort in expressing sexual preferences than the coitally-active group. It may be the case that continued interest in sexual activities as one ages is at least partially dependent on having enjoyed satisfactory sexual exchange earlier in life. Past discomfort or guilt regarding sexual feelings may have a low but significant relationship with current sexual frequency and enjoyment of both sexual intercourse and non-coital touching and caressing [7]. In this study, when compared to the coitally active women, significantly fewer abstinent women gave high ratings to the importance of sexual satisfaction in their life, suggesting that they might have been willing to abandon coital activities because of their lack of past sexual enjoyment and comfort and the belief that sex was not very important in their lives. It is also possible that disappointment with their partners past and present sexual performance or the couple's sexual 'script' may have contributed to their lack of sexual enthusiasm. Sexual satisfaction may be at least somewhat related to marital satisfaction, as those women who were coitally active obtained higher ratings on marital satisfaction.

It is interesting that these women reported high levels of partner sexual disinterest, whereas the men themselves did not report sexual disinterest; the men reported high level of erectile and ejaculatory problems. Possibly, older women assume lack of partner interest when men do not engage in intercourse; however, it appears that the men- may be having erectile difficulties and therefore shun intercourse even though they may have continued desire. From this study it appears that there is a lack of sexual communication between older couples.

Finally, the prevalence of sexual difficulties in this sample of older couples is high and is consistent with other reports (7,28-30). However, this high percentage of sexual problems should not be interpreted as the older couple's desire to abandon sexual exchange as interest in sexual activity, although at reduced levels, persisted for most of the sample. With an available partner continued sexual activity was enjoyed by the majority of couples.

In summary, although sexual activity is no longer considered taboo in the later years, sexual dysfunctions are prevalent and many older couples enter these years lacking the sexual knowledge and skills to communicate their sexual needs and desires to their spouses and to address their sexual problems. Physicians should not be reluctant to obtain a sexual history for fear of patient embarrassment since most older men and women consider sexual activity acceptable across the adult life cycle and do not view sexual exchange as deviant behavior.

Physician intervention for these older couples should consist of encouraging the couple to communicate their sexual needs and problems to their partner and educating them regarding the physiologic and anatomic changes that occur with aging [31,32]. Suggestions on changing sexual scripts so that coitus is not considered the only acceptable sexual activity and information on the use and benefits of hormones and/or vaginal lubricants in appropriate cases can make a significant difference in older couple's sexual well-being. Sexual activity does not have to stop at a specific chronological age and most older men and women desire continued sexual exchange.

References

1 Sarrel PM: Sexuality in the middle years. Obstet Gynecol Clin North Am, 14 (1987) 49-62.

2 Kobosa-Munro L: Sexuality in the aging woman. Health Soc Work 1977; 2: 70-88.

3 Hallstrom T: Sexuality in the climacteric. Clin Obstet Gynaecol 1977; 4: 227-239.

4 Tsai CC, Semmens JP, Semmens EC, Lam CF, Lee FS: Vaginal physiology in postmenopausal women: pH value, transvaginal electropotential difference and estimated blood flow. South Med J 1987; 80: 987-990.

5 Morrel MJ, Dixen JM, Carter CS, Davidson JM: The influence of age and cycling status on sexual arousability in women. Am J Obstet Gynecol 1984; 148: 66-71.

6 Leiblum S, Bachmann G, Kemmann E, Colburn D, Swartzman L: Vaginal atrophy in the postmenopausal woman. The importance of sexual activity and hormones. J Am Med Assoc 1983: 249: 2195-2198.

7 Easley EB: Sex problems after the menopause. Clin Obstet Gynecol 1978; 21: 269-277.

8 Cutler WB, Garcia CR. McCoy N: Perimenopausal sexuality. Arch Sex Behav 1987; 16: 225-234.

9 Maoz B, Durst N: The effects of oestrogen therapy on the sex life of Maturitas 1980; 2: 327-336.

10 Detre T, Hayashi TT, Archer DF: Management of the Menopause. Ann Intern Med 1978; 88: 373-378.

11 Sarrel PM: Sex problems after menopause: a study of fifty married couples treated in a sex counseling programme. Maturitas 1982; 4: 231-237.

12 Sherwin BB: Changes in sexual behavior as a function of plasma sex steroid levels in post-menopausal women. Maturitas 1985; 7: 225-233.

13 Sherwin BB, Gelfand MM, Brender W: Androgen enhances sexual motivation in females: a prospective, crossover study of sex steroid administration in the surgical menopause. Psychsom Med 1985; 47: 339-351.

14 Persky H, Dreisbach L, Miller WR, et al: The relation of plasma androgen levels to sexual behaviors and attitudes of women. Psychosom Med 1982: 44: 305-319.

15 Sherwin BB, Gelfand MM: The role of androgen in the maintenance of sexual functioning in oophorectomized women. Psychosom Med 1987; 49: 397-409.

16 Hagstad A: Gynecology and sexuality in middle-aged women. Women Health 1988; 13: 57-80.

17 Channon LD, Ballinger SE: Some aspects of sexuality and vaginal symptoms during menopause and their relation to anxiety and depression. Br J Med Psychol 1986; 59: 173-180.

18 Bachmann GA, Leiblum SR, Kemmann E, Colburn DW, Swartzman L, Sheldon R: Sexual expression and its determinants in the post-menopausal woman. Maturitas 1984; 6: 19-29.

19 Lauritzen C: Biology of female sexuality in old age. J Gerontol 1983; 16: 134-138.

20 Fede T: Sexual problems in elderly women. Clinical experiences. Clin Exp Obstet Gynecol 1982; 9: 252-253.

21 Steger RW, Peluso JJ: Sex hormones in the aging female. Endocrinol Metab Clin North Am 1987; 16: 1027-1043.

22 Bachmann GA, Leiblum SR, Sandler B, et al: Correlates of sexual desire in post-menopausal women. Maturitas 1985; 7: 211-216.

23 McCoy NL, Davidson JM: A longitudinal study of the effects of menopause on sexuality. Maturitas 1985; 7: 203-210.

24 Bottiglioni F, De Aloysio D: Female sexuality activity as a function of climacteric conditions and age. Maturitas 1982; 4: 27-32.

25 Bungay GT, Vessey NP, McPherson CK: Study of symptoms in middle life with special reference to the menopause. Br Med J, 281 (1980) 181-183.

26 McCoy N, Cutler W, Davidson JM: Relationships among sexual behavior, hot flashes and hormone levels in perimenopausal women. Arch Sex Behav, 14 (1985) 385-394.

27 Rentzsch W, Boblan W: Health and sexual behavior of employed women in the menopause phase. ZFA 1982; 37: 349-358.

28 Wise TN, Rabins PV, Gahnsley J: The older patient with a sexual dysfunction. J Sex Mar Ther, 1984; 10: 117-121.

29 Wallis LA: Management of dyspareunia in postmenopausal women. J Am Med Womens Assoc 1987; 42: 82-84.

30 Bachmann GA, Leiblum SR, Grill J: Brief sexual inquiry in gynecologic practice. Obstet Gynecol 1989; 73: 425-427.

31 Huffman JW: Counseling the menopausal patient. Postgrad Med 1979; 65: 211-212, 214-215.

32 Gruis ML, Wagner NN: Sexuality during the climacteric. Postgrad Med 1979; 65: 197-201, 204, 207

Section XI

SEXUALLY TRANSMITTED DISEASES

There are numerous diseases that can be transmitted by close or physical contact. We normally refer to these as Sexually Transmitted Diseases (STDs). These include a variety of viral and bacterial infections. One category of these, also popularly called venereal diseases, are caused by microorganisms (viruses, bacteria, or protozoa) and transmitted between partners by sexual contact. These diseases can also be transmitted to the unborn (through the maternal placenta) or the neonate (through an infected birth canal). Instrumental in the spread of sexually transmitted diseases is the mixing of body fluids therefore also including blood and blood products.

The first use of the term venereal disease is traced to Jacques de Bethercourt in 1527. Legally today it refers only to syphilis, gonorrhoea and chancroid. Syphilis may have been taken back to the Old World by Columbus and his men after their first visit to America in March 1493 (Gregersen 1983). It soon gained a nomenclature identifying it with its host. Originally it was called: "Indian measles", but as European traders spread eastward Portuguese navigators introduced "the Portuguese disease" to Chinese and Japanese women, while the Turks feared contracting "the Christian disease". There is evidence that gonorrhoea was present in Old Testament times (Leviticus 15) and among the Romans and Greeks in classical times. In fact, its name derives from Greek meaning "flow of seed" and was coined by the Greek physician Claudius Galen in the second century AD. It was only in 1879 that the bacterium *Neisseria gonorrhaea* was discovered by Albert Neisser.

Bacterial sexually transmitted diseases can generally be cured by a single shot of penicillin, though some strains of these diseases have become resistant to drugs, or have mutated into new strains. An example is a particularly virulent strain of gonorrhea brought back from Vietnam by returning American service men. This penicillin-resistant strain, known as Penicillinase Producing Neisseria Gonorrhea produces an enzyme which destroys penicillin. In men it is concentrated in the urethra but in women it is also associated with Pelvic Inflamatory Disease and may result in sterility. Though normally treatable by penicillin a disease like chlamydia, one of the fastest spreading STDs, requires a weeklong treatment with tetracycline or erythromycin and this will cure 95 percent of the cases.

Diseases which are caused by viruses, specifically Herpes Simplex Viruses (Herpes), Human Papilloma Viruses (Warts) and Human Immunodeficiency Viruses (AIDS) are normally non-responsive to the curing aim of drugs. The herpes family of viruses are responsible for such infections as cold sores, chicken pox and shingles. However in the sexual context herpes virus type 1, responsible primarily for cold sores and fever blisters, and herpes virus type 2, responsible for genital herpes, have now become confused. Perhaps due to oral-genital contact a crossover has taken place and today between 10 and 20 percent of genital herpes are caused by herpes virus type 1 (Masters, Johnson and

Kolodny 1992). Contrary to popular opinion, it is now known that women who have no outward signs of the disease can spread the virus.

Human Papilloma Virus (HPV) is spreading rapidly. There are 56 papilloma viruses known to cause warts and scientists have been able to link 25 to cervical cancer. Recently "an international research team studying cervical cancer tumors of women from 22 countries has found overwhelming evidence for a single cause for all those cancers. The culprit is a common sexually transmitted virus known as the human papilloma virus, or HPV" (Discover 1995:23). In fact, they found the HPV in 95 percent of the tumors.

Of all the diseases transmitted primarily or exclusively by sexual contact, none is as lethal or as catastrophic in its effects as AIDS. In the United States and many western countries, the AIDS virus was initially associated with homosexual and bisexual men, intravenous drug users, and—in large part due to these factors—with certain sub-groups in the population. Much of that has now changed. A whole issue of Science (Vol. 239, February 1988) dealt with this topic and public health policies and programs have increased awareness among the general public.

In many Third World countries, and particularly in Africa the position is quite different. This is due in part to the presence of other members of the human retrovirus family namely HTLV-IV and HIV-2, cultural practices allowing for blood contact by traditional practitioners, sexual values, and behaviors leading to widespread heterosexual transmission, as well as the poverty of many countries preventing thorough blood screening and requiring multiple use of needles. Lastly, and perhaps the most important factor in the devastation of AIDS, is its slow incubation period. Thus persons who are seropositive, but symptom-free, can pass the virus to unsuspecting persons.

The two readings in this section are quite diverse. The first deals with a practical question involving immediate (pregnancy) versus long term (testing positive for HIV) effects. It also deals with real practical observed effects as opposed to something which is believed to not really happen to young people. These questions were included in an extensive questionnaire administered to 10th graders in eight public high schools in Dade County, Florida. The second paper is one of the most thorough recent surveys of the spread of HIV through out the world. In conclusion the report distinguishes two major types (as well as different strains within each type) of the virus, which also imply different transmission modes.

References

Discover. 1995. *The Cervical Cancer Virus.* Vol. 16, No. 9.

Gregersen, Edgar. 1983. *Sexual Practices. The story of human sexuality.* New York: Franklin Watts.

Masters, William H., Virginia E Johnson and Robert C. Kolodny. 1992. *Human Sexuality,* Fourth Edition. New York: Harper Collins Publ.

Science. 1988. Vol.239, No. 4840

WHICH IS MORE IMPORTANT TO HIGH SCHOOL STUDENTS: PREVENTING PREGNANCY OR PREVENTING AIDS?

Lilly M. Langer, Rick S. Zimmerman and Jennifer A. Katz

A sample of about 2,900 high school students in greater Miami, Florida, was surveyed to determine their attitudes toward pregnancy prevention vs. AIDS prevention and how these attitudes affect condom use. Female, Hispanic and black respondents were the most likely to consider pregnancy and AIDS prevention to be equally important. White non-Hispanics and males were relatively more likely to believe that preventing pregnancy is less important than preventing AIDS, whereas males and females involved in a steady relationship placed more emphasis on pregnancy prevention than AIDS prevention. The more knowledge about HIV and AIDS a respondent had, the less importance he or she placed on pregnancy prevention, and as the importance of preventing pregnancy declined, so did the frequency of condom use. Males who were in a steady dating relationship and perceived pregnancy prevention as more important than AIDS prevention were the most likely to report using condoms often. (Family Planning Perspectives 26: 154-59, 1994)

As of March 1993, 56,287 cases of AIDS have been reported among teenagers and young adults aged 13-29 years in the United States.[1] Several factors contribute to the risk for HIV infection among adolescents, including the fact that young people are becoming sexually active at increasingly earlier ages and have more sexual partners than their predecessors.[2] Among 15-year-olds, nearly one-fourth of females and one-third of males have engaged in sexual intercourse.[3] Susan Millstein and colleagues found that 21% of some 560 adolescents aged 11-14 from a variety of social, racial and ethnic backgrounds were sexually active; almost half had had their first intercourse prior to 11 years of age.[4] Although 50-60% of adolescents have experienced intercourse by 17-18 years of age, condom use is not routine.[5] The high rates of sexually transmitted diseases (STDs) other than AIDS among adolescents are indicative of the potential for HIV transmission in this age-group.[6]

More than one million teenage girls become pregnant in the United States each year—approximately one out of every ten girls under the age of 20.[7] One-quarter of all babies born to U. S. teenagers are not first births.[8] Approximately 40% of pregnancies to both white and nonwhite 15-19-year-olds end in abortion, and 25% of abortions in the United States are obtained by adolescents.[9]

Condom use and other "safe sex" behaviors remain the only methods of protection against both pregnancy and STDs for sexually active adolescents. Recent studies have identified several barriers to condom use among adolescents.[10] One is that pregnancy may be the primary concern of sexually

From The Alan Guttmacher Institute, 120 Wall St., New York, NY 10005.

active adolescents due to the perceived low prevalence of HIV infection among their peers. They may use oral contraceptives, diaphragms, or other methods of birth control in lieu of condoms, thereby placing themselves at increased risk for STDs.

Barnard and McKeganey found that adolescents often find issues relating to sex embarrassing, and therefore may find it easier to have unprotected sex than to discuss STD prevention.[11] In addition to needing effective interpersonal skills to negotiate condom use, there may be tremendous social difficulties for adolescents in purchasing and carrying condoms. Two such barriers to condom use were identified in a study of about 1,700 high school students. When students were asked why they personally did not use condoms, 42% reported they didn't have them at hand and 34% felt that condoms interfered with the pleasure of sex.[12] A French study of 1,500 students suggests that those who are sexually experienced use condoms less and have a more negative attitude toward condom use than those who are sexually inexperienced.[13]

Unprotected sex among adolescents may be the result of unstable sexual relationships.[14] Thus, whether or not the adolescent is in a steady dating relationship may have important implications regarding interpersonal trust and the perceived importance of condom use. Regular sexual relations with one individual may result in an increase in concern for pregnancy prevention, but a diminished concern for prevention of HIV infection. In this sense, even the practice of serial monogamy among adolescents may increase their risk for HIV.

A study of midwestern high school students revealed that sexual responsibility—including condom use—was positively correlated with knowledge about HIV and AIDS.[15] On the other hand, misperceptions concerning sexual activity and safe sex practices are associated with increased risk for HIV among adolescents.[16] For example, 21% of inner city adolescents listed oral contraceptive pills as a way to decrease risk of AIDS infection.[17] However, the findings from a number of studies designed to change risky AIDS-related sexual attitudes, beliefs and behaviors among adolescents clearly indicate that HIV and AIDS knowledge does not necessarily translate into behavioral changes.[18] The primary purpose of this investigation was to describe the perceived relative importance of preventing pregnancy vs. preventing AIDS by various background characteristics and behaviors of adolescents. We hypothesize that the frequency of condom use varies among respondents by attitude regarding the importance of preventing pregnancy vs. preventing AIDS, and that adolescents who are more concerned with preventing pregnancy than AIDS are less likely to use condoms. The results of the study may help in the development of HIV risk-reduction programs for adolescents.

Methods

Sample and Design

The study was a panel design, in which a questionnaire was used to collect data at four time points over a five-month period. Waves I and II were collected in November and December of 1988; waves III and IV were collected in January and April of 1989. The entire study collected data on HIV and

AIDS-related attitudes, beliefs, skills and behaviors, as well as on the effectiveness of different methods of teaching HIV and AIDS education; the material presented in this article represents only some of the information gathered, and only the first wave of data collection.

The data were obtained from a sample of 2,896 10th-grade students in eight public high schools in Dade County (greater Miami) Florida. The main criteria for a school's participation in the study were a relatively balanced racial and ethnic distribution in the student body and the approval of the principal for the school's participation in the study. (About 26%-58% of students at each school were white, about 21%-66% were Hispanic and approximately 15%-40% were black.) Parental consent forms in English, Spanish and Haitian Creole, outlining the objectives of the research, were sent to all parents two weeks before the study began.

The total nonparticipation rate was 17.5%. Of this total, 16.3% did not return their consent forms and another 1.2% refused to participate. Of those who refused participation or did not return the consent form, 40% were male, 32% were black and 30% were Hispanic. Statistical analysis revealed significant racial and ethnic differences between those who participated in the study and those who did not: Whites had higher refusal rates than Hispanics.

The 198-item questionnaires, which were at a seventh-grade reading level, were self-administered and were completed by the participants following a brief introduction by a trained member of the research staff. There were few queries by the students during data collection; thus, we concluded that confusion or misunderstanding regarding the questions was low.

Measures

The questionnaire was in part a compilation of items from previous studies that had been used to obtain information on HIV and AIDS-related knowledge, attitudes, beliefs, skills and behaviors among different social and demographic populations.[19] In addition, a large number of questions were newly developed for the study. Background information was obtained on age, grade-point average, whether or not the respondent was in a steady dating relationship, sexual experience (whether the respondent had had vaginal, anal or oral sex, the respondent's frequency of vaginal sex, and how many partners he or she had had), and if she or he had used any type of contraceptive method.

The main dependent variable in the study was measured by a Likert-type scale; respondents were asked "Which of the five statements best describes how you feel about preventing pregnancy and AIDS?" Responses ranged from "Preventing pregnancy is much more important than preventing AIDS" (coded one) to "Preventing pregnancy is much less important than preventing AIDS" (coded five).

The five responses actually represented three categorically different phenomena rather than one continuous variable, so we collapsed responses 1 and 2 and responses 4 and 5. This categorized respondents into three groups: those who answered that preventing pregnancy is much more or somewhat more important than preventing AIDS; those who said that preventing pregnancy and preventing AIDS are equally important; and those who responded that preventing pregnancy is somewhat less or much less important than preventing AIDS.

Frequency of condom use, an independent variable, was also measured by a Likert-type scale. Responses were "often" (coded one), "sometimes" (coded two), "rarely" (coded three) or "never" (coded four).

Other independent variables used scales of 1-4 to measure parents' mean years of education, and respondent's level of worry about AIDS and about pregnancy. Race and ethnicity were assessed by two dummy variables, one for black and one for all other races, and one for Hispanic as opposed to all others. Family structure was measured by a single dichotomous variable that indicated whether or not the respondent lived with two parents.

A measure of interpersonal skills related to sexual relationships assessed the perceived likelihood of being able to buy a condom, discuss the topic of AIDS prevention with a partner, ask a potential partner about previous sexual and drug experience, refuse a proposal for unwanted sex, and alter their behavior if potential sexual partners said they had been sexually active or had used drugs. (Five point responses ranged from "Definitely can do it" to "Definitely can't.")

Knowledge about AIDS was measured by an 11-item scale. Five items asked such questions as whether teenagers could become infected and whether it is always possible to tell if a person has the virus. (Responses were coded one if they were "sure it's true" and two if they were "sure it's false.") Six items specifically about transmission of HIV asked such questions as how likely a respondent thought it was that the virus could be acquired by eating food handled by an infected person or by donating blood. (Responses ranged from one for "very likely," to four for "very unlikely.") Finally, respondents were asked how many people with AIDS they thought were homosexual men. Response categories ranged from one for "almost none" to four for "almost all."

The maximum possible score on the scales related to interpersonal skills and AIDS knowledge was 59. All scales were constructed using factor analyses and reliability analyses designed to determine unidimensionality and internal consistency. The interpersonal skills scale and the AIDS knowledge scale were both tested for internal consistency with Cronbach's alpha. (An alpha of .68 was found for the former and .58 was found for the latter.) Chi-square analyses and analysis of variance tests were performed to make comparisons by various characteristics among respondents who were and were not in a steady dating relationship. Loglinear analysis was conducted with the dependent variable, in order to identify significant differences between observed and expected frequencies for two- and three-way interaction effects.

Results

The sociodemographic data for the total sampl—eas well as for subgroups composed of those who were in steady dating relationships and those who were not—are reported in Table 1. Of the total sample, 40% were Hispanic, 29% were black, and 31% were white. The respondents' mean age was 15.5 years.

TABLE 1: Sample means or percentages of high school students, by whether or not respondent was in a steady dating relationship, according to background characteristics, Dade County, Florida, 1988.

Characteristics	All (n=2,896)	Yes (n=1,095)	No (n=1,449)
All students			
Gender***			
% Male	47.5	39.0	52.3
% Female	52.5	61.0	47.7
Race			
% Hispanic	40.1	41.3	39.0
% Black	28.7	32.9	25.5
% White	31.2	25.8	35.5
Age	15.5	15.6	15.4***
Grade Point Average#	5.1	4.9	5.3***
Parents' Education°	2.9	2.9	2.9
% living with two parents	50.0	44.7	55.2***
HIV/AIDS knowledge	51.5	51.3	52.1***
Interpersonal sexual skill	23.6	24.3	23.2***
Worry about AIDS score	2.7	2.8	2.7
Worry about pregnancy score	2.5	2.7	2.4***
% who had ever had oral, anal, or vaginal sex	49.9	65.1	36.5***
Those who had ever had sex			
Age at first sex	13.4	13.6	13.2***
% who had ever had vaginal sex	90.0	91.9	90.0
Number of times respondent had vaginal sex in past 3 months	3.1	2.3	3.9***
% who had ever had anal sex	14.8	13.8	15.1
% who had ever had oral sex	52.6	52.9	54.7
Number of lifetime sexual partners	3.1	3.0	3.0
Condom use during vaginal intercourse+		2.7	2.9*
Used contraceptive methods other than condoms		29.2	22.5

*P<.05; ***p<.001; #GPA values: 1=F; 2=D; 3=C- or D+; 4=C; 5=B- or C+; 6=B; 7=A- or B+; 8+A.
° Parents' education: 1=< high school; 2= high school; 3= some college; 4 = college. + 1 = often; 2 = sometimes; 3 = rarely or 4 = never. *Note*: 352 respondents did not answer when asked if they were in a steady relationship. For gender, statistical significance indicates difference between male and female students, whereas for all other categories, it indicates difference between students in a steady relationship and those who are not.

Relationship Status

Table 1 shows that respondents in a steady dating relationship were significantly more likely to be female, older than average, and have lower than average grades, and to be less knowledgeable about HIV and AIDS, to perceive themselves as having better interpersonal skills with regard to sexual relationships, and to worry more about pregnancy than those who were not in this type of relationship. In addition, respondents in a steady dating relationship were less likely to report living with two parents. No significant differences were found between respondents who were dating someone steadily and those who were not with regard to their parents' education level, or the respondent's degree of worry about AIDS.

Approximately 84% of our sample—both those who had had sexual intercourse and those who had not—perceived their risk for HIV infection as very or somewhat unlikely (not shown). One would hypothesize that AIDS would be a greater concern for students who were not in a steady relationship than for those who are. In an attempt to explain this finding, further analyses were performed to compare those in a steady relationship with those who were not on measures of sexual experience, frequency of vaginal intercourse, and condom use during vaginal intercourse.

As also shown in Table 1, a significantly greater proportion of students in a steady dating relationship were sexually active, and they were older when they had their first sexual experience than those not in a steady dating relationship. Among students who had had sex, those who were not steadily dating one person had a significantly higher frequency of vaginal intercourse in the past three months than those who were. This is a behavior that would seemingly lead to increased worry about AIDS; indeed, respondents not in a steady relationship reported using condoms during vaginal intercourse significantly more often than those in a steady dating relationship. No significant differences were found between these two groups with regard to type of sex (vaginal, anal or oral), number of lifetime partners, or use of contraceptives other than condoms.*

Preventing Pregnancy vs. AIDS

Table 2 shows the relative importance of preventing pregnancy versus preventing AIDS by gender, dating relationship status, sexual experience, race and ethnicity. Significant differences were found by gender: A greater proportion of females (55%) than males (46%) reported that preventing AIDS and preventing pregnancy are equally important. Conversely, a greater proportion of males than females reported both that preventing pregnancy is more important than preventing AIDS (7% vs. 4%), and vice versa (48% vs. 41%).

TABLE 2: Percentage distribution of students, by attitude toward preventing pregnancy vs. preventing AIDS, according to background characteristics.

Characteristic	N	Preventing pregnancy is more important	Preventing AIDS is more important	Both equally important	Total
ALL STUDENTS					
Gender***					
Male	1316	6.5	47.9	45.5	100.0
Female	1436	4.4	40.9	54.7	100.0
Have had sex of any kind					
Male	788	6.3	47.7	45.9	100.0
Female	496	5.4	42.5	52.0	100.0
Have not had sex of any kind***					
Male	430	5.6	49.3	45.1	100.0
Female	871	3.3	41.1	55.6	100.0
Vaginal sex					
Yes	1100	5.5	46.1	48.4	100.0
No	104	6.7	47.1	46.2	100.0
Anal Sex					
Yes	156	9.0	40.4	50.6	100.0
No	908	4.8	46.5	48.7	100.0
Oral sex**					
Yes	593	5.7	50.1	44.2	100.0
No	521	5.4	40.5	54.1	100.0
Race or Ethnicity***					
White	761	2.6	54.5	43.0	100.0
Hispanic	1033	6.4	39.1	54.5	100.0
Black	746	7.2	42.0	50.8	100.0
IN A STEADY DATING RELATIONSHIP					
Gender					
Males	413	7.7	44.1	48.2	100.0
Females	649	5.2	42.8	51.9	100.0
Sexual Experience					
Had not had vaginal intercourse	365	6.0	41.9	52.1	100.0
Had had vaginal intercourse	677	6.4	44.5	49.2	100.0
NOT IN A STEADY RELATIONSHIP					
Gender***					
Males	733	4.0	52.0	44.1	100.0
Females	675	2.4	40.6	57.0	100.0
Sexual Experience					
Had not had vaginal intercourse	506	2.5	45.6	51.9	100.0
Had had vaginal intercourse	881	4.5	47.2	48.2	100.0

**Difference significant at $p<.01$.   ***Difference significant at $p<.001$.

Significant differences were found by gender within the subgroup of respondents who reported never having engaged in any type of sex. Females who had not had sex were significantly more likely than sexually inexperienced males to say that preventing pregnancy and AIDS were equally impor-tant; there was no significant difference on this measure between males and females who were sexu-ally experienced. Significant differences in the relative importance of preventing pregnancy and preventing AIDS were found according to whether or not the respondents had engaged in oral sex; however, contrary to expectations, those who had engaged in oral sex were less likely (44%) to con-sider AIDS and pregnancy prevention equally important, compared to those who had not had oral sex (54%) Further, those who reported having had oral sex were more likely than those who had not to re-port that preventing pregnancy was less important than preventing AIDS (50% vs. 41%).

Both males and females who were in a steady relationship were more likely than those who were not to consider pregnancy prevention more important than AIDS prevention. Differences were sig-nificant only among those not in a steady dating relationship: Females were significantly more likely to consider pregnancy and AIDS prevention equally important, paralleling other gender differences reported above.

Significant differences were also revealed among racial and ethnic groups; white respondents were least inclined to report that preventing pregnancy is more important than preventing AIDS, or that the two are equally important, and were most likely to say that preventing pregnancy is less im-portant than preventing AIDS. Responses of Hispanics and blacks were similar to one another—and in contrast to responses of whites—as they tended to say that preventing pregnancy is equally or more important than preventing AIDS.

An examination of knowledge about AIDS (not shown) revealed that whites had significantly more knowledge about AIDS (mean knowledge score of 53.7) than did Hispanics and blacks (50.8 and 50.4, respectively) and, as knowledge increased, relatively less importance was placed on preventing preg-nancy. Furthermore, when asked, "Of all the people with AIDS, how many do you think are homosex-ual men," Hispanics and blacks suggested significantly greater proportions than did whites.

In order to identify significant differences between expected and observed frequencies for two—and three-way interaction effects, log-linear analysis was performed; the importance of preventing pregnancy vs. preventing AIDS was the dependent variable. This analysis (not shown) revealed sig-nificant differences for two subgroups (likelihood ratio χ^2=18.66, df=23, p=.721): Among those who were not in a steady dating relationship, black males who were not yet sexually active and sexually active black females were both more likely than other subgroups to believe that preventing AIDS is more important than preventing pregnancy (adjusted residuals were -2.23 and -2.46, respectively). In other words, these subgroups placed more value than others on preventing AIDS. These subgroups were also more likely than others to indicate that preventing AIDS and preventing pregnancy were equally important (for males, the adjusted residual was 2.09; for females, 2.16).

Table 3 shows how the frequency of condom use is affected by whether preventing pregnancy or preventing AIDS is more important to the respondent; the data are examined by gender and whether or not the respondent was dating someone steadily. A statistically significant difference was found only for males involved in a steady dating relationship: Those who perceived preventing pregnancy as more important than preventing AIDS were most likely to use a condom always or often during vaginal intercourse (86%), followed by those who perceived pregnancy and AIDS as equally important to prevent (64%) and those who perceived preventing pregnancy as less important than preventing AIDS (53%). While the trend was very similar for females not in a steady relationship, because of the smaller sample sizes, the differences were not significant. The relationship between attitude toward prevention and condom use was also nonsignificant for females in a steady relationship, and males not in a steady relationship.

TABLE 3: Percentage of sexually active students who always or often use condoms, by type of relationship, gender and attitude toward preventing pregnancy vs. preventing AIDS

Relationship status, gender and attitude	N	%
STEADY RELATIONSHIP		
Male		
Preventing pregnancy is more important	21	86**
AIDS and pregnancy prevention equally important	132	64
Preventing pregnancy is less important	133	53
Female		
Preventing pregnancy is more important	16	50
AIDS and pregnancy prevention equally important	166	55
Preventing pregnancy is less important	134	45
NO STEADY RELATIONSHIP		
Male		
Preventing pregnancy is more important	14	79
AIDS and pregnancy prevention equally important	146	67
Preventing pregnancy is less important	176	67
Female		
Preventing pregnancy is more important	5	80
AIDS and pregnancy prevention equally important	45	47
Preventing pregnancy is less important	28	43

**$p < .01$

Discussion

To explain why both respondents who were in a steady dating relationship as well as those who were not were equally worried about AIDS, we speculate that although individuals who were not in a relationship reported more vaginal intercourse than those who were, their relative worry about AIDS was probably mediated by their more frequent use of condoms. For persons in a steady relationship, on the other hand, as partners become more familiar with each other, a sense of trust (real or perceived) develops that may in turn mediate worry about HIV and AIDS.

Overall, more than 90% of the sample indicated that they thought preventing pregnancy is much less, somewhat less, or equally as important as preventing AIDS. However, significant differences in attitudes about the relative importance of pregnancy and AIDS prevention were found among gender groups, racial and ethnic groups, those with varying levels and types of sexual experience, and those who were and were not in a steady dating relationship. Females were found to be more likely than males to believe that preventing pregnancy and preventing AIDS are equally important, while males were more likely than females to indicate that preventing AIDS is more important than preventing pregnancy. Certainly, since females bear the greater burden of unwanted pregnancy in our society, one would expect to find females—although asserting the importance of AIDS—to be less inclined to disavow the relative importance of pregnancy.

Whites were less likely than Hispanics or blacks to indicate that AIDS and pregnancy prevention are of equal importance, and more likely to indicate that pregnancy prevention is of lesser importance; Hispanics were the least likely to indicate that preventing AIDS is more important than preventing pregnancy. Compared to whites, Hispanics indicated that homosexual men were the most likely to have AIDS, indicating that Hispanics in this sample may view AIDS as primarily a "gay disease" and as a consequence, may be relatively less inclined to assert the importance of preventing AIDS over preventing pregnancy.

Males in a steady dating relationship were significantly more concerned about the importance of preventing pregnancy than those who were not in a relationship, with one exception: black males not in a steady relationship. These men, especially those who had not yet had sex, were more likely than their counterparts to place greater importance on preventing pregnancy. This was also true of black females who had had sex, although the majority of both groups indicated that preventing AIDS and preventing pregnancy were equally important. It may be that a history of pregnancy among the peers of black females makes the possibility of pregnancy more real for those who are sexually active. And as a result, this subgroup of females may hold stronger beliefs regarding the importance of pregnancy prevention. With regard to a similar finding for black males who had not had sex, this subgroup may be less confident of their personal skills with regard to contraception and, hence, more concerned about preventing pregnancy.

Males and female students who were involved in a steady relationship were more likely to perceive pregnancy as a concern than those not in a relationship. These findings support our hypothesis that the relative importance of preventing pregnancy vs. preventing AIDS differs across demographic variables, sexual experience level, and whether or not the respondent is in a steady relationship.

Most of the sample (84%) perceived their risk for HIV as very or somewhat unlikely. Unfortunately, when perception of low risk is combined with a relatively diminished concern for preventing pregnancy, the consequence may be even less vigilance in the use of condoms and, concomitantly, an increase in risk for HIV.

One of the most interesting findings of this study is the differences in attitudes about the relative importance of preventing pregnancy versus preventing AIDS between those who had engaged in oral sex and those who had not. The former were significantly more likely than the latter to indicate that preventing pregnancy is less important than preventing AIDS. One possible explanation is that those who had had oral sex had had vaginal intercourse less often. However, this was not the case. There were no significant differences in frequency of vaginal intercourse or use of condoms during vaginal intercourse between those who had had oral sex and those who had not. On the other hand, those who had had oral sex were significantly more likely than those who had not to report other behaviors that put them at risk for HIV, which could explain the greater importance they place on the prevention of AIDS as compared to pregnancy.**

Is frequency of condom use differentially associated with attitudes about the relative importance of preventing AIDS versus preventing pregnancy? The findings indicate that when attitudes about the relative importance of pregnancy vs. AIDS prevention were compared to condom use during vaginal intercourse, a significant association was revealed only for males in a steady relationship. That is, the more important these males believed preventing pregnancy to be, the more they used condoms. This suggests that for males with a steady partner, the motivation for frequent use of condoms lies in the importance of preventing pregnancy rather than AIDS.

Significant differences were not found for the other relationship and gender subgroups; however, there was an overall tendency for the frequency of condom use to decrease as the importance of preventing pregnancy decreased. This also suggests that the use of condoms among adolescents is associated with preventing pregnancy, rather than preventing AIDS.

In an attempt to understand these findings, we examined the use of other contraceptive methods as a possible mediating effect on condom use. However, we found that the more frequent the use of methods other than condoms, the more frequent the use of condoms. Conversely, the less frequently females used other methods. the less frequently they used condoms. (In fact, of those who reported not using condoms, approximately 77% of the sexually active females and 86% of the sexually active males reported using no contraceptive method at all.)

This study did have some limitations. In particular, since race and ethnicity were stratified rather than homogenous within schools, it may be that the students who attended the schools in our study were of a higher socioeconomic status overall. A further limitation is our inability to determine long-term changes in pregnancy attitudes and condom behavior. That is, it would be informative for intervention purposes to be able to determine how these attitudes and behaviors change over a student's entire high school experience.

AIDS risk-reduction interventions are generally aimed at increasing knowledge about HIV and AIDS while stressing the importance of preventing HIV infection through the regular use of condoms. Most HIV and AIDS education interventions are separate units within "life management" or health classes, apart from units that teach about the importance of and methods to prevent unwanted pregnancy. The findings of this study suggest that perhaps HIV and AIDS risk-reduction interventions should be structured within the context of family planning or pregnancy prevention education to help adolescents bridge the gap between the importance of preventing pregnancy and the importance of preventing HIV and AIDS.

Notes

*An additional item asked, "How often do you engage in behavior that puts you at risk for getting AIDS?" Responses ranged from "all of the time" (coded one) to "never" (coded four). Students who had not had any type of sex were excluded from this analysis. Those who had engaged in oral sex reported a higher mean number of HIV-related risky sexual behaviors than those who had not had oral sex (3.4 vs. 3.3; p<.003).

**The data presented in this study are cross-sectional and current attitudes were measured at the time of data collection, yet reported behaviors took place at some point in the past. Thus, no attempt is being made to establish causality.

References

1. Centers for Disease Control, *HIV/AIDS Surveillance: U.S. AIDS Cases Reported Through March 1993*, 5:11,1993.

2. S. L. Hofferth, J. R. Kahn and W. Baldwin, "Premarital Sexual Activity Among U. S. Teenage Women Over the Past Three Decades," *Family Planning Perspectives*, 19:4-53, 1987; S. L. Hofferth and C. D. Hayes, eds., *Risking the Future Adolescent Sexuality, Pregnancy and Childbearing*, Vol. 11, National Academy Press, Washington, D. C., 1987; M. L. Belfer, P. K. Krener and F. B. Miller, "AIDS in Children and Adolescents," *Journal of the American Academy of Child and Adolescent Psychiatry* 27:147-151, 1988; and D. Prothrow-Smith, *Journal of Adolescent Health Care*, 10:5-55-75, 1989.

3. W. Baldwin, "Adolescent Pregnancy and Childbearing: Rates, Trends, Research Findings from the Center for Population Research of the National Institute of Child Health and Human Development," National Institute for Child Health and Human Development, March 1990; and F.L. Sonenstein, J. H. Pleck and L. C. Ku, "Sexual Activity, Condom Use and AIDS Awareness Among Adolescent Males, *Family Planning Perspectives*, 21:152-158,1989.

4. S.G., Millstein et al., "Health-Risk Behaviors and Health Concerns Among Young Adolescents," *Pediatrics*, 3:422-428, 1992.

5. H. G. Miller, C. E Turner and L. E. Moses eds., *AIDS: The Second Decade,* National Research Council, Washington, D. C., 1990.

6. S. O. Aral and K. K. Holmes, "Epidemiology of Sexual Behavior and STDs," in K. K. Holmes, P.A. Mardh and E.P. Sparling, eds., *Sexually Transmitted Diseases* , McGraw Hill, New York, 1990.

7. S. K. Henshaw and J. Van Vort, "Teenage Abortion, Birth and Pregnancy Statistics: An Update," *Family Planning Perspectives* 21:85-88,1989.

8. The Alan Guttmacher Institute, "Teenage Sexual and Reproductive Behavior," *Facts in Brief,* January 4, 1993.

9. J S. Turner and L. Rubinson, *Contemporary Human Sexuality,* Prentice Hall, Englewood Cliffs, N.J., 1993, p. 433.

10. R. J. DiClemente and J. D. Fisher, "Social Influence Factors Associated with Consistent Condom Use Among Adolescents in an HIV Epicenter: Communication and Perceived Referent Group Norms," *Journal of Adolescent Health,* 12 385-390,1992.

11. M. Barnard and N. McKeganey, "Adolescents, Sex and Injecting Drug Use: Risks for HIV Infection," *AIDS Care,* 2:103-116, 1990.

12. J. H. Skurnick et al., "New Jersey High School Students' Knowledge, Attitudes and Behavior Regarding AIDS," *AIDS Education and Prevention*, 3:21-30, 1991.

13. S. Malavaud, F. Dumay and B. Malavaud, "HIV Infection: Assessment of Sexual Risk, Know ledge and Attitudes Toward Prevention in 1,586 High School Students in the Toulouse Education Authority Area," *Journal of Health Promotion*, 4:260-265, 1990.

14. S. Kippax et al., "Women Negotiating Heterosex: A Study Using Memory Work," unpublished manuscript.

15. T. Andre and L. Bormann, "Knowledge of Acquired Immune Deficiency Syndrome and Sexual Responsibility Among High School Students," *Youth and Society*, 22:339-361, 1991.

16. R. Hingson et al, "Beliefs About AIDS, Use of Alcohol and Drugs, and Unprotected Sex Among Massachusetts Adolescents," *American Journal of Public Health*, 80:295-299,1990; and R.J. DiClemente, ed., *Adolescents and AIDS: A Generation in Jeopardy,* Sage Publications, Beverly Hills, Calif., 1992.

17. E. Goodman and A. T. Cohall, "Acquired Immunodeficiency Syndrome and Adolescents: Knowledge, Attitudes, Beliefs and Behaviors in a New York Adolescent Minority Population," *Pediatrics*, 34:36 42,1989.

18. S. M. Kegeles, N. E. Adler and C. E. Irwin, "Sexually Active Adolescents and Condoms: Changes over One Year in Knowledge, Attitudes and Use," *American Journal of Public Health* 78:460-461, 1988; K. P. Bettinghaus, "Health Promotion and the Knowledge-Attitude-Behavior Continuum," *Preventive Medicine*, 15:475-491,1986; R. J. DiClemente, J. Zorn and L. Temoshok, "Adolescents and AIDS: A Survey of Knowledge, Attitudes and Be fiefs about AIDS in San Francisco," *American Journal of Public Health,* 76:1143-1145, 1986; and R. J. DiClemente, "The Emergence of Adolescents as a Risk Group for Human Immunodeficiency Virus Infection," *Journal of Adolescent Research*, 5:7-17,1990.

19. R. J. DiClemente, ed., 1992, op. cit. (see reference 16); R.J. DiClemente, J. Zorn and L. Temoshok, 1986, op. at. (see reference 18); and R.J. DiClemente, 1990 op. cit. (see reference 18).

SYMPOSIUM 1996
THE STATUS AND TRENDS OF THE
GLOBAL HIV/AIDS PANDEMIC

organized by
The AIDS Control and Prevention (AIDSCAP) Project of Family Health
International, The Francois-Xavier Bagnoud Center for Health and
Human Rights of the Harvard School of Public Health, The Joint
United Nations Programme on HIV/AIDS (UNAIDS)

Global Overview

In mid-July 1996, an estimated 21.8 million adults and children worldwide were living with HIV/AIDS, of whom 20.4 million (94 percent) were in the developing world. Of the adults, 12.2 million (58 percent) were male and 8.8 million (42 percent) were female (For more details, see "The HIV/AIDS Situation in mid-1996, Global and Regional Highlights. Fact Sheet 1 July 1996," UNAIDS and WHO, Geneva, Switzerland). Close to 19 million adults and children (86 percent of the world total) were living with HIV/AIDS in sub-Saharan Africa and in South and Southeast Asia.

Worldwide during 1995, 2.7 million adult HIV infections occurred in adults (averaging more than 7,000 new infections each day). Of these, about 1 million (an average of nearly 3,000 new infections per day) occurred in Southeast Asia and 1.4 million infections (close to 4,000 new infections per day) were in sub-Saharan Africa. The industrialized world accounted for about 55,000 new HIV infections in 1995 (nearly 150 new infections per day; about 2 percent of the global total).

In 1995 approximately 500,000 children were born with HIV infection (about 1,400 per day); of these children 67 percent were in sub-Saharan Africa, 30 percent in South and Southeast Asia, and over 2 percent in Latin America and the Caribbean.

From the beginning of the pandemic until mid-1996, an estimated 27.9 million people worldwide have been infected with HIV. The largest numbers of individuals ever infected with HIV were in sub-Saharan Africa, totaling 19 million (68 percent of the global total), and in South and Southeast Asia, totaling 5 million (18 percent of the global total).

Since the beginning of the pandemic, the majority of HIV infections—26 million (93 percent)—have occurred in the developing world. The number of HIV-infected people in South and Southeast Asia is now more then twice the total number of infected people in the entire industrialized world.

The global cumulative number of HIV infections among adults has more than doubled since the beginning of the decade, from about 10 million in 1990 to almost 25.5 million by mid-1996. Of these, 14.9 million were men (58 percent) and 10.5 million were women (42 percent).

More than 6 million adults have developed AIDS from the beginning of the pandemic to July 1996, and of these 4.5 million (close to 75 percent) were in sub-Saharan Africa; 0.4 million were in Latin America and the Caribbean (7 percent); and 0.75 million were in North America, Europe and North and South Pacific combined (12 percent). In South and Southeast Asia, where the pandemic gained intensity more recently, it is estimated that 330,000 adults have developed AIDS. Of the 1.6 million children with AIDS, the majority—1.4 million (85 percent)—were in sub-Saharan Africa.

By July 1996, 5.8 million people (4.5 million adults and 1.3 million children), 75 percent of all people with AIDS, are estimated to have died from AIDS worldwide.

In summary, the HIV/AIDS pandemic is as powerful as ever. This report will show that the pandemic is now composed of distinct epidemics each with their own features and force, and disproportionately impacting on the developing world. The following sections of this report will show that as the HIV/AIDS epidemics within each region and country have become increasingly diverse and fragmented, they have created a multifaceted and devastating pandemic.

Africa and the Middle East

Sub-Saharan Africa by mid-1996, 13.3 million adults were living with HIV in sub-Saharan Africa, representing about 60 percent of the world's total. Three broadly defined geographic areas, which include countries with severe epidemics and others with epidemics at their intermediate stages, account for almost 90 percent of all current HIV infections in adults and adolescents in Africa. Within these three areas, 18 countries have at least 100,000 people living with HIV. In central/eastern Africa, Cameroon, Ethiopia, Kenya, Rwanda, Sudan, Uganda and Zaire have 37 percent of all current HIV infections on the continent. A similar proportion is contributed by a second group of countries in southern Africa: Botswana, Malawi, Mozambique, South Africa, Tanzania, Zambia and Zimbabwe. Finally, West African countries, including Burkina Faso, Cote d'Ivoire, Ghana and Nigeria, contribute about 15 percent to the total number of adults and adolescents living with HIV in Africa.

In Kenya, Malawi, Rwanda, Tanzania, Uganda, Zambia, Zimbabwe (countries where HIV began to spread widely in the early 1980s), more than 10 percent of women attending antenatal clinics surveyed in urban areas have been found to be HIV-infected, with rates which may exceed 40 percent in some surveillance sites. In these populations, transmission of HIV occurs mainly through heterosexual contact, beginning in early teen years and peaking before age 25. Following similar patterns of spread and intensity, HIV epidemics have recently expanded in Botswana, Lesotho, Swaziland and South Africa. The observed high rates of HIV in women of reproductive age have resulted in high numbers of HIV-infected newborns. Of the 3 million HIV-infected infants born in the world with HIV infection since the beginning of the pandemic, over 90 percent have been born in Africa. Many of these children typically develop AIDS and die within a few years.

In other sub-Saharan countries (mostly in west and central Africa) HIV epidemics are currently passing through their intermediate stage where between 1 and 10 percent of women attending urban antenatal clinics are HIV-infected. A few of these countries still have relatively low levels of HIV prevalence, but these have begun to rise in several countries such as Nigeria and Cameroon, which earlier had been relatively spared. HIV-2 is primarily found in West Africa, but HIV-2 infections also have been confirmed in African countries elsewhere, including Angola and Mozambique. The highest prevalence of HIV-2 infection is found in Guinea Bissau and in southern Senegal. In contrast to the increasing spread of HIV-1, the prevalence of HIV-2 has remained rather stable in West Africa. This is thought to be the result of the higher transmissibility of HIV-1 compared to HIV-2. The likelihood of transmission of HIV-1 through heterosexual intercourse is estimated to be about three times higher per exposure than for HIV-2. In addition, perinatal transmission rates of HIV-2 are reported significantly lower (less than 4 percent for HIV-2 compared with 25 to 35 percent for HIV-1).

Under circumstances that are not yet fully understood, epidemics may suddenly explode, with rates of infection increasing several fold within only a few year as has been observed recently in Botswana and South Africa. HIV prevalence in pregnant women in South Africa has grown dramatically. From 1993 to 1995, HIV prevalence increased from 4.3 to 11 percent, and from 9.6 to 18 percent, in the provinces of Free State and Kwazulu/Natal, respectively. Population mobility, patterns of sexual behavior, and societal factors are likely to influence the potential for such explosions.

The presence of sexually transmitted diseases (STDs) suggests a marked risk of concurrent HIV infection for at least two reasons: (1) the modes of transmission of HIV and other STDs are similar; and (2) the role of STDs in facilitating the transmission of HIV has been clearly established. STDs are affecting young adults, especially women, with direct serious consequences. For women, these consequences include pelvic inflammatory disease, cervical cancer, infertility and post-partum endometritis. For infants, maternal STDs may lead to low birth weight, neonatal syphilis and gonococcal opthalmia. The lack of circumcision in mates has been shown to add to the risk of acquiring STDs. The World Health Organization estimates that in 1995, 65 million new cases of curable STDs occurred in Africa.

Populations Affected

The transmission of HIV in adults and young people in sub-Saharan Africa occurs essentially through heterosexual contact. Rates of HIV infection among sex workers are now found as high as 80 percent in Nairobi and 55 percent in Abidjan. HIV antibody testing of blood donations remains incomplete in most countries in sub-Saharan Africa. Transfusions continue to play a role in the spread of HIV to those most likely to receive them: women of reproductive age and children.

Within each country, HIV epidemics have progressed with different velocity in various population groups. Early in the evolution of the epidemics, urban populations and rural communities located along highways were more rapidly affected. Among them, young adults with multiple sexual partners acquired high rates of infection. Urban and trading centers generally continue to have substantially higher prevalence of HIV infection than rural areas. But, this pattern is by no means universal: population displacement, armed conflicts, proximity to highways or intense migration and population mobility for economic reasons influence strongly the spread of HIV.

As a result of a combination of these factors, some rural communities of Kenya, Tanzania and Uganda have higher infection rates than those observed in neighboring urban populations. In some countries where HIV epidemics were initially found in urban areas, rates of HIV infection in some rural populations have increased steadily over recent years. In other countries, perhaps with poorer transport networks, this has not been the case.

As epidemics mature, they tend to spread into younger populations, especially young women. The rates of newly acquired HIV infections are highest in the 15- to 24-year-old group among both females and males in most of sub-Saharan Africa. The peak of new infections occurs several years earlier in young women than in young men. In Masaka, Uganda, for example, HIV prevalence in 13- to 19-year-old females is over 20 times higher than in males of the same age. Most of the infections in 15- to 19-year-olds are in females, although as young men get older, their prevalence increases as well.

Apart from possible biological factors, there are at least two reasons for the disproportionate risk of young women acquiring HIV infection early, including: (1) an earlier age of sexual initiation of girls (in Masaka, the median age at first sexual intercourse is 15 for females and 17 for males); and (2) the patterns of sexual mixing, wherein young women tend to have sex with older men in the context of marriage or in exchange for money or advantages, whereas young men tend to have sex with young women. But for many women, the major risk factor for HIV is the behavior of their spouse or regular sexual partner. Monogamous women are at a disadvantage in protecting themselves against HIV when spouses are engaged in high-risk behavior.

Populations on the Move

Major political, social and demographic changes have occurred in sub-Saharan Africa over the last few decades and have resulted in important population displacement, migration and rapid urbanization. The improvement of transportation and communication networks, the increased exchange of goods, and the creation of large-scale development programs have stimulated the movement of young men and women within and across national boundaries. Open conflicts, environmental degradation, natural disasters and low-intensity wars have also led millions of Africans to leave their places of residence and, in some situations, to turn to survival strategies that have increased the practice of unsafe sex. Consequences of political and civil unrest and subsequent population displacement have led to an increased spread in HIV transmission; populations displaced from Ethiopia, Mozambique, Rwanda and Liberia are examples. In addition, the movement of troops from West Africa to Angola and Mozambique has been linked to the spread of HIV-2 to these countries.

Migration within countries, across borders, and urbanization (e.g., from rural areas to urban centers or Industrial sites) have led to high concentrations of predominantly male communities and increased participation in commercial sex. Professional groups characterized by mobility, for instance, truck drivers, traders and military personnel, have also been associated with a higher risk of HIV infection. Population mobility facilitates the spread of STDs, including HIV.

Economic development programs (the construction of highways, dams, and the creation of new industries or agriculture projects, for example) need to include an initial appraisal of the potential impact of these projects on the vulnerability of the labor force and the local population to HIV infection and other STDs. Measures to minimize this impact, such as reducing gender imbalance in the labor force, enabling workers to be joined by their families, allowing for regular contacts with distant spouses, and incorporating HIV/STD programs in development schemes, need to be built into the project design. But even with such initiatives, the sheer dynamic of transition towards increasingly urbanized society brings with it changing behavior mores that create new needs and present new opportunities for HIV transmission.

All of these social and demographic changes need to be addressed by well-designed national and inter-country HIV/STD prevention programs based on epidemiological, behavioral and social determinants research.

Burden of Disease

Although the constantly growing HIV/AIDS care needs have already overwhelmed the coping capacity of urban health systems in hard-hit countries, demands for care will increasingly fall on poorly equipped and under-funded rural services, households and individuals. Already, 80 percent of hospital beds in an infectious disease hospital in Abidjan, Cote d'Ivoire, and 50 percent in a hospital in Kampala, Uganda, are occupied by people with HIV.

Demographic surveys in several countries have already noted significant increases in infant and child mortality. Projections for Zambia and Zimbabwe indicate that AIDS may increase child mortality rates nearly threefold by the year 2010. Other estimates point to a more modest impact. In either case, due to high levels of fertility, populations will generally continue to grow, but critical deficits will affect the economically active ages. Studies in areas where 8 percent of the adult population is HIV-infected have measured a doubling of mortality due to HIV and a decrease of 5 years in life expectancy. Some HIV epidemics will have severe effects on the population age structure, indenting the population pyramid in young adults, the main contributors to social and economic development, but this may not occur in all areas.

Successes in Prevention

To date in sub-Saharan Africa, there has been a lack of rigorous evaluation of intervention strategies, especially for the behavioral interventions designed to reduce the sexual transmission of HIV. Without good behavioral, social and contextual data, however, it is difficult to attribute observed changes in HIV prevalence rates to specific program efforts. STD control programs, through early diagnosis, treatment and the promotion of safer sexual behavior, have been shown to reduce significantly the rates of STD infections. Successful programs have been documented in Zambia and Zimbabwe. In a research study in Mwanza, Tanzania, early treatment of STDs in a rural population has been associated with a 42 percent decline in the rate of newly acquired HIV infections. Emerging data also show substantial decline in some STDs. This important finding supports the revitalization of STD control programs benefiting from new approaches that have already been initiated in several sub-Saharan countries.

Treating Sexually Transmitted Diseases Reduces HIV Incidence—Result of the Mwanza, Tanzania Trial: One of the key advances in HIV/AIDS research over the past year has been the confirmation that treating sexually transmitted diseases (STDs) reduces the incidence (rate of new infections) of HIV. This evidence arises from the Mwanza trial, the first randomized controlled trial to demonstrate the impact of preventive measures against HIV in a general population setting.

The aim of the Mwanza trial was to implement improved STD treatment services for the rural population of this northern Tanzanian region. These services were fully integrated into the primary health care system based on the syndromic treatment method (not requiring laboratory diagnosis) recommended by the World Health Organization. The services were designed to be affordable and replicable on a large scale in resource-poor settings, and their impact was measured in a randomized trial: six communities with the improved STD services (the intervention group) were compared with six matched comparison communities with pre-existing STD services (the comparison group).

A random sample of 12,000 adults in Mwanza was followed over two years to record HIV incidence and the prevalence (proportion of infections in a population) of selected STDs. HIV prevalence at baseline was about 4 percent in both the intervention and comparison groups. Incidence of HIV infections over two years was 1.2 percent in the intervention communities, compared with 1.9 percent in the comparison community, showing a reduction of about 40 percent from the intervention. Reductions were seen in all age and sex groups.

Data from Mwanza, also show a substantial impact from the intervention on some of the STDs targeted by the treatment program: active syphilis was reduced by 30 to 40 percent, and in men the prevalence of symptomatic urethritis was reduced by 50 percent.

There was little effect from the Mwanza intervention on asymptomatic STDs, which are common in both women and men in this population. Because symdromic treatment services rely on patients perceiving STD symptoms, the significant impact on symptomatic but not asymptomatic STDs is not surprising.

A detailed economic evaluation showed that the annual cost of the Mwanza intervention program for a population of 150,000 was about US $68,000, or about 45 cents per capita. The cost per case of HIV infection averted was about $250, or $11 for each year of healthy life saved. This compares favorably with child immunization programs and other highly cost-effective health interventions.

Results from Mwanza suggest that a large proportion of HIV infections in this population are due to the enhancing effects of other STDs, particularly when these are symptomic. This may help to explain the very rapid spread of HIV in some parts of Africa and other regions of the developing world. The Mwanza trial has shown that providing effective treatment services for such STDs can significantly reduce their prevalence and the number of new HIV infections.

The economic data from Mwanza show that improved STD treatment services are not only effective, but highly cost-effective and should, therefore, be promoted as an essential component of HIV/AIDS control activities wherever STDs are highly prevalent. Large-scale implementation of STD treatment services could have a major impact on the HIV pandemic worldwide.

Hope that the number of new infections occurring may have decreased comes from studies of the epidemic in Uganda, a country with one of the older epidemics in Africa. A study of recent trends in HIV infection in women attending several antenatal clinics in Uganda shows significant declines in HIV prevalence. Between 1990-93 and 1994-95, overall HIV prevalence in pregnant women at sentinel site decreased 29 percent (from 21 to 15 percent), and decreased 35 percent in both 15- to 19- and 20- to 24-year-olds. Since infection levels (prevalence) in this young age group reflect more recent patterns in new infections (incidence), these data suggest a substantial reduction in the incidence of HIV infection in young people over time.

Declines in HIV Incidence and Prevalence in Pregnant Women and their Relationship to HIV Risk Reduction in Uganda from 1989 to 1995: In Uganda, recent trends in HIV prevalence (proportion of people infected) in pregnant women detected by sentinel HIV surveillance in urban areas indicate that a substantial decline has occurred in recent HIV incidence (proportion of new infections) in young women.

From 1990 to 1993 and from 1994 to 1995, HIV prevalence in pregnant women at sentinel sites in Uganda decreased overall by 29 percent (from 21 percent to 15 percent), and by 35 percent in both 15- to 19-year-olds (from 17 percent to 11 percent) and in 20- to 24-year-olds (27 percent to 17 percent). These findings are consistent with a reduction of 30 to 50 percent in HIV incidence in female adolescents and young women in Uganda since 1988.

Population surveys to assess the determinants of declining HIV incidence in Uganda suggest that changes could be due largely to a reduction in high-risk behavior, including: increased monogamy; reduction in numbers of sexual partners; condom use in sexual relationships at risk of HIV infection; and later age of sexual debut. For example, in 1995 in Kampala, 22 percent of male respondents reported sex with a non-regular partner, of whom 63 percent reported use of a condom in the last sexual encounter at risk of HIV infection.

A decline in HIV incidence is the most plausible explanation for the observed trends in Uganda, and such changes could result from a reduction in high-risk sexual behavior. These findings provide evidence that prevention strategies to change high-risk sexual behavior in Uganda may have had a direct impact on reducing the rate of new HIV infections in some areas of the country. Additional studies are required to better identify the determinants of such sexual behavior change in Uganda and assess the extent to which these findings can be applied to other HIV epidemics in sub-Saharan Africa.

Similar declines in HIV prevalence in young adults are reported from another study in the Masaka district in Uganda. These findings could indicate that the growth of the epidemic has been blunted, perhaps transiently, by behavioral changes resulting in decreased spread of HIV in younger age groups. Surveys of such populations suggest that behavior change might have led to these apparent declines; however, more rigorous qualitative and quantitative behavioral and social data will be required to help interpret these results.

Notwithstanding these encouraging signs, new infections remain high, especially in young people. The combination of reductions in levels of infection and continuing evidence of new infections should provide additional impetus for enhancing prevention efforts.

North Africa and the Middle East

This region represents 22 countries ranging from Morocco in the west to Pakistan in the east. Information on HIV infection in the region is sparse. Information available from mandatory screening of blood donors indicates low HIV prevalence in these populations, except for Djibouti.

The highest levels of HIV infection have been documented in Djibouti (9.3 percent in pregnant women and from 2 to 20 percent in STD patients). HIV prevalence among STD patients rose from 1.3 to 5 percent in Sudan; this pattern has also been seen in Yemen, Pakistan and the Syrian Arab Republic. Seventy-five percent of reported AIDS cases are from five countries in the region: Morocco, Sudan, Saudi Arabia, Tunisia and Djibouti.

The future size and trends of the epidemic in this region are difficult to predict. There is anecdotal evidence of high STD rates and risk behaviors. The region is characterized by late introduction of the virus, the status of women in society, the highly stigmatizing nature of STDs, and the difficulty of conducting effective sexual health programs.

Asia

This region includes Bangladesh, Bhutan, Brunei Darussalam, Cambodia, China, India, Indonesia, Hong Kong, Japan, DPR Korea, Republic of Korea, Laos, Malaysia, the Maldives, Mongolia, Myanmar, Nepal, the Philippines, Singapore, Sri Lanka, Thailand and Vietnam. It is home to over 60 percent of the world's adult population, hence what happens in the region will have a major impact on the global pandemic.

The general epidemiology and estimated prevalence rates for these countries are extremely diverse, ranging from countries with low HIV prevalence rates (Mongolia, DPR Korea) to countries with high HIV prevalence (Cambodia, Myanmar and Thailand).

There has been substantial variation in the timing and rate of growth of the epidemic. In some countries, e.g., Cambodia, India, Myanmar and Thailand, HIV spread has been extensive, with extremely rapid growth in some geographic areas. In others, e.g., DPR Korea and the Republic of Korea, the Philippines and Singapore, only limited spread has occurred to date and the rate of growth appears to be substantially lower.

The epidemic in Thailand is among the best documented in the world, with an estimated three-quarter of a million people living with HIV. Nationally, HIV prevalence among injecting drug users rose quickly in 1988 to approximately 35 percent. HIV among brothel-based sex workers rose from 3.5 percent in 1989 to 33 percent by late 1994. Infection levels in males at STD clinics grew from 0 percent to 8.6 percent over the same time period. HIV prevalence in women attending antenatal clinics has continued to rise steadily from 0 percent in 1989 to 2.3 percent in 1995. This trend is expected to continue for several years. However, there is evidence that prevention efforts are taking effect; HIV infection levels in military conscripts have dropped from 3.6 percent in 1993 to 2.5 percent in 1995.

In India HIV seroprevalence is high in the south and west. For example, in Bombay prevalence went from 2 to 3 percent in STD clinic attendees before 1990 to 36 percent in 1994. HIV prevalence in sex workers rose from 1 to 51 percent between 1987 and 1993, and antenatal clinic women tested positive at a 2.5 percent rate in 1994. There is great geographical variation in India. HIV seroprevalence in the central, eastern and northern parts of the country are generally lower than in the rest of India. Studies among sex workers in Calcutta have shown a clear and consistently low prevalence of 1.2 percent. In Vellore rates among women attending antenatal clinics have been steady at 0.1 percent, although STD clinic rates there grew from 4 percent to 15 percent between 1993 and 1995. Injecting drug use has been a problem in Manipur State, with prevalence reaching 60 percent by 1992. This geographic variability and the size of the country have made estimation of the actual number of infections difficult. At the end of 1994, WHO estimated 1.75 million HIV infections, while evidence suggests an estimate of between 2 and 5 million in mid-1996.

HIV/AIDS in India: India is experiencing rapid and extensive spread of HIV. This is particularly worrisome since India is home to a population of over 900 million. As a single nation it has more people than the continents of Africa, Australia and Latin America combined.

There are an estimated 2 to 5 million people infected with HIV in India today, and 50,000 to 100,000 cases of AIDS may have already occurred in the country.

This epidemic is fueled by both married and unmarried men visiting sex workers. The most rapid and well-documented spread of HIV has occurred in Bombay and the State of Tamil Nadu. In Bombay HIV prevalence has reached the level of 50 percent in sex workers, 36 percent in STD patients and 2.5 percent in women attending antenatal clinics.

Certain regions, such as eastern India (Calcutta area) and northern India (New Delhi region), still show a lower prevalence of HIV (1 to 2 percent) among sex workers.

Contrary to traditional belief, sexually transmitted diseases and sex with multiple partners are common in the country, both in urban and rural areas. An estimated 3 to 4 percent of some rural populations have a sexually transmitted disease.

Injecting drug use is a problem in Manipur, which is in North East region, where 55 percent of drug users are HIV-infected and 1 percent of women attending antenatal clinics are infected with HIV.

HIV is rapidly spreading to rural areas through migrant workers and truck drivers. Surveys show that 5 to 10 percent of some truck drivers in the country are infected with HIV.

An estimated 1 to 2 million cases of tuberculosis occur in India every year. In Bombay 10 percent of the patients presenting with tuberculosis are HIV-positive. Tuberculosis is the presenting symptom of AIDS in over 60 percent of AIDS cases. A major international and governmental effort is necessary to respond effectively to this severe epidemic.

In Cambodia the HIV/AIDS data indicate that the current extensive HIV epidemic started during the late 1980s or early 1990s and is predominantly occurring among heterosexuals with multiple sex partners. To date, there has been no evidence of a significant problem of injecting drugs in Cambodia. Levels among blood donors in Phnom Penh have risen from less than 0.1 percent in 1991 to about 10 percent in 1995. Dramatic rises have also been seen in sex workers, the police, the military, STD patients and pregnant women.

The epidemic in Myanmar is one of the most serious in the region. There are an estimated half a million people with HIV in this country in 1996. The epidemic began with the infection of large numbers of injecting drug users in the late 1980s, with a prevalence of 60 to 70 percent since 1992. HIV prevalence in sex workers has steadily risen from 4.3 percent in March 1992 to 18 percent in March 1995. There is substantial geographic variability, with infection rates in pregnant women varying according to region between 0 and 12 percent in 1993. High levels of other STDs, low levels of condom use, the clandestine nature of commercial sex, and limited blood screening due to cost constraints are contributing factors to HIV spread.

In Malaysia, HIV infection levels in IDUs have grown rapidly from 0.1 percent in 1988 to 20 percent in 1994. In female sex workers, rates have gone from 0.3 percent in 1989 to 10 percent in 1994. A behavioral study conducted nationwide in 1992 found that almost one in three sexually active men and one in ten married men reported having had casual sexual contact in the previous month. Reported condom use in commercial sex is low. This implies serious potential for heterosexual transmission. The rapid growth in prevalence in IDUs and sex workers in Malaysia in the last three years is similar to that seen in Thailand and Myanmar in the early stages of their epidemics.

In Vietnam there is some evidence that the HIV epidemic is now growing rapidly. High levels have been demonstrated in IDUs in treatment (32 percent in 1992-95), and recent evidence suggests increasing levels among young men and women in the south of Vietnam. Rates in some sex worker populations rose from 9 to 38 percent between 1992 and 1994-95.

In China the majority (about 70 percent) of reported HIV infections and AIDS cases have been among IDUs in Yunnan Province. HIV infections are believed to be increasing among heterosexual populations in southern China, especially in the areas surrounding Hong Kong. The Chinese Academy of Preventive Medicine has estimated that there were 10,000 HIV-infected persons in China as of the end of 1993, growing to 100,000 by the end of 1995.

Limited HIV/AIDS data for Laos suggest that HIV transmission may be starting in the heterosexual population. Additional data are needed to confirm the beginning of an HIV epidemic in Laos.

In Bangladesh, Indonesia, Nepal and Sri Lanka the situation must be assessed based upon relatively limited testing, low rates of HIV detection in most populations, and low numbers of reported HIV and AIDS cases. These limits to our knowledge of the situation make any estimates of total prevalence or incidence quite speculative. However, most of these countries appear to have high levels of other STDs in their populations, implying a strong potential for extensive HIV spread.

In Hong Kong, Japan, Mongolia and the Republic of Korea, extensive spread has not been documented. In DPR Korea and Bhutan no AIDS cases or HIV infections have been reported, but only limited surveillance has been carried out.

In the Philippines there appears to be slower growth of the epidemic, with much lower levels (less than 1 percent) of HIV among sex workers. Early AIDS cases indicated some spread of HIV among men having sex with men. The lower number of clients and more indirect nature of sex work in the Philippines may help to explain the more gradual evolution of the situation.

In Singapore, infection levels in sex workers have been growing quite slowly. The rapid growth of HIV infection in sex workers seen elsewhere in the region has not been seen there, perhaps as a result of prevention efforts.

Populations Affected

The epidemics in Asia are predominantly spreading through heterosexual contact. On a regional basis, infected men probably outnumber infected women by a factor of 3 to 1 or more, since commercial sex clients, injecting drug users and men having sex with men have contributed most strongly to the rapid initial growth of the epidemic. This male/female ratio is expected to drop as the epidemic spreads into the general population through spread of HIV from clients of sex workers to their regular partners and spouses.

The HIV/AIDS epidemics in Asian countries have been strongly influenced by gender inequality and the frequent practice of men visiting sex workers. Since sexual expression for females is typically more limited than for males, the small population of sex workers has large numbers of clients, and consequently high rates of other STDs, which enhance HIV transmission. As a result, most epidemics begin with rapid prevalence increases in sex workers and their clients (as seen through STD clinic data). This growth can be quite explosive. Annual incidence in sex workers as high as 25 percent and in clients of almost 10 percent have been seen in India. High growth rates have also been well documented in numerous studies in Thailand and Cambodia.

Sharing of needles among injecting drug users, given its high efficacy for HIV transmission, has also played a significant role early in the epidemics, particularly in the Golden Triangle region (from Thailand and Vietnam, across southern China, to Myanmar, to Manipur) and in northern Malaysia. As the epidemics mature, transmission from sex worker clients and IDUs to their wives or girlfriends becomes the most important route of female infection, although this transmission occurs at slower rates than that between sex worker and client.

The ultimate size to which the epidemic might grow in most countries is difficult to assess because few studies of risk behaviors in the general population are available. Only Hong Kong, Malaysia, the Philippines, Singapore and Thailand have done national studies of risk behavior. Indicating that the total number of men engaging in sexual risk behavior is lower in Hong Kong, the Philippines and Singapore than in Thailand and Malaysia, these studies may help to explain the slower growth of the epidemic in those countries.

Pediatric HIV infection is also difficult to assess in this region, given the wide geographic variability in antenatal clinic infection levels. In Thailand it is now estimated that 6,400 children are infected annually, approximately 10 percent of total new HIV infections.

Impact of Prevention Programs

The extent of behavior change in the region has varied greatly from country to country. Thailand has best documented the most extensive behavioral change, the result of an active multi-sectoral national effort. In national surveys conducted in 1990 and 1993, the percentage of men visiting sex workers in the last year declined from 22 percent to 10 percent. Condom use in commercial sex transactions is now the norm. As a consequence of these behavioral changes STD rates have fallen precipitously, with reported cases dropping to one-fourth of their initial levels. Male HIV incidence is estimated to have fallen by an even greater factor. While there has been substantial success of HIV prevention in commercial sex trade, the situation in non-commercial casual sex remains of concern. Current levels of condom use between boyfriend/girlfriend or with other longer-term partners remains low, on the order of 10 percent. Another area in which there has been only limited success has been slowing HIV transmission within HIV-discordant married couples in which the husband is HIV-infected and the wife is not. As these women become infected, rates found in antenatal clinics continue to climb.

The slow growth of the epidemic in Singapore may largely be attributable to general awareness and programs promoting condom use at STD clinics and in brothels. It is reported that condom use by sex workers has reached fairly high levels, although commercial sex by Singapore residents traveling overseas remains an important avenue of HIV transmission.

Efforts to produce behavior change have been less effective in other countries of the region. In India, no formal studies have been done on the large-scale impact of prevention programs. From focus group discussions, however, it appears that fear of acquiring HIV has risen among the educated and the higher socioeconomic classes. This may lead to higher condom use in these populations, but this is not yet documented. Unfortunately, in the lower socioeconomic classes and rural areas there is still a gross lack of awareness and knowledge of HIV prevention methods, suggesting that behavioral change has probably been minimal. There still appears to be low use of condoms in many sex worker populations, especially among those who have many clients per day. Condoms continue to be the exception rather than the rule for most premarital and extramarital sex in India. Sexually transmitted diseases continue to be a major problem in this country, a fact not well recognized prior to the HIV epidemic.

In the Philippines, behavioral surveys in 1990 and 1994 in Metro Manila have shown fairly constant levels of casual and commercial sex, implying little behavioral change during that time. The levels of condom use, while rising somewhat in Metro Manila, remain quite low. STD rates are lower than in many other countries of the region, but as mentioned earlier, are high in certain populations, including sex workers.

Myanmar and Malaysia's effectiveness in inducing behavioral change is difficult to evaluate because no periodically collected data on risks is available there. However, extensive NGO efforts in Malaysia and grass-roots efforts in Myanmar may be reducing risk behaviors and increasing the use of condoms.

For those countries in the early stages of HIV epidemics (e.g., Bangladesh, Bhutan, Brunei Darussalam, Indonesia, Nepal, the Maldives and Sri Lanka), national efforts at HIV control have been fairly limited and major nationwide behavioral change is unlikely to have yet occurred. Non-governmental organization and governmental program efforts targeted at commercial sex may have raised condom use somewhat in more heavily populated urban settings, e.g., Jakarta, Kathmandu and Colombo.

Impact of Care Programs

Because the epidemics in the region are comparatively young, many doctors fail to properly diagnose AIDS and, in addition, medical care is often difficult to access or limited in scope. As a result, what little data are available on issues of survival and the effect of care show somewhat shorter survival after diagnosis with AIDS than in the industrialized world. In one study in Thailand, median survival time after a diagnosis of AIDS was only 7 months, much shorter than in many industrialized countries, possibly because cases were only diagnosed when illness was quite advanced. In the Philippines, a small study following HIV-infected sex workers found survival times of one and a half years after the recognition that the immune system was seriously compromised. In Thailand, approximately one-fifth of children infected at birth were found to have developed AIDS after 6 months. However, the findings of these small preliminary studies can hardly be generalized. Studies of accessibility to and use of care, and its impacts on disease progression and survival are urgently needed throughout the region.

AIDS: the Eruption in Asia

It is critical to recognize the sheer numbers of people living in South and Southeast Asia, a region that contains more than 60 percent of the world's adult population. In particular the evidence gathered in India suggests rapid, extensive and uncontrolled spread in many parts of the country. There is an urgent need for a comprehensive synthesis of the state of the epidemic in India. It is clear that there is a critical need, in this country as elsewhere in the region, to gather more credible HIV/AIDS data on rural populations.

China, too, because of its size and rapid changes in social and sexual behaviors, potentially represents a major focus of the epidemic in the region.

The different rates of spread within and between countries must be acknowledged and better understood. For example, why is the spread of HIV in the Philippines and Indonesia apparently slower than in Malaysia and Thailand? Is it related to later introduction of the virus, to lack of reliable information or differences in behavior?

Some governments (Hong Kong, Malaysia, Singapore, Thailand) have committed extensive resources to responding to the epidemic. However, the majority of governments in the region are relying heavily on external financial support to prevent epidemics occurring within their own borders. In addition, there continues to be a serious problem of denial and reticence about releasing surveillance and behavioral information by some governments in this region.

Latin America and the Caribbean

Latin America and the Caribbean region is heterogeneous and diverse, with a total of 44 countries and territories, an estimated population of 470 million people with a variety of ethnic backgrounds, and four main languages (English, Spanish, French and Portuguese). The rate of spread of HIV/AIDS has been slower than in other developing regions of the world, but the pandemic is well established and there is a wide variation in the level of HIV infection and the speed of the many epidemics among sub-regions and countries.

The dominant modes of transmission vary from one country to the next, ranging from some epidemics that are predominantly related to homo- and bisexual behaviors, to epidemics connected to injecting drug use, and to others that are primarily determined by heterosexual transmission. In spite of this epidemiological diversity, sexual transmission of HIV/AIDS accounts for 80 percent of overall transmission in the region, ranging from 64 percent in Brazil to as high as 93 percent in the Andean sub-region (Bolivia, Colombia, Ecuador, Peru, Venezuela). Although data are limited and sometimes spotty, they reflect an increasing pandemic that is progressively affecting heterosexual populations and non-urban areas.

As of June 10, 1996, Latin America and the Caribbean accounted for 26 percent (176,930) of the cumulative total of cases reported in the Americas to the Pan American Health Organization (PAHO) and 13.4 percent of the cases reported worldwide to the World Health Organization (WHO). It is estimated that 1.6 million people in the region have already been infected with HIV and that some countries are at particular risk of rapid dissemination of HIV from traditional "at-risk" groups (sex workers, men who have sex with men [MSM], men with multiple partners) and to other vulnerable groups in the general population (women, youth and children).

Sexual behaviors across the region reflect patterns that place the population at risk for HIV. These behaviors include early onset of sexual behavior, cultural acceptability of multiple partners, especially for males, and low levels of condom use. In this region, however, despite the relatively high proportion of men who have sex with other men, patterns of homo- and bi-sexual behavior are still poorly understood. Bisexual behavior is more prevalent than exclusively homosexual behavior, while self-identification with a gay lifestyle or culture is not common. Consequently, targeting messages likely to reach MSM is difficult.

The current epidemiological profile of HIV/AIDS in Latin America and the Caribbean is driven by high-risk situations favorable to a rapid spread of the HIV infection. Slowly but steadily the pandemic is taking hold of communities rendered doubly vulnerable due to their socioeconomic disadantage and lack of information. Migration, both between countries and from rural to urban areas, contributes to the continued spread of HIV/AIDS and creates additional challenges to HIV prevention. The epidemiological evidence signals a rapid shift of new infections to younger ages, particularly toward people between 15 and 24 years old. In addition, there are marked tendencies for HIV infection to increase among the general population and among specific populations, in particular women, children, the poor, rural communities and, generally, those who have lower socioeconomic status and those who lack access to basic educational and health services.

Mexico, the Isthmus of Central America and the Latin Caribbean

The number of new HIV infections in Mexico, the Central American Isthmus (Guatemala, Belize, El Salvador, Honduras, Nicaragua, Costa Rica and Panama) and the Latin Caribbean (Cuba, Dominican Republic, Haiti and Puerto Rico) continues to rise. As of June 10, 1996, 60,564 cases were reported to PAHO. This represents 8.7 percent of the total number of cases reported for the Americas and 4.6 percent of the cases reported worldwide to WHO. However, the estimated "true" incidence of AIDS is substantially higher than the number of cases reported by 20 to 70 percent, with a one- to two-year lag in data collection.

There is evidence of continued increasing HIV incidence among MSM in Mexico, although the rise is not as rapid as it was in the 1980s. Transfusion-associated HIV infection and AIDS cases have drastically declined in this country as in the rest of the region due to effective blood screening. In Mexico this has resulted in an apparent slowing of AIDS cases among women, but there is, in fact, a much younger epidemic of heterosexually acquired HIV infection emerging among women. Consequently, in this country two epidemics are observed: an urban epidemic, more mature and affecting predominantly MSM and an emerging rural epidemic, which is predominantly spreading through heterosexual transmission.

The Central American Isthmus and the Latin Caribbean reflect epidemics with increasing HIV/AIDS incidence and accelerated heterosexual transmission. Honduras accounts for 57 percent of AIDS cases diagnosed in Central America, while it has only 17 percent of its population.

HIV seroprevalence levels among sex workers in Honduras have reached as high as nearly 40 percent. Sentinel surveillance of pregnant women in the city of San Pedro Sula has documented prevalence of up to 4 percent. Commerce, migration patterns and communication within this subregion suggest that HIV is spreading within each country in well established local epidemics and, externally, across international borders.

In the Latin Caribbean, Haiti is of particular importance because, perhaps alone in the region, it represents a case of a relatively mature epidemic. Due to social, economic and political instability, among other factors, HIV prevalence rose from 2 percent in 1989 to an estimated 5 percent of the adult population in rural areas in 1994. In urban areas the prevalence was estimated at 10 percent in 1994. HIV prevalence is particularly high among sex workers, STD clinic attendees and tuberculosis (TB) patients. High rates of HIV prevalence found by recent studies among pregnant women aged 14 to 24 are of particular concern.

Within this sub-region, there is diversity in the structure and organization of commercial sex, ranging from informal networks to thriving sex industries. The latter involve countries from which sex workers in other countries within and outside this region originate and others that have organized sex tourism. In the Dominican Republic, HIV seroprevalence among Dominican population subsets reached levels up to 11 percent among sex workers, 5 to 8 percent among STD patients and, by 1993, 1.2 percent among women attending antenatal clinics. International and intra-regional travel, including tourism and employment seeking, also exert major influences on the dynamics of the epidemics in the Caribbean, enhancing the potential for spread of HIV.

The English-Speaking Caribbean

The predominant mode of transmission for HIV in the English-speaking Caribbean is heterosexual, but estimates of HIV transmitted through homo/bisexual contacts account for 14 percent of all new infections. Inter-country variation exists in AIDS incidence rates and in the underlying HIV infection levels but, in general, the number of cases is increasing in all countries. As of June 10, 1996, this region accounted for 4.6 percent (9,399) of the cumulative total of cases reported in the Americas to PAHO and 0.7 percent of the cases reported worldwide to WHO. The doubling time for the annual number of new AIDS cases in this sub-region is four to five years. Some Caribbean countries report AIDS incidence rates that are among the highest in the world. Among the many small countries of the Caribbean, the presence of countries with very high and very low rates of HIV incidence indicates that there are many different epidemics and not one regional pattern.

The male-to-female ratio of incident AIDS cases has fallen dramatically over the past 10 years, standing at just less than 2 men to 1 woman in 1994. Women aged 15 to 19 now have higher annual incidence rates than men of the same age. Pediatric AIDS cases have been steadily rising and now account for 5 percent of all incident cases. AIDS has become the leading cause of death among young adult men in some Caribbean countries. There is an urgent need for increased surveillance of behavioral risk factors for AIDS and HIV infection, although the small size of most Caribbean countries makes the confidentiality issue an important obstacle to data collection and analysis.

Among the heterosexual population in the Caribbean, increasing numbers of persons from marginalized groups are becoming infected, including migrant workers, sex workers and users of crack cocaine. The extremely low incidence of HIV infection through contaminated blood represents a partial success story for the Caribbean region. Available data from sentinel surveillance indicates increasing HIV prevalence rates among pregnant women, sex workers, applicants for visas to the U.S. and migrant farm workers in some Caribbean countries.

South America

The number of HIV infections and AIDS cases in South America is rising steadily. As of June 10, 1996, South America accounted for 15.5 percent (106,841) of the cumulative total of cases reported in the Americas to PAHO and 8.2 percent of the cases reported worldwide to WHO. However, as in other sub-regions, the true incidence of AIDS is believed to be substantially higher due to under reporting and difficulties in data collection. Within this specific region, Brazil accounts for 75 percent of all cases of AIDS reported to PAHO/WHO, followed by the Andean Region (15 percent) and the Southern Cone (10 percent). Sexual transmission of HIV accounts for 74 percent of all reported AIDS cases (51 percent homo/bisexual and 23 percent heterosexual), injecting drug use for 19 percent and blood and vertical transmission and undocumented cases, 7 percent.

The HIV/AIDS epidemics in the region are at differing levels of maturity, but are well established in most countries. There is considerable transmission of HIV/AIDS due to injecting drug use in Brazil (27 percent) and the Southern Cone countries of Chile, Argentina, Uruguay and Paraguay (30 percent), although recent data in Brazil suggests that the HIV transmission through injecting drug use seems to be leveling off. The pandemic in this region has progressed since the early 1980s from one predominated by homo/bisexual transmission to one with accelerated heterosexual transmission. In addition, there is an emerging transition from epidemics centered in major urban areas to increasing involvement of smaller urban centers and rural areas. Epidemics are increasingly taking hold in specific population subsets, including adolescents, marginalized communities, and others characterized by low socioeconomic status and lack of basic socioeconomic, educational and health services.

High HIV seroprevalence levels have been reported among specific South American populations: 27 percent among sex workers in Santos City, Brazil; 30 to 60 percent in several studies of urban IDUs in Brazil and Argentina, 23 percent in MSM in Rio de Janeiro, and 1 percent to 3 percent among pregnant women in Santos City, Brazil. The impact of HIV/AIDS on morbidity and mortality is already seen in major urban centers in Latin America and the Caribbean. In the city of Sao Paulo, Brazil, for example, AIDS deaths are now the leading cause of mortality in women of reproductive age.

Challenges for Prevention

A significant increase in knowledge, attitudes, practices and behaviors (KAPB) about HIV/AIDS has occurred in the region in the past ten years. Behavior changes are most visible among sex workers, MSM and health care providers involved in AIDS management. The behavior changes observed invariably coincide with prevention interventions. However, in spite of these trends, knowledge of the relationship between HIV and AIDS and of asymptomatic transmission is still very limited in the region as a whole. Knowledge of sexually transmitted diseases and their relationship to HIV is limited, too. This is further compounded by the fact that although awareness of HIV/AIDS has substantially increased to levels over 80 percent in many countries, there are still many misconceptions regarding the transmission of HIV through casual contact. Surveys on knowledge, attitudes, practices and behavior (KAPB) have documented the coexistence of high levels of knowledge of HIV/AIDS in many populations with myths and misconceptions, unsafe practices and low self-perception of risk.

Immediate and targeted attention to specific population subsets (women, adolescents and children) is needed as these populations are expected to become most vulnerable in the next phase of the epidemic. While attention has been given effectively to partner reduction, non-penetrative sex, and the increase and correct use of condoms, programs have not fully capitalized on and need to be complemented with realistic prevention messages addressing abstinence, delayed sexual initiation and monogamy.

In brief, as the pandemic escalates in Latin America and the Caribbean, affecting larger segments of the population, the social, economic and demographic impacts of HIV/AIDS are likely to exacerbate the burden on individuals, communities and countries, threatening the development and stability of the region as a whole. Hence, the need for continued and increased support and an expansion of HIV/AIDS prevention and control programs is critical to effectively combat the pandemic in this region.

North America

The growth of the AIDS epidemic in North America has slowed in recent years and is approaching stable incidence, largely due to the decline in sexual transmission between men. However, current AIDS incidence is at an unacceptably high level and it must be recognized that this leveling off should in no way be considered reason for complacency. AIDS data do not reflect current HIV infections, and HIV infection continues to occur at an alarming rate in a number of sub-populations and geographic areas. The characteristics of persons with HIV infection and AIDS continue to change, reflecting the evolving patterns of transmission.

Populations Affected

Estimates from a statistical model show that in 1992 in the United States about 750,000 persons were living with HIV, and that year about 60,000 persons became infected with HIV. In Canada an estimated 34,000 adults were living with HIV in 1994, and 2,500 to 3,000 persons were newly infected with HIV each year in the period from 1990 to 1994. Recent estimates based on surveys of childbearing women indicate that approximately 3.2 per 10,000 children born in Canada and 15.1 per 10,000 children born in the United States carried HIV antibodies. In the U.S., an estimated 12,000 children are currently living with HIV. Since the start of the epidemic, from 1 to 1.5 million cumulative HIV infections have occurred in North America.

HIV infection has become one of the major causes of death for individuals between the ages of 25 and 44. Among men in this age group, it was the leading cause of death in the U.S. and the second leading cause of death in Canada in 1994. In that same year, HIV infection was the third leading cause of death among 25- to 44-year-old women in the U.S.

Through December 1995, 513,486 persons had been reported with AIDS in the United States; 13,291 had been reported through March 31, 1996 in Canada. Overall AIDS incidence in North America has been slowing progressively. Although there were large increases in the number of persons annually diagnosed with AIDS-related opportunistic illnesses (AIDS-OIs) through the early 1990s, the annual increase since 1993 has been less than 5 percent. In 1995, after adjustment for delays in reporting, approximately 62,000 persons were diagnosed with AIDS-OIs (29 per 100,000 population) in the United States and 2,166 in Canada (9 per 100,000 population).   In North America, although there has been an overall slowing in the increase in AIDS incidence, there has been substantive variation in the populations affected. For example, in the United States, the increase in AIDS incidence in the 1990s has been greatest for women compared to men, blacks and Hispanics compared to whites, and persons infected through heterosexual contact compared to those infected through other modes of transmission. As a result of these trends, AIDS incidence in 1995 was 6.5 times greater for blacks and 4 times greater for Hispanics than for whites, 20 percent of persons diagnosed with AIDS were women, and 15 percent were infected heterosexually.

The HIV infection rates are also high among certain groups, such as incarcerated persons. In 1994, 2.3 percent of nearly 1 million prisoners in the United States were known to be infected with

HIV, the rate of AIDS among prisoners was 7 times the rate of the non-incarcerated population, and AIDS was the second leading cause of death among prisoners. Among Canadian prisoners, HIV prevalence is higher in women, between 2 and 10 percent versus 1 to 4 percent for men; for both sexes, transmission is primarily related to injecting drug use.

In the United States, AIDS incidence among children less than 13 years of age has declined annually. For example, while there were 938 cases in 1992, there were approximately 600 cases in 1995. Only 21 Canadian children were diagnosed with AIDS in 1995. This decline may well reflect such factors as lower conception rates in women diagnosed with HIV and the possible impact of maternal and neonatal zidovudine therapy on HIV transmission.

In North America, syphilis incidence has declined, yet 1994 rates in the U.S. were 60 times greater for blacks than for whites. The incidence of gonorrhea has also declined. In 1994, the U.S. rate was 168 per 100,000 and the Canadian rate was 21 per 100,000.

Estimates from statistical models and data from several cohort studies demonstrate that HIV transmission among men who have sex with men (MSM) has declined from the very high levels of the early 1980s. In Canada, HIV incidence among MSM has dropped from about 5 to 10 percent per year in the early 1980s to an estimated 1 to 2 percent per year in the early 1990s. The HIV seroprevalence rate among MSM attending STD clinics in the U.S. fell from over 30 percent in the late 1980s to 24 percent in 1995. However, the prevalence of HIV infection among MSM remains high in almost all areas of North America.

The declining trends in HIV infection and morbidity among MSM are consistent with trends in STD surveillance data, which show large decreases in the rates of syphilis and rectal gonorrhea. These declines are also consistent with behavioral survey results, which show decreases in the number of sexual partners and other indicators of sexual risk behaviors. There does, however, appear to be some variation in the risk behaviors of younger MSM in that relatively high rates of unprotected receptive anal intercourse (30 percent to 47 percent over a 6- to 18-month period) continue to be reported by this age group.

In the United States, HIV prevalence among injecting drug users has decreased in all areas. The largest decrease has been observed in the northeast among IDUs in drug treatment programs. Anonymous testing in drug treatment centers in 29 U.S. cities from 1988 to 1995 showed higher HIV infection rates in the northeast (median HIV prevalence, 23 percent) and lower in the west (median, 1.5 percent). AIDS cases related to injecting drug use has increased less than 5 percent annually since 1993. In 1995, more than three-quarters of the injecting drug users diagnosed with AIDS were black or Hispanic and one quarter were women. In Canada, HIV infection among IDUs is a major concern. For example, incidence in Montreal is currently estimated to be 5 per 100 person years; this rate is among the highest in North America.

Although some studies have shown a decrease in both unsafe injection practices and HIV incidence, new HIV infections continue to occur and the number of IDUs sharing injection equipment is high. Several studies have shown that 48 to 88 percent of IDUs continue to share injection equipment and that only 22 to 63 percent clean this equipment in any way. In Canada, sterile injection equipment for persons who continue to inject drugs is available in pharmacies and through numerous needle-exchange programs. In contrast, 45 of the 50 states in the United States prohibit the sale or possession of sterile needles or syringes without a medical prescription, and only a small number of legal needle exchange programs exist.

AIDS cases related to heterosexual contact represent an increasing proportion of cases in North America. Heterosexual contact is the most common mode of transmission among women diagnosed with AIDS in the U.S., and has doubled as a proportion of female AIDS cases in Canada since 1991. While a large proportion of these cases reported sexual contact with an IDU, a substantial proportion of women who acquired their infection heterosexually were unaware of their partner's risk status. In addition to injection drug use, the use of crack cocaine in the United States has been associated with an increased risk of HIV transmission through sexual contact in both urban areas and the rural South.

Between 1990 and 1995, the average HIV prevalence among heterosexual men and women attending STD clinics in North America changed little. However, the seroprevalence rates of heterosexual men and women in New York, Miami and Washington, DC, grew by 5 percent or more.

Changes in Behavior

General population surveys have shown that the level of HIV/AIDs knowledge is high in North America and that changes in sexual behavior have occurred. Among adolescents in U.S. schools, the use of condoms reported at last sexual intercourse increased from 46 percent in 1991 to 54 percent in 1995. In 1992, 50 to 65 percent of Canadian adolescents reported using a condom at last sexual intercourse. A study conducted in the U.S. from 1988 to 1991 showed that condom use by heterosexual adults with non-steady partners increased from 14 percent to 22 percent among whites and from 5 percent to 27 percent among blacks. In a 1994 Canadian survey, 26 percent of men and 19 percent of women aged 20 to 45 reported using condoms with non-steady partners.

Europe

The European region counts some 850 millions inhabitants living in 50 countries. For the purpose of this analysis, this region also includes countries of central Asia that have geo-political affinities with countries in eastern Europe. The analysis of the European AIDS epidemic reveals complex patterns and dynamics that cannot be reduced to a simple division between eastern and western Europe. However, this report uses the old political division because there are large differences in the timing and spread of the epidemic between eastern and western Europe, and the dramatic changes occurring in central and eastern Europe create specific situations of high vulnerability.

Long-Term Trends from AIDS Surveillance

By the end of 1995 a cumulative total of 160,982 AIDS cases, including 154,866 adult/adolescent cases and 6,060 pediatric cases, had been reported in the region. A total of 26,139 new AIDS cases were reported in 1995, an increase of less than 1 percent over the 25,986 cases reported in 1994.

Over the past 2 to 3 years, AIDS incidence appears to have stabilized in several countries in northwestern Europe. In contrast, there is no indication of the AIDS epidemic leveling off in countries in southwestern Europe.

In central and eastern Europe (with the exception of Romania) and central Asia, the HIV/AIDS epidemic is much more recent and AIDS incidence much lower than in western Europe. The highest rate per million (9.9) was found in the federal Republic of Yugoslavia in 1995. However, in some countries, a rapid spread of HIV is indicated, which is mainly linked with injecting drug use. In Poland and the Federal Republic of Yugoslavia (Serbia and Montenegro), where injecting drug users account for the largest proportion of cases, the incidence of AIDS is rising rapidly.

Before 1990, most AIDS cases were diagnosed in men who have sex with men. Since 1990, however, IDUs account for the highest proportion of yearly diagnosed cases in the region (43 percent of adult and adolescent cases in 1995). Among the 22,494 cumulative heterosexual AIDS cases diagnosed up to December 1995, persons originating from other regions accounted for 30 percent. The shift in transmission patterns was accompanied by an increase in the proportion of female cases, which rose from 11 percent in 1986 to 20 percent in 1995. Most women diagnosed with AIDS in 1995 were IDUs (46 percent) or had been heterosexually infected (40 percent), often by an IDU sex partner (accounting for 33 percent of non-IDU heterosexually infected women).

The epidemic among children is closely related to that among women. In most countries, the vast majority of children have been infected through mother-to-child transmission. However, in the region as a whole, the epidemic among children is dominated by the epidemic in Romanian hospitals, which was detected in 1989 and accounts for over 50 percent of the 6,060 pediatric cases reported in the European region. Another, though much smaller, epidemic among children in hospitals occurred in the Russian Federation in the late 1980s.

HIV Incidence and Prevalence

In western European countries, reconstruction of past trends of HIV incidence through back calculation models usually shows that the incidence of HIV infection peaked in the mid-1980s. The same method shows a low but steady increase of HIV prevalence among heterosexual populations. Trends for IDUs appear more variable and complex. Birth cohort analysis of AIDS cases suggest that HIV transmission through injecting drug use among young adults decreased in the early 1990s in France, Italy and Switzerland, but increased over the same period in Spain and Portugal.

Among eastern European countries, large outbreaks of HIV infection in IDUs have been observed in the late 1980s in the former Republic of Yugoslavia and Poland. Until recently, HIV reporting systems associated with systematic testing of large segments of the general population had not identified increasing trends of HIV incidence. However, Ukraine recently reported a dramatic increase of newly infected IDUs in cities bordering the Black Sea. For example, the percentage of HIV-infected IDUs in Nikolayev rose from 1.7 percent in January 1995 to 56.5 percent in December, eleven months later.

Back calculations performed in western Europe in 1996 estimate that 450,000 adults were living with HIV in western Europe at the end of 1993, a figure similar to that obtained by adding national "best" estimates. There is no indication of a rapid upward or downward trend in these countries. An annual incidence of around 40,000 since the beginning of the 1990s seems a plausible estimate. In many countries of eastern Europe, which are at a very early stage of the AIDS epidemic, estimates of HIV prevalence are more uncertain. Best estimates, according to national surveillance systems, gave a total of around 18,000 cumulative infections by the end of 1993. The possibility of recent rapid increases in HIV incidence in some of these countries, as demonstrated by the 1995 Ukraine outbreak, makes any estimate of prevalence or incidence for 1995 extremely hazardous.

In countries where local data are available, the HIV prevalence in pregnant women has been much higher in urban than in rural areas (England, Scotland, Italy). The highest prevalence (between 1 and 4 per thousand) is observed in women who give birth or in newborns in the regions of Paris, Rome, Milan, London, Madrid, Barcelona and Amsterdam. In northern and eastern Europe, where data are mostly limited to the national level, the prevalence among pregnant women appears much lower (between 0 and 0.1 per thousand). In 1995 systematic screening for HIV did not detect any infection among women in Bulgaria, Lithuania, Moldova, Norway or the Slovak Republic.

Rapid Spread of STDs in Eastern Europe and of HIV in Ukraine

Even as western Europe has experienced significant declines in the incidence of syphilis and gonorrhea, there has been rapid rise of syphilis reported in several countries in eastern Europe. From 1908 to 1991, the incidence of syphilis in western Europe dropped to below 2 per 100,000; it remained stable in Poland from 1986 to 1993, but rose sharply in several Newly Independent States, starting in 1989.

Countries of the former Soviet Union have experienced dramatic increases in the incidence of syphilis from a low 5 per 100,000 in 1990 to. a high 170 per 100,000 in 1995. The sharp increase in syphilis incidence prefigures the mounting vulnerability of the region to the sexual transmission of HIV.

In Ukraine, since the beginning of the HIV/AIDS epidemic in 1988, 40 to 80 new HIV infections were registered annually through extensive testing for HIV in various population groups. During the last year, however, more than 3,000 drug users have been found to be HIV-infected in Ukraine. The vulnerability of this country to the further spread of HIV is reflected in the more than tenfold increase of the number of syphilis cases between 1991 and 1995.

A European network of STD clinics from 17 countries (Czech Republic, Hungary, Norway, Switzerland and countries of the European Union except Luxembourg and Ireland) has collected data on HIV prevalence among STD patients since 1990. Among the 87,640 patients tested, 2.8 percent were HIV-infected. MSM had the highest HIV infection rate in most countries (between 30 and 50 percent in Denmark, France, Germany, Portugal and Spain, and 10 percent or less in the Czech Republic, Finland, Greece, Hungary, Norway, Scotland and Sweden). In Italy, Spain and Switzerland, the highest rates of HIV infection were found in IDUs.

Among the heterosexual STD patients who were not IDUs, HIV rates were below 1 percent in 11 countries, 10 to 30 times lower than among MSM. Higher rates (between 1 and 3 percent) were found in France, Germany, Italy, Portugal, Spain and Switzerland. No significant HIV prevalence trend has been observed in this population. Available results from systematic screening of STD patients in several countries in eastern Europe have shown very low rates of HIV infection. In Russia, HIV infections were identified in only 64 of nearly 6 million tests done between January 1987 and December 1993. In 1995, 2.3 per 100,000 STD patients tested in Russia were identified as infected with HIV. However, dramatic ongoing changes in STD incidence in these countries demonstrate a potential for a rapid change in HIV dynamics. Also in some countries of eastern Europe, where STD incidence rates are relatively low (as for example in Slovenia, where 2 early syphilis cases were reported per 100,000 population in 1995), HIV infections are already beginning to be detected among STD patients. In one of the regions of Slovenia that year, 1.4 percent of 294 STD patients tested unlinked anonymously for surveillance purposes were found to be infected with HIV.

In some countries in southwestern Europe the proportion of HIV-infected IDUs has been high for years. In Madrid, between 59 and 74 percent of IDUs entering drug treatment programs from 1986 to 1990 were found to be infected with HIV. In Italy, on a national level, HIV prevalence in IDUs was 31 percent and 39 percent in 1990 and 1991, respectively. In Poland, on a national level, the percentage of HIV-infected IDUs treated at health care settings ranged from 8.7 percent in 1988 to 2.9 percent in 1993. However, 46 percent of IDUs entering two drug treatment centers in Warsaw in 1993 were reported to be infected with HIV. In some eastern European countries, HIV infection seems not yet to have been introduced, although injecting drug use is on the rise and there is evidence of high-risk injecting behavior. In Slovenia, 80 percent of IDUs interviewed outside IDU treatment centers in 1991 admitted sharing injecting equipment during the previous year, although none of 115 unlinked anonymously tested IDUs entering methadone maintenance programs in two IDU treatment centers in 1995 tested positive for HIV infection.

Changing Behavior

In Europe, the lack of basic data on sexual behavior in most countries means that behavior change, condom availability and use are all difficult to monitor. A review of behavioral surveys carried out in western European countries between 1987 to 1990 shows that the reported numbers of sexual partners remained quite stable irrespective of the country, while condom use increased markedly, particularly for the most sexually active populations. Among people with casual partners, the percentage of those reporting using condoms regularly rose from 8 percent in 1987 to 48 percent in 1989 in Switzerland, and from 9 percent to 40 percent in the Netherlands during the same period. In the United Kingdom, the percentage of 18- to 24-year-olds who reported using a condom during their most recent sexual intercourse rose from 14 percent in 1986 to 31 percent in 1989. Such results, based on self-reported behaviors, are also partially supported by trends in condom sales. In Switzerland, wholesalers (representing 80 percent of the market) increased their sales from 7.6 million units in 1986 to 15 million in 1992. In France, the number of condoms sold in pharmacies and supermarkets rose from 38.6 million to 74.4 million between 1986 and 1993.

In contrast, very little is known about the condom market in central and eastern Europe. In Slovenia, condoms are available through pharmacies, petrol stations and supermarkets. In some countries, condom availability and low income levels can heavily restrict condom use. In Kazakhstan in 1995, condoms were available only in some pharmacies of Almati, the capital city. In Moscow that year, although condoms were available at most pharmacies and also could be found in some commercial kiosks, supermarkets and hotels, the price of a twelve-unit pack represented nearly one third of the minimum monthly salary.

The most worrisome information coming from STD surveillance arose recently from the independent republics of the former Soviet Union. Substantial increases in syphilis rates have been seen since 1990 in several of these states. In 1995, compared to 1994, syphilis incidence rates per 100,000 population rose from 81.7 to 172 in Russia (from 169.8 to 320.8 in St. Petersburg), from 72.1 to 147.1 in Belarus, from 116.6 to 173.6 in Moldova, and from 32.6 to 123 in Kazakhstan. These results indicate not only the likelihood of further spread of other STDs (including HIV infection), but also a potential for further spread to neighboring countries. This is already happening in Finland, where 118 new syphilis cases were diagnosed in 1995, as compared with 63 in 1994. Investigations have demonstrated close links between the Finnish and the Russian epidemics, through the increase of Finnish business/pleasure tourism in the St. Petersburg area, and migration from Russia to Finland.

Current and Future Trends

Transmission of HIV through injecting drug use has had and continues to play a major role in the dynamics of the epidemic in the region. Such transmission accounts for the majority of AIDS cases in some of the western countries with highest incidence (Spain and Italy), and is strongly associated with AIDS cases occurring among heterosexual adults and among children in the same countries. The sharp rise of AIDS incidence observed since 1992 in Portugal is mainly due to a rapid increase of cases among IDUs. In eastern European countries, the more serious HIV infection outbreaks reported until now (Poland and Ukraine) are also associated with IDU.

The relative proportion of homo/bisexual men among people with AIDS has steadily decreased in the past ten years in the region. This is mainly due to a comparatively rapid progression of cases among drug users and to a low, but steady, increase in the proportion of heterosexual AIDS cases. AIDS incidence among gay men appears to be moderately declining or quite stable in most of western Europe, while still increasing in Greece, Portugal and Norway. In the Baltic States, Slovenia and Hungary, homosexual men account for the vast majority of HIV infections reported so far among males. Homosexual men represent 77 percent of the 171 HIV infections reported in Hungary in the past 5 years. In Russia, male to male sex was considered the mode of transmission in 53 percent of the 587 HIV/AIDS cases reported among adult males up to December 1994. In Slovakia and Slovenia, 1996 data from unlinked anonymous HIV serosurveys using saliva tests performed in gay gathering places showed prevalence rates of around 3 percent, indicating a potential for further spread of the HIV epidemic in that population.

Moreover, information from the United Kingdom indicates that the declining trend of male-to-male transmission noted in the late 1980s may have begun to reverse, starting in 1990. Although of great importance, the relative increase of AIDS cases and HIV infections among non-injecting-drug heterosexuals, should not mask the fact that homosexual men and IDUs continue to experience the heaviest burden of the epidemic throughout the European region.

North and South Pacific

For the purpose of this report, North and South Pacific is defined as Australia, New Zealand, Papua New Guinea, the Territories and independent island countries of the Pacific. Populations range from 18 million people in Australia to less than 10,000 in some of the island states. By the end of 1995, around 7,400 cases of AIDS had been reported in North and South Pacific, of which over 7,000 were in Australia and New Zealand.

Australia and New Zealand's experience of the HIV epidemic has paralleled that of a number of industrialized countries, particularly those of Northern Europe. The major pathway of transmission has been through sexual contact between men, which occurred primarily in the early 1980s. This pattern also has been reflected in the French Territories of New Caledonia and French Polynesia. The HIV epidemic in Papua New Guinea has developed more recently, mostly as a result of heterosexual transmission. In a number of the small island countries in the region, HIV and AIDS cases have been reported, but populations and case numbers are really too small to define any clear patterns of transmission.

Overall, the per capita HIV prevalence and incidence of AIDS in Australia and New Zealand has been roughly in the middle of the range observed in industrialized countries in other regions of the world. Although AIDS incidence so far has been low in Papua New Guinea, it was estimated that by the end of 1994 there were 4,000 adults living with HIV infection in Papua New Guinea, overtaking Australia on a per-capita basis to give the highest prevalence in the North and South Pacific region. Some of the smaller countries of the region have relatively high rates, even though the number of reported cases is small.

Populations Affected

Cumulatively, over 85 percent of HIV infections in Australia and New Zealand are reported to have been acquired through sexual contact between men. In New Caledonia and French Polynesia, around two-thirds of cases with a reported mode of transmission were in men with a history of homosexual contact. Back-projection estimates from AIDS cases in Australia show that there was a peak in the homosexual transmission of HIV infection between men in the early to mid-1980s and a substantial decline in transmission rates during the latter half of the 1980s.

The incidence of AIDS has reached a plateau in Australia and actually appears to be declining in New Zealand. These patterns are essentially due to the drop in the rate of sexual transmission of HIV infection between men that occurred ten years earlier. This decline began well before any organized prevention program was implemented, but is likely to have been supported through the strong partnerships developed between gay community-based organizations and governments. Current trends in sexual transmission between men are unclear. Cohort studies, behavioral surveys and monitoring of rectal gonorrhea provide a basis for assessing changes in HIV risk.

In Australia and New Zealand, HIV has remained rare among people who inject drugs, apart from men who also have homosexual contact. In heterosexual injecting drug users, surveys have consistently found HIV prevalence below 2 percent. Both countries have adopted harm reduction policies, including extensive use of needle exchange. Although the low HIV rates indicate successful prevention efforts in this population, the transmission of hepatitis C continues to occur at epidemic levels among injecting drug users, with annual incidence rates of 15 to 20 percent being recorded in Australia. The ongoing hepatitis C epidemic indicates the continuing potential for a substantial outbreak of HIV through blood contact among injecting drug users.

On the basis of available evidence, heterosexual transmission of HIV has been infrequent in Australia and New Zealand. The pattern appears to be very different in Papua New Guinea, where heterosexual transmission accounts for the largest proportion of diagnosed infections. By the end of 1995, nearly 90 percent of the diagnosed cases of HIV in Papua New Guinea for which modes of transmission had been reported were attributed to heterosexual contact, and an equal number of males and females had been diagnosed with HIV infection.

In Australia, and to a lesser extent New Zealand, high rates of STDs other than HIV in indigenous people have led to mounting concern about the potential for a major heterosexual epidemic of HIV infection in these populations. Surveillance data so far indicate that the rate of HIV diagnosis is no higher among indigenous than non-indigenous people, but in Australia the rate of HIV diagnosis has increased in the past six years among indigenous people. In contrast, the overall rate of HIV diagnosis in the Australian population has declined substantially. There has also been a shift toward more heterosexually transmitted infections among the diagnoses of HIV among indigenous people in Australia.

Surveys among men who have sex with men show a substantial decline in Australia and New Zealand over the past decade in the frequency of unprotected anal intercourse with casual male sexual partners. There have also been major declines in the sharing of equipment by injecting drug users. There has been little longitudinal information on heterosexual risk behavior at a national level, but increased condom use has been reported among heterosexual university students.

HIV Care

Most of the need for HIV care in North and South Pacific has so far been in Australia and New Zealand. In these countries, there has generally been wide availability of good treatment services, access to appropriate therapy and a steadily improving climate in regard to discrimination. As the burden of HIV illness increases in Papua New Guinea and possibly some of the other smaller countries of North and South Pacific, it is likely that strain will be placed on existing health infrastructures, as has been the case in other parts of the developing world.

Symposium Conclusions

1. Remarkable progress has been achieved in reducing the spread of HIV in some developing countries and in certain populations in industrialized countries. Specifically, HIV incidence has declined in young men in Thailand.

    Impressive declines in HIV incidence and/or prevalence have been reported in gay men in the U.S., Australia, Canada and Western Europe. A decline in prevalence has also been observed in young women in Uganda, a country with one of the most mature HIV/AIDS epidemics. HIV prevalence has remained low in injecting drug users in a number of countries. In Australia, for example, major epidemics have been prevented in injecting drug users through timely prevention efforts. To a large extent, these successes in HIV reduction are attributable to education and prevention programs.

2. The HIV epidemic continues to expand in most developing countries, as well as in those European countries undergoing political stress and upheaval.

    The social, economic, demographic and health impacts of the HIV epidemics are increasing in most countries. Especially dramatic is the spread of HIV in young adults, adolescents and children in developing countries. In a number of industrialized countries, the spread of HIV is increasing rapidly in minority populations. There is also continuing spread of HIV to rural areas throughout the developing world. In many countries, the proportion of infected women is now roughly equal to that of men. Globally, heterosexual transmission continues to rise.

    Extensive commercial sex industries, high prevalence of sexually transmitted diseases and injecting drug use provide the potential for explosive epidemics in several countries, including Indonesia, China, and several countries in West Africa and Eastern Europe. In India, Cambodia and Myanmar, the explosion has already occurred.

3. The global pandemic is now composed of multiple epidemics in different stages of development. The characteristics of these epidemics include different viruses (HIV-1 and HIV-2), different strains of the same virus, differences in transmission modes and differences in incidence in population subsets, including young adults.

HIV Subtypes

Background

Advances in genetic technology in the 1980s made it possible to duplicate in the test tube - by a technique called polumerase chain reaction (PCR) - the RNA or DNA forms of the genetic "code" of HIV.

This revolutionary application made it possible to use the genetic information to distinguish the two major types of HIV, type 1 (HIV-1) and type 2 (HIV-2), as well as different strains within each type.

HIV-1 is more virulent than HIV-2 and is the predominant strain around the world. To date, HIV-2 is found principally in West Africa, and constitutes a small minority of infections in other parts of Africa, South America and West India.

Applications

As with other typable infectious diseases, the ability to compare and distinguish specific HIV virus isolates from individuals makes it possible to track the spread of virus from person, country to country and region to region.

Survellance and knowledge about the geographic extent of HIV-1 strains is important to confirm or rule out chains of transmission between individuals and to provide clues as to how the epidemic is spreading. Furthermore, the development and performance of AIDS vaccines and clinical prognosis may be affected by biological differences in the manifestations of infection with different subtypes.

HIV-1 and HIV-2 Subtypes

To date, two major groups of HIV-1 exist, "M" and "0" (for outlier). The virus that causes the great majority of HIV-1 infections diagnosed and studied in the world are in the M group. The 0 group includes a small number of isolates discovered in Africa (with one case found recently in the U.S.). These are genetically quite distant from the M group, and consequently may not show up on some standard laboratory tests for HIV-1.

HIV-2 is divided in the subtypes A and B, but further subtypes C through E have recently been characterized by DNA sequencing.

Geographic Distribution

In the predominant M group of HIV-1, 8 subtypes - A through H - have been identified to date. Most all are found in one area or another of Africa, while in other regions of the world, certain subtypes predominate.

In Europe, subtype B is predominant in men who have sex with men, while a variety of subtypes are found in the relatively small numbers of people infected through heterosexual contact in Europe and the countries of former Soviet Union. Subtype B has also been noted in Indonesia, the Philippines and Taiwan.

In India, subtype C predominates, with a small number of A and B infections. In Thailand, E predominates, while a minority of B infections occur in drug users, and this B strain has also been found in drug users in Myanmar (Burma), Malaysia and southeast China.

In the Americas (North, South and Central), as well as in Australia, New Zealand and Japan, subtype B is most common. Subtype F occurs in Romania, and along with subtype C also is found in a small proportion of strains in Brazil.

Biological Implications

Preliminary epidemiological work in Thailand suggests that subtype E may be more transmissible by the sexual route than subtype B, while preliminary clinical studies there suggested that subtype E infection may produce significantly lower levels of CD4+ T-cells than does infection with subtype B. Preliminary in vitro work in the U.S. suggests that subtypes C and E may more readily infect the Langerhans cells that line the sexual tract than subtype B.

It is not known whether an AIDS vaccine designed against one subtype of HIV-1 will work to protect the vaccine recipient against other subtypes to which they may be exposed. Knowledge of which subtypes exist in which proportions in specific geographic areas will be important for designing AIDS vaccine trials and determining which antigens might need to be included in future vaccines. Simple economical techniques have been developed for collecting HIV-1 in non-infectious dried blood spots that can be mailed safely without refrigeration to laboratories capable of performing PCR and subtyping.

Research-Needs and Implications

Some countries have multiple subtypes circulating in substantial numbers, such as E and B in Thailand, A and D in Uganda, and B and C in South Africa. Prospective studies among infected persons who continue to expose themselves to HIV (e.g., sex workers and injecting drug users) would be useful to determine whether infection with one subtype provides protection against "superinfection" with another subtype. Recent data from Senegal suggest that HIV-2 infection provides partial protection from HIV-1 superinfection. If superinfection does not occur as frequently as might be expected, this would bode well for the possibility that killed, whole-virus or live, attenuated vaccines might work if they can mimic the natural immune response to HIV.

4.   Epidemiological surveillance is an essential early component of a country's response to HIV. In most developing countries and in Eastern Europe, surveillance and evaluation data are insufficient to monitor adequately the status and interpret the changes in trends of the HIV epidemics.